THE AUSTRALIAN COLLECTION

The AUSTRALIAN COLLECTION

Australia's Greatest Books

GEOFFREY DUTTON

ANGUS
& ROBERTSON
PUBLISHERS

ANGUS & ROBERTSON PUBLISHERS

Unit 4, Eden Park, 31 Waterloo Road,
North Ryde, NSW, Australia 2113, and
16 Golden Square, London W1R 4BN,
United Kingdom

First published in Australia
by Angus & Robertson Publishers in 1985

Essays and biographies copyright ©
Angus & Robertson Publishers 1985

National Library of Australia
Cataloguing-in-publication data.

The Australian collection.

  ISBN 0 207 14961 5.

  1. Australian literature.
  2. Australia—Literary collections.
  I. Dutton, Geoffrey, 1922- .

A828'.008'3294

Picture research by Virginia York Dummett

Typeset in 10/12 Plantin by Midland Typesetters
Printed in Tokyo, Japan

You can make initial contact
with someone who does not speak
your language with signs or smiles, but to communicate
you need words.
So it is with a nation; to understand it
you have to read its books.

CONTENTS

Introduction 8

Watkin Tench
Sydney's First Four Years 9

Charles Sturt
*Two Expeditions into the
Interior of Southern Australia* 14

Edward John Eyre
*Journals of Expeditions of
Discovery into Central Australia* ... 18

James Tucker
Ralph Rashleigh 23

Raffaello Carboni
The Eureka Stockade 27

Rachel Henning
The Letters of Rachel Henning 31

Marcus Clarke
For the Term of His Natural Life ... 35

Rolf Boldrewood
Robbery Under Arms 39

Ernest Giles
Australia Twice Traversed 43

Louis Becke
By Reef and Palm 47

Ethel Turner
Seven Little Australians 51

David W. Carnegie
Spinifex and Sand 55

Ethel Pedley
Dot and the Kangaroo 59

Steele Rudd
On Our Selection and
Our New Selection 63

Henry Lawson
The Joe Wilson Stories 67

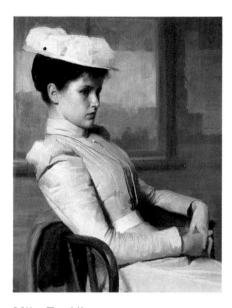

Miles Franklin
My Brilliant Career 71

Joseph Furphy
Such is Life 75

E. J. Banfield
The Confessions of a Beachcomber . 79

Mrs Aeneas Gunn
We of the Never Never 83

Mary Grant Bruce
A Little Bush Maid 87

Louis Stone
Jonah 91

Douglas Mawson
The Home of the Blizzard 95

May Gibbs
*The Complete Adventures of
Snugglepot and Cuddlepie* 99

Norman Lindsay
The Magic Pudding 103

William Gosse Hay
*The Escape of the Notorious
Sir William Heans* 107

C. E. W. Bean
The Story of ANZAC 111

Jack McLaren
My Crowded Solitude 115

M. Barnard Eldershaw
A House is Built 119

Katharine Susannah Prichard
Coonardoo 123

Lennie Lower
Here's Luck 127

Frederic Manning
Her Privates We or
The Middle Parts of Fortune 131

Henry Handel Richardson
The Fortunes of Richard Mahony .. 135

Frank Dalby Davison
Man-Shy 139

Ion L. Idriess
Flynn of the Inland 143

Myrtle Rose White
No Roads Go By 147

Brian Penton
Landtakers 151

H. V. Evatt
Rum Rebellion 155

Xavier Herbert
Capricornia 159

Francis Ratcliffe
Flying Fox and Drifting Sand 163

Christina Stead
The Man Who Loved Children 167

Eleanor Dark
The Timeless Land 171

Kylie Tennant
The Battlers 175

Eve Langley
The Pea-pickers 179

Martin Boyd
Lucinda Brayford 183

Ruth Park
The Harp in the South 187

Frank Hardy
Power Without Glory 191

Dymphna Cusack and Florence James
Come In Spinner 195

Russell Braddon
The Naked Island 199

Tom Hungerford
The Ridge and the River 203

CONTENTS

Judah Waten
Alien Son 207

Caddie
*Caddie: The Autobiography of
a Sydney Barmaid* 211

Tom Ronan
Vision Splendid 215

D'Arcy Niland
The Shiralee 219

Arthur W. Upfield
Man of Two Tribes 223

Nino Culotta
They're a Weird Mob 227

Patrick White
Voss 231

Cyril Pearl
Wild Men of Sydney 235

Olaf Ruhen
Naked Under Capricorn 239

Randolph Stow
To the Islands 243

Russel Ward
The Australian Legend 247

Mary Durack
Kings in Grass Castles 251

Robin Boyd
The Australian Ugliness 255

Kenneth Cook
Wake in Fright 259

Nene Gare
The Fringe Dwellers 263

Sumner Locke Elliott
Careful, He Might Hear You 267

Alan Moorehead
Cooper's Creek 271

Hal Porter
*The Watcher on the
Cast-Iron Balcony* 275

Colin Thiele
Storm Boy 279

Donald Horne
The Lucky Country 283

George Johnston
My Brother Jack 287

Thea Astley
The Slow Natives 291

D. E. Charlwood
All the Green Year 295

Colin Johnson
Wild Cat Falling 299

Ivan Southall
Ash Road 303

Geoffrey Blainey
The Tyranny of Distance 307

Peter Mathers
Trap 311

Joan Lindsay
Picnic at Hanging Rock 315

S. A. Wakefield
Bottersnikes and Gumbles 319

Eric Rolls
They All Ran Wild 323

Vincent Serventy
Dryandra 327

Hugh Stretton
Ideas for Australian Cities 331

David Ireland
The Unknown Industrial Prisoner . 335

Thomas Keneally
The Chant of Jimmie Blacksmith . 339

Frank Moorhouse
The Americans, Baby 343

George Farwell
Squatter's Castle 347

Patricia Wrightson
The Nargun and the Stars 351

Helen Garner
Monkey Grip 355

Manning Clark
A History of Australia, Vol. IV 359

Christopher Koch
The Year of Living Dangerously ... 363

David Malouf
An Imaginary Life 367

Roger McDonald
1915 371

Jessica Anderson
The Impersonators 375

Murray Bail
Homesickness 379

Shirley Hazzard
The Transit of Venus 383

Peter Carey
Bliss 387

A. B. Facey
A Fortunate Life 391

David Foster
Moonlite 395

Acknowledgements 399

Index of Authors 405

Index of Titles 406

INTRODUCTION

You can make initial contact with someone who does not speak your language with signs or smiles, but to communicate you need words. So it is with a nation; to understand it you have to read its books. However, a characteristic of civilisation is that it is as much a state of mind as the external evidence of art and science. The novels of Dickens or Tolstoy helped to shape nineteenth-century England or Russia, and not only gave the people who lived with them images of themselves but led to a deeper understanding of what they were.

Fortunately it is not only genius which exercises this authority. A nation's literature varies in ultimate quality, but it is thereby no less important in shaping and reflecting that nation's image, both to its own people and in the eyes of foreigners.

In 1983 publisher Richard Walsh asked me if I would make a selection of up to 100 classic Australian books, providing a descriptive and critical essay on each book, and a biographical account of each author. The project was daunting in its immensity but irresistible to any enthusiast for Australian literature.

We agreed on certain specific limitations. There were to be no more than 100 different writers, and only one book per author. Each book had to be a coherent whole, which ruled out collections of short stories. (Partial exceptions were made to this rule.) Poetry was to be the subject of a separate study; the emphasis in the reading of poetry is on individual poems, very seldom on books, unless an epic is under consideration. Again, in drama one looks to plays as complete in themselves, not as forming part of a book. The authors had to be Australian, or, like the explorers, had to have lived and suffered here. This ruled out visitors, however appealing, like D. H. Lawrence or Havelock Ellis.

The definition of "classic" should be relevant to both time and place. There are many books in each country's literature that are cherished as classics in their homeland but little known elsewhere. One thinks, for instance, of those by writers such as Constant or Mérimée in French, Grimmelshausen or Schnitzler in German, Saltykov-Shchedrin or Zoshchenko in Russian. A Frenchman, a German or a Russian could name you a dozen other writers who are important in their own countries but not known at all elsewhere except to specialists.

The history of a country is always being rewritten, but in one sense it has already been written in its literature. The fact that there may be conflicting versions, as for instance in Lawson's and Paterson's attitudes to the Bush, renders that history all the richer. A writer of relatively modest talent can be more important in the history of a country than in its literature, and thus worthy to be remembered.

The works discussed in *The Australian Collection* come from fiction, journals, histories, biographies, natural history, books of ideas, children's books and books of humour. They are all important to Australians, although some (like David Malouf's *An Imaginary Life*, for instance) are not on the surface about Australia at all. After all, *Hamlet* is not "about" England.

The problem of choice, of course, was acute. It was like making an anthology of poetry; every reader is bound to have complaints of favourites omitted or unworthy items included. Here many of my own favourites are missing, and the selection from individual writers was often very difficult. *Voss*, for instance, or *Riders in the Chariot*? And I would like to have included many more books of ideas, history and biography by such writers as Bernard Smith, John La Nauze or Geoffrey Serle.

Not all the books discussed here are of the highest literary merit. Such a standard would be impossible to attain in the literature of a young country. But they are all, in their different ways, classics. *The Magic Pudding* is as important as *The Fortunes of Richard Mahony*. A minor writer like Ion L. Idriess made a classic contribution to the development of the Australian consciousness. In the Australian landscape a pioneer's cottage is as evocative as the Sydney Opera House.

The first Australians have not been ignored — there is a strong Aboriginal presence in more than a third of the books chosen. Some of the books come complete with the prejudices of their times, such as the treatment of Aborigines in *Spinifex and Sand* or the Australian bias of the author of *Such is Life* or the loyal Britishness of *A Little Bush Maid*. Such complexities do not make a book less rich.

In making the choice of books there were some difficulties with short stories. Some of the best Australian writing is in short stories but, as with poems, short stories have an individual existence. In the case of Becke, Lawson and Moorhouse, there seemed sufficient unity of theme or character, of the "discontinuous narrative" Moorhouse claims for his work, to justify the books chosen.

Immediate popularity, of course, is no guarantee of merit in a book. But enduring popularity is; as long as Australians continue to read (a future by no means certain) most of these books will continue to be published. Many of them have been already made into feature films or television series. Such dramatisations always increase the sales of the original book; watching does not necessarily mean not reading.

Rereading the books and assembling the biographies for *The Australian Collection* I found that their Australianness could not be defined in any narrow national sense. It was more a question of an acceptance of a common environment, both human and natural, and an Australian use of language. For instance, these are already evident in the *Journals* of E. J. Eyre (1838), both in the subject matter and in the use of such an expression as "out back". This is not recorded by G. A. Wilkes until 1875. Again, suburban and urban Australia are as unmistakable in *Jonah* (1911) as in *Here's Luck* (1930) or *Monkey Grip* (1977).

There is also a characteristic Australian independence of mind evident in the work of writers as politically conservative as Boldrewood or as radical as Hardy, as fastidious as Manning or Boyd, as democratic as Lawson. Likewise the characteristics of Australian humour are unmistakable not only where they are allowed full play, as in "Steele Rudd" or Lower, but behind the scenes in nearly all the books, even in Patrick White, if not, alas, in Henry Handel Richardson.

The variety of *The Australian Collection* remains unassailable. It is quite remarkable for a country that is yet to celebrate the bicentenary of its white history. But in this variety of subject matter and technique there is also a depth of consciousness and a shared achievement that enable Australian writers today to feel no longer provincial but part of the literature of the world.

Watkin Tench

SYDNEY'S
FIRST
FOUR YEARS

SYDNEY 1961

During the intervals of duty, our greatest source of entertainment now lay in cultivating the acquaintance of our new friends, the natives. Ever liberal of communication, no difficulty, but of understanding each other, subsisted between us. Inexplicable contradictions arose to bewilder our researches, which no ingenuity could unravel, and no credulity reconcile.

Baneelon, from being accustomed to our manners, and understanding a little English, was the person through whom we wished to prosecute inquiry: but he had lately become a man of so much dignity and consequence, that it was not always easy to obtain his company. Clothes had been given to him at various times; but he did not always condescend to wear them: one day he would appear in them; and the next day he was to be seen carrying them in a net, slung around his neck. Farther to please him, a brick house, of 12 feet square, was built for his use, and for that of such of his countrymen as might chuse to reside in it, on a point of land fixed upon by himself. A shield, double cased with tin, to ward off the spears of his enemies, was also presented to him, by the governor.

November, 1790. Elated by these marks of favour, and sensible that his importance with his countrymen arose, in proportion to our patronage of him, he warmly attached himself to our society.

But the gratitude of a savage is ever a precarious tenure: that of Baneelon was fated to suffer suspension, and had well nigh been obliterated by the following singular circumstance.

One day, the natives were observed to assemble in more than an ordinary number, at their house on the point, and to be full of bustle and agitation, repeatedly calling on the name of Baneelon, and that of Dee-in (a woman). Between twelve and one o'clock Baneelon, unattended, came to the governor, at his house, and told him that he was going to put to death a woman immediately, whom he had brought from Botany Bay. Having communicated his intention, he was preparing to go away, seeming not to wish that the governor should be present at the performance of the ceremony. But his excellency was so struck with the fierce gestures, and wild demeanour of the other, who held in his hand one of our hatchets, and frequently tried the sharpness of it, that he determined to accompany him, taking with him Mr Collins, and his orderly serjeant. On the road, Baneelon continued to talk wildly and incoherently

of what he would do, and manifested such extravagant marks of fury and revenge, that his hatchet was taken away from him, and a walking-stick substituted for it. When they reached the house, they found several natives, of both sexes, lying promiscuously before the fire, and among them, a young woman, not more than 16 years old, who at sight of Baneelon, started, and raised herself half up. He no sooner saw her, than snatching a sword of the country, he ran at her, and gave her two severe wounds on the head, and one on the shoulder, before interference in behalf of the poor wretch could be made. Our people now rushed in, and seized him; but the other Indians continued quiet spectators of what was passing, either awed by Baneelon's superiority, or deeming it a common case, unworthy of notice and interposition. — In vain did the governor by turns soothe and threaten him; — in vain did the serjeant point his musquet at him; he seemed dead to every passion but revenge; forgot his affection to his old friends; and, instead of complying with the request they made, furiously brandished his sword at the governor, and called aloud for his hatchet to dispatch the unhappy victim of his barbarity. Matters now wore a serious aspect: the other Indians appeared under the controul of Baneelon, and had begun to arm, and prepare their spears, as if determined to support him in his violence.

It was an extraordinary piece of good fortune that one of the officers attached to the First Fleet should have been a humane man with a civilised and enquiring mind as well as a fine command of English. Among the various fairly rough eyewitness accounts of the settlement of New South Wales, Tench's *Sydney's First Four Years* is a work of art.

This book in fact makes available in one volume Tench's *A Narrative of the Expedition to Botany Bay* (London, 1789) and *A Complete Account of the Settlement at Port Jackson 1788-1791* (London, 1793).

Australia owes its birth as a nation to the transportation of a mere 760-odd convicts (about 568 men and 191 women), who were guarded by a force of officers and marines of 212

persons. Tench, like most of the marines, was a volunteer. The First Fleet came to an almost unknown country, with little or no knowledge of its resources. Today it seems incredible that the British officials gave so little thought to the need for the party to be self-sufficient. As it was, after finally settling at Port Jackson, the new colony was often on the brink of starvation, waiting for supplies to arrive by ship.

Governor Phillip had with him amongst the convicts three gardeners. Among the free members of the Fleet there was no gardener, farmer, botanist or mineralogist. Apart from vague hopes of finding flax for sails and timber for masts there was at this stage no thought in London of developing

New South Wales as a free colony and trading partner.

Consequently at first there was no commitment to Australia itself in any of those who landed there. The convicts had been sent there, and although their jailers had volunteered, most of them, like Tench, were waiting to go home again. The subsequent history of law and order in New South Wales may have been considerably influenced by this lack of any feeling of responsibility or permanent commitment to the new country.

Tench's book can be read on a number of levels, all immediately accessible in his excellent prose. It is a straightforward account of the settlement, and the hazards and discomfort undergone as supplies kept on running low, the soil failed to return good crops, and the animals either died or disappeared. After eight months only one out of 70 sheep remained. The only fresh protein available was kangaroos and fish. The kangaroos were not easy to shoot and the supplies of fish very erratic.

During the intervals of duty, our greatest source of entertainment now lay in cultivating the acquaintance of our new friends, the natives. Ever liberal of communication, no difficulty, but of understanding each other, subsisted between us.

Sydney's First Four Years is also, and perhaps most interestingly of all, a full and sympathetic account of the first deep interaction between the Aborigines and Europeans. Although Tench had read Rousseau, he neither expects nor finds the Noble Savage. His approach is that of the enlightened humanist, always prepared to acknowledge not only the common humanity between black and white but also demonstrations of courage, kindness or feminine delicacy. They may be savages, but they are human, and there is a responsibility for whites, from Governor Phillip

Native Family of NSW *Philip Gidley King (above)*

down, not to injure or rob blacks. Unfortunately, as later was to be true elsewhere, the convicts robbed and maltreated the Aborigines, and the clashes between black and white were nearly always the fault of the whites, as Tench impartially noted. There were also some mysterious and unprovoked attacks by the Aborigines, such as on the occasion when the Governor himself was speared. Phillip exercised admirable restraint, not to mention courage, over this episode, and did not even report it in his despatches home.

Finally, Tench's book can be read almost as a novel, as an account of the hero's state of mind and adventures. Modest, observant and cultured, Tench is devoid of egotism. His responses to New South Wales and its Aboriginal inhabitants are always fresh and unprejudiced. For instance, unlike many British arrivals for many years to come, Tench immediately appreciated Australian wildflowers: "a variety of flowering shrubs abound, most of them new to an European, and surpassing in beauty, fragrance, and number, all I ever saw in an uncultivated state: . . . The rare and beautiful flowering shrubs, which abound in every part, deserve the highest admiration and panegyric."

Tench has the acceptance of harsh punishment of an eighteenth-century officer, but he is always prepared to give the convicts credit when deserved. Besides, the harshness of the discipline did not extend only to the convicts. Convicts were sentenced to immediate death for robbery, or flogged (300 lashes for stealing potatoes, as well as being chained to two other convicts for six months and having their flour allowance stopped). But six marines were also hanged for thieving in March 1789.

Tench explored the country around Sydney, and studied the natural history. He suffered from the heat, felt hungry and admitted to boredom, the curse of New South Wales. "All is quiet and stupid as could be wished."

Tench's two journals give a beautifully balanced picture of two simultaneous enlightenments, of the Europeans getting to know entirely strange and "savage" people, and of the Aborigines, who had fragmentary associations with Cook and the French explorers, becoming aware that there was a European settlement that was going to be permanent. Although by the end of 1788, "Unabated animosity continued to prevail between the natives and us", caused mainly by the sorties of convicts robbing the Aborigines of weapons and food, each side behaved with remarkable restraint and dignity.

However, Phillip found the situation intolerable. Tired of "petty warfare and endless uncertainty" he had the astonishing idea of capturing a couple of Aboriginal men from whom it was hoped to learn the reasons for their attitude, and also by their good treatment, convey to the other Aborigines that they had nothing to fear from the whites who were in command.

On the last day of December 1788 a boat was sent to Manly Cove, and after "several Indians . . . were enticed by courteous behaviour and a few presents to enter into conversation", the marines rushed in and secured a prisoner who was fastened by ropes to the thwarts of the boat. Tench conveys both the emotions and the pragmatic acceptance of the captured Aborigine: ". . . when he saw himself irretrievably disparted from his countrymen, he set up the most piercing and lamentable cries of distress. His grief,

SYDNEY COVE, PORT JACKSON *William Bradley*

WATKIN TENCH
1758/9-1833

Watkin Tench was born in 1758 or 1759 at Chester, England. His father, Fisher Tench, ran "a most respectable boarding school" and instilled in his son the basis of not only a sound education but a love of reading. Tench was familiar with Latin and French literature as well as with English. At one stage of his early life Tench spent some time in France. In his own words, "I was no stranger, you know, to the customs of the French on land." Later, at Botany Bay, he took a special pleasure in the company of the French ships anchored there—*L'Astrolabe*, and *La Boussole*, under the command of La Pérouse.

For a prose writer it was indeed a fortunate time to be writing. Tench's works embodied the characteristic virtues of eighteenth-century English style—clarity, urbanity, balance and sensibility.

In 1776 Tench joined the Marine Corps as a second lieutenant, and served in various ships during the War of American Independence. When his second ship, the *Mermaid*, went aground he was captured, and for three months was a prisoner of war in Maryland. By 1782 he had become a captain-lieutenant (a captain-lieutenant, or lieutenant-captain, being the officer under a captain who commands the company in the captain's absence). Like so many officers, he was put on half-pay when there was no longer a war to fight.

In 1786, he volunteered for three years' service with the First Fleet that was being assembled to take convicts to Botany Bay. He sailed in the *Charlotte* on 13 May 1787 and arrived in Botany Bay on 20 January 1788.

Tench's equable and modest nature, and his cultivated mind, are obvious to any reader of his narrative. In the tiny settlement of Sydney where quarrels flared easily Tench was able to remain on good terms with almost everyone. He enjoyed the companionship particularly of William Dawes, another marine officer who had scientific interests, and of Surgeon Morgan, a musician who brought the first piano to New South Wales.

Tench made several exploratory expeditions around Sydney, in the course of which he discovered the Nepean River. He also kept a sharp eye on the shaky development of agriculture in New South Wales. As he himself said to a friend, "You know my fondness for agricultural pursuits."

His only trouble in Sydney occurred with Major Ross. Tench was President of a Court Martial which had given a soldier guilty of assault the choice of 100 lashes or making an apology. He and the other members of the Court Martial had refused to alter the verdict when Ross ordered them to do so and Ross then arrested them. Phillip intervened and the officers were restored to duty.

By the time Tench returned to England that country was at war with France. Tench was promoted to Brevet Major and went to sea with the Channel Fleet. In 1794 he was captured on his ship, *HMS Alexander*, and he then spent six months as a prisoner of war, mostly on parole in Brittany. Here he wrote a book, *Letters Written from France to a Friend in London*, which was published in 1796. He was released by exchange in 1795, and continued with the Channel Fleet until 1802.

He retired on half-pay with the rank of Major-General in the Army in 1816, but served again from 1819 until 1821, when he retired with the rank of Lieutenant-General in the Marines.

After his return from Australia Tench married, but there were no children of the marriage. He and his wife in 1821 adopted the four orphaned children of his wife's sister.

Tench died in England at Devonport in 1833.

The first instalment of Tench's journals, *A Narrative of the Expedition to Botany Bay*, was published in 1789 and went into three editions within a year. It was translated into French, German and Dutch. *A Complete Account of the Settlement at Port Jackson 1788-1791* was published in 1793 and was translated into German.

---

however, soon diminished: he accepted and eat of some broiled fish which was given to him, and sullenly submitted to his destiny."

Some extraordinary episodes followed, as the Aborigine at first called Manly but then by his own name, Arabanoo, settled down to live with his captors. His hair was cut off and the vermin removed from it (which he ate), and then he was put in a tub and washed by Tench among others. Tench wanted to see the real colour of his skin. He was "as black as the lighter cast of the African negroes". Arabanoo gradually regained his confidence, symbolised by the amount of food he ate, for example "for supper two Kanguroo rats, each of the size of a moderate rabbit, and in addition not less than three pounds of fish". Strangely, in view of the later sad history of the Aborigines, "strong liquors he would never taste, turning from them with disgust and abhorrence."

At this time reports started coming in of dead Aborigines being found around the harbour. It was an outbreak of smallpox, over the cause of which historians are still arguing. Certainly there was no smallpox amongst the members of the First Fleet. Perhaps it came from the French. Sadly, Arabanoo died from it. "He was, perhaps, the only native who was ever attached to us from choice."

Not long after this, two more natives were captured, Baneelon (Benelong) and Colbee.

The story of Baneelon, independent, passionate, courageous, a great fighter and lover, also fond of liquor, is one of the great achievements of Tench's journals. Tench also gives superb portraits of Barangaroo, wife to both Baneelon and Colbee, and of the "elegant and timid" female Gooreedeeana. He found in Barangaroo, as in Gooreedeeana, "as much feminine innocence, softness, and modesty (allowing for inevitable difference of education), as the most finished system could bestow, or the most polished circle produce. So little fitted are we to judge of human nature at once!"

In December 1790 when Phillip, after the murder by Aborigines of one of his men, abandoned his principle of friendship and organised a punitive party, Tench was put in charge of it. Tench obeyed his orders. Tench is not a humorous writer, although not lacking in a sense of humour, but his deadpan account of this "terrific procession" is pure comedy. The procession was, in the old sense of "terrific", meant to cause terror. Tench's macabre commission was to take two natives prisoner, and put to death 10 men. Women and children were not to be molested. Tench was ordered to cut off the heads of the slain and bring them in; "for which purpose, hatchets and bags would be furnished". Tench then persuaded the Governor to let him only capture six and not kill any. The Governor agreed, saying he would then hang two and send the rest to Norfolk Island. If Tench was unable to capture six, he was to shoot six.

So off went Tench with three officers, two surgeons, three sergeants, three corporals and 40 private soldiers, with three days' provisions, not forgetting ropes to bind the prisoners with, and the hatchets and bags.

The first day was typical in its lack of success of those that followed. "After having walked in various directions until 4 o'clock in the afternoon, without seeing a native, we halted for the night." The next day they saw some "Indians", as the early British visitors often called the Aborigines, but they ran away. The next day they found a native fishing in shallow water; it turned out to be their old friend, Colbee.

Farther to please him, a brick house, of 12 feet square, was built for his use, and for that of such of his countrymen as might chuse to reside in it, on a point of land fixed upon by himself.

After they had returned to base they set off on a second expedition. At the north arm of Botany Bay they tried to cross a creek when the tide was out. Soon they were up to their chests in mud, and could have perished in the bog had not those members of the party still on dry land managed to throw them boughs. Half of their firearms had now been made unserviceable by mud. Separating into three parties, and moving in silence, at dawn they rushed a "native village", but found no one there. So once more they returned to Sydney without catching a single Aborigine. No doubt the humane Tench was as relieved as Governor Phillip was disappointed.

Tench left for England with the marines in the *Gorgon* in 1791, still unconvinced that New South Wales, with its droughts and apparent lack of fertile soil, had any great future. In his journals, at least, he had chronicled its beginnings. But Tench is more than a journal writer lucky to have been present at an historic occasion. He is a true writer, and can be regarded as the father of Australian literature.

Aborigines Resting by a Camp Fire *Joseph Lycett*

Charles Sturt

TWO
EXPEDITIONS
INTO THE INTERIOR
OF
SOUTHERN AUSTRALIA

LONDON 1833

It was with considerable apprehension that I observed the river to be shoaling fast, more especially as a huge sand-bank, a little below us, and on the same side on which the natives had gathered, projected nearly a third-way across the channel. To this sand-bank they ran with tumultuous uproar, and covered it over in a dense mass. Some of the chiefs advanced to the water to be nearer their victims, and turned from time to time to direct their followers. With every pacific disposition, and an extreme reluctance to take away life, I foresaw that it would be impossible any longer to avoid an engagement, yet with such fearful numbers against us, I was doubtful of the result. The spectacle we had witnessed had been one of the most appalling kind, and sufficient to shake the firmness of most men; but at that trying moment my little band preserved their temper coolness, and if any thing could be gleaned from their countenances, it was that they had determined on an obstinate resistance. I now explained to them that their only chance of escape depended, or would depend, on their firmness. I desired that after the first volley had been fired, M'Leay and three of the men, would attend to the defence of the boat with bayonets only, while I, Hopkinson, and Harris, would keep up the fire as being more used to it. I ordered, however, that no shot was to be fired until after I had discharged both my barrels. I then delivered their arms to the men, which had as yet been kept in the place appropriated for them, and at the same time some rounds of loose cartridge. The men assured me they would follow my instructions, and thus prepared, having already lowered the sail, we drifted onwards with the current. As we neared the sand-bank, I stood up and made signs to the natives to desist; but without success. I took up my gun, therefore, and cocking it, had already brought it down to a level. A few seconds more would have closed the life of the nearest of the savages. The distance was too trifling for me to doubt the fatal effects of the discharge; for I was determined to take deadly aim, in hopes that the fall of one man might save the lives of many. But at the very moment, when my hand was on the trigger, and my eye was along the barrel, my purpose was checked by M'Leay, who called to me that another party of blacks had made their appearance upon the left bank of the river.

Turning round, I observed four men at the top of their speed. The foremost of them as soon as he got a-head of the boat, threw himself from a considerable height into the water. He struggled across the channel to the sand-bank, and in an incredibly short space of time stood in front of the savage, against whom my aim had been directed. Seizing him by the throat, he pushed him backwards, and forcing all who were in the water upon the bank, he trod its margin with a vehemence and an agitation that were exceedingly striking. At one moment pointing to the boat, at another shaking his clenched hand in the faces of the most forward, and stamping with passion on the sand; his voice, that was at first distinct and clear, was lost in hoarse murmurs. Two of the four natives remained on the left bank of the river, but the third followed his leader, (who proved to be the remarkable savage I have previously noticed) to the scene of action. The reader will imagine our feelings on this occasion: it is impossible to describe them. We were so wholly lost in interest at the scene that was passing, that the boat was allowed to drift at pleasure. For my own part I was overwhelmed with astonishment, and in truth stunned and confused; so singular, so unexpected, and so strikingly providential, had been our escape.

In 1826 at the age of 31 Captain Charles Sturt embarked in the *Mariner* with a detachment of troops in charge of convicts for New South Wales. He arrived at Sydney on 23 May 1827. To his surprise he was impressed with Sydney town, "The very triumph of human skill and industry over Nature", and cheered by the climate. "In a climate, therefore, so soft that a man scarcely requires a dwelling, and so enchanting that few have left it but with regret, the spirits must necessarily be acted upon, – and the heart feel lighter."

In Sydney Sturt was appointed Military Secretary to Governor Darling, but what he really wanted to do was lead an expedition into the unexplored interior. The recent explorations of Cunningham, Oxley, Hume and Hovell had established the existence of a number of important rivers all flowing westward. Oxley, who died in 1828, was one of those who believed that the rivers flowed into a great inland sea. In November 1827 Sturt was writing to a friend, "In February, I take an expedition into the interior to ascertain the level of the inland plains, and to determine the proposed existence of an inland sea."

Thomas Mitchell arrived in 1827 and took over control of the Surveyor-General's Department, following the death of Oxley. He wanted to lead the expedition himself and was bitterly jealous of Sturt, whom he denounced in the press as "never having travelled anywhere" and being without qualifications, "either as a scientific or practical traveller, to justify this appointment".

Nevertheless Sturt got together his party, which included Hamilton Hume as deputy leader, his old servant John Harris, two soldiers, Hopkinson and Fraser, and six convicts.

THE DEPOT GLEN *Charles Sturt*

They took with them a boat, to sail on the inland sea.

Sturt's account of his expedition opens with reference to the "Fearful drought" which was raging, and was to continue for two years. It was hoped that, by drying up the marshes, the drought would make it easier for Sturt to follow the rivers, and it would also indicate whether the supposed great lake filled up with salt water as well as fresh. Heading west beyond Bathurst, Wellington and Mount Harris the temperature rose to 129°F (53.8°C) in the shade and 141°F (60.5°C) in the sun.

The spectacle we had witnessed had been one of the most appalling kind, and sufficient to shake the firmness of most men; but at that trying moment my little band preserved their temper coolness, and if any thing could be gleaned from their countenances, it was that they had determined on an obstinate resistance.

After making separate reconnaissances, Sturt and Hume joined together, and after crossing what was later called the Bogan by Mitchell, they discovered the great river Sturt called after Governor Darling. Alas, it was salt. (Not from proximity to a salt sea, as Sturt later realised, but from salt springs in its bed.) This was a bitter disappointment, as the expedition was suffering from lack of water and the drought. As for game, it was so scarce that even the Aborigines were hunting in vain. "So long had the drought continued that the vegetable kingdom was almost annihilated, and the minor vegetation had disappeared: the largest forest trees were drooping, and many were dead." Sturt's and Hume's meetings with Aborigines were strictly non-aggressive. Sturt was determined to give no provocation, which especially meant keeping a strict control over his convicts. An early meeting between Sturt and Hume and a hunting party of Aborigines can be reduced to an image of extraordinary clarity and evocativeness; a symbolic picture of what might have happened between white and black if only all the whites had exercised the moral control of men like Sturt and Hume.

All the Aborigines disappeared except one man wearing a headdress of emu feathers. Hume also stood his ground. On seeing Sturt approaching, the Aborigine levelled his spear at Hume, who was closest to him. Hume unslung his rifle and offered it to the Aborigine, who lowered his spear. Hume then dismounted. As Sturt recorded, "He [the Aborigine] had evidently taken both man and horse for one animal . . . but when he saw him dismount . . . he stuck his spear into the ground, and walked fearlessly up to him." The centaur had become human.

Sturt's attitude to the Aborigines was as devoid of any patronising feeling of racial superiority as it was of panic or bluster, and this was to serve him in good stead on many later occasions.

After following the Darling downstream, they turned east around the edge of the Macquarie Marshes, and then carried out further exploration of the Macquarie, Castlereagh and Darling River junctions. They returned to their base camp at Wellington, reaching it on 21 April.

The discovery of the southwest-flowing Darling drew attention away from a possible inland sea (though Sturt continued to believe in it) and towards Spencer Gulf and the Gulf of St Vincent, charted by Flinders. Sturt had not found good country so far, but if the Murrumbidgee and the Darling joined, which seemed likely, there might well be rich country in the unexplored southern Australia.

Sturt's second expedition left on 3 November 1829. George Macleay, son of the Colonial Secretary, was deputy leader instead of Hume as he had to go back to his property for the harvest. As it was envisaged that the party would at some stage travel down the Murrumbidgee, Sturt took a whaleboat with the expedition. For a while they travelled through easy country, and on the Yass Plains, home now to some of Australia's finest merino studs, Sturt made an accurate prophecy: "Sheep I should imagine would thrive uncommonly well on these plains." Sturt was delighted with the Murrumbidgee, a real river with fast-flowing water. After following it by land, they stopped and the boat was assembled by the convict carpenter Clayton. ("It was impossible that I could do without Clayton," wrote Sturt.)

After difficulties with hidden logs in the river, and passing the confluence of the Lachlan, they found themselves one day "hurried into a broad and noble river". It was the river of which the Aborigines had told him, and which Sturt named in honour of Sir George Murray, Secretary of State to the Colonies. At last, Sturt considered, he was on the high road to success.

Sturt soon had his first full-scale meeting with the Murray River Aborigines. In the evening large numbers of them, painted and with shields and spears, appeared on the opposite bank to where Sturt's party was encamped. Sturt took a branch in his hand and waved to them. Some of them swam across the river, and Sturt gave them presents. Soon they were joined by others, and after a peaceful night, men, women and children accompanied Sturt down to the river.

Further down the river they made friends with several Aborigines, especially a very tall and powerfully built man, who allowed Fraser, one of the party, to shave him. Next morning, about 14 kilometres further on, they were confronted by hundreds of hostile blacks, who faced them with spears while the boat slowly ran aground on a sand bar. Thinking conflict was inevitable, Sturt brought out firearms, which he and two others were to use, while Macleay and the rest of the party were to defend the boat with bayonets. It was the most dramatic confrontation of Sturt's life, but the day was saved for him by the intervention of the very tall, powerfully built man whom Fraser had shaved the previous day. Soon friendly Aborigines were swimming around the boat "like a parcel of seals".

After a short journey the Murray was joined by a fine stream, undoubtedly the Darling. Sturt and his party rode upstream for a while, hoisted the Union Jack and gave three cheers.

After an uneventful trip downstream, the Murray ended in a large sheet of water he called Lake Alexandrina. On 12 February Sturt, Macleay and Fraser climbed the sandhills and saw the Murray mouth and the sea. Sturt considered it far too hazardous to attempt the fierce current and the double line of breakers. His supplies were running low and his crew was weak and there was no sign of, or possibility of joining, the ship which Darling was to have sent for them.

CHARLES STURT
1795-1869

Charles Sturt was born in India on 28 April 1795. He was the son of a Bengal judge and one of 13 children. Both the Sturts and the Napiers (Charles's mother's family) were old established Dorset landowners.

When he was four years old Charles was sent to England and at 15 he entered Harrow. He procured a commission in the 39th Regiment in 1813, and fought in the Peninsular War and in Canada against the Americans. After spending some years in France and Ireland on garrison duties, he arrived in New South Wales in May 1827 with a detachment of his regiment in charge of convicts.

After being appointed Military Secretary to Governor Darling, he led two expeditions (1828-29 and 1829-30) into western New South Wales, hoping to find an inland sea. Instead he discovered the Darling and, on the second expedition, the Murray. In a whaleboat, he followed the Murray down to its mouth. The party then had to row an epic 1450 kilometres back upstream, reaching the Murrumbidgee depot on 23 March 1830.

Sturt had troubles with his health, especially his eyes, probably as a result of vitamin deficiencies and the rigours of his journeys, and these culminated in blindness. He attributed the partial recovery of his sight to a course of a decoction of the leaves of sarsaparilla (*Smilax glyciphylla*), which in modern tests has been shown to have a high content of ascorbic acid. Nevertheless Sturt suffered from recurring poor eyesight for the rest of his life.

Sturt returned to England in 1830 and to some degree of esteem for his explorations. After many petitions to the Colonial Office, and the exercise of what influence his family possessed, he was promised a grant of 5000 acres in New South Wales and an army pension of £100 a year.

In 1834 he married Charlotte Green, a lady of fine character but, as he wrote to Sir Ralph Darling, with "neither youth nor beauty to recommend". He arrived with her in Sydney in 1835. His granted property of 2025 hectares was near the site of Canberra.

In 1835 he also purchased 790 hectares near Mittagong, where he lived. In 1837 he bought 405 hectares at Varroville, between Liverpool and Campbelltown.

Sturt's financial affairs did not prosper, and he sold his Mittagong property. He then joined a party overlanding stock to South Australia. In Adelaide Governor Gawler appointed him Surveyor-General in November 1838, but due to a misunderstanding, in September 1839 Lieutenant Frome arrived in Adelaide as Surveyor-General. Gawler then made Sturt Assistant Commissioner of Lands, and he worked in collaboration with Frome. Sturt did not get on with the new Governor, Grey, who arrived in 1841. He applied to lead an expedition into the interior, where he still hoped to find an inland sea.

In 1844 Sturt and his expedition left Adelaide for the unknown north, carrying a boat with them. In midsummer they were near the Grey Range, where they fortunately found a deep pool of water at Depot Glen on Preservation Creek. From 27 January to 16 July they were trapped there in terrible heat, and Sturt's second-in-command, James Poole, died of scurvy. The thermometer burst at 132°F (55.5°C) in the shade.

Heavy rain came on 12 July, four days before Poole died. Sturt made further reconnaissances north, but was driven back by the Simpson Desert. By November Sturt was suffering severely from scurvy and Browne the surgeon took charge of the party which brought Sturt back to the Murray, arriving in Adelaide on 19 January 1846.

In February 1846 Sturt was appointed Colonial Treasurer by another Governor (Robe). He was awarded the Gold Medal of the Royal Geographical Society, and went to England in 1847 where he published an account of the expedition. Returning to Adelaide in 1849, he was appointed Colonial Secretary, but his recurring blindness forced his retirement in 1851.

He returned to England in 1853 and died at Cheltenham in 1869.

Sturt was one of Australia's greatest explorers, a conservative and a gentleman, who suffered not only from ill-health but from his own lack of worldliness and financial ability. It is said that his friend George Macleay, who had been his second-in-command on the second expedition, had to pay for his funeral. Sturt was not a great writer, but his plain style, honesty and humanity are enough to carry the rich subject matter he had to convey.

There was no alternative to the terrible task of rowing about 1450 kilometres upstream to the Murrumbidgee depot. They re-entered the Murray on 13 February and arrived at the depot on 23 March, only to find it deserted. They battled on, finally taking to land, and arrived safely in Sydney on 25 May 1830.

With every pacific disposition, and an extreme reluctance to take away life, I foresaw that it would be impossible any longer to avoid an engagement, yet with such fearful numbers against us, I was doubtful of the result.

Sturt wrote in his journal, "I have the satisfaction to know, that my path among a large and savage population was a bloodless one." There was one occasion on the return journey when the record was nearly spoilt. Harris, on guard and watching two natives stealthily approaching the camp, called out:

> "The blacks are close to me, sir; shall I fire at them?"
> "How far are they?" I asked. "Within ten yards, sir."
> "Then fire," said I; and immediately he did so. M'Leay [Macleay] and I jumped up to his assistance. "Well, Harris," said I, "did you kill your man?" (he is a remarkably good shot). "No, sir," said he, "I thought you would repent it, so I fired between the two."

Sturt on these two expeditions was a great leader; even if on his third expedition and as an older and sick man, he was somewhat cantankerous. Those on his first expedition offered to go with him on the second, and the return boat journey was one of the most remarkable in the history either of boats or of exploration. He wrote good plain prose, he was an excellent observer of geographical detail as well as of flowers and fauna, and his humanity towards his own men and the Aborigines shines through all he wrote.

Edward John Eyre

JOURNALS OF EXPEDITIONS

OF DISCOVERY
INTO
CENTRAL AUSTRALIA

LONDON 1845

We were now many miles past these hills, and if we went back to examine them for water, and did not find it, we could never hope that our horses would be able to return again to search elsewhere; whilst if there was water there, and we did not return, every step we took would but carry us further from it, and lead to our certain destruction.

For a few minutes I carefully scanned the line of coast before me. In the distance beyond a projecting point of the cliffs, I fancied I discerned a low sandy shore, and my mind was made up at once, to advance in the line we were pursuing. After a little while, we again came to a well beaten native pathway, and following this along the summit of the cliffs, were brought by it, in seven miles, to the point where they receded from the sea-shore; as they inclined inland, leaving a low sandy country between them and some high bare sand-hills near the sea. The road now led us down a very rocky steep part of the cliffs, near the angle where they broke away from the beach, but upon reaching the bottom we lost it altogether on the sandy shore; following along by the water's edge, we felt cooled and refreshed by the sea air, and in one mile and a half from where

we had descended the cliffs, we reached the white sand-drifts. Upon turning into these to search for water, we were fortunate enough to strike the very place where the natives had dug little wells; and thus on the fifth day of our sufferings, we were again blessed with abundance of water, — nor could I help considering it as a special instance of the goodness of Providence, that we had passed the sandy valley in the dark, and had thereby been deterred from descending to examine the sand-hills it contained; had we done so, the extra fatigue to our horses and the great length of time it would have taken up, would probably have prevented the horses from ever reaching the water we were now at. It took us about two hours to water the animals, and get a little tea for ourselves, after which the boy laid down to sleep, and I walked round to search for grass. A little grew between the sand-drifts and the cliffs, and though dry and withered, I was most

thankful to find it. I then returned to the camp and laid down, but could not sleep, for although relieved myself, my anxiety became but the greater, for the party behind, and the more so, because at present I could do nothing to aid them; it was impossible that either the horses, or ourselves, could go back to meet them without a few hours' rest, and yet the loss of a few hours might be of the utmost consequence; I determined, however, to return and meet them as early as possible in the morning, and in the mean time, as I knew that the overseer and natives would, when they came, be greatly fatigued, and unable to dig holes to water the horses, I called up the boy, and with his assistance dug two large holes about five feet deep, from which the horses could readily and without delay be watered upon their arrival. As we had only some shells left by the natives to work with, our wells progressed slowly, and we were occupied to a late hour. In the evening we watered the horses, and before laying down ourselves, drove them to the grass I had discovered. For the first time for many nights, I enjoyed a sound and refreshing sleep.

At the end of all his Australian explorations, sailing from Adelaide to London in 1844-45 in the oddly named *Symmetry*, Edward John Eyre wrote up his *Journals of Expeditions of Discovery into Central Australia and Overland from Adelaide to King George's Sound in the Years 1840-1* (hereafter referred to as *Journals* for convenience), and the monumental "Manners and Customs of the Aborigines of Australia", the 375 pages of which were published at the end of his *Journals* in 1845. The *Journals* cover Eyre's explorations in 1840 in northern and western South Australia, and the final heroic journey around the Great Australian Bight to Albany in 1841. Eyre's journal of his early years and explorations still remains sadly unpublished in the Mitchell Library in Sydney.

The *Journals* are one of the most remarkable of Australian books, but are given added strength by the "Manners and Customs of the Aborigines of Australia", which, still neglected by scholars, was the first published comprehensive

account of the Australian Aborigine. It is more than an ethnographic work; it is a sympathetic study of an almost unknown race by one who always respected, and never injured, those people with whom he had so much contact.

When Eyre returned to Adelaide from a visit to Western Australia in 1840 he found the colonists planning an expedition to open up a stock route and new grazing country between South Australia and Western Australia. Funds had already been raised, and the idea had the approval of Governor Gawler. Ironically, in view of what later happened, Eyre persuaded the Governor and the colonists to divert the expedition into the northern regions. Charles Sturt was in sympathy with this, and Eyre was chosen to lead the expedition. In typical style, he poured most of his own money into the expedition. The outlay for the expenses was £1391 of which Eyre paid £680 15s 10d. He also provided three horses, at about £75 each.

The party consisted of a young man, E. V. Scott (his

assistant); his faithful overseer John Baxter who had been with him for many years, often in trouble for his fondness for the bottle; three white men; and two Aboriginal boys to drive the sheep, traps, etc. These were Neramberein and Cootachah, normally known as Joey and Yarry, who had been in Eyre's service, respectively, since 1837 and 1839. The expedition took thirty horses and forty sheep, and stores to last three months. The Government cutter *Waterwitch* was to be despatched to Spencer's Gulf and around the western coast with more stores, that would enable the expedition to stay out for nearly six months in all.

After the excitement of the public farewell, and the presentation to Eyre by Sturt of the flag, made by some of the ladies of Adelaide, to hoist in the centre of Australia, it was a solemn ride north. Eyre was thinking that he was now more isolated; his world now consisted only of his companions, all relying on his judgement. In front of him was the veil shrouding the mysteries of "the vast recesses of the interior of Australia".

We were fortunate enough to strike ... the very place where the natives had dug little wells; and thus on the fifth day of our sufferings, we were again blessed with abundance of water ...

Eyre led the expedition up to the Flinders Ranges and then around them to the north-west, making exhaustive reconnaissances out to Lake Torrens. Eyre looked on the glittering expanse of the salt lake with "feelings of chagrin and gloom ... the vast area of the lake was before me interminable as far as the eye could see to the northward". His only hope lay in trying to find a passage through to the north, but every time he climbed the ranges and looked out, or struck out across the plain on horseback, he found himself blocked. Reasonably enough, he assumed when he had his first view to the east of the Flinders Ranges, and saw a salt lake again, that there was one vast ocean lake going right around the Flinders Ranges which effectively blocked his journey north. He took his final view from a peak which he called Mount Hopeless.

Eyre now split his party, sending Baxter in charge of three men to Streaky Bay, and himself taking the remainder to Port Lincoln. From there he sent Scott back to Adelaide for stores and also to bring back Wylie, an Aborigine from King George's Sound whom Eyre had brought back with him from Western Australia. He intended now to strike out to the west. By 3 November, with the weather getting hot, the whole party, including Wylie, was reunited at a depot at Fowler's Bay. After three very difficult attempts, Eyre reached the head of the Bight. On his further reconnaissance he was the first white man to see from land the enormous cliffs of the Great Australian Bight. One of the wonders of the world, these abrupt limestone cliffs, 120-180 metres high and many kilometres long, fall sheer and crumbling away from the flat plain to the rollers of the Southern Ocean, and anyone looking at them will feel with Eyre, "a grandeur and sublimity in their appearance".

Eyre was never ashamed to include in his journals references to his emotions and to the deep response stirred in him by the country itself. His plain prose is thus constantly enriched by his poetic feelings.

The country he had discovered was so harsh and water was so short, that Eyre decided to take with him only Baxter and Wylie and the two other Aborigines in an attempt to reach Albany some 1450 kilometres away. With the laden packhorses, the small party left Fowler's Bay on 25 February 1841. On 12 March, after experiencing considerable privations, they reached good water at what is now Eucla, "after having passed over one hundred and thirty-five miles of desert country, without a drop of water in its whole extent, and at a season of the year most unfavourable for such an undertaking".

After Eucla the going was just as tough, and the weather began to get cold. This badly affected Eyre and Baxter as, to lighten the horses' load, they had had to throw away most of their clothing as well as other equipment. There were three sheep left, and some 64 kilograms of flour. To spare the horses, which were carrying the water, Eyre would let no one ride them, except on occasion the youngest Aboriginal boy. He wrote, "The aspect of the country before us was disheartening in the extreme."

After desperate difficulties, and "on the seventh day of our distress, and after we had travelled one hundred and sixty miles since we had left the last water", Eyre, digging for water in the sand, found abundant supplies in what is still known as Eyre's Sand-Patch. An overland telegraph station, called Eyre, was built near there in the 1870s; recently this was saved from the giant sand drifts and is now used as a bird observatory.

Eyre and Wylie Travel Along the Coast (*Picturesque Atlas of Australasia*)

EDWARD JOHN EYRE
1815-1901

Edward John Eyre was born on 5 August 1815 at Whipsnade, Bedfordshire, England, the third son of a vicar. When his father moved to Yorkshire he was educated at schools there. He had intended the Army as a career, however at his father's suggestion, aged 17 he used the purchase money for his commission to emigrate to Australia.

He arrived in Sydney on 20 March 1833, and after gaining some experience in the country he bought in July a flock of 400 sheep. In 1834 he took up about 510 hectares at Molonglo Plains near Queanbeyan, which he called Woodlands. In partnership with the Sydney merchant Robert Campbell, Eyre himself overlanded 3000 sheep from the Liverpool Plains to Woodlands. In January 1837 he raised money in Sydney to overland stock to Melbourne. On his arrival there on 2 August he sold his stock at a good profit.

Such bald accounts sound as if it were all quite easy, but it is really astonishing to think that these journeys were undertaken between the ages of 18 and 22 by a young man brought up in a Yorkshire vicarage. Eyre is often represented in illustrations as an old man with a long beard. All his travels in Australia were accomplished while he was still a young man.

The new Colony of South Australia was in urgent need of stock, and Eyre was determined to be the first to overland stock from Sydney to Adelaide. In January 1838 Eyre and a party, including his overseer Baxter who was to be his companion on all his explorations, set out with 300 cattle. He was defeated by the Wimmera scrub and lack of water in his attempts to find a direct route south of the Murray to Adelaide. He had to turn back and follow the tracks of another overlander, Hawdon, along the Murray to Adelaide.

After a short stay in Adelaide he returned to Sydney and then made a second overland trip, this time with 1000 sheep and 600 cattle. These were the first sheep to be overlanded to Adelaide. He bought half a hectare of land and built a cottage in Adelaide, but his energy and love of exploration would not allow him to stay put, and he made an exploratory expedition to the Flinders Ranges, where he first caught sight of Lake Torrens' "sterile and desolate shores".

Next he took ship to Port Lincoln, and on his twenty-fourth birthday left to cross the Peninsula which now bears his name. He was discouraged by having travelled over 965 kilometres of waterless country, except for "three solitary springs".

In 1840 he took sheep and cattle by sea to King George's Sound (Albany) and then drove them overland through to the Swan River settlement, at Perth. On his return to Adelaide he brought with him an Aborigine from King George's Sound, Wylie.

In 1840 and 1841 he led the expedition to the north and the west, the story of which makes up *Journals of Expeditions of Discovery into Central Australia and Overland from Adelaide to King George's Sound*. Back in Adelaide, he was appointed Resident Magistrate and Protector of the Aborigines at Moorundie on the Murray, for several years an area where whites had been in conflict with the Aborigines. No further attacks took place while he was there. Eyre had one of the most notable records among all Australian explorers of understanding of and success with the Aborigines.

Aged only 39, Eyre left Australia in December 1844, taking two Aboriginal boys with him to London.

In 1846 he was appointed Lieutenant-Governor of New Zealand, and in 1854 of St Vincent in the West Indies. In 1861 he became Acting-Governor of Jamaica, and in 1864 he was appointed Governor-in-Chief. On 11 November 1865 he was faced with a serious Negro riot at Morant Bay, which he interpreted, quite reasonably at the time, as a major rebellion. The excesses of the Armed Forces under martial law, and Eyre's court martial and hanging of the leader of the rebellion, G. W. Gordon, led to J. S. Mill, Thomas Huxley, Thomas Hughes and others twice bringing proceedings against him for murder. Eyre was defended by Carlyle, Charles Kingsley, Tennyson, Ruskin and others. The case of Edward John Eyre became a kind of intellectual civil war in England. The charges were dismissed.

Eyre lived in Devon in total seclusion for the rest of his long life. He died in 1901. He had been made a scapegoat for the English Victorian conscience, and he considered himself, with justification, to have been deeply wronged.

Eyre led the party on towards the west, but on 22 April Wylie and Joey deserted, taking their spears with them. Three days later they came back. Wylie apologised and asked to join the party again, while Joey sat sullenly by.

On the night of 29 April Joey and Yarry murdered Baxter and absconded with provisions and the two double-barrelled guns and ammunition.

Eyre lifted up the dead body of the faithful Baxter, who had been with him since 1834. Then:

The frightful, the appalling truth now burst upon me, that I was alone in the desert. He who had faithfully served me for many years, who had followed my fortunes in adversity and in prosperity, who had accompanied me in all my wanderings, and whose attachment to me had been his sole inducement to remain with me in this last, and to him alas, fatal journey, was now no more. For an instant, I was almost tempted to wish that it had been my own fate instead of his. The horrors of my situation glared upon me in such startling reality, as for an instant almost to paralyse the mind. At the dead hour of night, in the wildest and most inhospitable wastes of Australia, with a fierce wind raging in unison with the scene of violence before me, I was left, with a single native, whose fidelity I could not rely upon, and who for aught I knew might be in league with the other two, who perhaps were even now, lurking about with the view of taking away my life as they had done that of the overseer. Three days have passed away since we left the last water, and it was very doubtful when we might find any more. Six hundred miles of country had to be traversed, before I could hope to obtain the slightest aide or assistance of any kind, whilst I knew not that a single drop of water or an ounce of flour had been left by these murderers, the stock that had previously been so small . . .

About midnight the wind ceased, and the weather became bitterly cold and frosty. I had nothing on but a shirt and a pair of trowsers, and suffered most acutely from the cold; to mental anguish was added intense bodily pain. Suffering and distress had well nigh overwhelmed me, and life seemed hardly worth the effort necessary to prolong it. Ages can never efface the horrors of this single night, nor would the wealth of the world ever tempt me to go through similar ones again.

FIRST VIEW OF THE SALT DESERT – CALLED LAKE TORRENS *Edward Charles Frome*

Eyre and Wylie, who stayed faithful to Eyre, struggled on for over a month towards King George's Sound. At Thistle Cove (near Esperance today) they sighted a ship which turned out to be the French whaler *Mississippi*. Captain Rossiter gave them the warmest hospitality, and replenished their stores, as Eyre insisted on going on. Through heavy rains and cold they finally reached Albany on 7 July 1841.

Eyre had discovered nothing of immediate value – no rich land or flowing rivers – but for pure endurance and courage, his journey is the most heroic of all Australian explorations. It is astonishing that in the most extreme conditions, when he was close to death, Eyre still managed to write up his journal. His prose is always clear and vivid in detail, and when a great occasion presents itself, as in the murder of Baxter or the arrival at Albany and Wylie's welcome by his tribe, Eyre can always do it justice.

For a few minutes I carefully scanned the line of coast before me. In the distance beyond a projecting point of the cliffs, I fancied I discerned a low sandy shore, and my mind was made up at once, to advance in the line we were pursuing.

Eyre's "Manners and Customs of the Aborigines of Australia" was a courageous as well as informative work to have been published in 1845. He castigates the whites for their ignorance of the Aborigines and makes a most eloquent statement of the wrongs suffered by the Aborigines, whose character "has been so constantly misrepresented and traduced". He found them "frank, open and confiding".

> The more numerous the white population becomes, and the more advanced the stage of civilisation in which the settlement progresses, the greater are the hardships that fall to their [the Aborigines'] lot and the more completely are they cut off from the privileges of their birthright. All that they have is in succession taken away from them – their amusements, their enjoyments, their possessions, their freedom – and all that they receive in return is obloquy, and contempt, and degradation, and oppression . . .

> In addition to the many other inconsistencies in our conduct towards the Aborigines, not the least extraordinary is that of placing them, on the plea of protection, under the influence of our laws, and of making them British subjects. Strange anomaly, which by the former makes amenable to penalties they are ignorant of, for crimes which they do not consider as such, and which they may even have been driven to commit by our own injustice; and by the latter but mocks them with our empty sound, since the very laws under which we profess to place them, by their nature and construction are inoperative in affording redress to the injured.

Eyre had the stubbornness of the true hero. It is true that it would have been far more practical not to have attempted the journey around the Bight to Albany. It would also have been more pragmatic to have given a simple description of the manners and customs of the Aborigines and not to have spoken so eloquently in their defence. But Eyre was a true Victorian in doing his duty by his conscience, and this in turn became his destiny.

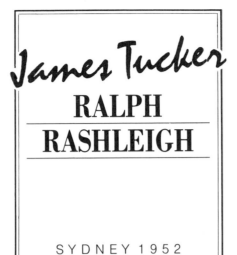

James Tucker
RALPH RASHLEIGH

SYDNEY 1952

Eighteen months had now elapsed since Ralph Rashleigh first joined the agricultural establishment at Emu Plains, during which period he had experienced full many an aching heart and full many an empty stomach. By far the greater part of that time he had neither shirt nor shoes to wear. In fact, his only garments consisted of a tattered frock of the kind just described and scarcely three parts of a pair of unmentionables, so much patched that, like the celebrated stockings of Sir John Cutler, hardly a particle of the original material remained. The nether extremities of these scanty apologies for decency looked as if his constant nightly companions, the rats—who maintained almost an equal right to his wretched bed of corn husks with himself— had nibbled them away piecemeal, until at last they had encroached upon those regions which ought to have covered the knees.

But the worst and most trying deprivation of all, to him, was the lack of shoes. For in the fields the sharply angular masses of clay, indurated almost to the hardness of flints by the arid sky, produced painful stone bruises, while on the "burning-off" ground or in the bush the frequent fires, having consumed all the inflammable portions of the grass, left nothing behind but the short stems, stiffened by flame, and as sharp as pointed stakes, which pierced, cut and tore the soles of his feet, until it was absolutely painful to him in the least degree even to stand erect upon them. If he walked at all it was necessarily at the rate of a snail's gallop, which procured for him a double portion of abuse from his overseers and the expressive but neither euphonious nor

honourable appellation of a crawler.

In the winter time, too, the torment produced by the hoar-frost, which agonised his very soul whenever his lacerated feet came in contact with it, produced many a bitter pang. But time enabled him at last to find a remedy for even these evils. He invented a sort of sandal similar to those of the Romans of old, the bottoms of which were formed of light wood, having a complicated arrangement of buckling straps to secure them. He also fabricated a kind of stockings from old woollen rags, which served the double purpose of warmth and security against thorns and briary vines which had so cruelly mangled him before. Besides, and better than all this, he was now getting so much inured to work that he no longer dreaded it, nor had his hours of rest broken by frightful dreams of cruelties perpetrated by the tyrannical overseers, as was too frequently the case at first.

In addition to all these causes of self-gratulation afforded to our exile, the drought which had so long oppressed the Colony broke up in the ensuing spring, and copious rains again blessed the earth with their fertilising effects, dressing the surrounding plains with nature's gayest livery—instead of the arid appearance they had so long presented—and affording promise of an abundant harvest to gladden the long depressed hearts of the starving settlers. Besides, Rashleigh was

now wealthy, his store having been increased by the unexpected liberality of the stranger to the sum of nearly two pounds—an amount which promised, with due economy, to afford him a moderate supply of extra food, sufficient to last him until the crops were ripe, when he hoped to earn a further supply.

Time now coursed rapidly on, until the month of November, when wheat reaping commenced. In compliance with an annual custom, instituted in order to afford the free settlers opportunities of acquiring additional labour to gather in their grain, which, in the then very limited population of New South Wales, would otherwise have been quite inaccessible, the superintendent of Emu Plains granted passes to such of the men under him as he thought deserving, each week upon Thursday evening; which documents entitled the holders thereof to be absent from camp and to work for themselves in the neighbourhood until the ensuing Sunday night—an indulgence which was so highly appreciated that all hands strained their nerves to the utmost to obtain it.

Ralph was among the fortunates, and having gotten his "pass", with a merry heart and full of joyful anticipations he hied across the river in search of work to do, being accompanied by one of his hut-mates. About ten o'clock that night they reached a part of the Nepean bank which was thickly occupied by small settlers, and where he had learned the wheat was now nearly ripe. The yellow lustre of the harvest moon illumined all the surrounding scenery with its mild radiance, and the hum of many voices told that the settlers were busy.

In the words of Colin Roderick, who discovered the identity of *Ralph Rashleigh*'s author, the convict James Tucker, *Ralph Rashleigh* "is the only novel of abiding stature to have been written by a man who during all his Australian life was never anything but a convict".

Interest in the breathless series of adventures that make up *Ralph Rashleigh* might flag if most of them were not so clearly and entertainingly authentic. The events of the book have not only, in Keats's phrase, been "proved upon the pulses", but also felt across the back in the cuts of the cat-o'-nine-tails. One wonders in *Ralph Rashleigh* that the mind can survive what the body endures.

This is a picaresque novel. One adventure follows another without Ralph's own character, after his initial falling into crime, being much affected. Unlike *For the Term of His Natural Life*, where Dawes's state of mind is always related to the conflict between fate and justice, *Ralph Rashleigh* attempts nothing more than a tale of horror and sometimes humour, in which some sort of humanity unaccountably survives. Rashleigh comes into usually violent contact with a great variety of villains, and is sustained by a few good men and women. He does not lose his basic decency, nor does he slip into self-pity. His sufferings bite like unslaked lime on a fresh-flogged back, but his hate is reserved for the system and its worst administrators. Quite unintentionally, the book is a tribute to human endurance and the human capacity for forgiveness. Rashleigh is generally unembittered at the end of the book, except for his attitude to the Aborigines, with whom he lives for some years. Although he makes friends with some of them, particularly with the women he lives with (no suspicion here of any love affair), he regards them as treacherous and less than human. At the very end of the book Tucker—for of course his attitudes are being revealed—has Rashleigh speared to death by Aborigines, "these bloodthirsty barbarians, whom the mock philanthropy of the age characterises as inoffensive and injured beings".

*E*ighteen months had now elapsed since Ralph Rashleigh first joined the agricultural establishment at Emu Plains, during which period he had experienced full many an aching heart and full many an empty stomach. By far the greater part of that time he had neither shirt nor shoes to wear.

Tucker's hatred and fear of the Aborigines are a convict's typical reactions. The woeful history of white–black relations in Australia is, at least in the earlier days, largely the history of assigned convicts maltreating the Aborigines. In *Ralph Rashleigh*, the Aborigines are always ambushing and attacking the whites in a manner that rarely applied in real life except when they had been provoked. For Rashleigh the Aborigines are just dangerous vermin to be shot. And even when he lives with them for a number of years after they have saved his life, he still regards them as treacherous and

A Chain Gang. Convicts Going to Work Near Sidney, N. S. Wales (*Narrative of a Visit to the Australian Colonies*) (*above*)

evil. This is both sad and ironic, in view of his intimate knowledge of the capacity of the white man for evil.

The style of *Ralph Rashleigh* changes as the book progresses, beginning in a sprightly, slightly ironic eighteenth-century manner that is reminiscent of Henry Fielding's *Jonathan Wild*. Later, perhaps under the weight of suffering, the irony disappears and sentiment sometimes takes over. But on the whole Tucker writes a most surprisingly clear and adequate prose, and he keeps up a pace that is essential for the chronicling of so many adventures.

The first 60 pages describe how Ralph, a well-educated son of decent London shopkeepers, gradually drifts into petty crimes during the 1820s. All the details are vivid and the slang authentic. Imprisoned in Newgate and sentenced to death, he escapes and is recaptured. He is placed in solitary confinement until the death sentence is to be carried out, but his penalty is commuted to life imprisonment. Awaiting the ship to New South Wales, Rashleigh is held in a hulk from which he escapes. He is taken and receives his first flogging, of 120 lashes. His naked back will receive over 1000.

In Sydney Rashleigh is assigned a soft job as assistant in a school, but he and some cronies are heard talking politics and Rashleigh is sent to work as an agricultural labourer at Emu Plains. From this point the book becomes a chronicle of cruelties, some of the worst of which are inflicted on the convicts by other convicts. The most hated tyrants are the convict overseers. The superintendent would select "from among the convicts under his charge the worst behaved and the most indolent of the number for his overseers and other subordinates, who, as he rightly judged, by being the most afraid of the hardships of work themselves, would exercise all manner of rigour towards their fellow-prisoners and exact as much labour as possible from each, in order to keep their places".

Apart from constant flogging, Rashleigh endures barbarities such as being thrown into solitary confinement in a kind of tiny yard in the open air with his hands handcuffed behind his back. For four days he is kept like this, having to eat his food from a dish like a dog.

"But the worst and most trying deprivation of all, to him, was the lack of shoes." In the heat his soles are cut by hot stones and pierced by the short stems of burnt-off vegetation; in the cold he suffers agonies from frost. He has no blankets or bedding.

Even so, the convicts manage to get up a theatre, under the auspices of one "Jemmy King, a most eccentric genius". Tucker himself organised such entertainments, for which he wrote the plays. Audiences ranged from the small settlers to the Chief Justice himself.

Eventually Rashleigh is assigned as a labourer to a settler, Mr Arlack. Tucker gives several entertaining descriptions of the settlers' crude houses, but the most vividly described is that of the Arlacks, whose life is almost indistinguishable from that of the animals wandering in and out of their dwelling. There are little touches from Rashleigh's educated past in his fastidious observation of it all. "The earthen floor of his *recherché* retreat was plentifully strewn with fowl's dung, *agreeably* chequered by petty lagoons of stinking water."

During an attack by bushrangers Rashleigh is captured

CONVICTS EMBARKING FOR BOTANY BAY *Thomas Rowlandson*

JAMES TUCKER
1803-1866

It is not absolutely certain that the convict James Tucker was the author of *Ralph Rashleigh*, but the evidence is sufficiently strong for it to be widely accepted. James Tucker was born at Bristol, England, in either 1803 or 1808. He was educated at the Catholic school, Stonyhurst College, from 1814. It is apparent from his books that he had a sound literary training and that he acquired a knowledge of Latin and French. However, there was little money in the family and he had to take work as a clerk; by 1826 he was unemployed, with the responsibility of supporting his mother.

He was befriended by a farmer cousin, Stanyford Tucker, near London, for whom James worked. In February 1826 there was a disagreement between the cousins and James left for London, Stanyford giving him £5 as security until he found work. Instead of being grateful, James sent Stanyford a blackmail letter alleging indecent assault and demanding another £5; he gave his name and address as Mr Rosenberg, the Bell, Exeter Street, Strand.

The result was that "James Rosenberg Tucker, 18, clerk", was charged with "feloniously, knowingly, and wilfully, sending a certain letter . . . threatening to accuse . . . James Stanyford Tucker with indecently assaulting him the said James Rosenberg Tucker, with intent to extort money from the said James Stanyford Tucker".

Tucker was sentenced to be transported for the term of his natural life. He arrived at Sydney in the *Midas* in 1827. Despite being a clerk he was sent as a field hand to the Emu Plains agricultural establishment. He was befriended by an overseer in the Roads Department, Alexander Burnett, who served as assistant surveyor with Major Mitchell on several of his exploring expeditions.

By 1835 Tucker was in Sydney, working without pay as a messenger in the Colonial Architect's office, where in 1836 he was promoted to first class messenger at 1s 9d a day. His ticket of leave was granted in 1835. He was employed as an overseer of works and favourably noticed by the Colonial Architect, Mortimer Lewis.

In 1839 Tucker lost his ticket for drunkenness and was sentenced to a fortnight on the treadmill. Back as a clerk at Hyde Park Barracks, he distinguished himself for bravery at a fire, and was granted another ticket of leave. Using this he began work at Maitland, making some unauthorised visits to Newcastle to see his friend Burnett. At Maitland, Tucker gathered the material for his stage comedy *Jemmy Green in Australia*. In 1841 he again lost his ticket and was sent as a storeman to Port Macquarie. There he organised a theatre, for which he wrote plays. He remained at Port Macquarie on another ticket of leave and wrote some picaresque stories. In 1849 he lost his ticket once more but received it back in 1850. In 1853 he went to Moreton Bay but returned to New South Wales and died in the Liverpool asylum in 1866.

At some stage Tucker gave several of his manuscripts to Alexander Burnett, who in turn gave them to his daughter Margaret. Her husband, Robert Baxter, brought the four manuscripts, all written on Government paper, to the Royal Australian Historical Society in 1920. One of the manuscripts was *Ralph Rashleigh or The Life of an Exile*, by Giacomo di Rosenberg. In 1929 a London publisher to whom it had been sent as a book of memoirs brought it out in a rewritten version with an introduction (written in considerable ignorance) by the Earl of Birkenhead.

The author's real identity was discovered, beyond reasonable doubt, by Colin Roderick, and the original manuscript was published for the first time in book form by Angus and Robertson in 1952.

---

and taken away as a kind of slave. Foxley the Murderer and his treacherous lieutenant O'Leary and the rest of the gang are some of the most appalling villains in any literature. Their cruelties and depravity are real enough, but rendered slightly more believable because their bitterness has been sharpened by the early tortures inflicted on them by cruel overseers and superintendents.

In the final shoot-out with the police Rashleigh survives, but of course the authorities do not believe his story that he has been a captive, and he is sentenced to death. On the very scaffold he is reprieved by the intercession of a woman he had helped save from Foxley.

But he might as well have died in view of what awaits him at Newcastle, where he works first in the coal mines and then in the lime kilns. The worst horrors in the book occur here, under the personal direction of the sadistic commandant, who not only ceaselessly flogs but starves his prisoners in order to break their spirits. The convicts far outnumber their keepers, but are too debilitated for mutiny.

Rashleigh and some companions escape in a canoe. Tucker never sentimentalises the convicts, presenting them as ruffians justly sentenced and not to be trusted. The injustice comes from the system that punishes them far in excess of their sentences and destroys in them any capacity for reform. Tucker's is the same message as that of Marcus Clarke in *His Natural Life*: the system is not only evil and corrupt, but monstrously wasteful.

Roberts, a former boatman who sails the canoe in which the convicts escape, is a rare example of a "good" convict, not only brave and resourceful but humane. After battles with the blacks and treachery from within, only Rashleigh and Roberts are left, and Roberts dies on the river in a flash flood.

Rashleigh is rescued by the blacks and initiated into the tribe. He wanders with them for four and a half years, until he avenges the murder of his gin, Lorra, and is forced to leave the tribe. Looking as well as acting like an Aborigine, Rashleigh wanders to the tip of Cape York, where he saves the lives of two women and a child in a wrecked ship. After many adventures they reach Sydney where the women are reunited with their father, Colonel Woodville.

Rashleigh once more dons European clothes. He throws himself on the mercy of the colonel who says, despite his anguish over his apparent ingratitude, that he must do his duty and give the runaway up. It seems that once more Rashleigh is to be sentenced to the dreadful treadmill of convict servitude. However, the colonel intercedes and Rashleigh is assigned as a servant to him. The governor promises that if he behaves himself for a year, he will be recommended for a pardon.

Rashleigh spends a few contented years managing properties on the Hawkesbury and in New England until he is murdered by Aborigines in 1844.

So many frightful things happen in *Ralph Rashleigh* that it should be a depressing tale, but it is not. Rashleigh has a kind of jauntiness of spirit, even in the worst adversity, that is reflected in the zest of Tucker's narrative. It is not the deepest, but it is the most entertaining of novels of convict life, all the more so for being written by a convict with a remarkable literary talent.

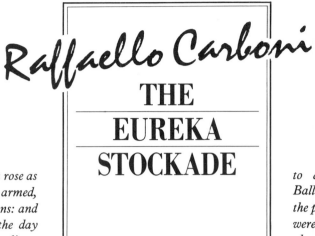

THE EUREKA STOCKADE

MELBOURNE 1855

On Friday, December 1st, the sun rose as usual. The diggers came in armed, voluntarily, and from all directions: and soon they were under drill, as the day before. So far as I know, not one digger had turned to work. It may have happened, that certain Cornishmen, well known for their peculiar propensity, of which they make a boast to themselves, to pounce within an inch of their neighbour's shaft, were not allowed to indulge in "encroaching". This, however, I assert as a matter of fact, that the Council of the Eureka Stockade never gave or hinted at any order to stop the usual work on the gold-field.

Towards ten o'clock, news reached our camp that the red coats were under arms, and there would be another licence-hunting.

The flames did not devour the Eureka Hotel with the same impetuosity as we got up our stockade. Peter Lalor gave the order: Vern had the charge, and was all there with his tremendous sword. "Wo ist der Raffaello! Du, Baricaden bauen," and all heaps of slabs, all available timber was soon higgledy-piggledy thrown all round our camp. Lalor then gave directions as to the position each division should take round the holes, and soon all was on the "qui vive."

Had Commissioner Rede dared to rehearse the farce of the riot-act cracking as on Gravel-pits, he would have met with a warm reception from the Eureka boys. It was all the go that morning.

No blue or red coat appeared. – It was past one o'clock: John Bull must have his dinner. Lalor spoke of the want of arms and ammunition; requested that every one should endeavour to procure of both as much as possible; but did certainly not counsel or even hint that stores should be pressed for it.

A German blacksmith, within the stockade was blazing, hammering and pointing pikes as fast as his thick strong arms allowed him: praising the while his past valour in the wars of Mexico, and swearing that his pikes would fix red-toads and blue pissants especially. He was making money as fast any Yankee is apt on such occasions, and it was a wonder to look at his coarse workmanship, that would hardly stick an opossum, though his pikes were meant for kangaroos and wild dogs.

Between four and five o'clock of same afternoon, we became aware of the silly blunder, which proved fatal to our cause. Some three or four hundred diggers arrived from Creswick-creek, a gold-field famous for its penny-weight fortunes — grubbed up through hard work, and squandered in dissipation among the swarm of sly-grogsellers in the district.

We learned from this Creswick legion that two demagogues had been stumping at Creswick, and called the diggers there to arms to help their brothers on Ballaarat, who were worried by scores, by the perfidious hounds of the Camp. They were assured that on Ballaarat there was plenty of arms, ammunitions, forage, and provisions, and that preparations on a grand scale were making to redress once for all the whole string of grievances. They had only to march to Ballaarat, and would find there plenty of work, honour, and glory.

I wonder how honest Mr. Black could sanction with his presence, such suicidal rant, such absurd bosh of that pair of demagogues, who hurried down these four hundred diggers from Creswick, helpless, grog-worn, that is, more or less dirty and ragged, and proved the greatest nuisance. One of them, MICHAEL TUEHY, behaved valiantly and so I shall say no more.

Of course something must be done. Thonen was the purveyor. The Eureka butcher on the hill gave plenty of meat, and plenty of bread was got from all the neighbouring stores, and paid for. A large fire was lit in the middle of the stockade, and thus some were made as comfortable as circumstances admitted; others were quartered at the tents of friends; the greater part, soon guessing how they had been humbugged, returned to their old quarters.

Arms and ammunition were our want. Men were there enough; each and all ready to fight; such was the present excitement; but blue and red coats cannot be driven off with fists alone.

It is a piece of literary good fortune that the most extraordinary conflict in Australian history should have had such an extraordinary chronicler as Raffaello Carboni. (For some reason he reversed his names on the title page of The Eureka Stockade and in later works published in Italy.)

His sprightly unconventionality is made clear on the original title page of the book, which he published himself. At the top is a Latin tag invoking the name of the Lord. Carboni was a Latin scholar who spoke at least five languages; his written English is entertainingly not quite perfect. Below the title are the enigmatic words, "The consequence of some pirates wanting on quarter-deck a rebellion". Underneath his name is the credit "By the Grace of Spy 'Goodenough,' Captain of Anarchists, but by the unanimous choice of his fellow-miners, Member of the Local Court, Ballaarat."

This appellation refers to the activities of the hated trooper Goodenough of the escort under whose protection "the traps" more and more frequently demanded to see the miners' licences. Carboni had been elected to the Local Court that adjudicated squabbles between the miners, a position of trust and responsibility not at all compatible with the label of "anarchist". There was a fascinating variety of foreigners among the English, Scots and Irish of the goldfields, of many colours and political sympathies, and Carboni was much in demand as interpreter.

Carboni's English might not have been perfect, but its effusiveness and staccato quality, its personal yet objective tone, forthrightness and erudition, exactly suit the character of the writer. He has a speaking style, and he makes the reader listen.

One fine morning (Epiphany week), I was hard at work (excuse old chum, if I said *hard*: though my hand had been scores of times compelled in London to drop the quill through sheer fatigue, yet I never before handled a pick and shovel), I hear a rattling noise among the brush. My faithful dog, Bonaparte, would not keep under my control. "What's up?" "Your licence, mate," was the peremptory question from a six-foot fellow in blue shirt, thick boots, the face of a ruffian armed with a carabine and a fixed bayonet.

Carboni enjoys his fellow diggers and Australia, but he thinks it a tough country. For a while he leaves the diggings and works as a shepherd on a run by the River Loddon, in the Western District.

One night lost the whole blessed lot of my flock. Myself, the shepherd, did not know, in the name of heavens, which way to turn . . .

He gets among a tribe of blacks, "what a rum sight for an old European traveller", and eventually finds his sheep, apart from those killed by dingoes, or wild dogs as he calls them.

Was satisfied that the Messiah the Jews are looking for will not be born in this bullock-driver's land; any how, the angels won't announce the happy event of his birth to the shepherds.

Peter Lalor

Like most of the diggers, Carboni is neither a rebel nor an anarchist, but a fierce opponent of injustice. The infamous Austrian rule in northern Italy drove him to emigrate. In the petty tyranny of the licences and the digger hunts, which are like sport to the ignorant, ex-convict troopers and traps, he sees a return of arbitrary rule and scorn for human rights. "'I came, then, 16,000 miles in vain to get away from the law of the sword!' was my sad reflection."

Carboni thinks talk of a rebel republic a farce, the program of the Reform League "worn out twaddle imported from old England" and the sentiments of the digger-orators Chartist blabber "bubbling with cant".

*O*n *Friday, December 1st, the sun rose as usual. The diggers came in armed, voluntarily, and from all directions: and soon they were under drill, as the day before. So far as I know, not one digger had turned to work.*

His friendship and loyalty are given without stint to those he thinks deserving, such as Peter Lalor. "More power to you, Peter! Old chummy, smother the knaves! they breed too fast in this colony." His descriptions of the individual diggers on the march to Eureka are vivid and full of humour, and there are other gems of character sketches, such as the German blacksmith hammering and pointing pikes before the battle of the stockade, "praising the while his past valour in the wars of Mexico, and swearing that his pikes would fix red-toads and blue pissants especially".

It is clear from Carboni's account that the aggression comes from the authorities, not the diggers, and that the huge numbers attending the public meetings are remarkably well behaved. This is all the more surprising as there are a number of hotheads in evidence. At the stockade itself, built for "defence against licence-hunting" there is also surprising moderation, especially when groups such as the 200-strong Independent Californian Rangers' Revolver Brigade arrive armed with large Colt's revolvers and with Mexican knives at the hip.

Part of the fascination of Carboni's book is that his is a far-from-simple narrative. Events seem to explode like mines around his ebullient self, so that the reader is simultaneously diverted by events and the author.

As the diggers' armed forces gather at the stockade, Lalor appoints Carboni to the inner committee in charge of all the foreigners; with his linguistic ability he can cope with them all. Tension grows with reports that large reinforcements of soldiers are on the way to crush the diggers.

Carboni worships Lalor and respects most members of the inner committee, but his fastidious and honourable nature is revolted by the riffraff who have joined the diggers more in hope of plunder than anything else. Going down to meet an "old mate" at the Prince Albert Hotel, Carboni meets a bunch of ten ex-convicts from Van Diemens Land, "armed to the teeth with revolvers, swords, pikes, and knives". Their idea of helping the diggers' cause is to demand free grog from the publican, Carl Wiesenhavern, "a man of noble character". Some of the best writing in *The Eureka Stockade* describes this incident and how the publican and his partner quietened the men.

THE EUREKA STOCKADE RIOT, BALLARAT   *J. B. Henderson*

RAFFAELLO CARBONI
1820-1875

Raffaello Carboni, or Carboni Raffaello as he called himself on the title pages of his books, was a fighter for Italian liberty (wounded in Garibaldi's campaign of 1849), a linguist proficient in five languages, an author of plays and a composer. Of all the men of Eureka, he was the most original, and his book *The Eureka Stockade*, published by himself and sold by "the fiery, lachrymose, faithful Raffaello" and his friends, is certainly one of the oddest and most appealing volumes in Australian literary history.

Carboni was born on 24 June 1820 at Urbino, Italy, and educated at the University of Urbino and the seminary of Santa Trinità in Rome. He always liked to refer to himself as a Roman. In 1840 he was imprisoned for suspected republican sympathies, and after his release he joined the Young Italy movement. Wounds in the leg received in Garibaldi's Roman campaign of 1849 troubled him for the rest of his life.

He wandered round Europe for three years improving his languages, then sailed for Australia in 1852 to look for gold. He began successfully, but was robbed and in 1853 became a shepherd.

He was not successful as a shepherd, and for a while he lived with an Aboriginal tribe.

He returned to the diggings at Ballarat and contributed his enthusiasm and his knowledge of languages to the cause of the diggers against the wrongs of the licensing system. Although he was not in the stockade at the time of the battle on 3 December 1854, he was arrested and was one of the 13 tried for high treason in February 1855 and acquitted.

In July 1855 Carboni was elected to the new Local Court at Ballarat. He wrote and published *The Eureka Stockade* in 1855 before sailing for the Northern Hemisphere in January 1856. For three years he travelled in the Middle East and Europe, returning to Italy where in 1860 he worked as a government translator and interpreter.

When Italy was unified after the idealistic struggles of the Risorgimento, so suited to Carboni's temperament, he settled in Naples for reasons of health. There he wrote and published a number of books, including plays and operas, with his own music.

Journalist and historian W. B. Withers of Ballarat described Carboni as "a shrewd, restless little man . . . under the middle height, with reddish hair and red beard cut short, and small hazel eyes that had a fiery twinkle beneath a broad forehead and rather shaggy eyebrows".

He died in Rome in 1875, and was described on his death certificate as "an unmarried man of letters".

Disgusted by other similar happenings, Carboni hurries back to the stockade to warn Lalor that their cause is being compromised by such scoundrels. It is nearly midnight on Saturday and Lalor is asleep. Tired out himself, Carboni retires to his tent outside the stockade.

Arms and ammunition were our want. Men were there enough; each and all ready to fight; such was the present excitement; but blue and red coats cannot be driven off with fists alone.

On the morning of the Sabbath, 3 December, he is woken by a discharge of musketry and shots whizzing by his tent. (It is established afterwards that 288 police and soldiers attacked the stockade in which on that Sunday morning there were slightly fewer than 150 diggers.) Carboni watches the progress of the battle from outside his tent. It is over in a few minutes. Lalor and other leaders are shot (but Lalor survives). In all, twenty-two diggers are killed and a dozen seriously wounded.

Carboni is arrested and then released. He goes into the stockade and helps the doctors and Father Smyth attend to the wounded and dying. Between eight and nine that night, "Spy" Goodenough rushes into the stockade, "panting, a cocked pistol in his hand, looking as wild as a raven, . . . pounced on me . . . and said in his rage, 'I want you.'"

Carboni is shackled to other prisoners, thrown into the lockup in appallingly overcrowded conditions, and left to languish. After four terrible months in gaol, he and twelve others are tried for treason in Melbourne before Judge Barry. All the prisoners are acquitted.

Carboni's natural optimism and hopes for humanity are sadly injured by the events of Eureka.

They were happy days in my youth, when I thought with Rousseau, that the heart of man is from nature good. It was a sad fatality now that compelled me to feel the truth from the prophet Isaiah, that the heart of man is desperately wicked.

The diggers on trial might have been acquitted, but the spirit of Eureka was broken. Nothing came of the day when, in Carboni's most moving description, some 500 diggers knelt under that "exclusively chaste and natural" Eureka flag, and said "Amen" to Lalor's words: "We swear by the Southern Cross to stand truly by each other, and fight to defend our rights and liberties."

THE LETTERS OF RACHEL HENNING

SYDNEY 1963

A few evenings ago I came nearer to a snake than I ever was before or ever wish to be again. I was walking by the creek, accompanied by my usual "tail" of two pet lambs, a tame emu and a bulldog, and one would have thought that all these creatures would have made disturbance enough to drive away any amount of snakes. The grass was rather long, and I noticed the lambs, which were trotting on in front, give a violent start, and, while looking at them, I all but trod on a large yellow snake that was literally under my feet. I only avoided him by giving a great spring to the right. He was coiled in the path so that I could not jump over him as people generally do. He slipped off into some hole, and I looked very carefully in the grass during the remainder of my walk, I assure you. Annie was not there. She never walks further than to the kitchen garden to cut vegetables for dinner.

It is getting hot now. Some days it has been very hot, but we get such frequent thunderstorms this year that the whole country is greener than an English spring. You should see the way convolvulus grows here this year. It climbs to the top of the veranda, and the beautiful pink, white and blue blossoms look so very pretty mixed with the passion-vines. But most of the flowers are over now for the summer. We shall have fresh blooms in autumn.

DECEMBER 2ND

I must finish my letter today, as there is a chance of sending to the Port. I wrote to Aunt Vizard and Sophy and sent their letters two or three days ago, but yours was not then finished. We hoped to have had your letters to answer. We heard from a Mr Grimaldi, who arrived yesterday afternoon, that a certain Mr Martin was bringing up the letters from the Port and would be here in the course of the evening. Later Beckford came in from the Nine Mile, and said that Mr Martin had been seen by the shepherds to pass both the Nine Mile and Two Mile sheep stations and ought to have been here before him [Beckford].

However, he never came last night nor this morning. It was a pitch-dark night and raining hard, and he must have got off the road between the Two Mile and this. We fired several guns last night and again this morning to guide him, if within hearing, and now the blackboy is gone out to try and track him, but it is almost hopeless to track, for the deluge of rain must have washed out every mark. He was an old bushman, however, and not likely to be lost so near the station, and in broad daylight. We think he may have camped out in the wet last night, and this morning struck the road somewhere past Exmoor and then gone to Mr Lack's, the next station—taking our letters with him.

Biddulph is rather disgusted at the wet weather we are having; thunderstorms every day, so that just as the sheep get dry enough to shear they get another soaking. It is a week since a whole day's shearing was done. This will delay our visit to Sydney till February, probably. If it was not for being out of everything in the garment line, I do not care about going at all this year.

Ever, my dearest sister, yours most affectionately,

RACHEL HENNING

The letters collected in this volume contain such strong threads of narrative, family life and revelation of character that they make excellent reading as a whole book, and, covering the period 1853-82, are as gripping as a good historical novel.

Rachel had three younger sisters, Henrietta ('Etta'), Annie and Amy, and a younger brother, Biddulph.

Biddulph and Annie arrived in Australia from England in 1853; he was 19 and she 23. Biddulph had an amazing capacity to settle into wild Australia and understand what Rachel calls "the mysteries of cows and sheep". In rapid succession Biddulph leased a farm near Appin, NSW, bought 73 hectares at Bulli Mountain, sold them and in November 1858 bought Marlborough Station, about 26,000 hectares, near Rockhampton, Queensland, for £900. In 1862 he moved further out to Exmoor Station, on the Bowen River near Port Denison.

Rachel's first letters are from Cheshire and Devon to "Dearest Annie and Biddulph" in Australia. They establish her as a sharp-eyed, well-read woman of 27, whose "principal employments" are "writing letters to a considerable extent, doing wool-work and reading Scott's Life". Etta marries the Reverend Boyce, and Rachel goes to Sussex to stay with them, writing to Biddulph and Annie to say that if they settle in Australia she will go out and join them, as "I would rather be anywhere with you than in the most beautiful place without you."

However, it does not work out quite so simply. The long posts go by—it takes six months or more to get an answer to a letter—until August 1854 when Rachel, with her sister Amy and cousin Tregenna Biddulph, leave England in the Calcutta for Australia. Established in Biddulph's cottage at Appin, her "principal employments" are drawing, mending stockings, reading aloud and walking in the bush. Rachel does not care for cooking, and is happy to leave it to Amy. But, alas, she finds, "I dislike this bush life extremely and find it sometimes difficult to amuse myself."

Rachel's homesickness is severe. "All parts of Australia are alike." "The soil is wretchedly poor." Australian wildflowers are of no interest to her, while "at Home every wildflower served like a friend to me". She longs to be in England again. When Mr Boyce sends her her fare, she is strongly tempted to leave, but not before Amy's wedding to Thomas Sloman. She goes to Sydney while Biddulph is building his house on that "accursed mountain", Bulli, and then has a most uncomfortable trip to Bathurst to see Amy. A young digger who helps her and her goods in and out of the coach is "not quite a gentleman, nor yet a common man". The two other women passengers, a shopkeeper and a domestic servant, are referred to as "ladies". In the Blue Mountains she has to admit that the scenery is very fine "for Australia". Bathurst and the plains are hot, dusty and awful.

Rachel at this time was the original "whingeing Pom", and Australia was well rid of her when she returned to England in 1856. It is not clear why, after five years at home, she decided to return to Australia, and sailed on the *Great Britain* in February 1861. Was she missing Biddulph? Was she bored with her life as a spinster in England? She does not say. However, in her letter of 19 May 1861, to Etta from Bathurst, she says, "I mean to be very happy at Bathurst this time, so don't think of me as otherwise."

*Y*ou should see the way convolvulus grows here this year. It climbs to the top of the veranda, and the beautiful pink, white and blue blossoms look so very pretty mixed with the passion-vines. But most of the flowers are over now for the summer. We shall have fresh blooms in autumn.

With that effort of will everything changed. She wrote of the Blue Mountains, "I wish I could give you the least idea of the beauty of the scenery here." Cobb & Co.'s coach is fine, and the driver "capital". She is the least tired of all the travellers. Servants, of course, are atrocious and the wages sky-high. "12s. a week and everything found." The Chinese are dreadful rascals but they didn't deserve to be massacred at Lambing Flat. It is good that the English cricketers have had a resounding victory, which "ought to take down the colonial 'bounce' a little". On the other hand, Sydney has

Exmoor Station, Queensland *Attributed to Rachel Henning* (above)

a very good opera company, better than in any provincial town in England.

She is quite happy to be travelling 1125 kilometres into the unknown to Exmoor, Biddulph's new station, for which they set out from Rockhampton on 24 August 1862. She loves her first night in the bush around the fire, listening to the horse-bells, with her and Annie very comfortable on "a sort of sofa made of a railway rug and the packs off the horses to lean against", with Biddulph reading the *Home News*, Mr Hedgeland making a damper and Mr Stewart boiling some more tea. And she adds, "We have 7 revolvers among the party, for which there is not likely to be any need."

Their dogcart is the first vehicle ever to penetrate this country. Fortunately Biddulph is a capital driver, but the springcart is smashed in one bad creek crossing. But life there is all enjoyable. And "Living in the open air and riding 25 miles a day is a great promoter of sleep."

She finds the Exmoor country very pretty, with fine natural boundaries of mountains on each side. The house and furniture are rough, but surprisingly good. Rachel writes to Etta, "fancy a long low building, built of dark-coloured slabs of wood with a veranda in front, and the doors and windows opening onto it. It contains 5 rooms." The kitchen, as usual with station homesteads, is in a separate hut.

The inmates consist of Rachel, Biddulph and Annie; Mr Hedgeland, a friend of Biddulph's who has been with him a long time, "Biddulph's right hand"; Mr Devlin, the Superintendent; Mr Taylor, the sheep overseer; and three other men. Usually most of the men are out riding around the property and seeing to the sheep. "Mr Hedgeland and Annie are great friends and may perhaps be more." Mr Taylor is English, a clergyman's son, well-educated, rather shy, "but with a good deal of fun in him".

The months that follow at Exmoor demonstrate the extraordinary capacity of young British men and women to adapt themselves to Australian conditions when their hearts are in it. On arrival at Exmoor Biddulph was still only 28 but he was already expert at coping, not only with the country and the stock, but with the men who worked for him.

It is fascinating to watch the transformation in Rachel from the discontented young woman of eight years before. She now loves the wildflowers, "so very handsome", "such beautiful flowers", and arranges a vase of them in the house every morning. Life in the bush flies by, "an easy, free sort of life". She rejoices in boiling the quart-pot by the Bowen river, and in riding. She has a number of pets, who make up what she calls her "tail" when she goes for a walk. They include two pet lambs, a tame emu and a bulldog. In short, she says, "I do greatly enjoy the lovely climate, good health and free outdoor life that we have here." She knows she would miss the bush if she was in Sydney. "I know I shall often wish I was feeding the lambs in the beautiful bush when I am grinding about the streets of Sydney shopping."

There are encounters with "wild blacks", but they are peaceful enough. It is interesting to note that any violence against the Aborigines comes from the station blacks, Alick and Billy, and not from the whites. When a shepherd's hut is robbed, Biddulph and Alick and Billy track the Aborigines to their camp, which they burn, and they take away all their weapons, "but Biddulph would not allow the boys to shoot them as they were very anxious to do".

THE DWELLING AT MOUNT KEIRA *Attributed to Rachel Henning*

RACHEL HENNING
1826-1914

Rachel Henning was the oldest of a family of four sisters and one brother. She was born at Bristol, England, in 1826. Her father was a clergyman, the Reverend Charles Henning, chaplain to the Duke of Cambridge, and her mother Rachel's family (Biddulph) belonged to the landed gentry. Her father died in 1840 and her mother in 1845. So at the age of 19 she assumed the responsibility of bringing up her younger sisters, Henrietta, Annie and Amy, and her brother Biddulph. As happened so often in the nineteenth century, the delicate boy (Biddulph had had a severe attack of scarlet fever, a disease which killed another brother and sister) was sent to Australia for his health and became a robust pioneer. Biddulph sailed for Sydney in 1853 with Annie in the *Great Britain*, and a year later Rachel and Amy followed in the *Calcutta*.

The story of her Australian life is told in her letters, written between 1853 and 1882, which were not intended for publication. They were mostly written to her sisters Etta and Amy and chronicled her life on Biddulph's stations in Queensland.

In March 1866 she married Deighton Taylor, 10 years younger than herself, who had for several years been Biddulph's overseer.

They lived at four places in the country in New South Wales until 1896 when they moved to Ryde. Rachel was not happy at moving to the city, but it had become necessary because of her husband's chronic asthma. Taylor died in 1900.

Biddulph had by this time prospered, and was living in a fine house called Euthella at Hunters Hill, where his wife died in 1902. He then bought an even more splendid house, Passy, also in Hunters Hill, and his two sisters moved there with him. There was a circular pattern to Rachel's life: the 19-year-old orphaned girl who had looked after her young sisters and brother became the widow in her seventies and eighties living with her brother and one sister again, albeit in considerably more comfort and style. The difference, of course, was that there were children. Biddulph had three, and Annie one; Rachel's nieces and nephews were somewhat scared of the old lady's wit and sharp turn of phrase. But she was a person of immense character, fond of poetry, with a great love of flowers (she made gardens at all the places where she lived) and animals. In her will she left legacies to the Animal Protection Society and the King Edward Home for Dogs.

Rachel died in 1914. The once-delicate Biddulph lived to be 94, dying in 1928. Amy died in 1891, Annie between Rachel and Biddulph, and Etta, in England, in 1919.

The letters of Rachel Henning were first published in the *Bulletin* in 1951 and 1952. They were edited by David Adams for publication in book form in 1952, with illustrations by Norman Lindsay.

Although there are occasions when the men are injured, everyone stays amazingly healthy, although in the Wet others on the low-lying stations tend to get ill. Rachel writes, "our treatment is of a highly experimental character. Mr Hedgeland swears by blue pills. Annie believes in castor oil. I generally consider that laudanum will be soothing, and Biddulph recommends quinine as strengthening. Nobody has been poisoned yet."

*B*iddulph *is rather disgusted at the wet weather we are having; thunderstorms every day, so that just as the sheep get dry enough to shear they get another soaking. It is a week since a whole day's shearing was done.*

After nearly three years at Exmoor Rachel writes to Etta with news that "will, I fear, seriously disarrange your hair if you have not a very tight elastic to your net". She is engaged! In fact she has been engaged, more or less, for the last six months to Mr Taylor, the sheep overseer. He has recently been rewarded by Biddulph with a very nice horse and saddle for getting the sheep out to Lara, another station further out that Biddulph has bought. Biddulph does not like Mr Taylor as a husband for Rachel, because he is merely an overseer, but Rachel blithely comments that "everybody cannot have stations". Mr Taylor has a good intellect, is a musician, a scientist and an astronomer, and he is kind, but "he is, unfortunately, a boy of little over 30, and I—well, the less said the better." (Actually she is 39, although in her letter of 24 June 1865, following her engagement, she says she is 37.)

Biddulph decides to sell Exmoor and move out to Lara, but in the end he sells Lara and keeps Exmoor. There are 320 square kilometres at Exmoor, and Biddulph has been asking £20,000 for it. Later he moves down to Sydney where in 1872 he marries Emily Tucker, daughter of a prominent business man. Eventually he becomes manager of Tucker & Co.

Rachel moves to Sydney in 1865, and on 3 March 1866 marries Deighton Taylor, a little over a month after Annie has married George Hedgeland. Rachel and Deighton move to Bulahdelah on the Myall River in the Hunter River district, where Deighton manages a logging business. Later they strike off on their own, buying a property called "The Peach Trees" of 60 hectares about 13 kilometres from Stroud. Later they move to a property a few kilometres beyond Wollongong. Her letters from this period are as vivid as those from Exmoor, though her life, as she says, has "none of the adventure and newness of station life".

The letters end in 1882 when she is 56, but she lived on until 1914, dying at 88 at Passy, a grand house at Hunters Hill, where as a widow she had been living with Annie, also widowed, and with Biddulph. When Biddulph died in 1928 at the age of 94, his life in Australia had spanned more than half of the country's history.

Rachel's letters are fresh with the youth of Australia last century, with its optimism and courage. They are also a notable document of the human will—once she had decided to make a success of her life in Australia, she did. She seldom talked about herself, and apologised when she did. She was conservative in politics and remained a bit of a snob. But she never lost her intellectual curiosity and her ability to enjoy life from day to day.

Marcus Clarke

FOR THE TERM OF HIS NATURAL LIFE

LONDON 1885

Three wooden staves, seven feet high, were fastened together in the form of a triangle. The structure looked not unlike that made by gipsies to boil their kettles. To this structure Kirkland was bound. His feet were fastened with thongs to the base of the triangle; his wrists, bound above his head, at the apex. His body was then extended to its fullest length, and his white back shone in the sunlight. During his tying up he had said nothing—only when Troke roughly pulled off his shirt he shivered.

"Now, prisoner," said Troke to Dawes, "do your duty."

Rufus Dawes looked from the three stern faces to Kirkland's white back, and his face grew purple. In all his experience he had never been asked to flog before. He had been flogged often enough.

"You don't want me to flog him, sir?" he said to the Commandant.

"Pick up the cat, sir!" said Burgess, astonished; "what is the meaning of this?"

Rufus Dawes picked up the heavy cat, and drew its knotted lashes between his fingers.

"Go on, Dawes," whispered Kirkland,

without turning his head. "You are no more than another man."

"What does he say?" asked Burgess.

"Telling him to cut light, sir," said Troke, eagerly lying; "they all do it."

"Cut light, eh! We'll see about that. Get on, my man, and look sharp, or I'll tie you up and give you fifty for yourself, as sure as God made little apples."

"Go on, Dawes," whispered Kirkland again, "I don't mind."

Rufus Dawes lifted the cat, swung it round his head, and brought its knotted cords down upon the white back.

"Wonn!" cried Troke.

The white back was instantly striped with six crimson bars. Kirkland stifled a cry. It seemed to him that he had been cut in half.

"Now, then, you scoundrel!" roared Burgess; "separate your cats! What do you mean by flogging a man that fashion?"

Rufus Dawes drew his crooked fingers through the entangled cords, and struck again. This time the blow was more effective, and the blood beaded on the skin.

The boy did not cry; but Macklewain saw his hands clutch the staves tightly, and the muscles of his naked arms quiver.

"Tew!"

"That's better," said Burgess.

The third blow sounded as though it had been struck upon a piece of raw beef, and the crimson turned purple.

"My God!" said Kirkland, faintly, and bit his lips.

The flogging proceeded in silence for ten strokes, and then Kirkland gave a screech like a wounded horse.

"Oh! . . . Captain Burgess! . . . Dawes! . . . Mr. Troke! . . . Oh, my God! . . . Oh! oh! . . . Mercy! . . . Oh, Doctor! . . . Mr. North! . . . Oh! Oh! Oh!"

"Ten!" cried Troke, impassibly counting to the end of the first twenty.

The lad's back, swollen into a hump, now presented the appearance of a ripe peach which a wilful child has scored with a pin.

Marcus Clarke's great novel was called *His Natural Life* in its original serialised publication. What an ironic title! Nothing could be more unnatural than the appalling lives of the convicts and their gaolers in this book. And there is a further irony provided by the physical presence of Australia, a natural prison from which it is almost impossible to escape, or even to survive in. A final thread of irony is that the hero, Richard Devine, alias the convict, Rufus Dawes, is a bastard, what was called a "natural son".

In his dedication to Sir Charles Gavan Duffy, Marcus Clarke says that he has "attempted to depict the dismal condition of a felon during his term of transportation", something he believed no writer had done before. (He could not know, of course, about *Ralph Rashleigh*, written in the 1840s but not published until 1929.)

The novel opens in England in 1827, with Richard Devine at liberty, but about to become the innocent victim of other people's misdemeanours and crimes. The 22-year-old Richard, just returned from travels abroad, is confronted by his father, millionaire shipbuilder Sir Richard Devine.

Sir Richard has learned that his wife was at one time the mistress of Lord Bellasis, and that Richard is in fact Bellasis' child. Only if Richard, his mother's only son, leaves the house and renounces his name forever, will Sir Richard refrain from making his wife's shame public. Moreover, Sir Richard will alter his will and leave his fortune to Richard's cousin, Maurice Frere. Richard, who detests Sir Richard Devine, accepts the terms. All this happens on the evening of 3 May 1827.

On that same evening Lady Devine's former lover, Lord Bellasis, walking towards Hampstead Heath, is set upon, murdered and robbed. Richard discovers the body and, having just seen the distraught Sir Richard returning home from the village, believes Sir Richard to be the murderer. However, Richard is apprehended as the murderer and robber. He cannot reveal his true identity and establish his innocence without exposing his mother. He gives his name as Rufus Dawes, and under this name is arrested. Sir Richard dies of apoplexy.

Dawes is sentenced to death, the sentence later being

commuted to transportation for life. Thus the whole story of horror and depravity that follows hangs on a point of honour, a son's refusal to betray his mother's secret. Dawes is not only innocent, but a sort of knight-errant carrying the banner of a woman's honour. Woman, virtuous and innocent or sexual and scheming, has an extraordinarily powerful part to play in *His Natural Life*. Lady Devine is a victim of passion who has atoned by a life of virtue.

The other two women in the book, the extremes of fair and dark, are introduced on the prison ship *Malabar* which is taking Rufus Dawes to Van Diemens Land. One is a child of six, Sylvia, the fair-haired daughter of Captain Vickers, ordered for service as Commandant in Van Diemens Land. The other is a black-haired sensual girl of 19, Mrs Vickers' maid, Sarah Purfoy. It soon becomes obvious that she is no ordinary lady's maid. In fact, she is secretly married to John Rex, one of the convicts.

Also on the ship, under Captain Vickers, is Lieutenant Maurice Frere, Dawes's cousin, though neither recognises the other.

Sarah's sexual presence, heightened by the admiration of the caged convicts, is so strong that both the ship's commander, Captain Blunt, and Maurice Frere are in love with her, not to mention the common soldier Miles, the sentry at the convict gangway, through whom she is able to obtain access to her convict husband in secret.

In the course of the voyage, the *Malabar* comes upon the blazing wreck of a ship, the *Hydaspes*. This is the very ship on which the young Richard Devine has allegedly set sail for Calcutta, to disappear from his mother's life. As Dawes watches the *Hydaspes* blow up and sink, he sees his former identity disappear forever.

Fever breaks out on the ship and there is also a convict mutiny, which the authorities are never to realise was organised by Sarah Purfoy. The attempt to seize the ship fails, and Gabbett and the other conspirators tell the authorities that Rufus Dawes planned the mutiny. Rex, the ringleader, is not caught.

On arrival at Hobart Town the mutineers are sentenced to death, but the sentence is commuted to six years at the penal settlement at Macquarie Harbour, of which Vickers is the Commandant. John Rex is also sent to Macquarie Harbour, having failed in an escape attempt when he was at partial liberty working as an assigned servant to Sarah Purfoy. She now has a house in New Town, having come into some money.

Six years pass, and Governor Arthur decides to break up the penal settlement at Macquarie Harbour. Two ships, the *Osprey* and the *Ladybird*, are to transport the party from Port Macquarie to the new penal settlement at Port Arthur. Captain Vickers is to take the *Ladybird*, and Frere is to follow with Mrs Vickers and Sarah in the *Osprey*. Before the ships sail, Dawes throws himself into the sea, hoping to end his sufferings, but he lives and is carried away by the current.

With John Rex as leader, the convicts seize the *Osprey*. Frere, Mrs Vickers and Sylvia, the wounded pilot Bates, and a soldier, Grimes, also wounded, are put ashore with some provisions. Both Bates and Grimes die, and Frere, Mrs Vickers and Sylvia are left alone in the wilderness. There on the beach Rufus Dawes, having wandered for weeks in the bush and now almost dead of hunger, finds them.

When Dawes recovers from his privations there is a strange reversal of roles. The prisoner is the one who knows how to find food, how to build a shelter and make the coracle of goat skins in which the party eventually makes its escape. "Rufus Dawes was no longer the brutalized wretch who had plunged into the dark waters of the bay to escape a life he loathed, and had alternatively cursed and wept in the solitude of the forest. He was an active member of society—a society of four—and he began to regain an air of independence and authority. The change had been wrought by the influence of little Sylvia." Clarke's basic criticism of the system of transportation is quite clear.

*R*ufus Dawes looked from the three stern faces to Kirkland's white back, and his face grew purple. In all his experience he had never been asked to flog before. He had been flogged often enough.

Dawes also learns, through talking to Frere, that Sir Richard Devine died before he could alter his will. Dawes is still the heir, and Frere has not received a penny. As Richard Devine he could be a rich man, but his identity as Richard Devine has been completely destroyed.

After tremendous difficulties and thanks entirely to Dawes's skills, the little party is rescued. Frere takes the credit, and denounces Dawes as an escaped convict who forced himself on the party.

Five years go by, and in the meantime the mutineers in the *Osprey* have got safely away to China and eventually London, where they are recognised. Two are executed, but Rex and three others are sent to Hobart Town for trial. Sarah Purfoy, as Frere's former mistress, threatens to blackmail Frere in order to try to save Rex's life. Frere agrees to speak up for Rex at the trial, and vouch for his kindness in giving provisions (which were very short) to the marooned party.

The trial, in which Dawes is called as a witness, is the crux of the book. Mrs Vickers has died of the hardships she has suffered, but Dawes firmly believes that his beloved Sylvia, who has married Frere, will tell the court of how he saved the lives of the stranded party. "The notorious criminal Rufus Dawes" is a potential hero in the witness box; despite all he has suffered, he is in magnificent physical condition, in the prime of life, with a natural elegance of attitude, and fierce, black eyes. But Sylvia has lost her memory and no one will believe the convict's version of the story against that of Frere. It is not only Dawes's hope of a reprieve that collapses; the sustaining vision of Sylvia, of merciful innocence, is also removed from him.

In a stupendous second effort to make contact with Sylvia, Dawes escapes from Port Arthur and waits in her garden to talk to her. But when he says his name to her, instead of a grateful smile of recognition of "Good Mr Dawes", Sylvia calls in terror to her husband for help and Dawes is apprehended.

The most terrible part of the book now follows, with Dawes incarcerated at Norfolk Island. He is befriended by the drunken parson James North, who in his diary describes Dawes as a "beetle-browed, sullen, slouching ruffian", with

THE FLOGGING OF CHARLES MAHER *From notebook of Robert Jones*

MARCUS CLARKE
1846-1881

Marcus Clarke, far and away the greatest of nineteenth-century Australian writers, led an irregular and often unhappy life and died, desperately short of money, in 1881, aged only 35. Perhaps only a doomed and harrowed man could have written *For the Term of His Natural Life*, a book of such melancholy grandeur. Yet Clarke could also be as witty a writer as his friends found him as a man.

Marcus Andrew Hyslop Clarke, the son of a successful if rather odd barrister, was born at Kensington, London, in 1846. His mother died of tuberculosis when he was three; he was an only child. Young Marcus was well educated and had a particularly good knowledge of French literature and spoke excellent French.

His father's health deteriorated and he eventually became insane; when he died it was found that his financial affairs were in total collapse. Instead of the expected large inheritance, Clarke was left with almost nothing. He had distinguished relatives in Australia, so he decided to try his luck in the colonies. He arrived in Melbourne on 7 June 1863.

After a not very successful year working in a bank, he took a job as a station hand—(he described himself as a "pupil")—in the Wimmera, in the west of Victoria. He spent much of his spare time reading and writing, and in 1866 four of his stories appeared in the *Australian Monthly Magazine*. Some of his early essays on Balzac and Doré appeared in the *Australasian*, the weekend magazine published by the *Argus*, on which newspaper he was given a job in 1867 as theatre critic. Later Clarke wrote some fine articles on aspects of Melbourne life, high and low, under the pseudonym of "The Peripatetic Philosopher", and a selection appeared under that title in 1869 as Clarke's first book. He continued to write, often for and about the theatre, and edited and published several magazines.

In 1870 Clarke went to Tasmania to research a series of articles on the convict system, abolished two decades before. What he learned there profoundly moved him, and his avowed purpose in *His Natural Life* was to expose the evils of the system. Many of the episodes of *His Natural Life* are based on fact. Of recent years it has been fashionable to say Clarke misrepresented the system, and that Port Arthur, for instance, was by nineteenth-century standards a modern and relatively humane institution. This may be argued, but it does not impugn the artistic truth of what Clarke wrote, nor the fact that the convict system was evil, both for convicts and gaolers.

His Natural Life first appeared as a serial in the *Australian Journal* in 1870-72. A revised and shortened version was prepared by Clarke for book publication in Melbourne in 1874 and London in 1875. The 1884 edition, retitled *For the Term of His Natural Life*, is the basis for most modern editions.

Clarke's patron in later years was Sir Redmond Barry, the judge, who was also the prime founder of the University of Melbourne and the Melbourne Public Library. Through his influence Clarke was appointed a clerk in the Library in 1870; in 1877 he was promoted to sub-librarian. He died bankrupt on 2 August 1881, leaving a wife and six children.

Clarke was a most gifted all-round writer, whose stories, essays and investigative journalism are still highly readable, although understandably completely overshadowed by the giant presence of *For the Term of His Natural Life*.

---

grey hair and a dejected carriage. He is far removed from the superb creature who appeared in the witness box in Hobart. All hope has left him, and his dehumanisation is symbolised by the frightful scene in which he is made to flog a young man who dies under the cat-o'-nine-tails.

Meanwhile Rex, with the connivance of the ingenious Sarah, has escaped again. In one of the most dramatic episodes in all fiction, Rex's life is saved by his being caught in a giant blowhole in the cliff, where a wave washes him to safety in a cave. Later, in England, taking advantage of his remarkable physical resemblance to the young Richard Devine, Rex passes himself off as the lost heir, Richard Devine, and claims the fortune.

It is now almost 20 years since the prison ship *Malabar* brought Rufus Dawes to Van Diemens Land. Frere is now the Commandant at Norfolk Island, and Sylvia is more and more unhappy in her life there. She rescues Dawes from one of her husband's tortures, but still does not recognise him as her childhood saviour. Eventually she prevails upon her husband to allow her to leave the island for a visit to her father, and it is arranged that she and the Reverend North will leave on the same ship.

With a rapid tightening of the plot, Clarke changes the scene to England, where it is revealed that it was Rex who killed Lord Bellasis, his "natural" father as well as Rufus Dawes's, and North who robbed him. Sarah tells Lady Devine that her son is a convict, Rufus Dawes.

Back at Norfolk Island, Dawes escapes his drunken gaoler, and rushes onto the ship disguised in North's cloak and hat. The climax of the book is imminent. The ship is caught in a cyclone and shattered. As it is sinking, Dawes appears in front of Sylvia and holds out his hands to her. Her memory returns and she calls out, "Good Mr Dawes", the words she wrote in the sand on the beach where they were marooned and Dawes saved them. Sylvia and Dawes are drowned in each other's arms, tangled in the rigging.

The Gothic melodrama of *For the Term of His Natural Life* is almost unique in Australian fiction. The strain of "weird melancholy" which Clarke found in the Australian bush permeates the whole book. Yet it is totally convincing and compelling to read. Translated into many foreign languages, it is a great novel of the nineteenth century.

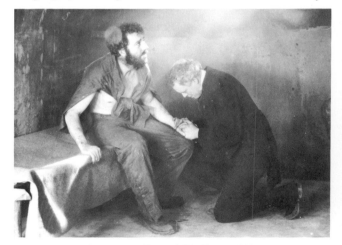

From the 1927 film *For the Term of His Natural Life*

Rolf Boldrewood

ROBBERY UNDER ARMS

LONDON 1889

Goring rides straight at Starlight and calls on him to surrender. He had his rifle on his hip, but he never moved. There he stood, with his hand on the mane of the old horse. "Keep back if you're wise, Goring," says he, as quiet and steady as if he'd been cattle-drafting. "I don't want to have your blood on my head; but if you must—"

Goring had taken so many men in his day that he was got over confident-like. He thought Starlight would give in at the last moment or miss him in the rush. My right arm was broken, and now that Jim was down we might both be took, which would be a great crow for the police. Anyhow, he was a man that didn't know what fear was, and he chanced it.

Two of the other troopers fired point blank at Starlight as Goring rode at him, and both shots told. He never moved, but just lifted his rifle as the other came up at the gallop. Goring threw up his arms, and rolled off his horse a dying man.

Starlight looked at him for a minute.

"We're quits," he says; "it's not once or twice either you've pulled trigger on me. I knew this day would come."

Then he sinks down slowly by the side of the old horse and leans against his fore leg, Rainbow standing quite steady, only tossing his head up and down the old way. I could see, by the stain on Starlight's mouth and the blood on his breast, he'd been shot through the lungs.

I was badly hit too, and going in the head, though I didn't feel it so much at the time. I began to hear voices like in a dream; then my eyes darkened, and I fell like a log.

When I came to, all the men was off their horses, some round Goring—him they lifted up and propped against a tree;

but he was stone dead, any one could see. Sir Ferdinand was on his knees beside Starlight, talking to him, and the other saying a word now and then, quite composed and quiet-like.

"Close thing, Morringer, wasn't it?" I heard him say. "You were too quick for us; another day and we'd been out of reach."

"True enough. Horses all dead beat; couldn't raise a remount for love or money."

"Well, the game's up now, isn't it? I've held some good cards too, but they never told, somehow. I'm more sorry for Jim—and that poor girl, Aileen, than I am for myself."

"Don't fret—there's a good fellow. Fortune of war, you know. Anything else?"

Here he closed his eyes, and seemed gone; but he wakes up again, and begins in a dreamy way. His words came slowly, but his voice never altered one bit.

"I'm sorry I fired at poor Warrigal now. No dog ever was more faithful than he has been to me all through till now; but I was vexed at his having sold Dick and poor Jim."

"We knew we should find you here or hereabouts without that," says Sir Ferdinand.

"How was that?"

"Two jockey-boys met you one night at Calga gate; one of them recognised Locket by the white patch on her neck. He

wired to us at the next station."

"So you were right, after all, Dick. It was a mistake to take that mare. I've always been confoundedly obstinate; I admit that. Too late to think of it now, isn't it?"

"Anything else I can do?" says Sir Ferdinand.

"Give her this ring," he pulls it off his finger, "and you'll see Maddie Barnes gets the old horse, won't you? Poor old Rainbow! I know she'll take care of him; and a promise is a promise."

"All right. He's the property of the Government now, you know; but I'll square it somehow. The General won't object under the circumstances."

Then he shuts his eyes for a bit. After a while he calls out—

"Dick! Dick Marston."

"I'm here," says I.

"If you ever leave this, tell Aileen that her name was the last word I spoke—the very last. She foresaw this day; she told me so. I've had a queer feeling too, this week back. Well, it's over now. I don't know that I'm sorry, except for others. I say, Morringer, do you remember the last pigeon match you and I shot in, at Hurlingham?"

"Why, good God!" says Sir Ferdinand, bending down and looking into his face. "It can't be; yes, by Jove, it is—"

He spoke some name I couldn't catch, but Starlight put a finger on his lips, and whispers—

"You won't tell, will you? Say you won't?"

The other nodded.

He smiled just like his old self.

"Poor Aileen!" he says, quite faint. His head fell back. Starlight was dead!

Australia's greatest novel of bushranging, *Robbery Under Arms*, is a rollicking good yarn about outlaws sticking up mail coaches. But it is also far more than that. It has an extraordinary zest and immediacy of action, a feeling of excitement and daring, a love of the skills of fine horsemanship, so that while the book opens in a prison with the narrator under sentence of death, what emerges is a paean of praise for the freedom of the Australian countryside. Boldrewood was a countryman who understood his subject, and his work has the clarity of figure and landscape of the

Impressionist painters who followed him.

But Boldrewood was, as well as a novelist, a magistrate who had seen good men go wrong, and he wanted his book to be a warning to all those young men who might be a bit bored with the straight life and thinking of doing something "on the cross". His main characters, Dick and Jim Marston and Captain Starlight, are, despite their misdeeds, good men gone wrong—thoroughly decent characters who would never do anything dastardly like shooting a man in cold blood or molesting a woman. In fact, women play a major part in *Robbery Under Arms*, the good ones as a constant reference to moral values, the bad ones as betrayers.

The novel opens with the zest of life and the morning sun crossed with the shadows of prison bars. This image sets the tone of the whole book, for Dick, the single survivor of a bushranging gang, under sentence of death, and his brother Jim and Starlight have always been conscious of impending doom. They would get out of the bushranging life if they could, cross the sea to America and begin again. Not so the boys' father, old Ben, who is an ex-convict with scars on his soul, as well as on his back, and a grudge against the world for the injustices he has suffered.

Then he sinks down slowly by the side of the old horse and leans against his fore leg, Rainbow standing quite steady, only tossing his head up and down the old way. I could see, by the stain on Starlight's mouth and the blood on his breast, he'd been shot through the lungs.

The reader is early introduced to the Marston boys and their sister Aileen and their near neighbours, the Storefields. Gracey Storefield, their daughter, owes her life to Dick, who saves her from drowning. This theme of chivalry is repeated later when, in a splendidly vivid episode, Jim saves Miss Falkland, a rich neighbouring squatter's only daughter, from certain death as her bolting horse carries her towards a cliff top. Both these episodes happen very early in the story, but they establish the Marstons' good qualities, and the Storefields and the Falklands never cease to be grateful to Dick and Jim.

Dick and Jim are excellent farm workers and can fence and ride and cope with all aspects of country life. They go wrong almost by chance, helping Dad brand some cattle he has duffed. Dick remembers thinking "like many another young fool, I suppose, that I could draw back in time, just after I'd tackled this job". And later, when they have joined their father's cattle-duffing friend, Starlight, and are undecided whether or not to go on with the job he puts up to them, the decision is made on a toss of a coin. "There was a heavyish stake on that throw, if we'd only known. Only ruin—only death. Four men's lives lost, and three women made miserable for life."

There is a profound melancholy under the galloping adventure of *Robbery Under Arms*, even under the debonair mask of the aristocratic Starlight. Starlight is always imperturbably in control of events, especially when, as a wanted man, he is dancing with the belle of the ball in the presence of the Police Commissioner, or winning the Turon Handicap with his great horse Rainbow. But at the same time he is a double exile, outlawed like Dick and Jim not only from ordinary blameless life, but also far removed, for some never-to-be-revealed misdemeanour, from his aristocratic English birthright.

The Marston boys look up to Starlight, as the conservative Boldrewood himself looked up to the Old Country. But Starlight is by no means the only gentleman in the book. In a key passage, when Dick is working for "the big squatter", Mr Falkland, Boldrewood makes clear his admiration for the Englishman who has worked his way up to become Boldrewood's ideal, the Australian gentleman.

Boldrewood found a perfect natural symbol of the bushrangers' knowledge and skill, and at the same time of their need to hide from the world, in Terrible Hollow, the hidden valley to which they retreat and where they get together the huge herd of duffed cattle which they drive down to Adelaide and sell in triumph. But Terrible Hollow is a secret that can eventually be found out, and in fact a secret within a secret, hiding as it does the skeletons of old Ben and Warrigal at the end of the book.

Warrigal, Starlight's dangerous but devoted Aboriginal offsider, is at one with the country, as even native-born bushmen like Dick and Jim can never be. He has a compass in his head when striking out through trackless country. He can appear and disappear like a shadow. There is a deep vein of bitterness, partly due to jealousy, between him and the otherwise amiable Dick, that leads, in the end, to Warrigal's unintended betrayal of his beloved master. He has been in his own way a servant, but the wrongs suffered by his race give him an untamable ferocity.

Starlight is an immediate success with women, but no particular one ties him down. He treats Aileen "just as if she was a real lady; but he was the same to all women". The Marston boys are also free spirits, while under the constant threat of disaster, but are firmly tied both to certain women and to the ideal of woman as pure, constant and loving. Aileen, their mother Mrs Marston, Jim's wife Jeanie, Gracey Storefield, whom Dick eventually marries, the unattainable Miss Falkland, are absolutely essential not only to the story, but as moral pointers to the state of Dick's and Jim's souls. Even when Dick is under sentence of death, the women who care for him do not desert him. The threat of exposure and capture gives a melancholy and dramatic edge to the bushrangers' lives, but it is the women in the book who give it depth and poignancy. And it is the cursed passion of Kate, Jeanie's sister, for Dick that simmers vengefully on until her ultimate betrayal.

As an exciting yarn *Robbery Under Arms* could not be bettered. The audacity, always inspired by Starlight, with which the bushrangers enjoy themselves in the society they are robbing manages temporarily to negate morality. It is a sort of game, made infinitely more exciting because the penalty is death. Starlight, of course, always passes himself off as a slightly effete English swell, and hobnobs with the highest in the land—at Adelaide when they are selling the great herd of stolen cattle, in the ballroom, or at the racecourse at the Turon goldfields.

Even when they are first caught, and are sentenced to five years in Berrima Gaol, Starlight does not lose his

BUSHRANGERS ON ST KILDA ROAD *William Strutt*

ROLF BOLDREWOOD
1826-1915

"Rolf Boldrewood", whose real name was Thomas Alexander Browne, was born in London in 1826 and arrived in Australia in 1831. His father, Sylvester Brown (without the "e") was an adventurous character who at one time was a ship's captain with the East India Company. He was in charge of a shipload of convicts sent out to New South Wales and he then became a whaler; later he moved down to Port Phillip and prospered.

This prosperity ended in the depression of 1841, when Sylvester Brown's financial affairs collapsed. Three years later, at the age of 17, Boldrewood took up for £10 32,000 acres near Port Fairy, in the Western District of Victoria. Later he wrote in *Old Melbourne Memories*: "Pride and successful ambition swelled my heart on that first morning as I looked round on my run. My run! my own station! How fine a sound it had . . ."

In the late 1850s he sold his successful run and moved to a sheep station by Lake Boga near Swan Hill. In 1861 he married Margaret Maria Riley, later the author, under her maiden name, of *The Flower Garden in Australia* (1893).

It was disastrous to leave the rich, high-rainfall Western District for Lake Boga, and ultimately a series of droughts forced Boldrewood to sell up. With his two brothers-in-law he took up a property, in their names, of 28,160 acres on the Murrumbidgee, where he acted as manager. But another four years of drought forced him to move on again, and in 1870 he went to live in Sydney with his family. His finances were now so low that he went droving, and also began to write in the hope of making some money. He took the penname Boldrewood from Scott's *Marmion*.

In the next four years he had articles on life in the Australian countryside published in England in the *Cornhill*, a magazine of literature and travel, and in Australia in the *Australian Town and Country Journal*.

Although he was really not qualified for the job, in 1871 Boldrewood was appointed Police Magistrate and Clerk of Petty Sessions at the goldmining town of Gulgong in New South Wales. He was probably helped to the post, and was certainly helped financially, by another brother-in-law, (Sir) Frederick Darley, later Chief Justice and Lieutenant Governor of New South Wales. In 1881 he was transferred to Dubbo as Police Magistrate.

By 1882, when he began to write *Robbery Under Arms*, he had had published seven serials in the *Town and Country Journal*, the best of these probably being *The Miner's Right*. The first two chapters of *Robbery Under Arms* were rejected by the *Australasian* and the *Town and Country Journal* as being too gloomy. Finally the *Sydney Mail* agreed to run the serial, which appeared for a year between 1882 and 1883. At the same time *Old Melbourne Memories* was being published in the *Australasian*, an indication of Boldrewood's popularity at the time.

In later life Boldrewood moved to Melbourne, where he led an active social life. Boldrewood did not approve of the democratic Australian nationalism of the 1890s, and always refused to write for the *Bulletin*. His last work was a condemnation of the Aborigines for their "treachery" in their dealings with the whites. Yet as a writer of fiction Boldrewood was not narrow-minded. As his own life was healthy and straightforward, so too was his love for Australia, but he was of the breed that still looked back to the "Old Country" and he was bewildered by the nation that Australia was becoming. He died in 1915.

Since its first appearance in book form in London in 1888, *Robbery Under Arms* has never been out of print. It is immediately recognisable as Australian, told as it is in Dick Marston's vernacular. "I claim to know what I write," said Boldrewood, and the authenticity of *Robbery Under Arms* is always evident.

---

panache. When Dick and Jim are waiting by the outside wall to escape: "I heard a man's step coming up softly; I knew it was Starlight. I knew his step, and thought I would always tell it from a thousand other men's; it was so light and firm, so quick and free." That "free" is ultimately ironic, yet Starlight, up to the end, lives out a freedom of the spirit that makes clods of the men he is fooling. He has dreams of a further freedom, as he says to Aileen: "To be free, and have a mind at ease; it doesn't seem so much . . . and yet how we fools and madmen shut ourselves out of it for ever, for ever, sometimes by a single act of folly, hardly crime. That comes after."

But Starlight is never melancholy for long. His greatest triumph – dining with the Police Commissioner and winning the race at Turon – is "about the best practical joke I ever carried out, and I've been in a good many . . . There's nothing like adventure."

It is very different with old Ben Marston. The injustices of Australia's convict past still lie heavy as fetters on him.

I was thrashed and starved, locked up in a gaol, chained and flogged after that, and half the time for doing what I didn't know was wrong, and couldn't know more than one of them four-year-old colts out there that knocks his head agin the yard when he's roped, and falls backward and breaks his neck if he ain't watched. Whose business was it to have learned me better? That I can't rightly say,

but it seemed it was the business of the Government people to gaol me, and iron me, and flog me. Was that justice? Any man's sense'll tell him it wasn't.

But the old bitterness is deep in Australia's past, and Dick and Jim will have none of it. They just say: "Father had got into one of his tantrums." Their sights are on the future.

Finally, helped by George Storefield who has a string of stations that stretches up into Queensland, Dick, Jim and Starlight head for the north with the idea of getting a boat to take them to freedom in America. They are betrayed by Kate, whom they meet on the beach, and by Warrigal, vengeful after being beaten in a fight with Dick. But even without those betrayals, they have already been identified by the white patch on the neck of Starlight's beloved Rainbow, and the troopers are waiting. Dying, Starlight admits: "So you were right after all, Dick. It was a mistake to take that mare. I've always been confoundedly obstinate, I admit that. Too late to think of it now."

Robbery Under Arms ends in tragedy for Starlight and Jim, who are both shot, but happily for Dick, whose death sentence is commuted after representations by Mr Falkland, George Storefield and others who point out that there was "no distinct evidence of you having personally taken life". Dick serves out his sentence of 15 years, marries Gracey and at last achieves what he and his companions' lives have symbolised but never achieved – freedom.

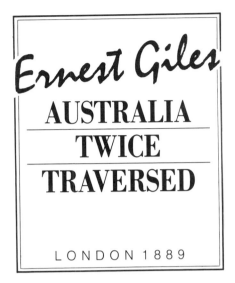

Ernest Giles

AUSTRALIA
TWICE
TRAVERSED

LONDON 1889

To the north was the main chain, composed for the most part of individual high mounts, there being a valley between them and the hill I was on, and meandering along through this valley from the west I could trace the course of the Finke by its timber for some miles. To the east a mass of high and jumbled hills appeared, and one bluff-faced mount was more conspicuous than the rest. Nearer to me, and almost under my feet, was the gorge through which the river passes, and it appears to be the only pass through this chain. I approached the precipice overlooking the gorge, and found the channel so flooded by the late rains, that it was impossible to get the horses up through it. The hills which enclosed it were equally impracticable, and it was utterly useless to try to get horses over them. The view to the west was gratifying, for the ranges appeared to run on in undiminished height in that direction, or a little north of it. From the face of several of the hills I climbed to-day, I saw streams of pure water running, probably caused by the late rains. One hill I passed over

I found to be composed of pudding-stone, that is to say, a conglomeration of many kinds of stone mostly rounded and mixed up in a mass, and formed by the smothered bubblings of some ancient and ocean-quenched volcano. The surface of the place now more particularly mentioned had been worn smooth by the action of the passage of water, so that it presented the appearance of an enormous tessellated pavement, before which the celebrated Roman one at Bognor, in Sussex, which I remember, when I was a boy, on a visit to Goodwood, though more artistically but not more fantastically arranged, would be compelled to hide its diminished head. In the course of my rambles I noticed a great quantity of beautiful flowers upon the hills, of similar kinds of those collected in the Glen of

Palms and these interested me so greatly, that the day passed before I was aware, and I was made to remember the line, "How noiseless falls the foot of Time that only treads on flowers." I saw two kangaroos and one rock wallaby, but they were too wild to allow me to approach near enough to get a shot at them. When I said I walked to-day, I really started on an old favourite horse called Cocky, that had carried me for years, and many a day have I had to thank him for getting me out of difficulties through his splendid powers of endurance. I soon found the hills too rough for a horse, so fixing up his bridle, I said, "Now you stop there till I come back." I believe he knew everything I said, for I used frequently to talk to him. When I came back at night, not thinking he would stay, as the other horses were all feeding within half a mile of him, there he was just as I had left him. I was quite inclined to rest after my scrambles in the hills. During the night nothing occurred to disturb our slumbers, which indeed were aided by the sounds of the rippling stream, which sang to us a soothing song.

Giles liked to refer to himself as "the last of the Australian explorers". He was certainly the most poetic and one of the finest bushmen of the great explorers. Although, as in the case of Eyre, his journeys did not open up immediately rich country, the vast areas in central and western Australia he penetrated became part of white consciousness of Australia as a result of his travels.

Giles was unusual in always seeing the beauty of the harsh country he journeyed through.

The birds delight him. When he reaches a pleasant place he does not want to move. "The country was so agreeable here we had no desire to traverse it at railway speed; it was delightful to loll and lie upon the land, in abandoned languishment beneath the solar ray."

When, torn, sweaty and hot, he reaches water among the rocks he calls the place "The Fairies' Glen".

Poetry was always in his mind and he saw nothing incongruous in making it at home in the Australian desert. Giles always stopped to look at things. When he finds "a great quantity of beautiful flowers" near the peak in central Australia he remembers the line "How noiseless falls the foot

of Time that only treads on flowers". In the harsh desert beyond the Mann Ranges, with the shade thermometer in thundery air between 43 and 44.4°C, driven to the point of madness by frightful hordes of ants, sand in the eyes from fierce, hot winds, eaten alive by flies, ill with the fever, he thinks of Shakespeare, "Like Othello, I am perplexed in the extreme—rain threatens every day, I don't like to go and I can't stay."

Giles always keeps his sense of humour, and sees the comedy in people and events. One of his men, Jimmy Andrews, has curious habits, such as biting dogs on the nose. Then there is Saleh the camel-driver, who says he will pray to Allah to give Giles a rockhole full of water by the morning. Giles replies there is not time for Allah to make one, but anyhow if Saleh can get what he wants by praying, "let me have a fresh-water lake, or a running river, that will take us right away to Perth". Then Saleh says solemnly, "Ah, Mr Gile, you not religious."

Giles loved horses, and gave them all names which often matched their characters. His lists of horses make wonderful reading, horses such as, "an iron-grey colt, called Diaway, having been very poor and miserable when first purchased, but he was a splendid horse"; or "Terrible Billy . . . falling into holes . . . without the slightest confidence in himself"; or "Giant Despair, a perfect marvel . . . old, large-framed, gaunt, and bony, with screwed and lately staked feet. . . . He was dreadfully destructive with his pack-bags, for he would never get out of the road for anything less than a gum-tree." Then there was his own riding horse, "West Australian – shortened to W.A., but usually called Guts, from his persistent attention to his 'inwards'." He was heartbroken when, in the Rawlinson Range, he lost four horses in dry country, and he "called the vile mountain which had caused me this disaster, Mount Destruction".

No wonder Giles is the most entertaining to read of all Australian explorers.

Giles's one blind spot was regarding the Aborigines, though rumour has it that he left several mixed-blood children in his wake. He had no appreciation of the Aborigines' customs or beliefs. He considered their cave paintings the scribblings of "cave-dwelling, reptile-eating Troglodytes". It was not until he had as guide on his Third Expedition, Old Jimmy, "a very agreeable old gentleman", that he realised the "Really marvellous" abilities of the Aborigines. On several occasions, and most notably in what he interpreted as a major attack from the Aborigines at Ularring, Giles fired at and wounded (and probably killed) Aborigines.

Giles's First Expedition was fitted out by the botanist Baron von Mueller, Giles's brother-in-law G. D. Gill, and himself. His assistant, Samuel Carmichael, also contributed. The expedition, with horses, left Chambers Pillar, between Charlotte Waters and Alice Springs, to head west into unknown country. Giles farewelled the remarkable natural monument of Chambers Pillar with a deliberate misquotation from Tennyson, "clothed in white sandstone, mystic, wonderful!" Giles followed the Finke Valley and then went out towards the Great Sandy Desert, south of the MacDonnell Ranges until waterless country drove him back. Turning south, he was repulsed by Lake Amadeus which he named. The extraordinary mountain in the distance he named Mount Olga.

On his return to Charlotte Waters there was bitter news

Giles at Queen Victoria Springs (*Australia Twice Traversed*)

waiting for him. Colonel Peter Egerton Warburton was already there with a strong expedition furnished with camels, waiting to cross to the north-west, sponsored by Sir Thomas Elder and Captain Hughes, and another expedition was under way, commanded by W. C. Gosse, sponsored by the South Australian Government.

*O*ne hill I passed over I found to be composed of pudding-stone, that is to say, a conglomeration of many kinds of stone mostly rounded and mixed up in a mass, and formed by the smothered bubblings of some ancient and ocean-quenched volcano.

Giles hurried back to Adelaide and got together another expedition, this time joined by his old friend William Henry Tietkens and collecting on the way a young man called Alfred Gibson. With 20 pack horses, four riding horses and two little dogs he headed west for the Alberga and far Mount Olga on 4 August 1873. Here, reaching a paradisal valley with running water, which he called Glen Ferdinand (after von Mueller), Giles had his first serious brush with the Aborigines, actually firing at them. Blithely he wrote, "it is next to impossible in Australia for an explorer to discover excellent and well-watered regions without coming into deadly conflict with the aboriginal inhabitants. The aborigines are always the aggressors, but then the white man is a trespasser in the first instance, which is a cause sufficient for any atrocity to be committed upon him." Eyre and Sturt would have agreed with the second half of the last sentence but not the rest of Giles' sentiments. When on 12 September they reached the strange wonders of Mount Olga, Giles was startled to find marks of a wagon and horses and camels. Gosse had been there before him, and discovered and named Ayers Rock. Actually the two parties were now only about 48 kilometres apart, and Gosse was retreating homeward.

Giles went on and explored out to the Warburton Ranges then up to the Rawlinson Range. From there in April Gibson volunteered to go on a reconnaissance 160 kilometres or so to the west. They rode out into what Giles later called "Gibson's Desert". After several days they were in desperate trouble, out of water, with only one horse left. Giles stayed in the desert and told Gibson to ride back to the kegs, where they had left the main water supply. He was to water the mare and then bring back water for Giles.

Gibson never returned. Almost dead with thirst, Giles reached the kegs on 24 April 1874. His only hope was to carry the kegs (which with other vital equipment made a load of about 22 kilograms) and walk back to the Rawlinsons. All he had to eat was a few sticks of dried horsemeat.

He staggered on, punctured all over by the dense, high spinifex, often falling down and waking later from unknown hours of unconsciousness. About 29 April he had emptied the keg, and there were still over 32 kilometres to go to the Circus, where they had left water. However he plodded on there and drank; he caught a tiny wallaby and ate it, "fur, skin, bones, skull, and all".

Somehow or other he went on, and in the morning of 1 May he reached the camp at the Gorge of Tarns and woke Tietkens. Gibson had not returned. "I was the only one of

THE OLGAS, THE NORTHERN ASPECT *Lloyd Rees*

ERNEST GILES
1835-1897

Ernest Giles was born in 1835 at Bristol in England. He was the son of a merchant, William Giles, and his wife Jane Elizabeth. He was educated in London at Christ's Hospital school, famous as the Blue Coats School because of its uniform. It must have been a good school, for he had a sound classical and literary education by the time he emigrated to Australia at the age of 15, to join his parents, brother and five sisters who had gone to Adelaide the previous year.

Young Ernest followed the gold rush to Victoria, but had no luck and had to find work as a clerk in the Melbourne GPO. In his early twenties he left the city and took various jobs on stations along the upper Darling River. Thus, almost alone amongst Australian explorers, he had had proper training as a bushman. In 1864 Giles was in Melbourne again, and there he met another old Blue Coat boy, William Henry Tietkens, who became his lifelong friend and companion on his explorations.

Giles had a passion to be the first person to penetrate into the unknown regions of Western Australian and western South Australia. He made friends with the great botanist, Ferdinand von Mueller, who agreed to be one of the backers of a small expedition. Giles himself put his own money into it. By 22 August 1872 Giles and his expedition were crossing the Finke River and undergoing the first tortures of the sharp spines of "that abominable vegetable production, the so-called spinifex or porcupine grass—botanically, the *Triodia* or *Festuca irritans*". This was to be Giles's cruel

adversary over thousands of kilometres and many years.

Giles's five expeditions, the last two with camels, led to the discovery of Lake Amadeus and Mount Olga, and the naming of the Gibson Desert and the Great Victoria Desert. Giles crossed Australia from the Overland Telegraph Line to Perth, and back, on routes 500–800 kilometres apart, in conditions of the utmost harshness.

Giles was a great bushman, who seldom made the impulsive errors committed by so many other Australian explorers. Although awarded the Gold Medal of the Royal Geographical Society, he was not given land, money or employment in recognition of his services by either the South Australian or Victorian Governments, except for the South Australian Government's offer of a lease of 5330 square kilometres in the Northern Territory which Giles could not afford to take up. In 1881 Governor Jervois refused him an official appointment, writing, "I am afraid that he gambles and that his habits are not always strictly sober."

Giles held some minor clerical appointments in Victoria and Western Australia, but then in the 1890s joined the gold rush at Coolgardie. He became a clerk, for £3 a week, in the office of the Chief Inspector of Mines. In November 1897 he contracted pneumonia; he died on 20 November.

There was talk of a State funeral, but the Western Australian Government did no more for him than had the South Australian or Victorian Governments. At least the inhabitants of Coolgardie turned out, and the local paper stated that "The attendance was very large." He wrote his own epitaph at the end of his book: "though I shall not attempt to rank myself amongst the first or greatest, yet I think I have reason to call myself, the last of the Australian explorers." He also wrote, which is true to his heart, "An explorer is an explorer from love, and it is nature, not art, that makes him so."

---

six living creatures—two men and four horses—that had returned, or were now ever likely to return, from that desert." Only a day later Giles was being helped on to his horse by Tietkens. They nearly perished again in their unsuccessful efforts to find Gibson, who had disappeared into the parallel sandhills, even though he had taken with him Giles's Gregory's Patent Compass.

When Giles returned to Adelaide he learnt that a fourth expedition was in the field, led by John Forrest from Western Australia. In an excellent season Forrest got through from Perth to the Overland Telegraph Line, with water all along the way. Such is the luck of the exploring game. Forrest was given over 2000 hectares by the West Australian Government. The South Australian Government gave Giles and Tietkens nothing.

Now his patron von Mueller introduced him to Sir Thomas Elder, who had the only available camels in Australia. Under Elder's patronage, with these unknown creatures, camels, Giles set off on his Third Expedition to the edge of the Nullarbor Plain, and along the coast to Eucla and back. On his Fourth Expedition Giles took with him Tietkens, James Young and Alec Ross, Peter Nicholls and two Afghans; he was joined a little later by an Aboriginal boy, Tommy. The route of the expedition, looking for pastoral land for Elder, took him to Ooldea (Youldeh) and Fowler's Bay, and then across the Great Victoria Desert, then beyond it to Perth in 1875.

Going with the camels, Giles was able to cover prodigious distances between water holes, but even so, over 480

kilometres out into the desert it seemed that they were all about to perish. The only cheerful member of the party was Tommy. Giles had a small leather bag containing necklaces, pocket knives and oddments as gifts for the Aborigines. When Giles made a joke to Tommy about them all dying, " 'If we all die,' said Tommy quickly, 'could I have the bag of trinkets?' "

On the sixth day out from Boundary Dam, Tietkens sent Tommy to look out for water after seeing signs of Aboriginal and emu tracks, and Tommy found water, a miniature lake surrounded by grassland and pines, which Giles called Queen Victoria's Springs, now known as Queen Victoria Springs. The desert he called the Great Victoria Desert.

After that the remainder of the journey to Perth was relatively easy. Given a hero's welcome, and a hero's send off, Giles took his Fifth Expedition up to Geraldton and from there across to the Ashburton, from where, despite being temporarily blinded by ophthalmia in what he called the Ophthalmia Range, he crossed the Gibson Desert to his old camp at Fort Mueller, at one stage being 10 days without water. Giles had achieved a double crossing of the western half of the continent.

Giles's exuberant style well conveys that even in the extremities of suffering and the nearness of death, in his own words, "the burning charm of seeking something new, will still possess me". Inside the wiry, humorous bushman was the soul of a poet. Although on several occasions the country he crossed nearly killed him, he loved it and that love gives warmth and depth to his writing.

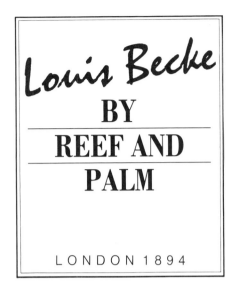

Louis Becke

BY REEF AND PALM

LONDON 1894

"What a stroke of luck," he writes to Doris. "Had I gone back to Sydney, where would I be now?—a mate, I suppose, on some deep-sea ship, earning £12 or £14 a month. Another year or two like this, and I could go back a made man. Some day, my dear, I may; but I will come back here again. The ways of thy people have become my ways."

He laid down his pen and came to the door and stood thinking a while and listening to the gentle rustle of the palms as they swayed their lofty plumes to the breezy trade wind.

"Yes," he thought, "I would like to go and see Doris, but I can't take Luita, and so it cannot be. How that girl suspects me even now. When I went to Tahiti to buy the schooner I believe she thought she would never see me again. . . . What a fool I am! Doris is all right, I suppose, although it is a year since I had a letter . . . and I—could any man want more? I don't believe there's a soul on the island but thinks as much of me as Luita herself does; and by G—d she's a pearl—even though she is only a native girl. No, I'll stay here: 'Kapeni Paranili' will always be a big man in the Paumotus, but Fred Brantley would be nobody in Sydney—only a common merchant skipper who had made money in the islands . . . and perhaps Doris is married."

So he thought and talked to himself, listening the while to the soft symphony of the swaying palm-tops and the subdued murmur of the surf as the rollers crashed on the distant line of reef away to leeward. Of late these fleeting visions of the outside world—that quick, busy world, whose memories, save for those of Doris, were all but dead to him—had become more frequent; but the calm, placid happiness of his existence, and that strange, fatal glamour that for ever enwraps the minds of those who wander in the islands of the sunlit sea—as the old Spanish navigators called Polynesia—had woven its spell too strongly over his nature to be broken. And now, as the murmur of women's voices caused him to turn his head to the shady end of the veranda, the dark, dreamy eyes of Luita, who with her women attendants sat there, playing with her child, looked out at him from beneath their long lashes, and told him his captivity was complete.

Although *By Reef and Palm* is a collection of short stories, it has such a powerful unity of place, theme and style that it becomes a whole, a book about the Pacific. There is, of course, no obvious unity in such a vast subject, except physically: the reef, the palm, the brilliant clear water inside the reef, the surf breaking against the reef—these tie the Pacific region together, from the mountains of Tahiti to the flat atolls of the Marshall Islands. The people, too, are obviously very different from each other: Polynesians, Micronesians, Melanesians. Yet the formality of their societies, albeit accompanied by attitudes towards sexual morality somewhat different from those of nineteenth-century Europeans, is something they have in common. This is especially so when concerned with keeping control over blood lines in small communities, and in paying respect to the gods and the elements relevant to their island lives.

Into these structured communities came the white man, and often the worst of white men; then came the missionaries who, in one of Becke's most brilliant stories, are symbolised by sharks tearing the old ways and lives limb from limb. Experts on the region agree that of all European writers it is Becke who knows most about the Pacific. James Michener has said that if someone is claiming to be knowledgeable about the Pacific, don't ask him about the names of islands or local government in Samoa, just ask him if he has read the stories of Louis Becke.

Naturally Becke has his limitations. You do not read him to understand the complexities of Samoan society, beside which even the formality of European court life seems almost relaxed, but to experience something of the sometimes happy, but more often tragic, relationship between white men and the Pacific islanders. Becke's subjects are usually white men rather than white women; the white men who roamed the Pacific were often only too pleased to see the last of white women, and it was not in the nature of Pacific society that a man should live alone.

Yet loneliness is common to most of Becke's characters, even when they are surrounded by amiable islanders. They may have "gone native", but often they remain European in sensibility. The classic case is probably that of Captain Brantley who has settled on Vahitahi island in the Paumotu Archipelago after a shipwreck. Although he still has visions of the outside world he has been captivated by island life.

So he thought and talked to himself, listening the while to the soft symphony of the swaying palm-tops and the subdued murmur of the surf as the rollers crashed on the distant line of reef away to leeward. Of late these fleeting visions of the outside world—the quick, busy world, whose memories, save for those of Doris, were all but dead to him—had become more frequent; but the calm, placid happiness of his existence, and that strange, fatal glamour that for ever enwraps the minds of those who wander in the islands of the sunlit sea—as the old Spanish navigators called Polynesia—had woven its spell too strongly over his nature to be broken. And now, as the murmur of women's voices caused him to turn his head to the shady end of the veranda, the dark, dreamy eyes of Luita, who with her women attendants sat there, playing with her child, looked out at him beneath their long lashes, and told him his captivity was complete.

Doris is, in fact, his sister, who is lonely in Auckland and wants to come to live with him. Brantley fears that she will be shocked to find that he is living with Luita, by whom he has had a child. As Brantley is returning in his schooner from a pearling voyage, he sights another vessel, a brig from Tahiti, the captain of which is a friend. From him Brantley learns that he has brought his sister Doris, dying of consumption, to Vahitahi. The next night Luita and the child disappear in a whaleboat. Brantley guesses that she has gone to the island Tatakoto, her "mother's land", now uninhabited. Doris tells Brantley how fiercely Luita looked at her, and Brantley confesses that he has never told Luita that Doris is his sister. Luita had thought Doris was his wife.

Brantley finds Luita on Tatakoto. She is dying, and the child is already dead. She calls herself "a fool that fled from his house . . . because I thought that he lied to me". She

He laid down his pen and came to the door and stood thinking a while and listening to the gentle rustle of the palms as they swayed their lofty plumes to the breezy trade wind.

dies on the island; Doris dies on the schooner. Brantley tells his crewmen to leave him there and call back in a week. When they return they find him dead, in the shade of a puka-tree, with a bullet-hole in his temple.

This story, the last in the book, contains both the joyous and tragic elements of most of Becke's work. It is noteworthy that Brantley buried Doris under the puka-tree, while the site of Luita's grave is not specified. In the end the deepest ties are with his own race, however much he has been in love with the Pacific and its people.

In "Challis the Doubter", the first story in *By Reef and Palm*, the white man's loyalties take a different direction. On reading a love-letter sent to his beautiful, violet-eyed wife

of less than a year, and after a bitter scene, Challis leaves both his wife and Australia and sails for the islands of the North-West Pacific. Four years later he is living on a "lonely and almost forgotten island" in the Tokelaus, with a native girl, Nalia, who takes her status as white man's wife very seriously. In a conversation between Challis and a native boy the sexual ethics of Polynesia are succinctly explained. The boy says that no other woman will come inside the door while Nalia is away visiting the other white man on the island. But Challis asks, is he not trusting, to let Nalia visit a single white man? "True," answers the boy. "But, then, he is old and feeble, and thou young and strong. None but a fool desires to eat a dried flying-fish when a fresh one may be had."

Challis asks another question: if he were old and withered, would not Nalia be false to him in the house of a younger white man? No, answers the boy, because that man would have a wife who would watch her. "And if he had not, and were *nofo noa* (single), would he be such a fool to steal that which he can buy—for there are many girls without husbands as good to look at as that Nalia of thine. And all women are alike . . ."

The beauty and the sensuality is part of the world of Gauguin's South Sea paintings. And yet a further element always intrudes into this world in Becke's stories: the white man's sensibility or, on other occasions, his crude brutality. In this story, after the beautiful young Nalia returns, Challis suddenly flushes hotly as he thinks: "By God, I can't be such a fool as to begin to *love* her in reality, but yet . . ." Then he asks her:

> a question that only one of his temperament would have dared to ask a girl of the Tokelaus.
>
> "Nalia, dost thou love me?"
>
> "Aye, *alofa tumau* (everlasting love). Am I a fool? Are there no Letia, and Miriami, and Elinë, the daughter of old Taiki, ready to come to this house if I love any but thee? Therefore my love is like the suckers of the *fa'e* (octopus) in its strength. My mother has taught me much wisdom."

Becke is a romantic in that he is highly susceptible to the beauty of the Pacific and its islanders, and understands their fascination for the lonely white man. But he is also a realist, the tough trader who has sailed with the pirate "Bully" Hayes, and the adventurer who has worked on the goldfields and been wrecked in the Gilbert Islands. The most terrible story in *By Reef and Palm*, and indeed a classic horror story is "The Revenge of Macy O'Shea—A Story of the Marquesas". Macy O'Shea is an escaped convict, one of the few who got away from the chain gangs of Port Arthur. He has since been a beachcomber, pirate and "Gentleman of Leisure" in Eastern Polynesia. "And of his many known crimes the deed done in this isolated spot is the darkest of all. Judge of it yourself."

O'Shea has a young wife, Sera, who is part Tahitian and a quarter Portuguese, who hates him. When the story opens she is recovering from being beaten up by him. O'Shea, to her fury (even though she loathes him, with her white skin, she does not think of herself as a native and cannot tolerate polygamy), buys another wife, the 16-year-old daughter of a trader, and brings her home and forces Sera to shake hands

POINSETTIA GARDEN *Ray Crooke*

LOUIS BECKE
1855-1913

"Louis" Becke (George Lewis Becke) was born in 1855 at Port Macquarie in New South Wales, the son of a police magistrate. Perhaps he inherited his love of the sea from his mother's father, Charles Beilby, who had been private secretary to the Duke of Cumberland and who had bought a small vessel and sailed with his family to Australia.

At 14 Becke was sent with his brother to a mercantile firm in San Francisco. Their voyage across the Pacific in a dilapidated old barque was a frightful one; the crew mutinied, the vessel was almost wrecked, they took 90 days to reach Honolulu and another 40 to make San Francisco. Becke soon escaped from his desk in San Francisco and for years wandered around the Pacific as a supercargo, shark-catcher and trader. In one interlude he joined the goldrush to North Queensland.

After this he returned to Samoa and set up on his own as a trader for the first time. Later he sailed a trading vessel under sealed orders to the Marshall Islands. There he found that he was to hand over the ship to the notorious pirate, "Bully" Hayes, who was waiting on his infamous brig the *Leonora*. Becke spent some months cruising with Hayes until they were wrecked on Kusaie Island, where he quarrelled with Hayes. Becke then spent several years living in the Eastern Pacific, on the Gambiers, the Paumotus, and Easter and Pitcairn Islands. Going north again, he was wrecked on Peru, one of the Gilbert Islands, and lost all his possessions.

He married and lived in Sydney in the early 1890s. Here he was encouraged by Archibald and Stephens to write for the *Bulletin*. He made his reputation with his collection of short stories, *By Reef and Palm*, published in London in 1894. His finest work is contained in this book and in the collections of stories that followed in quick succession, which were also published in London: *The Ebbing of the Tide* (1896); *Pacific Tales* (1897); *Rodman the Boatsteerer* (1898) and *Ridan the Devil* (1899). Altogether he published over 30 books, including short stories, novels, biography and reminiscence.

Towards the end of the century he went to London, living there and in France for 11 years. Returning to the South Seas, he lived in New Zealand and then in Sydney, where he died in 1913.

The Earl of Pembroke, co-author of one of the minor classics of the Pacific, *South Sea Bubbles*, by "The Earl and the Doctor", wrote the introduction to the first edition of *By Reef and Palm*. He wrote, with truth, from his first-hand knowledge of the subject and from his friendship with the author, that Mr Becke

> . . . knows the Pacific as few men alive or dead have ever known it. He is one of the rare men who have led a very wild life and have the culture and talent necessary to give some account of it. As a rule, the men who know don't write, and the men who write don't know.
>
> Everyone who has a taste for good stories will feel, I believe, the force of these. Everyone who knows the South Seas, and I believe many who do not, will feel that they have the unmistakable stamp of truth.

Pembroke was right about Becke's "culture and talent". The raw material of his stories would be fascinating enough by itself, but Becke has shaped it into works of art.

---

with her. This she does, but left-handed. What she does with her right hand is best left to Becke to tell.

> *The calm, placid happiness of his . . . existence, and that strange, fatal glamour that for ever enwraps the minds of those who wander in the islands of the sunlit sea—as the old Spanish navigators called Polynesia—had woven its spell too strongly over his nature to be broken.*

Becke is no sentimentalist. The cruelties and the brutalities of the white men are accepted by the natives. "The Methodical Mr Burr of Majuru" (in the Marshall Islands) shoots his wife Le-jennabon's would-be lover, cuts off his head and throws it into the middle of her kinsfolk, pushing her after it. Ned Burr denies it's a bad business to the narrator of the story, "It's just about the luckiest thing that could ha' happened. Ye see, it's given Le-jennabon a good idea of what may happen to her if she ain't mighty correct. An' it's riz me a lot in the esteem of the people generally as a man who hez business principles."

Becke writes in a deceptively simple style, but there is a great deal of technical skill behind the pared-away clarity of his stories. Novels could be made of what lies behind most of them. But Becke is not interested in drawing out the complexities of psychological analysis. He leaves that to the reader's imagination. The vivid precision of vital detail is what appealed to Becke, and perhaps also the challenge of compressing the fluidity of life around the greatest of oceans into something as compact as a short story.

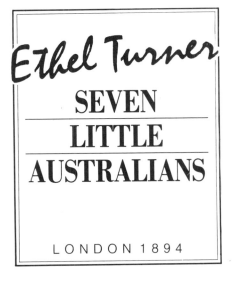

Ethel Turner

SEVEN
LITTLE
AUSTRALIANS

LONDON 1894

Everyone offered Judy everything on the table, and spoke gently and politely to her. She seemed to be apart from them, a person not to be lightly treated in the dignity of this great trouble. Her dress, too, was quite new—a neat blue serge fresh from the dressmaker's hands; her boots were blacked and bright, her stockings guiltless of ventilatory chasms. All this helped to make her a Judy quite different from the harum-scarum one of a few days back, who used to come to breakfast looking as if her clothes had been pitchforked upon her.

Baby addressed herself to her porridge for one minute, but the next her feelings overcame her, and, with a little wail, she rushed round the table to Judy, and hung on her arm sobbing. This destroyed the balance of the whole company. Nell got the other arm and swayed to and fro in an access of misery. Meg's tears rained down into her teacup; Pip dug his heel in the hearthrug, and wondered what was the matter with his eyes; and even Bunty's appetite for bread and butter diminished.

Judy sat there silent; she had pushed back her unused plate, and sat regarding it with an expression of utter despair on her young face. She looked like a miniature tragedy queen going to immediate execution.

Presently Bunty got off his chair, covered up his coffee with his saucer to keep the flies out, and solemnly left the room. In a minute he returned with a pickle bottle, containing an enormous green frog.

"You can have it to keep for your very own, Judy," he said, in a tone of almost reckless sadness. "It'll keep you amused, perhaps, at school."

Self-sacrifice could go no further, for this frog was the darling of Bunty's heart.

This stimulated the others; everyone fetched some offering to lay at Judy's shrine for a keepsake. Meg brought a bracelet, plaited out of the hair of a defunct pet pony. Pip gave his three-bladed pocket-knife, Nell a pot of musk that she had watered and cherished for a year, Baby had a broken-nosed doll that was the Benjamin of her large family.

"Put them in the trunk, Meg—there's room on top, I think," Judy said in a choking voice, and deeply touched by these gifts. "Oh! and, Bunty, dear! put a cork over the f—f—frog, will you? it might get lost, poor thing! in that b—b—big box."

"All right," said Bunty. "You'll take c—c—care of it, w—won't you, Judy? Oh dear, oh—h—h!—boo—hoo!"

Then Esther came in, still troubled-looking.

"The dogcart is round," she said. "Are you ready, Ju, dearest? Dear little Judy! be brave, little old woman."

But Judy was white as death, and utterly limp. She suffered Esther to put her hat on, to help her into her new jacket, to put her gloves into her hand. She submitted to being kissed by the whole family, to be half carried downstairs by Esther, to be kissed again by the girls, then by the two good-natured domestics, who, in spite of her peccadilloes, had a warm place in their hearts for her.

Esther and Pip lifted her into the dogcart, and she sat in a little, huddled-up way, looking down at the group on the veranda with eyes that were absolutely tragic in their utter despair. Her father came out, buttoning his overcoat, and saw the look.

"What foolishness is this?" he said irascibly. "Esther—great heavens! are you making a goose of yourself, too?"—there were great tears glistening in his wife's beautiful eyes. "Upon my soul, one would think I was going to take the child to be hanged, or at least was going to leave her in a penitentiary."

A great dry sob broke from Judy's white lips.

"If you'll let me stay, Father, I'll never do another thing to vex you; and you can thrash me instead, ever so hard."

It was her last effort, her final hope, and she bit her poor quivering lip till it bled while she waited for his answer.

"Let her stay—oh! do let her stay, we'll be good always," came in a chorus from the veranda. And, "Let her stay, John, please!" Esther called, in a tone as entreating as any of the children.

But the Captain sprang into the dogcart and seized the reins from Pat in a burst of anger.

"I think you're all demented!" he cried. "She's going to a thoroughly good home, I've paid a quarter in advance already, and I can assure you good people I'm not going to waste it."

This book was the first of the great Australian children's classics to appear, being published in 1894, five years before *Dot and the Kangaroo* and 16 years before *A Little Bush Maid*. *Seven Little Australians* is both a powerful and entertaining story about children and a penetrating study of their father that is worthy of a major novel.

Captain Woolcot has had six children by his first wife, who must have died (although it is not explicitly stated) having the girl who is always called Baby. Unusually for Victorian times, within a year Captain Woolcot has married again—a beautiful young girl, Esther. When the book opens she is 20, and her eldest step-daughter, Meg, is 16.

The different characters of the children are very clearly delineated. Meg is dreamy, romantic, and suspected of writing poems and stories and even a diary, which are locked in her old tin hat-box. Pip is a handsome, tall boy of 14 who doesn't think much of girls. Judy, 13, "without doubt was the worst of the seven, probably because she was the cleverest". Her name is really Helen, which is used by the father when he is being severe with her; Pip likes to call her Fizz, which she certainly does. Judy is very thin, freckled, quick and eager. Nell is a 10-year-old beauty. Bunty is six, "fat and very lazy . . . and I don't think had ever been seen with a clean face". Baby is a cuddlesome girl of four, given to teasing the real baby, Esther's boy, who is always called the General, and who is about 18 months old.

Captain Woolcot used to live in the officers' quarters in the barracks in Sydney, but his fellow officers found the children so troublesome that he has moved them all to a house on the Parramatta River, in a "big wilderness of a garden" with lots of sheds and two or three horse paddocks. It used to be called The River House, but is now always known as Misrule. Most early Australian children's books were set in the country; life in *Seven Little Australians* is more spacious than the city, but it is in strong contrast to the bush, where the final chapters take place at Esther's parents' station, over 530 kilometres out of Sydney. There are also some lively episodes in Sydney itself.

Ethel Turner makes it clear from the first page that this is not to be a story about "goody-goody" children, and also that it is emphatically to be an Australian story. The title makes that obvious enough, but Ethel Turner is aiming for

Judy sat there silent; she had pushed back her unused plate, and sat regarding it with an expression of utter despair on her young face. She looked like a miniature tragedy queen going to immediate execution.

a subtler depiction of Australia than the usual gum tree and kangaroo variety. She maintains firmly that the Australian character is different, and that it is intimately related to Australian nature and history. Not one of the seven children, she says, "is really good, for the very excellent reason that Australian children never are . . . In Australia a model child is—I say it not without thankfulness—an unknown quantity."

> It may be that the miasmas of naughtiness develop best in the sunny brilliancy of our atmosphere. It may be that the land and the people are young-hearted together, and the children's spirits not crushed and saddened by the shadow of long years' sorrowful history.

Nursery Tea (*Seven Little Australians*) (*above*)

There is a lurking sparkle of joyousness and rebellion and mischief in nature here, and therefore in children.

She also speaks of "the utter absence of veneration" of Australian children for their parents, again a daring proposition to advance in the 1890s. It is certainly true of the young Woolcots.

Later in the book, in reference to Meg's first experience of "sweethearting", Ethel Turner maintains that "Australian girls nearly always begin to think of 'lovers and nonsense', as middle folks call it, long before their English aged sisters do". She is of the opinion that Australian girls lose their bloom too quickly.

From the first episode in *Seven Little Australians* when the children, led by Judy, go down one by one from their nursery tea to beg pieces of chicken from the grown-ups' dinner party, it is apparent that Captain Woolcot has no coherent plan for, or ability to impose, discipline. Also Esther is clearly more an ally than a stern mother-figure. All the Captain can do in a crisis is to impose drastic punishments— beating the boys with a strap or a riding-whip, cutting off privileges. After which, Meg's "Couldn't you get round him, Esther?" is the theme-song of the children.

Esther will do her best, on the occasion of the chicken, but only on condition that the children are "preternaturally good and quiet all day", an injunction that leads to some comical efforts at goodness and one very moving scene that is recalled later in tragedy.

Judy's attempt at virtue is to mow the grass outside the house with a scythe that is imperilling not only the rose bushes but her legs. The image of her that the Captain sees is as vivid as a painting by Tom Roberts. "The little girl looked so comical, standing there in her short old pink frock, a broken-brimmed hat on her tangle of dark curls, her eyes sparkling, her face flushed, the great scythe in her hands, and the saucy words on her lips."

But, being Judy, the mowing is well done, and the Captain lets her continue, while he goes back to the house. "Judy always mystified him. He understood her the least of any of his children . . . It gave him an aggrieved kind of feeling when he thought about it, which was not very often."

The Captain's tragedy is that he cares less for his children than for his cigars. Ethel Turner states explicitly that he does not understand his children. He is happiest when they go away for two months to Esther's parents; he walks down the railway platform "with a jaunty air".

His erratic and intermittent attempts at authority, and Esther's easy-going youth, cause difficulties for some of the children. *Seven Little Australians* is, on the deepest level, a powerful analysis of the varying ways in which different children need parental help and guidance.

Bunty, for instance, is not an attractive boy; greedy, a fibber, lazy and a tell-tale. But it is not altogether his fault. When he lames his father's horse with a cricket ball he retires in dejection to a shed. "If ever a little lad was in need of a wise, loving, motherly mother it was this same dirty-faced, heavy-hearted one."

The children, who spend so much time together, are in fact very much alone when it comes to a crisis. Meg, led into a little bit of "sweethearting" by her obnoxious friend Aldith, has no one to confide in. Hence she writes two foolish

UNTITLED *Frank Mahony*

ETHEL TURNER
1872-1958

Ethel Turner came to Australia when she was seven, with her two sisters and her twice-widowed mother. She was born in Yorkshire in 1872; her father was a merchant, George Burwell, who died when she was two years old. Her sister Lilian and she took the name of her mother's second husband, Henry Turner, a businessman, by whom Ethel's mother, Sarah Jane, had another daughter, Rosie.

Ethel Turner wrote two autobiographical novels about the family, *Three Little Maids* and *The Little Larrikin*. *Seven Little Australians* and *The Family at Misrule* she described to A. G. Stephens as "really the most fanciful things I have done". Her mother seems to have been beautiful and high-spirited, and her house full of books. In 1881 they were living in Woollahra, and from 1885 to 1890 in Oxford Street, Paddington.

From 1889 Ethel kept a diary. It is apparent from it that although she enjoyed parties and clothes she was also interested in both writing and publishing. She started a magazine, the *Iris*, at Sydney Girls High School, and obtained excellent results in her public examinations. Ethel and her sister Lilian followed the *Iris* with another magazine, the *Parthenon*, which published essays and romantic fiction. The sisters wrote most of their sixpenny monthly themselves. They needed a children's page, and Ethel "sat sulkily down and began to write a story for children".

Ethel used the pseudonym "Princess Ida", and she agreed with the ideals of Tennyson's poem from which she took the name, that "the most highly cultivated women are those whose homes are happiest". Her diary for 12 October 1890 shows that on that day she read *Hamlet*, made a cake, a blancmange and jelly, and began Rolf Boldrewood's *The Squatter's Dream*, which is a nice mixture

of the practical, feminine, intellectual and Australian. Her heavily romantic serial novel in the *Parthenon* had, perhaps unexpectedly, a Sydney setting. Boldrewood himself contributed to the *Parthenon*. The magazine was by no means just an indulgence; it sold about 1500 copies a month out of a print run of 2000, carried a number of advertisements and made the sisters about £50 a year. Ethel's children's page developed until it supported a serial, *Bobbie*, which reappeared in the *Illustrated Sydney News* and achieved book publication in 1897.

Herbert Curlewis and Ethel became engaged in 1891, but as Ethel was only 20 and Curlewis was still reading for the Bar, they had to wait.

Ethel had her first story published in the *Bulletin* in 1893. She began *Seven Little Australians* in January 1893 and finished it nine months later. Ward, Lock accepted the novel, and after some haggling (for Ethel had learned about literary business on the *Parthenon*) the publishers agreed to pay her £15 and 2½ per cent royalty. They asked for a sequel; she wrote *The Family at Misrule* in less than five months.

Seven Little Australians and *The Family at Misrule* were well received critically and sold well. The *Bulletin* did not discuss them as children's but adult novels, and placed them in the great Australian tradition, with "Louis Becke, Ethel Turner and 'The Banjo' well-arrived, and with Lawson and Daley and Montgomery approaching the goal". In 1895 Ethel made £377 from her books and other writings, and her stories were appearing in Australian and English periodicals. George Meredith and Mark Twain wrote to her, praising *Seven Little Australians*.

Ethel Turner and Herbert Curlewis were married at Gordon, Sydney, in 1896 and went to live at Mosman Bay. They had a daughter, Jean, and a son, Adrian. Jean became a writer and Adrian a judge. Ethel continued to write novels, articles and plays, as well as leading a vigorous public life.

Her beloved Jean died in 1930 of tuberculosis. Herbert died in 1942, and Ethel in 1958. *Seven Little Australians* was made into a film in 1939, and into a television series in 1980.

---

letters that go astray and cause her a lot of embarrassment.

Judy, the most interesting of all the children, suffers the most; partly because she is always the ringleader, partly because her father cannot understand her. In what is admittedly a ripe piece of wickedness, Judy persuades Pip to leave the General in the Captain's room at the Barracks for a couple of hours so that they can go to the Bondi Aquarium. After all, says Judy, to Pip's great uneasiness, "his father [is] the proper person to watch over him". The appalling rumpus that follows ends in Pip being thrashed and Judy sent to boarding school. Despite the protests of all the family, the Captain is inflexible, and Judy goes.

Judy runs away, taking a week to cover the 120 kilometres, and arrives weak and starving to hide in the loft at Misrule, where the other children secretly bring her furniture and food and drink. One of the most touching scenes in the book is the description of Pip kneeling by her bed feeding her with "morsels of chicken and sips of wine".

In an unpleasant chapter, "Swish, swish", Bunty is thrashed by the Captain for laming the horse, and divulges Judy's secret. When the Captain finally discovers his daughter sleeping in the loft, the scene could not be more different from that with Pip. He cannot think about her, only about himself. ". . . a great anger and irritation rose

within him as he watched her sleeping so quietly there. Was she always to be a disturber of his peace? Was she always to thwart him like this?" He is too angry to notice how sick she is, and tells her that she will be sent back to school on the next train. She is only saved by a violent fit of coughing which brings up blood and reveals she has consumption.

During her convalescence the whole family goes to stay at Yarrahappini, Esther's parents' station, where all the children enjoy the station life. In those idyllic (and unexpectedly well-evoked) surroundings, Judy is killed saving the General from a falling tree.

The tragedy of clever, wilful and lovable Judy's wasted life deeply affects all the family except the Captain. He is certainly moved, he never smokes his cigars at the end of the verandah any more, because he can still see Judy mowing the grass. But he has not basically changed at all. "Judy's death made his six living children dearer to his heart, though he showed his affection very little more."

Seven Little Australians is a profound and moving Australian novel as well as being a successful children's book, with five new editions in the last 10 years. In the history of Australian literature it is a psychological study far ahead of its time.

David W. Carnegie

SPINIFEX
AND
SAND

LONDON 1898

I do not wish to institute comparisons, but it is often said that a prospector, or pioneer, who explores with the hope of gain to himself, cannot be deserving in an equal degree of the credit due to those who have risked their lives in the cause of science. I may point out that these latter have not only been at no expense themselves, but have been paid salaries for their services, and have, in addition, been rewarded by grants of money and land—and deservedly so. Yet a man willing to take the same risks, and venture the fruits of perhaps years of hard work, in equipping and bearing all the expenses of an expedition, is credited with no nobler incentive than the "lust of gold"—because he hopes, with a vague chance of his hope being realised, to be repaid by compelling Nature to part with some of her hidden treasures.

The prospector in his humble way slowly but surely opens up the country, making horse or camel-pads, here, there, and everywhere, from water to water, tracks of the greatest service to the Government road-maker and surveyor who follow after. He toils and labours, suffers, and does heroic deeds, all unknown except to the few. He digs soaks and wells many feet in depth, makes little dams in creeks, protects open water from contamination by animals, and scores of other services, primarily for his own benefit, it is true, but also for the use of those who come after. Very few recognise the immense value of the work carried out by prospectors who are not actuated only by the greed for gold, as I, who know them, can assert. Some wish to satisfy a longing to determine the nature of new country, to penetrate where others have never been; others work for love of adventure and of the free bush life; while many are anxious to win what distinction may fall to the lot of successful travellers, though reward or distinction are seldom accorded to prospectors. But beyond all this, there is the glorious feeling of independence which attracts a prospector. Everything he has is his own, and he has everything that is his own with him; he is doing the honest work of a man who wins every penny he may possess by the toil of his body and the sweat of his brow. He calls no man master, professes no religion, though he believes in God, as he cannot fail to do, who has taken the chances of death in the uphill battle of life "outside the tracks," though he would perhaps be annoyed if you told him so; and it is only by intimate acquaintance with him that you can know that his God is the same as the other men's, though called by another name. For the rest, he lives an honourable life, does many acts of kindness to those in need, never leaves his mate in the lurch, and goes "straight" to the best of his ability. For him, indeed,

"Two things stand like stone:
Kindness in another's trouble,
Courage in his own."

David Carnegie was the last Australian explorer to achieve journeys that were comparable in heroic scale with those of explorers before him who had drawn their thin and dangerous lines across the empty map of Australia. To have crossed the deserts of Western Australia from Coolgardie to the Kimberley Range in 1896, then to have returned, on a different route, in 1897, took a degree of courage and skill that alone would make Carnegie a memorable figure in Australian history. But as well as possessing these attributes, this young Scottish aristocrat wrote one of the most fascinating books in Australian literature, one equally interesting as history and as a salute to the eternal qualities and cruelties of the Australian desert.

Modest, humane, sensitive and an observer of great insight, an educated man with a sound literary style, Carnegie would seem a paragon, an ideal example of the nineteenth-century all-round gentleman. But Carnegie had a fatal flaw, which was his inability to accept the Aborigines as fellow human beings. When he needed something from them he treated them like animals, except that he had far more feelings and sympathy for his camels and dogs than he had for the "savages". He decided that the only way he could find waterholes and natural wells in the desert was to capture an Aborigine, male or female, sometimes more than one, and chain them up until they led the caravan to water.

Sometimes he fed them extra salt beef, in order to make them more thirsty. On other occasions he behaved perfectly correctly towards the tribes he met, using his medicines to heal their sores and infected eyes. In fact, on his return trip he was treated by one tribe as a benefactor and given presents in thanks for restoring the eyesight of a child.

It is to Carnegie's disadvantage to compare him with Sturt or Eyre or Grey in relation to the Aborigines, but in all other respects he is their equal. Indeed he is superior to Grey in relation to other white men. There is no trace of upper-class British patronising of Australians in Carnegie. He gets on well with every type of honest Australian, and has a deep feeling of loyalty and friendship towards his mates, those working with him on his prospecting trips and his explorations. He weeps when burying Charlie Stansmore, "as only men can weep". There is no more bogus male toughness about Carnegie than there was about Achilles or Hector.

The book begins with the arrival of Carnegie and his friend Lord Percy Douglas in Western Australia in 1892, and their departure for the goldfields of Coolgardie. Immediately the reader is aware of being with a traveller who is not only adventurous but who has a sense of humour. They arrive at the Southern Cross to find the bank the scene of an all night party. "Since that time it has been my lot to witness more than one such evening of festivity!" However, Carnegie is later at pains to point out the "four bottles of good brandy" on his list of stores for his major exploring journey are there "for medicinal purposes only".

He toils and labours, suffers, and does heroic deeds, all unknown except to the few. He digs soaks and wells many feet in depth, makes little dams in creeks, protects open water from contamination by animals, and scores of other services, primarily for his own benefit, it is true, but also for the use of those who come after.

From his arrival on the goldfields Carnegie is made aware of the terrible scarcity of water in Western Australia, something that was nearly to cost him his life on more than one occasion. His book might well have been called *Spinifex and Sand and Looking for Water*. He is also, being the sort of man he is, immediately on good terms with the diggers. One old fossicker watches him "belting away" at a solid mass of quartz and then shows him how to do twice the work at half the expenditure of labour. Carnegie adds "I never remember a real digger who was not ready to help one." He in turn would on a cold night give one of his blankets to a shivering digger. He also notices a teamster "apostrophising his horses with oaths that made my flesh creep, to help them up a steep hill. The top reached, he petted and soothed his team in most quaint language."

Lord Percy left the goldfields and returned to London to raise money, while Carnegie worked for wages. On Percy's return to Western Australia, Carnegie undertook a prospecting journey for the Hampton Plains Pastoral Company out into the Queen Victoria Desert, with camels, watering at Giles's famous Queen Victoria Spring. Percy remained at Coolgardie with their partner Mr Driffield to work the mines they already had. It was Carnegie's first experience of the animals he came to love: on this trip they were once without water for 12 days and covered 320 kilometres. The camels belonged to a remarkable man from Alsace called Luck, who taught Carnegie a lot about the bush and about camels.

They discovered a reef and Carnegie also experienced the charm of travelling in the Australian desert; the silence, the first little noises that herald the dawn, the cold nights after the fiery days.

"There is a charm about the bush—the perfect peace in the 'free air of God'—that so takes hold of some men that they can never be happy anywhere else."

When they returned to Coolgardie on 22 June 1894 they had been 90 days out and had been reported dead.

On 10 November 1894 Carnegie started out on another expedition for Hampton Plains Pastoral Company. On this expedition they found gold. Fired with enthusiasm Carnegie set off for Coolgardie with two camels, riding Satan and leading Misery, to apply for a lease. The journey nearly cost him his life, as he contracted typhoid fever. He was so weak that he would not let the camels go free at night in case he couldn't catch them in the morning: they slept on either side of him and kept the cold wind off him. His route was blocked by a salt lake and for the first time he knew despair. He would have died but for his extraordinary will and reserves of strength. But he finally reached Coolgardie, and later Perth, where he spent several weeks convalescing.

With his share of the money from the sale of the mine he returned to London in 1895, and came back to Western Australia in 1896. He then achieved his ambition to outfit his own exploring and prospecting expedition. His aim was to explore the country between Coolgardie and the Kimberley Range, cutting north across the tracks of the only other white men, Warburton, Giles and Forrest, who had been there on their east-west journeys.

As companions he had Big Joe Breaden and his black boy Warri, Charlie Stansmore and Godfrey Massie. He had nine camels, including his old friends Satan, Misery and Czar, a little fox terrier called Val, and provisions for six months. They left Coolgardie on 9 July 1896.

Before long they were only too well acquainted with that "accursed vegetation", spinifex, whose needle-like prickles torture both man and beast. However, Carnegie was too good an observer not to see that it was the spinifex that held the country together and stopped it blowing away.

Carnegie had to cross three types of desert: the rolling sands, the gravel with granite outcrops of the Gibson Desert (named by Giles after his companion who died there), and the terrible parallel sandhills. On one occasion they traversed at right angles some 105 sand ridges in seven hours, some of them considerably more than 30 metres high. All in all, on the north and south journeys they crossed 1400 kilometres of these sand hills. Carnegie analyses the psychological effect of the physical fatigue from which they suffered. "I found it really impossible to restrain myself from breaking out into blind rages about nothing in particular."

After entering the desert they soon found themselves in desperate need of water, and in the first of several reprehensible actions, Carnegie captured a "buck" as he calls an Aboriginal man, who would supposedly lead them to water. Carnegie tied him up with a rope at night and took turns to watch him. "King Billy", as they christened him, led them to a pool in a deep cave. This was a permanent spring. Defending himself, Carnegie said "without the aid of natives we could not hope to find water . . . I felt myself justified, therefore, in unceremoniously making captives from what wandering tribes we might fall in with." On one occasion they "treed a buck", who beat Carnegie over the head and arms with a stick as he climbed up the tree and chained the Aborigine's ankle to the trunk. The Aborigines the expedition captured seemed to settle down quite amicably with their captors; and their tribesmen made no attempt to rescue them.

CAMPSITE 1. SADDLE AND EQUIPMENT FOR THE PRIMARY SURVEYOR (WITH AXE) *Tim Storrier*

DAVID CARNEGIE
1871-1900

David Wynford Carnegie was born on 23 March 1871 in London, fourth son of the Earl of Southesk. He was educated at Charterhouse and at the Royal Indian Engineering College, Staines.

For a time he worked on a tea plantation in Ceylon, but he found this type of existence uncongenial. He was after adventure, and when gold was discovered in Western Australia at Coolgardie in 1892 he joined the rush. In September 1892, with his friend Lord Percy Douglas, he arrived at Albany, and set off for the goldfields via Perth, Northam and Southern Cross. As he said, they were lucky in comparison with many other diggers, for they had a riding horse and a packhorse each.

They did not strike it rich, and Carnegie for a time worked for wages while Douglas returned to England to organise funds for further gold-seeking. When Douglas returned they formed a partnership with a Mr Driffield and with a camel-man from Alsace called Luck, and with his camels they joined the rush to the new diggings at Kurnalpi, again without success.

Carnegie then led a prospecting expedition for the Hampton Plains Pastoral Company across the Hampton Plains north-east of Coolgardie into the desert. He left on 24 March 1894 with Luck and three camels and provisions for three months.

Later in that year, after he had returned to Coolgardie, a syndicate asked him to organise another prospecting expedition. This time he took two experienced diggers with him. Although he found auriferous country on this expedition, he fell dangerously ill on his return to secure the claim, and had a falling out with the syndicate, who would not even defray the cost of his illness. Returning to Lake Darlôt he supervised the sale of the mine, and with his share of the profit visited London in October 1895.

Back again in Western Australia he organised his own expedition to explore the country from Coolgardie to the Kimberley Range. With four men, nine camels and a dog he left on 9 July 1896, reaching Halls Creek on 4 December. He left on the return journey on 22 March 1897.

He again returned to England in 1897, and was awarded the Gill Medal of the Royal Geographical Society. *Spinifex and Sand*, the record of his time in Western Australia, was published in 1898.

In December 1899 he went to Northern Nigeria as assistant resident under Sir Fredrick Lugard. He was much respected by the Nigerians. While based at Lokoja he was killed by a poison arrow in a skirmish, dying on 21 November 1900. His letters from Nigeria were published in 1902 with an introduction by his sister.

In *Spinifex and Sand* he made some remarks about Australians which not only show how well he had come to understand Australians, but are remarkably prophetic of Gallipoli and France in World War I. "A common subject of speculation is whether or no Australians would make good soldiers; as to that my belief is, that once they felt confidence in their officers none could make more loyal or willing troops; without that confidence they would be ill to manage, for the Australian is not the man to obey another, merely because he is in authority—first he must prove himself fit to have that authority."

Establishing Friendly Relations (*Spinifex and Sand*)

Carnegie reached Halls Creek on 4 December 1896 after a journey of 2274 kilometres, having lost several camels from poison weed. Charlie Stansmore had also died, having been accidentally shot by his own gun. On an even more difficult return trip, they had with them horses as well as camels, which seemed nothing but a hindrance. Carnegie and his men left Halls Creek on 22 March 1897 and arrived at Coolgardie after an absence of 13 months and a journey of a little over 4800 kilometres. In the last stages they would have died of thirst if it had not been for a stroke of luck. They were down to their last 11 litres of water when they found footprints which led them to a creek and water.

On this, his major expedition, Carnegie found neither gold nor country which would support a stock route. At least, he says wryly, he demonstrated "to others that part of the interior that may best be avoided". He said good-bye to his "brave and true men" and ended by saying, "I verily believe that so large an extent of country, good or bad, has never been travelled through by a more cheerful party, or by one, the members of which were more in accord."

Carnegie's book is always easy to get on with, like the man himself, but it is also imaginative and surprising. For instance, on one expedition Carnegie sat up with his camel, Misery, who seemed to be dying from eating poison plant. Carnegie dosed Misery and with Misery's head in his lap, he read *Vanity Fair* for hour after hour, every now and then getting the camel to his feet and making him walk, and then reading some more *Vanity Fair*. Misery lived.

It is strange that from the harshest and most aloof regions of Australia Carnegie wrote one of the most companionable of Australian books.

Ethel Pedley
DOT AND THE KANGAROO

SYDNEY 1899

All this time the Kangaroo had been speaking, only Dot had been too surprised to listen. But now the gentle, soft voice of the kind animal caught her attention, and she found that the Kangaroo was in the middle of a speech.

"I understood what was the matter with you at once," she was saying, "for I feel just the same myself. I have been miserable, like you, ever since I lost my baby kangaroo. You also must have lost something. Tell me what it is?"

"I've lost my way," said Dot; rather wondering if the Kangaroo would understand her.

"Ah!" said the Kangaroo, quite delighted at her own cleverness, "I knew you had lost something! Isn't it a dreadful feeling? You feel as if you had no inside, don't you? And you're not inclined to eat anything—not even the youngest grass. I have been like that ever since I lost my baby kangaroo. Now tell me," said the creature confidentially, "what your way is like. I may be able to find it for you."

Dot found that she must explain what she meant by saying she had "lost her way", and the Kangaroo was much interested.

"Well," said she, after listening to the little girl, "that is just like you Humans; you are not fit for this country at all! Of course, if you have only one home in one place, you must lose it! If you made your home everywhere and anywhere, it would never be lost. Humans are no good in our bush," she continued. "Just look at yourself, now. How do you compare with a Kangaroo? There is your ridiculous sham coat. Well, you have lost bits of it all the way you have come today, and you're nearly left in your bare skin. Now look at my coat. I've done ever so much more hopping than you today, and you see I'm none the worse. I wonder why all your fur grows upon the top of your head," she said reflectively, as she looked curiously at Dot's long flaxen curls. "It's such a silly place to have one's fur the thickest! You see, we have very little there; for we don't want our heads made any hotter under the Australian sun. See how much better off you would be, now that nearly all your sham coat is gone, if that useless fur had been chopped into little, short lengths and spread all over your poor bare body. I wonder why you Humans are made so badly?" she ended, with a puzzled air.

Dot felt for a moment as if she ought to apologize for being so unfit for the bush, and for having all the fur on the top of her head. But, somehow, she had an idea that a little girl must be something better than a kangaroo, although the Kangaroo certainly seemed a very superior person; so she said nothing, but again began to eat the berries.

"You must not eat any more of these berries," said the Kangaroo, anxiously.

"Why?" asked Dot. "They are very nice, and I'm very hungry."

The Kangaroo gently took the spray out of Dot's hand and threw it away. "You see," she said, "if you eat too many of them, you'll know too much."

"One can't know too much," argued the little girl.

"Yes, you can, though," said the Kangaroo, quickly. "If you eat too many of those berries, you'll learn too much, and that gives you indigestion, and then you become miserable. I don't want you to be miserable any more, for I'm going to find your 'lost way'."

All the great children's books can be read by people of all ages, for what comes naturally as fantasy to a child can also liberate the imagination in an adult fed all day on harsh reality. However, *Dot and the Kangaroo* is most unusual in that it quite deliberately refers fantasy back to reality. It is meant to make both children and their parents think about what today is considered to be a very modern issue—conservation. The message of the book does not come across with a heavy thud; rather it infiltrates and then settles in the mind gently, like the effect of the berries the little lost girl Dot is given to eat by the kangaroo who saves her life, "the berries of understanding". By eating these she can understand the language of the bush creatures and enter into their world, which is often so cruelly assaulted by humans, both white and black.

Ethel Pedley meant the dedication of *Dot and the Kangaroo* to be taken very seriously. "To the children of Australia in the hope of enlisting their sympathies for the many beautiful, amiable, and frolicsome creatures of their fair land, whose extinction, through ruthless destruction, is being surely accomplished."

It is a remarkable dedication for a book published in 1899. At this time most Australians thought that animals and birds could be shot indefinitely for pleasure, as well as for their skins or meat, that the forests were inexhaustible and that the bush was simply there to be cleared.

Ethel Pedley was quite right to protest against the white man's despoliation of untouched Australia. She was less kind to the Aborigines, whom she dismisses as hideous savages who hunt kangaroos with their dogs and spears. She even makes fun of the corroborees, when a kangaroo dance is performed. But the Aborigines were conservationists, and, when they did kill the native birds and animals, it was for food, not for sport.

Although Ethel Pedley does have some of the prejudices of her day, *Dot and the Kangaroo* is a book that has scarcely dated at all. The poems are sometimes a little arch, but Dot is a most convincing child, and all the animals have clean, separate characters which are often expressed with a wit and word play that is very much to the point.

"Oh, don't think!" pleaded the kangaroo; "I never do myself!"

"I can't help it" explained the little girl. "What do you do instead?" she asked.

"I always jump to conclusions!"

Later the Kangaroo says, when Dot asks whether they will get safely to the bottom of an alarming descent, "I never think, but I know we shall."

" *I* wonder why all your fur grows
. . .upon the top of your head," she said
reflectively, as she looked curiously at Dot's long
flaxen curls. "It's such a silly place to have one's
fur the thickest! . . ."

The behaviour of the bush creatures is based on knowledge and instinct. The Kangaroo thinks it absurd that Dot should just have one home, which means that she can get lost when she leaves it. For the Kangaroo everywhere is home. The tragedy that haunts the Kangaroo is that she has lost her baby, her joey, not because he has wandered away but because she had to hide him when she was fleeing from human hunters, and he was not there when she returned. At the end of the book the mystery is explained. One of the men from the selection found Joey and took him back to the house – human interference again.

Ethel Pedley is a serious but not a solemn writer. The theme of bush knowledge is given an arcane twist by the Platypus, who is like an old scholar who knows everything but whom nobody can understand. Dot asks the Kangaroo whether the Platypus could help them find the way back home.

"I *never* think," said the Kangaroo, "but as the Platypus never goes anywhere, never associates with any other creature, and is hardly ever seen, I conclude it knows everything – it must you know." This quiet satire of the knowledge that resides in an ivory tower is typical of the way in which, in classic style, Ethel Pedley uses her animals to make fun of human traits.

The Platypus, who always refers to himself pompously by his proper name, *Ornithorhynchus paradoxus*, does give them good advice, which is to go and talk to the Willy Wagtail, who is always fraternising with humans. In pleasure Dot cries "Oh Platypus, how clever you are!" But this compliment is quite inadvised. She has referred to him as Platypus, and he explains severely to her that this is a very insulting name, for it means *broad-footed*, whereas when contracted his feet are very elegant. When his feelings are hurt, there is nothing for it, the Platypus has to sing. His Lewis Carroll-like song is full of long names like Iguanadon and Ichthyosaurus and impossibly erudite words like "flammivomous" and "neocomian".

"Dear Kangaroo" said she, "what was that song about?"

"I don't know", said the animal wistfully, "no one ever knows what the Platypus sings about."

The bush creatures have instinctual knowledge, which Dot also learns, such as how to survive in the bush, where to find water, and how to differentiate between the characters of the various animals. The Opossums are quarrelsome. When Dot asks the Koala why, he answers "Because they live in the same tree, of course. . . . If they lived in different trees, and never quarrelled, they wouldn't like it at all. They'd find life dull, and they'd get sulky. There's nothing worse than a sulky possum."

As for the Koala himself, who likes to sleep but also enjoys from time to time making the most hideous noises, when Dot asks, "As you don't like being waked yourself, why do you wake others then?", he simply answers "Because this is a free country."

One of the most successful characters is the rude Bittern who helps save the Kangaroo's life after the terrifying chase when she finally escapes from the Aborigines and the dogs with Dot in her pouch. The Kangaroo tells Dot to yell and scream. The Bittern joins in and the Aborigines are scared away by what they take to be a Bunyip. But then the Kangaroo collapses. Dot thinks she is dying. The Bittern shows her how to get water from the moss so she can give the Kangaroo a drink, and wet her fur, which saves her life.

When Dot thanks the Bittern for this, "The Bittern was greatly pleased at this praise, and in consequence it got still ruder, and making a face at Dot, exclaimed 'Yah!' and stalked off." Then it stops, and roughly directs them to a nice warm cave. The psychology is brilliantly realised. It immediately makes you think of someone you know.

Ethley Pedley also handles Dot skilfully. She is not sentimentalised; yet she can be enchanting as well as a figure of pathos. When she and the Kangaroo are following the Willy Wagtail's directions they go through some very pretty country where trailing creepers hang down like swings. Dot immediately climbs into one of the loops and swings and sings, and the Kangaroo comes to the conclusion that "Dot was certainly quite as nice as a Joey Kangaroo".

From D O T A N D T H E K A N G A R O O an original illustration by Frank Mahony

ETHEL PEDLEY
1860-1898

The daughter of a fashionable London dentist who practised in Hanover Square, Ethel Pedley was born at Acton, England in 1860. Her mother, Eliza (née Dolby) was the sister of the famous contralto singer, Madame Sainton-Dolby.

Ethel showed an early aptitude for music, and began to learn the piano at the age of five; at seven she decided to be "an Artist like Auntie". She studied with Mr Foghill, the bandmaster of Crystal Palace, and went to the concerts at the Crystal Palace. It was arranged that she would be enrolled in the Royal Academy of Music as a pianist, but in the year she was going to enter, her father's ill health forced the whole family to move to Australia in search of a warmer climate.

They settled in Sydney, where Ethel was fortunate in finding a fine teacher in Mr Paling. She took up the violin, and gave some public concerts, before being sent to England to study singing.

In London she studied at the well-known vocal school of her aunt, and at the Royal Academy of Music, where she learned the violin under M. Sainton. She was a medallist in 1881. She was asked to stay on and give concerts in England, but her health had been affected by the very cold winter of 1881, and she returned to Australia in 1882.

In Sydney she gave concerts and taught music. Much of her time was spent in training choruses, and she was instrumental in founding St Cecilia's Choir. In 1888 she conducted a concert in which, for the first time in Australia, all the performers were women.

She was initially associated with the composer Emmeline Woolley. In 1895 soloists of the St Cecilia's Choir gave the first performance of a cantata, *The Captive Soul*, with music by Emmeline Woolley and libretto and verses by Ethel Pedley. It was well received by Sydney critics and the public. The story concerns a fay (fairy) who, longing for human love, captures a soul on its way to earth and becomes a human maiden. However, her human life is not a success, and eventually she is burnt as a witch. The soul returns to Paradise.

Dot and the Kangaroo was published in London in 1899 and was an immediate and lasting success. It was adapted for stage presentation and published under the same title in Sydney in 1924.

Ethel Pedley died aged 38 in 1898.

After further adventures with the gossipy Bower-Birds and the shrewd Emus, Dot has to appear before an Animal Court, charged with all the wrongs the "Bush creatures have suffered for the cruelties of white Humans". Dot's natural innocence and incapacity to believe that any harm can be done to her is beautifully contrasted with the very adult satire on the idiocies of human law which the bush creatures are so sedulously copying. It is an episode of great subtlety which can be read on several entertaining different levels, like a medieval Parliament of Birds.

"*If you eat too many of those berries, you'll learn too much, and that gives you indigestion, and then you become miserable. I don't want you to be miserable any more, for I'm going to find your 'lost way'.*"

The happy ending, the reunion of Dot and her parents, is almost marred by tragedy when her father lifts his gun to shoot the Kangaroo, who has Dot in her pouch. Jack, the station hand, knocks the gun up and saves Dot's and the Kangaroo's lives. The point goes home, that even good men like Dot's father will kill the bush creatures.

Never again, of course, after Dot has told her story. Even so, the Kangaroo does "not like to be stroked by a man who let off guns". The happy ending is assured by the appearance of little Joey, who had been found by Jack.

Humans and animals are both happy, but the Kangaroo will not again allow Dot to eat the berries of understanding. It is not right that she should learn too much.

They reached the house just as Dad arrived at the steps on the mare.

"Don't! See if he knows me," Dan said, silencing Bill, who began yelling to announce the home-coming of the heir.

Dad stared hard from the party approaching him to the horses left unprotected in the dray, scowled, and looked ugly.

Dan separated himself from the others.

"Doesn't know me from a crow – told y' he wouldn't," he said, saluting Dad as though Dad were a colonel with gold lace and a wooden leg.

"I don't know who y' are man," Dad answered gruffly and was about to revile Dave for wasting time when Dan bowed like a man winding water and said, "Your fust-born . . . Daniel, sir – Daniel Damascus Rudd."

Dad nearly fell off the mare.

"Dan!" he blurted out and urged the old mare towards the prodigal and stretched out his hand. But all at once he checked himself. He remembered he had kicked Dan out and never wanted to see him again. He changed colour.

Then it was that Dan showed himself a strategist.

"Not a word – not one syllable," he said in grave tones, seizing Dad's hand without a blush. "I know what's in your mind, exactly. Say nothing -- it's past. Let it slide . . . You turned me out, that's true, but I don't mind – I deserved it. But I went – I obeyed like a man, didn't I? And now – " Dan paused, so that Mother and all standing round her might hear – "and

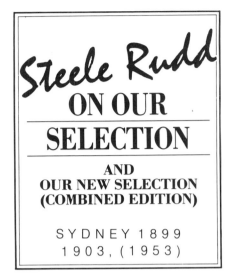

Steele Rudd
ON OUR
SELECTION

AND
OUR NEW SELECTION
(COMBINED EDITION)

SYDNEY 1899
1903, (1953)

now I'm back – " paused again – "back a wiser – " another pause – "a better – " here Dan smote himself hard on the thigh where his pocket had been, before he tore it out to wear on his foot – "and – " elevating his voice – "a richer man – wanting no one's favour, fearing nobody's frown!"

Dan was a rare speaker.

Dad never before displayed so much agility in dismounting, except when he fell off. He gripped Dan by both hands. Large tears like hailstones gathered and broke in his big eyes, and one smothered sob like a colt choking was all we heard. It was too much for us. We stared at our feet and felt we should have been dead. If there was one thing more than another we couldn't stand it was Dad blubbering.

"Never mind," Dan said in tones of forgiveness, holding a hand high above Dad's head. "Never mind! Fer me own part it's fergotten long enough ago, 'n' I'm back. 'N', as I hinted before, well off, Dad, well off – independent!" And he looked down on Dad and smiled.

Dan was an object lesson in filial affection.

Dave smiled, too, and went back to work. Dave smiled because he knew what a beautiful liar Dan was.

Dan followed Dad inside and had something to eat. He ate everything Sarah placed before him. Then he sat back, and all the rest of the afternoon talked to Dad and Mother, and admired the furniture, and smoked and spat. But he didn't spit on the floor. He rose every time and went to the door and did it on the clean boards of the veranda that had just been scrubbed.

Dan confided to Dad his plans for the future. He'd had enough outback life, he said, and intended putting a bit of money into a farm and settling down. If he could get a suitable place, about eighteen hundred acres with water, he'd start dairying, milk a hundred cows, feed them on lucerne, and fatten wethers and steers beside.

Dad said there was a big thing in it, and knew the very place Dan required – "Curry's," he said, "joining me. Two thousand acres, creek runnin' right through it, two pounds ten an acre."

"We'll have a look at it," Dan said reflectively.

Just before tea-time Dan apologized to Mother for the sad condition of his clothes. "Fact is," he remarked, "me wardrobe's comin' down be train, so I'm afraid y'll have to put up with me as I am till it's here."

Mother said if he liked he could put on some of Dave's for a change. Dan thought he would. He put on a full suit of Dave's, besides a shirt and collar, and came to tea a new man. He put them all on the next day, too, and never took them off any more.

Steele Rudd's immensely popular stories about the farm where Dad, Mother, Dave, Sal, Dan, Kate, Joe and the other children work, nearly starve, and eventually prosper, are often misinterpreted as being only "knockabout" humour. There is certainly plenty of humour in them and sometimes Rudd goes for little more than slapstick. But the stories are the stuff of human comedy, and as such, carry a great deal of anguish in them. Rudd meant them as a tribute to small selectors like his own family. In a broadcast late in his life he said that he had wanted "to tell faithfully all I knew of the life our family and neighbouring families had lived".

Rudd's immense respect for Mother underpins the stories. (She is *never* referred to as 'Mum'.) She is never made fun of, as the other characters are. Nor does she ever say much, though some of her remarks are very telling. "She said she had shaken the [flour] bag to get enough to make scones for the morning's breakfast, and unless some was got somewhere there would be no bread for dinner." The loneliness of the selection is expressed through her. Although there is always some communal effort, frequently comic, involving Dad and the boys and the smaller children, the loneliness is left for her to bear by herself.

"I often wonder how the women stood it the first few years, and I can remember how Mother, when she was alone, used to sit on a log where the lane is now and cry for hours. Lonely! It *was* lonely."

"It" is a selection (a small farm used for agricultural purposes) adjoining a sheep run on the Darling Downs in Queensland. Rudd wrote half a dozen books of stories about the old and the new selections, and together they make what today would be called a "discontinuous narrative", which is held together by a continuing family of characters. These remain as they always were, except perhaps for Dan. Their comfortable familiarity to the reader is part of their charm.

The first story, "Starting the Selection", brilliantly gives the essence of it all, the harshness, the simplicity, the struggle to tame the wilderness and make the farm work. "No mistake, it was a real wilderness—nothing but trees, goannas, dead timber, and bears; and the nearest house, Dwyer's, was three miles away." The timber is the enemy that has to be cleared before corn, and later wheat and barley can be planted. Then the kangaroos and wallabies become the enemy. No wonder the Rudds are not conservationists. To begin with they have no draught horse. All the water they have is the small supply in Dad's well, and the springs two miles away, which are likely to have a few dead animals in them, so that the water has to be purified through charcoal.

The returns from the first harvest do not even clear the storekeeper's account. Kangaroos and wallabies and the neighbours' cattle get into the crops; a fire destroys the fence. The hardness of the life demands humour to make it bearable. This equation should never be overlooked in any assessment of Rudd's writing. And if the humour is sometimes cruel, so was life. Yet there is often a great tenderness in the humour, as in one of the best stories, "The Night We Watched for Wallabies", when Dad, cursing and threatening, gets all the children out of the house on a bitter cold night to protect an almost non-existent crop from hordes of wallabies, leaving at the house only Mother and Sal and the strange woman who has been staying for several days. Late at night Sal comes and tells Dad to return to the house. "At dawn he appeared again, with a broad smile on his face, and told us that mother had got another baby—a fine little chap. *Then* we knew why Mrs Brown had been staying at our place."

As the stories progress the characters become more clearly defined. Dad is a hard worker, tough and determined, and flies off the handle easily; he is always respectful to Mother, and does not waste soft words on the children. He has no ear for music, though all the children are good concertina players. He is determined to see the best of things. When there is no tea, ". . . Dad showed Mother how to make a new kind. He roasted a slice of bread on the fire till it was like black coal, then poured the boiling water over it and let it draw well. Dad said it had a capital flavour—*he* liked it!"

"*D*an!" he blurted out and urged the old mare towards the prodigal and stretched out his hand. But all at once he checked himself. He remembered he had kicked Dan out and never wanted to see him again. He changed colour.

When Dad and Dave are grubbing stumps to clear a new paddock, with the temperature over the Fahrenheit century, "Dad wished to be cheerful and complacent. He said, putting the pick down and dragging his flannel off to wring it, 'It's a good thing to sweat well.' Dave didn't say anything."

Nobody holds it against Dad that every now and then he gets drunk, as when his old horse Emelina comes back home with Dad's swag, having left him at the pub, "wanting to fight the publican for a hundred pounds". Though he does once go up the bush, working to earn money, he resists his son Dan's pleas for him to leave the farm and make easier money elsewhere.

Dave is the silent one, and a great worker. Eventually he tires of being sworn at and treated as a child and decides to leave home and work for someone else. But after eight days he can't stand the loneliness and goes home again. On another occasion Dave breaks out and gets drunk with the thresher in his tent. Dad is furious, "looking across at Dave like a Chief Justice". He storms out to speak severely to the thresher, while Mother listens anxiously for the sounds of a fight. But McPhee the thresher comes from Dumfries, and it seems Dad does too, especially when the bottle of Scotch comes out. "They talked of Scotland, at least McPhee did. Dad didn't know anything about Scotland."

Joe, who stutters, is a born clown and a naturalist, terrifying the household with snakes. Kate, in one notable story, gets married. Sal becomes Sarah, and on the new selection, "We saw that changed circumstances had made a new girl of Sarah. She had an abundance of leisure time now and revelled in reading the *Family Herald* and other intellectual papers; took a keen interest in fashions; studied etiquette hard, and wherever she visited took stock and learnt things."

Dan, to begin with, is the dashing one who leaves the farm to go shearing and comes home with money when Dad has none. Dad loves Dan and stays up all night talking to him. But the love changes to exasperation when Dan just stands around watching everyone else work. Dad shouts, " 'Out of this!'—placing his hand on Dan, and shoving him. 'You've loafed long enough on me! Off y' go t' the devil!' " In the end, after 14 years, Dan returns again, but he is a broken man, all his charm gone.

UNTITLED *Percy Lindsay*

STEELE RUDD
1868-1935

Arthur Hoey Davis ("Steele Rudd") was born in 1868 at Drayton, near Toowoomba in Queensland, of Welsh and Irish extraction. His father ran the smithy at Drayton before following the tin-mining rush to Stanthorpe. He then took up a selection at Emu Creek, where "with a small paddock of brothers and sisters" Steele Rudd grew up.

He was educated at the local school. Writing to A. G. Stephens of the *Bulletin* in 1897 Rudd says, "When I wasn't watering cows or driving horses in the plough or hunting kangaroos or bears, I was at school up to about the age of 12. I do not know if I was very bright there. But I remember the school-master telling me I was the smartest boy in my class. I also remember being the only one in the class."

At 15 Rudd went to work as a junior stockrider at Pilton station, where he loved the horse work but hated slashing Bathurst burr.

At 18 he became a clerk in the office of the Curator of Intestate Estates in Brisbane, and was later transferred to the Sheriff's Office. He was an enthusiastic oarsman, and contributed a column on rowing to a weekly called the *Chronicle*. Wanting a pseudonym for his writing, he adopted the name of the English eighteenth-century essayist Steele, and needing some reference to rowing, added "Rudd" as a shortening of "rudder". Rudd was always a keen sportsman, and later became an outstanding polo player.

In 1894 he married Christina Brodie, who had attended the Emu Creek school at the time he did. In 1895 his first stories began to appear in the *Bulletin* where over the years he became a favourite with Stephens and Archibald. The technical demands of the *Bulletin* help to explain the shortness of the stories of Rudd and other writers of the time. The attitudes of the times, and of the editors of the *Bulletin*, also help to explain the moral proscriptions contained in those stories.

In 1903, the year of publication of *Our New Selection*, Rudd resigned his job at the Justice Department. He started up the monthly *Steele Rudd's Magazine*. Although it succeeded at first in Brisbane, it then failed in Sydney, leaving him with heavy financial losses.

In 1912 *On Our Selection* was dramatised by Bert Bailey and taken on tour by his company, and was an immense success in Adelaide, Brisbane, Sydney and Melbourne. The first film of *On Our Selection* was made in 1920 by Raymond Longford and starred Bert Bailey as "Dad". Later, in 1932, Bailey made *On Our Selection* into one of the most successful of Australian films.

Steele Rudd was described as "a tall, ruddy-faced man of mercurial temperament, kind of heart, fiery of temper, an excellent talker and a charming companion". A. G. Stephens called him a "shrewd, genial native of the bush". He dressed elegantly and once said to Bill FitzHenry of the *Bulletin*, when criticised for wearing a dinner suit: "How did he expect me to turn up? In moleskin trousers, with a cabbage-tree hat and blucher boots?"

In 1917, after living again on the Darling Downs, the Rudds went to Clayfield in Brisbane; Christina Rudd had a nervous breakdown, and by 1926 she was living permanently in an institution. Rudd, after a period of illness, died in Brisbane in 1935. His biography was written by his friend of later years, Winifred Hamilton.

There are, of course, other characters as well as the Rudds. The parson, Mr Macpherson, though not a bad chap, is of a breed that Dad does not care for. When they were poor, on the first selection, they had to eat kangaroo meat, but when visitors come they hide the kangaroo leg hanging on the veranda, to keep up appearances. In more prosperous times, on the new selection, Dad hangs a kangaroo leg up conspicuously when he sees the new parson coming, as he knows he will then not stop for a meal.

Perhaps the most interesting character of all is the "hatter" who comes to work for them, Cranky Jack, and the story of that name is in some respects the finest of all. Here the humour takes on a wild, almost apocalyptic quality unlike anything else in Rudd's writing.

Rudd's serviceable prose always rises to the occasion when his keenness of observation demands it.

A sweltering summer's afternoon. A heat that curled and withered the very weeds. The corn-blades drooping, sulking still. Mother and Sal ironing, mopping their faces with a towel and telling each other how hot it was. The dog stretched out across the doorway. A child's bonnet on the floor, the child out in the sun. Two horsemen approaching the slip-rails.

The living room at the first selection has an earth-and-cow-dung floor. After an all-night dance, "you couldn't stay inside, because the floor broke up. And talk about dust! Before morning the room was like a draughting-yard."

One of the most engaging qualities of the Rudds and their neighbours is their cheerfulness, and despite all their hardships they still love to dance. Neighbours drop in for a surprise party. And Kate's wedding is of course a great occasion. There is an unforgettable episode just before the wedding when Dave practises his dancing at evening in the horse paddock, bowing to the saplings and the stumps. Young Johnson, watching, races to the house to tell everyone that Dave has gone mad.

And then there is the occasion when Dave falls in love. "Dave was always the unlucky one. When he wasn't bitten by a snake or a dog he was gored by a cow or something. This time it was a woman. Dave was in love." Poor Dave! The conventions of the time demanded such delicacy that it is only by reading between the lines that one realises that Dave's Fanny has become pregnant by Dave's rival, who is forced to return to marry her. Another such scene behind the scenes occurs at the very end of *Our New Selection* when, after Dan has married Mary MacSmith, Mrs Geraghty drags her daughter Polly, "into MacSmith's place, and, within hearing of the whole family, told Dan he wasn't a man or he would have married Polly, and asked him what he meant to do. "Dan was imperturbable. He laughed and said, 'Git out!'" But his wife leaves him and, worse, goes to the store and buys "a cart-load of goods in his name".

The *Bulletin*, which gave Rudd his start in writing, called him the first Australian humourist. So he was, and he is still one of the best. He is also a deep and sympathetic observer of pioneering life, in which humour was as essential as flour.

THE
JOE WILSON
STORIES

SYDNEY 1901

The first turn we got with Jim was the worst. I had had the wife and Jim camping with me in a tent at a dam I was making at Cattle Creek; I had two men working for me, and a boy to drive one of the tip-drays, and I took Mary out to cook for us. And it was lucky for us that the contract was finished and we got back to Gulgong, and within reach of a doctor, the day we did. We were just camping in the house, with our goods and chattels anyhow, for the night; and we were hardly back home an hour when Jim took convulsions for the first time.

Did you ever see a child in convulsions? You wouldn't want to see it again: it plays the devil with a man's nerves. I'd got the beds fixed up on the floor and the billies on the fire—I was going to make some tea, and put a piece of corned beef on to boil overnight—when Jim (he'd been queer all day, and his mother was trying to hush him to sleep)— Jim, he screamed out twice. He'd been crying a good deal, and I was dog-tired and worried (over some money a man owed me) or I'd have noticed at once that there was something unusual in the way the child cried out: as it was I didn't turn round till Mary screamed "Joe! Joe!" You know how a woman cries out when her child is in danger or dying—short, and sharp, and terrible. "Joe! Look! Look! Oh, my God, our child! Get the bath, quick! quick! it's convulsions!"

Jim was bent back like a bow, stiff as a bullock-yoke, in his mother's arms, and his eyeballs were turned up and fixed—a thing I saw twice afterwards and don't want ever to see again.

I was falling over things getting the tub and the hot water, when the woman who lived next door rushed in. She called to her husband to run for the doctor, and before the doctor came she and Mary had got Jim into a hot bath and pulled him through.

The neighbour woman made me up a shake-down in another room and stayed with Mary that night; but it was a long while before I got Jim and Mary's screams out of my head and fell asleep.

You may depend I kept the fire in, and a bucket of water hot over it for a good many nights after that; but (it always happens like this, there came a night, when the fright had worn off, when I was too tired to bother about the fire, and that night Jim took us by surprise. Our wood-heap was done, and I broke up a new chair to get a fire, and had to run a quarter of a mile for water; but this turn wasn't so bad as the first, and we pulled him through.

You never saw a child in convulsions? Well, you don't want to. It must be only a matter of seconds, but it seems long minutes; and half an hour afterwards the child might be laughing and playing with you, or stretched out dead. It shook me up a lot. I was always pretty high-strung and sensitive. After Jim took the first fit, every time he cried, or turned over, or stretched out in the night, I'd jump: I was always feeling his forehead in the dark to see if he was feverish, or feeling his limbs to see if he was "limp" yet. Mary and I often laughed about it—afterwards. I tried sleeping in another room, but for nights after Jim's first attack I'd just be dozing off into a sound sleep, when I'd hear him scream, as plain as could be, and I'd hear Mary cry, "Joe!—Joe!"—short, sharp, and terrible—and I'd be up and into their room like a shot, only to find them sleeping peacefully. Then I'd feel Jim's head and his breathing for signs of convulsions, see to the fire and water, and go back to bed and try to sleep. For the first few nights I was like that all night, and I'd feel relieved when daylight came. I'd be in first thing to see if they were all right; then I'd sleep till dinner-time if it was Sunday or I had no work. But then I was run down about that time: I was worried about some money for a wool-shed I put up and never got paid for; and besides, I'd been pretty wild before I met Mary.

I was fighting hard then—struggling for something better. Both Mary and I were born to better things, and that's what made the life so hard for us.

The stories collected in Henry Lawson's two volumes *Joe Wilson* and *Joe Wilson's Mates*, though not all strictly related, form a coherent group in Lawson's work. And in the eight *Joe Wilson* stories Lawson's own character, both appealing and weak, is exposed as nowhere else in his writing. Some of his finest stories are in the two collections, from the pain and the stark lack of alternatives in "Water Them Geraniums" to the explosive humour of "The Loaded Dog".

It is interesting to read *Joe Wilson* after Steele Rudd's *On Our Selection*. The stories in both books are about selectors and the tough times they went through. There is sadness and cruelty behind both, but survival in Lawson is a kind of broken poetry, while in Steele Rudd it is energised by humour. Thus life is desperate for the Wilsons and their neighbours, while it is ebullient for the Rudds. It was not that Lawson was incapable of humour (far from it—he is the author of "The Loaded Dog") nor that he did not understand the vital essence of humour for survival in bush life. "They had a sense of the ridiculous, most of those poor sundried Bush-women. I fancy that that helped save them from madness." There is never any thought that the Rudds, or their neighbours (except for the hatter, Cranky Jack) are ever anywhere near madness.

There are several vital differences between the Rudds and the Wilsons, which in turn illuminate the work of Steele Rudd and Henry Lawson. The Rudds form a sturdy, absolutely unbreakable family group. Dan may splinter off, and Dad in later years sometimes thinks more of money than Mother, but the familiy is a force that not even the Australian bush can withstand. The Wilsons on the other hand, are a slightly misfitted young couple whose baby has convulsions. Joe says of himself, "I was not fit to 'go on the land'. The place was only fit for some stolid German, or Scotsman, or even Englishman and his wife, who had no ambition but to bullock and make a farm of the place. I had only drifted here through carelessness, brooding and discontent."

Joe and his wife Mary have both had lonely childhoods without, especially in Joe's case, the inner resources to welcome the freedom of being alone. Mary's father had been the younger son of a well-to-do English family who was sent with £1000 to Australia to make his way. He drank his money and died young. Her mother was the daughter of a German immigrant. The children "were adopted around". As for Joe, "I'd had no boyhood to speak of." More dangerously, "I was not a healthy-minded, average boy; I reckon I was born for a poet by mistake, and grew up to be a Bushman, and didn't know what was the matter with me—or the world." The result for both of them is a fatal inability to accept the world around them, with no compensating energy to erupt into ambition to change that world. "Both Mary and I were born to better things, and that's what made the life so hard for us."

I had had the wife and Jim camping with me in a tent at a dam I was making at Cattle Creek; I had two men working for me, and a boy to drive one of the tip-drays, and I took Mary out to cook for us.

Joe's drinking and Dad Rudd's, or even Dave's rare outbreaks are totally different. Dad drinks to blow off steam and soon sobers up. Joe drinks "because I felt less sensitive, and the world seemed a lot saner and better and kinder when I had a few drinks: I loved my fellow-man then and felt nearer to him." One of the most interesting things about the Rudds is that there is precious little need for mateship among them. The family is sufficient. But for Joe, and of course for Lawson himself, mateship is essential, but all too often it

is a prop for personal inadequacy. And Joe is incapable of contributing his share of the sturdy central support that is the basis of marriage, a relationship more demanding than mateship. Joe will not let down his mates, but he is only too aware of how often he lets down Mary.

In the happiness of the first story there is little thought of such unhappy endings. "*Joe Wilson's Courtship*", in fact, begins with a little essay on happiness, although there is something ominous in the repeated injunction, "Make the most of your courting days, you young chaps, for they will never come again." Joe may have been born for a poet, but Lawson gives a most engaging picture of him as a wild young man, as "a fool of a bushman". He would never have got anywhere with Mary, though she was keen enough, if it had not been for his mate Jack. "I reckon it was all on account of that blasted Jack working me up."

Mary works in the house of the squatter Black, but on the basis of helping out rather than as a servant, for her father had been a friend of Black. Black is an important figure in Lawson's work, as he transcends the usual glib myth about the hostility between the bushman and the boss. He belonged to Australia as his English wife never did. (What a lot of harm those unconverted English women did!)

> He was a good sort, was Black the squatter: a squatter of the old school who'd shared the early hardships with his men, and couldn't see why he should not shake hands and have a smoke and a yarn over old times with any of his old station-hands that happened to come along. But he'd married an Englishwoman after the hardships were over, and she'd never got any Australian notions.

Joe, somewhere in his twenties, and his old mate Jack go to do some building and fencing for Black, and it is Jack who is determined to get Joe off with Mary, a nice little dumpling called Possum because of her bright eyes. Joe bumbles around, and despite Jack's efforts it might have come to nothing if it were not for a rather sinister shearer, a nasty character called Romany, who speaks disrespectfully of Mary. Joe fights him. It is a wonderfully described fight, for Joe's consciousness of not only his lack of ability as a fighter but of his active horror of it. "I hated the idea of hitting a man. It seemed brutal to me. I was too sensitive and sentimental." After being knocked down a few times, "I had the bushman up in me now, and wasn't going to be beaten while I could think."

Indirectly, Joe wins Mary as a result of winning the fight, although he is so bashful he forgets to propose to her even after the seal of the kiss.

"Brighten's Sister-in-Law", the two stories of "Water Them Geraniums", and the four stories "A Double Buggy at Lahey's Creek", chronicle the later lives of Joe and Mary, from their first two years in a weatherboard shanty at Gulgong, where Joe does odd jobs, to the small selection where they take up farming at Lahey's Creek. They have a child, Jim, who has convulsions, and who, Joe thinks, is too "intelligent for his age". Already one of Joe's inadequacies is being revealed in that, in Jim's words, "You never has time to know Jim at home," and in his inability to communicate with Mary. "Why don't you talk to me, Joe?" she says.

Brighten's sister-in-law is a "big hard looking woman" who has been a hospital matron. She saves young Jim's life.

THE PIONEER (Detail) *Frederick McCubbin*

HENRY LAWSON
1867-1922

Henry Lawson was always inclined to make the worst of things, especially of anything in relation of himself. Although his parents were certainly poor, they were both highly intelligent, and his mother (however difficult to get on with) was one of the most remarkable of Australian women.

His father, Peter Larsen, born in 1833, was a Norwegian ship's officer (he held a master's ticket) who jumped ship to go to the goldfields. His mother Louisa, the daughter of a store and shanty keeper at Gulgong, was born in 1846 near Mudgee, the granddaughter of early settlers. The first son, Henry, was born at Grenfell on 17 June 1867, and his name was registered as "Lawson". When Henry was a few months old they moved to Pipeclay, later to be called Eurunderee, where Henry's earliest memory was of a tent with a forked tree in front of it. After a spell looking for gold at Gulgong they retired to Eurunderee in 1871, to the hated poor selection that symbolised rural poverty and misery in Lawson's stories and poems.

He went to a number of local schools. He was a shy, delicate boy who at nine began to suffer from deafness, which became acute at 14. He suffered much from the fights between his intellectual, sensitive mother and his happy-go-lucky, odd-job father. He idealised his father, but received little affection from his mother.

In 1883 Louisa took the children to live in Sydney, where she published and edited two magazines, first the *Republican* and then *Dawn*. The latter was one of the first outlets for feminist writers in Australia. Henry worked from the age of 13 as a labourer and painter, his experiences forming a background for the story "Arvie Aspinall's Alarm Clock".

In 1887 his first published work, "Song of the Republic", appeared in the *Bulletin*. In 1890 he went to Western Australia with his brother Peter and worked there for a year. He was beginning to write stories as well as poems, and he was well supported by A. G. Stephens and the *Bulletin*; he also wrote for the Sydney *Worker*. In 1893 he went to New Zealand, where he had a job in the South Island as a telegraphic linesman. This was probably the happiest period of his life. Offered a job on the new paper, *Daily Worker*, he returned to Sydney; the paper went out of business, and Lawson was driven back to poverty. His heavy drinking probably dates from this time.

In 1895 Angus and Robertson published a verse collection, *In the Days When the World was Wide*. In 1896 he married Bertha Bredt, whose stepfather ran a radical bookshop. In 1900, by which time they had had two children, Lord Beauchamp, the governor of New South Wales, arranged for their fares to be paid to London. Here Henry did little more than drink. Using an advance from the publisher, Blackwood, Bertha took the children back to Sydney. Apart from a few months in 1902, Henry and Bertha did not live together again.

The rest of Lawson's life was a dismal downhill slide of drinking and cadging, and self-pity and treatment in hospital. Occasionally he rallied, as when with E. J. Brady on holidays in Victoria at Mallacoota Inlet. In A. G. Stephens's words, "At thirty he had worked out his alluvial field of youth; his mind lost vigour." He was granted a literary pension in 1920. He died in 1922, honoured by a brass band (something that he would have enjoyed) at his funeral.

But there is a gentleness beneath her strength, and she sees Joe as only a boy himself. After visiting Brighten's sister-in-law, "Mary was extra gentle for the next few days."

"Water Them Geraniums" is, in a way, a sequel to "The Drover's Wife". Together they make up Lawson's finest study of the lonely bushwoman, Mrs Spicer, who is alone up to 18 months at a time when her husband is away droving. In her rough way she does her best for her children. Mary every now and then has them over to teach them something. How well Lawson understands her difficulties! "I think the saddest and most pathetic sight on the face of God's earth is the children of very poor people made to appear well."

In the end, "a bit ratty" from "the heat and the dullness", she is truly "past carin'". Her last words to her daughter echo her frequently voiced injunction—"Be sure to water them geraniums." Mrs Spicer gives a further dimension to the despair that afflicts Joe.

The first stories of "A Double Buggy at Lahey's Creek" show Joe with more spark in him, even if the original impetus, as in the matter of planting spuds at Lahey's Creek, often comes from Mary. Mary, too, longs for a buggy, especially a double buggy which will take two horses or which can be converted back to one. As Mary's sister in Gulgong says to Joe, "Now if Mary had a comfortable buggy, she could drive in with the children oftener. Then she wouldn't feel the loneliness so much." It is Joe's greatest triumph when he drives home with the double buggy for Mary. This occurs after they have had their worst quarrel, and Joe has thought of his treatment of her as leading her to become a Mrs Spicer. Now Mary dashes out and says,

"Joe! Whose buggy is that?", and Joe answers, in typical laconic style, "Well I suppose it's yours." And the sense of friendship and human kindliness that Joe always longs for is for once triumphantly revealed in what Mary finds under the seats—boxes of goodwill presents from everyone at Gulgong.

The companion volume to *Joe Wilson*, *Joe Wilson's Mates*, contains three of Lawson's greatest stories, "The Loaded Dog", "A Bush Dance", and "Telling Mrs Baker", as well as the hilarious episodes of the bushmen getting the best of that dreadful publican, Poisonous Jimmy, whose speciality is using a pretty barmaid as bait and turning on free drinks so that the bushmen will cut out their cheques in his pub. There is also in that very funny story, "The Golden Graveyard", one of the most notable women in Australian literature, that "awful woman" Mother Middleton, an ex-convict who once "pulled a mounted policeman off his horse, and half killed him with a heavy pick-handle, which she used for poking down clothes in her boiler. She had said that he had insulted her."

But *Joe Wilson's Mates* is most notable for the delicate, characteristically oblique portraits of the mates, Dave Regan, Jim Bentley and Andy Page. It is Andy and the narrator who have to break the news of her husband's death to Mrs Baker, and to disguise the fact that it was the drink that did it.

Lawson's sympathy, humour and mastery of the laconic idiom and indirect narration are at their finest in *Joe Wilson* and *Joe Wilson's Mates*, with the addition, in the first selection, of an extraordinarily honest self portrait.

MY BRILLIANT CAREER

Miles Franklin

EDINBURGH 1901

He approached me and was stooping to kiss me. I cannot account for my action or condemn it sufficiently. It was hysterical – the outcome of an overstrung, highly excitable, and nervous temperament. Perhaps my vanity was wounded, and my tendency to strike when touched was up in arms. The calm air of ownership with which Harold drew near annoyed me, or, as Sunday-school teachers would explain it, Satan got hold of me. He certainly placed a long strong riding-whip on the table beneath my hand. As Harold stooped with the intention of pressing his lips to mine, I quickly raised the whip and brought it with all my strength right across his face. The instant the whip had descended I would have smashed my arm on the door-post to recall that blow. But that was impossible. It had left a great weal on the healthy sun-tanned skin. His moustache had saved his lips, but it had caught his nose, the left cheek, had blinded the left eye, and had left a cut on the temple from which drops of blood were rolling down his cheek and staining his white coat. A momentary gleam of anger shot into his eyes and he gave a gasp, whether of surprise, pain, or annoyance, I know not. He made a gesture towards me. I half expected and fervently wished he would strike. The enormity of what I had done paralysed me. The whip fell from my fingers and I dropped on to a low lounge behind me,

and placing my elbows on my knees crouchingly buried my face in my hands; my hair tumbled softly over my shoulders and reached the floor, as though to sympathetically curtain my humiliation. Oh, that Harold would thrash me severely! It would have infinitely relieved me. I had done a mean unwomanly thing in thus striking a man, who by his great strength and sex was debarred retaliation. I had committed a violation of self-respect and common decency; I had given a man an ignominious blow in the face with a riding-whip. And that man was Harold Beecham, who with all his strength and great stature was so wondrously gentle – who had always treated my whims and nonsense with something like the amused tolerance held by a great Newfoundland for the pranks of a kitten.

The clock struck eleven.

"A less stinging rebuke would have served your purpose. I had no idea that a simple caress from the man whose proposal of marriage you had just accepted would be considered such an unpardonable familiarity."

Harold's voice fell clearly, calmly,

cuttingly on the silence. He moved away to the other end of the room and I heard the sound of water.

A desire filled me to tell him that I did not think he had attempted a familiarity, but that I had been mad. I wished to say I could not account for my action, but I was dumb. My tongue refused to work, and I felt as though I would choke. The splash of the water came from the other end of the room. I knew he must be suffering acute pain in his eye. A far lighter blow had kept me sleepless a whole night. A fear possessed me that I might have permanently injured his sight. The splash of water ceased. His footfall stopped beside me. I could feel he was within touching distance, but I did not move.

Oh, the horrible stillness! Why did he not speak? He placed his hand lightly on my head.

"It doesn't matter, Syb. I know you didn't mean to hurt me. I suppose you thought you couldn't affect my dark, old, saddleflap-looking phiz. That is one of the disadvantages of being a big lumbering concern like I am. Jump up. That's the girl."

I arose. I was giddy, and would have fallen but for Harold steadying me by the shoulder. I looked up at him nervously and tried to ask his forgiveness, but I failed.

This is a most outstanding Australian book. Miles Franklin was a girl of only 16 when she wrote it. A. G. Stephens of the *Bulletin* called it "the very first Australian novel to be published". Henry Lawson, who wrote the Preface to it, said "the book is true to Australia – the truest I ever read". More than 75 years after its publication it was made into a memorable film.

But what makes *My Brilliant Career* so out of the ordinary is the fierce emotional and intellectual conflict in the 16-year-old heroine of the book, Sybylla Melvyn. When she turns 17 she has not been kissed (except by Everard Grey, "a kind of uncle and brother") and she is certainly not sweet. She longs for the sweetness of love but cannot help her natural

tartness. She wants above all to be a woman with an independent career but she also loves the station life of her well-off relations. She is always telling herself that she is short (as if that mattered) and ugly but in her first evening dress ("one of the prettiest and most idiotic customs extant") she cannot help looking at herself in the mirror and admiring what she sees. Such a bundle of contradictions can be infuriating, but one always forgives Sybylla for her honesty and the intensity of her feelings. It seems neither Sybylla nor Miles Franklin is aware of the conflicts of sexuality raging inside the girl. Her anger is not bad temper but a defence against her uncertainties. On the occasions when she is "content merely to be young" she is as lovable as she is intolerable when discontent gnaws at her again.

There is no autobiographical novel quite like *My Brilliant Career* in the literature of any country, both for the fire of the revelation of Sybylla's character, and for her love of her country which so appealed to Lawson. Turgenev is one of the very few great masters who could understand the intensity and purity of a 16-year-old girl's feelings, but he could never have coped with Sybylla's perversity—a girl who, having just agreed to become engaged to Harold Beecham, an extremely eligible and admirable young man, switches him across the face with a riding whip when he tries to kiss her.

The scene is totally convincing, but Sybylla and her creator are at one in their incapacity to recognise Sybylla's sexual motivation. Sybylla says, "my tendency to strike when touched was up in arms" and "Satan got hold of me". A moment later,

> The whip fell from my fingers and I dropped onto a low lounge behind me, and placing my elbows on my knees crouchingly buried my face in my hands; my hair tumbled softly over my shoulders and reached the floor, as though to sympathetically curtain my humiliation. Oh, that Harold would thrash me severely! It would have infinitely relieved me.

Some 20 pages later, having provoked the quiet, self-controlled man into angry jealousy, crying, "How dare you touch me!" she still allows him to seize her so tightly that she can "feel the heat of his body, and his big heart beating wildly".

He has become "splendidly alive". And when she goes to bed that night,

> I discovered on my soft white shoulders and arms—so susceptible to bruises—many marks, and black.
> It had been a very happy day for me.

No wonder Henry Lawson said nervously in his Preface, "I don't know about the girlishly emotional parts of the book—I leave that to girl readers to judge."

He approached me and was stooping to kiss me. I cannot account for my action or condemn it sufficiently. It was hysterical—the outcome of an overstrung, highly excitable, and nervous temperament. Perhaps my vanity was wounded, and my tendency to strike when touched was up in arms.

Havelock Ellis, who wrote monumental works about the psychology of sex, should have been able to judge better than "girl readers", but in a review that appeared a couple of years after the book's publication he wrote, "Something more than emotion is needed to make fine literature, and here we are minus any genuine instinct of art or any mature power of thought, and are left at the end only with a painful sense of crudity."

Pain can be very crude, and there is a great deal more than emotion in *My Brilliant Career*. It is odd that Havelock Ellis could not see how transparently and powerfully Miles Franklin portrays both Sybylla's physical needs and her revulsion at being touched.

More than anything else in the world Sybylla wants independence. In her introduction Miles Franklin proclaims her independence from the romantic novel of plot and description. In fact *My Brilliant Career is* romantic, is possessed of a plot that makes the reader want to know what is going to happen as a result of what has happened, and is the vehicle for a number of fine descriptions. The first of the latter is in fact on page one, Sybylla's faint recollections of life at the age of three, with her father on "a distant part of the run".

This was the idyllic time when Sybylla's father was still a fine bushman, "a swell" owning several stations totalling 81,000 hectares up in the high country of southern New South Wales. It is interesting that Henry Lawson admired *My Brilliant Career* so much, as Sybylla is of the squattocracy; her mother's pedigree is impeccable though her father's "included nothing beyond a grandfather". Sybylla's happiest days are on her very well-off relations' stations.

In no time Sybylla's father has sunk into drink and the squalor of a mortgaged farm, Possum Gully, near Goulburn. Sybylla despises her father, and does not get on well with her mother, whom she calls "unjust and cruel".

> There never was any sympathy between my mother and myself. We are too unlike. She is intensely matter-of-fact and practical, possessed of no ambitions or aspirations not capable of being turned into cash value. She is very ladylike, and though containing no spice of either poet or musician, can take a part in conversation on such subjects, and play the piano correctly, because in her young days she was thus cultivated; but had she been born a peasant, she would have been a peasant, with no longings unattainable in that sphere. She no more understood me than I understand the works of a watch.

Fortunately for Sybylla she is invited to stay with her grandmother on Caddagat station; she loves her grandmother and her aunt Helen. Sybylla has such talent for playing the piano and for singing that a friend of the family, a competent judge of such things, wants to take her to Sydney so she can be trained. Grannie will not think of such a career for Sybylla. Sybylla still has her writing, though that cannot release her from captivity. At least there are books at Grannie's, and she falls with rapture on Lawson and Paterson, "actually countrymen, fellow Australians!"

At 16 she is "a cynic and an infidel", convinced that love is not for her because she is ugly and clever, a hopeless combination. This is obviously one of her delusions. Despite

WAITING *Gordon Coutts*

MILES FRANKLIN
1879-1954

Miles Franklin's home country – the country of the stations in *My Brilliant Career* and the "Brent of Bin Bin" novels which she wrote under that pseudonym – is the high wild uplands west and south-west of Canberra. It is unspoiled still, with the freedom of the mountains, the forests and the rivers. A taste for freedom was bred in her from that country, and it was accentuated by her passionate desire to be an independent woman, something so difficult to achieve for an Australian girl born in 1879.

Miles's father, John Franklin, was the son of an early settler who had been running stock along the Goodradigbee River in 1847 and who had taken up Brindabella station in 1863. Her mother, Susannah Lampe, who married John Franklin in 1878, was descended from the Miles family, which went back to the First Fleet. Susannah's father, a German, ran his father-in-law's property of 12,000 hectares on the Tumut River at Old Talbingo.

Shortly before Miles was born in 1879, her mother rode 100 kilometres from Brindabella to Old Talbingo to have her baby. Miles was the oldest of seven brothers and sisters. In 1889 the family moved to a property near Goulburn, which Miles found very dull after the mountains.

My Brilliant Career was published in 1901. Although it was a work of fiction, the novel was autobiographical in form, and caused an uproar amongst Miles's family and friends. She withdrew the book from sale, left home and went to live in Sydney where she had a number of feminist friends.

In 1902 and 1903 she wrote a sequel to *My Brilliant Career*, *My Career Goes Bung*, but no publisher would handle it and it remained unpublished until 1946.

In 1905 she joined another Australian feminist, Alice Henry, in Chicago, and altogether she stayed away from Australia for 30 years. In Chicago, Miles managed the office of the Women's Trade Union League and edited their magazine, *Life And Labor*.

In 1915 she moved to England to help in the war effort, doing social work and joining in the Scottish Women's Hospital Unit. For a while she served in Macedonia as an orderly with the Serbian army, returning to London after the war to work for the National Housing Council.

In 1928 the first of six novels by "Brent of Bin Bin" was published. Her real identity was not discovered for many years, although the background of the high-country aristocracy and the style were unmistakably Miles Franklin's. After two visits home in 1928 and 1930, she settled permanently in Sydney in 1933.

She won the *Bulletin* Prior Memorial Prize in 1936 with *All That Swagger*, a family saga covering four generations. The most notable character in the novel is Danny Delacy, modelled on her father's father, Joseph Franklin, who had emigrated to Australia from Ireland in 1839 and settled near Yass.

In 1944, with Kate Baker, she wrote *Joseph Furphy – The Legend of the Man and his Book*, based on her early friendship and correspondence with Furphy. In her seventies, she wrote a sparkling and poetic autobiography, *Childhood at Brindabella*, which was not published until 1963. For many years she was a resolute, if somewhat narrow-minded, champion of Australian literature. The prestigious Miles Franklin Award for Australian fiction which bears her name was funded from her estate.

She died in Sydney in 1954 and her ashes were scattered in the creek at Talbingo.

---

her lack of belief in herself, Everard Grey proposes to her (and is rejected). The favoured son of the district, the rich Harold Beecham, is soon declaring his love; not to mention the unfortunate Frank Hawden, whom she rejoices in humiliating.

When her uncle Jay-Jay Bossier twits her with "the game" that she and Harry Beecham have been up to, her real wishes emerge. She declares roundly, "I never intend to marry. Instead of wasting so much money on me in presents and other ways, I wish you would get me something to do, a profession that will last me all my life, so that I may be independent." But her uncle thinks she is just joking.

Sybylla is still tempted by marriage and love. She accepts Harry's ring on the occasion she used the riding whip, but insists on a trial engagement of three months. Later she throws it to his feet in the orchard of Caddagat, but in a reconciliation shortly afterwards cries, "Oh Harold, I'm afraid I very nearly love you, but don't hurry me too much! You can think me sort of secretly engaged to you if you like, but I won't take your ring."

A catastrophe befalls Harry. He loses his money and his properties, and tells Sybylla she is free, that she is not to marry a poor man. Of course her reaction is absolutely the opposite, and she tells him he is to come back in four years. In the meantime she will look at no other man.

An even worse catastrophe is about to befall Sybylla. She is sent to the dirty farm of the frightful M'Swats to work as a governess and help pay off her father's debts to M'Swat. It is not just the fall from the culture and luxury of Caddagat

to the squalor of Barney's Gap that humiliates Sybylla; it is the blow to her pride and her hopes of independence. M'Swat is crude but not a bad fellow; Mrs M'Swat and the children are intolerable. There is no intellectual conversation. One day she attempts conversation with Mrs M'Swat.

"A penny for your thoughts."

"I wuz just watchin' the rain and thinkin' it would put a couple of bob a head more on sheep if it keeps on."

Sybylla falls sick and finally is allowed to return to Possum Gully, where she is not happy, especially when Grannie offers to take one of the girls at Caddagat and mother sends Sybylla's rather silly sister, Gertie, instead of her.

Then fortune makes her its most tempting offer. Harry recovers his fortune and stations and is richer than ever before. He comes back to Possum Gully to ask her to marry him. She refuses him, finally telling him in a letter "I like you better than any man I have ever seen, but I do not mean ever to marry."

The book ends with a song of praise to Australia. Sybylla does not know what the future holds for her, and she has been unable to reconcile love and life with a man with her independence. But she can openly and wholeheartedly admit that she loves Australia, that she is "a child of the mighty bush", and that she loves and respects her brother Australians, and loves and pities her sister Australians. "I love you. I love you," she repeats as she could never say it to a man, "I am only a – woman!"

Joseph Furphy

SUCH IS LIFE

SYDNEY 1903

Mary O'Halloran was perfect Young-Australian. To describe her from after-knowledge—she was a very creature of the phenomena which had environed her own dawning intelligence. She was a child of the wilderness, a dryad among her kindred trees. The long-descended poetry of her nature made the bush vocal with pure gladness of life; endowed each tree with sympathy, respondent to her own fellowship. She had noticed the dusky aspect of the ironwood; the volumed cumuli of rich olive-green, crowning the lordly currajong; the darker shade of the wilga's massy foliage-cataract; the clearer tint of the tapering pine; the clean-spotted column of the leopard tree, creamy white on slate, from base to topmost twig. She pitied the unlovely balah, when the wind sighed through its coarse, scanty, grey-green tresses; and she loved to contemplate the silvery plumage of the two drooping myalls which, because of their rarity here, had been allowed to remain in the horse-paddock. For the last two or three springs of her vivacious existence, she had watched the deepening crimson of the quondong, amidst its thick contexture of Nile-green leaves; she had marked the unfolding bloom of the scrub, in its many-hued beauty; she had revelled in the audacious black-and-scarlet glory of the desert pea. She knew the dwelling-place of every loved companion; and, by necessity, she had her own names for them all—since her explorations were carried out on Rory's shoulders, or on his saddle, and technicalities never troubled him. To her it was a new world, and she saw that it was good. All those impressions which

endear the memory of early scenes to the careworn heart were hers in their vivid present, intensified by the strong ideality of her nature, and undisturbed by other companionship, save that of her father.

This brings us to to the other mark of a personality so freshly minted as to have taken no more than two impressions. Rory was her guide, philosopher, and crony. He was her overwhelming ideal of power, wisdom, and goodness; he was her help in ages past, her hope for years to come (no irreverence intended here; quite the reverse, for if true family life existed, we should better apprehend the meaning of 'Our Father, who art in heaven'); he was her Ancient of Days; her shield, and her exceeding great reward.

A new position for Rory; and he grasped it with all the avidity of a love-hungered soul. The whole current of his affections, thwarted and repulsed by the world's indifference, found lavish outlet here.

After tea, Rory took a billy and went out into the horse-paddock to milk the goats—Mary, of course, clinging to his side. I remained in the house, confiding to Mrs. O'Halloran the high respect which Rory's principles and abilities had always commanded. But she was past all that; and I had to give it up. When a woman can listen with genuine contempt to the

spontaneous echo of her husband's popularity, it is a sure sign that she has explored the profound depths of masculine worthlessness; and there is no known antidote to this fatal enlightenment.

Rory's next duty was to chop up a bit of firewood, and stack it beside the door. Dusk was gathering by this time; and Mrs. O'Halloran called Mary to prepare her for the night, while Rory and I seated ourselves on the bucket-stool outside. Presently a lighted lamp was placed on the table, when we removed indoors. Then Mary, in a long, white garment, with her innocent face shining from the combined effects of perfect happiness and unmerciful washing, climbed on Rory's knees—not to bid him good-night, but to compose herself to sleep.

"Time the chile was bruk aff that habit," observed the mother, as she seated herself beside the table with some sewing.

"Let her be a child as long as she can, Mrs. O'Halloran," I remarked. "Surely you wouldn't wish any alteration in her."

"Nat without it was an altheration fur the betther," replied the worthy woman. "An' it 's little hopes there is iv hur, consitherin' the way she's rairt. Did iver anybody hear o' rairin' childher' without batin' them when they want it?"

"You bate hur, an' A 'll bate you!" interposed Rory, turning to bay on the most salient of the three or four pleas which had power to rouse the Old Adam in his unassertive nature.

"Well, A 'm sure A was bate—ay, an' soun'ly bate—when A was lek hur; an 'iv A did n't desarve it then, A desarved it other times, when A did n't git it."

In a now famous letter to Archibald of the *Bulletin*, Furphy wrote, "I have just finished writing a full-sized novel: title, *Such is Life*; scene, Riverina and Northern Vic; temper, democratic; bias, offensively Australian." A. G. Stephens, having read the bulky manuscript, declared it "fitted to become an Australian classic, or semi-classic".

Such is Life is really several books at once. It is an investigation of the nature and texture of life itself, as well as being an account of the life of the Riverina bullockies, sundowners and squatters of the 1880s. It is an essay on the need for Australian independence from old-world (and particularly English), class-ridden ways. It is a multi-layered study of the art of writing fiction, and of the relationship of structured fiction to unpredictable life. It is an exercise in literary self-parody, for the alleged author, Tom Collins, is the very type of the "learned bushman" whom life has a tendency to cut down to size. Although realistic, democratic and Australian, *Such is Life* teems with literary allusions, parallels and parodies. It is all the more remarkable for being written by a 50-year-old (Furphy was 60 when it was published) ex-bullocky, manual worker, who was self-educated, a great reader of the Bible, Shakespeare, Byron and Fielding, and largely out of reach of any literary advice or intellectual company on any professional level.

The opening words, "Unemployed at last!" introduce Tom Collins, formerly "a Government official of the 9th class . . . A Deputy-Assistant-Sub-Inspector", and a bushman and bullocky. Tom proposes taking certain entries from the 22 volumes of his diaries, and "amplifying these to the minutest detail of occurrence or conversation. This will afford to the observant reader a fair picture of Life." Never was a title more carefully chosen than Furphy's for his novel.

Mary O'Halloran was perfect Young-Australian. To describe her from after-knowledge—she was a very creature of the phenomena which had environed her own dawning intelligence. She was a child of the wilderness, a dryad among her kindred trees.

Yet at the same time warning has already been given, on the first page of the book, that Tom Collins is a philosopher given to expressing himself sententiously and elaborately, with many a literary flourish to show how well he knows Shakespeare. One of his bullocky friends, Thompson, says "He calls himself a philosopher . . . but his philosophy mostly consists in thinking he knows everything, and other people know nothing." This device of a highly fallible narrator allows for several levels to operate between reality and imagination.

Opening the diaries at random, Collins begins with 9 September 1883. On that day he was riding across the black-soil plains of the Riverina, and fell in with five bullock teams carting wool, "Thompson's twenty; Cooper's eighteen; Dixon's eighteen; and Price's two teams of fourteen each".

Steve Thompson, a Victorian, is an old friend, "scarcely a typical bullock driver, since fifteen years of that occupation had not brutalised his temper, nor ensanguined his vocabulary nor frayed the terminal 'g' from his participles". He is "tall and lazy, as bullock drivers ought to be".

Cooper is a stranger from Port Phillip, "three inches taller, three stone heavier, and 30 degrees lazier, than Thompson".

Dixon is an old friend, "a magnificent specimen of crude humanity".

Old Price is a man of "prudence and sagacity" who was carting goods from Melbourne to Bendigo in 1852. His second team is driven by his son Mosey, "a tight little fellow, whose body was about five-and-twenty, but whose head, according to the ancient adage, had worn out many a good pair of shoulders".

Camped with the bullockies is Willoughby, a sundowner and remittance man. He is an Englishman with a university degree and, "notwithstanding his rags and dirt, a remarkably fine-looking man".

Collins comes upon the bullockies as they are yarning around their dinner and he joins them as they are discussing the possibilities of grass—"a vital question in '83, as you may remember". The problem is where to open a fence and get feed for the bullocks and not be caught by the station management. The next station is a very tricky one. "You dunno what you're doin' when you're foolin' with this run. She's hair-trigger at the best o' times, an' she's on full cock this year. Best watched station on the track."

This is a favourite device of Furphy's. He introduces his story, or stories, very casually, so that they grow out of the yarning of the bullockies, with Tom Collins being involved both as commentator and interpreter, his interpretations frequently being wrong. Collins is sometimes also a participator and even an instigator of the action.

The bullockies live in a state of war with most of the squatters who grudge them both grass and water. But actions like opening a fence are just one of life's "dirty transactions". There is one Christian squatter, Stewart of Kooltopa, who according to Collins (and, in this case, surely Furphy also) is a democrat and not a gentleman, despite being born one. Furphy had a fierce if illogical loathing of the English gentleman. Quite rightly, he was appalled at such novels as *Geoffry Hamlyn* where the young imported gentleman is depicted as superior to the rough Australian bushman.

Furphy was also justly annoyed at the idea that it was right for a gentleman not to work. But of course he quite forgot that in Australia there were countless examples of gentlemen who had worked hard, whether on the goldfields or the station. And nearly all the explorers (so admired by Furphy) were English gentlemen.

Collins says approvingly, "Stewart, it must be admitted, was no gentleman" despite being "the younger son of a wealthy and aristocratic Scottish laird". He had worked hard, and believed in democracy, and ". . . there is no such thing as a democratic gentleman; the adjective and noun are hyphenated by a drawn sword". Moreover, according to Collins, ". . . there is no such thing as a Christian gentleman". There is Folkestone, for instance, who is ". . . a gentleman by the grace of God and the flunkeyism of man". Stewart, on the other hand, is the sort of man who will give a swagman a lift in his buggy.

When Stewart and Collins get together, they not only share cigars and a bottle of Scotch but quotations from Shakespeare, the Bible and Dr Johnson. A good half of *Such is Life* consists of bush conversations and yarns, conducted on every level of literacy.

Such is Life may appear plotless and shapeless (like life), but embedded in it are a number of stories with a beginning, a middle and a sort of an end, though not always in that order. The most important of these, the romance of Molly Cooper, is less interesting in itself than in the manner of its telling, for Tom Collins does not realise how involved in it he is.

Taking the dates from his diary at random, Collins hears how Molly Cooper's face was disfigured by a kick from a horse, and as a result she was jilted by her lover who, after a disastrous marriage, is now bullock-driving in the north of the Bland country. In Chapter IV Collins finds the drover Warrigal Alf, sick in his wagon. They have long discussions about the behaviour of lovers, and jealousy. As Collins

THE BULLOCK TEAM *Frank Mahony*

JOSEPH FURPHY
1843-1912

Joseph Furphy's father was a tenant farmer from Northern Ireland, who, with his wife, migrated to Victoria in 1841 and found work on a station near Yarra Glen. Joseph was born there on 26 September 1843. As well as being a farmer, Joseph's father worked as a shoemaker and hay and corn merchant.

As a boy Joseph took farm jobs, paid an unsuccessful visit to the goldfields, and operated a steam threshing machine near Daylesford, trying to educate himself all the time. He remained a prodigious reader all his life, "half bushman and half bookworm", in his own words.

In 1866 he married 16-year-old Leonie Germaine, who was of French extraction. Together they took up a selection near Stanhope in northern Victoria, "the worst selection in Rodney Shire". After some years, he had to sell up because of poor seasons. In 1877 Joseph and his family moved to Hay. He became a bullock-driver, working in the Riverina. Leonie remains a shadowy figure, with Furphy away with his bullock team, sometimes for months on end. He was a teamster for seven years. In 1884 he had to give up his bullocks because of drought and disease, and he went to work as a labourer in his brother's foundry at Shepparton.

For the next 20 years he lived at Shepparton. With regular hours of work during the day he was able to concentrate on his books and writing at night. He began by selling stories, anecdotes and poems to the *Bulletin*, and worked for many years on the first version of *Such is Life*.

Furphy was a Socialist and a Christian, but was firmly opposed to wowserism, respect for Old England and the gentry, and "Churchianity" as personified by his employer, his "right reverend elder brother". He described this brother to A. G. Stephens as an "intolerant Conservative, an enthusiastic loyalist, a valued contributor to the *War Cry*, and a local preacher of eminence". Furphy did not care for respectable people, much preferring his old bullocky and droving friends.

Furphy made the fullest use of the Shepparton Mechanics' Institute library. He read widely in philosophy and history as well as in literature. Miles Franklin's biography of Furphy shows that the family had always been great readers, and that even as a child Furphy had a talent for parody.

He exchanged letters with William Cathels, a Melbourne blacksmith of a literary bent, and derived support from these. From 1887 a young schoolteacher, Kate Baker, helped him with his writing. Furphy said that *Such is Life* could not have been written without her advice. He also corresponded with Miles Franklin for many years.

He spent several years "loosely federating these yarns . . . till by-and-by the scheme of *Such is Life* suggested itself". He sent 1125 pages of longhand manuscript to Archibald of the *Bulletin* in 1897. To their eternal credit, Archibald and his editor Stephens admired the manuscript and eventually published it in 1903. Two long sections were cut from the original manuscript, *The Buln-Buln and the Brolga* and *Rigby's Romance*, and were later published separately. *Such is Life* was reissued in 1917 with a preface by Vance Palmer, who also edited an abridged version which appeared in 1937. Furphy used the name "Tom Collins" for his *Bulletin* contributions and developed Collins more fully as a character and narrator in *Such is Life*.

In 1904 Furphy joined his two sons and daughter in Fremantle, Western Australia. The house he built at Swanbourne is now a National Trust memorial, Tom Collins House. He died in 1912.

---

saddles up to go he hears Warrigal Alf repeating, in a low and monotonous voice, the words, "O Molly! Molly, my girl!—my poor love!—my darling!"

In his meeting with Stewart, over whisky and Shakespeare, Collins gives an erroneous account of Warrigal's life to Stewart, before Stewart goes off to rescue the sick man.

In Chapter VI, Collins hears about the misogynist boundary rider, Nosey Alf, who can play the piano and the violin and is reputed to have a beautiful voice but will not sing in company. Nosey Alf's hut is clean and bright, surrounded by flowers in kerosene tins. Also the ground around the hut has been swept with a broom. Sullenly Nosey Alf gives Collins, who has brought him a parcel and the newspaper, a cup of tea, keeping "his disfigured face averted as much as possible". Apart from the scar, his face is "more beautiful than a man's face is justified in being"; his gait is "lithe and graceful", he has no whiskers, and his figure is "tapering the wrong way". He is "the most interesting character within the scope of these scrappy memoirs". They discuss poetry, and dress materials, about which Nosey Alf is strangely knowing.

Collins mentions that he has met another Alf, Warrigal Alf, name of Morris. Collins says, "Widower". "'Widower?' repeated Alf, almost in a whisper." More talk about Morris leaves Nosey Alf shaking, so that Collins asks if he is sick. When Collins reveals that not long ago Alf Morris fed his bullocks just near Nosey Alf's hut, Nosey stares with "a wild, shrinking look". Finally Nosey Alf plays the violin for Collins and then sings—"and such a voice!"

In Chapter VII there is a reference to Nosey Alf being seen north of the Darling, heading for Queensland. So Molly Cooper/Nosey Alf's whole sad love story has passed through Collins' expansion of his diary notes, not only without Collins putting the clues together, but without him being actually involved in it.

The subtlety with which Molly Cooper's story is revealed gives an idea of the complexity of Furphy's narrative method, and of his method of demonstrating "such is life". However, if he wishes, Furphy, through Collins, can use another narrator to tell a story directly and with the maximum of pathos. The finest example occurs in Chapter V with the tough but decent bullocky, Thompson, telling the story of the lost child, Mary O'Connell. Mary is a little five-year-old who walks 40 kilometres to her death. Thompson was one of the many who turned out to search for her. His plain style is skilfully contrasted with that of Sanders, telling the story of another lost child. Sanders cannot stick to the point, and the whole story becomes absurd.

Such is Life is a most original novel. Stylistically and formally it has links with Sterne and Fielding, but Furphy was attempting something entirely new to him. Indeed, far off, in isolation in Australia, he was exploring some of the possibilities of the novel which, at more or less the same time, were concerning Henry James, Joseph Conrad and James Joyce.

The drongo-shrike is another permanent resident; glossy black, with a metallic shimmer on the shoulders, long-tailed, sharp of bill and masterful. He has a scolding tongue, and if a hawk hovers over the bloodwoods he tells without hesitation of the evil presence. He is the bully of the wilderness of leaves, bouncing birds vastly his superior in fighting weight and alertness of wing, and chattering his jurisdiction to everything that flies. When the nest on the nethermost branch of the Moreton Bay ash is packed with hungry brood, his industry is exhilarating. Ordinarily he gets all the food he wants by merely a superficial inspection; but with a family to provide for, he is compelled to fly around, shrewdly examining every likely looking locality. Clinging to the bark of the bloodwood, with tail spread out fan-wise as additional support, he searches every interstice, and ever and anon flies to the Moreton Bay ash and tears off the curling fragments of crisp bark which afford concealment to the smaller beetles, grubs and spiders.

With the loose end of bark in his bill, tugging and fluttering, using his tail as

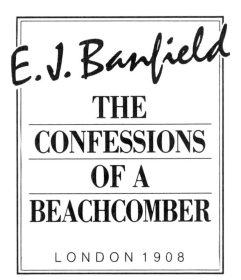

THE CONFESSIONS OF A BEACHCOMBER

LONDON 1908

a lever with the tree as a fulcrum, and objurgating in unseemly tones, as the bark resists his efforts, the drongo assists the Moreton Bay ash in discarding worn-out epidermis, and the tree reciprocates by offering safe nesting-place on its most brittle branches.

The drongo is a bird of many moods. Silent and inert for months together, during the nesting-season he is noisy and alert, not only the first to give warning of the presence of a falcon, but the boldest in chivvying from tree to tree this universal enemy.

He is then particularly partial to an aerial acrobatic performance, unsurpassed for gracefulness and skill, and significant of the joy of life and liberty and the delirious passion of the moment. With a mighty effort, a chattering scream and a preliminary downward cast, he impels

himself with the ardour of flight—almost vertically—up above the level of the tree-tops. Then, after a momentary, thrilling pause, with a gush of twittering commotion and stiffened wings preternaturally extended over the back and flattened together into a single rigid fin, drops—a feathered black bolt from the blue—almost to the ground, swoops up to a resting-place, and with bowing head and jerking tail gloats over his splendid feat.

The spangled drongo has no rival in the peculiar character of the notes and calls over which he has secure copyright. The shrill stuttering shriek which accompanies his aerial acrobatic performances, the subdued tinkling tones of pleasure, the jangle as of cracked china, the high-pitched tirade of jarring abuse and scolding at the presence of an enemy, the meek cheeps, the tremulous, coaxing whistles when the young first venture from the nest—each and every sound, totally unlike that of any other bird, indicates the oddity of this sportive member of the crow family.

This book is more than just an account of Banfield's experiences after he and his wife settled on Dunk Island, four kilometres off the northern Queensland coast. It is also a natural history of the island, a sympathetic survey of Aboriginal life on and about the island, and a resumé of its history since Captain Cook gave it the rather plain name that derived from the family name of the Earl of Halifax; the Aborigines called it Coonanglebah.

Banfield has been called Australia's Thoreau, a misleading comparison that is, however, given some impetus by the fine and relevant quotation from Thoreau which Banfield placed on the title page of his book. "If a man does not keep pace with his companions perhaps it is because he hears a different drummer. Let him step to the music which he hears." Banfield was a journalist, and having suffered a physical and mental breakdown, had the wisdom to see that a change of pace was essential for his well-being. But he was unlike Thoreau in that he did not wish to step alone to the music of nature. With him were his wife Bertha and, later, her old housekeeper, Essie McDonough; up to four Aborigines

worked on his gardens; he paid frequent visits to his neighbours on the mainland, and he did not mind visitors. It must also be said, of course, that he was not as great a writer as Thoreau, although he is always capable of rising far above the highly competent journalism which was his métier.

In his foreword he says plainly that he sought "an unprofaned sanctuary . . . and there dwelt in tranquillity, happiness and security". He does not recommend that people rush to follow him and become beachcombers. The life would only suit a certain type of personality, and "Besides, there are not enough thoughtful islands to go around".

He then gives what is the best account of his own book:

My chief desire is to set down in plain language the sobrieties of everyday occurrences—the unpretentious homilies of an unpretentious man—one whose mental bent enabled him to take but a superficial view of most of the large, heavy and important aspects of life, but who has found light in things and subjects homely, slight and casual; who perhaps has queer views on the pursuit of happiness, and who above all has an inordinate passion for freedom and fresh air.

"Sobrieties" is an odd word to use, though in the context a pleasing one, and in one crude sense accurate enough, for Banfield is well aware that gin and rum have been the downfall of many a beachcomber. In the dictionary sense of "avoidance of excess or extravagance . . . soundness or saneness of judgement", the word is apt, and Banfield is well aware that his island has restored his threatened sanity. Yet "sobrieties" remains too modest a word to describe the zest and whole-hearted love Banfield gives to his island and its inhabitants. Of the latter, he says later that it is "a sentimental regard for the welfare of birds and plant life" that has given him the idea of retiring to an island. Having seen what damage man can do to the environment, and how man in turn suffers from "the blows that nature inflicts as she recoils", he is determined that on his island there should be "more of example than precept". So, far ahead of his time, Banfield in a miniature and private way declares Dunk Island a national park.

The drongo is a bird of many moods. Silent and inert for months together, during the nesting-season he is noisy and alert, not only the first to give warning of the presence of a falcon, but the boldest in chivvying from tree to tree this universal enemy.

One of his first ordinances is that there should be no interference with the birdlife. This, unexpectedly, causes him some anguish, and teaches him that the way of the conservationist is not altogether easy. One of his plans for survival, apart from planting vegetables and fruits, is to produce honey, and accordingly he brings with him some hives of Italian bees. A honey of quality begins to flow, and there is a good prospect of making "a modest profit from one of the cleanest, nicest, most entertaining and innoxious of pursuits".

However, in this minor disruption to the ecosystem, he has not reckoned with the pretty little wood-swallow, with its "graceful, soaring flight and cheerful chirrup". These marauders settle comfortably by the hives and take hundreds of bees every day. How is he to protect the bees when he has sworn to protect the birds? Besides, the birds are so useful in controlling insects. "It took no long time to make up my

mind. Gladly came the determination to abandon the enterprise rather than do violence to the birds."

This decision in favour of birds over bees is typical of his resolution that in settling on the island "our interference should be considerate and slight". With the periodic help of the four Aborigines he clears one and a half hectares of jungle and plants fruits and vegetables that bear in abundance. "Be it understood that we depended almost solely on the aid of the blacks." Fortunately Banfield is in sympathy with the Aborigines, and is content that they should work in their own way and time. He does not complain if they go walkabout or do not feel in the mood for work. His attitude, and its results, is reminiscent of that of Jack McLaren, living at much the same time in his "crowded solitude" on Cape York.

Everything that has been planted grows splendidly, as well it might on an island where 309 centimetres of rainfall was recorded in a year. Banfield has a special regard for the pawpaw; there is nothing of sobriety in his rapturous chapter on the tree, whose fruit he claims, is not only delicious to eat but, if you are a woman, by eating it "your complexion will become more radiant. If a mere man, you will be the manlier". The leaves wrapped around meat will make it tender, the milk of the branches has many medicinal qualities. The seeds and the flowers can also be eaten. Banfield's writing in praise of the pawpaw is both sensuous and delicate.

> The stalk must be carefully cut, and the spice-exhaling fruit borne reverently and immediately to the table. The rite is to be performed in the cool of the morning, for the pawpaw is essentially a breakfast fruit, and then when the knife slides into the buff-coloured flesh of a cheesy consistency, minute colourless globules exude from the facets of the slices. These glistening beads are emblems of perfection.

While rejoicing in all the manifestations of nature on the island, Banfield remains realistic, aware of the bite of the green ant, and the cruel spines of the lawyer vine. There is humour as well as rapture in Banfield's observations, as when he watches the birds getting drunk on the melaleuca blossom which flowers in super-abundance, "pale yellow spikes, odorous to excess". He is particularly good on that comical bird, "the bibacious drongo", sober and drunk. After all, Banfield has come to Dunk Island for liberty, and "this is not a prohibition district . . . Are not the tenses of intoxication infinite?" So why should the spangled drongo not get drunk? It is all a part of "the small liberties" that are the delight of the beachcomber's life.

What Banfield modestly calls his "casual and unprecise" observations are immensely satisfying, not only to the nature-lover but to anyone who responds to the small joys and tragedies of life. While there is harmony, more or less, on land, Banfield finds the coral reefs very different, "gorged with a population of varied elements viciously disposed towards each other. It is one of nature's most cruel battlefields." What Banfield sees under water has, in his view, ominous implications for human beings with their ever growing population. In this microcosm, cannibalism and perpetual war are results of chronic overcrowding. Nevertheless, Banfield is deeply responsive to the

TROPICAL GARDEN *Sali Herman*

E. J. BANFIELD
1852-1923

Edmund James Banfield was born in Liverpool, England, on 4 September 1852, the son of a printer, Jabez Banfield, who emigrated to Victoria two months before Edmund's birth. Mrs Banfield and her four children remained behind in Liverpool until 1855, while Jabez found work and eventually established himself as one of the partners producing the Ararat *Advertiser*. In 1861 he became the sole proprietor.

Ed, as Edmund was always called, was educated at the Ararat Church of England Denominational School. His father was a lover of the English classics, and Ed was brought up on Shakespeare and Dickens in particular. He developed an interest in the great nineteenth-century American books of natural history, philosophy and poetry, and read deeply in Thoreau, Emerson and Whitman. Banfield took a work by Thoreau with him when he went to seek employment in Melbourne. Later he worked in Sydney on the *Daily Telegraph* before going to Townsville to work for editor Dodd Clarke on a new daily newspaper, the *Bulletin*, which was launched in January 1883.

During this time, Banfield had been having severe trouble with one of his eyes, the result of a boyhood accident, and a friend, the visiting English journalist J. T. Critchell, persuaded him to go to London to consult a specialist. He left in 1884, his fare paid by Robert Philp in exchange for articles about the voyage up the Queensland coast and through Torres Strait. The Townsville *Daily Bulletin*'s "Travelling Correspondent" wrote seven articles about the voyage to England.

In London the specialist removed Banfield's infected eye and fitted a glass one. Banfield made an excellent recovery from the operation. While recuperating, he stayed in Liverpool with the Goldings, friends of his mother, and there met his future wife, Bertha Golding.

By 1885 Banfield was back in Townsville, and the seven "Homeward Bound" articles and the seven "Erratic Rovings" he had written as the "Travelling Correspondent" were issued as pamphlets by his father in Ararat. In the following years Banfield wrote a prodigious number of articles under such general titles as "Rural Homilies" and "Southern Scenes Revisited" for the Townsville *Bulletin* and the *North Queensland Register*.

In 1886 Banfield proposed to Bertha Golding by letter, and she came out to Queensland to marry him at Townsville on 3 August 1886. The marriage was to be childless. For the next 10 years Banfield continued his journalistic career, as well as carrying out an immense reading programme he had set himself. But his health was not at all good and he was also having troubles with his managing editor, Dodd Clarke, who was an alcoholic. More and more Banfield began to feel the need of retiring to live in close contact with nature in order to restore his physical and mental health. After a camping trip to Dunk Island with Bertha, he applied for a lease of the island. By 1897 he was so ill, losing weight and unable to sleep that as Bertha wrote in a letter to Alec Chisholm: "He was absolutely worn out with day and night work and want of sleep, and I believe it was slowly but surely killing him."

Banfield gave up his Townsville job, and on 28 September 1897 Bertha and he landed on Dunk Island for a trial period of six months, abandoning "the heat, the clatter, the stuffy odours, the toilsomeness, the fatigue of town life". Within three months Banfield had made up his mind that they should remain on the island. Later they were joined by Bertha's old housekeeper, Essie McDonough.

In 1905 Banfield was appointed Ranger of Dunk and the neighbouring islands, which had been gazetted as a reserve. This position was of great importance to him, as it gave him the authority to carry out his dream of protecting the bird life, in particular, of the islands.

The Confessions of a Beachcomber was published in London in 1908, followed by *My Tropic Isle* in 1911 and *Tropic Days* in 1918; Alec Chisholm edited a posthumous volume, *Last Leaves from Dunk Island* which was published in 1925. Banfield gained fame but pitifully little income from his books.

Given six months to live in his 40s, Banfield survived in excellent health until he was 70, dying on Dunk Island in 1923. Bertha survived him by 10 years.

---

extraordinary beauty of the reef and its inhabitants, and some of his best writing is on this large theme.

He is also at his best in describing the huge flights of butterflies that cross the water at certain times from the mainland to the island.

> This was a day of gushing sunshine and myriads of butterflies. They flew from the mainland, not as spies but in battalions—a never-ending procession miles broad. You could fancy you heard in the throbbing stillness the movement of the fairy-like wings—a faint, unending hum. From the odorous jungle they came, flitting in gay inconsequence, steering a course of "slanting indeterminates", yet full of the power and passion of the moment. They flitted between the idle boom and the deck, and up the gleaming sky, in all the sizes that distance grades between nearness and infinity.

The last section of the book is about Aboriginal life on the island and in the district. A man of his time in that he cannot see much aesthetic worth in the paintings he discovers in caves, nevertheless he writes with humour and affection about the Aborigines, and especially about their extraordinary bush-craft. In fact, throughout the book in discussions of nature Banfield frequently refers to Aboriginal responses to plants, birds or places.

The world of *The Confessions of a Beachcomber* is complete in itself, and Banfield's presence in it is that of a custodian, not a conqueror. It is the first great book of natural history by an Australian writer, and full of the author's own "inordinate passion for freedom and fresh air".

Mrs Aeneas Gunn

WE
OF THE
NEVER NEVER

LONDON 1908

Within a week we returned to the homestead, and for twenty-four hours Cheon gloated over us, preparing every delicacy that appealed to him as an antidote to an out-bush course of beef and damper. Then a man rode into our lives who was to teach us the depth and breadth of the meaning of the word mate—a sturdy, thick-set man, with haggard, tired eyes and deep lines about his firm, strong mouth that told of recent and prolonged tension.

"Me mate's sick; got a touch of fever," he said simply, dismounting near the verandah. "I've left him camped back there at the Warlochs"; and as the Maluka prepared remedies—making up the famous Gulf mixture—the man, with grateful thanks, found room in his pockets and saddle-pouch for eggs, milk, and brandy, confident that "these'll soon put him right," adding, with the tense lines deepening about his mouth as he touched on what had brought them there: "He's been real bad, ma'am. I've had a bit of a job to get him as far as this." In the days to come we were to learn, little by little, that the "bit of a job" had meant keeping a sick man in his saddle for the greater part of the fifty-mile dry stage, with forty miles of "bad going" on top of that, and fighting for him every inch of the way that terrible symptom of malaria—that longing to "chuck it," and lie down and die.

Bad water after the fifty-mile dry made men with a touch of fever only too common at the homestead; and knowing how much the comforts of the homestead could do, when the Maluka came out with the medicines he advised bringing the sick man on as soon as he had rested sufficiently. "You've only to ask for it and we'll send the old station buck-board across," he said; and the man began fumbling uneasily at his saddle-girths, and said something evasive about "giving trouble"; but when the Maluka—afraid that a man's life might be the forfeit of another man's shrinking fear of causing trouble—added that on second thoughts we would ride across as soon as horses could be brought in, he flushed hotly and stammered: "If you please, ma'am. If the boss'll excuse me, me mate's dead set against a woman doing things for him. If you wouldn't mind not coming. He'd rather have me. Me and him's been mates this seven years. The boss'll understand."

The boss did understand, and rode across to the Warlochs alone, to find a man as shy and reticent as a bushman can be, and full of dread lest the woman at the homestead would insist in visiting him. "You see, that's why he wouldn't come on," the mate said. "He couldn't bear the thought of a woman doing things for him"; and the Maluka explained that the missus understood all that. That lesson had been easily learned; for again and again men had come in "down with a touch of fever," whose temperatures went up at the very thought of a woman doing things for them, and always the actual nursing was left to the Maluka or the Dandy, the woman seeing to egg-flips and such things, exchanging at first perhaps only an occasional greeting, and listening at times to strange life-histories later on.

But in vain the Maluka explained and entreated: the sick man was "all right where he was." His mate was worth "ten women fussing round," he insisted, ignoring the Maluka's explanations. Had he not "lugged him through the worst pinch already?" and then he played his trump card: "He'll stick to me till I peg out," he said—"nothing's too tough for him"; and as he lay back, the mate deciding "arguing'll only do for him," dismissed the Maluka with many thanks, refusing all offers of nursing help with a quiet "He'd rather have me," but accepting gratefully broths and milk and anything of that sort the homestead could furnish. "Nothing ever knocks me out," he reiterated, and dragged on through sleepless days and nights, as the days dragged by finding ample reward in the knowledge that "he'd rather have me"; and when there came that deep word of praise from his stricken comrade: "A good mate's harder to find than a good wife," his gentle, protecting devotion increased tenfold.

This is the story of Jeannie Gunn's arrival in the Northern Territory in the Wet Season as wife of the manager at Elsey Station, 400 kilometres south-east of Darwin, and the year she spent there in 1902.

On a close reading, however, *We of the Never Never* reveals itself to be two books in one. Firstly, it is a classic account of bush life at the turn of the century and of the characters that lived and worked in the far outback. Second, it is one of the great classics of women's writing in Australia. It is the most powerful account we have of the impact of a highly educated, city-bred young woman on the Aborigines and the white men at an isolated station where the nearest white woman is 160 kilometres away. With great skill Jeannie Gunn links her own startled reactions with those, often horrified, of the men. Her love and understanding, both of the Never Never and of its few inhabitants, give the book a sense of unity.

At first Jeannie is by no means made welcome. By the time she and her husband, called the Maluka, leave Darwin for the 240-kilometre rail journey to Pine Creek, and the further 160 kilometres by horse and cart and on horseback over flooded rivers to Elsey, the telegraph is already humming. Mac, the Sanguine Scot, leads the opposition which is determined to "block" her. A "missus" on the Elsey would not be appreciated. The fear is that she will be a big, bossy "snorter", "a goer", and not "the right sort". She is, in the Maluka's words, "the Unknown Woman".

Fortunately for her the word soon gets around that she is "a little-un". "The little-uns are all right." A great burly bushman, an old friend of the Maluka's, boards the train and sees Jeannie and laughs. "Is that all there is of her? Gimme the little-uns . . . you can't beat-em for pluck."

And when finally at Pine Creek she meets the opposition, Mac, "at the sight of the 'Goer' reduced to a meek five feet, all the wrath died out of him." With a sharp eye Jeannie notes that "we thoroughly understood each other, being drawn together by a mutual love of the ridiculous. Only a mutual love of the ridiculous, yet not so slender a basis for a lifelong friendship as appears, and by no means an uncommon one 'out bush'." It is this particular aspect of a sense of humour, "the mutual love of the ridiculous", which underlies any successful acceptance of life in the bush.

Jeannie certainly needs that sense of humour. She has to cross the flooded Fergusson on a wire, the Edith in the Katherine publican's tiny rowing-boat, and the King at full gallop in the buckboard. As for the homestead, there is scarcely anything of it, as most of it had been demolished by the 1897 cyclone. Jeannie especially relishes the dog's

From the film *We of the Never Never*

prints on the wall and ceiling, the muddy paw-marks having been left on the planks when the house was built, nobody thinking to remove them.

The cast of *We of the Never Never* is altogether memorable, with the idealised Maluka as the lightest drawn, as if Jeannie's love for him made her want to keep him to herself. The men may be scared of her, but in her presence they soon forget their resentment.

Then a man rode into our lives who was to teach us the depth and breadth of the meaning of the word mate—a sturdy, thick-set man, with haggard, tired eyes and deep lines about his firm, strong mouth that told of recent and prolonged tension.

The Sanguine Scot is the first to be tamed; but he soon goes off on his own with bullocks and wagon (22 to a wagon). Then there is shy Tam, whose confidence comes back immediately he is on horseback. Dan, the Head Stockman, with the dog "old Sool 'em", is a bushman of the old type. Jack, the Quiet Stockman, is going to clear out of the sight of a woman. Mac says he will stay, and that, "You can't beat Jack by much, though, when it comes to sticking to a pal".

The Dandy sums her up on arrival and approves; she is not "that other woman" he had been dreading. As Mac says, "bushmen have a sixth sense, and know a pal when they see one." Fortunately Jeannie understands their ways. "Bushmen will risk their lives for a woman—pal or otherwise—but leave her to pick up her own handkerchief."

Jeannie realises how much importance instinct plays in the lives of the bushmen. Things are not written down to be learned. You need to have instinct: instinct about horses, cattle, the weather, the lie of the land, the movement of game, and, above all, about people. Jeannie's friendship with Jack is sealed by her instinct for picking the best horse in the mob that is to be broken in. When the Dandy politely suggests that it might be knowledge, the Quiet Stockman says, "it never *is* anything *but* instinct . . . No one ever *learns* horses."

Jeannie shows no trace of condescension towards those who are illiterate. She knows how much they really know— the knowledge that does go with instinct. She uses that same judgement in relation to the Aborigines on the station, including the lubras who after their own fashion help around the house.

Above all she relishes Cheon, the Chinese cook and gardener whose fat presence and vivid language are one of the great attractions of *We of the Never Never*. From the moment Cheon rises at cock-crow ("fowl-sing-out") "there was nothing he could not and did not do for our good". She uses her instinct once again and accepts that "he knew what was best for us" and does not try to order him around. She even has the tact not to order him away when, after weeks of delay, her trunks arrive and he sits and watches her unpack them. She finally sends him off ecstatic to the kitchen with a lot of new utensils, with the aid of which wonderful sponge cakes and other delights later emerge.

HOUSE *Sidney Nolan*

MRS AENEAS GUNN
1870-1961

Jeannie Gunn, née Taylor, was born in Melbourne on 5 June 1870 to Thomas and Anna Taylor. She was educated at home (the best education, she often said), and then at Melbourne University. For some time she was a teacher in private schools. One of her pupils later recalled that "travelling with Miss Taylor was as exciting as setting off for the moon". Another always remembered her "light springing footstep".

In 1901 she married Aeneas James Gunn. He had worked in the far outback and, with Joseph Bradshaw, established Victoria River Downs Station. He returned to civilisation and for two years was Librarian of the Prahran Library. It was at that time that Jeannie and Aeneas met. She recalled that their first "unorthodox introduction" was when she was alighting from a buggy, the horses backed and she was thrown literally into his arms.

Early in 1902 she accompanied her husband, now manager of Elsey Station in the Northern Territory, to Darwin and then on the difficult journey (it was in "the Wet") down to Elsey Station. There she lived and worked with her husband for the next year.

Aeneas Gunn, whom the local Aborigines called the Maluka (meaning "the boss"), died of malarial dysentery early in 1903. The Dandy, who was later to become one of the characters in Jeannie Gunn's book, *We of the Never Never*, drove her back to the Pine Creek rail terminal from where she returned to Melbourne. She lived with her father at Monbulk in Victoria until his death in 1909. There she wrote *The Little Black Princess* and *We of the Never Never*. *The Little Black Princess* was published in London in 1905. Although ostensibly a story for children about Bett-Bett, an eight-year-old Aboriginal girl, niece of Old Goggle-Eye, an elder of the local tribe, it is a charming and sympathetic study of the Aborigines around Elsey Station. She was, however, influenced by the attitudes of her time and believed that the Aborigines should change their ways and copy the behaviour of whites. The great anthropologist, Baldwin Spencer, wrote: "I know of nothing comparable to it in any writings on Australian Aborigines. Only one who really understood and liked the natives, and who, at the same time, was liked by them, could possibly have written it."

We of the Never Never, an account of the author's life at Elsey Station, was rejected by six publishers in three months. Since its publication in London in 1908 it has been one of the most consistently popular of Australian books, having sold over 400,000 copies. It was translated into German.

After her father's death, Jeannie Gunn toured Europe for three years, then settled in Melbourne with her two sisters. In 1932, she moved to Hawthorn with one of her sisters. During both world wars she was much occupied with welfare work with soldiers. She died, aged 91, on 9 June 1961.

Cheon's finest achievements come at Christmas. " 'No good two-fellow dinner longa Clisymus,' he said. And the blacks, too, must be regaled in their humpy. 'Must have vealer, longa black fellow Clisymus,' Cheon ordered."

On the day the food is lavish. "Duck Cully and lice", "close up sausage" (no skins available), six pullets in a row, a ham (a present from Mine Host at Katherine), and finally the pudding with two threepenny bits, all that could be found, but "Must have money longa poodin'!"

" *If you please, ma'am. If the boss'll excuse me, me mate's dead set against a woman doing things for him. If you wouldn't mind not coming. He'd rather have me. Me and him's been mates this seven years. The boss'll understand.* "

One of the great characters of the book is The Fizzer, the mailman who brings the eight mails they are allowed in a year. The Fizzer thinks nothing of his 1600-kilometre-ride "on me Pat Malone", travelling over dangerously long dry stages, always arriving on time, an expert with horses and a fountain of news. Jeannie Gunn's eight-odd pages of description and evocation of the Fizzer's mail route is one of the great Australian tributes to the finest type of men of the outback. (The Fizzer, alas, was drowned in 1911 while attempting to cross the Victoria River with the mail.)

One of the most poignant passages in the book occurs when a man arrives at the Elsey to say that his mate is very sick and needs help. The Maluka immediately offers to send the buckboard to bring him in to the station, or else he and the Missus will go out. The man "flushes hotly" and says that he could not possibly allow a woman to look after his mate. Not even when Jeannie offers to stay completely out of sight will the bushman accept the offer to bring his mate in. Finally the Dandy does bring him in, but the man dies. The bushman and he had been seven years mates, but he could tell little of his mate's life except his name and that he came from Wollongong. (The bushman himself was to perish on the Tanami Track in 1919.)

By the end of the year Jeannie is completely at home in the peace of the bush. She has solved the problem of occupying time that so worried her city friends who were always asking "What will there be for you to do all day?" For a start, there were many visitors that year, including a man who had not seen a cabbage or a woman (he put it in that order) for five years. Time is full, either at the Elsey or out on the mustering camps, yarning with the men in time off from work. Jeannie found that, contrary to expectations, the bushmen enjoyed talking with a woman.

Then, accepted and accepting, thoroughly at home in the Never Never, Jeannie has to accept the unacceptable. The Maluka dies of fever. The Afterword is only half a page. The end of "the best Boss that ever a man struck" is the end of Jeannie Gunn's life in the Never Never.

We of the Never Never is a record of what happened in one year, but it is far more than a record. It is a recreation of what it was like to be a woman at the Elsey in 1902, and of what lay behind the lives of those who could survive in the Never Never.

Mary Grant Bruce

A LITTLE BUSH MAID

LONDON 1910

The old man walked across to his fire and, kneeling down, carefully raked away the ashes. Then he drew out a damper—Norah had never seen one before, but she knew immediately that it was a damper. It looked good, too—nicely risen, and brown, and it sent forth a fragrance that was decidedly appetizing. The old man looked pleased "Not half bad!" he said aloud, in a wonderfully deep voice, which sounded so amazing in the bush silence that Norah fairly jumped.

The old man raked the ashes together again, and placed some sticks on them, after which he brought over the billy, and hung it above the fire to boil. The fire quickly broke into a blaze, and he picked up the damper again, and walked slowly back to the tent, where he paused to blow the dust from the result of his cookery.

At this moment Norah became oppressed with a wild desire to sneeze. She fought against it frantically, nearly choking in her efforts to remain silent, while she wildly explored in her pockets for a non-existent handkerchief.

As the water bursts from the dam the more violently because of its imprisonment, so Norah's sneeze gained intensity and uproar from her efforts to repress it. It came—

"A—tish—oo—oo!"

The old man started violently. He dropped his damper and gazed round.

"What on earth's that?" he said. "Who's there?"

For a moment Norah hesitated. Should she run for her life? But a second's thought showed her no real reason why she should run. She was not in the least frightened, for it never occurred to Norah that anyone could wish to hurt her; and she had done nothing to make him angry. So she modestly emerged from behind a friendly tree and said meekly, "It's me."

"'Me', is it?" said the old man, in great astonishment. He stared hard at the little figure in the blue blouse and serge riding-skirt—at the merry face and the dark curls crowned by the shady Panama hat. "'Me'," he repeated. "'Me' looks rather nice, I think. But what's she doing here?"

"I was looking at you," Norah exclaimed.

"I won't be unpolite enough to mention that a cat may look at a king," said the old man. "But don't you know that no one comes here? No young ladies in blue dresses and brown curls—only wombats and wallabies, and ring-tailed 'possums—and me. Not you—me, but me—me! How do you account for being here?"

Norah laughed. She decided that she liked this very peculiar old man, whose eyes twinkled so brightly as he spoke.

"But I don't think you know," she said. "Quite a lot of other people come here—this is Anglers' Bend. At least, Anglers' Bend's quite close to your camp. Why, only to-day there's Jim and the boys, and black Billy, and me! We're not wallabies!"

The essentials of Mary Grant Bruce's Billabong books are set out in the first few pages of her first novel, *A Little Bush Maid*. There is Billabong, "a big station in the north of Victoria" (actually based on stations in Gippsland) where, according to Norah Linton, you can "ride all day and never see any one you didn't want to see". Norah has never known her mother, who died when she was a baby. "She had grown just as the bush wild flowers grow—hardy, unchecked, almost untended; for, though old nurse had always been there, her nurseling had gone her own way from the time she could toddle. She was everybody's pet and plaything; the only thing who had power to make her stern, silent father smile—almost the only one who ever saw the softer side of his character."

Mr Linton is an old-style grazier with a passion for horses. When he took over Billabong the stables were in poor shape. He has made them the pride of the station, and by the time Norah is nine one of the horse boxes is hers, for her horse Bobs, whose name her brother Jim has carved over the door.

Jim is Norah's elder brother, and they are "tremendous chums". He is "growing up straight and strong and manly, able to make his way in the world". Norah "mopes sadly" when he is sent away to Melbourne Grammar School.

Norah is happy to spend "two-thirds of her waking time on horseback". She does not care for girls or girl talk; she has "all the dread of being thought 'silly' that marks the girl who imitates boyish ways". She is much respected by the boys Jim brings home in the holidays, who begin by patronising her and end by realising she "could teach them more of bush life than they had dreamed of".

"But Norah's principal mate was her father." In the long and complex history of Australian mateship, Norah has claims to be the first woman, apart from Sybylla in *My Brilliant Career*, who calls a man her mate, the man in both cases being the father. Certainly in Norah's case all the qualities of mateship are there in the relationship between her and her father. Norah wishes for no other company when Jim is away and she is not likely to get any, with the nearest township, Cunjee, 27 kilometres away. Their mateship is not just working together and riding around the station, but doing things like camping out: "just you and me, Daddy". Mary Grant Bruce tapped an immensely rich vein in describing this relationship of a young girl with her father. It is, however, very proper indeed. When they go swimming in the river, Mr Linton leaves Norah at her waterhole, "and himself went a few yards further up, round a bend in the creek".

On Mr Linton's side, acceptance of Norah as his mate leads him to neglect her as a daughter. "I won't have her bothered with books too early", Mr Linton says to her nurse when she is eight, and as a result Norah's education "was of the kind best defined as a minus quantity". Even her natural gift for music is given only minimal encouragement, a few piano lessons from Mr Groom, the young English bookkeeper. Near the end of the book, to Norah's horror, Mr Linton tells her that a tutor will arrive to teach her Latin, French, drawing, grammar and other accomplishments so that she will not grow up "altogether a bush duffer".

Then he drew out a damper—Norah had never seen one before, but she knew immediately that it was a damper. It looked good, too—nicely risen, and brown, and it sent forth a fragrance that was decidedly appetizing.

Norah's obvious problem is that she could easily be spoiled—"if spoiling consists in rarely checking an impulse". The discipline of station life and the demands of mateship save her. Under such circumstances it is impossible for her to become either selfish or neurotic. Her flaws are more likely to be those of ignorance and intolerance resulting from a lack of education and intellectual discipline, the limitations of mere day-to-day healthy work in preventing a greater breadth of mind.

Mary Grant Bruce was a feminist, but it is impossible to tell from *A Little Bush Maid* whether she is implying that Norah's lack of culture results from her loss of her mother when she was a baby, women usually being the bearers of culture. For instance, if Norah had had a mother, undoubtedly her gift for the piano would have been encouraged. At the same time, Mary Grant Bruce does less than justice to the male world of station life, where many of the men, both squatters and station hands and even boundary-riders, were avid readers, especially of the English novelists and poets, and, long before 1910, of the *Bulletin* and its writers of prose and verse. Such a horse lover as Mr Linton would surely have learned "The Man from Snowy River" off by heart. But there is no sign in the Billabong books of Mr Linton having read a word of "Banjo" Paterson. It appears that Norah has read Adam Lindsay Gordon. Jim does not read anything; instead he excels at all sports.

Norah is not only fearless but she can scarcely believe that anyone would want to harm her. When a ruffian of a swagman tries to take her gold watch, she simply laughs. But the man means business, and almost robs her before her Irish terrier intervenes and sinks his teeth in the swagman's leg. Swaggies are almost the only messengers of evil in *A Little Bush Maid*. Another swaggie, ordered off the station by Mr Linton, starts a grass fire that threatens Billabong and the neighbouring station; he gets three years in the Melbourne gaol.

Other important people at Billabong are Hogg the gardener and Lee Wing, the Chinese who looks after the orchard and the vegetable garden; these two are mortal enemies. Mrs Brown, the housekeeper, is enormous, amiable and much loved by Norah. Black Billy, the 18-year-old Aboriginal station hand, is very much a part of the family life, and is a good friend of the 12-year-old Norah. Mr Linton says, "He's the best hand with horses we ever had on the station." Billy can catch fish, when Norah cannot. Mary Grant Bruce makes fun of his poor command of English. Every time he opens his mouth out comes the word "Plenty!"

Norah's quiet life is enlivened when Jim brings his friends Harry and Wally back for the Easter holidays. On a fishing expedition with the boys to Anglers' Bend, Norah discovers an old hermit, with a long white beard and dressed in wallaby skins, living in a tent by the river. She befriends him and brings him back to meet the boys. He is even closer to the Australian earth than Norah; the birds come down and hop about him. Moreover, he cooks an excellent damper, something Norah has never tasted.

Shortly afterwards, on a trip to Cunjee with Mrs Brown, Norah hears about a local murder. The dreadful thought occurs to her that the hermit may be the murderer, the man who has poisoned his mate. But she cannot believe it, remembering "his two honest eyes". "Why, Bobs made friends with him." That gives her fresh confidence; her horse Bobs always knows "a good sort". However, it is disturbing when the trooper comes out to the station, looking for a "big fellow—old—plenty of white hair and beard".

Meanwhile, something altogether new comes into Norah's life with the arrival of a circus at Cunjee, to which Mr Linton takes her. Norah's visit to the circus could be rather unexciting, with its descriptions of the clown, the tiger and so on, but in fact it is one of the most appealing episodes in the book because of Norah's reactions, her naive excitement. Until then Norah has always been shown as in command of her familiar environment, young of course but mature in her dealings with nature, animals and men. At the circus, she is a child, and Mary Grant Bruce gives special emphasis to this. "It is something to possess nowadays, even at twelve, the unspoiled, fresh mind that Norah brought to her first circus." (Especially when one remembers how scruffy most country town circuses are.)

One of the rare scenes in which Mr Linton is emotionally involved outside the family is when the old hermit turns out not to be the murderer, of course, but, in Mr Linton's words, "the best friend I ever had", long presumed to be dead. Norah finds him desperately ill in his tent; she fetches her father, who recognises his old friend Jim, after whom he had called his son, and then Norah rides 24 kilometres to get the doctor. When she arrives at the station she meets the new tutor; he is Dick Stephenson, old Jim's son. Jim is innocent of the crime for which he had been ostracised by his wife and society, he recovers from his sickness (typhoid, correctly diagnosed by Mr Linton), and all ends happily with his coming to live at Billabong and help with the book-work.

Some of the limitations of the Billabong characters have already been mentioned, but Mary Grant Bruce's positive achievements were prodigious in 1910, opening a whole new world to young readers. *Seven Little Australians* is a greater novel than *A Little Bush Maid*, and *Dot and the Kangaroo* has a greater poetic sympathy with the bush, but "fresh,

MIDDAY *Sydney Long*

MARY GRANT BRUCE
1878-1958

Mary Grant Bruce was born, suitably in character, on Empire Day, 24 May 1878, at Sale, in the Gippsland district of Victoria. Her father, Lewis, was a surveyor who had arrived in Australia from Dublin in 1854. Her mother Minnie was the daughter of William and Louisa Whittakers and came from a remote station in the Snowy River country. Minnie's family were gentry who firmly kept up cultural standards; she was an accomplished pianist.

Mary's childhood (she was one of six children) was spent amongst friends and relations in Sale, riding and exploring in the bush. One of the stations they visited was "Heyfields", managed by her uncle Charles Whittakers for the millionaire "Hungry" Tyson. They also visited the Walhalla gold mines. Minnie's formidable great-aunt Martha lived with them, having brought her fine furniture with her, until her death in 1858 at the age of 91. Great-aunt Martha's seventeenth-century walnut table frequently appears in Mary's books.

When Mary was seven, her favourite brother Paddy died in a shooting accident. Otherwise her childhood was happy, except for her resentment at the "unfortunate accident" of not being born a boy. Mary did not care for sewing, cooking or housework, or for clothes; she preferred riding, especially stock work, and reading and writing. At seven she wrote her first long poem, an epic about the mad Tsar of Russia.

She went to a private school in Sale, where she was dux, and for two consecutive years won the Melbourne Shakespeare Society's prize examination. The president of the Society, Dr Neild, encouraged her to write stories and her first published story appeared in the Melbourne *Leader* in 1898.

Mary continued to live at home until the depression of the 1890s forced her father to sell the Sale house and move to a smaller one at Traralgon. At the age of 20, despite the strong opposition of her father, she went to seek work in Melbourne, "with a heart full of assorted ambitions, and five pounds in my pocket".

Dr Neild eventually found her a job as editor of the *Leader's* children's page and at the same time she wrote articles and stories on every imaginable subject for other newspapers around Australia. She also owned a three-speed bicycle on which she rode the 160 kilometres from Melbourne to Traralgon to visit her parents. She became engaged to the son of a Gippsland landowner; the engagement was broken off after a year.

Back in Melbourne, Mary's journalistic career flourished. She was an ardent feminist for her time, and wrote long articles on women's rights and sex education, denouncing the idle gentility that was the female ideal in the early 1900s. She also wrote children's stories that were fresh and unsentimental, and that above all had authentic Australian settings. These led to serials, and to her first book *A Little Bush Maid*, published in London in 1910 and based on these stories. The book was an immense success, and Mary was launched on her Billabong books, of which she wrote 15, the last being published in 1942. Altogether she wrote 38 children's books, which have sold over 3,000,000 copies.

In 1913 Mary went to Britain where she met her cousin George, whom she married in Australia in 1914. They returned to England where George served as a major in the army during World War I. Returning to Australia in 1919, they settled in Traralgon until 1927, when they went to live in Ireland and England for 12 years, returning to Australia in 1939. They had two sons. George died in 1949, and Mary in 1958 on a visit to England.

Mary Grant Bruce loved Australia and the idea of Australian country life. She once said that she would like to write for grown-ups, "if only to give a less sordid view of our country than Henry Handel Richardson's books gave".

Norah and Bobs (*A Little Bush Maid*)

unspoiled" Norah and her vivid station life, with its simple, positive values, had an enormous effect on generations of Australian children, from country children who recognised for the first time their own environment in a novel, to city children who—again for the first time—had set before them a convincing picture of a coherent, deeply satisfying and distinctive Australian country life.

Perhaps the clearest account of the impact that Mary Grant Bruce's Billabong books had on Australian children of several generations comes from an article by Mary Walker in the *Bulletin*, published on 16 July 1958, four days after Mary Grant Bruce's death.

We grew up with Norah, from her first appearance as *A Little Bush Maid* in 1910. She was so much more than a character in the pages of a book—she was *Us*, as we liked to fancy ourselves in supreme moments of idealism.

Mary Grant Bruce had a lot to answer for. She and Norah did more to mould our characters than home and church, State and school combined . . .

They were not *our* station-breds we mustered, but the Billabong Shorthorns. We are proud of our bearded fathers, regarding them as counterparts of David Linton . . . *Vale*, Mary Grant Bruce, but you have left us Norah!

Louis Stone

JONAH

LONDON 1911

He lit a cigarette and stared at the candle, smiling with the pride of a good workman at the thought of his plan that had worked so neatly. The Push was secure, and the blame would fall on the Ivy Street gang, the terror of Darlington. For a moment he regretted the active part he had taken in the stoushing, as his hunchback made him conspicuous. He wondered carelessly what had happened after the Push bolted. These affairs were so uncertain. Sometimes the victim could limp home, mottled with bruises; just as often he was taken to the hospital in a cab, and a magistrate was called in to take down his dying words. In this case the chances were in favour of the victim recovering, as the Push had been interrupted in dealing it out through Jonah's excessive caution. Still, they had no intention of killing the man; they merely wished to teach him a lesson.

True, the lesson sometimes went too far; and he thought with anxiety of the Surry Hills affair, in which, through an accident, a neighbouring push had disappeared like rats into a hole, branded with murder. The ugly word hung on his tongue and paralysed his thoughts. His mind recoiled with terror as he saw where his lawless ways had carried him, feeling already branded with the mark of Cain, which the instinct of the people has singled out as the unpardonable crime, destroying the life that cannot be renewed. And suddenly he began to persuade himself that the man's injuries were not serious, that he would soon recover; for it was wonderful the knocking about a man could stand.

He turned on himself with amazement. Why was he twittering like an old woman? Quarrels, fights, and bloodshed were as familiar to him as his daily bread. With a sudden cry of astonishment he remembered the baby. The affair of the bricklayer had driven it completely out of his mind. His thoughts returned to Cardigan Street. He remembered the quiet room dimly lit with a candle, the dolorous cry of the infant, and the intoxicating touch of its frail body in his arms.

His amazement increased. What had possessed him to take the brat in his arms and nurse it? His lips contracted in a cynical grin as he remembered the figure he cut when Chook appeared. He decided to look on the affair as a joke. But again his thoughts returned to the child, and he was surprised with a vibration of tenderness sweet as honey in his veins. A strange yearning came over him like a physical weakness for the touch of his son's body.

His eye caught his shadow on the wall, grotesque and forbidding; the large head, bunched beneath the square shoulders, thrust outwards in a hideous lump. Monster and outcast was he? Well, he would show them that only an accident separated the hunchback from his fellows. He thought with a fierce joy of his son's straight back and shapely limbs. This was his child, that he could claim and exhibit to the world. Then his delight changed to a vague terror—the fear of an animal that dreads a trap, and finds itself caught. He blew out the candle and fell asleep, to dream of enemies that fled and mocked at him, embarrassed with an infant that hung like a millstone round his neck.

The great Australian novel of the larrikins and "The Push", *Jonah*, did for Sydney what C. J. Dennis was to do for Melbourne four years later, though it should be remembered that two of the *Songs of a Sentimental Bloke* had appeared in the *Bulletin* two years before the publication of *Jonah*.

Although the vicious fire of the unregenerate larrikin can flare up in Jonah himself to the end, more than half of the book is about the personal lives of the larrikins, about Jonah and Chook and their wives and the other women with whom they are involved. Oddly enough, the larrikins are not promiscuous. Chook is always faithful to his beloved Pinkey. Although Jonah's Ada becomes a drunken slut and he falls in love with the bourgeois Clara, and would like to set her up as his mistress, in the end he returns to Ada. The Push would cheerfully kick a man to death, but they would never be false to their "donah", their special girl.

Jonah is held together by the strength of Stone's observation of Sydney's poor, by the clarity of his portrait of their lives in the streets and markets and in their squalid houses. The book opens with the mob surging through Waterloo doing the Saturday night shopping, the carnivores seeking their prey at the butcher's or staggering home like ants with their plunder from the greengrocer's. The Push is "gathered under the veranda at the corner of Cardigan Street, smoking cigarettes and discussing the weightier matters of life—horses and women." Chook, Ada and Pinkey and the hunchback Jonah are introduced immediately. Chook's dubious compliments to Pinkey's beauty and subsequent insults are repaid smartly, much to Chook's admiration. "She kin give it lip, can't she?"

The Push, as always, are up to no good. They begin to break up a Salvation Army meeting, but flee when a policeman appears. Their lives appear to be entirely on the surface—a matter of clothes and pointed boots and random violence. But in Jonah's case something deeper is at work.

Ada has had his baby, and Ada's widowed mother, Mrs Yabsley, is determined to arrange a marriage between Jonah and Ada. Jonah of course is very wary of the idea, but the huge Mrs Yabsley is as deft as a dancer in getting around Jonah without his knowing. Mrs Yabsley, this "unwielding jester" to whom the poor women bring their troubles, is a connoisseur of the characters of the street. The street life, says Mrs Yabsley, is what people "if their eyesight was good would be able ter see fer themselves instead of readin' about it in a book".

He turned on himself with amazement. Why was he twittering like an old woman? Quarrels, fights, and bloodshed were as familiar to him as his daily bread. With a sudden cry of astonishment he remembered the baby. The affair of the bricklayer had driven it completely out of his mind.

Mrs Yabsley is always worth listening to.

"Well," said Mrs Yabsley, reflectively, "an 'usband is like the weather, or a wart on yer nose. It's no use quarrelling with it. If yer don't like it, yer've got ter lump it. An' if yer believe all yer 'ear, everybody else 'as got a worse."

However, it is not the wiles of Mrs Yabsley that manoeuvre Jonah into marriage with Ada, but the innocent responses of his own baby, which he is very reluctant to see. Finding himself by chance alone in the house with it, he cannot help going and looking at it when it cries. When it touches him this tough larrikin realises that it is "flesh of his flesh".

Then he remembered his deformity, and, with a sudden catch of his breath, lifted the child from the cradle, and

Larrikin and Donah *George Ashton* (*above*)

felt its back, a passionate fear in his heart: it was straight as a die. He drew a long breath, and was silent, embarrassed for words before this mite, searching his mind in vain for the sweet jargon used by women.

"Sool 'im!" he cried at last, and poked his son in the ribs.

It is typical of the rhythms of the book that at this moment of tenderness, in comes Chook to demand Jonah's presence at the stoushing of a bricklayer who has betrayed a man to the police. At first "the velvety touch of his son's frail body" makes Jonah indifferent to the coming stoush, but he soon "pulls himself together" and joins the Push.

The police do not catch the Push, who nearly kick the bricklayer to death, but the baby has caught Jonah—the only creature that does not see his hump. Indirectly he confesses as much to Mrs Yabsley.

"I knowed all along", she answers, "the kid 'ud fetch yer, Joe. I knowed yer'd got a soft 'eart." And skilfully she leads him to work and a steady job.

At the wedding, which goes magnificently well on green peas, hot pies, saveloys and beer, Chook and Pinkey are formally introduced. Chook, the hardened Lothario, immediately falls in love. With unerring insight into his characters, Louis Stone recognises that there is in Chook "a surprising virginity of emotion that his facile, ignoble conquests left untouched".

Pinkey is the most attractive character in the book, but she is not in the least sentimentalised. Her native idiom is always ready for insult or jest, but she has a delicacy beneath the tongue and the red-headed beauty. It is not surprising that Bernard Shaw admired *Jonah*; Pinkey and Eliza Doolittle are sisters.

Jonah had worked with the old bootmaker, Hans Paasch, and Mrs Yabsley, from her secret savings under the floor, stakes Jonah the £7 needed to buy a bootmaker's tools and set up his own shop. In a beautifully realised scene Mrs Yabsley lifts the floorboard in the kitchen under which she has buried her coins, wrapped in paper, only to find them gone. As she wails in despair Jonah grabs the axe and sets about demolishing the floor. He finds the sovereigns and the remains of the paper, rolled away by rats and mice looking for lining for their nests.

Jonah is a born trader. Before long he has put poor old Paasch out of business, selling shoes as well as mending them. He goes to night school where he reveals a remarkable talent for figures.

Meanwhile Chook's and Pinkey's love affair slowly prospers, despite the hazards of her household which consists of her father, William Partridge, and stepmother, Sarah. Mr Partridge will not have a young man in the house since his eldest daughter, Lily, was seduced and eventually became a prostitute. Chook, however, brazens it out, enchanted with Pinkey in her domestic setting, having known his other conquests only in the streets. "For the first time in his life he understood why men gave up their pals and the freedom of the streets for a woman."

Chook, like Jonah, gradually becomes aware of his kinship with ordinary people, instead of clinging to the larrikin hostility. Though the larrikin can do terrible things, and of course he regards all policemen as enemies, he is not

MORNING IN THE MARKETS *Normand Baker*

LOUIS STONE
1871-1935

Louis Stone was born in 1871 at Leicester, England; his father was in the Royal Navy. In 1884 he migrated with his parents to Australia, settling first in Brisbane and a year later in Regent Street, Redfern, in Sydney.

Stone became a pupil-teacher with the Department of Public Instruction and taught at Waterloo, where he lived in Raglan Street. Thus from his earliest days in Sydney he was familiar with the territory of *Jonah*, with the cottages and lanes where the larrikins and their girls (their "donahs") lived when they were not on the streets.

In 1893 and 1894 he held a teacher training scholarship at Fort Street School, and matriculated at the University of Sydney in 1898. He began an Arts degree but did not graduate. He taught in Sydney and then went to the country, teaching at Cootamundra and Wagga. By 1904 he was back in Sydney again, teaching at Leichhardt. There he met his future wife Abigail Allen. They were married in 1906 and set up house in Waverley, near Bondi Junction, on his salary of £156 a year.

Stone worked on *Jonah* for four years, writing and re-writing. He spent hours in Waterloo and around the Paddy's Market, studying the larrikins and listening to their speech. Stone described Jonah as "composite of the Waterloo larrikin", but he said the final impetus to the character came from the discovery on one of his night prowls of a hunchback hard at work at a small bootshop. "He was mine! I stood gloating over him through the window. It was Jonah—complete, a gift from the Gods."

Although Stone finished *Jonah* in 1909, it was not until 1911 that it was published, in London by Methuen. There it was praised by H. G. Wells and Galsworthy. George Bernard Shaw also read it. A. G. Stephens reviewed it warmly in *The Book Fellow*. But critical acclaim did not sell copies, and the book was not a financial success. Nor was Stone's next book, *Betty Wayside*, which was serialised in the *Lone Hand* and published, after some moralistic cutting, in book form in London in 1915. Stone also wrote seven plays, only one of which had even a mild success.

He suffered much from ill-health, and was retired from the Department of Education in 1931. The Inspector wrote that he was compelled to retire Stone "because of the complete breakdown of mental and physical strength", and regretting it because "he is a cultured man and a gentleman".

Norman Lindsay first read *Jonah* in 1914 and befriended Stone from this time. Stone and his wife often stayed with him at Springwood. Lindsay wrote of "tall, lank, dyspeptic Lou, with his tragically depressed eyes and his fastidiously tormented mind. A tragic figure he remains for me, for he had not the stuff in him to sustain the endurance-test of work unrewarded by money or recognition."

It was not until the 1960s and 1970s that *Jonah* at last achieved the popularity it deserved. It was also made into a television series by the ABC in 1981.

---

necessarily a criminal. The Push and its activities are a sort of team game it is possible to give up, though the larrikin retains some innate ferocity, which may emerge if he is taunted or provoked.

Chook is worried by Pinkey's skinniness. His mother had been a cook before she married; whatever other hardships the family had to endure, the children always had plenty to eat. Not so in the Partridge household. So Chook appears at eight one Sunday morning with two plates wrapped in a towel.

"But wot is it?" cried Pinkey, in astonishment.

Chook removed the upper plate, and showed a dish of sheep's brains, fried with eggs and breadcrumbs—a thing to make the mouth water.

"Mother sent these; she thought yer might like somethin' tasty fer yer breakfast," he muttered gruffly, in fear of ridicule. Pinkey tried to laugh, but the tears welled into her eyes.

"Oh, Sarah will be pleased!" she cried.

"No, she won't," said Chook, grimly. "Wot yer can't eat goes back fer the fowls."

The "feeding up" of Pinkey continues and inevitably leads to marriage.

Jonah's shoe business prospers, but Ada takes to drink and neglects the boy Ray. One day a beautiful young woman comes to Jonah's Silver Shoe Emporium. The particular brand of shoe she wants is no longer made. Jonah is enchanted by her; he is drunk just with looking at her. He offers to make her shoes like the ones she wants, and kneels before her to measure her foot. The woman, Clara Grimes, is the daughter of a family which has come down in the world; her father was a country bank-manager and is now a derelict alcoholic. She gives piano lessons, and she takes on Ray as a pupil. Gradually Clara and Jonah come together, taking ferry rides to the North Shore. There amongst the rocks and trees Jonah, like Pan, plays to her on his mouth organ, on which he has always been a remarkable performer.

As Jonah prospers, Chook and Pinkey are being ground down by poverty. Pinkey, skinny again, lumps heavy bags of vegetables in the rain from the market for their shop; Chook watches in shame, too poor to buy a cart. In desperation he gambles all their savings at a brilliantly described two-up game and wins £15. He can now afford the horse and cart that will make their lives comfortable.

Jonah's two passions in life, for Ray and for Clara, are foiled by his drunken wife, Ada. Clara refuses to be set up as his mistress, her fatal flaw being her bourgeois gentility. However she does have the sensitivity to persuade Jonah to secretly give the derelict old Paasch, the bootmaker who had taught him his trade, an annuity of £50 for life.

Clara, wanting Ada out of the way, gives Ray the money Ada needs for a bottle of brandy. Ada drinks it, falls down the stairs and breaks her neck. But this does not solve Clara's problems. Jonah finds out how Ada got the brandy. With a strange loyalty to Ada (which in the context is entirely convincing), Jonah denounces Clara and refuses to see her again.

The humanity beneath the harsh surface of *Jonah* gives the book its deepest strength. Jonah is not an habitual criminal, and thus is a more interesting character than Frank Hardy's John West, whom he resembles in many ways. The women are all brilliantly portrayed—a rare achievement in Australian fiction before 1911. But none is better realised than Pinkey, who does not lack toughness in a tough world. She is one of the most appealing women in Australian fiction.

Douglas Mawson

THE HOME OF THE BLIZZARD

LONDON 1915

A start was made at 8 a.m. and the pulling proved more easy than on the previous day. Some two miles had been negotiated in safety when an event occurred which, but for a miracle, would have terminated the story then and there. Never have I come so near to an end; never has anyone more miraculously escaped.

I was hauling the sledge through deep snow up a fairly steep slope when my feet broke through into a crevasse. Fortunately as I fell I caught my weight with my arms on the edge and did not plunge in further than the thighs. The outline of the crevasse did not show through the blanket of snow on the surface, but an idea of the trend was obtained with a stick. I decided to try a crossing about fifty yards further along, hoping that there it would be better bridged. Alas! it took an unexpected turn catching me unawares. This time I shot through the centre of the bridge in a flash, but the latter part of the fall was decelerated by the friction of the harness ropes which, as the sledge ran up, sawed back into the thick compact snow forming the margin of the lid. Having seen my comrades perish in diverse ways and having lost hope of ever reaching the Hut, I had already many times speculated on what the end would be like. So it happened that as I fell through into the crevasse the thought "so this is the end" blazed up in my mind, for it was to be expected that the next moment the sledge would follow through, crash on my head and all go to the unseen bottom. But the unexpected happened and the sledge held, the deep snow acting as a brake.

In the moment that elapsed before the rope ceased to descend, delaying the issue, a great regret swept through my mind, namely, that after having stinted myself so assiduously in order to save food, I should pass on now to eternity without the satisfaction of what remained—to such an extent does food take possession of one under such circumstances. Realizing that the sledge was holding I began to look around. The crevasse was somewhat over six feet wide and sheer walled, descending into blue depths below. My clothes, which, with a view to ventilation, had been but loosely secured, were now stuffed with snow broken from the roof, and very chilly it was. Above at the other end of the fourteen-foot rope, was the daylight seen through the hole in the lid.

In my weak condition, the prospect of climbing out seemed very poor indeed, but in a few moments the struggle was begun. A great effort brought a knot in the rope within my grasp, and, after a moment's rest, I was able to draw myself up and reach another, and, at length, hauled my body on to the overhanging snow-lid. Then, when all appeared to be well and before I could get to quite solid ground, a further section of the lid gave way, precipitating me once more to the full length of the rope.

There, exhausted, weak and chilled, hanging freely in space and slowly turning round as the rope twisted one way and the other, I felt that I had done my utmost and failed, that I had no more strength to try again and that all was over except the passing. It was to be a miserable and slow end and I reflected with disappointment that there was in my pocket no antidote to speed matters; but there always remained the alternative of slipping from the harness. There on the brink of the great Beyond I well remember how I looked forward to the peace of the great release—how almost excited I was at the prospect of the unknown to be unveiled. From those flights of mind I came back to earth, and remembering how Providence had miraculously brought me so far, felt that nothing was impossible and determined to act up to Service's lines:

"Just have one more try—it's dead easy to die,
It's the keeping-on-living that's hard."

My strength was fast ebbing; in a few minutes it would be too late. It was the occasion for a supreme attempt. Fired by the passion that burns the blood in the act of strife, new power seemed to come as I applied myself to one last tremendous effort. The struggle occupied some time, but I slowly worked upward to the surface. This time emerging feet first, still clinging to the rope, I pushed myself out extended at full length on the lid and then shuffled safely on to the solid ground at the side. Then came the reaction from the great nerve strain and lying there alongside the sledge my mind faded into a blank.

Sir Douglas Mawson was a geologist, and he always thought of his Antarctic explorations primarily in terms of science. The aim of the publication of *The Home of the Blizzard* was not a literary one, but to record the story of the Australasian Antarctic Expedition of 1911-14, of which Mawson was the leader. Yet, as is the case with some of the other Australian explorers and their journals, the quality of the experience was so rich, and the strength of character of the individual so great, that an almost instinctive art emerged to produce many passages of the highest literary merit. Mawson was a well-educated man who read poetry and had a profound respect for words; as a scientist he was a trained observer. At the same time his almost superhuman courage and powers of endurance enabled him to view his own experiences with a further detachment. All is clear as in the Antarctic light, and no dust of loose emotion flows over the firm outlines of events.

And, as with the explorers, the two volumes of *The Home*

of the Blizzard are based on diaries written on the spot, an extraordinary achievement, especially in the case of Mawson's solitary journey back to the base camp after the death of his two companions.

All literature is a sharing of experience, and a kind of noble simplicity, both in Mawson himself and in his prose, gives the reader a vision of one of the strangest and certainly the harshest regions of the world. It was a triumph for human beings to exist at all in such conditions, especially in Adelie Land where the winds are the highest in the world, frequently blowing at 150 kilometres per hour and on one occasion even reaching 197 kilometres per hour. Physical strength and endurance were obviously called for, but strength of mind and character were even more essential.

Mawson said that what he looked for when choosing men for the expedition was mental stamina which came from a man's outlook on life. Long periods of inactivity, cooped up in a flapping tent or in a silent ice-cave, tested a man's capacities to the utmost. One member of the expedition, the wireless operator, did in fact go mad.

Anyone who thinks that the arts are mere decorations to the serious structure of life would do well to read *The Home of the Blizzard* and the diaries and letters of members of the expedition. Mawson himself thinks of poetry at some of the worst moments of his journey. Bickerton records in his diary that, when he and Whetter and Hodgeman were lying up in their bags in the tent while the blizzard raged outside, Whetter read to them from Thackeray's *The Virginian*. When the sound of the wind and the flapping of the tent made listening impossible, they divided the book and each read a part. Hodgeman was an architect and gave them mini-lectures on architecture. He also had a small book of pictures of the art collection in the Louvre which was passed around; Bickerton records that each time they studied these they found something they had not noticed before.

The Australasian Antarctic Expedition was made up of the youngest body of men under the youngest commander ever to visit Antarctica. Mawson was 38 when the *Aurora* left Hobart on 2 December 1911 under Captain J. K. Davis, who was second-in-command of the expedition, a modest and remarkable man. As Mawson wrote in his Preface to Davis's book *With the* Aurora *in the Antarctic*, "In him I had every

trust and confidence . . . the ship's company performed wonders with the good old vessel."

Mawson had some remarkable companions in the expedition, and one of the charms of *The Home of the Blizzard* is the revelations of human fellowship which it contains. Mawson was a great leader, as all his team acknowledged; they affectionately called him D.I., short for *Dux Ipse* ("the leader himself").

Mawson's intention, after establishing the main base, was to send out six sledge parties. Two were to do special scientific work to the south, around the South Magnetic Pole. One party was to examine the coastal highlands to the west, and another two to the east. Finally, the most difficult journey was to be undertaken by the Far Eastern party, consisting of Mawson himself, with Lieutenant Ninnis and Dr Mertz.

A start was made at 8 a.m. and the pulling proved more easy than on the previous day. Some two miles had been negotiated in safety when an event occurred which, but for a miracle, would have terminated the story then and there.

The whole of *The Home of the Blizzard* is of great interest, but particularly fascinating are the descriptions of those calm and comical inhabitants of the polar wastes, the penguins; or of the habits and characters of the teams of sledge-dogs; or of the extraordinary beauty of the icescape; or of the building of Aladdin's Cave in the ice, in which on one occasion several men nearly died of foul air. But undoubtedly the greatest passages of *The Home of the Blizzard* are in Mawson's account of the return journey of Ninnis, Mertz and himself, the Far Eastern party.

They had passed the most difficult terrain, where they and the dogs had all at various times fallen into crevasses. They were experiencing fine weather, after appalling blizzards (in one of which they had had to lie up for three days) when on 14 December, on a sunny day with the temperature at 16°C, Mawson saw Mertz, who was ahead, signal. When Mawson reached the spot he saw faint signs, nothing serious, of a crevasse. Busy on his sledge with his tables, he looked up to see Mertz halted in his tracks, anxiously gazing beyond Mawson. Mawson turned round. There was no sign of Ninnis. Hurrying back, Mawson found:

> . . . a gaping hole in the surface about eleven feet wide. The lid of the crevasse had broken in; two sledge tracks led up to it on the far side but only one continued on the other side.
>
> Frantically waving to Mertz to bring up my sledge, upon which there was some alpine rope, I leaned over and shouted into the dark depths below. No sound came back but the moaning of a dog, caught on the shelf just visible one hundred and fifty feet below . . .

They were 507 kilometres from Winter Quarters at Cape Denison; with Ninnis and his sledge and dogs they had lost most of the food and necessities including the tent.

As they trudged back, always hungry, they began to eat the dogs, which were so skinny that the meat was tough and

Pushing Against a Gale, Winter Quarters, Cape Denison *Frank Hurley*

SLEDGING IN ADELIE LAND *Van Waterschoot van der Gracht*

DOUGLAS MAWSON
1882-1958

Douglas Mawson was born at Bradford in Yorkshire in 1882. His father was a farmer and wool agent who emigrated with his family to New South Wales when Douglas was a small child. The family lived for a while in the country near Rooty Hill, where Douglas had to walk over six kilometres to school, and then moved to Sydney where Douglas went to Fort Street High School.

He studied physics, chemistry, geology and mineralogy at the University of Sydney, and in 1901 he graduated Bachelor of Engineering (Mining).

In 1903 he spent six months in the New Hebrides (now Vanuatu) and his report is the first scientific record of those islands.

After he had taken his Bachelor of Science Degree he was recommended by Professor Edgeworth David for the appointment of junior demonstrator in chemistry. In 1904 he was appointed lecturer in mineralogy and petrology at the University of Adelaide, later becoming Professor of Geology.

In 1907 he was appointed "route surveyor, cartographer and magnetician" to Shackleton's Antarctic Expedition, sailing in the *Nimrod* whose first officer was J. K. Davis, later Captain of the *Aurora*. Also on board was Professor David, who intended to return with the *Nimrod* but in fact stayed on with the explorers.

Mawson returned from the Expedition to Adelaide in 1909, and began negotiations to organise an Australasian Antarctic Expedition to explore the unknown segment of Antarctica due south of Australia. He visited London, where the Royal Geographical Society contributed £500 to the expedition costs. In 1911 he became engaged

to be married to Paquita Delprat, daughter of the General Manager of the BHP, and left shortly afterwards for Antarctica as leader of a large scientific expedition.

The events of the Australasian Antarctic Expedition are described in *The Home of the Blizzard*. After Mawson's return in 1914 Paquita and he were married on 31 March 1914. His wireless message of April 1913, offering to release her from the engagement after his epic journey back to Cape Denison, minus the soles of his feet and his hair, had gone round the world:

> Deeply regret delay stop only just managed to reach hut stop effects now gone but lost most my hair stop you are free to consider your contract but trust you will not abandon your second hand Douglas.

The Mawsons went to London where Douglas was knighted and lionised both by scientists and society, in between working hard on the editing of *The Home of the Blizzard*, to be published by Heinemann.

During World War I Mawson worked for the Ministry of Munitions, returning to Australia in 1919. In 1921 he was appointed Professor of Geology at Adelaide University; he made many trips with students to the outback, particularly in the Flinders Ranges area. He was a leading pioneer in the study of uranium.

Mawson returned to the Antarctic in 1929 to command the British Australian New Zealand Antarctic Research Expedition (BANZARE). Working from the *Discovery*, the Expedition extended over two years, returning to Australia for the winter of 1930. An immense amount of scientific data was collected on the Expedition and some 3¾ million square kilometres claimed as British territory.

Mawson retired from his chair at Adelaide University in 1952, but continued his scientific work and was much involved in the planning of the International Geophysical Year and the Australian National Antarctic Research Expedition. He died in 1958.

---

stringy. By New Year's Day 1913 Mertz was sick and weak, and they had to keep stopping. Mawson was pulling the sled on hands and knees, too weak to stand even with the wind behind him. On the night of 7 January Mertz died. Mawson wrote: "In his life we loved him; he was a man of character, generous and of noble parts."

For the rest of the night in the makeshift tent, with Mertz's body beside him, Mawson lay awake in his sleeping-bag. "Outside, the bowl of chaos was brimming with drift snow and I wondered how I would manage to break and pitch camp single-handed." His own physical condition was very bad, and he saw little hope of reaching the hut. Late that evening he buried Mertz's body in the snow and made a cross from the runners of the sledge which he had cut in half to save weight.

On 11 January his feet were so painful that he examined them and found that his soles had separated from them. He bandaged them up with lanoline and continued. On 17 January he found himself:

> ... dangling fourteen feet below on end of rope in crevasse—sledge creeping to mouth—had time to say to myself, "so this is the end" expecting the sledge every moment to crash on my head and all to go to the unseen bottom.

With enormous effort he slowly hauled himself up the rope and reached the top of the crevasse, only to be immediately thrown down into it again as the snow on the edge of the

crevasse gave way. "Exhausted, weak and chilled", he almost succumbed to the temptation to end it all, to slip out of his harness and fall into the black chasm. But he made "one last tremendous effort. The struggle occupied some time, but I worked slowly upward to the surface."

He struggled along, sometimes too weak to leave his tent for a day, until on 29 January, by an incredible fluke he found a cairn erected by some of his comrades who had been looking out for him, with food and the bearings of Aladdin's Cave, 37 kilometres distant. When he finally reached the Cave, only eight kilometres from Winter Quarters, such a blizzard was raging that he had to wait in the cave for a whole week.

The *Aurora* had sailed the very morning of the day he reached the hut at Winter Quarters. Mawson and the six men who had waited to look for him had to spend another winter in the Antarctic. It was not until December 1913 that the *Aurora* was able to return and pick them up.

It was not until many years later that the theory was advanced that Mertz's death and Mawson's symptoms of bodily decay were due to an excess of Vitamin A in the livers of the dogs they had eaten.

There has been no greater feat of human endurance in history than Mawson's solitary return journey. *The Home of the Blizzard* could be a classic for that alone. But it is much more; it is fine record of human companionship and scientific discovery in an "accursed country".

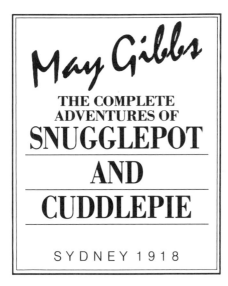

THE COMPLETE
ADVENTURES OF
SNUGGLEPOT

AND

CUDDLEPIE

SYDNEY 1918

Now it happened that just under the tree where they were sitting hidden by a bush lay a friend of Mr Lizard. When he heard Mr Lizard's name he cocked his head and listened, and when he heard what they said about drowning the Nuts he crept softly away till he was out of sight; then he dashed along as fast as he could to find Mr Lizard and tell him.

But alas! his warning was never given. Just hear what comes of being greedy. Many people, when they go to big dinner parties, eat and drink more than is good for them—because the things are good and they are greedy.

Mr Lizard was one of those "Greedies". He ate and drank so much at Mr Pilly's party that he had to stay in bed all the next day; and his head ached, and the flies worried him, and he was so cross that no one could go near him; so when he saw his friend coming he shouted, "Go away! I'm sick! Go away!" And he lashed his tail and wouldn't listen to a word. Naturally his friend was offended and went away.

So it happened that, while Mr Lizard lay moaning and groaning, all sorts of things were afoot and he knew nothing about them.

A big ship was lying in the harbour, and the Captain had come ashore, and had invited Ragged Blossom and Snugglepot and Cuddlepie to go on a long

journey with him, and see new countries.

Quite a lot of other Nuts and Blossoms said they would like to go too, so it was arranged that The Snag should sail at once, and everybody was busy packing; and all the time Mr Lizard lay tossing and grumbling on his bed.

Now, in their excitement, Snugglepot and Cuddlepie forgot all about Mr Lizard; and it was not until the ship was towing out into the stream that Mr Lizard, hearing the shouts of the crowd on the wharf, sprang out of bed and rushed wildly down, calling, "Stop! Stop! Wait for me!"

All the crowd took up the cry and shouted, "Stop!"

Snugglepot and Cuddlepie saw Mr Lizard and ran to the Captain, begging him to put back. But the Captain, who was a big stern man with a great beard and bushy eyebrows, frowned at them, and said, "The tide's going out and we must go with it."

Then were Snugglepot and Cuddlepie very sad, and Ragged Blossom dropped tears into the sea as she hung over the side

waving to poor Mr Lizard.

"Oh, why did we forget him?" moaned Snugglepot.

"He was so kind to me," wailed Ragged Blossom.

"Our dear old friend," sobbed Cuddlepie.

Mr Lizard, frantic with distress, jumped into a little boat and rowed after them. He pulled with all his might, and the Nuts on the ship shouted, "Come on!" The people on the wharf shouted "Hurrah!" as they saw his little boat get nearer and nearer to the big ship.

But alas! just as he was nearly touching the side the breeze caught the big green sails, filling them, and away went The Snag out to sea, leaving Mr Lizard in his little boat far behind, like a speck in the distance. Mr Lizard sat stiff as a tree trunk, staring after The Snag; his eyes looked as if they would pop out, and he ground his teeth with rage.

"Oh, Gum! Gum! Gum!" he groaned. Then he fell in a heap and rocked the boat in his grief and anger, for he had seen the Captain and he knew!

That big Captain, with his scrubby beard and bushy eyebrows, was—who do you think? He was the biggest and baddest of the Banksia men. "And no one knows," cried Mr Lizard.

Was there ever a children's book, or indeed any book, in which as much happens as in *Snugglepot and Cuddlepie*? The pace might be too hectic, even for the most eager child, were it not for May Gibbs's wonderful illustrations. These not only give an added dimension to the text but also demand time for their enchanting detail to be explored.

Like *Dot and the Kangaroo*, *Snugglepot and Cuddlepie* begins with a message, a plea for conservation. "Humans—please be kind to all Bush Creatures and don't pull flowers up by the roots." Also like *Dot and the Kangaroo*, humans are immediately seen as hostile to the bush creatures, amongst whom there is a bond of communication and acceptance unsuspected by crude humans. And once again, the Snake is not admitted to the happy company of nature.

Snakes, it seems, are always evil.

But one of May Gibbs's major achievements in *Snugglepot and Cuddlepie* is the creation of one of the most potent images of evil in all children's literature, the bad Banksia men. Unpleasant enough in their talk and their actions, they are most frightening in May Gibbs's illustrations, so dark and hairy. Many adults who read *Snugglepot and Cuddlepie* as children still cannot walk past a banskia tree without shuddering.

Children love to be safely frightened, as is borne out by any number of great books from the brothers Grimm and Hans Andersen in the past to Maurice Sendak today. The malevolence of the Banksia men is quite clear and consistent. It is impossible to imagine a nice Banksia man. And they are diabolically cunning, experts at disguise, at listening behind doors and at setting up false clues and traps.

The bad Banksia men provide the strongest presence of evil in *Snugglepot and Cuddlepie*. May Gibbs is not sentimental about nature and the bush creatures, but balances good against evil. The unfailing goodness of Snugglepot and Cuddlepie, Ragged Blossom and their friends on land or in the sea is offset by the bad Banksia men, the Snakes, the Octopus and other monsters. John Dory is different again; he is in the end a reformed character, a greedy, cruel creature purified and softened by his love for Ann Chovy.

So, although there are good and bad characters amongst the bush creatures, we are told firmly at the very beginning of *Snugglepot and Cuddlepie* that humans are bad. The wise Mr Kookaburra, respected by all, says early in the book: "These Humans are as bad as bad, but there must be bad things in this world as well as good. It would be very awkward for me if there were no snakes to eat."

The world of *Snugglepot and Cuddlepie* is very much a predatory one, which of course makes for many of the more alarming of Snugglepot and Cuddlepie's adventures. Being so tiny, the gumnut babies are eminently edible, delicious morsels to be snapped up. The greedy Owl takes Snugglepot for a pink mouse, pounces, and flies away with him. With appealing camaraderie, Cuddlepie immediately screams, "Take me! Take me! I don't want to be left. I would rather be eaten with Snugglepot than live alone without him." But Snugglepot, in typical Australian manner, does not like to show his feelings. When they are reunited, thanks to Mrs Fantail, Cuddlepie gives Snugglepot a great hug. "Snugglepot did not like kissing in public, so he said, 'We must thank kind Mrs Bird.' "

Not long after this they are nearly eaten by a cat. In their underwater adventures Snugglepot nearly has his head bitten off by John Dory, and then they are in great peril from the Giant Octopus. Their worst humiliation, if not danger, is when they are caught by humans and put in a specimen bottle. "Every now and then the big people shook the bottle to make them move, and their poor little heads were quite sore with being bumped against the sides."

"*Oh, Gum! Gum! Gum!*" *he groaned. Then he fell in a heap and rocked the boat in his grief and anger, for he had seen the Captain and he knew!*

That big Captain, with his scrubby beard and bushy eyebrows, was — who do you think? He was the biggest and baddest of the Banksia men. "And no one knows," cried Mr Lizard.

Respect for all creatures (except Snakes, Banksia men and the Giant Octopus), however small, is one of the major themes of the book. This is established early in the action, when the evil of humans is redeemed by the good human who releases the Possum from the trap and flings the trap into a stream. So when at the end Snugglepot and Cuddlepie are captured, one does not fear for their safety, as we know that not all humans are bad.

Snugglepot and Cuddlepie's friend Ragged Blossom shares many of their adventures. They first meet little Blossom at a dance. "Her dress was torn, and she was very dirty and sad — nobody danced with her." Snugglepot crawls through a crack in the wall near her and they dance. "Everybody" looked crossly at them because they couldn't dance and because Blossom is dirty and Snugglepot has no clothes. Little Blossom has an uncle who sells cheap clothes. The fore-and-aft gumleaves that frequently blow off or twist around form some of the most entertaining details in May Gibbs's illustrations. She has a genius for drawing fat little bare bottoms; the finest selection appears in the drawing of the Football Scrum.

The old Lizard is a faithful, if not always reliable, friend to Snugglepot, Cuddlepie and Ragged Blossom. He acts both as transport and as an ally against the machinations of the bad Banksia men and the Snakes. But Mr Lizard has his faults, one of which is gluttony. If he had not been sleeping off a dinner party, he would not have missed going to sea on *The Snag* with Snugglepot, Cuddlepie and Ragged Blossom, and a crowd of other Nuts and Blossoms, and would have been able to protect them. For the Captain of *The Snag* is in fact the worst of the Banksia men, and Mr Lizard would have recognised him.

They are in fact saved by the ingenuity of the sad little Jerboa, Winky, but only temporarily, for "the great wicked Captain" catches up with Snugglepot and Cuddlepie and Ragged Blossom. In a dramatic incident, accompanied by quite the scariest drawing in the book, he breaks down the door that Snugglepot is trying to hold shut against his great black hairy arm and grasping hand with long claws.

But the wicked Banksia man is not as clever as he thinks he is. Cuddlepie escapes while the villain puts Snugglepot

From S N U G G L E P O T A N D C U D D L E P I E an original illustration by May Gibbs

MAY GIBBS
1877-1969

Cecilia May Gibbs was born at Sydenham, Kent, England, in 1877. In June 1881 her father migrated to Australia, and May's mother, her brothers and she followed, arriving in Adelaide on the *Hesperus* in October 1881. Later the family moved to Perth, where May went to Amy Best's girls' school.

At an early age she showed a remarkable talent for drawing, and in 1901 went to England to study art. She spent three years at various night schools, the Cope and Nichol School, the South-Western Polytechnic at Chelsea and the Henry Blackburn School of Black and White Art.

She returned to Perth in 1904, and contributed many illustrations and cartoons to the *Western Mail*. Her special Christmas full-page covers are particularly imaginative and witty. She had a strong talent for political cartooning, and a number of her works show her sympathies for the early feminist movement.

She felt, however, that Perth was confining her talents, and she returned to England in 1909, continuing her studies, working for the publisher George Harrap and drawing cartoons for the suffragette journal, *Common Cause*. In 1912 she published a fantasy about the chimneys of London called *About Us*.

The English climate did not agree with her, and she returned to Australia in 1913, settling at Neutral Bay in Sydney. In Sydney she contributed to the *Lone Hand*, the *Sydney Mail* and the London *Tatler*. She also earned her living illustrating for the NSW Department of Public Instruction, and doing sketches of AIF soldiers leaving for overseas.

Her lovely original characters, the gumnut babies, first reached the general public with *Gumnut Babies*, published in 1916, and she followed this up with calendars, bookmarks and novelties. *Snugglepot and Cuddlepie* appeared in 1918 and 17,000 copies were sold.

In 1919 on a trip to Perth she married a mining agent, James Kelly, and then returned to Neutral Bay. *Little Ragged Blossom* appeared in 1920, and *Little Obelia* in 1921. She had begun to design strip cartoons. The first of the incredibly popular and long-lived *Bib and Bub* series appeared in 1924 in the *Sydney Sunday News*. The strip ran until September 1967, and five books of Bib and Bub cartoons were issued.

May Gibbs was awarded the MBE in 1955.

She died childless in 1969, and left all her papers and copyrights to the NSW Society for Crippled Children and the Spastic Centre of NSW. Many of her drawings, illustrations and political cartoons remain unpublished.

Perhaps May Gibbs's greatest achievement is that she invented a uniquely Australian fairy story tradition for children. Based firmly on the Australian natural environment, it owes little to the English or European fairytale traditions.

---

and Ragged Blossom into a big bag, throws them into the sea and roars, "Ha! Ha! . . . Now they'll be drowned!" But they are not at all. A curious eagle catches the bag, but they fall out, right to the bottom of the sea, and are soon on the best of terms with the Fish Folk.

Snugglepot and Cuddlepie saw Mr Lizard and ran to the Captain, begging him to put back. But the Captain, who was a big stern man with a great beard and bushy eyebrows, frowned at them, and said, "The tide's going out and we must go with it."

The sea adventures that follow form some of the most original and enchanting episodes in the book. Australia is of all nations the most intimately involved with the sea. By far the largest proportion of its population live within a short distance of a sea that is part of life as it cannot be in cold countries. England may have produced a nation of mariners, but certainly not of swimmers and surfers.

Snugglepot and Ragged Blossom's underwater adventures may owe something to Hans Andersen's Little Mermaid or Charles Kingsley's Water Babies. They seem very natural, once one is prepared to accept that Snugglepot and Ragged Blossom have no trouble in breathing under water.

May Gibbs's story is so impetuous that one has no trouble over this willing suspension of disbelief, although it is frequently pointed out that none of the sea creatures can live out of water. The terrible consequence will be that "They will dry."

Splitting the original team means that May Gibbs can keep two sets of adventures going at once, with Cuddlepie still on land and Snugglepot and Ragged Blossom under the sea. She also introduces a new character, Little Obelia, named after a certain type of seaweed. Part of the universal appeal of Snugglepot and Cuddlepie and Ragged Blossom is that they are so little; Little Obelia is, when introduced, even smaller. Led by their fishy friend Frilly, they come to "a wonderful pearly white flower, and resting asleep in the middle of its petals was a tiny pale baby". The legend about Little Obelia is that she is the soul of a beautiful unhappy woman who was the slave of a wicked king. She flung herself into the sea and was turned into a pearl, which will become a baby when live Land Folk come near it.

Little Obelia is a most unusual character, for she grows very fast, is highly intelligent and possesses magic powers. It is not surprising that she fulfils the prophecy and becomes Queen of the Fish Folk.

In the final rout of the bad Banksia men, those on land are whacked over the head by Mr Lizard and those under the sea are blown up by Little Obelia in a sea quake. In a happy ending Snugglepot and Cuddlepie and Ragged Blossom are reunited. But it is also a bitter-sweet ending, for, to many a child's dismay, Little Obelia has to stay below the sea. For all the fantasy, Snugglepot and Cuddlepie and Ragged Blossom are real, vulnerable creatures, involved in the life of the Australian bush, and except for Cuddlepie, the life of the sea. It was a stroke of genius to invent Little Obelia, for she supplies a further dimension of magic and beauty.

Norman Lindsay

THE MAGIC PUDDING

SYDNEY 1918

Bill was a small man with a large hat, a beard half as large as his hat, and feet half as large as his beard. Sam Sawnoff's feet were sitting down and his body was standing up, because his feet were so short and his body so long that he had to do both together. They had a pudding in a basin, and the smell that arose from it was so delightful that Bunyip Bluegum was quite unable to pass on.

"Pardon me," he said, raising his hat, "but am I right in supposing that this is a steak-and-kidney pudding?"

"At present it is," said Bill Barnacle.

"It smells delightful," said Bunyip Bluegum.

"It is delightful," said Bill, eating a large mouthful.

Bunyip Bluegum was too much of a gentleman to invite himself to lunch, but he said carelessly, "Am I right in supposing that there are onions in this pudding?"

Before Bill could reply, a thick, angry voice came out of the pudding, saying —

"Onions, bunions, corns and crabs,
Whiskers, wheels and hansom cabs,
Beef and bottles, beer and bones,
Give him a feed and end his groans."

"Albert, Albert," said Bill to the Puddin', "where's your manners?"

"Where's yours?" said the Puddin' rudely, "guzzling away there, and never so much as offering this stranger a slice."

"There you are," said Bill. "There's nothing this Puddin' enjoys more than offering slices of himself to strangers."

"How very polite of him," said Bunyip, but the Puddin' replied loudly —

"Politeness be sugared, politeness be hanged,

Politeness be jumbled and tumbled and banged.
It's simply a matter of putting on pace,
Politeness has nothing to do with the case."

"Always anxious to be eaten," said Bill, "that's this Puddin's mania. Well, to oblige him, I ask you to join us at lunch."

"Delighted, I'm sure," said Bunyip, seating himself. "There's nothing I enjoy more than a good go in at steak-and-kidney pudding in the open air."

"Well said," remarked Sam Sawnoff, patting him on the back. "Hearty eaters are always welcome."

"You'll enjoy this Puddin'," said Bill, handing him a large slice. "This is a very rare Puddin'."

"It's a cut-an'-come-again Puddin'," said Sam.

"It's a Christmas steak and apple-dumpling Puddin'," said Bill.

"It's a —. Shall I tell him?" he asked, looking at Bill. Bill nodded, and the Penguin leaned across to Bunyip Bluegum and said in a low voice, "It's a Magic Puddin'."

"No whispering," shouted the Puddin' angrily. "Speak up. Don't strain a Puddin's ears at the meal table."

"No harm intended, Albert," said Sam, "I was merely remarking how well the crops are looking. Call him Albert when addressing him," he added to Bunyip Bluegum. "It soothes him."

"I am delighted to make your acquaintance, Albert," said Bunyip.

"No soft soap from total strangers," said the Puddin', rudely.

"Don't take no notice of him, mate," said Bill, "That's only his rough and ready way. What this Puddin' requires is politeness and constant eatin'."

They had a delightful meal, eating as much as possible, for whenever they stopped eating the Puddin' sang out —

"Eat away, chew away, munch and bolt and guzzle,
Never leave the table till you're full up to the muzzle."

But at length they had to stop, in spite of these encouraging remarks, and, as they refused to eat any more, the Puddin' got out of his basin, remarking — "If you won't eat any more here's giving you a run for the sake of exercise," and he set off so swiftly on a pair of extremely thin legs that Bill had to run like an antelope to catch him up.

"My word," said Bill, when the Puddin' was brought back. "You have to be as smart as paint to keep this Puddin' in order. He's that artful, lawyers couldn't manage him. Put your hat on, Albert, like a little gentleman," he added, placing the basin on his head. He took the Puddin's hand, Sam took the other, and they all set off along the road. A peculiar thing about the Puddin' was that, though they had all had a great many slices off him, there was no sign of the place whence the slices had been cut.

The great early classics of Australian children's literature are, with one exception, all by women: Ethel Pedley, Mary Grant Bruce, Ethel Turner, May Gibbs. The exception is, of course, *The Magic Pudding*.

It is ironic that Norman Lindsay, notorious for his paintings and drawings of voluptuous (if hardly ever erotic) women, should have in this, his greatest literary work, almost entirely excluded female characters. It is very much a male book, with a boyish zest to it. Norman Lindsay once remarked that he chose a pudding as his subject because food was one topic that always appealed to boys. Nevertheless, Lindsay wrote such an entertaining book that it has a universal appeal.

The Magic Pudding is a perfect demonstration that, if handled with sufficient skill, one entirely original idea can sustain a whole book. As in many of the best stories, the idea does not immediately appear, the characters have to be introduced first.

The most appealing is undoubtedly the good-natured dandy, Bunyip Bluegum, a thoroughly atypical Australian bear (koala) in that he is full of movement and humour. He is also an innocent. He cannot solve the problem of what to be when he leaves home, where he has lived with his whiskered Uncle Wattleberry in a tree house that is far too small for two bears *and* whiskers. "You can't go about the world being nothing, but if you are a traveller you have to carry a bag, while if you are a swagman you have to carry a swag, and the question is: Which is the heavier?"

A peculiar thing about the Puddin' was that, though they had all had a great many slices off him, there was no sign of the place whence the slices had been cut.

He goes for counsel to the Poet who sums up Bunyip Bluegum as "A Gentleman of Leisure" who should take to the road not with bag or swag but simply with a walking stick. Off goes Bunyip Bluegum and thoroughly enjoys the world until he begins to feel hungry; he forgot to bring any food. *The Magic Pudding* is about magic, but it is basically a very practical book.

Bunyip Bluegum, in the extremity of hunger, comes upon Bill Barnacle, and his mate Sam Sawnoff, the penguin bold, having lunch together by the road. Bunyip Bluegum is tantalised by the aroma of steak and kidney pudding. But it is no ordinary pudding in the basin that Bill is holding.

For a start, it is odd, on being courteously asked by Bunyip Bluegum whether it is a steak and kidney pudding, that Bill should reply, "At present it is." It is even odder that the pudding then talks, angrily telling Bill to offer the stranger a slice. " 'There you are,' said Bill. 'There's nothing this Puddin' enjoys more than offering slices of himself to strangers.' "

The story of the Puddin' begins to emerge. " 'It's a cut-an'-come-again Puddin',' said Sam. 'It's a Christmas steak and apple-dumpling Puddin',' said Bill." Eventually Bill explains the secret of the Puddin', which is the basic idea of the book. It is a Magic Puddin'—"The more you eats the more you gets . . . me an' Sam has been eatin' away at this Puddin' for years, and there's not a mark on him." They call the Puddin', a very rude fellow who is apt to run away, Albert.

A lot of the rollicking quality of *The Magic Pudding* is due to the poems and songs which are interspersed with the text. W. S. Gilbert would have enjoyed them, particularly the ballad which tells the story of how, in very dubious circumstances, Bill and Sawnoff obtained the Puddin' from a Chinese cook on an iceberg after a shipwreck. There are other excellent songs of the sea such as "Spanish Gold", and,

delivered in fragments, the ballad of "The Salt Junk Sarah", one of those songs that go on forever. Anyone who has seen Lindsay's beautiful and extraordinarily detailed ship models will know that, landlubber though he was, he had an intricate knowledge of the sea and everything to do with it.

Of course, anyone owning a Magic Pudding is likely to be haunted by Puddin' thieves, and that in turn presents an opportunity for fighting, which boys are supposed to like next best to eating. Bill and Sam rout the pudding thieves, the Possum and the Wombat, and the wanderers travel on until it is time for the evening meal. Now the Puddin' comes into his own, as they regale themselves on steak and kidney and then boiled jam roll and apple dumpling "as the fancy took them, for if you wanted a change of food from the Puddin', all you had to do was to whistle twice and turn the basin round". After such a dinner, it is time for a story. Out comes a mouth organ, and Bill leads off with "Spanish Gold", Sam following with "The Penguin Bold".

Then, with fine solemnity, Bill invites Bunyip Bluegum, "a young intelligent feller, goin' about seein' the world by yourself", to "become a member of The Noble Society of Puddin' Owners". "Done!" says Bunyip Bluegum, and together they sing "The Puddin'-Owners' Anthem".

It adds to the fun that Bunyip Bluegum, Bill and Sam are not just friends on the road, but are bound together by puddin'-eatin', a rewarding occupation that also involves considerable responsiblity in protecting the pudding, and various bonuses, such as "songs, roars of laughter, and boisterous jests" for breakfast.

The dangers of puddin'-ownin' are soon apparent. When they all go off to help a Fireman fight a fire, hiding the Puddin' in a hollow log, the thieving Wombat is suddenly observed by Bunyip Bluegum in the act of making off with it. It was all part of a put-up job, the Fireman being exposed as none other than "that snooting, snouting scoundrel, the Possum", who is smartly hit on the snout, knocked into the fire and somewhat singed. In the melée both Wombat and Possum get away with the Puddin'.

Bunyip Bluegum rallies his dejected friends and they set off to find the Puddin', so that the book now becomes a detective story with a frustrating hunt for clues. They have no success with a Horticultural Hedgehog, a Parrot Swagman and a Bandicoot carrying a watermelon, but a loquacious Rooster puts them on the track leading to the Wombat's house in a tree, where the thieves are feasting themselves on illicit Puddin'.

Until now Bunyip Bluegum has played a quiet part, a dapper and companionable fellow, but not as vigorous as Bill or Sam. His style of speech is quite different from that of Bill or Sam. Bill is not too good at grammar, but he has a splendidly inventive turn of abuse. Sam's speech has a Cockney perkiness to it. But Bunyip Bluegum's has a Dickensian ornateness, excessive elegance making fun of itself.

Bunyip Bluegum comes into his own with a ruse which revives the despondent friends. Disguising himself as a commercial traveller with a grass moustache and Bill's hat and a bag, with a fine spiel he persuades Possum and Wombat to bring the Puddin' outside so they can see how his commodity, Pootle's Patent Pudding Enlarger, will swell the Puddin' to twice his size. It is a nice satire on gullibility

From T H E   M A G I C   P U D D I N G an original illustration by Norman Lindsay

NORMAN LINDSAY
1879-1969

Norman Lindsay was born in 1879 at Creswick, a small town 17 kilometres from Ballarat, where his father Robert was the local doctor. It was a most remarkable family; Norman, his brothers Lionel, Daryl and Percy, and his sister Ruby all became artists, and Norman was also a novelist and writer of autobiographies and essays. Dr Lindsay was much loved by Norman. "He was the best of all possible parents, a father who let his offspring develop as their temperaments and faculties dictated . . . he rejected any interdiction on his right to get all the fun out of life that came his way." Norman's mother does not seem to have had the same zest for life; he describes her as "a harried woman, incessantly driven by the tyranny of a large family, and with no intellectual or social releases from its drab monotony".

The best guide to Norman's youth in and around Creswick is his trilogy of novels, *Saturdee, Half Way to Anywhere* and *Redheap*. Like his drawings of urchins that appeared in the *Bulletin*, these books did their best to dispel, in Lindsay's words, "the notable illusion that childhood is the era of sweet and guileless innocence". Lindsay also wrote an autobiography, *My Mask*, which reveals a lot about his Creswick days.

Norman went to the local state school at six, and then to the Grammar School, which he left at 17 to join his brother Lionel in his studio in Little Collins Street, Melbourne. He did enough commercial drawings to keep him alive, and otherwise luxuriated in idleness in the artistic life of Melbourne.

In 1900 Norman married his first wife Katie; two sons, Jack and Ray, were born in 1901 and 1903. In 1901 J. F. Archibald invited him to draw for the *Bulletin*, and he left for Sydney. His marriage was breaking down, and at this time he met the 16-year-old model, Rose, who later became his second wife.

It was a very exciting time to be working on the *Bulletin* and living in Sydney. In *Bohemians of the Bulletin* and elsewhere he wrote about some of the writers and artists he knew: Lawson, Steele Rudd, Banjo Paterson, Louis Stone, Christopher Brennan and many more. Hugh McCrae was a particular friend. Lindsay's intellectual and aesthetic frame of reference was narrow (he hated modern art and most modern literature) but he had an enormous ability to stimulate people which went with a great capacity for friendship and for helping other artists and writers.

In 1910 Lindsay went to London. On his return he bought for £500 an old stone house and 17 hectares of land at Springwood in the Blue Mountains. There he painted and drew, wrote his nine novels and the immortal *The Magic Pudding*, created cement sculptures in the garden, and worked on his extraordinarily detailed ship models. These are on exhibition at Springwood, which is now a National Trust museum. Kenneth Slessor, Douglas Stewart and other writers have recalled the atmosphere of Springwood, the talk and the stimulus given to Norman's disciples, presided over by Norman's elf-like figure. Although Lindsay's ideas about art may have been violently reactionary, there was never any doubt about his inexhaustible enthusiasm for the creative process and his encouragement of those whom he considered to be furthering it.

Lindsay also wrote three books of philosophical and artistic essays, the less said about which the better, and three volumes of autobiography. He died at Springwood in 1969.

---

and greed, for why would anyone want a Magic Pudding any larger than its ever-renewable self? At the prearranged signal Bill and Sam spring out from behind the tree and after brisk fisticuffs the Puddin' is secured, and that night there is feasting and songs.

They take to the road again, Bill and Sam closely examining all passers-by in case they are Puddin'-stealers in disguise. They think that one whiskered character is Watkin Wombat and are in the painful process of trying to pull his whiskers off when Bunyip Bluegum appears and tells them they have got hold of his Uncle Wattleberry. Uncle's exasperation is so acute that it can only be relieved by "bounding and plunging" and singing a song of rage.

Thinking that there is nothing to do but leave Uncle Wattleberry to bound and plunge, and get on the road again, they set off. To their astonishment they meet Possum and Wombat, undisguised, carrying a bag in which there is a present for them. As gullibility had been the thieves' downfall, so it is now of the three friends, who are induced to put their heads in the bag which is smartly drawn tight so they cannot get out. Possum and Wombat again steal the Puddin'.

Rescued by an elderly dog, Benjimen Brandysnap, a market gardener, whose bag it is, stolen by Possum and Wombat, they set off on the search, accompanied by Benjimen. Again Bunyip Bluegum's superior intellect comes to the rescue. He writes out a notice, "A Grand Procession of the Amalgamated Society of Puddings will Pass Here at 2.30 Today".

The thieves will find this irresistible. All the friends have to do is hide and confront them. In just 15 minutes the Possum and the Wombat appear, but the problem is that the Wombat has the Puddin' under his hat and there is no way, except by breaking the law, say the Possum and the Wombat, by which the hat may be removed. Bunyip Bluegum, the intellectual of the party, solves the problem by striking up the National Anthem, and off come all the hats, and the Puddin' is revealed sitting furiously on the Wombat's head. After punishment and the singing of moral songs, the thieves promise repentance and are allowed to go.

The Puddin' himself is unimpressed: "Puddin'-thieves never suffer from remorse. They only suffer from blighted hopes and suppressed activity."

Reaching the town of Tooraloo they meet two persons in bell-topper hats, again the Possum and the Wombat in disguise; the Mayor and the Constable arrive in the midst of the fracas, and the Puddin' is arrested as the cause of the trouble.

A trial scene is usually a success in a book, but in this case it goes on a little too long. It is the only flaw in *The Magic Pudding*; intended as a satire on the law, it is outside the scope of the book. However, the friends are soon outside the court, and the book ends happily with a building of a magnificent tree-house in Ben's garden, with a special platform for a "little Puddin' paddock".

By this time, a complete mythology of Puddin'-fanciers has been established, and the custodians of the sacred, if rude, Puddin' may well go on eating and singing for ever.

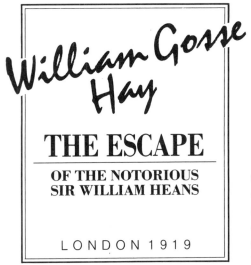

THE ESCAPE

OF THE NOTORIOUS
SIR WILLIAM HEANS

LONDON 1919

At something in what he said, Heans' nerve seems to have failed him, and even while he was speaking, he left the window — too pale for mere indignation — and putting himself before the fire (Daunt being at the bottom of the table) removed a pair of grey cotton gloves, and laid them somewhat aimlessly on the mantel-piece beside one of the marble figures. Had he recollected who was there speaking so pleasantly — one of the sharpest policemen in Tasmania? With a hand leaning by them, he turned inward a little to the fire, a varnished boot upon the fender, yet standing in a grey chilled way, as if his shrunken finenesses of costume were too thin for this windy weather.

"Indeed," he said, in a hoarse yet gracious voice, which he seemed to strive in vain to keep steady and aloof, "you are right of my resignation of mind. I would cut and run to-morrow if I could. Well, sir" (with a short, trembling laugh), "take the room if you desire. Take my pretty ornaments for your bal paré and deck the old Chamber with them. Take my clock, my bird, my green lustres, my two ladies with the doves." He catalogued them, staring at them one by one. Afterward he turned and looked at Daunt, very cowed, grey and gracious. "Yes, let them have the room, sir," said he. "Take anything you want."

Daunt gave a little glance up at him — a sort of mournful, bitter glance. "Come, I know you, Heans," said he, "better than you know yourself. You are an irreconcilable man. 'Pon my faith, sir, you hug it to yourself! I should never be surprised at any sudden recklessness from you. A report! A catastrophe! Ah, it is Sir William Heans! Just as A said — just as B prophesied! Tut — tut — it delights you, I think, not to be circumspect, and help yourself. I am persuaded you shall not pleasure yourself with a fresh mortification and hug a new reason for reckless speaking — not by my word, if we can fob Tipton off! Come, sir, you will be yet frank enough to admit with your old master Oughtryn that our care of you is as just as our punishment. Here is one who is rich from his firm belief in our good intentions." He turned to Oughtryn, adding: "Still quite unassailable, Oughtryn, I am sure?" And he laughed gravely, but how sternly he said it, with a parting glance into the room and round at the two windows, his pale little hand upon the table! Suddenly, while he spoke, the noise of someone knocking rattled into the wind, and Oughtryn, while he backed to the door, remarked, "since Mr. Daunt was pleased to ask, he was the same as ever he was". But as he felt for the handle, his air was puzzled and pale. He added, in his shrill voice: "I look for highness from my masters, Honours, but a gentleman cannot always show his hand. I've suffered little and gained much from my masters, gentry, but by them as to which my masters delegates their mastering I've suffered hell. A gentleman cannot give his mastering."

The title of William Gosse Hay's finest novel suggests adventure and the horrors of convict life in Tasmania, another version of Marcus Clarke's *For the Term of His Natural Life*. Nothing could be further from the truth. Although Hay minutely researched the details of the transportation system in Tasmania and the geographical background, he wrote a highly idiosyncratic novel about passion and pride and the preservation of human dignity. His hero, William Heans, is unique in Australian fiction because he is an Anglo-Irish aristocrat, and the preservation of the aristocratic style is as essential to him as breathing. The morality of the book is in the redemption of the gentleman in Heans, so that in certain key actions, Heans's gentlemanly style, as in the old proverb, "is the man himself".

Sir William Heans has been transported, in 1836, for abducting a married woman. We are told that women are inclined to forgive him for this crime, and men, if resentful of the implied threat to property, do not take it all that seriously. Hay himself, not wanting to follow Marcus Clarke in having his hero wrongfully transported, admitted that, "I had to find a crime that I could bear in a man for hero."

When the book opens Heans has been nearly four years in Hobarton, as Hay always calls Hobart. Owing to his wealth and aristocratic connections, and a somewhat tenuous reputation as an architect, he is allowed to work as an architect and to enjoy a number of privileges. Wearing his beautiful clothes, he leads a comfortable life that in someone of another temperament would have led to acceptance of his lot.

These privileges do not lead him into any acceptance of or even much curiosity about Australia. His life is described as both "exile and boredom in a wild island at the bottom of the world".

His unremitting adversary, the Superintendent of Police, Mr Daunt, has a very thorough understanding of Heans's character. Two-thirds of the way through the novel Daunt says, "Come, I know you, Heans . . . better than you know yourself. You are an irreconcilable man." Daunt says Heans has been fortunate in many ways, but he has not been granted resignation. Heans answers, "You are right of my resignation of mind. I would cut and run to-morrow if I could."

Heans's proud and aristocratic spirit cannot be reconciled with his life as a convict, however gentlemanly that is allowed to be. Heans mingles with the best of society in the colony, from the Governor, Sir John Franklin, down. (Hay allows several historical figures to appear in his story, but treats them as fictional characters when he wants to.) Heans is made especially welcome by a staff officer, Captain Hyde-Shaxton (mostly called Shaxton), and his beautiful young wife Matilda.

Mr Daunt, "a dark man, quick and neat . . . with a hearty, silent laugh" insulted Heans on the hulk before he left England, and now humiliates him by the strictness of the watch he keeps on him. Daunt is in love with Matilda, and hates Heans because of the obvious fact that she is in love with the Irish aristocrat.

At the beginning of the book, Heans does not restrict his acquaintances to those at the top of Hobarton society. He gambles and mixes with bad characters, while Matilda tries to get Lady Franklin to use her influence to get Heans appointed to some post where he would be "bound among a better set".

Heans's determination to escape gives the novel its structure. Book I, "High Water", carries him through his life among the gentry of Hobarton to the day he not only intends to escape with Captain Stifft in the *Emerald*, but, reverting to his original crime, also tries to persuade Matilda Shaxton to elope with him. After an anguished dialogue, she refuses. Daunt foils his attempt to escape, and Heans loses his privileges and is assigned as a "pass-holder servant-man" to Charles Oughtryn, a freed prisoner. Daunt will not allow Heans to work at Oughtryn's country property at Bagdad; he has to remain in Hobarton.

In Heans's own words, "My pride, under raw supervision, is wearing bare. It has long passed the standing capacity of just anger." Heans goes on to speak of "my once dear friends, the Hyde-Shaxtons". Oughtryn has a near-blind daughter, Abelia; one of Heans's duties is to teach her to ride. A tender and selfless side of his character is revealed in his kindnesses to Abelia.

Thus in Book II, "Neap Tide", Heans's fortunes are sinking, but his moral situation begins to improve. He clears

Hobart from McGregor's Gardens (*Picturesque Atlas of Australasia*)

Matilda's name in a sinister scene between Daunt, Shaxton and another officer when her name is never actually mentioned. Daunt has been overheard by the officer maligning "the wife of an officer" who gave Heans money taken from her husband to pay for his attempted escape. In fact, Heans points out, he had used his own money, which was hidden in her house. In the taut situation of Daunt and Heans both being in love with Matilda, to the knowledge of her husband Shaxton, it is Daunt the policeman who comes off worst.

Heans's next attempted escape is foiled by his own gentlemanly actions, another stage of his moral redemption. At the very moment he is making his escape with great difficulty, through the cave behind Oughtryn's house, he hears the soldier Spafield attacking Abelia. In the most ornate set piece of the book, Heans turns back to help her, and, using a small poniard against Spafield's bayonet, kills him and saves Abelia.

He turned inward a little to the fire, a varnished boot upon the fender, yet standing in a grey chilled way, as if his shrunken finenesses of costume were too thin for this windy weather.

Meanwhile, Shaxton has challenged Daunt to a duel. Daunt shoots first and Shaxton is wounded; then, as Shaxton is lifting his pistol, Daunt has a heart attack and dies.

As a result of his attempted escape and killing of Spafield, Heans is sentenced to that final prison, Port Arthur. He is still allowed some privileges and can wear his own clothes, but the elegant image is sorely tarnished. He now looks like an old man, and is dressed "in a second-class suit of smooth cords, a sort of collar, and that sort of clever cravat which tries to hide a linenless shirt. No cane. No glass. No gloves. A black peaked cap a little rain-loosed."

At the opening of Book III, "Low Water of Spring Tides", the reader is immediately told that on 2 December 1842 the prisoner Heans "had either escaped or been lost in the forests about Port Arthur". Reports followed that Heans is living in France: "But it was not until his demise in the year of the Franco-Prussian War that the rumour of his survival is privately confirmed."

Hay obviously wants the emphasis of his last 50 pages to be not on suspense but on the state of Heans's soul, which is at first paradoxically refreshed by the beauty of the freestone and pink brick buildings of Port Arthur. Captain Shaxton, who has designed the new prison (in which work Heans has helped him before his first attempts at escape), meets Heans. A kindly man, Shaxton has agreed to help carry out the plan evolved by his wife, Oughtryn, Abelia and Captain Stifft to help Heans escape. Shaxton tells Heans that the old Australian Aborigine, Conapanny, who is known to both Shaxton and Heans, is prepared to guide Heans across the 13 kilometres of mountains to the bay where Captain Stifft and the *Emerald* will be waiting, and to provide food for him. "The audacity of it—the unlikeliness of it!" The quotation is apt enough.

Heans gets out to sea in a boat and reaches a beach where

PORT ARTHUR *Artist unknown*

WILLIAM GOSSE HAY
1875-1945

William Gosse Hay was born in 1875 at "Linden", his parents' home in what is now the Adelaide suburb of Linden Park. His father, Alexander, was a successful businessman who had arrived as an assisted emigrant boy in 1839. William's mother was Agnes Gosse (sister of the explorer William Christie Gosse, who discovered Ayers Rock).

William spent much of his childhood at the magnificent mansion, "Mt Breckan", at Victor Harbour, which his father built for his mother. William and his elder brother Alexander were sent as boarders to Melbourne Grammar School in 1889, and in 1895 William followed Alexander to Trinity College, Cambridge, where he read for the law. When he was at Cambridge, William resolved to become a writer. There was plenty of precedent for this in the family. His mother wrote memoirs and biographies. She was also related to the critic and essayist Edmund Gosse. Other relatives connected with literature included the publisher Arthur Waugh, father of Alec and Evelyn.

However, William's family expected him to live in the country and become a grazier. His father died when he was at Cambridge; after taking his BA he proposed to Mary Williams, returned to Australia and announced that he was going to become a writer.

He bought a large stone house with a tower in Beaumont in the Adelaide foothills, and built himself a room in the garden, where, protected by Mary, he wrote. The withdrawn, unworldly, almost hermetic style of his books reflects this secluded and comfortable life.

His first novel, *Stifled Laughter*, appeared in 1901. Others followed, almost all dealing with Australia's convict past, and all written in a sometimes excessively wordy style.

In 1909 "Mt Breckan" was burned down while William's mother and sister Helen were staying there. They escaped but went to England on the *Waratah*, which mysteriously vanished off the coast of Africa. These two events caused William to have a sort of nervous breakdown; Mary took him to Tasmania to recuperate, and the result of this visit and others was *Captain Quadring* (1912) and *The Escape of the Notorious Sir William Heans* (1919), both set in Tasmania in convict times.

In his search for privacy, Hay built an ornate house by the ocean at Seacliff, but after a few years decided that beach had become too public, so built another on a bare windy hill at Marino. He also thought Beaumont was becoming too crowded, so he bought a farm near Victor Harbour where he ran sheep and dairy cattle. Mary, who had hoped to be married to a farmer, at last achieved her aim, though of course Hay was never a working farmer; his entire life was still given to writing. As if the farm were not remote enough, Hay built a cabin for himself a few kilometres away on the hills above "Mt Breckan".

When he was 69 he over-exerted himself helping to fight a bushfire at Victor Harbour, and died shortly afterwards in 1945.

In his personal life, as in his books, Hay is one of the oddest, most atypical, of Australian writers, and all the more worth reading for that reason.

Conapanny is waiting for him. These last few pages of the book are quite unlike the rest. Heans gives up all his graces and pride and surrenders himself to the old Aborigine and her knowledge of nature. She catches fish and snakes, cooks them for him and brings him to the rendezvous with Stifft and the *Emerald*. Only the gentleman's code of honour and kindness remain; all the graces have gone.

> "*Indeed,*" *he said, in a hoarse yet gracious voice, which he seemed to strive in vain to keep steady and aloof, "you are right of my resignation of mind. I would cut and run to-morrow if I could . . .*"

There are three sub-plots in the book, all of which impinge on Heans's own story. The first is the attempt of the Earl of Daisley, disguised as Captain Homely O'Crone, to rescue a woman prisoner, Mme Ruth; the second is the life-story of old Conapanny; and the third the (unhistorical) murder of Governor Collins in the house where Oughtryn lives.

Hay's narrative method is always extremely complex. Amazingly enough, though there seems to be no record of his ever having read *Such is Life*, there are a number of affinities between Furphy's and Hay's approach to narrative, although Furphy is writing about bullockies and Hay about a gentleman—a member of a class that Furphy detested. Neither story proceeds in a simple chronological fashion. Hints are given out, the narrative flashes out and jumps ahead, characters are not aware of actions that are apparent to other characters, the narrator is not omniscient, and so on. Both books require a lot of concentration from the reader, who must put the story together himself from the clues offered.

The intricacies of Hay's style and narrative method make *The Escape of the Notorious Sir William Heans* a difficult book to read, but one can see why fellow writers, such as Katherine Mansfield, and critics, such as R. G. Howarth, thought so highly of it. Heans's distinction is unmistakable. Other characters such as Oughtryn, Franklin or Conapanny stand out against what Hay saw as the trend of life, "our wild equalising", "a drab end of formlessness". Hay wanted to get Australian literature away from what he called "fifth-rate tales of the 'paddock and stockyard variety'". He wanted it to deal with "Australia's own romantic, deeply enthralling, and in many cases heroic history", "tragic, ballad-like". (He meant the Scots border ballads, not bush ballads.) Influenced by Meredith and Hawthorne, his style is sometimes too deliberate, but there is no doubt that with this book, Hay brought a new richness of texture into Australian literature.

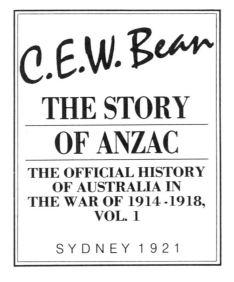

C.E.W. Bean

THE STORY
OF ANZAC

THE OFFICIAL HISTORY
OF AUSTRALIA IN
THE WAR OF 1914-1918,
VOL. 1

SYDNEY 1921

The work of a stretcher-bearer often prevented him from taking cover which others could seek. Thus on April 26th and the following days the Turks poured down Shrapnel Gully the rain of shells which gave it that name. The whine of the small salvoes could always be heard approaching, and most passers through the valley were able to take some cover during the heavier spasms. But the stretcher-bearers carried their burdens through it, erect. Four of them were taking an officer to the Beach, when, under a particularly hot burst of shell fire, one suggested that they should lower the stretcher and wait. The senior of the party, Private Blackburn, a big Lancashireman of the 3rd Battalion, would not consent. "It's no good dropping the stretcher now," he said. "If we're going to be hit, we shall be, whether walking or crouching." That was the spirit of the men. Many became fatalists. If the shell "had their name and number marked on it," as they said, they would be hit. Until that shell arrived, it was best to let others see them going proudly rather than flinching.

One bearer there was whose name has become a tradition in Australia. A number of donkeys with Greek drivers had been landed on April 25th for water-carrying. The Greeks were soon deported, and after the first days the donkeys ceased carrying and fed idly in the gullies, till they gradually disappeared. Private Simpson, of the 3rd Australian Field Ambulance, was seized with the idea that one of these might be useful for moving men wounded in the leg. On the night of April 25th he annexed a donkey, and each day, and half of every night, he worked continuously between the head of Monash Valley and the Beach, his donkey carrying a brassard round its forehead and a wounded man on its back. Simpson escaped death so many times that he was completely fatalistic; the deadly sniping down the valley and the most furious shrapnel fire never stopped him. The colonel of his ambulance, recognising the value of his work, allowed him to carry on as a completely separate unit. He camped with his donkey at the Indian mule-camp, and had only to report once a day at the field ambulance. Presently he annexed a second donkey. On May 19th he went up the valley past the water-guard, where he generally had his breakfast, but it was not ready. "Never mind," he called. "Get me a good dinner when I come back."

He never came back. With two patients he was coming down the creek-bed, when he was hit through the heart, both the wounded men being wounded again. He had carried many scores of men down the valley, and had saved many lives at the cost of his own.

Though time and the release of further evidence have slightly modified some of Bean's judgements in *The Story of ANZAC*—though few of the facts—the book remains as the greatest of all tributes to the fighting qualities of the Australian volunteer soldier. Bean profoundly knew the character of the young Australians who made up the battalions of the first AIF, from his experiences in the country that provided the material for his books *Along the Wool Track* and *The Dreadnought of the Darling*, and from having lived in Bathurst and in Sydney, where he was a journalist on the *Sydney Morning Herald*.

If he idealised the Australian soldier, it was not because he was unaware of the "bad egg" or the outright criminal, of whom there were certainly some in the first AIF. However, the qualities of the Australian soldiers often led the British generals to put them into the most demanding and dangerous sectors. The proof of this is in the casualties, which were a cruel 52 per cent of enlistments for Australians compared to 42 per cent for the British, 30 per cent for Canadians, and 25 per cent for New Zealanders.

Bean's six volumes in *The Official History* are altogether a stupendous achievement, but none is more important or better written than the first. In this volume, as well as recounting in extraordinarily intimate detail the Gallipoli fighting up to 4 May 1915 (363 pages for 10 days!), he gives in the first four chapters an invaluable survey of what the outbreak of World War I meant to Australians at the time, and also of the men who had enlisted.

Although it may seem outrageous now that faraway Australia and New Zealand were dragged in to fight England's war in Europe and the Middle East, Bean maintains that there was a "distinct idealism" in Australia's response, that was associated with both the family of the British Empire and with the recent unification of the Australian people into the Commonwealth of Australia. He writes, "The faith which upheld the allied cause was nowhere more sound and pure than among the peoples of Australia and New Zealand. Their very distance from the centre of the struggle made more distinct the idealism of their motives. The emotion which stirred them was purged of the local pettiness of the days before the War. For the first time Australians of all the States in the Commonwealth, and of all sections in those States, were a united and unanimous people."

Bean points out that Australians already had "markedly divergent qualities of mind and character" from the average Englishman. (The boy from Bathurst knew what he was talking about, having being educated at two English schools and Oxford; he had also travelled on the Continent, especially Germany, and he spoke both German and French.) Bean saw Australians as physically bigger and tougher than the English. "If there was in them something of aggressiveness, there was also a vigorous and unfettered initiative. Many of them who lived in lonely places learnt to hold no practicable problem insoluble." They did not care for social differences. "The grown man was unaccustomed to commands untempered by the suggestion of a request." Bean saw the Australian soldier's reputation for lack of discipline more than balanced by his capacity for "swift individual decision" and self-control in moments of crisis.

"*It's no good dropping the stretcher now,*" *he said. "If we're going to be hit, we shall be, whether walking or crouching." That was the spirit of the men. Many became fatalists.*

Absolutely vital to the Australian's strength in battle was his prevailing romantic creed, "that a man should at all times and at any cost stand by his mate". Out of his own diaries, as proof of this, he produced an incident from Gallipoli. "In the last few moments before the bloody attack on Lone Pine in Gallipoli, when the third Australian Infantry Battalion was crowded on the fire-steps of each bay of its old front-line trench waiting for the final signal to scramble over the sandbags above, a man with rifle in hand, bayonet fixed, came peering along the trench below. 'Jim here?' he asked. A voice on the fire-step answered 'Right, Bill; here.' 'Do you chaps mind shiftin' up a piece?' said the man in the trench. 'Him and me are mates, an' we're goin' over together.' The same thing must have happened many thousands of times in the Australian divisions."

Bean faced up honestly to the charge of lack of discipline, admitting that it was at first by no means certain that the Australian soldiers would obey their officers' every order. There was also the distinct possibility that unpopular officers might be despatched by their own troops. However, the officers proved themselves (and they were not from a rich or privileged class), and the men accepted what was required of them. Bean was well aware of the notorious behaviour of the AIF in Cairo, and did not excuse the excesses, mostly committed by a criminal minority who were sent home in

the greatest disgrace. Like General Birdwood himself, Bean could not help laughing at incidents such as the one when Birdwood's own staff car was taken from the front of his headquarters and found some hours later abandoned on the sand in the heart of Mena camp. On another occasion, when Lieutenant-Colonel Elliott, a big, tough disciplinarian, "issued a stern order that any man appearing on parade without the wide-brimmed Australian hat would be severely punished, he found, a minute before leaving his Headquarters for the parade ground, that his own hat was missing. Some of his men had filched it."

Nor did Bean's intense respect for the bush traditions which he thought to be at the heart of the AIF lead him to forget the quality of the ex-larrikin soldiers from Woolloomooloo.

Bean's love of the English and their traditions did not lead him to lift any of the blame from Winston Churchill for the failure of the Dardanelles campaign. Churchill's impetuous enthusiasm carried away both Asquith and Kitchener, and as First Lord of the Admiralty overruled his own admirals, who warned that the whole of naval history was against setting ships to fight land defences. The naval bombardment of Gallipoli did little but warn the Turks that a major attack was on the way. And as for the terrain and the plan of attack, a Turkish staff officer told Bean four years later, as they were walking across the heights, "It would have been almost impossible to reach those objectives even in an operation of peacetime." Just to look at the photos in *The Story of ANZAC* is enough now to reduce one to impotent fury that such impossible tasks should have been set so many brave men. Bean, the most moderate of men, who risked his life continually throughout the campaign, declared that the lightheartedness with which the operation was conceived seemed "almost madness".

The bulk of *The Story of ANZAC* deals with what happened after the Navy began putting the troops ashore, in the wrong place, at 4.30 a.m. on 25 April 1915. His narrative is full of fascinating, immediate detail. For instance, the lines on the left of the grotesquely named Baby 700 were exposed on several sides to the fire of the Turks. "Close shaves" were so numerous that men ceased to reckon them. Thus Private R. L. Donkin of the First Battalion had two bullets in his left leg, the third pierced the top of his hat and cut his hair, one ripped his left sleeve, three hit his ammunition pouches and exploded the bullets; another struck his entrenching tool. Sadly and ironically, after surviving all that, Private Donkin was killed in action on 15 August 1915.

Bean's astonishingly detailed account is never dry to read. On the contrary, any sensitive reader must always be near tears at the forlorn nature of the struggle and the butchery of the finest young men of a young country. The vividness of his style takes the reader into the thick of it. "The 400 Plateau", where the Second Brigade was trapped, "stood out like a stage in a Greek amphitheatre". Four Turkish batteries were firing from the heights of the semi-circle. "Every shot went home. The gunners had only to increase or shorten the range in order to play on the backs of the Australians on the Second ridge as a fireman plays with a hose . . . incessantly hour after hour, the salvoes of four shells recurring every minute or half minute [firing nothing except

THE BEACH AT ANZAC *Frank Crozier*

C. E. W. BEAN
1879-1968

The intense feelings which C. E. W. (Charles Edwin Woodrow) Bean always retained towards England, mingled with an idealism and total identification with Australia, are reflected in his parentage. He was born on 18 November 1879 at Bathurst, New South Wales. His mother Lucy was born in Hobart in 1852, of parents who had arrived in the colony in 1824. Her father was a merchant who settled in Hobart as a solicitor. Bean's father Edwin, a clergyman and schoolteacher, was an Anglo-Indian, born in Bombay in 1851, who after Oxford came to Hobart as a tutor in 1873. Later he became headmaster and then proprietor of All Saints College at Bathurst. He sold the school in 1888, and took Lucy and Charles and his two brothers to England in 1889.

In the following two years, spent in England and on the Continent, Charles Bean became proficient in both French and German. In England he went to Brentwood school, where he was a friend of Virginia Woolf's brother Thoby. He won a scholarship to Oxford (which was fortunate as his father suffered severely in the Australian bank crash in the 1890s). As well as taking his BA, Charles studied law.

In 1904 he returned to Australia. He had had teaching experience and had been admitted to the NSW Bar, but he wanted to write. He had articles accepted by the *Sydney Morning Herald* and by the *Evening News*, of which A. B. Paterson was editor. He became associate to Mr Justice (later Sir William) Owen and travelled with him around New South Wales. In 1908 he went to work at the *Herald*, where he became a much-admired journalist. Montague Grover described his work as of "incandescent clearness". While with the *Herald* Bean made the journeys that were later written up in his books *The Dreadnought of the Darling* and *Along the Wool Track*, which contain some of the finest of all writing on outback Australia.

On the outbreak of World War I Bean was appointed Official War Correspondent with the AIF. No one could have been better suited to the job than he, with his knowledge of city and country life and of the sorts of men who made up the AIF. To this knowledge were added his personal courage and his expanding skills as a journalist and writer, backed by a rare quality of mind and a depth of human sympathy.

Bean's six volumes of *The Official History of Australia in the War of 1914-1918* are like no other war histories, for he was above all concerned with the true story of the front-line soldiers' engagements. Official reports were never enough for him, and he revealed many errors in them. He accompanied the soldiers and risked his life on countless occasions. Bean was the first to elucidate the complexities of the Anzac landing, and such appalling muddles as the battle of Lone Pine.

He worked on *The Official History* for 25 years after 1918, both as writer and editor, and he also visited the battlefields and talked to Turkish and German soldiers. One of Bean's great advantages was that he was universally respected by all ranks for his own bravery at the front. General Sir Brudenell White said, "That man faced death more times than any other man in the AIF, and had no glory to look for either."

Bean was also very much involved with the planning and foundation of the National War Memorial. Bean married Effie Young in Sydney in 1921. In 1959 he became an Honorary Doctor of the Australian National University. Three times he refused a knighthood. After some years of illness, he died in Sydney in 1968.

---

shrapnel] as automatically as the shower of some giant garden-spray."

Those who were there and commanding troops, like Colonel Brudenell White and General Bridges, the commander of Australian and New Zealand troops ashore, both of whom Bean very much admired, against all their fighting instincts decided by the night of 25 April that the troops should withdraw. Birdwood also, unwillingly, agreed, but the British commander-in-chief, General Sir Ian Hamilton, when wakened from his sleep aboard the *Queen Elizabeth*, listened to Admiral Thursby, who said an evacuation was impossible, and wrote to Birdwood that "there is nothing for it but to dig yourselves right in and stick it out . . . P.S. You have got through the difficult business, now you have only to dig, dig, dig, until you are safe."

"Got through the difficult business!" "Safe!" Thus are tragedies made. Bean makes no comment; he simply continues to chronicle Mustafa Kemal's counter-attack and the subsequent fighting. He makes it clear that often nothing was clear to those who were shooting and being shot. For instance, at Lone Pine there was an attack that had never been ordered by General Bridges. Only the receipt of a chance note penned by (Major) Macnaghten (shot in the chest and the neck) from his stretcher, "gave the Staff its first hint that, without orders and without objective, a full-dress attack had been delivered, one of its finest battalions decimated, and two of the finest leaders—Saker and Onslow Thompson—killed."

By 29 April, on overcrowded Anzac Beach, no one was paying "heed to shell fire even by so much as turning a head or lowering the pannikin from which he was drinking". This complete indifference to shellfire, says Bean, was "simply the natural expression of the men's self-respect . . . That careless, easy manner and apparent indifference to shellfire marked the Australians on every battlefield."

The Story of ANZAC is as much an analysis of the character of the Australian soldier as it is of the appalling hour-by-hour events at Gallipoli. Bean says that the failure of the plans, both at Helles and at Anzac, was due to "the enormous extent of the objectives which were set for the covering force, and the contempt in which the Turkish Army was held by those who made the plans . . . It needed one hundred and fifty thousand men to effect at that time what Hamilton sought to do with seventy thousand."

The cost of the landing to Australia and New Zealand was 9000, of whom at least 2500 were killed. Bean ends the book with an analysis of the motives for the troops' bravery and concludes, in two pages which contain some of the greatest of Australian historical writing, that "the dominant motive" lay in the mettle of the men themselves. "Life was very dear, but life was not worth living unless they could be true to their idea of Australian manhood."

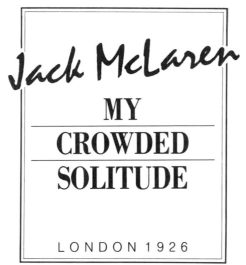

Jack McLaren

MY CROWDED SOLITUDE

LONDON 1926

In a clear space near the back of the house lived a ground-spider whose home was a tube-like hole fitted with a door on a hinge—the door being composed of grass cut into diamond-shaped fragments and bound with an intricacy of silver web. He was a little, grey person, that spider, with small eyes wrinkled like those of a querulous old man; and often did I watch him come home from his hunting of leaf-insects and the like, lift the door and close it after him, exactly as a man lifts and closes the door of a cellar. And as often I would tap the door with a tiny stick, get back out of sight and watch; whereupon the door would open a bit and the little grey person put out his head, turn his wrinkled eyes in all directions as though wonderingly, and then, apparently concluding he had been mistaken about hearing a knock, go down indoors again. After which I would give a further knock; and this time the little grey person would come right out and make an exhaustive investigation of the neighbourhood, going even to the grass edging of his cleared space and looking behind the tufts, moving quickly, jerkily, like a man exasperated and exceedingly annoyed, the while seeming vehemently to exclaim: "Drat those boys!" and when at last he returned to his home it was as though he had determined not to be fooled again, for no amount of knocking would bring him forth once more.

There was a lizard with whom I became quite intimate, even to the extent of naming him George. He was a grey-brown slip of a thing, four or less inches in length, delicately graceful of body and movement both; and each morning, as I breakfasted on the verandah, he would climb the leg of the table and perch at the edge of the cloth, his head high and arched and his tongue showing from between his lips like a triangle of thin pink paper; and there he would remain without stirring—taking no heed of the various noises and movements I made—till the meal was done and I had pushed back my chair. Then he would immediately set to work cleaning up the crumbs, with almost incredible swiftness darting over the plates and between them, circling the saucer and the cup, making diagonal traverses of the table's whole width, flashing this way and that, his slim body twisting and curving and doubling, and the pink triangle of his tongue a skeltering spot of colour—and never once pausing a moment, but taking the food in his stride. George's exhibition of nimbleness put me always in good humour for the day, and when at last some accident befell him and he came again no more, I missed him as I would have missed any highly entertaining friend.

I became intimate with the habits and manners of many such creatures as these—creatures which hitherto I had scarcely thought of as possessing habits and manners at all. They became to me companions almost as satisfying as any humans could have been. It was not that I was interested only in the spectacular and peculiar; others of these companions of mine led lives as dull and drab as the lives of men can be dull and drab—small animals which went about their daily food-hunting quietly and without display; birds which sat unobtrusively among the trees and picked humbly at whatever fruits and berries they could find; insects which performed their commonplace tasks in a commonplace kind of way. Nor was it of any great importance to me that it was only by the exercise of the imagination that the doings of the others were as the doings of humans—that the little ground-spider was not really annoyed, that "The School Kids" were not really at school as they sat in a row on their limb. It was merely that I was viewing Life in another—and maybe truer—perspective, understanding and sympathizing where hitherto I had not thought there was need to understand and sympathize at all. If only I could have attained the perspective in which the birds and insects and things saw Man, my vision of Things As They Are would have been complete.

My Crowded Solitude is the true story of the establishment, by Jack McLaren in 1911, of a coconut plantation in virgin rainforest near the tip of Cape York. It is exactly what its title implies, a book about his solitude, but a solitude full of the manifestations of life, human, animal, and natural, that crowd in on it. Few men have the capacity to cope with such an experience, let alone to recount it. Jack McLaren, a young adventurer, was physically, spiritually and mentally tough enough to survive, and he was also blessed with the command of a clear and sensitive prose style. *My Crowded Solitude* can be read both as an adventure and as a profound comment on life.

McLaren goes into partnership with a friend, who is to put up the money while McLaren establishes the plantation. He knows at the beginning he is sentencing himself to eight years of solitude. This is the time it will take to select the site, clear the rainforest, plant the trees, and wait for them to mature. In those days a would-be settler in that area simply found the land he wanted and bought it from the Lands Department. In his innocence of the nomadic life of the Aborigines, McLaren thinks that he will have no difficulty in finding Aborigines who will work for him in clearing the land and planting the coconuts.

After sailing unsuccessfully up and down both sides of

Cape York in a battered lugger with a rather disreputable crew, McLaren finds an ideal site with the unromantic name of Simpson's Bay. This is a harbour and a long beach, sheltered by several islands, with streams of fresh water and rich vegetation, which indicate good land.

Here he is finally put ashore with his stores and equipment, and here, on a huge tree, he carves his initials J. M., and the date, 7/10/11. He is alone. McLaren has already had some experience of solitude, on an occasion when he was left on Turtlehead Island, on the west coast of Cape York, and the vessel that was supposed to call for him after three days failed to arrive. (In fact, it went aground on a reef, and did not pick him up for two weeks.) Apart from his alarm at being stranded without supplies, he found he enjoyed being alone. For the first time in his life, he later wrote, he gave his attention "wholly to Nature and natural things. Hitherto I had carelessly generalised with regard to Nature. Now I particularise. I noted individuals and individual characteristics."

He was a little, grey person, that spider, with small eyes wrinkled like those of a querulous old man; and often did I watch him come home from his hunting of leaf-insects and the like, lift the door and close it after him, exactly as a man lifts and closes the door of a cellar.

At Simpson's Bay, however, McLaren finds himself in a new situation. He has to act as well as exist, create as well as observe. He rapidly discovers the need for a new set of personal priorities as a result of his aloneness. Wandering around the South Seas and New Guinea he has lived as a typical white man of his time; that is, he has expected, and found, indigenous people to do manual and domestic work for him. He has been "a White Man among a multitude of black men, and therefore a Master and a Superior Person. Here it was very different. Here I was master and labourer too." Here he is a "Superior Person" cut down to size. Just as he is learning to cope with the situation a tribe of Aborigines arrives, and again he has to learn something new. These amiable human beings (he had been warned of treachery and ferocity) are not at all like the black people he has known around the South Seas. They are nomads, and it is these people in whom he is to try and inculcate regular habits so that they will work for payment.

At first he cannot get used to their sleeping habits. They like to talk and dance and sing at night and sleep in the morning, not wake up at dawn ready for a hard day's work. At first, naturally enough, they are not interested in working at all. But they like his tobacco and trade goods, so eventually they begin to co-operate. Their idea of work, however, is not his, and they will stop at any hour to go hunting or fishing or simply to fall asleep.

If McLaren has to teach them new ways, they are also capable of teaching him old ways. He discovers that they know more about their environment than any other indigenous people he has met. In New Guinea or the Solomons a man may know about one aspect of nature and one area. But these Aborigines, he finds, have a highly systematised and regulated knowledge of animals, plants, weather, and the sea over a wide area, and moreover relate that knowledge to myths and poetry and religion. Although, according to their sexual standards (and apart from adultery), there is no sin in promiscuity, he reports that if an unmarried woman bears a child she is speared to death and the child's brains dashed out with a club. This is all part of a complex system of laws pertaining to marriage and social behaviour which guard against inbreeding. However, the Aborigines' knowledge of the abortifacient qualities of certain herbs and plants is such that, in all McLaren's eight years on the plantation, only two girls have illegitimate children and these are both born dead, thus saving the mother and child from destruction.

McLaren soon establishes excellent relationships with the tribe. For an Australian of his time, he was unusually open-minded and tolerant. Although he believed in progress and thought the Aborigines had not "reached the stage of ethical and moral distinctions", he learned from their knowledge and respected their virtues. He found them rarely dishonest, and noted their kindness to their dogs, although perhaps he was startled to see women suckling a baby on one breast and a pup on the other.

An old woman called Mary Brown comes to look after him, and he feels that without her cheerfulness there were times when he might not have survived. Before long she brings home a man and asks McLaren to marry them. When he says he cannot, she answers that this does not matter, as she does not think much of the white man's marriage ceremonies anyway. They are too gloomy. Her consort is apparently called Alligator, and he asks McLaren's permission to change his name, now that he is living with Mary Brown, to Willie.

Then, to McLaren's dismay, the whole tribe goes walkabout for three and a half months, just when they have almost succeeded in fighting back the rainforest's regrowth over the plantation. McLaren's crowded solitude takes on another dimension. Although he has a lot of books and is a great reader, he decides to learn more about "the vivid truths of nature". He observes birds, spiders, lizards and snakes. As well as noting down their exact habits, he invents lives for them. He attains understanding and sympathy, where before he has not even been aware of a need for them. He goes further. "If only I could have attained the perspective in which the birds and insects and things saw Man, my vision of Things As They Are would have been complete."

After 14 weeks the Aborigines return, and McLaren's dog

RAIN FOREST *Sidney Nolan*

JACK McLAREN
1887-1954

Jack McLaren was born in Melbourne in 1887 and educated at Scotch College where, as the son of a clergyman, he was able to be enrolled at reduced fees. He grew up in poverty in a working-class suburb.

His father was a fiery, puritanical Scot who frequently told his congregation to heed their ways, lest they be cast into hell, "hats, coats, boots and all". Young Jack, in his school uniform, was ordered to accompany his father on his street corner evangelical preachings. His father played the harmonium, his mother (much younger than his father) sang, and Jack "squeaked out the hymns on a fiddle". He always hid his cap, intensely embarrassed that he might be seen by any of his schoolfellows. His father intended him to be a medical missionary.

His father also learned Chinese (to the end of Jack's life he could repeat the Lord's Prayer in Chinese) and went regularly to the Chinese quarter in Melbourne in an attempt to convert the heathen. Jack was interested in other things. Allowed neither to gamble nor to go to the theatre, he would slip away after school to the Chinese gambling shops, and he even managed to visit theatres. Having been betrayed to the Scotch College headmaster after one of these excursions, he was given a ferocious dressing-down. Not only was he "a Scotch College boy in a Chinese gambling den, but the son of a preacher". When the headmaster was called out for a few minutes, Jack threw his cap on the floor and ran away. He was 16, with one shilling in his pocket.

Young Jack got a job with a horse trader, then went into the country as a bush worker, and finally he went to sea. For the next 19 years he wandered around the South Seas. He was a sailor, a diver for pearls and pearl shell; he prospected for gold in New Guinea, traded copper in the Solomons and planted coconuts in Fiji. He was the skipper of a sailing cutter which was wrecked on the New Guinea coast, and his life and that of the only other survivor was saved by a tribe who had recently been in trouble with the police for murdering white men.

In 1911 he returned to Australia and started a coconut plantation on Cape York (the story of which is told in *My Crowded Solitude*). He began writing paragraphs for the *Bulletin*, and his first novel, *Red Mountain*, was accepted by the New South Wales Bookstall Co. for £35. He wrote a dozen more South Sea yarns for the New South Wales Bookstall Co. Four autobiographical books, including *My Odyssey* and *My Crowded Solitude*, were published in London in the 1920s and 1930s. The last years of his life he lived in England, and during World War II he worked for the Ministry of Information. He died in 1954.

Vance Palmer wrote of him: "One of the most likeable of men, romantically innocent in his outlook, devoid of malice or envy, he yet seemed strangely shut in on himself; not, I think, from any anti-social feeling but because as a boy he had never learnt the ways of intimacy . . . he was more at home with natives than those of his own race."

Togo is soon forgetting his aloofness and playing with the native dogs. At first all seems well again, but trouble comes with the arrival of other coastal people, who try to turn his friends against him. One evening all the males of the tribe assemble in front of McLaren's house with their spears and demand that he go away. They tell him it is their land, and that the white man has no right to clear it and plant his coconuts. McLaren aims his rifle at one of the men, but does not fire. They go away, and he passes a dreadful night wondering if they will attack. They do not, and in the morning he goes to them, tells them it was wrong for the government to have given him the land, and that he would like to buy it from them himself. This they are happy to do, on immediate payment of tobacco, sheath knives, cloth and other things.

There was a lizard with whom I became quite intimate, even to the extent of naming him George. He was a grey-brown slip of a thing, four or less inches in length, delicately graceful of body and movement both . . .

A change begins in the life of both the Aborigines and McLaren. The Aborigines begin to see the advantages of staying in one place, and more and more people come to live near the plantation. Then McLaren himself, having ceased to be a wanderer, begins to enjoy the comfort and ease of the agricultural life. "I developed the agricultural habit," he notes.

But he is a complete failure at arousing the agricultural habit in the Aborigines, who will not wait for plants to ripen. They dig up the yams as soon as they are formed, and complain that it is much harder work than hunting.

To give himself more freedom, he takes on an Aboriginal overseer from outside the tribe, as no one in the tribe has the necessary sense of authority. And at last the first palm comes to bear fruit. McLaren sees himself as the planter, playing host, "A Settled and Respectable Person". And indeed many interesting people come to see him, from penniless vagabonds to famous scientists. It seems that McLaren is well and truly ensconced in his way of life.

After eight years he decides to take a holiday. He goes to Darwin and then joins a party on a cruise around Arnhem Land. He rediscovers indolence, and begins to long for the adventurous wandering life again. He returns to Cape York, and decides that plantation life is "delightful and satisfying no longer". But the welcome from all his Aboriginal friends unsettles him yet again. "To give it all up would be like giving up a part of myself."

The offer of a good price for his shares decides him. The wanderlust takes over and he sets out over the seas again.

McLaren has reverted to his original self, albeit a much wiser man. The Aborigines, on the other hand, have been corrupted, giving up their free nomadic life for one of settled dependence. McLaren passes a harsh judgement on himself, as guilty of a social wrong. Thinking naively that he was uplifting them from their primitiveness, he has destroyed their peace of mind.

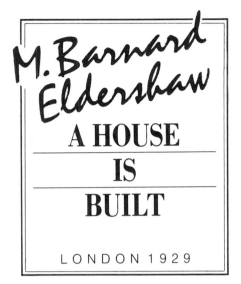

M. Barnard Eldershaw

A HOUSE IS BUILT

LONDON 1929

"Is it not strange, I have been in New South Wales for more than a year, and yet I know very little about it? The climate is different, of course, and it is very hard to get used to Christmas in the summer. I have seen a few aborigines, and everything is very new and raw. Of course, there are a lot of differences, but we live much the same sort of lives as we did in England. I thought it would be so different."

"I have striven to reproduce our English life as far as possible," said William, with pride and complacency. "I think it is the duty of every Englishman to reproduce English conditions as far as possible wherever he may happen to be. The man who does not is, I don't scruple to say it, a renegade. If I thought the conditions of a new country had deflected me a hand's-breadth from the decent and decorous standards I was brought up to I should be grieved indeed."

Adela wanted to laugh but she saw it would not do. "But are we not a little ridiculous sitting here on the coast all dressed up, pretending we are in England, when only a few miles away life is so difficult and there is so much to be done? I have heard Papa and Fanny talk of the pioneers—and really it does seem mean of us to let them do all the work."

"We are not pioneers, my love, but we are just as necessary. Where would they be without us? And I certainly cannot see anything ridiculous in our mode of life. What finer thing can we do for Australia than make it like another England? Australia of itself is nothing. I have seen much of the surrounding country, and it is unprepossessing—large tracts of wooded country that does not deserve or receive the name of forest but is very properly called 'bush'—brown, drought-parched grass-land. A man must own hundreds of acres to make a living. Parts of the coast, I admit, are pleasing, but untutored. It is a country that belonged to no one. The natives are a poor scattered people, they do not often give trouble on the mainland. The country is, if I may use a Latin expression, a tabula rasa—a blank sheet, dear Adela. It has no personality of its own, only a resistance. It is for us with British perseverance to break down that resistance, to plant English life here in its entirety. Who are we to edit the greatest civilization the world has known? It is our duty to behave here exactly as if we were in England. I shall never abate one jot or tittle of our good old English ways. Ours is a race of empire-builders because no Englishman worthy of the name ever yields to climate or environment. But there, my love, you need not trouble your pretty head with these deep questions."

Adela had sat through this oration with twitching lips and modestly downcast eyes. She saw an Empire built up on antimacassars and top-hats, Australia a brand snatched from the burning to the glory of gentility.

"Dear William, how wise you are!" she murmured, and came to stand beside him, slipping her arm through his. She loved him best when he was a little ridiculous. He looked down at her kindly. He had feared a little while ago that she was going to be unreasonable, when, if they took things quietly, life could be so smooth and pleasant. He wanted a sleek untroubled domestic life of almost mathematical calm, and did not see why he should not have it. He was a reasonable man, and never, he prided himself, asked more of his family than they could easily and happily perform. He looked at Adela in her meek and wifely pose, gentle and quiet, yet able to engage him in intellectual conversation; he looked about him at the substantial but ornamental furniture, the gilded clock, the marble urns; he thought of James upstairs in his bassinet—and he was content. It was as it should be. He had tamed matrimony, as the English were to tame Australia.

The "house" of *A House is Built* is a business house, the merchant and shipping firm that James Hyde establishes, with its own wharf, at Windmill Street, in Sydney in 1839. For James and his family (his son William and his son's wife Adela, his elder daughter Fanny, and William's sons, James and Lionel), the store and the business is their world in which their own lives are inexorably set. Even Lionel, an artist at heart, a pianist and a lover of beauty rather than commerce, cannot leave the firm when the opportunity offers. Only Fanny's little sister Maud, flirtatious and rather silly, escapes the House of Hyde.

Yet, although prosperity and finally riches are the result of watching the ledgers and making wise decisions about whale oil, butter or real estate, *A House is Built* is not at all a money-grubbing chronicle.

A House is Built was written by two women in collaboration, Marjorie Barnard and Florence Eldershaw. These two remarkable women had an eye for accumulated detail and a passion for getting the facts right that they shared with their characters, the Hydes. They also had a joy in life and an instinct for quality that enabled them to create in the character of James Hyde an amiable fountainhead of gusto and good sense that flows right through the book. James had been a quartermaster in the Royal Navy. Throughout the book he is always referred to as "the Quartermaster" and he always retains the spacious philosophy of the adventurous sailor. Early in the book he refers to himself in disgust as a "money-grubber".

> But though he could not have put it into words he knew in his heart that it was not the money he wanted, that these were only steps toward the ideal, that there can be the splendour of courage in merchant-venturing, and that a nation might be built by such men as he more honourably and more securely than by the swords of conquerors.

He has bred a dull stick in his son William, albeit a godsend to the firm as he is so good with figures. Old James is always involved with the life of the Colony, but not so William, the typical permanent Englishman, who wishes to make Australia another England.

> I have striven to reproduce our English life as far as possible . . . I think it is the duty of every Englishman to reproduce English conditions as far as possible, wherever he may happen to be . . . What finer thing can we do for Australia than make it like another England? Australia of itself is nothing . . . It has no personality of its own, only a resistance. It is for us with British perseverance to break down that resistance, to plant English life here in its entirety.

This attitude may seem absurd today, but it ruled the lives of many "Australians" for many years; it has never been more succinctly expressed.

*A*dela had sat through this oration *with twitching lips and modestly downcast eyes. She saw an Empire built up on antimacassars and top-hats, Australia a brand snatched from the burning to the glory of gentility.*

Barnard and Eldershaw are in fact writing not only about the House of Hyde but about the building of a nation, and of how (with the exception of such as William) English men and women become Australians. There is also a parallel in the family's moves from house to house. They begin in rooms over the store, down by the waterfront. Then they come to "a commodious gentleman's residence of brick" in the Parramatta Road. Finally they move to Firenze, the enormous, ornate Italian-built mansion in Hunters Hill. It is significant that none of these houses is built by the Hydes.

The houses themselves are an extension of Australian history, something already existing which is taken up by these vigorous newcomers. There is even the hint that, as aristocratic French and Italians built such houses as Firenze at Hunters Hill, the Australian tradition need not be exclusively British.

The action of *A House is Built* is cleverly balanced between the characters and the more abstract fortunes of the firm. The lifestyle of the family is entirely dependent upon the success of the firm. For some family members it is salvation; for others a calamity, curtailing the development of their own individual lives.

Apart from the old Quartermaster himself, Fanny is the most interesting character in the book. She is as complex and withdrawn as he is simple and outgoing. The relationship between her and her sister Maud is exceptionally well drawn at the beginning, when they arrive from England to take up residence in one of the rooms above the store, overlooking the Harbour. From the Harbour comes the whaling captain, Hildebrand, with whom Fanny falls in love. "Almost everything that happened to her in the years of her making was important, just as nothing that happened to Maud seemed important at all, because it happened so easily and naturally."

Hildebrand keeps away from Maud—"too obviously labelled 'Fire'"—and strikes up a "pure and sentimental dalliance" with Fanny. She is not sophisticated enough to understand such a game and attempts to elope with him on his ship, to his intense embarrassment. "Now run back home like a good girl", is his comment, after which Fanny's life is never the same. When Maud successfully elopes with Mr Humphrey Gillam of Gillam Park, to be married in secret at Cobbitty, Fanny is furious. For some time there is an estrangement between the sisters, caused basically by Fanny's "secret bitterness" over Hildebrand, and by her being "constitutionally unable to achieve an impulsive and generous gesture".

On top of this, in May 1844, William's fiancée, Adela, sails from London to marry him, and Fanny will no longer be the female head of the household, which is to move to Parramatta Road. She wants to work in the store, but the Quartermaster won't hear of such a thing as a woman working. It is not until 1851, when the Quartermaster leaves Sydney to set up branches of the business at the goldfields, that Fanny is allowed to work in the store. "So for a few brief years Fanny found satisfaction."

That satisfaction is based on the similarity between her and her father's attitudes to trade.

> She had thought of work at the store as providing her with occupation and independence, but she found in it romance as well. She did not know it, but the Quartermaster's feelings towards his life work were being reproduced in her. She saw their business as a plastic living thing, and she admired it as she could never have admired any work of art.

She even comes to admire William, "as a good workman may admire a fine machine". Fanny is undoubtedly a success in the firm, but she is still an unmarried woman living in Victorian times, and her future is outside her own control. Her sister Maud comes breezing in covered with finery and

CIRCULAR QUAY *Frederick Garling*

MARJORIE BARNARD AND FLORA ELDERSHAW
1897-   , 1897-1957

Barnard *(top)* and Eldershaw *(bottom)* were both born in New South Wales in 1897. They met as students at the University of Sydney during World War I.

Barnard did not go to school until she was 10. Her father was a chartered accountant, and they lived in the bush at Eastwood, a Sydney suburb. She says: "I was my mother's girl. My father didn't like me and I didn't like him."

She went to Sydney Girls' High School, and later studied history at Sydney University under Professor G. A. Wood. She took first-class honours, won the University Medal and a scholarship to Oxford, which her father would not let her take up. She became a librarian, first as a member of the staff at the Public Library of New South Wales and then as librarian of the Sydney Technical College and the National Standards Bureau at the University of Sydney. She was an only child, and continued to look after her parents. She lived in the family home at Longueville for nearly 80 years.

Eldershaw was born in Sydney and went to school at Wagga, where her parents lived. Her knowledge of the Riverina provided the background for Barnard and Eldershaw's *Tomorrow and Tomorrow and Tomorrow*. After university she became a school teacher and finally senior mistress at the Presbyterian Ladies' College, Croydon. Later she worked in Canberra for the Commonwealth Department of Labour and National Service. She then moved to Melbourne where she was an industrial consultant.

Barnard and Eldershaw together wrote six novels, several historical studies and a book of essays on Australian writers. Their collaboration was extraordinarily successful. Eldershaw said that either could draft a chapter in their combined style which needed scarcely any alteration when it was received by the other in another city.

Barnard says: "We talked and talked and talked. And then we precipitated. I did most of the writing, she did most of the talking. And we never fell out—it was always a happy relationship. She was very *certain*, and that was a great help to me. She had the critical ability."

At one stage, to give them some independence, both ladies took a flat at Point Piper. Frank Dalby Davison lived with Barnard there for a number of years. She describes it as "a very happy interlude".

A House is Built tied with *Coonardoo* for first prize in the *Bulletin* novel competition in 1929. It was serialised in the *Bulletin* under the title of *The Quartermaster*.

Barnard Eldershaw's novel *Tomorrow and Tomorrow and Tomorrow* is set in the twenty-fourth century. It is the story of Knarf (F. D. Davison's first name spelled backwards), a philosopher, who has written a novel about Sydney 400 years before, when the city was burned and obliterated. The book was censored when it first appeared in 1947, and was issued in its entirety in 1983.

Flora Eldershaw died in 1957. Marjorie Barnard lives near the coast, north of Sydney.

---

trailing children; they are long since reconciled, but their lives have diverged. "Fanny, to whom nothing had happened, was changed, and Maud, who had borne six children, was essentially the same."

The Quartermaster has flourished on the goldfields, and the firm is a leader in the general prosperity of the 1850s. So the family moves again, this time to the grand Italianate mansion in Hunters Hill; a shipload of ornate, tasteless furniture is brought out from England. William is vexed that his sister should still be working in the business when it is no longer necessary. He feels it is not proper. But Fanny will not be budged.

The excuse to dislodge her for the sake of gentility comes when Adela falls sick after nursing Lionel through scarlet fever. The Quartermaster says Fanny must see to the running of Firenze. "Besides," he says, "she is not needed any more." She forgives her father as always, but there is "a hard, unbreaking core of bitterness against William for many years".

Young James, in the meantime, after being educated at King's, enters the business with the world before him, handsome and agreeable. He falls in love with Laurel Franklin, of the rival firm to the House of Hyde. Laurel persuades James to betray the secret of Hyde's bid for the Red Funnel contract, and Franklin underbids Hyde and gets the contract.

In a swift and dramatic climax to the book James sails his skiff out in a storm and is drowned. His body is brought back to Firenze and the Quartermaster falls down by it with a stroke, holding in his hand a note from Franklin telling him that James had betrayed him.

Lionel is forced to enter the firm. When William also dies, Lionel is only 24 and unprepared for the role of owner and manager of the vast enterprise. Adela urges her son to sell the business. "It is killing you," she says. But Fanny persuades Lionel that it is his duty as a Hyde to remain in the business. He settles down to live a double life, active and busy in the store, contemplative and aesthetic at home.

Adela dies of cancer and of all the Hydes only Fanny and Lionel are left. Mary Bardon, daughter of their cousin Esther, who had been living for some years at Firenze, is asked by Lionel to marry him. He does not love her, but she will bring peace and affection to the house.

The novel ends on the sombre note of Lionel, who does not feel himself a Hyde, a builder and a maker, alone in the splendour of his surroundings. The House of Hyde has been built, but there is no room in it, and not yet in the nation that has been built, for the man of culture.

Katharine Susannah Prichard

COONARDOO

LONDON 1929

All happy, indeed they were sitting there singing and smoking while thunder rumbled and cracked among far hills of the To-Morrow ranges, lightning flashed and threw glittering mysterious koodgeedas across the sky. Warieda's new song was a great success. For days men and women went singing. Thin and high, through the nose, fretted and quavering, fragments drifted:

"Perandalah gnunga, willy-willeree, wilbee-wilberee . . ."

In the distance somebody would tune up and go on:

"Wonga coolah, kangee, weerungunoo babba, bookerilla munda . . ."

The rain had made a great inland sea of the place where Mumae's house stood. The house and the trees were like a little island in it. But still the white cockatoos roosted there, screeching wildly. "She's afraid what the water will do to the house," Coonardoo thought, knowing how Mumae had loved the white roof and walls of her home.

Long ago this place had been all water. There was a song about it. Wytaliba homestead reared itself from the floor of a dead sea really. There were hills all round still, and the sea had been made from waters draining out of them. Pebbles on the ground were still water-worn.

Coonardoo sang and played with her children under the roof of the buggy shed until the sun shone again and rain water disappeared, soaking down into the earth, where it whispered to seeds of the grass. Soon there was green down everywhere on the plains.

Did Youie know there had been rain? If he knew there had been rain on Wytaliba, he would come quickly, Coonardoo guessed. Soon he would be coming.

White cockatoos had taken possession of the homestead. Always they were shrieking and flying restlessly about it. Feeding in drifts in the garden, they rose with that swift silken flash of wings against the light, so that Coonardoo was dazzled, afraid, and cried "Yukki!" as they turned and wheeled in the air past her.

The day came when, about sunset, Coonardoo's glad cry roused the uloo.

"You comin'!"

Dogs flew out barking; men and women, young and old, ran down to the gate.

Dust at the creek crossing swirled and swung in.

Coonardoo stood where she had first seen it. The Wytaliba buggy which had been waiting for Hugh at Lala threw off its clouding red dust. Coonardoo knew the horses Hugh was driving, the bound and swing of Nessus and Paris, the punch and plodding sway of Demeter and Saturn.

Wanna and Mick flung the lower gate open and the buggy drove on. Coonardoo's head swam and her eyes would not see. Then they got Hugh in mass and outline. He was not alone. She had known he would not be. The woman she had thought he would bring was there beside him — Youie's woman.

White cockatoos feeding in the garden flew up and away, whirling against the sky with their thin shrieking cries. They would feed no more in the garden, roost no more in the gum-tree beside the veranda, Coonardoo knew.

As she went down to the house, her cooboo in her arms, the joy of her life was pressed into this moment. Youie had come again; she would see him. He was well and strong; she could hear him shouting out to Joey and Meenie, as people from the uloo came swarming up to the garden in front of the veranda to meet him, a dirty draggled crowd, their clothes in rags.

Coonardoo was pleased to remember she had been to the shower-house under the big windmill that morning. Every morning lately she had been down to the shower-house because she knew Hugh might come any day now, and he would not like to find she had not washed, or soaped her hair and dried it in the sun, as Mumae made the gins do every day before they went into the house.

Katharine Susannah Prichard's finest novel, *Coonardoo*, is the subtlest and most moving of all Australian books about Aboriginal–white relationships. It is also remarkable in having a vibrant sexuality that was almost non-existent in Australian literature at the time.

As soon as the novel opens on Wytaliba station in northern Western Australia, a web of affection is established between Mrs Watt, also called Mrs Bessie, or Mumae (which, interestingly, means *father* in the local Aboriginal dialect), her son Hugh and the Aboriginal girl Coonardoo. The children are both about nine years old. Coonardoo is Hugh's playmate, with fair hair "soft, and wavy when it had just been washed, . . . dull golden, like wind grass out on the plains". Mrs Watt has taught Coonardoo to help her and old black Meenie in the house, but she is also "really fond of the little girl", who later fills the place in her heart left when Hugh goes to boarding school. She recognises that, in her own way, Coonardoo suffers a desolation in missing Hugh that is as deep as her own.

Coonardoo is already promised to the most valued Aboriginal worker on the station, Warieda, Meenie's tribal husband (Meenie is old enough to be his mother) who will soon take Coonardoo to be his woman. Mrs Bessie bribes him with a horse to wait until Coonardoo is 16. She sees a happy future for Coonardoo, looking after Hugh. "He'll marry some day, I suppose, but even so, I'd like to think he had some good faithful soul to look after him."

But with exquisite tact Prichard has already, at the very beginning of the book, hinted at deeper problems beneath the innocence. Coonardoo's name means "the well in the shadows"; she is called after the dark well by the hut in which she was born. She is "old Joey Koonarra's kid", and nobody talks about her dead mother, Maria, who was fatally injured by Hugh's drunken father.

The other warning note is sounded by the description of the neighbouring station owner, Sam Geary, who calls to take Hugh to school. Nothing much is said, but he is an unattractive, powerful man who may be neither honourable nor kind.

Coonardoo's head swam and her eyes would not see. Then they got Hugh in mass and outline. He was not alone. She had known he would not be. The woman she had thought he would bring was there beside him . . .

By 16, Coonardoo is highly marriageable, but everyone knows the bargain struck between Mrs Bessie and Warieda. "Desirable, unattainable, Coonardoo had enjoyed herself very much in those years." Mrs Bessie is furious when Sam Geary, who cohabits with Aboriginal women, offers old Joey Koonarra a rifle, blankets, tobacco and whisky for the girl. He even tries to kidnap her. Unruffled by Mrs Bessie's anger, Geary ominously says, "I thought you'd be glad to get the baggage off your hands before Youie comes home." But Coonardoo is safely married to Warieda and within a year has a baby girl.

Hughie comes back with Jessica, his intended bride in white muslin, white shoes, pink sunshade and all, to find his mother a sick woman. She tells Meenie the housekeeper and Coonardoo that they must look after Hugh, otherwise she will haunt them like a white cockatoo.

On a visit, Sam Geary, coarser and cruder than ever, bets Hughie "a new saddle you take a gin before a twelvemonth's out—if ever you're in the country on your own". But Hughie intends holding on to what he had said: "I'm goin' to marry white and stick white."

It is not Jessica he marries. She is a silly little creature, scared of the loneliness and simplicity, and she wants to go home. Mrs Bessie is relieved as well as disquieted for she has overheard Geary's bet with Hugh, and Hugh is now going to be alone.

Mrs Bessie has cancer of the stomach. It is a hopeless case. As she is dying she urges Hugh to get married—but not to someone like Jessica; she says, "I'd rather a gin than a Jessica." She dies and Hugh is left in charge. He has become a strange man, wandering about at night with Coonardoo his shadow, keeping him from harm.

One night Hugh wanders so far away that he is lost, bushed. Coonardoo materialises out of the shadows. "Show'm track, Youie," she offers. But he tells her to sit down, while he lights a fire. They make love, drawn "to the common source which was his life and Coonardoo's".

Then Hugh suddenly falls desperately ill, and is nursed by Coonardoo. He is finally roused back to life when he opens his eyes to see Sam Geary, the man who had always wanted Wytaliba and Coonardoo. Determined to live so that Sam Geary shall get neither, Hugh recovers, and goes 800 kilometres down to the coast to a doctor for treatment.

It is the rhythm of the book that Hugh comes and goes, but that Coonardoo, like the spirit of the place, always remains. It will be disastrous, and not only to her, if she ever leaves. The varying strength of links between whites and blacks and the soil is one of the most subtly explored themes of the book. But this time when Hugh returns he brings a wife with him, "a sonsy young woman". As they get down from the buggy Coonardoo comes up with her new baby, a boy. Hugh immediately knows that it is his.

Coonardoo is not jealous of Hugh's woman, Mollie; she is simply happy that he is home. She also senses that Hugh is not in love with Mollie, that he wants a good, sensible girl for a wife. Mollie is rather genteel, and she wants the Aborigines to call her "Ma'am". The cheerful facade is cracked by a visit from Sam Geary, who immediately realises that Hugh is the father of Coonardoo's baby, and demands payment of his bet, to Hugh's fury. Mollie does not suspect, but is disgusted by Sam Geary's flaunting his gin, Sheba. "You'd never be a gin's man, Hughie?" she asks. "No," Hugh lies.

Soon Mollie goes down to the coast, and returns with a baby, a girl. Hugh loves this little white creature, "but she was less real, much less his own than that son of a whirlwind", Winni, Coonardoo's child. He feels the same about the four daughters who follow, Hugh's "poker hand". And while Coonardoo is always her patient, laughing, beautiful self, Mollie turns into a grouse, a nag, a white woman who wants Hugh to sell Wytaliba so they can go and live in a white town. After a final row, Hugh gives Mollie all the money he has and tells her to go. But she does not go, and instead works on her suspicion that Winni is Hugh's son. The solution comes pat to her small, vicious, jealous mind. She will stay only if Hugh orders Coonardoo and Winni to leave Wytaliba.

She presents her intolerable ultimatum. Coonardoo and her child and Warieda, the pride and mainstay of the station, must go. Surprisingly, Hugh has the strength to send Mollie and his daughters away instead.

Strangely, however, when Hugh is alone at the station he does not want Coonardoo to share his bed. He has "no passion or desire, except to beat the drought". The first

LEITMOTIF *Elizabeth Durack*

KATHARINE SUSANNAH PRICHARD *1883-1969*

Katharine Susannah Prichard was probably better known overseas than any other Australian writer before Patrick White, and her books have been translated into 13 languages. Her first book, *The Pioneers*, won an award in London, and she worked as an occasional journalist there for several years, but she always returned to Australia. All her novels are founded firmly on her Australian experiences, which were remarkably wide-ranging.

She was born in 1883 in Fiji, where her father was editing the *Fijian Times*. Her mother was Australian, and her father had come to Australia as an infant; they were of mixed Irish, Scottish, Welsh and English ancestry. Katharine was the oldest of four children. When she was three her father brought the family to Melbourne, where he edited a weekly, the *Sun*. Her father also published verse and a novel that appeared in 1891. Katharine went to various schools in Victoria and Tasmania; she was especially fortunate because her headmistress at South Melbourne College, J. B. O'Hara, was a poet who encouraged her to write.

There was not enough money in the family to send her to university, so she worked as a governess in Gippsland (which gave her the material for *The Pioneers*) and then on a station out from Broken Hill. Before her twentieth birthday, magazines had published articles and her first short story.

In 1907 her father committed suicide; she was to be haunted by such tragedies, as her husband also killed himself in 1933. In 1908 she went to London, where she worked as a journalist, returning to become social editor of the Melbourne *Herald*, the first women's page in a Melbourne daily newspaper. There, she said, "My political consciousness began to wake." She returned to London, where she won the £1000 Hodder and Stoughton literary prize with *The Pioneers*, which was published in 1915.

She came back to Australia in 1916, the war and the extremes of rich and poor in England having converted her to socialism. Soon after the end of the war she married Captain Hugo Throssell, VC, (whom she called Jim) and settled with him at "Greenmount" in the Darling Ranges about 20 kilometres out of Perth. Their son Ric later became a playwright and wrote a biography of his mother.

Her novel *Working Bullocks* (1926) was written after visits to the forests of giant kauri in south-west Western Australia; Miles Franklin said it marked "the breaking of the drought in Australian fiction".

Coonardoo, her finest novel, won a *Bulletin* competition and was published in book form in 1929. It came from a nine-month residence at Turee, a cattle station in the Ashburton and Fortescue river country of northern Western Australia. She wrote to Nettie Palmer from Turee, "I'm overflowing with stories, delighted and quite mad with the beauty and tragedy of them." Her story *The Cooboo* and her play *Brumby Innes* also came from her stay at Turee. Her other successful books included *Black Opal* (1921), *Haxby's Circus* (1930) and *The Roaring Nineties* (1946).

Katharine Susannah Prichard helped to found the Australian Communist Party, and was always an ardent worker for the communist cause; when she died her coffin was draped with a red flag. After living in Sydney and Canberra, she returned to "Greenmount" in 1947 and lived there until her death in 1969.

---

tragedy comes with the death of Warieda after a bone has been pointed at him. The malevolent aspect of Aboriginal life hints at what is to come, an inevitable destruction.

Coonardoo was pleased to remember she had been to the shower-house under the big windmill that morning. Every morning lately she had been down to the shower-house because she knew Hugh might come any day now, and he would not like to find she had not washed, or soaped her hair and dried it in the sun . . .

To save Coonardoo from being taken by Warieda's brother, Hugh tells her to sleep on his verandah, as his woman. "Only she could not imagine why Hugh did not take her as his woman . . . Sheer cussedness, Hugh thought, deterred him from doing what everybody expected of him." And anger grows in Coonardoo, while the drought continues for four years and Hugh grows gaunt like his cattle. There is a drought inside Hugh, too; he cannot pour out his seed for Coonardoo and, like the parched earth, she is sterile and longing for moisture.

Then, quite unexpectedly, Hugh's daughter Phyllis arrives to live at Wytaliba. She is a modern girl, tired of her stupid mother and longing to be born again at Wytaliba. Welcomed by Coonardoo and the blacks, she settles into station life, "happy to be sex-free". This does not last for long; to Hugh's dismay she marries the rough Billy Gale from Catchy-Catchy Downs.

In a terrible scene, while Hugh is away, Sam Geary and another man come over to Wytaliba and get drunk. Like a bird before a snake, Coonardoo yields to him "half dead in her sterility" because of Hugh, while Geary, whom she loathes and fears, is "male to her female, and she could not resist him".

Later, by the campfire out mustering, Bardi, the fat gin, lets the secret out. Hugh attacks Coonardoo verbally and physically, beyond himself with fury, and she falls into the fire.

Coonardoo disappears and Hughie's bond with the blacks is broken. For years he searches for Coonardoo, but he cannot find her. Finally in the pub at Roebourne he meets drunken Sam Geary, who has seen Coonardoo, rotten with disease, hanging around the Chinese quarters at Port Hedland.

The curse has worked—Mrs Bessie's spirit has seen to it that Wytaliba and Hughie are finished because Coonardoo has been driven away and can no longer look after her Youie. The banks take over Wytaliba, and Hugh goes off prospecting. The book ends with the dying Coonardoo wandering back to the deserted homestead, singing the song she had crooned at the opening of the book.

A theme of *Coonardoo* is crudely expressed by Phyllis's husband Bill: "Cripes! . . . A man doesn't love a gin, not a white man." The tragedy of the novel is in Hughie's inability to acknowledge and accept Coonardoo's love.

Lennie Lower

HERE'S LUCK

SYDNEY 1930

Chatswood is one of those places that are a stone's throw from some other place, and is mainly given over to the earnestly genteel. Here, respectability stalks abroad adorned with starched linen and surrounded by mortgages. The clatter of lawn-mowers can be heard for miles on any sunny Saturday. Sunday evenings, the stillness of death descends on the place, but if one listens very attentively one may hear the scraping of hundreds of chewed pens as they travel the weary road of principal and interest and pay-off-as-rent.

Agatha's mother's home tucked its lawns about its feet and withdrew somewhat from the regular line of houses in the street. It had been paid for. My mother-in-law's chief occupations were writing letters of complaint to the municipal council, and calling upon God to look at our so-called democratic government and blight it. She also laid a few baits for the neighbours' dogs, kept a strict eye on the morals of the whole street, and lopped off any branch, twig or tendril which thrust itself from the next-door garden over the fence and so trespassed on her property. What spare time she had left was used up by various communings with God about the water-rates, and the only really light work she indulged in was when she seated herself behind the window-curtain and watched for small boys who

might be tempted to rattle sticks along the front fence. Altogether, she was a busy woman. And then, of course, there was the parrot. The parrot was also an opponent of governments, cursed the municipal council, squawked miserably over the water-rates and was withal highly religious. Whether this spiritless subservience to local opinion was due to force of example or merely a desire for a quiet life, I do not know. In this description of my mother-in-law's mode of life I think I have written with a certain amount of tolerant restraint. She is an old lady and the age of chivalry is not dead while a Gudgeon lives. Perhaps a different son-in-law might have described her as a senseless, whining, nagging, leather-faced old whitlow not fit to cohabit with the rhinoceros beetle. But I wouldn't.

Arriving at the house, I paused. The lawn needed mowing. I crossed the road and stood regarding the place. That the grass of the front lawn needed mowing may seem a very little thing and not sufficient to make any one pause, but I

had bitter memories of my infrequent visits to this place in my earlier days. I would enter and be given a cup of tea, then — "Ha! Now we have a man in the house."

In other words: "Ha! Here is a work-beast. Let him paint the tool-shed; let him mend the wheelbarrow; bring out the hedge-clippers and the lawn-mower and point out to him the location of the axe and the woodheap."

That, of course, would be when I was comparatively welcome.

And now?

As I gazed across at the place, a window-curtain quivered. I had been seen. I could not now retreat with dignity so I crossed the road, took a deep breath, and knocked at the door. Wiping my feet industriously on the mat, I waited. I could imagine the scurrying and the whisperings that were going on inside. I knocked again. I had expected this sort of thing, and after waiting a few moments longer I turned and made for the gate as though about to leave. The strategy was successful. The door opened a few inches and the hideous beak of my mother-in-law protruded from the gap.

"Well," she snapped, "what do you want?"

I doffed my bowler.

"I've come to see my wife."

"**A**ustralia's funniest book", Cyril Pearl called *Here's Luck*, and that is a compliment, coming as it does from one of Australia's wittiest writers.

The unfailing delight of *Here's Luck* is that it mocks all that is most sacred in Australian suburban life. Cleanliness, getting up early and going to work, care with money, punctuality, sobriety, the sacredness of matrimony, getting on with one's relations, keeping out of trouble with the police, respect between father and son, avoidance of vulgarity and noise are all roasted. The comedy is in the unspoken promise that all these things will be respected in the end. Mere anarchy may be loosed upon the world, but only until the end of next week.

Jack Gudgeon, the anti-hero, is 48, "called fat by envious persons less kindly treated by nature", and out of a job. He

has a son Stanley, 18 or 19 years old (Jack is not sure), who looks much older than his years, and has all the makings of someone who will get on in the world but who is not in a regular job. He shares most of the riotous action of the book with Jack. The unfortunate Jack is burdened with a wife called Agatha and is ground down by her sister Gertrude. He is also persecuted by various debt collectors from whom he escapes to Flannery's saloon bar.

Jack Gudgeon is disillusioned with life, but his world-weariness can always be routed by such unfailing remedies as a jug of whisky, steak and eggs, a win at the races or witnessing a good fight. Steak and eggs are more than what they seem in *Here's Luck*. After a falling out with Agatha, who refuses to cook their dinner, Jack and Stanley (who live in the Sydney suburb of Woollahra, obviously not quite as fashionable then as it is now) go out for steak and eggs in the Greek restaurant. Stanley has already fallen out of love, after protesting a deathless passion for Estelle; he has just seen her in the sidecar of Oscar Winthrop's new motorcycle. (There is delicious period flavour to all of *Here's Luck*.) The proof of his quick recovery is his immediate eye for two pretty girls in the restaurant. He asks Jack who they are.

I raised my face from my plate.

"They, it would seem, are known to their intimates as Steak and Eggs. The one with the red hair I should say is Steak, and the one with the legs, is Eggs."

This seemed to puzzle him for a while, but he came at me again.

"But who are they, dad?"

"They are Gimmes," I said, "their names I do not know."

"Gimmes?"

"Gimmes. Yes, Gimmes. Gimme this and gimme that. Human leeches. They'd extract a fur coat from a marble statue of Harry Lauder. Don't smile or we're lost."

But it is already too late. Stanley has smiled. The girls join them. Jack is rather taken with Steak, whose name is Daisy. "She had red hair and blue eyes, and a wide mouth. Not a hard mouth, but a mouth that knows its way around." Stanley is distinctly taken with Eggs, or Maureen, "a beautiful chemist's blonde".

The morning after, when they eventually reach home, Stanley lets out the story of Steak and Eggs during the day while Jack is at Flannery's. Agatha and Gertrude leave for their mother's house in Chatswood. Jack and Stanley are left at home (when they are home) to fend for themselves.

My mother-in-law's chief occupations were writing letters of complaint to the municipal council, and calling upon God to look at our so-called democratic government and blight it.

There is no plot in *Here's Luck*; it is furious narrative that takes light from itself. The departing ladies turn off the gas, so Stanley chops up the kitchen cupboard to light the wood stove. He then organises a party, at which Steak and Eggs are the first arrivals, followed by Stanley's friends The Boys, and others like "an alleged female of the ultra-modern type, who could not be definitely placed as a boy or a girl and was best classified as a Boil".

The action of *Here's Luck* is fast enough, but Lower's prose style is like the bangs of the jumping-jack—wisecracks, descriptions, repartee, invocations. The timing is always impeccable, the idiom unmistakably Australian but never forced. To give the flavour of *Here's Luck* there is no substitute for a few samples of Lower's style.

Women, of course, are a prime target. This is no cause for anxiety, as not only is the situation as old as Noah and his wife, but the women, especially Steak and Eggs, give back as good as they are given. A rather crude male called Woggo Slatter asks Steak (Daisy) if she married him when he was unconscious after a fight. "'Blow in your ear and wake yourself up,' exclaimed Daisy contemptuously, 'I wouldn't send in the coupon if you were a free sample.'"

Jack is bitterly opposed to marriage, and is dismayed to see signs of incipient matrimony in his brother-in-law George, who has come down from the bush to stay with the Gudgeons. He shakes his head sadly.

"Tell me, George. Does she catch hold of your coat lapels and look up at you? Does she pick little threads off your suit in a motherly kind of way, and straighten your tie? Does she catch hold of your hand when she crosses the road?"

George stared at me and nodded wonderingly.

I slid down in my chair and smirked bitterly at my fingernails.

Here and now I would like to say that of all the refinements of female technique there is none to approach the subtlety of "picking the thread". The reason for the infallible success of this method is deep-rooted in psychology, and it is not for me to go into it. It is a combination of the "motherly" and "clinging vine" that has led more men to a one-suit-for-life existence than any other of the legitimate holds.

Neither Lennie Lower nor Jack cares for the more respectable suburbs such as Chatswood.

Chatswood is one of those places that are a stone's throw from some other place, and is mainly given over to the earnestly genteel. Here, respectability stalks abroad adorned with starched linen and surrounded by mortgages. The clatter of lawn-mowers can be heard for miles on any sunny Saturday. Sunday evenings, the stillness of death descends on the place, but if one listens very attentively one may hear the scraping of hundreds of chewed pens as they travel the weary road of principal and interest and pay-off-as-rent.

One thing leads to another in *Here's Luck*, and it is impossible to give a coherent account of the book without taking as many pages as the original, but there are some splendid scenes where the various characters are brought together. During a day at the races Jack first meets a friend of Steak and Eggs, "Call me Woggo" Slatter, "not the type of man I normally associate with". He is tall and very broad. "His features reminded me of the cliffs at South Head, and his nose, which had evidently been broken at some time, had a disposition to lounge about his face." Slatter appears to be pursuing Jack throughout most of the rest of the book with what Jack takes to be ill intent.

At Randwick, thanks to Steak, Jack backs King Rabbit

From H E R E'S L U C K an original illustration by WEP

LENNIE LOWER
1903-1947

Lower's comic *persona* is still so powerful that it seems one of his own jokes that he should have been christened Leonard Waldemar Lower. He was born in Dubbo on 3 September 1903. It is also in character that on that occasion his father was on a bender and failed to register his birth.

His father died when Lennie was seven, his mother remarried and the family went to live in Sydney. Lennie attended Barcom Avenue State School, Darlinghurst, but was not a notable scholar. Lennie then joined the Royal Australian Navy, but the mutual relationship was not a success and Lennie left, reputedly by the simple method of deserting. He took odd jobs such as road mending and also rural work when he could get it, but often slept in the Sydney Domain or in trains.

His first published piece appeared in 1926 in a scandal sheet called *Beckett's Budget*. He then wrote a daily column under the name of T. I. Red in the *Labor Daily*.

Gradually he established a reputation as a humorous columnist, and then the publication of *Here's Luck* in 1930 made him famous.

He was so much in demand that at one time he was writing no fewer than eight columns a week of what someone called his "slapstick surrealism" for the *Daily Guardian*, the *Daily Telegraph*, *Smith's Weekly*, the *Sunday Telegraph* and the *Australian Women's Weekly*. He was a heavy drinker and not always regular in his hours, and it is said that a copyboy had sometimes to be despatched to bring Lennie to the office, where he would arrive still dressed in his pyjamas. Frank Packer sacked him from the *Daily Telegraph* (allegedly for the 111th time) after an interview with Noel Coward in which he used some intemperate epithets.

One cannot imagine how he passed the medical examination, but he succeeded in joining the AIF in World War II and saw service at Dubbo and some other country towns before being discharged in poor health.

He died of throat cancer in 1947. An anonymous writer on *Smith's Weekly* (Kenneth Slessor?) wrote after his death, "The great secret of Lower's humour is that he was always himself, he never let anyone or anything get in the way of his natural genius. Editors could tell him what to write about, he would go away and come back with something entirely different."

As well as *Here's Luck* he published *Here's Another* (1932), *Life and Things* (1936) and *The Bachelor's Guide to the Care of the Young and Other Stories* (1941). A selection of his columns has recently been published.

---

and wins £136. With some other wins and a few losses, he clears over £250 for the day, so for the rest of the book is assured of drinking money, although he has to watch Stanley closely, his son being a firm believer in boys being supported by their fathers.

Stanley succeeds in getting his own motorcycle and sidecar, which he parks in the sitting room of the house, and eventually manages by crashing it into Oscar's bike to take his revenge on the faithless Estelle and her lover. The result is that Estelle comes back to him, charmed. "You beautiful, ruthless brute," she says.

What spare time she had left was used up by various communings with God about the water-rates, and the only really light work she indulged in was when she seated herself behind the window-curtain and watched for small boys who might be tempted to rattle sticks along the front fence. Altogether, she was a busy woman.

"Stanley: the blight of my life" is as keen as Jack to welcome Uncle George when he arrives from Split Rock to stay, taking off his enormous boots and shaking out a roll of notes that he is hiding from the sharks of Sydney, unaware that two of the worst are watching. Stanley's last words, in unexpectedly affectionate tones, to his father at bedtime are "Dad, you'll go halves with me in Uncle George, won't you?"

George is as innocent and likable as Bazza MacKenzie, and is an unexpected asset when late at night Stanley crashes his motorcycle into a police station. George has already fallen out of the sidecar a few kilometres back. Jack, George and Stanley are thrown into the cells for the night by the constable on duty, but when the sergeant hears the case in the morning he realises that George is the son of his old mate from up the bush. The sergeant shouts them all drinks and a meal and will not even let them pay for the broken fence.

As the frantic days go by, a note of melancholy sounds in Jack, and despite the beauteous Steak, Jack has thoughts of Agatha, who is after all only about 38. "Not an unattractive age. Not at all unattractive." Life has been ruined by the presence of Gertrude, who has always "taken charge" and come between him and Agatha. Agatha, he reflects, "really was a good wife, in a way. She could make pea soup to a degree of excellence that has never been surpassed on land or sea." Jack's trouble is that he is lonely; "left alone, misery romps all over me".

Nevertheless, he is still horrified to find both George and Stanley contemplating matrimony, and warning them of the worst, "I pulled the stopper out of the vials of wrath and splashed the wrath around like ginger-beer at a Sunday school picnic."

But it is all bravado. At a final stupendous party, as Jack strolls out to see if the police are about, there at the gate is Agatha. For once he is lost for words. Finally, with a courtesy based on years of marriage, he says, "Come inside and sit on the gas-box for a while." She has left her mother and Gertrude. She sobs. Jack puts his arm around her. "After all is said and done, it's nice to put your arm around the same old waist after a holiday away from it."

They all happily watch as the house burns down. Slatter was only trying to borrow money, not beat Jack up. George's girl Mary turns out to be none other than Maureen, known as Eggs. George sets Jack and Agatha up in a ham and beef shop. Jack has written to the Secretary of the Department of Navigation, recommending Stanley for a job "on the staff of some fairly remote lighthouse". All ends happily.

Frederic Manning

HER PRIVATES WE

OR
THE MIDDLE PARTS OF FORTUNE

LONDON 1930,
1929

"Mr. Clinton died of wounds this afternoon. Do you know, he told me some days ago he had a feeling that he would be killed if he went into the line here? I think he told me, because in a way he was rather ashamed of it: when he did go up, he went quite cheerfully, as though he had put it out of his mind."

Bourne shrank from talking about the incident with the Padre, even though the Padre was one of the best. He could only say, in some confusion, how sorry he was: it was odd to think he could speak more frankly about the matter with Sergeant Tozer.

"I don't know how you can go on as you are, Bourne," said the chaplain, abruptly changing the subject. "I suppose even the luckiest of us have a pretty rough time of it out here; but if you were an officer, you might at least have what comfort there is to be found, and you would have a little privacy, and friends of your own kind. I wonder how you stick it. You haven't anyone whom you could call a friend among these men, have you?"

Bourne paused for quite an appreciable time.

"No," he said finally. "I don't suppose I have anyone, whom I can call a friend. I like the men, on the whole, and I think they like me. They're a very decent generous lot, and they have helped me a

great deal. I have one or two particular chums, of course; and in some ways, you know, good comradeship takes the place of friendship. It is different: it has its own loyalties and affections; and I am not so sure that it does not rise on occasion to an intensity of feeling which friendship never touches. It may be less in itself, I don't know, but its opportunity is greater. Friendship implies rather more stable conditions, don't you think? You have time to choose. Here you can't choose, or only to a very limited extent. I didn't think heroism was such a common thing. Oh, it has its degrees, of course. When young Evans heard the Colonel had been left on the wire, he ran back into hell to do what he could for him. Of course he owed a good deal to the Colonel, who thought it a shame to send out a mere boy, and took him on as servant to try and give him a chance. That is rather a special case, but I have seen a man risking himself for another more than once: I don't say that they would all do it. It seems to be a spontaneous and irreflective

action, like the kind of start forward you make instinctively when you see a child playing in a street turn and run suddenly almost under a car. At one moment a particular man may be nothing at all to you, and the next minute you will go through hell for him. No, it is not friendship. The man doesn't matter so much, it's a kind of impersonal emotion, a kind of enthusiasm, in the old sense of the word. Of course one is keyed-up, a bit over-wrought. We help each other. What is one man's fate to-day, may be another's to-morrow. We are all in it up to the neck together, and we know it."

"Yes, but you know, Bourne, you get the same feeling between officers, and between officers and men. Look at Captain Malet and the men, for instance."

"I don't know about officers, sir," said Bourne, suddenly reticent. "The men think a great deal of Captain Malet. I am only talking about my own experience in the ranks. It is a hard life, but it has its compensations, the other men have been awfully decent to me; as they say, we all muck in together. You know, Padre, I am becoming demoralized. I begin to look on all officers, N.C.O.s, the military police, and brass-hats, as the natural enemies of deserving men like myself . . ."

Manning's great novel of World War I has had a curious publishing history. Peter Davies issued it in a two-volume limited edition as *The Middle Parts of Fortune* in 1929; an expurgated commercial edition appeared as *Her Privates We* in 1930. (The expurgations consisted mainly of soldiers' swear-words.) In both cases no author's name was given; all that appeared on the title page was "Private 19022". It became best known in the second edition.

The two titles both came from *Hamlet*, Act II, Scene 1.

Hamlet: Then you live about her waist, or in the middle of her favours?
Guildenstern: Faith, her privates we.
Hamlet: In the secret parts of Fortune? O! most true; she is a strumpet.

The sexual innuendo is hardly taken up in the book, which has remarkably little soldiers' bawdry, and only touches lightly on the love affairs between the soldiers and the French village girls.

Every chapter is headed by a Shakespearian quotation, and it is clear that Manning intends them as pointers to a more serious level of meaning in his novel. Its profundity and power appealed immediately to readers. A number of eminent critics and authors, such as E. M. Forster, Arnold Bennett, Ernest Hemingway and T. E. Lawrence, declared it to be the finest of novels about World War I. What is most amazing is that Manning, an aesthete and recluse and asthmatic, who suffered all his life from ill-health, should have been able to survive life as a private soldier in the trenches during the battles of the Somme.

Since Manning left Australia when he was 15 and returned only for two short visits, it may be regarded as debatable whether *Her Privates We* qualifies as an Australian novel. It is reasonable to conclude that it does, for it could not have been written by an Englishman. By education and birth Manning was of a different class from the privates of the King's Shropshire Light Infantry with whom he fought. (Indeed, in the book, the character Bourne, obviously a self-portrait of the author, is always being asked by his officers why he did not take commissioned rank; in the end it is forced on him.) In 1916 an upper-class Englishman's capacity to communicate with his fellow-soldiers would have been crippled by class-consciousness. Manning's more democratic Australian instincts allowed him full access to the minds of privates, sergeants and officers. As his publisher, Peter Davies, wrote in his introduction to the 1943 edition, the first to carry Manning's name on the title page, *Her Privates We* "is a profoundly democratic book".

"*I have seen a man risking himself for ...another more than once: I don't say that they would all do it. It seems to be a spontaneous and irreflective action, like the kind of start forward you make instinctively when you see a child playing in a street turn and run suddenly almost under a car . . .*"

Manning's Australian blood gave him a double advantage. He was, as has already been stated, an instinctive democrat in the classic Australian style. He had also, as T. E. Lawrence acutely observed, an outsider's detachment of observation by virtue of being both Australian and having been distanced from ordinary life by his sufferings from asthma and other illnesses.

Bourne, the hero, is a highly educated man with affluent friends in England who send him parcels, one of which contains a bottle of whisky hidden in a loaf of bread. In the *estaminets*, he shouts champagne for sergeants as well as privates. He does not wish for promotion at all, not even to lance-corporal (although this does come to him at the end of the book, before his commission). "Bourne had no ambition to become an acting lance-corporal, unpaid. He preferred the anonymity of the ranks."

Her Privates We is about the individuals who emerge from that anonymity, and how they behave when they go into action. At the very beginning of the book Bourne, after taking part in an attack, reflects that "every impulse created immediately its own violent contradiction". As the soldiers move forward there is a "sense of unreality, and dread", but at the same time there is "some restoration of balance as one saw other men moving forward in a way that seemed commonplace, mechanical". While he is just "an act in a whole chain of acts" at the same time "every sense was alert". Again, "the extreme of heroism, alike in foe or friend, is indistinguishable from despair".

The toy-like men are running beside him towards the enemy trenches under a rain of shells; at the same time, he is undergoing a "moral and spiritual conflict, almost superhuman in its agony". A bullet or a piece of shrapnel hits Bourne's helmet, "knocking it back over the nape of his neck so that the chin-strap tore his ears". The blow actually fractures the steel.

Death is active, but Bourne is still alive. "Death, of course, like chastity admits of no degree; a man is dead or not dead. Nothing in the world is more still than a dead man."

The living say of the dead, "I shall not be like that", but when a man's mate is killed alongside him, all that he is left with is the knowledge of his own feelings. These may produce a terrible anger in battle, but tears, even in a strong man, after battle.

No wonder the soldiers drink, when they can. Bourne is admired, even by the Regimental Sergeant Major, for his ability to hold his liquor. Some of the best episodes occur when the soldiers are eating and drinking in the French villages that have survived so strangely close to the firing line. This presence of the villagers—Bourne helping a French girl to write a letter to her lover in the British army, Bourne befriended by an old peasant, the soldiers singing music-hall songs in the *estaminets*—all this makes more poignant the other reality of battle.

Bourne loves his fellow-soldiers, particularly little Martlow, and Shem, and the wonderfully portrayed Weeper Smart, but in most of them he sees "very little reason or sense of responsibility". After being in action their mood has changed:

In the last couple of days their whole psychological condition had changed: they had behind them no longer the moral impetus which thrust them into action, which carried them forward on a wave of emotional excitement, transfiguring all the circumstances of their life so that these could only be expressed in the terms of heroic tragedy, of some superhuman or even divine conflict with the powers of evil; all that tempest of excitement was spent, and they were now mere derelicts in a wrecked and dilapidated world, with sore and angry nerves sharpening their tempers, or shutting them up in a morose and sullen humour from which it was difficult to move them.

About halfway through the book, Bourne, Shem and Martlow are transferred to the Signals Section. They have a new commanding officer, Colonel Bardon, who is free of that "romantic swagger and arrogance to which, in the past couple of months, they had become accustomed and indifferent".

There is an attack imminent, and Bourne wants to be sent back to his company, away from this "cushy job" with

DEAD BEAT, TIRED OUT *Frank Crozier*

FREDERIC MANNING
1882-1935

Frederic Manning was born in Sydney in 1882 to a family well known in the legal circles. He was the fourth son of Sir William Patrick Manning, and brother to Sir Henry Manning, Attorney-General of New South Wales.

Frederic suffered severely from asthma and attended Sydney Grammar School for only six months. He once stated that he was chiefly self-educated in England and Italy; he was also much influenced and helped by Arthur Galton, a scholar and clergyman who had been private secretary to the Governor of New South Wales. Manning went with him to England when he was 15, and when not travelling, lived with Galton, near Bourne in Lincolnshire, until Galton's death in 1921. (Bourne is also the name of the hero of *Her Privates We*.)

Manning published three volumes of poetry between 1907 and 1917, but he made his literary reputation with *Scenes and Portraits* (1909), a series of imaginary conversations and stories in prose, somewhat after the style of Landor. Max Beerbohm said he knew of no better stories in English. On reading the stories T. E. Lawrence also became an admirer of Manning's work – an admiration which grew with the appearance of *Her Privates We*. Of one of the stories, "The King of Uruk", E. M. Forster said, "Perhaps it is the most exquisite short story of our century."

Manning, despite his recluse-like life in the English countryside, had a number of literary friends, including Ezra Pound and his wife Dorothy Shakespear, W. B. Yeats, Laurence Binyon, T. E. Lawrence and the artist Sir William Rothenstein. Rothenstein described him as having "the worn look, as of carved ivory, due to constant ill-health". Dorothy Shakespear said he seemed to belong to the nineteenth rather than the twentieth century.

From 1907 to 1914 Manning was the principal reviewer for the *Spectator*, and later he reviewed for T. S. Eliot's *The Criterion*.

During World War I, he served in the King's Shropshire Light Infantry as a private soldier in a number of campaigns. *Her Privates We* is set in the Somme offensive of 1916. Those who knew him said it was amazing that a man who was an asthmatic and in very delicate health could even have got into the army, let alone survived in the trenches.

Her Privates We (1930), by Private 19022, was the commercially oriented, expurgated version of *The Middle Parts of Fortune*, which had been published in a limited edition by Peter Davies in 1929. It is said that Davies had to lock Manning up to make him complete the book.

Her Privates We was reprinted five times in 1930, and went through four more editions by 1964. It was highly praised by English critics but not reviewed at all in Australia, although the *Age* reprinted some of the favourable English reviews. T. E. Lawrence wrote, "I am sure it is the book of books as far as the British Army is concerned." Arnold Bennett called it, "A major document in war literature". E. M. Forster considered it, "The best of the war novels". *The Middle Parts of Fortune*, complete with the original soldiers' language, was reissued in a commercial edition in 1979.

On Manning's death Peter Davies wrote, "Constant ill-health, combined with an extreme fastidiousness, curtailed the literary output which might have been expected from so fine and penetrating a mind, and the modesty and aloofness which prevented him from putting his name to the most successful of his books robbed him of the personal fame which would have been his had he cared to claim it."

Manning paid two visits to Australia, and lived in Italy for some years. He died of pneumonia in London in 1935.

---

the sigs. This is not allowed. Instead, in the signals class, he meets an extraordinary man, Weeper Smart: ugly, huge, a cross between an ape and a vulture, and "such a spectacle of woe" that some cruel wit has called him Weeper. Bourne, respecting him, always addresses him by his name, something Smart does not forget.

The soldiers discuss the war and death and the enemy with a simultaneous gravity and humour that recalls Shakespeare's *Henry V*. Weeper says, "A've no pride left in me now." He just wants to go home. As for the enemy, "A tell thee . . . there are thousands o'poor beggars, over there in the German lines, as don' know, no more'n we do ourselves, what it's all about." And yet, as Manning says elsewhere in the book "all responsibility . . . is borne eventually by private soldiers in the ranks". The most tragic element is that they are at the disposal of some inscrutable power, using them for its own ends, and utterly indifferent to them as individuals.

Manning reaches the height of his narrative as Bourne moves from his "cushy job" to taking part in a major attack. The terrible waiting, the unimaginable storm of steel when the attack commences, the effect of it all on the ordinary soldiers, is brought together with frightening, unstoppable momentum. Three-quarters of the way through Chapter XV there is a passage which is perhaps the finest tribute to the front-line soldier, and his faith in the men on either side of him, in the literature of war.

A great anger mounts in Bourne, overtaking the gusts of fear and rising to a frenzy when his gentle young friend Martlow, an innocent country boy, is killed. After it is all over, and Bourne has survived, he tells the others about Martlow's death. Weeper puts out his hand: "'A'm real grieved,' was all he said."

Shortly afterwards Brigade orders a small raid "to secure identifications". Volunteers are called for. Bourne is more or less pushed into it by an unpleasant officer. Weeper stands up. "'If tha go'st, a'm goin',' he said solemnly."

After the successful conclusion of this raid, as they are returning through a path cut through the wire, Bourne is shot through the chest and falls. With his dying words he tells Weeper to go on. "'A'll not leave thee,' said Weeper." With his huge strength he carries the dead man back and collapses with the body on the duck-boards of the dug-out.

Bourne was a queer chap, thinks Sergeant-Major Tozer, looking at the dead body. "There was a bit of mystery about him; but then, when you come to think of it, there's a bit of mystery about all of us."

Tozer's words apply to Manning as well as to Bourne, both to his individuality and to his sense of the common man.

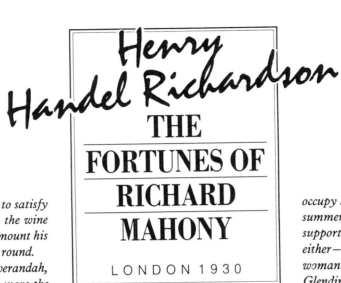

Henry Handel Richardson

THE FORTUNES OF RICHARD MAHONY

LONDON 1930

Mahony promised to do his best to satisfy her, and declining, very curtly, the wine she pressed on him, went out to mount his horse which had been brought round.

Following him on to the verandah, Mrs. Glendinning became once more the pretty woman frankly concerned for her appearance. "I don't know how I look, I'm sure," she said apologetically, and raised both hands to her hair. "Now I will go and rest for an hour. There is to be opossuming and a moonlight picnic tonight at Warraluen." Catching Mahony's eye fixed on her with a meaning emphasis, she changed colour. "I cannot sit at home and think, doctor. I must distract myself; or I should go mad."

When he was in the saddle she showed him her dimples again, and her small, even teeth. "I want you to bring your wife to see me next time you come," she said, patting the horse's neck. "I took a great fancy to her—a sweet little woman!"

But Mahony, jogging downhill, said to himself he would think twice before introducing Polly there. His young wife's sunny, girlish outlook should not, with his consent, be clouded by a knowledge of the

sordid things this material prosperity hid from view. A whited sepulchre seemed to him now the richly appointed house, the well-stocked gardens, the acres on acres of good pasture-land: a fair outside when, within, all was foul. He called to mind what he knew by hearsay of the owner. Glendinning was one of the pioneer squatters of the district, had held the run for close on fifteen years. Nowadays, when the land round was entirely taken up, and a place like Ballarat stood within stone's throw, it was hard to imagine the awful solitude to which the early settlers had been condemned. Then, with his next neighbour miles and miles away, Melbourne, the nearest town, a couple of days' ride through trackless bush, a man was a veritable prisoner in this desert of paddocks, with not a soul to speak to but rough station-hands, and nothing to

occupy his mind but the damage done by summer droughts and winter floods. No support or comradeship in the wife either—this poor pretty foolish little woman: "With the brains of a pigeon!" Glendinning had the name of being intelligent: was it, under these circumstances, matter for wonder that he should seek to drown doubts, memories, inevitable regrets; should be led on to the bitter discovery that forgetfulness alone rendered life endurable? Yes, there was something sinister in the dead stillness of the melancholy bush; in the harsh, merciless sunlight of the late afternoon.

A couple of miles out his horse cast a shoe, and it was evening before he reached home. Polly was watching for him on the doorstep, in a twitter lest some accident had happened or he had had a brush with bushrangers.

"It never rains but it pours, dear!" was her greeting: he had been twice sent for to the Flat, to attend a woman in labour. — And with barely time to wash the worst of the ride's dust off him, he had to pick up his bag and hurry away.

This novel is a record of contradictions and incompatibilities, especially of its main character, Richard Mahony. Mahony is Irish, but Protestant and loyalist. He is a highly qualified doctor, but so fastidious and outspoken as to be devoid of anything approaching a bedside manner. He marries a down-to-earth English girl who fits happily into Australian life, while he cannot abide the growing republican spirit. He has a deep need for spiritual sustenance, but is profoundly dissatisfied with the Christian God. He is a kind, loving and considerate man, but will make his own (often foolish) decisions without consulting those most involved in them. He is a man of considerable intellect and learning, but is a fool amongst the worldly. Not altogether by luck, he makes a fortune, but altogether by his own ineptness he loses it.

The book itself is missing one main ingredient of Australian life—humour. While it chronicles the disastrous impact of Australia and Australian life on this proud Irishman, and gives a vivid picture of mid-nineteenth-century Ballarat and Melbourne, it is almost totally humourless.

Excessive pride is Mahony's deadly sin, and of course excessive pride is incompatible with humour. The ominous signs appear very early in the book, when Dr Mahony is somewhat unsuitably running a store in Ballarat, in the belief that more money is to be made out of store-keeping than doctoring. At a meeting shortly before the violence at the Eureka Stockade (which later Mahony calls that "pitiful little forcible-feeble rebellion"), Mahony antagonises the diggers by calling them "gentlemen" and telling them to show their loyalty by giving three cheers for the British Flag. "Not so much gentlemanning, if *you* please . . . *Men's* what we are—that's good enough for us," one of them calls out.

Mahony is touchy and irritable, but basically sweet-natured, sensitive, and ready on the instant to be propitiated. His fastidiousness does not stop him having a scapegrace friend, Purdy Smith, who is shot in the ankle (by mistake, by another digger) at the Eureka Stockade. It is through Purdy that he goes to Beamish's Family Hotel, near Geelong, to meet Purdy's sweetheart, Tilly, and her sister, Jinny. Also at Beamish's is Polly (just turned 16 and just out from

England, though there is a dark un-English strain in her), who is regarded as a treasure by all.

For once in his life Mahony acts quickly and sensibly. Within a few days he asks Polly to marry him. When she accepts, he goes into Melbourne to ask final permission from her elder brother John Turnham, a rich merchant, with whom he almost immediately has an argument. John maintains that what the colony needs is good workmen, not gentlemen, and Richard replies that "a leaven of refinement" is essential. However they part on good terms, especially as the marriage has the blessing of John's beautiful wife, Emma. John's only misgiving is that Richard has no intention of remaining in Australia – he will return to England as soon as he has enough money.

Richard sees Polly as the "busy, willing little woman" who will help him and be the mother of his children, "neither too rare nor too fair for her woman's lot". He is not discouraged when he finds she has no feeling for poetry or music. After all, she is only a child, and he will teach her.

*B*ut Mahony, jogging downhill, said to himself he would think twice before introducing Polly there. His young wife's sunny, girlish outlook should not, with his consent, be clouded by a knowledge of the sordid things this material prosperity hid from view.

It is in fact Mahony who will be revealed to be the child, and Polly – later Mary – the wise and practical one, although Mahony will always patronise her for her lack of interest in cultural matters.

Within the first eight chapters many of the themes of the book are clear, including the relationship between Australia and the white people who have invaded it with "loveless schemes of robbing and fleeing". But the "ancient barbaric country" . . . "held them captive" and will have her revenge. The best that Mahony can ever allow Australia is to call it "An unlovely country, yes, as Englishmen understand beauty: and yet not without a charm of its own."

The first book of the trilogy, *Australia Felix*, covers Mahony's troubles in Ballarat, his abandonment of the store and setting up as a doctor, and his success with the local gentry despite a lack of response with the ordinary people, who find him stiff and standoff-ish. His old friend Purdy returns, full of his adventures. Polly finds she can talk

Ballaarat Post Office and Township from Government Enclosure
S. T. Gill (above)

uninhibitedly to him about her husband's odd ways. Tilly marries old Mr Ocock, after "hoping against hope, Poll, that a *certain person* [Purdy] would come to the scratch at last".

Then some shares of Richard's come good. Suddenly (as was so typical of the economic climate in the Australia of the day) the Mahonys are lifted out of poverty. "The suddenness of the thing was what staggered him." They take a new house and Polly has a new piano. About this time she ceases to be Polly and becomes Mary, as her brother Ned's new wife is Polly. Everything goes happily, until at a ball – or rather, in a little room off the main hall during the ball – Mary has "a very unpleasant experience" with Purdy. Richard's reaction is straight from melodrama. First he almost accuses Mary of encouraging Purdy. Then he dashes off a note: "You damned scoundrel! If ever you show your face here again, I'll thrash you to within an inch of your life." But then, being Mahony, he cannot bring himself to deliver the note.

This is the crux of Mahony's inability to cope with life. "He had no talent for friendship, and he knew it." And in this country easy intimacy is essential. But his black Irish pride will not allow it. Apart from Mary, "in Purdy, the one person he had been intimate with passed out of his life . . . hence the break with Purdy was a real calamity".

Mahony has a breakdown. In a fit he falls off his horse. He is found and brought back and Mary nurses him back to health, but "never . . . would things be quite the same again". Since the night she told him about Purdy, she has begun to doubt Mahony's wisdom. Mahony is now a success, but she has come to feel "deeply sorry for him with his patent inability ever to be content". His crowning folly is that he blames Australia for his own hollowness. He is becoming an old man yet he is not yet 45. He decides to sell his practice and go to live in England. In anguish Mary falls in with his plans, resigned "with the best grace she could muster, to the inevitable".

In the second volume, *The Way Home*, the Mahonys reach England and, after a disastrous beginning in Leicester, Mahony buys a practice by the sea at Buddlecombe.

In Australia Mary had maintained people were the same anywhere, so why go to England? Richard had replied, "No, by God, they're not! . . . This sordid riff-raff! These hard, mean, grasping money-grubbers!" Mary had been appalled that he could forget all the kindness and generosity shown them in Australia. Ironically, it is the English who now prove to be snobbish, rude, hard, ungenerous and altogether intolerable. The Mahonys decide to return to Australia. Mahony has "hated the Motherland . . . from the first moment of landing".

Now the rejected Australia welcomes them again, with good fortune. Some shares he had bought and rather unwillingly kept have suddenly boomed. He is now a rich man. He is even willing to admit to the kindness with which their old Australian friends welcome them.

Time and money are no longer his enemies. He retires from medicine. He has time for books and music, and money for a fine house and to pay for Mary's "rampageous hospitality". However, he still cannot forgive his old friend Purdy, now "a common, shoddy little man, already pot-bellied and bald", who is going to marry Tilly, now a rich widow. Mary chides him. People change, he says; ironically, he is unaware that he himself is changing.

UNTITLED *Robert Ingpen*

HENRY HANDEL RICHARDSON
1870-1946

Those of Henry Handel Richardson's books which are set in Australia show that, for a writer, childhood experiences are a sufficient basis on which to build. She was born in Fitzroy, Melbourne, in 1870 and christened Ethel Florence Lindsay Richardson. In 1887, only 17 years later, she left Australia with her mother for Europe, and returned only once in 1912 for "a flying six-weeks' visit to test my memory". Her memory was sound enough, but the lack of sympathy with Australia and Australians demonstrated in *The Fortunes of Richard Mahony* does not lie only in the nature of Mahony himself. Henry Handel Richardson appreciated the vulgar kindness and good spirits of Australians: but having left Australia at an early age, she grew up without an understanding of the nation's own growth towards maturity. What she did understand, completely, was the character, and the slow physical and mental degeneration of Mahony himself, which were based on her own father's life and misfortunes. However, it must be remembered that a novelist is not a biographer. In Richardson's autobiography, *Myself When Young* (1948), she wrote: "The person who knew me best always maintained that, in my imaginary portrait of Richard Mahony, I have drawn no other than my own."

Richardson's father was an Irish doctor. Her mother, an English girl "of yeoman stock", was aged 14 when she and her parents migrated to Australia. In her autobiography Richardson wrote "to these two widely differing parents I was born some fifteen years after marriage when my father was forty-four, my mother thirty-three".

Her father prospered and eventually retired from medicine, and when she was four he took the family on a grand tour of Europe.

But while they were away his investments failed, and he had to bring the family back to Melbourne and begin again as a general practitioner in Hawthorn. The practice was not a success, and the family moved to Chiltern in north-east Victoria (on which Barambogie was based). Here Doctor Richardson's mental decline became more obvious. "My father we saw only at mealtimes. When not out on his rounds he remained shut up in the tiny room known as the surgery." At Chiltern his practice also failed. In 1878 Doctor Richardson secured the job of Acting Health Officer at Queenscliff. For a while they were all happy living by the sea, but it soon became necessary for Mrs Richardson to support the family. In the same year she took work in the Post Office at Koroit in Western Victoria. Doctor Richardson died there in 1879, "a gentle broken creature who might have been a stranger".

In 1880 Mrs Richardson was promoted to post-mistress at Maldon, a gold-mining town in northern Victoria, where she stayed until 1886. Meanwhile young Ethel was sent as a boarder to the Presbyterian Ladies' College in Melbourne; her experiences there were the basis of her book, *The Getting of Wisdom* (1910).

In 1887 Mrs Richardson took Ethel to Europe to study music in Leipzig. She was not sufficiently talented to become a concert pianist, but her experiences in Leipzig and as a musician gave her the background for her two novels, *Maurice Guest* (1908) and *The Young Cosima* (1939). In 1895 in Dublin, Henry Handel Richardson married J. G. Robertson, later the first Professor of German Language and Literature at the University of London.

In 1912, at her home in Regent's Park, London, she began work on *The Fortunes of Richard Mahony*. The trilogy took her almost 20 years to research and write. Little notice was taken of the first two volumes in England or Australia, but the third, *Ultima Thule*, was a success and gradually an interest grew in all three books. This was much helped in Australia by the enthusiasm of Nettie Palmer.

In 1933, J. G. Robertson died. Henry Handel Richardson then lived with her friend and housekeeper, Olga Roncoroni, in Sussex, until her death in 1946.

Mary has a child, Cuthbert, called Cuffy, and twins, Lallie and Lucy. The Mahonys have reached the top of the social ladder, although Richard is never a happy man. But at least he can count his blessings, when Mary's brother John dies of cancer. Richard still has his health and his wealth. Then, while visiting England in style and travelling on the continent, a telegram reveals that a man called Wilding has absconded with all Richard's money.

Volume Three, *Ultima Thule*, opens with Richard's return to Australia, feeling "doubly alien", a ruined man of 49. He goes back to medicine, first at Hawthorn in Melbourne, and then, to Mary's dismay, in an awful little country town called Barambogie in the Ovens District. Mary has said they lived "like a pair of hermit crabs" in Hawthorn, but it is worse in Barambogie. Here Richard simply wishes to "forget and be forgotten". Once again, he cannot be friendly with the people in the town, and his practice falls off. After an agonising illness, Lallie dies. Good-natured Tilly has Mary and the other two children to stay at Lorne. During this time Mahony falls into a boundless depression, which ends in another fit. On Mary's return he tells her that the practice has collapsed, that he has a hidden debt of £800, and that he fears he is going mad.

On one level, *The Fortunes of Richard Mahony* is the chronicle of Richard's inexorable downhill slide into

madness. It is made all the more poignant through being viewed, particularly later in the book, through Cuffy's eyes. Mahony's slow decay is partly due to his inability to put down succouring roots in Australian soil. His deterioration is a slow process which needs the 928 pages of the trilogy to convey all its heartbreak and complexity. Richard's character is always offset by that of the sturdy Mary, who stands strong and unchangeable in her strength and love.

Richard has to be sent to a nursing home and then to an asylum, while Mary supports the family by taking a job as a postmistress in a Western District town. Eventually, thanks to Mr Ocock's son Henry who is now in parliament, Mary gets permission to take her wreck of a husband home and he dies there in peace. The last words of the book are "the rich and kindly earth of his adopted country absorbed his perishable body, as the country itself had never contrived to make its own, his wayward, vagrant spirit".

The Fortunes of Richard Mahony is recognised as one of the greatest of Australian books, but it is a European tragedy, devoid of Australian literary influence. Its hero is essentially an unreconstructed European. Henry Handel Richardson's greatest achievement is that she, an expatriate living in England, demonstrates, from the last lines of the Proem to the last words of the book, how the unloved country taking its revenge could in the end be "rich and kindly".

[At] the scorch of the iron, [the heifer] bellowed and wrenched her body in one convulsive effort to free herself; but the pull of the ropes and the weight of the men had been applied in just such a way as to cope with that. She was helpless.

To the touch of the second and third iron she lay quiet, except for a painful quivering of her muscles.

The ropes were slipped from neck and heels. The weight of the men was lifted from her body. Not realizing that she was now free, the heifer lay still, stretched out.

One of the men slapped her with his hat.

"All over, now, Jemima!"

The heifer scrambled to her feet. A gate opened before her. She jumped through it, banging one hip against a post in her haste, and found herself back among the calves in another yard.

Usually, an animal finding itself released and returned to its kind would settle quietly. But not the red heifer! Her one idea was flight. Not merely escape, but the satisfaction that would come with putting distance between herself and her tormentors.

She went straight across the yard at a trot. The men, looking through the rails, watched her. The rails of the yard enclosing the heifer were five feet high— but that would hold her! It would hold most horses.

The heifer went straight up to them and stopped. Raising her head, and snuffing, she tested the height of the top one. Then she jumped—a standing cattle jump.

None of the stockmen quite knew how she did it—but an involuntary shout went up from them as she hung across the top rail, balanced, like a beast in a sling. A space of convulsive kicking during which she edged her body forward an inch or two. Then gravity came to her assistance and she fell in a heap on the outside of the yard. She untangled herself and jumped to her feet.

The stockmen climbed the rails, laughing to watch her go.

She went down the slope and out across the flat, flying. Not with the lumbering, swag-bellied trot of an old milker, but galloping like a wild thing, her head out and her tail up—the plume flying like a pennant on a lance, and her limbs swinging long and free. She passed out of sight behind a clump of box-trees—still travelling.

The men got down from the rails.

"There'll be more fun with that one before she's turned into beef," one of them prophesied.

This is a novel about a red heifer which breaks away from a domestic herd and joins a band of wild scrubbers in the Queensland hills. It is a book about animals, but it is also about men. Davison is no sentimentalist, and although in the novel he reveals more faults among the humans than the brutes, the scales of his sympathies are not tipped either way.

Davison does not disapprove of raising beef cattle for the market, but with his shrewd eye he notes that the stockmen galloping after cattle have qualities not often found among those concerned only with following the profit motive.

Man-Shy opens with mustering a herd for drafting and branding. The cattle are no match for the skilful stockmen, with their highly trained horses and blue heeler dogs. Beyond this annual disturbance, the cattle accept the routine of their lives, peaceful enough except for the occasional tremor of nervousness when a mounted stockman and his dog approach and make a half-circle around the mob and ride away. Otherwise there is "nothing but the wide earth, the herd life, the elements, and the seasons".

However, among these thousands of docile beasts there are a few which want their independence from man. These drift off in twos and threes to the ranges, where they join up and form a wild mob in the stony hills, with their own waterholes and grazing grounds. The scrubber band of Man-Shy has been in existence for over 60 years. They have regained the bond with nature shared by the wild creatures. They are free.

The red heifer first appears as a four-day-old calf with her old, feeble mother, who has gone down with the rest of the domestic herd to drink at the Washpool. The cow, nervous of the steep banks and the mud in her feebleness, waits till the boisterous mob has drunk before she ventures near the water. All Davison's skills as a writer are apparent in the economy and understated pathos with which he describes her cautious descent to the water, her backward looks and calls to her sleepy calf left in the shade of a bush, her falling into a mud-hole, her frantic efforts to get out, and her settling deeper into the muddy water until she drowns.

Normally a four-day-old calf deprived of its mother would be certain to die of lack of milk or to be killed by a dingo. But in the red heifer calf there is an extra quality of persistence, often allied with luck, that distinguishes her throughout her life as calf, heifer and cow. In a convincing episode the usual law of rejection is abnegated, and a strange cow mothers her along with her own calf.

When the stockmen arrive for the annual muster the two

little calves are too young to keep up with the mob, and so escape the branding irons. In a pungent aside, Davison contrasts the life of beef-on-the-hoof with its destiny as beef-on-the-hook, and the associated terrors of yarding, trucking and slaughtering.

Next year at mustering the stockman who had earlier observed the two young calves, recognises the red heifer, a fine young yearling with satiny skin, broad back and deep body. She is already independent-minded, disturbed by the abject submission of the rest of the mob. She heads off on her own, but soon suffers her first experience of the teeth of a blue heeler. Breaking away again, she is again driven back to the mob by the dog. She never forgets this experience.

The next morning she is in a yard of round rails, which are "lashed with wire to posts as high as a man's head", among the calves waiting to be branded. But she stands higher than them because she escaped branding the year before. Determined to get out, she finds the rails too high to jump and too low to crawl under. The men leave her till last, knowing that they will have a battle on their hands, but they are too clever and tough for her, and so she is roped and branded. Even so, she arouses the admiration of the men. "She's one out of the box, all right."

Put back amongst the calves, she should have settled down in the usual style of cattle. "But not the red heifer! Her one idea was flight. Not merely escape, but the satisfaction that would come with putting distance between herself and her tormentors." By a prodigious leap she gets herself over the top rail; balances, kicking; and then heaves herself off and gallops for the hills while the stockmen climb the rails and laugh to see her go.

Usually, an animal finding itself released and returned to its kind would settle quietly. But not the red heifer! Her one idea was flight. Not merely escape, but the satisfaction that would come with putting distance between herself and her tormentors.

Eventually, after wandering through the brigalow, she finds the scrubber mob. Davison beautifully handles her relations with the scrubbers. These begin with her rejection by the leader of the mob (always a cow, by the way, not a bull), the challenge from another heifer of the same age and weight, the fight, her victory and her acceptance by the bull and thus the mob. She will not submit to the indignities forced on her by men, but she is obedient to the rules of the wild mob. Nevertheless, she is homesick for her old Washpool mob, and leaves the scrubbers to join them again. Davison traces the double instinct in her: the allegiance to the domestic herd and the call of the wilderness.

She is away again with the scrubbers when the next mustering takes place, but is caught with the domestic herd the next year. The stockman again recognises her, and sees in her fidgety, nervous behaviour sure signs that she has been with the scrubbers. He decides to send her down to market. He sees her already as beef-on-the-hook. Up in the hills the scrubbers hear the sounds of the muster, and are ready for flight. But the old bull is angry and goes along the ridge until he can see the mob crossing the plain and hear the distressed calls of the cows. He bellows out his answering call.

This is the climax of the book. At the bull's bellow, "Something in the heifer snapped—the bond of fear!" She gallops off for freedom. Some of Davison's most vivid descriptions follow, as two dogs and then the horseman with his whip try to head her back. But despite the pain, and being brought to her knees, she responds to one more trumpet-blast from the bull. To the stockman's astonishment she lurches to her feet and gallops off into the scrub.

She does not know it, but war has been declared. The boss tells the head stockman to get his men together and clear the scrubbers from the range. A breaker is sent up to find them. After a long and cautious ride he finds their hidden waterhole, and counts the mob. He recognises a young, blood-red cow as the heifer who had leaped the railings and escaped mustering.

The battle that follows is as vivid as the chase in "The Man from Snowy River". After a wild gallop through the timber-covered hills the stockmen capture the wild cattle and yard them. The rails baffle them, but not the red cow. She remembers those other rails, and these are lower. With a great leap she again drops on the top rails, kicks and is free.

The fenced-in scrubbers will not feed or drink in captivity. Despite the men's indignation, Black the boss is determined to break the mob's spirit. But he cannot, and the cattle begin to die. Rather than release them, he decides to shoot them for their hides. Then the old bull comes down to join them. He is easily yarded, but once he decides that no posts or rails are going to stand between him and freedom, he breaks the rails down with his great weight and the whole mob escapes into the ranges.

The cycle is complete: the red cow has a calf. Once again life seems peaceful in the freedom of the ranges. However, the scrubbers are now exposed to a new danger: a shooter, who is making money by bringing wild beef down to the new settlers on the plains. Tracking the mob to their waterholes, he soon shoots four, including the leader. The red cow takes her place.

Caught by the drought and drying waterholes, the scrubbers are forced into long marches down to the waterholes of the plains. But the open run is now fenced into farms and selections, where many of the scrubbers are trapped and shot. The red cow leads the remains of the mob back to the Washpool.

It is typical of Davison's even-handed approach that the new settler whose tent is pitched by the Washpool should

UNTITLED *Frank Mahony*

FRANK DALBY DAVISON
1893-1970

Born at Glenferrie, Victoria, on 28 June 1893, Frank Dalby Davison was the son of a printer. At the age of 12 he left Caulfield State School to work on a farm and stayed there for three years.

In 1908 his father moved the family to the United States, where they lived in St Louis and Chicago, and young Frank was apprenticed to the printing trade. He started writing poems and stories very early in his life, and printed some of his own work while working in New York as a printer.

Always broke, he was caught riding a train without a ticket and sentenced to a fine or gaol at Albany, US. He took 10 days in gaol, which gave him some firsthand insights into the lower levels of humanity.

After making several voyages to the Caribbean as Ship's Printer on a tourist vessel, he went to Canada. In 1914 he travelled from there to the United Kingdom in charge of a number of cavalry horses. In England he joined the British Cavalry, and saw service in France before retiring to England, where he was commissioned.

In 1915 he married his first wife Kay Ede.

In 1919 he returned to Australia and took up a Soldier's Settlement block in the Maranoa district of south Queensland, where he spent four years clearing the bush and grazing cattle. Ultimately beaten by bad seasons he had to leave the property.

Davison joined his father selling real estate in Sydney, where his father was also editing and printing his own magazine, the *Australian*. Frank contributed to this, and also had paragraphs published in the *Bulletin*. In 1923 he published five short stories in the *Australian*. His novel *Man-Shy* was also initially serialised in the *Australian*. Later *Man-Shy* was bound in wall-paper and Davison sold it from door to door for sixpence. The Depression saw the end of his father's real estate business, and he took to printing and selling books full-time. Frank's next novel, *Forever Morning*, was sold for two shillings. This business also failed, and father and son ended up on the dole.

In the 1930s Davison worked freelance for the *Sydney Morning Herald* and other papers, and for a while edited the "Red Page" of the *Bulletin*. *Man-Shy* was published by Angus and Robertson in 1931, after the Australian Literature Society had given it a gold medal as the best novel of the year. It subsequently sold over 300,000 copies. *The Wells of Beersheba*, a short but powerful book about the Australian cavalry in the Middle East, was published in 1933.

In the early 1930s Davison was awarded the MBE, but had to borrow tuppence for the ferry fare to collect the medal. A Commonwealth Literary Fund grant later enabled him to write his collection of stories, *The Woman at the Mill*, which was published in 1940.

His first marriage was dissolved during the war and in 1944 he married Edna Marie (Maree) McNab. Soon after, out of his early experiences and also his life with her, he began what he considered the most important book of his life, a long study of human sexuality called *The White Thorntree*.

His novel *Dusty*, published in 1946, won the £500 *Argus* competition. In the late 1940s he bought a small farm near Arthur's Creek where the Davisons settled in 1951. Only 40 kilometres from Melbourne, he lived there until his death in 1970. *The White Thorntree* was published in 1968.

Davison was a writer of classical economy and simplicity. His most successful works were the animal stories, *Man-Shy* and *Dusty*, and the miniature war epic, *The Wells of Beersheba*. Critics still argue over the putative success or failure of *The White Thorntree*, an immensely ambitious book, marred by lapses in style and characterisation.

---

be sympathetic; a man who loves wild creatures and wild land, and who wishes the scrubbers no harm. But there are only two alternatives: either fence the cattle out so that they die of thirst in the ranges, or fence them in and shoot the full-grown beasts. All the scrubbers are captured, but the red cow with her unbreakable will again bursts out, torn by the barbed wire, and takes her calf with her.

Fenced off from all water, she leads her calf to the last and highest of the old camps, where the pool is now dry.

On top of the ranges she waits to die.

Man-Shy is above all an analysis of the urge for freedom, and the courage and independence of spirit that must support it. It is a tragedy, but in common with the great tragedies of literature, it is a tragedy of events but not of the spirit. At the end the fences and the drought are symbolic. To choose freedom is to choose death. But the red cow has no doubts. Death is preferable to submission.

Ion L. Idriess

FLYNN
OF THE
INLAND

SYDNEY 1932

Triumph came to Flynn and Traeger—the latter had discovered the wireless link that welded his Chain of Dreams! In desperate anxiety they hurried to test out the completed instrument. They took it to the Centre, and when it "worked", their overstrained faces glowed, and with wild shouts they threw their hats in the air and joined hands in an hilarious "merry-go-round" with the little machine in the centre. The old Dodge, packed with its boxes, its swags and dusty tarpaulins, its tools and mats and water-bags—their tried and trusty old friend was forgotten. Eagerly they rapped the little instrument again, and the morse shot out to the distant amateurs who were listening in to the test. The Baby Wireless Transmitting and Receiving Set was a fact! Very materialistic the little instrument looked, squatting on the sand; hard to realize that it was actually built by the thoughts of men.

The machine could be easily carried, easily installed: it could be easily mastered by the bush mother. It was worked by pedal. The generator was simplicity itself and a marvel of efficiency. It could be phoned up from any mother station, but transmitted its own messages by morse. Those technically interested might like to know the following details:

The generator which supplies the power for the transmitter is operated by foot, like a bicycle, and can generate a power of about 20 watts at a pressure of 300-400 volts. The gears are enclosed in an oil-tight casing filled with oil: thus minimizing wear.

The transmitter is "crystal controlled", the crystal maintaining the wave-length at a definite value, and keeping the note steady; thus making the signals easy to read even if the generator is driven unevenly.

The receiver is a two-valve regenerative circuit usually known as the P.1.—Tetrode valves being used. The "A" battery is a 1.5-volt dry cell, and the "B" battery consists of two 4.5-volt "C" batteries connected in series; thus giving nine volts. One set of batteries gives from four to six months' service. By plugging a larger coil into the receiver, broadcast programmes can be received. Ear-phones are used. A small loud-speaker can be used. The cost of the instrument is under £60.

The experimenters hurried back to Adelaide. Here Scott joined them. Arrangements were made to make some of the machines immediately. Then Traeger and Scott hurried to Cloncurry to install the Mother Station.

Flynn's dream was realized. Australia in her most isolated areas girdled by Nursing Homes; a Flying Doctor established at a Base Station; and now the perfected wireless machine to link the doctor with his patients!

Six more flying doctors, each at their base station, and all isolated Australia would be under the Flying Red Cross!

The reaction had come for Flynn, the old fighting light left his eyes. With their blessing and the necessary cash the Board sent him overseas on a twelve-month holiday.

For generations of readers, Ion Idriess's books were invaluable guides to the vast outback and its stories, about which most city-dwelling Australians knew so little. Sometimes a few of his "facts" were fiction, but he was always true to his real subject, the Australian bush. He had been a bushman himself, and he had wandered all over the tough country of outback Queensland, the Northern Territory, the Channel country and the Kimberley area.

The best of his books, still selling well 50 years after its first publication in 1932, is *Flynn of the Inland*. This is partly because the facts are accurate, but mostly because the nature of the hero's work enables Idriess to take the reader all over his beloved bush, from Blinman to Darwin, from Birdsville to Wyndham, as he follows the dream of Flynn, the outback padre, in his travels by camel, then by motor car and finally by aeroplane over areas where Idriess lovingly describes the land and with a journalist's ear picks up the stories that are waiting to be told.

Flynn's mission is to bring the word of God to men who "don't go much on religion", but his dream is also a practical one—of bringing medical help to the isolated men, women and children on the stations and the mines of the inland. Idriess is always refreshingly idealistic about the inland. He clearly sees the harshness of the terrain and the climate, the dust and the distance, the primitive nature of most human settlement, and the desperate lives that many are forced to live. But he looks to the day when improved communications and facilities will enable people to live in reasonable comfort and safety thousands of kilometres from the cities. How Flynn would be cheered by the existence of today's mining towns, such as Mt Tom Price, or oil and gas installations, such as Moomba! It was not only Flynn who had his dream.

In one respect Idriess was too optimistic. Improved services, road trains for instance, and improved living and health conditions, have not led to the great expansion of productivity that Idriess hoped for. The country and the climate will not allow great increases in the carrying of cattle and sheep, and as for crops, the Ord River scheme has still not paid off. Handing over stations to the Aborigines has meant a dramatic falling off in cattle and sheep numbers on those properties. Idriess understood a great deal about Aborigines, their beliefs and customs, but he was of that generation of Australians who still talked about "niggers". He was not aware that they have been the greatest beneficiaries of the Flying Doctor Services. For Idriess, the Flying Doctor Service came into existence for the benefit of the isolated whites; after all, the Aborigines had gone along without the white feller's medicine for thousands of years.

Eagerly they rapped the little instrument again, and the morse shot out to the distant amateurs who were listening in to the test. The Baby Wireless Transmitting and Receiving Set was a fact!

Idriess always had a fine instinct for drama. *Flynn of the Inland* opens with a mysterious figure, the Camel-man, alone in the inland immensity. "He had a thousand miles to go, but Central Australia shrugs at distances." The Camel-man has knowledge and a dream, both centred on the word "if":

If the wife gets sick! If . . . that "If" of the Inland spoilt the security, the strength and happiness of Inland life. No man in all Australia knew more of that "If" than the Camel-man. It was his job to blot it out: it was his life's work. Dearly he loved the happiness of the Inland, the brightness, the hope, the feeling of "life" in everything, from the insects' song and mountain range and sunlit plain to the laughter and the dry humour of its people. All would be like that "if—"

The realities are enough to breed a family of "ifs".

Twenty days' rough travel necessary to transport a sick person from Alice Springs to Oodnadatta railhead, for instance. Even then a hospital was six hundred miles farther south. The lonely tracks of the Kimberleys with two doctors in an area of 137,294 square miles! One tiny school at each of the three little ports, none inland. The Northern Territory with one doctor and one school in an area of 523,600 square miles! No wonder the sick ones seldom arrived. Distances—distances—distances.

It is chastening to think that this was written about Australia after Federation, when life was thriving in big cities and comfortable country towns. One of Flynn's, and Idriess's, great contributions was to make Australians aware of these uncomfortable realities.

Chapter II introduces the bush padre, who of course is the Camel-man, and Idriess skilfully describes his arrival at an inland station so that, from the authentic welcome from young and old, the reader is immediately aware of Flynn's special qualities. He follows this with an encounter between Flynn and a pioneer cattleman near Lake Eyre, who is astonished to hear that Flynn is "a parson on the wallaby". Flynn has an opportunity to explain what he wants to do for such a man. "Just to give you a hand in any way we can. Just to be a wandering link between you and civilisation as it were—might come in handy sometime."

Flynn's dream was a practical one in that it could be realised. He saw that isolation and distance could be defeated by communication. In 1911 the Home Missions Board of the General Assembly of the Presbyterian Church sent him for a year into Central Australia to prepare a report on the establishment of hospitals and nursing homes across inland Australia. His superiors and Flynn believed "that the greater Outback would welcome Christianity when it came as Christ came, with healing for the body as well as for the soul". Flynn established a spider-web of communication and nursing homes in this country the size of the whole of Europe, with a population of 50,000 whites and an unknown number of Aborigines.

With Flynn as organiser, and in charge of Field Operations, his Board set up the Australian Inland Mission. (As Idriess points out, the name was a little unfortunate, as the Mission serves thousands of miles of coastline as well as the inland.)

Idriess uses Flynn's travels to tell astonishing stories of bush life such as an operation carried out by a man with only a little medical knowledge, with a penknife and razor, under instructions over the telegraph from a doctor in Perth 3670 kilometres away by wire. But two more operations were necessary, and these were beyond the skills of the man at Hall's Creek, so the doctor set out from Perth by steamer and road. Twelve and a half days later the doctor arrived; the day after the man had died.

Flynn succeeded first in setting up patrols and nursing homes in four huge territories in Western Australia, the Northern Territory and South Australia, and Queensland. The story has still not been fully told of these incredibly heroic nurses who would ride hundreds of kilometres to attend to sick or injured people.

PLANE OVER DUNLOP *Sam Fullbrook*

ION L. IDRIESS
1890-1979

Ion Llewellyn Idriess was one of Australia's most popular authors (his books have sold over 3,000,000 copies in Australia alone) and probably the most travelled all over Australia. Before becoming a professional writer he worked at different times as a gold prospector, an opal gouger, a pearl diver, a station hand, a horse breaker, a wharf labourer, a builder's labourer, a miner and a drover.

He was born in 1890 in the Sydney suburb of Waverley. His father was a Welsh seaman who married an Australian girl and settled in Australia, taking a variety of jobs around the country before becoming a mining inspector and sheriff's officer in Broken Hill.

Ion Idriess, or Jack as his friends always called him, left home at 17 and got a job as a boatswain's mate on the paddle steamer *Newcastle*, a berth he shared with innumerable bugs and fleas. When opal was found at Lightning Ridge he moved there, opened up the Deadman's Claim deposit and made some money. A friend there suggested he write something for the *Bulletin*. A reply came in the Answers to Correspondents column: "Stick to your pick and shovel; they're the pen that suits your style!" However, he kept trying, and eventually had a number of paragraphs and sketches accepted.

When war was declared in 1914 he was on Cape York Peninsula and stowed away on small steamers until he reached Townsville, where he enlisted. He served in the Light Horse at Gallipoli and in Sinai and Palestine, and was wounded three times.

After hearing Idriess tell stories of his experiences mining tin and wolfram on Howick Island, North Queensland, Alec Chisholm persuaded him to take his diaries to George Robertson of Angus and Robertson. His first book, *Madman's Island*, is based on the diaries and was published in 1927. It was a flop, probably because of the love interest he was persuaded to write into it.

In 1931, unemployed, he offered to write a prospector's handbook for George Robertson, and the success of *Prospecting for Gold* (1931) was followed by *Lasseter's Last Ride* (1931), *Flynn of the Inland* (1932) and *The Desert Column* (1932), which is about his war experiences, and has an introduction by General Chauvel. Idriess was established as a professional author. He wrote his books in a room at Angus and Robertson's office, standing up, with dozens of lead pencils on quarto sheets. Two hours in the morning was enough, by which time he had written 20 pages. It took him two or three months to write a book, and often he published two a year. In all he wrote 56 books; some of them have gone into 40 or 50 editions.

A review of *Flynn of the Inland* said that Idriess had been a Boswell to John Flynn. Next time Idriess saw George Robertson he asked, "Who's this bastard Boswell?" George Robertson gave him *The Life of Samuel Johnson* to read. When an interviewer mentioned the episode to Idriess some 40 years later, Idriess was still not sure what the reviewer and George Robertson had been up to. "This Boswell was a literary figure of the day," he said. "He didn't do any bushwhacking."

Idriess died at the age of 88 in Sydney in 1979.

Flynn then succeeded in establishing, through his Board, hospitals in Birdsville and Victoria Downs. But Flynn was already chasing his next dream, that of a baby wireless that would enable the stations to communicate with the base, a "Baby Wireless Transmitting Set, so inexpensive, light, and simple that every bush mother could handle it". He enlisted the aid of E. T. Fisk, Kauper and others of Amalgamated Wireless Australasia (AWA) and it was through Kauper that Flynn was able to interest Alfred Traeger, a young genius in Adelaide.

Idriess brilliantly handles the story of the "successful failures" of Traeger and the ways in which he and Flynn tried out his ideas in Hermannsburg and other remote settlements, until finally the pedal wireless transmitter was evolved, revolutionising communication in the inland.

At the same time another dream of Flynn's was being realised, following the foundation of QANTAS in 1920. The establishment of three more hospitals by 1926 meant that the new airline could bring in sick people who would previously have died because of slow communication, but Flynn saw the real solution lay in the conjunction of doctor, aeroplane and pedal wireless. The first experiment, supported by Flynn's board for a year as a trial, was at Cloncurry in Queensland, where an aeroplane capable of being used as an ambulance, with room for a pilot, a doctor, a nurse and a patient was to be available in a radius of 480 kilometres. This was inaugurated in 1928, and two years later the service was being used in conjunction with the pedal wireless. Flynn's dream was working.

*F*lynn's dream was realized. Australia in her most isolated areas girdled by Nursing Homes; a Flying Doctor established at a Base Station; and now the perfected wireless machine to link the doctor with his patients!

Idriess's book is a tribute to a great man, and a hymn of love both to outback Australia and to man's ingenuity. Idriess is no great writer—his work has clichés galore—but he was always able to respond to the greatness of his theme.

Myrtle Rose White

NO ROADS GO BY

SYDNEY 1932

On the day that I came into the world myself, one of the worst dust-storms known in the history of the Barrier was blowing. But that fact did not endow me with a love for dust, which, in view of the many pecks I found I was to swallow in later life, was something of a pity.

The dust-storms of the West Darling are something extra special of their kind, but those of the "open country"—well, you, who know the Darling Showers, can picture just how much worse they would be, released in a country where there is no tree-growth worth mentioning, and only sand, sand and again sand. The blinding, stinging, infinitesimal specks sear the flesh with a million hot pin-points; a thick yellow fog completely obscures the world. Day after day, night after night, it blows, and blows—north, south, east and west. From all points of the compass it comes; and oh! the horror of living through it.

Food is prepared with dust sifting down from every crack and crevice; food is cooked with dust pouring down the chimney into the pots and pans; food is left waiting until there is a sufficient lifting of the reddish-yellow blanket in which to serve it. Dishes freshly washed are filmed with dust and grit as they are laid on the table; follows a meal with grit, and the one and only flavouring from start to finish.

Quite often the lamps are lit at two o'clock, although the sun does not set until seven and after, but as an illumination a lamp would be only a farce. In a dark room, there is a lightening towards the centre, a nimbus of fog around the flame.

The thought comes that the crust over Hades has broken, and that the orange-red, sulphur-yellow fumes have drifted through. At times when the wind drops, an uncanny silence grips the dust-choked world. For a fleeting moment, sheds, harness-room, meat-house, and kitchen are seen, unfamiliar and indistinct shapes through the gloomy pall. Then with terrible venom the wind sweeps down the depressions between the sandhills. Such ungovernable fury is released as will surely brush one from the face of the earth. Timber creaks and strains, roof-iron begins to lift and flap, and window-sashes rattle and shake as if in the grip of ghostly hands. A noise of rending wood, a strange boom, boom, boom, and a new ten thousand gallon rain-water tank is rolling ahead of the storm to be crumpled up like tinfoil before it reaches the second sandhill. Satisfied with the destruction of its plaything the wind again drops, this time to a thin haunting whine; all the lost and lonely souls in the world send their plaint on that lowering note. First it is under this corner of the roof, then under that; the saddest, weirdest, soul-shaking whisper that ever was. Meanwhile, the dust thickens and deepens to a dull dead black and closes in, closer, closer, and closer, until one stifles and feels that all hope is lost.

A week of this and one emerges fit for a full course of the latest nerve treatment. Nature knows that and provides her own cure. If you can take it with a Christian spirit, thankfully, uncomplainingly, you are the salt of the earth. Personally I never could.

Picture a house camouflaged from floor to ceiling with red sand; your curtains, that you stencilled with such pride, deep red with sand; the soft moss-green carpet that rests your tired eyes when there is no living green for miles and miles, buried under barrow-loads of sand; sheet, pillow-cases, quilts, blankets, crockery, and walls all covered with sand; the corrugations in the iron roofs running sand; the six-foot iron fence that borders the garden enclosure, buried, absolutely buried, beneath the sand. There is no longer need to open a gate, a nice sloping bank leads to the top of the fence, a nice sloping bank leads down the other side. If you can put in a week wielding a broom, and battling with a wheel-barrow which pours hour-glass sand from six or seven holes and as many cracks, while hot suds gradually bring back a semblance of your old home—if you can do that and come up smiling—well, then, it's hats off all round. You are something more than human, you are divine.

With *We of the Never Never, No Roads Go By* is one of the two best-known classics of women keeping house in the bush. Myrtle Rose White was spared the tragedy of losing her husband, but otherwise she had a much harder time than Jeannie Gunn.

In 1915, Myrtle Rose White and her five-year-old daughter, known as the Little'un, accompanied Con White to the station he was to manage in the sandhill country, where the far north of South Australia borders New South Wales, between Lake Frome and Milparinka, about 240 kilometres from Broken Hill. Noonameena, as Mrs White calls it, was about 12,900 square kilometres of open country and in a good season carried 5000 cattle. The government had put down a number of artesian bores in this otherwise waterless country, "opening it up": that wonderfully vague phrase which disguises infinite hazards and tests of patience, ingenuity and courage. A house had to be built, and in the meantime the Whites lived at an old homestead at Mirrabooka, some 80 kilometres away.

The story opens simply. "The Head of the Family decided that the bush was the place for us, and so, of course, to the bush we went." There is no question that Con White is The Boss, but also no question of the respect due from him and all the station hands to Myrtle Rose White and the children. (As well as the Little'un, Mrs White had two boys in the seven years they lived there, arriving back from Adelaide with the first when he was only five weeks old.)

Like most bushmen of the time, Con White is a lover of poetry, quoting selections from Gordon, Kendall, Paterson, Boake and other Australian poets to the cattle at night. During moments of desperation, Mrs White is also comforted by poetry.

However, her presence is more than a comfort; it is a reassurance that standards will be kept up, no matter what the difficulties. These begin at home, when the house is built and they move in. Mrs White has a succession of married couples, women and girls to help her with the house and children, but the activities of some of these could scarcely be called "help". The most startling incident concerns Ruth; her fellow houseworker Bertha passes on something a certain station hand has said about her just as Ruth is cutting down the meat. In walks the very station hand and Ruth slashes him across the face with the knife, almost taking his nose off.

*F*ood is prepared with dust sifting down from every crack and crevice; food is cooked with dust pouring down the chimney into the pots and pans; food is left waiting until there is a sufficient lifting of the reddish-yellow blanket in which to serve it.

Domestic life becomes a little more gracious when a young girl, whom Mrs White calls Miss Seventeen, arrives as cook and housemaid. The station hands' clothes and manners improve miraculously, and Miss Seventeen is much persecuted by the Little'un asking why Tim was kissing her behind the kitchen door. She is an expert at playing the men off against each other until Tim secures the inside running. But Tim transfers his affections to her successor, Miss Dimple, and they marry. It often seems that the only permanent residents at Noonameena are the Whites themselves.

In *We of the Never Never*, Jeannie Gunn says that life on the Elsey was not lonely, despite her remoteness from any other white woman. There was a constant stream of visitors to the Elsey, but nobody travels through Noonameena. Mrs White admits to being much troubled by loneliness, for The Boss has to be away for long spells with the cattle.

The epigraph to *No Roads Go By* is a quotation from A. B. "Banjo" Paterson.

Out in the wastes of the trackless west,
Wandering ever he gives the best
Of his years and strength to the hopeless toil . . .

This was more or less what The Boss did for seven years in that most difficult country, struggling against drought with limited equipment, and fighting a continual battle with nature, even to continually pushing back the sand which gradually creeps up on the homestead. But there is a difference between man's loneliness and woman's. The Boss is responsible for the men, black and white, who work for him, and for the cattle, the horses and the camels. The difficulties are often acute; once the drovers taking his prize fat cattle to a seller's market all go down with gastric troubles, leaving one man to take the whole mob through to water.

Mrs White is responsible for three small children as well as for the running of the homestead, often in dust storms so bad that the only clean places in the house are where the children's heads have been on their pillows. The Boss is always with other men: she desperately misses other women in the same position as herself. But in the early years of this century, however close husband and wife were, the wife's duty was to support her husband, to sympathise with him about his troubles and to keep quiet about her own.

The children don't hanker for contact with the outside world; they have each other. While the Little'un's life is full of games with her cattle dog Bluey, with horses, with harnessing ants to pull a matchbox, with imaginary playmates, Mrs White is left with solitude. "I will not try to convey the loneliness of those days, the loneliness of the nights, save to say when the shadows of evening crept from the sandhills, the solitude was at times almost more than I could bear." Elsewhere she says:

I ached, just ached, for the touch and voice of a fellow human being as I stood there in the terrible, frightening dark. It was a feeling never entirely erased in all the years I lived in the bush. I was to feel it always—that terrifying oppression of the infinite solitude, the eerie silence that can crush the bravest spirit, and mine was never that.

Mrs White is too modest. Through her heartrending account of her little boy's illness and the appalling journey over the sandhills to get him to the doctor 240 kilometres away, it is clear that hers was indeed a very brave spirit.

She says that perhaps she had a foretaste of that journey on the occasion when she first went to Noonameena bore (the depot) before the house was built. She was travelling with the owner, J. D. D., who said cheerfully to a cattle buyer who asked her what she thought of it, "At least she will have the distinction of being the first white woman to live out here, and the Little'un will certainly be the first white kiddie to leave footprints in the sand."

All day, that first day, they climb up and down the sandhills, seeing fresh vegetation at the base of each one after the rain, few trees, only stunted mulga, beefwood or box trees along the beds of dead swamps.

Indeed, it was a curiously dead country to my thinking. Every wind-waved sandhill was like a dead, dead sea, the waves frozen and still.

WOMAN AT A WINDOW *Russell Drysdale*

MYRTLE ROSE WHITE
1888-1962

Myrtle Rose White was born in 1888 during a dust storm at Acacia Vale, near Broken Hill. She spent her childhood in softer country – South Australia's Barossa Valley. But she came from hardy stock: both her maternal and paternal great-grandparents had been early pioneers of South Australia; her great-grandmother lost her husband on the voyage out and gave birth to Myrtle's grandmother on board ship.

Born Myrtle Rose Kennewell, she married Con White and went with him when he was appointed manager of the 12,900-square-kilometre cattle station, Lake Elder, in the sandhill country of far north-east South Australia. In extreme isolation, 80 kilometres from a telephone, 160 kilometres from a doctor, she brought up three children through sickness and drought.

No Roads Go By, her book about her experiences in the homestead surrounded by drifting sandhills, was published in 1932 in an edition of 1500 copies. It was reprinted twice in the same year, and again in 1933, 1934 and 1936. In 1938 Angus and Robertson wrote to her to say they intended to publish it again in a cheap edition "to give it a new lease of life". This was not done and on 27 October 1939 W. G. Cousins of Angus and Robertson wrote to say that the type had been melted down and it would not pay to include the book in their 3s 6d edition, as a sure sale of 5000 copies was needed. "I do not think *No Roads Go By* in a cheap edition would reach this figure as it took us a long while to sell the remainder of the 6/- edition at 3/6. If you were to sell us the copyright of the book for £25 we will include it in our 3/6 series." Sensibly, Mrs White refused to sell the copyright.

It was reprinted in 1954 and 1956 with illustrations by Elizabeth Durack. Mrs White "hated" the illustrations.

The book was accorded high critical praise in Australia and very favourably reviewed in the *Times Literary Supplement* and the *New York Times Book Review*. Flynn of the Inland described it as "a most potent force" in assisting him in his drive for funds to establish and maintain the Flying Doctor Service, so improving the quality of life for people living in the outback.

After leaving Lake Elder, Con White took the family to live at Morden and Wonnaminta stations west of the Darling River, some 320 kilometres north-east of Broken Hill. Myrtle Rose White wrote *Beyond the Western River* about the family's experiences there.

Her husband died in 1940, and her two sons joined the RAAF; one of them was posted missing in Malaya. Mrs White went to Adelaide with her daughter, where she ran a boarding house. In 1950 she wrote to Angus and Robertson asking for their support in a grant application to the Commonwealth Literary Fund as "I have had to drop writing for 10 years in order to earn a living."

Mrs White lived for many years at Aldgate in the Adelaide Hills. She died in 1962 on a visit to her son at Lalla Rookh Station near Port Hedland in Western Australia.

Over this country, her nearest woman neighbour is 56 kilometres away. While living at the depot, she finds a second woman neighbour, a smiling young woman with a family of nine children, happy and serene. Mrs White arranges for both women to come and visit her, and one of the most touching episodes in *No Roads Go By* is when the women get together and talk, voicing "thoughts that women can voice only one to the other, and then only when they know where waits understanding, and sympathy, and love".

Noonameena is so remote that even the cheerful mother of nine says on seeing it, "How dreadfully lonely you must be! . . . I don't think I like it. It is too far out." How relative is such a definition of "too far out"!

During the seven years the Whites live at Noonameena, the place changes hands. The new owner buys it without even seeing it. Years later Mrs White meets him after he has seen it, and he says:

> "I don't know how you stood it so long. It's a terrible, terrible place. No place for a woman."
>
> I told him the woman did not mind so much for herself, but she agreed it was no place for children.

There is no doubt that the worst thing for Mrs White is the ceaseless worry about the children. She is pregnant when she has her long fight to save her son, called Boy, and he remains a delicate child. The youngest seems, when he is born, to have been affected by her troubled pregnancy. Despite the nine months they spend in the city, Little Brother turns out to be "a nervous, irritable, highly strung child". She worries that in her fight to save the elder boy she has not thought enough of the new life for which she is responsible. Then there is The Boss: she has not been giving him a square deal. So she goes back to Noonameena and to the worst drought of all.

As they are in the Australian bush, a great many new problems come when at last it rains. The water fills the house to a depth of seven centimetres and with it come centipedes, scorpions, spiders and snakes. Then the sandy country turns green, "and with the green growth came hordes of mosquitoes and swarms of flies. With the flies came barcoo, dysentery and other illnesses."

Finally, The Boss says that it is time to go. Always conscientious to a fault, he will not leave in a drought. Now he says, "The place is all shipshape" and it is all right to leave. "Life here is only an existence," he says. "They have been wasted years – these seven. We are no nearer our goal now, no better off, than we were when we first came to the bush." There is grey in black hair, faces look older, the sandhills have taken their toll. Later Mrs White hears that the sand has almost smothered the house, which can only be entered through the top half of a window.

The extraordinary achievement of *No Roads Go By* is that it is not a harsh, rancorous or self-pitying book. Mrs White is very conscious of the strange beauty of her environment, the flowers and birds that come after rain, the freshness of the winters when they have log fires in the house, the wasps with their wonderful nests (one such, with six rooms, contained 63 spiders), and the butterflies. But most of all this book is a moving portrait of a woman in dreadful isolation, not afraid to admit her fears, doing what is expected of her without complaining, leaving nothing permanent behind her except her book.

Brian Penton

LANDTAKERS

SYDNEY 1934

And still another seven years. Now, looking back on the seven years that had gone, what an immensity of time this was! Seven more years of heat, dust, rats, ants, mud, drought and lamb-marking.

Seven more years to endure the eternal, unconquerable stupidity of sheep. How he hated them! Resigned, fatalistic, always ready to lie down and die, always being lost, bogged, picked to death by crows, gutted by dingoes, only kept on their feet by the constant, exhausting expenditure of his will. Pale from the operation in the scrub, he came back to the job of driving a mob to the yards for crutching—the cutting away of wool from the rump to save the animals from being blown by flies. As usual, it was a struggle to get them through the gate. They stood stock still and stared into the yard, bleating timidly, while he danced about in the dust with wild falsetto shrieks; the side of his face was swollen out as big as an apple and bands of pain stiffened the jaw. As usual, he had to seize the leaders and carry them into the pens—sixty pounds apiece—and, of course, they ran out again as soon as he turned his back, and the flock scattered. He brought them up once more, once more shrieked with his cracked, sore voice, once more staggered into the pen with the leaders one by one, the hot panting bodies clutched to his, the sunlight pressing on his shoulders like a sheet of hot metal. The leaders started to escape a second time. He met one in the gateway and punched at it blindly—a blow straight between the eyes. It sagged down, scrambled to its forefeet in the dust, to rise again, then rolled over with a little bleat, its quick, pitiable breath expiring, jerked convulsively—dead. He rubbed his bruised fist in his hand and suffered a revulsion as he gazed at its upturned, helpless eyes. He was ashamed and hid the body under the woolshed, felt uneasy all that day and the next, wondering if anybody had seen. The jangle of his nerves softened into self-pity.

He harboured resentment against Gursey, who would not let him talk in the hour between supper and turning in. He wanted the small comfort of reciting all these woes aloud, but every evening Gursey got up from the table and went down to Peters in the men's hut. He found that most of all he missed Gursey's passionate upflarings of rage, prophesying scornfully his return to England as a rich man. He could have drawn a lot of consolation from this. But Gursey withheld himself, brooding with Peters over a dark secret.

Thrown back on himself, he sought relief in his daydreams, but whatever fantasy he manufactured turned into a girl in a dripping wet dress, and sooner or later they were together in a dark shed and he was running his hand over the soft skin of her back. "Beastly," he thought, pushing the image aside, and called up the ever-vivid memory of his mother to protect him from it, but imperceptibly the darkness fell, the soft flesh grew up under his hand. He ground his forehead against the frame of the bunk till his eyes smarted. Then he fell asleep and dreamt again.

He disappeared for the fourth time. The evening he returned, dark and silent, Gursey said, "McFarlane was here."

Cabell turned his eyes away. "Yes?"

"Wants us to run his sheep for a while. He's going down to Moreton Bay to meet his old woman on the boat."

"He's bringing a woman?"

"Yes, why not?"

Cabell frowned. Suddenly he burst out, "The man must be a monster. The man who brings a woman into this loneliness and filth and disorder ought to be horsewhipped." He spoke angrily, yet it was easy to see that he was not thinking of McFarlane, but of something quite different altogether.

That process called pioneering, by which Englishmen were turned into Australians and Australia itself into ploughed paddocks and grazing ground for sheep and cattle, has never been more harshly described than in Brian Penton's novel, *Landtakers*. Derek Cabell, a young man of good family from Dorset, who has come to Australia at the age of 21 to make his fortune and go home again, eventually finds that home in Australia. In less than 25 years he makes his fortune, but he loses his youth, his looks, his morals and his sensitivity. He becomes one of "that mob in at Pat Dennis's pub" he so scorns when the reader first meets him at Moreton Bay in 1844:

Their harsh voices, their ungracious gestures, their watchfulness uncovered for him suddenly the surface of a life in which men had not yet made the social contract that softens the brutality of "everyone for himself".

The social contract is never drawn up in Cabell's lifetime, which, like the country, is of unremitting harshness, broken only by some deeper glimpses of peace and beauty in the Australian light and landscape. About halfway through the book, when Cabell has completed his superhuman journey of 151 days from his station to Moreton Bay with his first wool clip, there is an ironic reference to some slim signs of culture in "the little world held in the claws of two bends of the river". Cabell learns that the Moreton Bay Reading Circle will be meeting to discuss the latest of Miss Maria

Edgeworth's novels. What could be more remote from the rigours of his own existence?

Landtakers is mostly told in a simple, chronological direct narrative. But a personal narrator sometimes interrupts, for example, early in the book when he explains that "very little of this story is imaginative". He has pieced its events together from memoirs and Cabell's own letters, with the strongest impulse coming from the fact that he had known Cabell as a "very old and lonely man", "a battered old relic". The narrator thinks that the life of Cabell and his generation will explain the roots of the new Australian people.

The roots go down into anger and cruelty, loneliness and madness. The first words of the book are, "Derek Cabell glared". He looks with "undisguised contempt" at a detachment of convicts and soldiers assembled for floggings. A Mrs Duffy brings her own husband in every month to be flogged. Amidst this brutality Cabell is waiting to return to Murrumburra station, about 64 kilometres north of Moreton Bay, where he is overseer and is running 1000 ewes of his own. McGovern, the superintendent of convicts there, who is to haunt Cabell's life for the next 20 years, is a greedy, swaggering bully who mocks the tall Cabell as "the little limejuicer". The reader first meets McGovern in a significant episode, when Cabell has to force his way past the superintendent's huge body which is blocking the door of the house. McGovern pins him to the door jamb and then forces him, chest bleeding, to the floor. "Cabell never forgot it."

Seven more years to endure the eternal, unconquerable stupidity of sheep. How he hated them! Resigned, fatalistic, always ready to lie down and die, always being lost, bogged, picked to death by crows, gutted by dingoes, only kept on their feet by the constant, exhausting expenditure of his will.

Amongst the convicts working on Murrumburra is Joe Gursey, an old man of 35, hair and beard white and body bent from 15 years of flogging and two years of working in the Coal River mines. Gursey has been transported for agitating for higher wages in the new mills at Manchester. There is a strange love-hate bond between Gursey and Cabell which, as well as causing some of the most important actions in the book, gives rise to some fundamental discussions about Australia and its future. Cabell is still nostalgically looking back to England. Gursey and the convicts look to a future in Australia, however badly the system has treated them; the system, after all, is English.

After a scene of appalling violence between McGovern and the convicts, Cabell helps Gursey escape. The next section of the book, "Wastelands", shows Cabell and Gursey and two other men taking Cabell's stock out beyond the furthest settlement, seeking "uninhabited" land. Of course, "myalls", wild Aborigines, are already there, wandering through and beyond the beautiful valley the white men find on 5 March 1847, where Cabell establishes his station.

Cabell and the men are entirely occupied with the hard work this entails, but Cabell himself is still haunted by "images of that far, far world, clearer and more real to him than the world at hand, where all was still fantastic in its crude, wild ways". It is Gursey who has the dreams of the great future of Australia. " 'What a people!' Cabell interjected, 'a mob of despairing immigrants.' "

> Gursey brushed this aside. "People don't immigrate in despair. They immigrate in hope," he said.
> "I've got my own hopes," Cabell said. "You know what they are." Gursey's nagging voice jumped half an octave. "Ay, like the rest of them—pick the eyes out of the country and leave it."

In fury, he denounces Cabell for his attitude to Australia.

But not long after this, one night under the moon, Cabell almost unwillingly begins to surrender to the country. "He felt at once calm and exalted", looking at the beauty of the country under the moon.

> It was as though he had momentarily let go his hold on everything that had kept him alive in the land and had become part of its wild fantasy—to him, for that moment, no longer strange, no longer fantastic. He felt content.

It is too good to last. The blacks are gathering for ceremonies, and in the middle of a corroboree, a mad shepherd, Dan, shoots three of the natives. This leads to further violence with natives attacking the cattle, and finally to a massacre, ironically committed in "the blossoming miracle of an Australian dawn". As it is happening, Cabell realises to his horror and dismay that his new life has quite changed him; as the shooting starts all other emotions are flushed away, "filling him with a mad vigour". Some irrevocable thing has happened to Cabell, something has ceased, "some fine bright thing that was precious above everything else to him".

Cabell's terrible journey to Moreton Bay with the first wool clip seems almost like a penance for the massacre.

While at Moreton Bay Cabell officially takes up a lease of 240 square kilometres, including a 16-kilometre front on each side of the river, rich country where, as Gursey says, he could carry 40,000 sheep and 2000 cattle. Although Gursey is always nervous of being discovered, and especially of McGovern turning up, the future on the station looks good: ". . . Cabell was content. A dangerous condition, which invites thunderbolts."

They come, not from flood or fire or disease, but from a new group which settles on his boundary, made up of the horse thief Jem, a young man, Dick Surface, and his sister Emma. Cabell is driven into a sexual frenzy by the presence of this woman; she also disturbs Gursey, who is afraid that she will move in and throw him out. With the aid of a bottle

THE CHARCOAL BURNERS (THE SPLITTERS) *Tom Roberts*

BRIAN PENTON
1904-1951

Brian Penton was born at Ascot in Brisbane on 21 August 1904 and educated at Brisbane Grammar School and the University of Queensland.

He began as a journalist in Brisbane, then moved to Sydney as a political columnist on the *Sydney Morning Herald*. Penton had a wide-ranging mind, wrote on a large variety of subjects, and travelled and worked overseas, but the centre of his life remained in Sydney, and his chief passion (apart from his novels) was undoubtedly the political and social life of Australia. When he died, in 1951, it was said, "As a political commentator he was without equal in the Commonwealth."

In 1929 he went to London and worked on the *Daily Express* and, while there, he helped Jack Lindsay run the Fanfrolico Press which printed some remarkable and scandalous books. He returned to Australia as a reporter on the Sydney *Daily Telegraph*. At the age of 37 he was appointed editor of that newspaper, a post he held until his final illness.

Penton was an extremely energetic man with both the reporter's questioning mind and the creative writer's synthesising imagination. He assaulted the problems and faults of Australia in his newspaper articles (he wrote his own leaders) and pamphlets, *Think—or Be Damned* (1941), *Advance Australia—Where?* (1943) and *Censored* (1947). He tried to interpret the history and soul of Australia in his two novels about the career of Derek Cabell, a nineteenth-century pioneer, *Landtakers* (1934) and *Inheritors* (1936).

Penton was particularly interested in training young journalists and he produced several pamphlets for cadets which are model textbooks of journalism.

He was a great opponent of censorship and interference with the freedom of the press, and he was in the front line of the notorious clash between the press and the Minister of Information, Arthur Calwell, when in 1944 the government attempted to close down all Sydney newspapers on an alleged breach of censorship. He told the story in his pamphlet *Censored*.

Penton was an enthusiastic blue water yachtsman, and twice won the Montague Island race in his yacht *Josephine*, which he also raced in the Sydney-Hobart race.

When he died in 1951 a rival newspaperman, Sir Keith Murdoch, wrote: "I would class Brian Penton as a great Australian editor. Original and provocative, and certainly sincere in his thinking, he imparted to his paper his own vision and interesting character. I would describe his training system for young men as the best in Australia."

Norman Lindsay described Penton as "the most brilliant man we have ever had in daily journalism in Australia. He was also one of the best talkers I ever knew."

(urged on by Emma) Cabell wins a fight with Jem, and Emma comes to live with Cabell. She hankers after peace, "Not happiness, not anything great." She "released him from a prison. His heart welled over with gratitude."

But there are tensions between them, especially because of Gursey, and she goes back to Jem's place. Cabell cannot stand life without her, and rides over to bring her back, promising her to set Dick up with 1000 ewes and some cattle.

He finally marries her and they have a child. Any possible atmosphere of domestic bliss is shattered by Jem, who has come through rain and floods to see Emma. He tells Cabell Emma's story—she is an ex-convict who has been publicly flogged and who lived with the drunken old Major Mowlatt on the Murray for three years. Gursey of course, has known this all the time. In fury Cabell sacks him and drives him out; Gursey and his horse plunge into the flooded river and are swept away, apparently drowned.

The next section of the book is called "Change". The first change is in Cabell himself; he becomes a "rusty guts", a sour, mean man who lives in love and hate with Emma and her quiet determination, building a house for her, unwillingly becoming an Australian.

Without quite understanding, he felt the destructive power of the comfort she brought to Cabell's Reach—destructive to that part of him which lived most vitally in discontent.

By 1859 he has achieved a long-sought goal and made a clear £10,000. A new type of settler is arriving after the gold rushes, in love with the poetry and beauty of Australia. Even Cabell and Emma, with her "shrewd and fibrous strength", come closer together. "He felt at peace with the world."

As always with Cabell, something goes wrong. He has boundary and stock trouble with his neighbours. A law case about his boundaries goes against him. Gursey is alive after all, and returns to the station. There are rumours that McGovern is also alive and in the district, and Cabell fears that one or other of them may blackmail him about Gursey's escape. Even Nature, which had seemed to bring him contentment, is neither kind nor merciful. Everything has been "stolen from him by this land of sin, sweat, sorrow and treachery". His doubts and fears are finally understood by Emma, who does not share them. "She began to feel a tolerant contempt for one less strong and cunning than herself."

In the last section of the book McGovern comes back to haunt Cabell. He is overseer at the neighbouring station, a different McGovern, fat and soft and wanting to settle down, but still a vicious man and a threat. Gursey is unwillingly fascinated by him, wondering whether McGovern will betray him, "driven by the necessity to know what McGovern was thinking".

In two terrible final scenes the old McGovern emerges, and in a fight temporarily blinds Cabell with a stockwhip. Cabell has his revenge, despite his blindness, by pushing McGovern face first into a fire. The maddened McGovern, however, is about to murder Cabell when Emma hears them fighting, comes in the door and, after calmly watching them for a while, kills McGovern with an axe as the scattered coals of the fire take hold and burn down the homestead.

The book ends with Cabell, his sight restored in one eye, at last accepting Australia, and seeing Emma and Gursey in a new light. " 'Perhaps I always meant to stay,' he thought." The reconciliation has been hard won, although it is more like a truce than a triumph. The landtaker has himself been taken by the land.

H.V. Evatt

RUM
REBELLION

SYDNEY 1938

It is a most fortunate circumstance that the recent publication by the Golden Cockerel Press of the Log of the "Bounty" not only supports the inference that it was this longing to return to Tahiti which inspired the mutineers, but also explains nearly all of Bligh's objects and motives during the voyage. The log shows conclusively that the few disciplinary measures taken by him, though appearing somewhat harsh to the present generation, were not harsh when judged, as they should be, by contemporary standards. The Log of the "Bounty" openly reveals Bligh's qualities as master, as navigator, as seaman and as leader of men. He had been given a very important commission to execute and he was inflexibly resolved that it should be executed. Subject to this overriding duty, he made every possible effort to safeguard the health and well-being of all on board. Indeed, Bligh stands out as one of the first great sea captains whose policy it was to obtain results, not by punishment and terror, but by unremitting care and attention to the daily needs of all engaged in a great common enterprise. It is impossible to give an adequate summary of Bligh's log, but it is an inspiration to all who will read it in full.

Bligh regards the sailors as requiring the same care and protection as little children, and makes this entry:

> Seamen will seldom attend to themselves in any particular and simply to give directions that they are to keep themselves clean and dry as circumstances will allow, is of little avail, they must be watched like Children, as the most recent danger has little effect to prevent them from the same fate.

Bligh had been instructed to enter the Pacific by rounding Cape Horn. But the winds were most unfavourable, and, again and again, fierce north-westerly gales drove the vessel back. But, again and again, he refused to give up, showing leadership, seamanship and courage of the highest order. He became nearly exhausted with fatigue but never failed to display consideration for the men who were sharing in the great ordeal of manoeuvring so small a sailing vessel against so turbulent an ocean. Thus the log reads:

> My next business was to see after my People who had undergone some fatigue, and to take care that a proper fire was kept in and that no one kept on Wet Cloathes. This being done and seeing them all comfortably dry, I ordered a large quantity of Portable Soop . . . which made a Valuable and good dinner for them.

When Bligh finally gave up his attempt to round the Horn and, turning back, reached the Cape of Good Hope five months out from England, he wrote: "The Grand Object now became the refreshment of my People, about which I heartily set to Work."

He had taken elaborate precautions against scurvy, following the example of Cook. He had even engaged a fiddler in order that by dancing the men should obtain regular exercise. He insisted on hot breakfasts; he introduced the system of three watches, arguing that it was conducive to health and: "not being Jaded by keeping on Deck every other four hours, it adds much to their Content and Chearfulness." He insisted upon absolute cleanliness on board. Incidentally, his log shows that the science of discovery was more than his profession, it was his passion. As he approaches an island first described by Captain Cook, though discovered earlier by Captain Wallis, he decides that as both his predecessors had passed the island on the south, he must pass it on the north.

In the dreadful storms encountered near the Horn, Bligh surrendered his own cabin, to repeat his own words, "to the Use of those poor fellows who had Wet Births." It is impossible to refrain from a reference to Bligh's position when he was faced with the necessity of making a decision either to pursue his attempted westing or to make the Pacific via South Africa. His written account of his reasons is masterly, not only for its inherent logical soundness, but for its magnificent form and style. To quote just a sentence of it would be doing injustice. His capacity for scenic description is revealed by his log entries while the Bounty was at Tahiti, which he called "the Paradise of the World". His account of the islanders' method of using surf boards is most striking. One is continually lost in wonder at the simplicity and eloquence which seem to pervade every reasoned statement he wrote. It is impossible to put the log book down without a deep sense of respect and admiration, even of affection, for the man responsible for it. In my opinion, Bligh's log is a triumphant vindication, not only of his particular actions, but of his general character.

The so-called Rum Rebellion was one of the most extraordinary episodes in Australian history. In 1908 John Macarthur, and Major Johnston and the officers of the New South Wales Corps deposed Governor William Bligh, arresting him and holding him in confinement at Government House in Sydney for more than a year, after which he departed for Tasmania.

At the time Evatt was writing *Rum Rebellion* Bligh was

still, in the popular imagination, the cruel and tyrannical commander of the *Bounty* so brilliantly misrepresented by Charles Laughton in the film *Mutiny on the Bounty*. Bligh was certainly hot-tempered, with a command of swearing that astonished even his fellow naval officers. However, Evatt was right in pointing out not only his heroic qualities, but the temperance of his personal habits (as distinct from his "very colourful language"), and the quality of his mind and reading. Evatt writes:

> It seems almost miraculous that a boy who left school so early should in his manhood have been able to write the beautifully direct . . . flowing English which often characterises Bligh's letters and speeches.

*T*he Log of the "Bounty" *openly reveals Bligh's qualities as master, as navigator, as seaman and as leader of men. He had been given a very important commission to execute and he was inflexibly resolved that it should be executed.*

During the Napoleonic Wars Bligh served with great gallantry, earning the praise of Nelson at Copenhagen in 1801. In 1805 Joseph Banks obtained for him the post of Governor of New South Wales at a salary of £2000, double that of his predecessor, Governor King. Banks thought that only a man of Bligh's strength of character and personal bravery would be able to handle the turbulent population of New South Wales, where John Macarthur, George Johnston, and his fellow officers of the New South Wales Corps had, to use Evatt's word, already "subverted" the governments of Hunter and King. Bligh left his wife and five of his six daughters behind, but was accompanied by his eldest daughter Mary and her naval husband, Lieutenant Putland.

Evatt should have placed more emphasis on the women involved with the three main actors in the Rum Rebellion. They were all devoted and all remarkable women. Esther Abrahams was a beautiful Jewish convict who lived with Johnston from 1788; he married her in 1814. They had seven

William Bligh (*Picturesque Atlas of Australasia*) (*above*)

children. Elizabeth Macarthur was not only a brilliant manager of Macarthur's flocks but the focal point of the family loyalty which supported that tormented man. Bligh had only his wife's letters, and his daughter's presence, to succour him.

Certainly Bligh needed every means of support he could find when he ventured into the vicious world of New South Wales. The officers of the New South Wales Corps of whom Macarthur was the daemonic guiding spirit, held a monopoly of "all the necessaries of life which are brought to the Colony", and also of rum, from which they not only made gigantic profits but which they also used as a bribe, handing it out when support was needed. As a witness in a later enquiry said, "The officers did not exactly sell it themselves, but they kept women, and those women used to dispose of it, which was the same thing. Immense quantities instead have been sold in that way." The officers also smuggled convicts away from government to private service; even sergeants, corporals and drummers were given convict servants.

Evatt gives a number of examples of the officers' attempts "to sabotage the civil administration". Macarthur, proud, violent, scheming and highly intelligent, also fell foul of his Commanding Officer, Lieutenant-Colonel William Paterson, who was in effect the military dictator of New South Wales. Paterson, corrupt but not as daring as Macarthur, refused to agree to Macarthur's plan to boycott Governor King. In Evatt's words:

> . . . Macarthur turning his resentment against Paterson, the result was a duel between them, Paterson receiving a bad wound.

Macarthur was then arrested by Governor King and sent to England for trial. Oddly enough, the vital despatch giving the background to the case was stolen on the voyage. Owing to Macarthur's influence in England, the case was dropped and Macarthur resigned his commission and obtained from Lord Camden a land grant of over 2000 hectares to develop the Australian wool industry, with a promise of a further 2000 hectares if tangible results were forthcoming.

In 1805 "the perturbator", as King had called Macarthur, returned to Port Jackson, so he had a year to consolidate his political and agricultural schemes before Bligh arrived. Macarthur, of course, was implacably convinced that the welfare of the colony and the development of his land holdings were synonymous, especially if his land was selected from the richest pastures in the colony.

A few months after Bligh's arrival, 369 free settlers from the Sydney and Hawkesbury areas presented an address to him, thanking him for rescuing them from "the dreadful crisis of general calamity" of military rule that had existed on his arrival. They wanted freedom of trade, the right to buy and sell goods on an open market, an end to the rum monopoly and, most important and most dangerous for Macarthur and his officer friends, justice to be administered by the free settlers, as well as the military.

Bligh was to be the champion of the small settlers, the agriculturists, against the graziers of cattle and sheep. In this he had the somewhat confused support of the British government. Towards the end of 1807 Bligh was writing to Banks: "This sink of iniquity Sydney, is improving in its

MAJOR JOHNSTON ANNOUNCING THE ARREST OF GOVERNOR BLIGH *Raymond Lindsay*

H. V. EVATT
1894-1965

One of the most gifted and controversial of all Australians, Herbert Vere Evatt was a brilliant writer as well as a distinguished lawyer and politician. He represented Australia at the United Nations, and was President of the UN Assembly.

He was born in New South Wales at East Maitland, on 30 April 1894. His father died when he was six. His mother, who greatly influenced him, brought her family up in humble circumstances.

Evatt went to Fort Street High School in Sydney in 1905 and was dux or second in every class until he left in 1911. He was also captain of the school, captain of the football XV and captain of the cricket XI. At the University of Sydney he took his BA in 1914, his MA in 1917 and his LlB in 1918, all with first-class honours. He began practice at the Bar in 1920, and was appointed lecturer at the Sydney Law School in 1924.

He entered the NSW State Parliament in 1925. From 1930 to 1940, when he was elected to the Federal Parliament, he was a Justice of the High Court. He was Federal Attorney-General and Minister for External Affairs from 1941 to 1949. He led the Australian delegation to the United Nations from 1946 to 1948 and was President of the United Nations Assembly in 1948-49.

He was Leader of the ALP in the Federal Parliament and Leader of the Opposition from 1951 to 1960. His most difficult year was 1954, with the defection of the Petrovs from the Soviet Union and the split in the ALP which led to the formation of the Democratic Labor Party (DLP).

It is extraordinary that Evatt found time to write several solid, well-researched books, the most notable being *The King and his Dominion Governors* (1935), *Rum Rebellion* (1938), and *Australian Labour Leader* (1940), which was a study of W. A. Holman, the Premier of New South Wales, 1913-20.

Evatt always had a passionate sense of injustice, and the verdict of history that Bligh was a villain and Macarthur a hero prompted him to argue the case for an appeal in *Rum Rebellion*.

Evatt maintained his interest in football and cricket throughout his life. He was also involved with the State Library of New South Wales and the University of Sydney for many years. Evatt and his wife Mary Alice (who was a Trustee of the National Gallery of New South Wales) were notable patrons of modern art in Australia. He died in 1965.

---

manners and its concerns. Government is securing a substantive dignity and producing in consequence good effects on the whole."

With his trained legal mind, Evatt is an excellent guide to what happened next. The criminal court of the colony consisted of the Judge-Advocate and six officers (if possible from both the army and navy) nominated by the Governor.

On 15 December Bligh, through Richard Atkins, ordered Macarthur's arrest in connection with his various dealings with his ship the *Parramatta*. Atkins was a magistrate who, in Governor Hunter's attempt to reduce the power of the military in 1796, was given Captain John Macarthur's post of Inspector of Works in the Parramatta District. By the time Bligh arrived, a feud of unimaginable ferocity had developed between Atkins, now Judge-Advocate, and Macarthur. (Atkins also had little knowledge of the law.) When Oakes, the chief constable at Parramatta, presented the warrant, Macarthur wrote out the following remarkable paper and handed it to them.

> Mr Oakes — You will inform the persons who sent you here with the warrant you have now shewn me, and given me a copy of, that I never will submit to the horrid tyranny that is attempted until I am forced; that I consider it with scorn and contempt, as I do the persons who have directed it to be executed.
>
> J. McArthur [sic]
> Parramatta, 15 December, 1807.

As if this were not enough, Oakes was told that "if he came a second time to come well armed, for that he [Macarthur] would never submit until there was bloodshed".

As soon as Atkins had received Macarthur's message and had heard Oakes' report, he called together three magistrates, who issued a second warrant for Macarthur's arrest. He was granted bail until the next day, 17 December, and committed for trial for sedition. In Evatt's reasoned view, a jury would have found Macarthur guilty of the charge.

In a coincidental case of a stolen document, Macarthur "found" a copy of the indictment to be used against him. Evatt quotes from a contemporary poem:

> . . . very strange tales
> Are told of gentlemen of New South Wales.

Next, an illegally constituted court of six officers (set up by the military) granted Macarthur bail. Bligh arrested him and put him in gaol, whereupon Johnston released him and ordered Bligh's arrest, and as Lieutenant-Governor assumed control of the colony. A special post of "Colonial Secretary" was created for Macarthur.

Strong complaints inevitably arose from the small settlers, whereupon Macarthur arranged for his own mock trial, at which he was, as Evatt puts it, "acquitted".

After more than a year under arrest, Bligh was allowed to leave for England. In fact, on 17 March 1809 he sailed for Van Diemen's Land where he waited until his replacement, Macquarie, arrived in Sydney. He sailed for England on 12 May 1810. In a later despatch Macquarie wrote that he could not discover " 'any act of his [Bligh's] which could in any degree form an excuse for' the mutiny".

Johnston was brought back to England, court-martialled and found guilty; in 1813 he returned to New South Wales to his properties and family.

Macarthur left the colony for England in 1809. Macquarie had been directed to arrest Macarthur and bring him to trial, thus making it impossible for Macarthur to return safely to New South Wales for almost nine years.

Rum Rebellion is a fascinating brief by a great advocate rather than balanced history. Although Evatt, as a judge, tries to be impartial and to be fair to Macarthur and to Johnston, Bligh's faults of personality are somewhat glossed over. But as a guide through the complex pseudo-legal shenanigans of New South Wales in the early nineteenth century, Evatt is superb.

CAPRICORNIA

SYDNEY 1938

Oscar pondered for a while, then said, "Oh, but halfcastes don't seem to be any good at all. All the men here are loafers and bludgers, the women practically all whores—"

"Do the men get a chance to work like whitemen? Look, the only halfcastes of all the thousands in this country who are regularly employed are those who work on the nightcart in Town. Occasionally others get a casual labouring job. When it peters out they have to go back to the Old People for a feed. They get no schooling—"

"There's a school in the Halfcastes' Home."

"Bah! A kindergarten. A hundred children of all ages crowded into one small room and taught by an unqualified person. I'll tell you something. Once I had a look at that school, hoping to get the job of running it, knowing that the teacher barely taught 'em more than A.B.C. and the fact that they're base inferiors . . . Just think of it—when those kids leave that lousy school they have no-one to go to but the Binghis; and so they forget even the little they learn. The language of Compounds and Aboriginal reserves is Pidgin. A few score of words. No wonder such people come to think like animals! You said the women were whores. What chance have they to be anything else? Moral sense is something taught. It's not taught to halfcaste girls. They're looked upon from birth as part of the great dirty joke Black Velvet. What decent whiteman would woo and marry one honestly? It wouldn't pay him. He'd be looked upon as a combo. Look at Ganger O'Cannon . . . with his halfcaste wife and quadroon kids . . ."

"Oh I don't see much difference between a black lubra and a yeller one. Anyway, Tim O'Cannon's lubra's father was a Chow, which makes her a full-blood and his kids halfcaste. But this is a distasteful subject. I don't like this Black Velvet business. It makes me sick."

"You're like the majority of people in Australia. You hide from this very real and terrifically important thing, and hide it, and come to think after a while that it don't exist. But it does! It does! Why are there twenty thousand halfcastes in the country? Why are they never heard of? Oh my God! Do you know that if you dare write a word on the subject to a paper or a magazine you get your work almost chucked back at you?"

"I wouldn't be surprised. Why shouldn't such a disgraceful thing be kept dark? Is that what you're writing about in this book of yours?"

"No fear! I've learnt long ago that I'm expected to write about the brave pioneers and—Oh bah! this dissembling makes my guts bleed! But talking about Tim O'Cannon, Oscar—most of the men in this district go combo, mainly on the sly. How can they help it? There are no white women. Would moralists prefer that those who pioneer should be sexual perverts? Well, if there are any kids as the result of these quite natural flutters they are just ignored. The casual comboes are respected, while men like O'Cannon and myself, who rear their kids, are utterly despised. Take the case of your brother Mark for instance. A popular fellow—"

"All this talk about Mark has got to be proved."

"There's plenty more examples— popular and respected men, their shortcomings laughed over, while Tim O'Cannon's been trying for years to get a teacher sent down to Black Adder for a couple of days a month to get his kids schooled a bit. The Government tells him again and again to send them to the Compound School—"

"Well, if he's so keen on getting 'em schooled—"

"Better have 'em ignorant than taught humility, the chief subject on the curriculum of the Compound . . ."

There is more of Jonathan Swift's savage indignation in *Capricornia* than in any other Australian novel, with perhaps the exception of the same author's *Poor Fellow My Country*. The story of the half-caste, Norman Shillingsworth, is central to the book, but it is only one of many stories incidentally told. The maltreatment of so-called half-castes, or mixed-blood people in the Northern Territory; the failure of the whites to give any rights to the binghis, the full-blooded Aborigines; the moral degeneracy of white leadership; the kowtowing of Australians to the British and the eagerness to fight their wars; the general inhumanity of man to man—all stoke the fire in Herbert. The danger in savage indignation, for a novelist, is that it can lead to a general contempt for humanity, as happened with Swift. A novelist cannot allow the balance of good and evil in human beings to go awry in his work.

Apart from *Capricornia*'s enthralling gusto, variety, humour and tragedy, its greatness as a novel is firmly based on the preservation of this balance of good and evil. There is no question of the wronged half-castes being all virtuous and the whites all vicious. And when there is a character of transparent goodness, such as the railway worker Tim O'Cannon, Herbert's uproarious sense of humour and of human fallibility preserves the character's reality as a human being.

One difficulty has to be faced up to in *Capricornia*, and that is Herbert's use of invented names. To avoid petty identifications he christened the Northern Territory Capricornia, for example, and Darwin Port Zodiac. Then to identify his characters and at the same time give them all allegorical significance, which would make them a type as well as an individual, Herbert distributed some outrageous names amongst them, as well as some clever ones. Norman is an anglicism of Nawnim, which is an Aboriginal way of saying no-name, a name the Aborigines give to dogs they do not love but haven't the heart to kill.

Norman's father is Mark Shillingsworth, his uncle (who rears him) is Oscar. There are characters with normal names—the evil Charles Ket; Humbolt Lace, protector of Aborigines, who sires the wonderfully drawn quadroon girl, Tocky; and Fat Anna, the washerwoman.

Then there are the obviously satirical and allegorical names, especially of the police, O'Crimnell, O'Theef, Robbrey, McCrook; or of the law, Judge Pondrosass, the barrister Caesar Bightit ("The Shouter"), lawyers Nawratt and Nibblesom; or of the missionaries, the Reverend Hollower and the Reverend Bleeter; or of the publican Rotgutt, or the railwaymen, O'Pick and Pickandle. The names of the Aborigines, such as Bootpolish or Muttonhead, are different again, being typical stockmen's names at the time of the book, roughly from 1910 to the 1930s.

All the names of the principal characters and a very brief description are given at the beginning of the book, as in the novels of the Victorian period. This is fortunate for the reader, as the pace of the book is terrific. *Capricornia* is one of the most energetic of modern novels. And it *is* a modern novel, despite its straightforward narrative technique and style and being set in the past, with characters whose names recall Bunyan or Dickens. It is modern because it impinges on contemporary consciousness. The issues it deals with are as relevant today as they were in 1938 when it was first published.

Nawnim is sired on Flying Fox island by Mark Shillingsworth, an educated and, to a certain extent, sensitive young man who was already a boozer and drifter. The baby, in a brilliant image, is "the colour of the cigarette stain" on the finger with which Mark was prodding his son's tiny belly. Mark goes away trepang-fishing with his partner Chook Henn, more or less abandoning Nawnim, who grows up in filth with the dogs of the roaming Yurracumbunga tribe.

Nawnim is given to a drunken grazier, Jock Driver, to be trained as a stockman, but is left in a cattle-truck at the 80-Mile Siding, and unwillingly adopted by his uncle, Oscar Shillingsworth, who runs cattle on the 965-square-kilometre Red Ochre station. Oscar has two legitimate children, Roger and Marigold, by his wife Jasmine Poundamore. Roger dies and Nawnim, or Norman as he comes to be called, is brought up with Marigold. Oscar has previously tried to hand him back to Mark, his father, who on being warned in advance, fled to sea in his pearling boat, *The Spirit of the Land*. It is a disgrace for a man to be a "combo", that is to live with a female Aborigine or half-caste—Oscar finds it difficult to accept Norman, proof of such disgrace. But Oscar is a good man, and Norman grows up a Shillingsworth.

Norman's father, Mark, is becoming more and more disreputable, and disappears after unintentionally murdering the Chinese, Cho See Kee.

During World War I Oscar sublets Red Ochre and goes down to Batman (Melbourne) with Marigold and Norman. The emphasis of the book shifts to the O'Cannon family, to Tim and his part-Chinese part-Aboriginal wife, Blossom, "The Bloody Parrakeet", and his six quadroon children. Tim is the son of a soldier and has served himself, but although he is a "sooler", a propagandist for the war, he forgoes the pleasure of fighting in order to look after his children, who will be classified as half-castes and removed to the compound in Port Zodiac if he cannot support them.

The events leading up to the shotgun wedding, and the wedding itself, of his 15-year-old daughter Maud to a white grazier, Cedric Callow, make some of the funniest episodes in the book. The invitation to the wedding is a masterpiece, culminating in the promise of "420 Imperial Gallons of Beer"! "The response was wonderful. Out of the 118 guests invited, 317 arrived, most of them, fortunately for the happiness of all, bringing some food and liquor."

The good-natured O'Cannon rescues the sick Connie Differ and her little daughter. Connie is the once beautiful half-caste daughter of Peter Differ, a settler and author and a neighbour of Oscar's. There is a fine irony in his efforts to get Connie in to the hospital. "There's a woman here dyin'." The policeman says, "She is not a woman, she's a lubra." Tocky, as O'Cannon christens the baby, grows up with his children for the next seven years.

The action of *Capricornia* is periodically cut through by fate, chance, bad luck. Some of these imponderables are of natural origin, such as the Wet, some are caused by humans, such as the Great War or the malfunctionings of the railway. There are two bloody episodes where people are accidentally run down by a train. The second involves O'Cannon himself, trundling his tricycle up the track to his homestead, only to be mown down by an engine.

After the war, Oscar resumes Red Ochre, and an elegant and highly intelligent Norman comes back with him, trained as a fitter. Oscar has told Norman that he has Javanese blood, but he is instantly picked in Port Zodiac as a "yeller-feller", a half-caste. He is refused work on the railways, even though he has proven his skills by getting a stranded engine going. He is refused a drink in a hotel. His own "sister", Marigold, won't go for a walk in town with him because he is coloured.

There are no such bars when he meets Tocky, who is now "close-up fourteen, I tink", an enchanting waif who lives and works at the Halfcastes' Home. They meet happily, but Tocky is always misbehaving and is sent to Flying Fox island, now a Mission, which is ferociously satirised by Herbert. The pace of *Capricornia* slows down, deliberately, when Norman goes to work at Red Ochre and wanders off from time to time, on a sort of walkabout in the country. This is the deep heart of the book, Norman's relations with the Spirit of the Land (ironic echo of the name of his father's boat) and his Aboriginal heritage. As some of his old full-blood friends tell him, "Proper good country, dis one . . . number-one good country."

But in conversation with whites he repudiates his links with the Old People. The grazier, Andy McRandy (like Peter Differ, a spokesman for Herbert's own beliefs about the Territory and the Aborigines) chides Norman for his failure to acknowledge publicly the virtues of the Old People. Norman is a true "yeller-feller" caught between the Old People who accept him and the whites who reject him; he is attracted to the mystique of one and the skills of the other.

In the last part of the book the threads are drawn together. Frank McLash and Charles Ket murder Con the Greek and go bush, where they join with Jack Bramble (Mark

THE OUT-STATION *Russell Drysdale*

XAVIER HERBERT
1901-1984

Xavier Herbert's birth was never registered and his parents never married. However, it appears that he was born on 15 May 1901 at Port Hedland, Western Australia.

His father was an engine-driver and a former prospector. Herbert grew up amidst the raw material of *Capricornia* and *Poor Fellow My Country*, riding beside his father in the engine, with the full-blood Aborigines and mixed-blood fringe dwellers, seeing drunkenness and fights. In fact, his own nose was broken in 1919 when he went to the aid of a policeman in a riot.

In 1913 the family moved to Fremantle and Xavier was there educated at the state school, then the Technical School, and finally the Christian Brothers College, which he left at 17 to study pharmacy. He qualified, and in 1923 became a pharmacist at the Melbourne General Hospital. He also attended the Medical School in Melbourne, and worked at a VD Clinic in Little Lonsdale Street. His first short stories appeared at this time, under the name of Herbert Astor, in *The Australian Journal*.

Between 1925 and 1930 he worked at various jobs in Sydney, Queensland and the Northern Territory, where he worked on a Darwin newspaper before becoming a railway fettler (more grist for *Capricornia*'s mill) in the Rum Jungle area, inheriting, he says, "a harem of young lubras from my predecessor who died of a surfeit". He then went to the Pacific, and worked as a sailor.

For 10 years he struggled to write a novel, "Black Velvet", about white men and black women. With the help of a Jewish milliner, Sadie Nordern (later his wife), this became *Capricornia*. He sometimes wrote for 32 hours at a time and then slept for 16. The book was rejected by Jonathan Cape.

In 1932 he returned home, and P. R. Stephensen agreed to publish it in the Endeavour Press if Herbert re-drafted the novel.

In 1933 he did this. The novel was actually being typeset when Stephensen went bankrupt and the type was melted down. Herbert went bush. In 1935-36 he was temporary Superintendent of Aboriginals in Darwin, and later was involved in mining and in a native co-operative.

In 1937 Stephensen again took on *Capricornia*, and published it in 1938 in time to enter it for the Commonwealth Sesquicentenary Literary Competition. It won the novel section.

Of the book he said, "My only great feeling is my love for this good earth; hence that must have been the greatest feeling expressed in *Capricornia* . . . It is a hymn-book in adoration of Australia."

He also wrote to Miles Franklin about his reaction to the news of winning the prize. He was in Darwin at the time.

> When the news came I was stunned for a moment; but only for a moment; for I promptly bought a case of beer & called in all the bums and bagmen and Greeks and Chows and Yeller fellers about, and got well and truly tanked.

In 1940 Herbert was awarded the Gold Medal of the Australian Literary Society for *Capricornia*, and was given one of the first Commonwealth Literary Fund awards. During the war he joined the AIF. In 1945 he went with Sadie to live near Cooktown before moving down to Redlynch, near Cairns, his home for many years. After Sadie's death in 1979, he went on a number of long trips around Australia and was in Alice Springs when he died in 1984.

Although Herbert produced several more books before *Poor Fellow My Country*, none repeated the success of *Capricornia*, partly perhaps because of his ambivalent attitude towards writing and writers. He often said that living comes before literature, and once had the temerity to claim that flying a light aircraft is more difficult than writing a book.

In 1964, while doing a locum as a pharmacist in Atherton, he started to sketch *Poor Fellow My Country*, which eventually, all 850,000 words of it, was published in 1975 to much acclaim.

"Any fool," Herbert once said, "can write one good book. It takes a good man to write two good books." Herbert was a good man.

Shillingsworth) and Joe Mooch (Chook Henn), not telling them about the murder. Norman, on a walkabout, meets Tocky, who has fled the Mission. Despite her highly irregular life, her poor command of English and her superstition, there is something irresistibly attractive about Tocky. She and Norman almost immediately become lovers, but he grows bored with her and leaves her. She shoots Frank McLash when he attempts to rape her. Norman, returning, is ignorant of the shooting, but takes pity on Tocky and installs her as housekeeper at Red Ochre, which he has been managing since Oscar's death.

Mark, now a pitiable old man, turns up at Red Ochre and Norman takes him in. This necessitates sacking the cook, Cho Sek Ching, the brother of the man Mark murdered. Cho informs on Mark, who is arrested and tried for the murder. Thanks to the Lawyer Bightit, "The Shouter", Mark is found not guilty.

Norman is then tried for abducting Tocky (who is now pregnant). After a superb denouncement of the missionaries, he is sentenced to three months' imprisonment, while Tocky is locked up in the Halfcastes' Compound.

Later Tocky escapes from the Compound and goes back to Red Ochre, whence she intends to go bush to have her baby. Norman sees troopers coming and, thinking they have come for her, tells her to go off with the wild binghis, or else to hide in the old broken tank. In fact the troopers have come to arrest him for the murder of Frank McLash. The police have found his skeleton and the rifle he used, which was stolen from Norman, who thought he had lost it. At Norman's trial, again thanks to "The Shouter", Norman is found not guilty.

Returning happily to the station, with the promise of good times ahead, Norman goes up to the stock tanks. He sees the flutter of blue cloth by the old broken tank.

> He climbed the ladder, looked inside, saw a skull and a litter of bones. He gasped. A human skull. No—two—a small one and a tiny one. And human hair and rags and clothes and a pair of bone-filled boots. Two skulls, a small one and a tiny one. Tocky and her baby!

It is the end of the book, another tragedy of mischance. In *Capricornia*, the patterns of the human will are crossed by human weakness. The unlucky ones are wiped out by fate. Herbert's savage indignation is against human prejudice, stupidity, hypocrisy and greed, not against fate.

His prodigious comic sense saves him from blind railing or crippling bitterness. Despite the incidental and final tragedies, and the revealed wrongs, *Capricornia* is not a tragedy. It belongs with the great books of what Balzac called the "Human Comedy".

FLYING FOX
AND
DRIFTING
SAND

LONDON 1938

Droughts, like deserts, are rather hard to define, and in this part of the world especially so. Theoretically a drought can be measured by comparison with a normal year; but there is no such thing as a normal year or normal rainfall here: an average rainfall perhaps, but normality is a matter of opinion. (When an average annual rainfall of 8 inches is derived from these figures for successive years, 12, 3, 6, 14, and 5 inches, what is a normal year?) Moreover, in practice, one is forced to conclude that the measure of a drought depends on the number of stock carried on a property. As this will undoubtedly be a novel idea to most people, I had better explain it more fully.

The most important features of the climate of the semi-desert pastoral country of South Australia are infrequent rains and an exceedingly dry atmosphere. The latter means excessive evaporation, especially in the summer when temperatures of over 100° are far from rare. This in turn means that the lighter falls, which merely moisten the surface of the soil, are valueless to promote the growth of plants. Plant growth, and thus stock feed, depends in fact on a very small number of "good" or effective rains.

Many a time I have been told that the total rainfall for the year means little or nothing: "Sometimes when it is above the average things are tight all the time". Usually my informant would go on to declare that he could do splendidly on five inches a year, if he could select how and when it was to fall. "I'd have a couple of inches," he would say, "in November, and another inch three weeks later. That would give me summer feed. Then I'd have the rest as a good, slow, steady fall in June or July when the weather was cool, and I'd be set like a jelly for the rest of the year."

A few rainless months hold no terror for the sheepman because the feed growing in that country is so persistent. It does not rot away and disappear after growth has stopped and the greenness gone, but remains highly nutritious. To anyone used to "better" country, the sight of fat and thriving sheep where the only visible fodder is the shrivelled and unappetizing-looking saltbush and a sparse grey prickly growth of bindi-eye always seems next door to the miraculous.

A certain amount of feed will grow after every good rain. Some of it will be provided by ephemeral plants, which thrive in the arid belt solely by virtue of their power to germinate, flower, and seed in an incredibly short space of time (in fact they are drought-escaping rather than drought-resistant). Much of it, however, will be persistent, and will hang on indefinitely, dormant or even dead.

Now it should begin to be clear why the intensity of stocking is so important. The sheepman is presented by mother nature with periodic supplies of fodder for his stock in a highly imperishable form. If he is cautious he will use them carefully, knowing that the next gift, like the dividend from speculative mining shares, may not appear when it ought to. If he takes a chance on regularity of payment, so to speak, and runs big numbers on his property, he may be badly caught out. He will then suffer from a drought which his neighbour may have escaped.

I had read a lot, and seen a little, of the recent drought in western Queensland, during which millions of sheep had perished. I was therefore rather surprised to discover that sheep were not dying, and had not died, wholesale in South Australia, which had apparently suffered an equivalent reduction in rainfall. The explanation of this seemingly topsy-turvy state of affairs—of almost-desert proving safer in a drought than a region with about twice its rainfall—is purely botanical. The plains of western Queensland are grass country, and grass will lose its nutriment, rot, and blow away in a relatively short time. South Australia, on the other hand, possessed in the perennial saltbush and bluebushes a reserve supply of fodder which would only disappear as it was eaten.

The fact that the "bush" had been eaten too much during the lean years when other feed had failed turned out to be the key to the problem of drift and erosion. Over-grazing had killed and destroyed the bush over thousands of square miles of country; and when the plant cover had disappeared, the soil lay unprotected at the mercy of the wind.

Economic biologist Francis Ratcliffe wrote this book as a result of his investigations of the habits and life cycle of the flying fox in Queensland and the problems of arid country erosion in South Australia. He observed the flying foxes in 1929-30, and the shifting sands in 1935.

As he says himself in the Preface to the first edition:

The two parts of this book may at first sight appear to have no relation to one another. Nevertheless they are related in that they portray different faces of one and the same country.

They are also related by the character of Ratcliffe himself and the people he meets, whether on the little dairy farms by the Queensland jungles or on the vast sheep and cattle stations of the South Australian saltbush and bluebush country.

Ratcliffe is further proof that scientists are among the

world's best writers when they address the general public. The eye both for detail and the whole, the ability to balance cause and effect, and the intelligence to draw reasonable conclusions are all evident in his plain but lively style. Ratcliffe, whether riding his motor cycle around Queensland, or going on a nightmare journey in the old Dodge utility with the Birdsville mail contractor, has the gift of companionship, an ability to respect all types of people he meets and to learn from those who have no academic qualifications.

He also has the benefit of extraordinarily interesting subject matter. Very little was known of the behaviour of the giant fruit-eating bats, of which there are four species in Australia, when Ratcliffe went to study them. He was amazed at their numbers; he estimated that one flock exceeded half a million, and learnt that there were bigger congregations of them on Cape York, which he did not visit.

Droughts, like deserts, are rather hard to define, and in this part of the world especially so. Theoretically a drought can be measured by comparison with a normal year; but there is no such thing as a normal year or normal rainfall here: an average rainfall perhaps, but normality is a matter of opinion.

There is an engaging spontaneity about Ratcliffe and his journeys. He writes, before the Queensland trip:

When I left Brisbane for the north I had no plan of campaign. I had no idea of how long I should be away, or where I should finish up. This is quite the best way of setting out on a journey.

Ratcliffe admits the failings of his English eyes in understanding the quality of Australian light and landscape, but he has no difficulty at all in making contact with local amateur naturalists. The remarkable John Schmieder, crippled by rheumatism, shares his inexhaustible flying-fox lore with Ratcliffe. Mrs Curtis of Tamborine Mountain teaches him about birds and shows him how to walk through the jungle. Even so, on a later occasion he brushes against a stinging tree, which causes him agony for several days and for three months after sets up a tingling itch every time he bathes his arm in cold water. Ned Sutton in the Border Ranges tells him about beetles and takes him into a remote area to talk to timber cutters felling hoop pine. Ratcliffe admires the axemen for their skill but takes Australians to task for the national recklessness in felling too many trees.

There are also dozens of sharply observed sketches, as of the two swearing urchins who take him on a battered old horse-drawn cart to look at a flying-fox camp. One of the boys, seeking to apologise for his mate's purple language, turns to Ratcliffe and says, "He swears bloody terrible, that bastard."

Some of the best portraits are of those who live in or traverse the desert. Men like the drover Alec Scobie, or the unbeatable father and son, Harry and George Williams, who carry the mail through burning sandhills or, when the drought breaks, the swamps of the Diamantina or the Cooper.

A young English scientist might be thought to have little in common with such people. Nothing of the sort; he enjoys them and they obviously like him. He has the advantage of realising the importance of machinery, of motorcycles, utilities (or buckboards as they were called then) and trucks. The trip up to Clifton Hills and Birdsville, and then back to Marree is far more real to the reader after the description of Harry Williams' Dodge. His new vehicle, a Ford V8, had been put out of action on the previous trip.

I had seen some warriors in my time, but that antiquated Dodge had them all licked hollow. I can best describe her by saying that there was not a single part of her . . . which had not been bashed and broken and rather obviously repaired. The sides of the bonnet had been discarded as unnecessary; one of the lamps was smashed, and from it a length of wire dangled hopelessly; the cap of the petrol-tank was a tobacco-tin held in place by a strap; and there was no sign of a spare wheel or tyre. Later I learned with something of a shock that she had no brakes—not merely bad brakes, but no brakes at all: the shoes had been taken out of the drums. What a vehicle, I thought anxiously, with which to tackle one of the longest, loneliest, and driest mail runs in Australia.

The essence of the Australian outback is in that car and the two men who keep it going.

Ratcliffe does not make *Flying Fox and Drifting Sand* the means of conveying his scientific conclusions, which were presented in two reports. He gives the essence of his findings which, in both the Queensland jungle and the South Australian semi-desert, are related to the vastness of Australia. Ratcliffe traces the migration of the flying foxes, from near the Victorian border to the north of Queensland, he studies their feeding habits, noting their fondness for the nectar in eucalyptus flowers, and pursues them into mangrove swamps with their "spider roots" and listens to the mangoes thudding on iron roofs as the bats feed in the trees. He shoots them for his work, in what seems rather excessive numbers (60 in 6 shots) and gets to know their sounds and smells. His conclusions are that it would be expensive and wasteful to try to control them, as some of the fruit growers wanted the Government to do. Moreover, they were in any case "in a process of natural and fairly rapid decline".

The vastness of the erosion problem also defeats him, although his findings today are as reasonable as they were in 1937. One of the most important of these concerns the inevitability of drought, and the stubborn refusal of the

DROUGHT(ARKABA) *Hans Heysen*

FRANCIS RATCLIFFE
1904-1970

Francis Ratcliffe was born in India in 1904 and educated in England. He studied biology at Oxford under Sir Julian Huxley, who later wrote an introduction to Ratcliffe's book, *Flying Fox and Drifting Sand*.

In 1929, in pursuit of his career as an economic biologist, working in the field of applied ecology, he came to Australia to spend two years studying flying foxes in Queensland for the Council of Scientific and Industrial Research (later the CSIRO). As he says: "By 1929 a considerable number of odd facts about the natural history of the Australian species of flying foxes had been accumulated, but anything like an accurate picture of their population as a whole and what might be called their economy was conspicuously lacking. It was my task to provide such a picture." After presenting his report, Ratcliffe returned to England for four years, but rejoined the CSIRO on his return to Australia in 1935.

This time he was sent to an entirely different area of Australia, to study the extent and causes of erosion and soil drift in the arid areas of northern South Australia. As he admits, he knew nothing about soil erosion at the time. He was soon to learn.

Professor A. E. V. Richardson, of the Waite Institute in Adelaide, had recommended him for the job, and briefed him on it. It was reported that the stock-carrying capacity of much of this area had been reduced by 50 per cent or more, and that whole blocks were being abandoned by farmers on account of drift. Professor Richardson commented: "It is a terrible country you are going into. You will be glad to escape from it; but it will get you, and ever after you will find yourself longing to go back . . . You are a biologist. It is quite on the cards that the problem will turn out to be a purely biological one, hinging on the rabbit. In that semi-desert country rabbits breed up to plague numbers every few years, and are very destructive to the vegetation . . . When we know exactly what is happening, and why it is happening, we should be able to decide whether the solution lies with botanists or soil experts, whether it must depend on the control of the rabbit, or is fundamentally a question of stock management."

Flying Fox and Drifting Sand was written following Ratcliffe's two missions. It was first published in London in 1938.

Ratcliffe stayed in Australia. He lived in Canberra and worked with the CSIRO. During World War II he joined the AIF, and served as a Major in New Guinea and the Islands.

He was asked by Angus and Robertson if they could bring out an Australian edition of his book. In October 1945 he wrote acidly from Bougainville to W. G. Cousins to ask, "Whether you have forgotten, or just diced, the idea of publishing my book, *Flying Fox and Drifting Sand*." In 1946 he was asking, if the reprint were in fact going ahead, if the Julian Huxley introduction could be dropped as it was "mostly extracts from my book". The Australian edition (with the introduction) eventually appeared in 1947, and has been reprinted seven times.

Ratcliffe was closely involved in the experimental stages of myxomatosis, and published a number of papers on rabbits. He was co-author of a book on Australian termites.

Dr Ratcliffe was awarded the OBE. He died in Canberra in 1970.

Australian people to recognise it.

The plain truth is that the pastoralist's existence will always be a gamble in the Australian inland, where the profits of the good seasons must be balanced against the losses of the droughts.

As he has already explained, the vital desert shrubs, the saltbush and bluebush, must not be overgrazed, otherwise the sand will start to drift. He also established that "sand does not make a desert" in the sandhill country. These enormous sandhills are not moving to take over other country, and after rain they are a swift and excellent source of good feed.

To anyone used to "better" country, the sight of fat and thriving sheep where the only visible fodder is the shrivelled and unappetizing-looking saltbush and a sparse grey prickly growth of bindi-eye always seems next door to the miraculous.

Anyone who has travelled frequently through the far north-east of South Australia, and has been haunted by its fierce beauty and its incredible transformation by flowers after rain, will be puzzled by Ratcliffe's fear of it. Time and again, despite his fascination with it and its inhabitants, he admits that the country gets on his nerves. "During my short visit [to Clifton Hills, a huge station on the Birdsville Track], I was jumpy as a cat." Admittedly there was a bad drought, and he was the prisoner of a sandstorm for several days, but later, after the breaking of the drought and travelling with difficulty by the Barcoo and the Cooper, he confesses:

I was back in a land which awakened in me an instinctive anxiety and distrust, deepening at times to a formless fear.

It is the honest admission of a man who, despite long residence in Australia, is still thinking as an Englishman.

The desert may have worried Ratcliffe, but he has a complete rapport with those who live there. One of the finest tributes to them is his description based on the people of Clifton Hills:

It is a strange thing, but the more desolate and cruel the land, the finer, in their simple way, are the people. I defy anyone to move among the folk who live in the Australian interior and come away without an unshakable belief in the fundamental decency and kindness of the human race.

It is heartening that this is the opinion of a scientist.

Christina Stead

THE MAN WHO LOVED CHILDREN

NEW YORK 1940

Sam hit her, with his open hand, across the mouth. Looking back madly at him over her shoulder, she raced into the hall, groped and found the stick in the dark and struck the gong, shrieking for the children to come downstairs and saying she would rouse the neighbours, that the beast was at her again. When she heard Bonnie on the stairs, she ran into the kitchen, seized the bread knife, and rushed at him, slashing him backwards and forwards across the arm and shoulder, and began slashing at his face before he had the presence of mind to knock it out of her hand and push her away. She stumbled and fell to the floor, where she lay exhausted and trembling.

Bonnie and Louisa, who had been brought up short in the hall, petrified with horror, rushed into the kitchen, crying and begging the man and woman to come to their senses. Blind with her tears, and sobbing loudly, Louie, tripping over her night-dress, went to help her mother, who was resting on her elbow as she got up slowly, weeping dejectedly. Louie began tugging at her, but Henrietta pushed her away, saying, "Don't touch me, I've had enough of everything!" while Bonnie was wiping the blood off Sam's face and arm with a damp cloth, crying and saying, "What happened, Henny? Whatever happened, Sam? Oh, it wasn't because of me? What did you do to her, Sam? The children—!"

Sam was unable to articulate, full of rage, fear, and astonishment. He pushed Bonnie away and finished the wiping himself. Then as he watched Henny, leaning, like the dying gladiator, on her arm, and brushing her hand across her mouth, he said in a strange, distant voice, "Leave us; go to bed and leave us!"

Bonnie looked at him, terrified, but said nothing.

Henny looked up at him, "I don't want to be left with the likes of you; I'm afraid for my life." She began to move like a creature broken with pain, and sniffing, still feeling her mouth with a drooping wrist, she stood up and pushed back her hair.

Sam said automatically, "The gas is on full!" and Henny turned to it, and turned it down under the bubbling kettle.

"Go to bed," Sam admonished Louie in an undertone. Louie and Bonnie moved out, full of doubt, but not daring to intervene, realizing that this was a conflict on another plane. Bonnie, pausing on the stairs, sent the little girl to bed, whispering to her, "I'll just wait for a while, darlin'; don't you fret: Bonnie will watch."

"Henny!" Sam said.

"Oh, what do you want?" she murmured mournfully.

"Look at me!" He held out his arm and turned his face, showing the cuts which were still bleeding.

She gave a swift glance and picked up the damp dishcloth which she handed to him again, "Here, wipe yourself off: don't stand there with that blessed martyred air like a saint in church!" She looked at him awkwardly and with much difficulty wrenched her ashamed gaze away.

He dropped the rag in the sink, dried his hands, and, looking at her sideways from the towel, said evenly, "The worst part of it is, Pet, that you love me still in a way; everything you do—even this!—shows me that. I know it!"

A novel of over 500 pages about a hopelessly mismatched married couple, their terrible rows, their lives of hate and rage, might seem too much to take. After all, one reads for pleasure, even a harsh book like *Crime and Punishment*.

Christina Stead's inimitable achievement is that *The Man Who Loved Children* is not only highly readable but endlessly fascinating. Sometimes it is the fascination that goes with horror, sometimes with pity, but mostly it is the fascination aroused by endless energy and exuberance. The sheer invention of Christina Stead's style cascades over the pages and sweeps the reader with it, even if, appalled at what is going on, he or she makes a feeble effort to stand back from it. The book is a triumph of language, to be compared in this respect with James Joyce's *Ulysses*—but not in imitation, as Christina Stead is an entirely original writer.

Exuberance can be tragic and manic as well as playful. All three varieties co-exist in *The Man Who Loved Children*. Although the subject of the book's title is Sam Pollit, it is his wife Henny (short for Henrietta, and somewhat symbolic of an early elegance lost and rough-handled), who begins the book and who emotionally and dramatically brings it to its climax. The book ends, however, with Sam's daughter Louisa, Louie (the Pollits never leave a name alone), going off alone on "a walk round the world". And Sam, Sam whose roots in the rich soil of self-esteem even the most frightful tempests have not shaken, lives optimistically on, with a new job as a biologist and beginning a new career as a broadcaster.

One cannot talk about *The Man Who Loved Children* without using the word "extraordinary". The Pollits and their six children are extraordinary, but the basic word "ordinary" is also part of their lives. The young children, apart from Louie, are perfectly normal, cheerful children. Like all children, they have imaginations which, when aroused, lead them easily into extraordinary worlds, happily set off by Sam's lectures or Louisa's stories. These are particularly good stories. Louie is surely going to be a writer, although she would love to be a dancer were she not so lumpish.

The Man Who Loved Children, for all the virtuoso performances from Henny and Sam and Louie, is like a triple concerto, firmly based on the orchestra. The children give the book its richness of tone, its solidity and its resonance. They hear their parents shouting insults at each other upstairs, they see and hear Louie rush weeping to her room, but to them it is the way the world is and still they love their parents and their half-sister. Their rowdy, riotous normality is sometimes overlooked in discussions of *The Man Who Loved Children*, but it is basic to the novel.

*H**e dropped the rag in the sink, dried his hands, and, looking at her sideways from the towel, said evenly, "The worst part of it is, Pet, that you love me still in a way; everything you do—even this!—shows me that. I know it!"*

Apart from the characters and the language, an important aspect of *The Man Who Loved Children* is that it is an Australian story set in the outskirts of Washington, DC. No book better demonstrates the ability of great art to rise above time and place than *The Man Who Loved Children*. *Anna Karenina*, for example, is unmistakably Russian, yet its subject is universal. Americans do, and are perfectly entitled to, regard *The Man Who Loved Children* as an American book. The details of the environment and the time (1936) when the book opens are lovingly realised. But Australians, and Americans, too, if they wish to know, can be told with certainty that Tohoga House, the rambling old place in Georgetown, DC, with its few acres of orchard, that Sam rents from his father-in-law for $50 a month, is in fact the Steads' house in Watsons Bay, Sydney. It is still standing in Pacific Street by the harbour. The house the Pollits move to in Annapolis, when Henny's father dies, his financial affairs in ruins, is "Lydham Hall", a beautiful property at Bexley in Sydney, that is now a tourist attraction.

In an interview with Graeme Kinross Smith, Christina Stead said:

I translated my family experience detail by detail to Annapolis and Washington. Bill [her husband] and I found the right setting there. We stayed in Annapolis and looked until we found a house that would match "Lydham Hall" and another that matched Watsons Bay. It became a sort of crossword puzzle to change it all over with details about trees, subsoil, salinity and so on supplied by the Washington government . . . you'd be surprised by the number of people who say it reminds them of home!

She also says *The Man Who Loved Children* shows "what the family could be".

You see, as a child I thought those stories about happy homes, happy families, were all conventionalities. It was a surprise later to find that some families actually got along. Our family got along in a way, I suppose. But my parents weren't ones to hold back, you see—they were melodramatic, voiced everything.

Christina Stead's mother died when she was two, and she was five years older than the oldest of the six children of her father's second marriage. In this, and other ways, she is exactly like Louisa, and also in her acceptance of her odd parents. She merely thought that all families were like hers. But like Louisa, Christina had to get away in the end, not only to live her own life, but to survive.

Henny is "an old-fashioned woman", "she belonged to this house and it to her", in her mid-thirties she already thinks of herself as old and worn out, a prisoner of marriage. She lives in a fury of hate and desolation. She gives out messages of death from the beginning of the book, putting her hands around Louisa's neck, then around her own, crying, "I ought to put us all out of our misery!"

Sam is 38, handsome, a scientist, a health fanatic (no alcohol), a moralist (no extramarital sex despite the fact that he and his wife do not sleep together), in love with himself as a god of love. He walks in the orchard at night.

"Mother Earth," whispered Sam, "I love you, I love men and women, I love little children and all innocent things, I love, I feel I am love itself—how could I pick out a woman who would hate me so much!"

On such occasions Sam seems as if he could be a poet, a disciple of Walt Whitman trapped into marriage. But in fact he has no poetry in him at all; in Whitman's word he "incorporates" nothing; all his fun and invention with the children, his baby-talk and nicknames are only an extension of his own will to dominate.

Henny does not want to dominate anyone; "she did not bother her head about her children". She sees them grabbing what they want and lets them get on with it, for she "belonged to a grabbing breed". But she has plenty of imagination, as her tirades and coupled curses show; she, in fact, is more like Whitman, for she understands death.

It is a mistake to look too gloomily and apocalyptically at *The Man Who Loved Children*. Its world does blow up in the end, but in the meantime, for the children, "There were excitement, fun, joy, and even enchantment with both mother and father," and it was just a question of whether one wanted to sing, gallop about and put on a performance ("showing off like all Pollitry," said Henny), or look for mysteries ("Henny's room is chaos," said Sam).

It would need a long quotation to convey the "excitement, fun, joy and even enchantment" of *The Man Who Loved Children*. It is an expansive book, and has been criticised for being too expansive, but without this torrent of exuberance Christina Stead could not have conveyed the quality of the Pollit household.

With Louie it is a different matter. She is always writing and telling stories. The little children love her stories, and one of them, "Hawkins, the North Wind", is so good that it is quite possible to believe in her talent with some of her own faith. Her play, *Herpes Rom*, or *The Snake-Man*, recited in an invented language and then in English, is a disaster with Sam but aesthetically a success. Her adolescence and her mental and creative development set her apart, but it is a household where no-one is allowed to be apart. There must be no secrets from Sam, loving Sam, Sam who adores his Loogoobrious LooLoo. In a dreadful scene late in the book Sam discovers Louie's hidden book of poems to her

THE PARENTS *Noel Counihan*

CHRISTINA STEAD
1902-1983

Christina Stead is perhaps the most international of Australian writers. She lived in Britain, Europe and the United States from 1928 to 1974, and only one of her novels, *Seven Poor Men of Sydney*, is wholly set in Australia. Yet, as she has cheerfully commented, "Australia formed me, I must be an Australian."

Stead was born at Rockdale, New South Wales on 17 July 1902, the only child of David Stead, a distinguished scientist and naturalist, and Ellen Stead. Her mother died when she was two. When her father remarried the family moved to a fine old stone house, "Lydham Hall" in Bexley. Its extensive outhouses and grounds provided room for her father's collections of birds, mammals and fish, and a small zoo. Christina describes her father as "an early twentieth-century Rationalist Press Association Fabian socialist humanitarian".

The young Christina attended Kogarah Intermediate High School, St George High School, and Sydney High School after the family moved to Watsons Bay in 1917. Watsons Bay is the Fisherman's Bay of *Seven Poor Men of Sydney*, and most of the first half of *For Love Alone* is set there. The house and grounds there provided the model for Tohoga House in *The Man Who Loved Children*.

Her early reading was avid and wide, and included Shakespeare, Milton, de Maupassant, Ethel Turner, Ethel Pedley, Steele Rudd, and "Banjo" Paterson "whom I have always loved".

Christina Stead completed a two-year course at Sydney Teachers College and in 1921 became a Demonstrator in Experimental Psychology there. She had trouble with her voice when teaching, and resigned in 1924 to work in an office to save enough money to go abroad, like Theresa in *For Love Alone*.

She arrived in London in 1928 and, through her future husband, William Blake, got a job with a firm of grain merchants. Sick and weak from overwork and malnutrition she wrote *Seven Poor Men of Sydney* as "something to leave behind". The publisher Peter

Davies liked it and asked for another book as well, so she wrote *The Salzburg Tales*. Both books were successfully published in 1934.

From 1929 she worked as a secretary at a bank in Paris. Her close involvement in the banking world (her husband was a banker as well as being a writer) gave her the knowledge to write *House of all Nations*.

She lived in the United States from 1937 until after the war, when she and her husband went to live in Antwerp. They later moved around Europe until settling in England in 1953. They were living at Surbiton when her husband died in 1968. By this time she had published 12 books of fiction in England and the USA.

In 1965-66 Angus and Robertson and Sun Books began, for the first time, to publish reprints of her books in Australia.

In 1967 the literature committee of the Britannica Australia Awards nominated her for the $10,000 literature prize. However the management committee decided she was not eligible as she had lived so long outside Australia. In 1974, the year she returned to live in Australia, she was awarded the Patrick White prize.

Of herself she has said:

> I write about events at which I've been present, either as actor or observer ... About myself,—no. I'm unimportant, an observer, a wandering minstrel.

Nevertheless, it is obvious that there is a great deal of Christina Stead in Teresa Hawkins of *For Love Alone* and Louisa Pollit of *The Man Who Loved Children*. The latter novel is her finest work and, without doubt, one of the major novels of the twentieth century.

Although she was a life-long supporter of the Left, none of her books is explicitly political. Her attitudes are well summed up by Michael Wilding in an obituary in *Australian Literary Studies* (October 1983).

> Her opposition to exploitation pervades all her work, whether the exploitation is economic, sexual or familial. She resisted the appropriation of her work to narrowly feminist readings. The capitalist, imperialist and military exploitations were the primary exploitations that had yet to be effectively confronted, resisted and removed.

Christina Stead died in 1983.

---

schoolteacher, Miss Aiden, and jestingly, mockingly, reads them out to the other children who for once think he has gone too far.

Louie shifts the whole emphasis of the book away from marital bickering, albeit on a superhuman scale, to a promise of true creativity (as opposed to fertility). She is the agent of destruction, though excused by her wrongs and her hopes. The change of focus she gives the book is a part of Christina Stead's brilliant construction of the novel. Like Shakespeare, Stead knows when to change the action or to introduce a minor character. Sam's months away in Malaya with a scientific expedition, Louie's visits to relations at Harper's Ferry, Henny's lover who possibly fathers her last baby and betrays her in the end, Aunt Bonnie who for a long time lives with them and herself has a baby by a faithless lover, the schoolteachers, the relations—they all impinge on the Pollit family and give a subtle new view of it.

Sam's loss of his job, their descent into poverty, Louie's increasing exasperation, Henny's descent into hopelessness, all give the last quarter of the novel an inevitable downward drive to disaster.

In an absurd last flourish, dragooning his children-slaves,

Sam orders everybody (except Henny) to assist in cutting up and boiling down a huge marlin and bottling the oil from its flesh. The fishy stink that permeates the house is like a parody of Sam's love, oil from the ocean.

Like everything in *The Man Who Loved Children*, Henny's ultimate fate—poisoning by cyanide—comes from mixed motives. It is bungled in action, half by luck, half design. Louie wants to kill them both, so she can get away, and so the children can have peace. She puts the cyanide and the tea in the cup, Sam comes blundering in with new cups, and her nerve fails. Louie warns her mother by signs not to drink, but her Mother, who knows her time has come, drinks it and dies. Sam, of course, survives. He would. But Louie is free. Sam does not believe her when she tells him the true story.

This is not a moral ending, but the essential story of the Pollits is profoundly moral. Basically *The Man Who Loved Children* is about communication and understanding. Despite their torrents of language, Sam and Henny never communicate. Louie is the one who does, and who will. Although her adult works are as yet unwritten, this is a most convincing portrait of the artist as a young woman.

Eleanor Dark

THE TIMELESS LAND

LONDON 1941

Now the white men, accompanied by Nanbarree and Booron, were landing. Aie! how ugly they were! They were coming forward, nodding, smiling, holding out their gifts as usual, and Bennilong was, also as usual, growing noisy and assertive in his excitement.

Barangaroo thrust her lower lip out and made a contemptuous noise. It was food which they were offering, and there was some of the strange drink, too, which Bennilong was always talking about. It was a magic drink, he said, which brought men strength and wisdom and ecstasy, and he had told her that he believed it to be by virtue of this drink alone that the Bereewolgal acquired their power. Barangaroo was prepared to believe anything of the white men, but she was not prepared to admit that her own people needed any greater strength than was already theirs, any deeper wisdom than that which their ancestors had bequeathed to them in their Law, any sweeter ecstasies than those provided by their tribal rites, by courtship and mating, by parenthood, by life itself.

Upon that occasion when the Be-anga had been speared Bennilong had drunk some of this magic fluid. Barangaroo's own opinion was that it had not made him strong, but only noisy and quarrelsome; not wise, but distinctly more foolish than usual; and as for ecstasy, she had, for the first time, repulsed him savagely that night, for there was a smell upon his breath which she did not like. Now, watching him advance with enthusiasm upon the bottle which Tench was holding out to him, she grunted scornfully, and turned her back.

Bennilong quaffed the wine, and loudly demanded bread and beef. He offered portions to his friends who stood about him, and they tasted the meat dubiously, but refused the bread. It was odd-looking stuff, they said to each other, eyeing it with aversion and squeezing it between their thumbs and forefingers— rather like fungus, pallid, spongy, and unwholesome. Bennilong, gulping down his last morsel with a greater display of relish than he really felt, demanded of Tench:

"You cut hair, beard to-day?"

Tench had brought not only a razor, but a barber, and Bennilong, seating himself upon a log, indicated with a lordly gesture that he was ready to be shaved. From her tree-trunk Barangaroo watched the operation with smouldering eyes. She did not want her man to display naked, woman-like cheeks, like those of the Bereewolgal. When the throng of men surrounding her husband, edging nearer and nearer to watch more closely, hid him at last from her view, she squatted cross-legged on the ground, struggling with a sense of oppression from which she was only aroused by the sound of her own name.

Booron was standing a few yards away, grinning shyly, and twisting the skirt of her straight blue garment between her fingers, nervous and ill at ease, but filled with a trembling sense of happiness. Here was a woman of her own race, the first she had spoken to for eighteen months. She stared wistfully, eagerly, as if in the dark, sullen eyes of Barangaroo she might find a solution of all the fears and desires which had tormented her in that long, long time.

They were quite kind people, the Bereewolgal, and her docile and affectionate nature had taught her to respect and obey them. Was it possible that one so great as Mr Dyon-ton, before whom even the Be-anga sometimes bowed his head, whose dignified gait and solemn mien marked him as apart from his fellows, who was obviously the chief sorcerer of the whole tribe, the leader of their weekly corroboree and the expounder of their Law, should speak other than the truth? She could not believe it possible. She listened attentively when he spoke, stored his words in her retentive memory, repeated them glibly when so instructed. At first, learning to understand their tongue, she had been astonished and delighted to find that new words may clothe an old, familiar story. For she found that these people were trying to teach her of the Maker-of-all, though they called him by a different name, and they pointed, as her own people did, to the Heavens as his dwelling-place. Eagerly she had nodded her comprehension when Mrs Johnson was instructing her. The Law of the white tribe, she had thought cheerfully, was evidently very much the same as her own Law, so she would get along very well with them. But no. It was the same, and yet not the same. There were incredible things in it. She repeated them dutifully, and tried to understand them, but could not. This heavenly Being of theirs, it seemed, expected that one should love one's enemies, which was, obviously, nonsense. The white people themselves considered it nonsense, for they were always quarrelling. Booron had never seen so much hatred and vindictiveness as she saw in their camp.

The new awareness of Australian national identity, and the changing attitudes to Aborigines that came with it, were anticipated to a remarkable degree in *The Timeless Land*. The first of a trilogy, this novel, which was begun in 1937 and finished in 1940, is usually regarded as a saga of the birth of the Australian nation, a re-creation of the events of the first settlement in Sydney from 1788 to 1792.

It certainly is that, but the concept of the book is more

far-reaching and its impact on the reader more profound than a mere retelling of historical events. Eleanor Dark saw the fateful events of those years as involving Australia itself—the timeless land—as well as the human protagonists. The Aborigines had to adjust to a new race of beings with their mysterious technology and their apparent lack of any understandable law. The white settlers had to suffer a strange and hostile country where "not even its seasons or its stars" were the same as they had known. And the convicts, the unwilling cause of the whole confrontation, were despised and feared by both the Aborigines and the free white men and women.

*N*ow the white men, accompanied by Nanbarree and Booron, were landing. Aie! how ugly they were! They were coming forward, nodding, smiling, holding out their gifts as usual, and Bennilong was, also as usual, growing noisy and assertive in his excitement.

To understand the full importance and achievement of *The Timeless Land* it is most important to get all these ingredients in focus. Her success in doing so is a measure of Eleanor Dark's skill, so interesting does she make the historical events which were so well documented by the letters and journals of men like Tench, Collins, White and Phillip himself. These are fascinating enough in themselves, but the great theme of conflict between Aboriginal and white, the land and the new settlers, rolls in like a river under the busy traffic of events.

To give the Aborigines such importance in the narrative took extraordinary powers of imagination and skill. It is worth remembering here that Eleanor Dark had already written four remarkable novels, as well as an undistinguished first novel, before she tackled *The Timeless Land. Prelude to Christopher* (1933) and *Return to Coolami* (1935) were both awarded the Australian Literature Society Medal and went through more than one edition in London. The writer was approaching her theme both as a professional novelist and an amateur historian. She and her husband had made deep studies of the works of Marx, Freud and other explorers of human behaviour. When she came to write about the Aborigines, she was able to do so not as an anthropologist, but as one whose imagination saw them as pre-eminent over the white man in their closeness to the origins of life, to nature and the mystery of things.

In writing in her Preface of the "great virtues" of the Aborigines, she says:

I do not want to be taken for a "back-to-nature" advocate, nor for one who, in these disillusioned times, regards our own civilisation as inevitably doomed; but I do believe that we, nine-tenths of whose "progress" has been a mere elaboration and improvement of the technique, as opposed to the art of living, might have learned much from a people who, whatever they may have lacked in technique, had developed the art to a very high degree. "Life, liberty, and the pursuit of happiness"—to us a wistful phrase, describing a far-away goal—sums up what was, to them, a taken-for-granted condition of their existence.

The events she narrates amply prove this point. The book opens with an unaffected and totally convincing picture of Aboriginal life around Sydney Harbour and Botany Bay before the arrival of the First Fleet. She does not shirk describing the less attractive features of Aboriginal life, particularly the harsh treatment of women; she does not fall into the trap of regarding the Aborigines as "noble savages". She creates an awareness, a waiting, a silence. "Out of silence mystery comes, and magic, and the delicate awareness of unreasoning things." But Wunbula, Bennilong's father, an elder, a teller of old tales and a maker of new tales, is also uneasily aware of the possibility, normally unthinkable, of change. He remembers the first "winged boat" that came (Cook's), and from it in smaller boats, "mysterious beings with faces pale as bones, who spoke an incomprehensible language, and wore coverings not only all over their bodies, but even upon their hands and feet". Wunbula knows that legends of such visitors already existed among his people, and it makes him uneasy.

The First Fleet arrives, consisting of 11 winged boats. Ironically Tirrawuul, an Aboriginal elder, and Governor Phillip both think the other incredibly ugly as they meet. The young, high-spirited Bennilong is soon a brilliant mimic of the white men's speech and gait. One of Eleanor Dark's best insights is the sense of humour of the Aborigines. As she says in the Preface, " . . . one cannot help suspecting that the early colonists had their legs frequently and diligently pulled." This sense of humour makes the Aboriginal tragedy all the more poignant.

The eminent anthropologist Professor Elkin vouches for the accuracy of her general presentation of Aboriginal life. There is no such thing as "the Aborigine" for Eleanor Dark. They are individuals, as are the white men. Barangaroo, the attractive laughter-loving girl who becomes Bennilong's first wife, is cunningly independent beneath the Aboriginal woman's traditional subservience. The historical characters Colbee, Arabanoo, and Gooroobarooboolo (Bennilong's second wife) and the fictional characters Tirrawuul, Wunbula and Cunnembeillee are clearly and sympathetically delineated.

It required less imagination, but a deal of judgement, to cope with the splendid cast of white characters. Governor Phillip, given the almost hopeless task of running the penal settlement, is a worrier. He is determined to do his duty, yet he is a humane man with a vision of what the new country might become, and he has a great respect for the Aborigines. Under him are many remarkable people. Captain-Lieutenant Watkin Tench of the Marines, elegant, intelligent, the writer of a remarkable journal; John White, the naval surgeon; David Collins, Deputy-Judge-Advocate; the cranky Major Ross, Lieutenant-Governor, always embarrassing and hindering Phillip; the fictional convict Prentice, his wife Ellen and his son Johnny who prefers the Aborigines to his own people; the arrogant landholder Stephen Mannion (also fictional)—there are many more.

The problems that faced the First Fleet and the others that followed were appalling. The colony was close to starvation on several occasions. Again and again Phillip appealed to the British Government to send him farmers, but only fresh shiploads of convicts arrived. Phillip kept his nerve with the Aborigines, even on the occasion when he

A DIRECT NORTH GENERAL VIEW OF SYDNEY COVE *Thomas Watling*

ELEANOR DARK
1901-

Eleanor Dark was born in Sydney on 26 August 1901. Her father, Dowell O'Reilly, had been a Labour member of the New South Wales Parliament from 1894 to 1898, and at the time of Eleanor's birth was an assistant master at Sydney Grammar School. He was the author of several books of fiction and poetry.

Eleanor was educated at Redlands, Neutral Bay, and although she had grown up in an atmosphere of intellectual and political awareness, she had not particularly thought about this until her marriage in 1922 to Dr Eric Dark. She has said that in her father's house she had taken "the political scene for granted equally with the literary atmosphere"; although her husband came from a conservative background they would go into a polling booth together, "he to vote Tory and I to vote Labour, quite naturally, without any feeling whatever arising from it".

The Depression years brought them both to the position of publicly supporting the ideals of the Communist Party, though neither of them joined it. Both were dismayed by the Soviet represssions of the 1930s. After the war Evatt recommended that Eric Dark be appointed Ambassador to the Soviet Union; Chifley vetoed the appointment because he believed the Darks were Communists.

Though social issues are important in the novels she published in the 1930s and the 1940s, Eleanor Dark was primarily interested in the psychology of the sexes, and in the social and biological trap which prevented women fulfilling themselves both intellectually and sexually. Her father had introduced the first bill for the extension of the franchise to women in New South Wales in 1894. Eleanor Dark in her first novel, *Slow Dawning* (1932), looked forward to a triumphant sequel.

By 1941, when *The Timeless Land* was a US Book of the Month Club choice, she had published five novels, four of them outside Australia. One of the latter, *Return to Coolami*, was translated into French and Italian. Even so she made very little money out of her books. "Without some other source of income," she told Drusilla Modjeska, author of *Exiles at Home*, a book about women writers, "Australian writers have had a thin time." Her husband always encouraged her writings. She had a studio in the garden of their house at Katoomba, but she was also a mother and a doctor's wife – "There was never enough *time* for writing."

In *The Timeless Land*, because of the nature of the subject, Eleanor Dark abandoned the complex narrative structures of her earlier novels. A further depth is given to the novel by the Aboriginal experience in the book which helps extend it far beyond a simple historical account. She partly explained what she was attempting to do with history in *The Timeless Land* in the course of an interview with Hazel de Berg in the 1950s. History, she said, is "to a community what memory is to an individual. Without memory we should be unable to learn from our past experience, and a knowledge of its history is in the same way indispensable to a nation."

Eleanor Dark's psychological studies of women and family and city life alone would have made her a remarkable novelist. It is an extraordinarily fine achievement to have written these and then something as different as her historical trilogy, *The Timeless Land* (1941), *Storm of Time* (1948) and *No Barrier* (1953). She was awarded the Order of Australia in 1977.

---

himself was speared as the result of a misunderstanding. However, the convicts continued to maltreat the Aborigines and misappropriate their possessions, and consequently there were reprisals. The imbalance of the sexes in the colony was acute. Above all there was no overall purpose or dignity to the whole settlement. Even before leaving England Phillip had said, "I would not wish convicts to lay the foundations of an empire", but once there in New South Wales he cannot help having visions of a future city and "the homes of a free and happy people". It is a recurrent theme, but by 1792 Phillip's concept of it has changed:

> To build a new nation! That had been his dream, and to that end all his efforts had been directed. But he saw now that when he had said "nation" he had meant "England", and that in meaning England he had brought himself into conflict with the land. For the land was not England, and nothing could make it so. It was, indeed, as different from England as any land could conceivably be; it shared with that country not even its seasons or its stars.

While such a problem is making Phillip "ghost-like", the escaped convict Prentice, a coarse, brutal fellow, has achieved some kinship with the land. He farms it and lives with an Aboriginal girl, Cunnembeillee, even though he has to hide from his own race. They have a healthy baby son who plays occasionally with the children of the tribe. With astonishment and joy Prentice finds that he feels satisfaction in ownership and success; he has rediscovered the earth. An illegal squatter, he is, in fact, a forerunner of Phillip's new nation.

Phillip, a remarkably humane man given the era and his background, conceived the idea (however odd it may seem now) of kidnapping Aborigines and using them as interpreters. Fettered by the wrist and ankle, some proved less tractable than others. One of them, Bennilong, enjoyed and understood the white man's ways to a remarkable extent. Eleanor Dark's portrait of him is superb. She never sentimentalises him or makes him a figure of fun, as did some of the early artists who drew him in the European clothes he wore with such panache. Phillip took him to England, and he survived even that, snow and all. Bennilong is the one, above all others, who understands that "Once there had been only one Law; now there was another, the Law of the Bereewolgal [literally, 'the men come from afar'], the law of personal power and personal possessions." And in the house Phillip built for him, where the Opera House now stands, he lives in a "misery of spiritual disunity", growing fonder and fonder of the white man's alcohol.

The book ends after Bennilong has returned from England on the *Reliance* with the new Governor, Hunter. He is sitting on a rock above the sea, drinking. He seizes a stone and scratches savagely over his father's (Wunbula's) rock-carving of the winged boat. He shakes his head and mumbles to himself, "I have forgotten how to be at peace."

It was to be a long time before the whites could learn to be at peace with either the timeless land or its Aboriginal people.

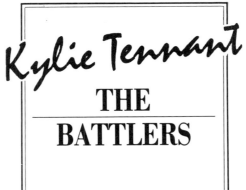

THE BATTLERS

LONDON 1941

She came round a bend where before her the road wound down and down, and then up the ample curves and swellings of another hill that soon she must climb. The Stray stopped to stare:

"'Strufe!" she said admiringly.

Through the rift in the clouds the sunlight poured down and lit the nearby hills, leaving those behind in a dimness of shadow; and in the flare of that light the hills showed a mass of purple flowers, a carpet of them, a brilliant torrent of flowers, pouring down the side of the road in colours of crimson and blue mauve, violet and opal, opening curious throated bells like snapdragons. They rushed up the far hill, overpowering everything—the paddocks, the pasture, the roadside grass. It was as though the clouds had rained crimson and blue and it had mingled in an indelible dye.

The Stray sat down on a rock and loosed her unwieldy pack. She simply sat and looked at the flowers. She also nursed her feet thoughtfully. "I won't forget," she thought gravely. "Not even when I'm old." Two nails had worked through the heel of her left shoe, but only part of her took note of it. She was busy glancing about, drinking in the shades of crimson and purple; pleasure and weariness making her a little unsteady, as though this beauty were some dangerous red wine. "I won't forget," she repeated. "When I get back to Sydney, I'll have this left." If she had

never come out on the track, she would never have seen this unknown flower flaunting its colours over miles of hilly ground.

She was still sitting there in a half daze as Snow and Jimmy and the turnout came clopping round the bend of the road.

"Get up," Snow commanded accusingly, sternly, as though she had done him some wrong.

"We seen you," Jimmy remarked. "And we shouted and waved and you didn't take no notice."

"You got the staggers like an old horse," Snow remarked, as she settled into place between them. "Sittin' down every few yards." His tone was censorious, as though she had, by her very sluggishness, forced him to overtake her. "What was yer sittin' there for?"

"I was looking at them flowers." The Stray had hardly greeted him. "What they called?" She waved her hand at the purple flowers.

Snow gave them a disparaging glance. "Patterson's Curse," he announced gloomily.

"Geeze, it's pretty!"

"That's you all over." Snow was determined to find fault. "It's a bloody weed. Sit there gawping at a weed that's driven many a man off his land. Ain't no use burnin' it." He was rather glad to have something to talk about besides the fact that they were there together again, sitting in the old van, just as they had sat many times. "Some farmer's daughter went out and picked a bunch of the stuff. Brought it home to stick in a vase. Chucked it out when it wilted, and of course it sprouts up lively. Next thing they knew they was fightin' it like it was a fire. Ends by drivin' them off the place."

The flowers flared up from the ground unconquerable. The unrepentant gaiety of the weed, the burning blues and crimsons, set the hills glowing.

"It's a plant that's struck it lucky," the Stray said thoughtfully. "It hasn't got no right, but it's there."

Oh! she was glad that she had come out into the country. She could never otherwise have seen the weed that ruined a land royally and like an army with a million bugles blowing. She would never have heard the lambs crying to the ewes; limping on white, bent legs, like four props that might buckle under them; trotting along painfully like a girl in high-heeled shoes.

The battlers are those who wandered the country roads in the 1930s, on foot or in sulkies or horse-drawn vans, sleeping by rivers or under bridges, sometimes in tents. They are mostly on the dole, but sometimes get seasonal work at a shearing-shed, orchard or cannery. They suffer the humiliations of the dole, having to produce papers for the police in country towns, being given vouchers for goods at the shops.

There is a strong camaraderie between them—although they might take a sheep, or a few sheaves of hay for their horse, or drop a few extra items into a sack at a shop, they will never rob each other. As Kylie Tennant observes, they are the third group in Australian society. The first is made up of the respectable people who have jobs or money; the second, the Aborigines; and the third, the battlers. One of her characters, Snow, reflects:

. . . how the travellers were getting to be like the blacks. They might pretend to despise them and look down upon them; but the travellers were just as much a separate race, distinct from the people who lived in towns, as the blacks were. The white "dolechasers" went about in families and little tribes, with a language of their own, or code of their own that forbade their refusing food or shelter to any like themselves. The women worked and sold things in towns, but the men hunted, or tended horses, or sat in the shade.

Snow, like many battlers, is a natural loner. Although he has a wife and children in a New South Wales country town he often goes nine months or more without seeing them. And when he does go home, "His return was never the scene of wild enthusiasm. One of his sons might stroll inside and announce: 'Hey, Mum, Dad's here.' And his wife would remark grimly: 'Hello! So you're back, are you?' and Snow would say: 'Yeah, I'm back.' "

Resting after his long trek over the black-soil plain in the biting westerly with his horse-drawn van and his dog, Snow makes the decision that alters his life. Instead of the track through Belburra, he takes the one through Currawong and meets the wild, dirty, hungry, almost illiterate Dancy who looks about 60 and turns out to be 19. Feeling sorry for her, he takes her along in the van. Then they meet young Duke, the busker, with his guitar; Miss Dora Phipps, with her airs and lost graces; and the ex-parson Harry Postlewaite, known as the Apostle, with his wife and children, and many more.

She came round a bend where before her the road wound down and down, and then up the ample curves and swellings of another hill that soon she must climb. The Stray stopped to stare:

"'Strufe!" she said admiringly.

The other battlers might drift in and out of Snow's life, but Dancy, despite his reluctance, becomes part of it.

Kylie Tennant has been accused of being sentimental, and in some of her books she comes close to it, but in *The Battlers* her basic optimism is not softened by sentiment. She believes, like the Apostle, in surrender to time, in the basic goodness of people, and in the harshness of God's designs. Snow and Dancy are certainly purged of any softness by their experiences.

Dancy is dirty and toothless; her skin is sun-blistered; and her history is appalling. Her father escaped from an asylum and murdered her mother and then cut his own throat. Dancy had to mop up the blood. She has had an illegitimate child which "the Welfare" took away from her. She has been "vagged" many times and her "husband" has just deserted her. Snow hasn't the heart to kick her out in the rain. "Courtesy to women had once been thrashed into him with a leather strap, and some of the scars still remained."

Snow and his dog, Bluey, are expert sheep-stealers when things get tough. Snow takes odd jobs droving, fencing, shearing, cleaning. He likes fighting and drinking and singing, but long sentences are beyond him. When things go bad for him, as when he finds his wife has taken a lover, he drinks himself blind. On this occasion he becomes very sick, not only from influenza but from being kicked in the face by a mare. While he is in hospital Dancy gets a job on a farm.

Troubles and adventures abound. There are fights between the bagmen and the Aborigines by the river; battles of wits, if not more, with the police; Duke and Miss Phipps singing with Black Olly's accompaniment; Duke hired at the Walfra Show as the yodelling drover; political talks under the bridges with Burning Angus, Snake and the Dogger, with plans to form a Bagmen's Union; and trouble with the Australian Workers' Union organiser, who wants to coerce the wanderers into a union when they are cherry-picking.

Angus expressed his views on the A.W.U. organiser, who, he claimed, was never to be seen except when he collected the ten shillings levy and the twenty shillings for the Union ticket; who hobnobbed with the bosses and drove round in a big car, and didn't care a hoot in hell what the conditions at a shed might be like.

One of the best episodes in the book, and a further revelation of the strange character of Miss Phipps, comes when she is working in a country pub (also a good opportunity for Tennant to satirise the rich young squatters). Phippsy, it is generally agreed, is a pain in the neck. She takes, and gives nothing in return. As the busker reflects:

Nothing, not the finest voice in the world, would persuade him to endure Miss Phipps' company again. She was the nearest thing to a vacuum he had ever met; and the busker, like nature, abhorred a vacuum. She drew everything into herself and gave nothing in return. She sucked all the good out of life, and her absence was a positive joy.

At the hotel where she is working she is similarly regarded and is snubbed by the staff. One night, while the young bloods are celebrating, Miss Phipps decides to go for a walk, away from the hotel "with its reek of drink and moral dirt". On her way back there is a call for help from the darkness at the bottom of the steps. It is "the drunken and abominable Tolly Sampson, the golden calf". Despite her distaste for him, she helps him up to his room. He staggers inside, and then comes swaying back and thrusts some notes into her hand.

Although indignant at the insult to her aristocratic blood, she takes the notes. She is broke as ever, having spent her wages on face-cream, cigarettes and stockings. Three pounds! Riches to her. Then to her astonishment she finds that they are £50 notes. It is true. She is holding £150. "A vivid exultation that was half fear seized her." Then she decides that she, as the future Ruler of the World Feminised State, has the *right* to confiscate wealth that was being put to undesirable ends.

But even as she is thinking this she is making her way to Tolly's father's room. Old Mr Sampson is a tough, hard-working squatter of the old school. She gives him the money, saying in her duchess tones that his son must have confused her with a member of the staff. After a touching conversation with the old man she leaves, not only the room but the hotel and her job, feeling free and unafraid.

When the story moves back to Snow, who is now recovered and going on his way again with his van and horse, the problem is still Dancy, the Stray. Snow is determined that she will not continue with him. "Pure cowardice on Snow's part induced him to bring Angus and the Dogger with him when he went up to the dairy to take away his van and his horse." He leaves Dancy, "sullen and desolate", but not whimpering or making a scene. Alone, she goes dully through her job, crying all night, repeating her old refrain,

UNEMPLOYED MARCHERS *Noel Counihan*

KYLIE TENNANT
1912-

Kylie Tennant was born at Manly, New South Wales, on 12 March 1912, of middle-class parents, and went to school at Brighton College. She refers to that time of her life as "dreary years of conventionality".

She left school at 16 and went into radio broadcasting as an assistant producer and writer of children's programmes. In 1930, when she was 18, she went to Melbourne with almost no money and got a job working in the Barker railway station kiosk. After paying board, she was left with two shillings and sixpence a week, for working days that often stretched to over 10 hours.

She went back to Sydney in 1931, matriculated, and went to university to study psychology and economics, but did not graduate. She took up chicken farming instead, and then went on the roads, dressed in slacks and sweater, jumping trains and hitching lifts, in company with the army of unemployed. In Coonabarabran she met a university friend, a school-teacher called Lewis Rodd, and within a few days they married.

The Rodds then lived in country towns and in slum areas of Sydney. During the 1930s Tennant made several more trips with the battlers on the roads, culminating, in 1938, with a journey in which she drove a horse harnessed to an old laundry cart. She began to write *The Battlers* in 1939. It was published in 1941.

By then she had already published *Tiburon* (1935) and *Foveaux* (1939), about the Sydney slums. Kylie Tennant says:

I've always been a bit of a radical, and I had a political interest in those people because as soon as I grew up I hated industrial civilisation with a hatred only equalled by today's beatniks and hippies. I gravitated naturally to unemployed people because they had been flung off the edge of the industrial wheel and I hated the wheel.

Tennant always immersed herself in the lives of those she portrayed, even to the extent of dyeing her hair, posing as a whore, pretending to be drunk and being arrested and sent to Long Bay Gaol. She did this for *The Joyful Condemned*, which was published in 1953 as a very abridged version of the full text, *Tell Morning This*, which finally appeared in 1967.

During her wandering years she wrote *The Honey Flow* (1956), a book about beekeepers.

During World War II the Rodds moved up to Laurieton on the New South Wales north coast where Rodd taught school and *Lost Haven* (1947) was written. *The Man on the Headland* (1971) is a tribute to a neighbour there.

Kylie Tennant worked for four years in Canberra and Sydney on her biography of H. V. Evatt, which appeared in 1970. The Rodds later moved to Hunters Hill. She was awarded the Order of Australia. She now lives on an orchard in the Blue Mountains, where she keeps bees.

The work people do, and the lives of those who cannot get work, the unemployed and the underprivileged, white and black, remain at the heart of Kylie Tennant's work. As she said of herself, she is a writer who "is not so much interested in emotions as in how people make a living, because I belong to the generation who couldn't get jobs."

"Ain't no damn man any good . . . I 'ates men." As for Snow on the road again, he is soon feeling lonely, missing his "three pests", "the busker, Phippsy, and, most of all, the Stray".

"*You got the staggers like an old horse,*" Snow remarked, as she settled into place between them. "*Sittin' down every few yards.*" *His tone was censorious, as though she had, by her very sluggishness, forced him to overtake her.*

Dancy's chance to rejoin Snow comes when she joins up with Jimmy, Snow's son, who is trying to find his father and travel with him. The scenes where Snow finally accepts her, and not just because of Jimmy, are some of the finest in the book.

There is some vigorous action when the travellers come together for cherry-picking at Orion, but a calamity overtakes Snow when he is revealed in a farmer's headlights—sheep-stealing. He is sentenced to gaol. A casual "So long, Stray" is all she has to hang on to.

"The most thoughtful, as far as her nature could allow," of the wanderers is Dancy. In a notable passage she wonders about the point of it all. Snow, who alone could hold it all together, is a cipher. After his release from gaol he does come back to her although he drunkenly turns on her. "Lemme alone . . . Dunno you, see? Don' want to." And he accidentally strikes her across the face. But she gets him back to the van, and Jimmy says sturdily, "Dad's never been a bloke what drunk much." When Snowy groggily revives, he says "Sorry, Stray . . . You know how it is."

This awkward apology makes all the difference to Stray. They take the road again, to a new mining field where there are lots of jobs. Snow meets Dancy's gaze and says, "Yeah. You an' me's mates. For always."

It is a happy, but not a sentimental, ending; for by this time not only Dancy but the reader "knows how it is".

Eve Langley

THE PEA-PICKERS

SYDNEY 1942

The hop-picking started that very afternoon. It was then that the unkindliness of work showed itself to me. To come here, like a child, and walk around, staring at the strangers, going from fire to fire, laughing and joking, that was the ideal life, although it held a certain deadness of expectancy in it. Sorrow, dullness, quietness and maturity began when the frames of the bins were put up and their bag bottoms shaken out in a paddock down near a broken maize crib where purple castor-oil plants stood around, tall and spiny.

The first thick and beautiful vine fell from the wire with a loud rustle like that of a flying serpent, and it was a pleasure to pick up. But soon, with quick greedy movements, it had to be picked to pieces, and the dark leaves had to be cleaned out of the bin, because if they were too thick there the measurer refused to touch the hops. And that attractive and elfin dampness which we had loved early in the morning became tropically hot and moist at noon, and a sickly inferno, a swampish vat, in the late afternoon. We shifted continually, one at each end of the clumsy heavy bin, trying to hide from the sun in the darkness of the hop shades.

Tired, languid and unhappy, I picked mechanically and tore down vines to the cries of "Pole-o!" around us. And the grim dark young pole-o shouted with an antic twinkle in his eye, "Pick up yer 'ops!"

"One!" the measurer shouted in the distance. "Two! Three! Four!"

"Pole-o!"

"Pick up yer 'ops!"

I felt the lack of humour and action, and my mind, filled with an Encyclopaedia Britannica of life, seethed and teemed. Sensations and thoughts fell on my body in a rich rain, so that I overran with romantic desires and poetry; but no one wanted to hear of it.

Ah, the Italians! They came over to us. They pitched their baggy bins-cum-tents right before us, and what joy enters into the heart at the sight of them. The Little Black Flea leapt over to us and performed on his head, with cries of joy, as he introduced a tall, womanish fellow, as handsome as Blue, and as lazy-looking as myself.

"Dis Salvatore Gallechio." The handsome one, golden-faced, blue-shirted, raised his torn cap lazily and said in an Australian cockney accent, "Ow are yer? Pleased ter meet cher."

"What? Are you Australian? Italian? What are you? Tell us, O golden face from the sun!"

"Oh, I came out from Italy wiv my people from Italy when I wuz young, you see? I lived in Fitzroy ever since. Picked up a bit of Italian from hearing them talking it at home. Of course I can't talk too well. There's a lot of Italians here.

This bloke's name's Toni. Ain't he got wonderful eyes? Dove sei, venga, Toni?"

"Dal Nord vicino al Tyrol," said Toni shyly, his mauve eyes with their fair lashes rolling laughingly as he came towards us. We had never seen eyes like his before. They were a light purple in hue.

"There yar! I knew he come from somewhere near Switzerland. What eyes, eh? Comme ti chiama tua mamma, Toni?"

Toni laughed again, modestly. "O, via, via."

"But she must have called you somethink! Well! See this little bloke 'ere," briskly pushing forward a short slender youth. "This is Pep. 'Ow are yer, Pep?"

"Arlright, thenk you," replied the lad, a mere child, with a serious honest face and the look of one destined to grow up in Australia, make money in her, marry in her and, in her bosom, carry forward a new race. He wore a huge hat, a light yellow felt, popular at that time, cocked on his head.

"Agiusta il cappello, Peppino!" said the Little Black Flea in a fatherly fashion.

"Che?"

"'Agiusta il cappello,' 'e said," answered Il Gallechio. "Fix yer 'at!"

Peppino fixed 'is 'at.

"Andiamo! Come on 'ome!" cried Gallechio and ran with the boys to the section, for it was now knock-off time. The measurer's hours were fixed, and any hops picked after the last measuring were left lying in the bins all night.

One of the richest, most densely packed books in Australian literature, *The Pea-pickers* is on one level the story of two high-spirited sisters who dress up in men's clothes and travel round the country working at picking peas, maize, hops or whatever offers. The girls take men's names, Steve and Blue. On another level it is the story of Steve's two passionate, if chaste, loves. At the same time the whole book is a poetic declaration of love — love of life, of youth and of Australia.

It is also a revelation to find today, some 40 years after it was written, and in a time when the ethnic balance of Australia has shifted from its traditional British base, that it is one of the earliest profound treatments in fiction of non-Anglo-Saxon immigrants in the Australian bush. The Italians in *The Pea-pickers* speak, sing and live as Italians, to the delight of the two girls. There is also an interesting portrayal of the Indian pea-grower, Karta Singh, and of other Indians and Afghans.

The complexity of the book is not only in its subject matter, but also in its style and tone. Sometimes it would

179

seem to be outrageously romantic, or alternatively mock-poetic, had not a sense of irony already been suggested. The balance is cleverly maintained. Steve laughs at herself for her love-frenzies, but at the same time she has a pure, poetic soul which is constantly seeking means of expression. In this she is profoundly Australian, a mixture of the sardonic and the sincere, which non-Australians often find difficult to understand.

Ah, the Italians! They came over to us. They pitched their baggy bins-cum-tents right before us, and what joy enters into the heart at the sight of them.

It was also daring of Eve Langley to allow Steve such a passionate love of Australia at a time when the national enthusiasm of the 1890s had long been soured by wars and the Depression. As it is, *The Pea-pickers* is one of the greatest hymns to the beauty and diversity of Australia.

However, it should not be thought that *The Pea-pickers* is all love, rapture and high-flown sentiment. Eve Langley can also be a stark realist when she wants. Her style is modulated to catch the authentic Australian voice.

There is no gentility about *The Pea-pickers*, and culture has to be tough to survive. Two examples will suffice. At the beginning of the book, when the girls are deciding which men's names they will adopt, one decides for Steve, because of Steve Hart in a bushranging song about the Kellys. The other sister is undecided. Steve suggests Jim, because Lawson in one of his stories says that, "There are a lot of good old mates named Jim, working around in the bush."

Just then there are shouts and rumbles in the night out the back and a voice yells, "To your left, Blue. . . . Back-trapdoor!"

It is the nightcart men. Steve says, "I think the name is Blue."

Again, when the girls who have in fact found a mate called Jim, settle in at Karta Singh's rough bush hut before picking his peas, Steve, who is in love with a young man called Macca, decides their new home needs a romantic name. Being educated in the Classics she decides on "Avernus", with its Virgilian overtones of hell and suffering. She has carved AVER over the door when Blue and Jim call her for a walk. When she returns Macca has continued it into AVERDRINK.

Macca is actually Steve's second love. Her beautiful sister, Blue, who draws and plays the violin, already has a long-standing love in their home town. Steve, plainer and more solid, adores poetry, so when her first love, Kelly Wilson, drives his buggy at a gallop down the track past the girls he is, to Steve, the incarnation of Gippsland and of Poetry. But though they kiss, "There was the cold but happy ideal of the virgin in my mind, forever, a joy and a torment to me." This may be a bit hard on Kelly, but Steve is rebelling against Tolstoy's epigram, "Women are like dogs. They have no soul." She is out to show him that they have, and not just any soul, but a poetic soul.

The girls travel around looking for work and finally find it in Karta Singh's peas. And there (unfortunately for Kelly) she meets Macca, "a poet . . . myself", but also a good, tough

Australian mountain boy. It is instant love. She adores his "heavy, languorous cynicism". They are, strangely, a well-matched pair, she with her virginal passion (although that might alter with some encouragement), he with his love for her non-sensual poetic quality.

"My love for you is pure. I do not need to touch you," he says. And elsewhere, "I fear the sensual, Steve, it clogs and destroys." Yet he is content to risk this elsewhere, but not with Steve. So they spend nights together in a bark hut, or another hut by the sea, but without making love.

The girls first meet the Italian pickers at Averdrink, when they come back to find the front room full of them. One immediately begins to sing "O Sole Mio" to Blue's violin. Steve's initial response is honestly recorded, and typical of a country-bred Australian of the time:

I felt half excited, half irritated to see these Italians in our room. We seemed to have descended another step in the ladder of our race. They really meant nothing to me, however, for I counted them as primitives, children, animals or deaf-mutes . . . Accepting their inferiority, they extended to their superiors many little courtesies that pleased.

One of the subtle developments of *The Pea-pickers* is the dawning of Steve's realisation that "racial ladders" are nonsense, and that Italians are not inferior. The first stage is reached instantly, when Peppino, with his green socks, begins to play the mouth-organ and stamp an accompaniment, and all the richness of old Italian folk songs fills the room.

The next night when they are together, Peppino introduces Domenic Gatto, immediately christened Tomcatto by Steve. He sings opera with tremendous gusto. Peppino immediately falls in love with Blue, and after the pickers have moved on to other jobs in other places Blue is pursued by hilarious love letters, some of them dictated, some of them in Peppino's own attempts at passionate English.

It is partly the unbridled emotions of the Italians that unleash Steve's love of her own country. She remembers the "grave face of Italia" they had once found in an old school book in a bark hut.

Out on a grassy hill, with the land veiled by the smoke of distant fires, in the mystical twilight, Steve cries out, "O Patria Mia! Patria Mia!" and her "naked brown feet kissed the dear earth" of Australia, and her "soul was pure with love of her". It is a most delicate moment, and the Italian words are easier to say in the moment of rapture than "My Country".

At the same moment, Steve thinks, "O, it is painful . . . to be a woman; to long for love and fame . . ." This is the same cry as has been uttered when walking in the bush with Macca: "When will my two great desires, to be loved and to be famous, be granted?"

Blue is quite different, and Eve Langley writes about her in a different style. Picking the 'Ardys' (as the sisters call them) peas with Macca, Steve is living in fairyland. But when Blue is with the 'Ardys, the style is more down to earth:

"Ar, Don't get married, Blue", cried Mrs 'Ardy dolorously to Blue who was always thinking about it, since she had

THE PEA PICKERS *Elaine Haxton*

EVE LANGLEY
1904-1974

Ethel Jane (Eve) Langley was born on 1 September 1904 on a cattle station near Forbes, New South Wales. Her father, Arthur Langley, was an itinerant labourer; her mother, Mira Langley (née Davidson), came from a land-owning family in Gippsland, Victoria. Eve's sister, June Lilian (Steve's mate Blue in *The Pea-pickers*) was born in 1905.

When Arthur Langley became ill with calcification of the bones, Mira took the two girls to Neerim South in Gippsland, where she managed the Sir Walter Scott Hotel at Crossover. Arthur died in 1915.

Eve was educated at Fiefield School, Crossover School, Brunswick Central and finally Dandenong State School. In 1920 she worked as a domestic servant in Dandenong, and later as a printer's devil for Walker and May's in Melbourne, while masquerading as a boy.

She read voraciously from a very early age, and fabricated a background—part Jewish, part Roman, part Greek and part Scythian—for her family.

In 1924, Eve and Lilian, dressed as boys, went apple-packing at Bairnsdale. For the next four years they worked seasonally at pea- and hop-picking. In February 1929 Eve rode over the Alps from Metung to Eurobin, where she met Ray Johnston. She worked with him picking the hops and peas in 1930 and 1931. In the meantime, Lilian had married and gone to live in New Zealand, accompanied by her mother.

Eve joined them in 1932 and took a live-in job at a girl's hostel in Wanganui, while also free-lancing for the Wanganui *Herald*. In 1933 she met a Maori, Ratana, and in 1934 went to live with him at his village. In 1935 she moved to Auckland, where she lived with other Maoris, and met a number of writers and artists, including the artist Hilary Clarke in 1936. Clarke and she were married in

1937 and had a daughter, Bisi. However, it was an erratic marriage, and her next child was not Clarke's. She later lived alone in a shack (what New Zealanders call a bach) at Birkenhead; then Clarke rejoined her and they lived in a bach at Chelsea where their child Karl Marx was born. Clarke supported the family by working as an art master at Elam School of Arts until 1941, when he joined the Royal New Zealand Air Force.

In 1940 Eve wrote *The Pea-pickers*, which won the S. H. Prior Prize for Literature. The conflicts (which form a part of that book) between the demands of being a creative artist and those of the role of wife and mother caused her acute depression, especially as she was attempting to put her husband's artistic work before hers.

In 1942 she was committed by Hilary to Auckland Mental Hospital, suffering from schizophrenia. She stayed there until 1949. She was re-committed for some months in 1950. Her three children were placed in foster homes and later in an orphanage.

In 1950 she took a job in the bindery at the Auckland Public Library and began writing her second novel, *White Topee*. In 1952 Eve and Hilary were divorced. In 1954 Eve changed her name by deed poll to "Oscar Wilde". In a letter to Nan McDonald on 12 April 1954, she wrote:

> As Oscar Wilde I can take anything and the rottenest rebuff and disappointment this world holds and remain myself inviolate, free white and twenty-one, with not a care in the world. But as Eve Langley I just collapse at the first blow into a vomiting fainting mass of death.

She lived alone in a rooming house in Auckland until she returned to Australia in 1957, and travelled from Gippsland up to Cairns. *White Topee* was published in 1954, but thousands of pages of her later work remain unpublished. In 1960 she bought a shack in the Blue Mountains near Katoomba which she called "Iona Lympus". She made an abortive trip to Greece in 1965, and was brought back to Australia through the efforts of Douglas Stewart and Joe Gullett, then Australian Ambassador to Greece.

She died in her shack in 1974; her body was not found until about a month after her death, by which time it had been gnawed by rats.

---

an importuning lover at home. Through the dry purple wings of the crop the warning flashed in glory. "Ar, Don't get married, Blue!"

"Go on," said her husband cheerfully, "I'd get married again tomorrow if I were single." Ah, how he smiled.

Later, when the girls are going home for a visit to their mother, Mia, there is a typically poetic farewell between Macca and Steve, and Macca says he would like to go with her. "Some day . . . when we are married," Steve says boldly, but the boldness is immediately tempered. "Ah, how wrong the words sounded when they were spoken!"

Later, when they are together again, they repeat to each other that neither will ever marry. "Our love has been pure," says Macca, "I've clung to that word ever since we spoke it together." And when Steve puts her arm around him he removes it, saying he lately has been with a girl in Bairnsdale, and he can get that sort of love from her. They part, promising to see each other next spring.

There is more picking, this time of hops in the mountains. There is dancing and singing with the Italians, not enough work, hunger, pilfering of food, maize picking, and no Macca. Steve recognises in herself "a strong, marriageable readiness", but certainly not to "Mrs Wallaby's

Charl", who is obviously on offer. Macca's beautiful letters cease coming. He, clearly, is lost to her.

When they return to Metung for the peas, there is still no Macca. Someone says he is up in the mountains, and "sweet on a cattle-owner's daughter".

Meeting Peppino again, and a friend of his, Leonardo, Steve enjoys their company so much, with "Their natures made open and free with wine", that she gives up her previous ideas about Italians and decides to love Italy. "For the first time in years I felt happy, truly happy. Love hurt me no more."

The book ends with Blue going home to be married, and Steve planning a life alone, writing to the wandering Macca, who perhaps will return to her when he is very old.

The Pea-pickers is a novel about youth, but particularly about two aspects of youth. One aspect it treats is youth as the time when the "young adventurers . . . are . . . fresh with the great goodliness of youth which age crucifies slowly". The other is the ignorance, the naivety, the misguided passions that go with "the narrow vision of youth". Uniting and transcending them both is Eve Langley's enthusiastic poetic imagination which, joined with her humour, gives *The Pea-pickers* its extraordinary freshness and richness.

LUCINDA BRAYFORD

LONDON 1946

"It was a very cheap present," declared Fred, "and my daughter is not anybody. She is somebody. Colman, fill the glasses. We must drink the health of my daughter, the Honourable Mrs Brayford."

While Fred was so assiduously drinking her health, Lucinda was sitting with Hugo under the ti-tree on the cliffs at Sandringham, about ten miles away. They had been lent a bungalow here for the first few days of their honeymoon. It was a wide-verandahed place built of jarrah with a bright-red roof. Ever since they had arrived there she had been surprised and reassured by Hugo's composure. When they had gone along to their rooms they had found Hugo's soldier servant unpacking his luggage.

"Out of here, Wilson," said Hugo, bland but authoritative, as one might speak to a faithful dog. No one in Australia would dare to speak to a servant in that tone.

One of the housemaids sent by Julie from Tourella came in with Lucinda's dresses on her arm. These familiar faces made Lucinda feel that somehow it was improper for her to be here alone with Hugo. When the bride and bridegroom had gone off from other weddings she had imagined them as somehow lost in a mysterious and intoxicating unknown. She had been nervous about her own disappearance into this region, but the commonplace business of settling into a bungalow at Sandringham and Hugo's matter-of-fact manner were both an anti-climax and a relief from her fear. He was now seated beside her, reading semi-facetiously an account of their wedding from the late edition of The Herald.

"A beautiful bride and a handsome husband," he quoted. "That's you and me, m'dear. Well, gettin' dark. Time to turn in."

He pulled her to her feet, gave her a warm hug and they strolled back under the stars to the outer-suburban bungalow.

"Might have a round of golf tomorrow," said Hugo.

Lucinda was a little hurt at his manner, but when they came indoors he amply made up for it. As the days of their honeymoon passed she became grateful for his lack of sentimentality. He showed an excellent sense of how life should be arranged. She had thought that he would be incapable of bothering about the colours of furnishings, but she found that he hated rooms that were in bad taste. He never became ruffled, and that also pleased her, so that by the time they returned to Melbourne she not only loved him with her body and soul, but her mind also approved him, so there was none of that discord which comes when the mind and the heart disagree.

There was one occasion when he did show anger. They were in the Sydney express, and were the first to come into the restaurant car. Hugo stayed by the door to ask the waiter about a table. This waiter was a curious-looking man with a massive and powerful forehead, though the lower part of his face was unpleasant and slightly negroid. Lucinda saw him take something from his pocket and show it rather furtively to Hugo. Hugo's eyes blazed, and he barked, "Get out of here!" with such compressed fury that she thought he was going to strike the man, who smirked and backed away.

"What happened?" she asked, when Hugo rejoined her.

"Nothing."

"What did he show you?"

"Postcards."

"Oh, I wanted some postcards. I promised to send one to Tony."

"They weren't fit to be seen. Please don't refer to it again."

Lucinda Brayford is a perfect vehicle for Martin Boyd's talents. An Australian girl whose father moves from poverty to riches, she marries an English aristocrat and is betrayed by him, though she is befriended by his family and others of his class. Later in the book Lucinda's place in the foreground is taken by her tragic son Stephen, a victim of the time in which he lives and the collapse of a society which once might have upheld his beliefs—he is a pacifist at the time of World War II. Boyd is too honest a writer not to make it clear that Stephen can be rather infuriating, although his weakness comes from bewilderment rather than lack of courage.

Lucinda Brayford begins vigorously. William Vane, a Cambridge undergraduate in the middle of the nineteenth century, organises the throwing into the River Cam of a divinity student, Aubrey Chapman, who is ill at the time and nearly dies of pneumonia. Vane just survives this episode without being sent down, but when his friend Brayford catches him cheating at cards, his reputation is lost. There is only one solution. "You'd better go to Australia," says his father. "You like horses." Ironically Chapman, for his health's sake, is also sent to Australia.

Vane marries the daughter of a station owner, and on his father-in-law's death, he becomes a rich man and builds a splendid house in Kew called The Pines. He again meets Chapman, whose disclosures blackball him from the Melbourne Club. In a further stroke of irony, of which there are many in the book, Vane's son Fred and Chapman's daughter Julie fall in love and marry. Julie imagines that she is going to be rich, but the death of William Vane at sea reveals that the Riverina property, Noorilla, and The Pines are both heavily mortgaged. Fred takes Julie to live at Noorilla in a desperate attempt to recoup the family fortunes.

Fred's attractions have diminished with his finances. Julie hates the rough station life, which becomes even less bearable after the birth of a daughter, Lydia. Miss Watson, the impoverished daughter of a country doctor, comes to live with them. Fred, who can't abide her, calls her "What-ho!" which is corrupted to "Watteau", which name sticks.

Lucinda was a little hurt at his manner, but when they came indoors he amply made up for it. As the days of their honeymoon passed she became grateful for his lack of sentimentality. He showed an excellent sense of how life should be arranged.

Caught by drought, the Vanes are in as desperate a situation as anything in the stories of Henry Lawson. Nevertheless, however vulgar Fred may be, there is strength and no self-pity in him. During the worst of the drought he buys several thousand sheep from his neighbour. Julie and Watteau think he has gone mad. At this stage Julie thinks of leaving him. But Fred has instinctively guessed that the drought must soon break, and it does. Rain pours down. In the midst of it, in the middle of the night, Fred rushes in from outside, wet and naked, and Julie's hatred of him melts at the sight of his beauty and happiness. Lucinda is born as the result of the reconciliation. It is perhaps the most memorable conception in Australian literature.

Fred again becomes rich and they go back to live at The Pines. Lucinda grows up in a confident atmosphere of vulgarity and success, though she is uncorrupted by it. Besides—the highest accolade for Boyd—she has "a composure and sensitive charm which had marked her as a natural aristocrat".

On a trip to Colombo by herself, Julie has an affair with Maitland, an Oxford anthropologist. As a result of this a son, William, is born. Somehow no one suspects that the child is not Fred's.

What is interesting about this affair is that Julie, a respectable Kew mother of two children, discovers for the first time that "the primal impulses of life" can be "at the same time both formalised and vitalised to a degree of passionate intensity . . . By daring to be 'fast' she had cracked her usual protective shell of convention." Such pleasures are supreme, and the aristocrat lives for pleasure, but they are also dangerous, even to the next generation. In a later ironic twist William wants to marry Maitland's daughter in England, and Julie has to tell Lucinda why they cannot marry.

Lucinda's chief ally in her life in Melbourne and by the beach is a young man-about-town who is also a talented amateur of architecture, Tony Duff. Their story is like a novella inside the novel; their public and private lives are observed and analysed with the greatest delicacy. Tony wants to marry Lucinda. Julie does not approve of Tony's attachment to Lucinda; he is 31 and she only 17. Julie wants Tony to tell Lucinda to be "sensible".

When Tony does propose, it is, disastrously, at a dance where Lucinda has booked three dances, including the supper dance, with Captain Hugo Brayford, the new ADC at Government House. Tony is refused. Lucinda marries Brayford, linking this generation again to the three young men portrayed in the book's opening. Julie has helped push her into his arms.

On a picnic to the Christmas Hills Hugo makes love to her:

> . . . the time and the place, the high and piercing sun, the stark earth, seemed to fire in her body in a wild desire . . .

> They never referred to this day again, nor mentioned this hill-top as long as they lived. They were both too conventional to care to think that they might be the passive instruments of forces outside themselves.

It is a curious fact about *Lucinda Brayford* that both Lucinda's and Stephen's conceptions take place in such elemental surroundings in Australia; one with drought-breaking rain pounding on the iron roof, the other under the rays of the sun in mid-heaven. Nothing like this happens in England, where three-quarters of the action of the book takes place. In England and in Europe there is flirting and some love-making, and one happy homosexual relationship and one sublimated one, but no child is conceived. It is as if the graces of civilisation are in England and Europe but they are sterile, while the elemental reproductive life is in Australia.

The pace of the novel is much more leisurely in England than in Australia. Lucinda's acceptance by Hugo's aristocratic relations is relatively quick. Lucinda gradually becomes disillusioned with Hugo. He leaves Lucinda while he goes grouse-shooting in Scotland, and reveals himself to be a compulsive gambler, and goes back to a former mistress. Boyd's portraits of the Brayford family—in particular, Hugo's uninhibited mother, Susannah, and Hugo's brother, Paul, who baffles Lucinda at first with the pungency of his talk about books and art and the Russian ballet—are masterly. She feels insignificant and uncomfortable when he says things like, "The artist and the aristocrat are the only people worthy of consideration . . . the rest of mankind should function merely to make their existence tolerable."

But they grow closer together at Crittenden House, where Lucinda and Paul go to stay with its present Lord, Arthur, and his wife, Marian, who was the daughter of Paul's housemaster at school. Paul says cheerfully that of course the marriage killed his father, the old Lord.

Arthur volunteers (with some cunning prompting from Marian) to refurbish the End House, which is the old dower house, for Lucinda. Paul helps her with the house, tells her the family history and about the neighbours.

The next section of the book is called "Invoking the Storm". But it is not until near the end that its implications are fully revealed, and then in a comment of Marian's to Lucinda and Paul, "We've only lived in a little oasis of bogus civilisation." As the peace of Crittenden is shattered by the storm of World War I, Lucinda has an affair with Hugo's friend, Pat Lanfranc. Hugo is badly wounded in France, most of his face being blown away. Although his brain is undamaged, he never goes out into society again. Lucinda

PORTRAIT OF FLORENCE *Tom Roberts*

MARTIN BOYD
1893-1972

Martin Boyd was a member of a family distinguished in many of the arts. His parents were both talented painters. His father, Arthur Merric O'Connor Boyd, had married Emma Minnie à Beckett, and they lived from 1890 to 1894 at the à Beckett family seat, Penleigh House, in Wiltshire, England. They both exhibited at the Royal Academy in 1891. Martin's brothers were Merric, a potter and painter (who was the father of painters Arthur and David, and sculptor Guy), and Penleigh, a painter (father of architect Robin). Martin was born in 1893 in Lucerne, Switzerland, and brought to Melbourne at the age of six months, thus forming an early link in his life between Europe and Australia. The dichotomy apparent in Boyd's life and work is reflected in his divided ancestry, which included a transported convict, members of the Irish gentry, and a Chief Justice of Victoria.

Boyd was educated at Trinity Grammar in Melbourne and studied architecture, but did not finish his course owing to the outbreak of World War I. It was typical of him that instead of remaining in Australia and enlisting in the AIF he went to England and obtained a commission in The Buffs. He later served with the Royal Flying Corps.

After the war he returned to Australia, but in 1921 he went back to England. There he wrote articles for *The British Australasian,* and began his first novel under the pseudonym "Martin Mills". The most notable of the novels that followed, written under that name, *The Montforts* (1928), was the first of his family sagas (which contained rather too many family scandals to please some of his relatives).

Between 1934 and 1938 four rather delicate, slight novels were published in London, followed by the somewhat enigmatic *Nuns in Jeopardy* in 1940. His first major success came with his fine novel *Lucinda Brayford*, in 1946. This was well received in New York as well as in London, though it took longer to find acceptance in Australia.

In 1948 he returned to Australia and settled outside Melbourne. He commissioned his nephew Arthur to paint a magnificent set of murals in his house; later the house was demolished after being sold to a quarrying company. His tetralogy *The Cardboard Crown* (1952), *A Difficult Young Man* (1955), *Outbreak of Love* (1957) and *When Blackbirds Sing* (1962) form a connected saga of the Anglo-Australian Langton family from 1860 to 1920. Together they make up his greatest achievement.

Boyd returned to Europe in 1951 and died in Rome in 1972. He never married.

Boyd is one of the very few Australian writers who can write with confidence about the wealthy and the gentry, without lapsing into scorn or losing a passion for justice, honesty and conservative moral values. Yet Boyd is a radical conservative. Again, this is a rare creature among writers of Australian fiction.

---

becomes, as it were, the prisoner of a prisoner until Hugo's death.

The title of the third section of the book, "The Leaves of the Fallen Tree", comes from a remark of Paul's to Marian and Arthur, that they are all yellowing leaves on the fallen tree of their class. Paul savages it out in England, flaying those he considers to be the betrayers of civilisation, and also enjoys himself in the South of France, where he now lives with Harry, a handsome young footman stolen from Crittenden House. Lucinda finds a new freedom in the South of France, but her lover Pat Lanfranc (a perfect portrait of the virtues as well as the limitations of an upper-class Anglo-Irish soldier) is unable to share it. In a gentlemanly way, he leaves Lucinda, marries and raises children on his estates in Ireland.

As for Lucinda, even when she is set free by Hugo's death there is no impetus for her to go back to Australia or to do anything more positive than to drift between London and Crittenden, and to look after Stephen. Before World War I Lucinda thinks that, if she had to choose between Australia and England, she would choose England, partly for the people, partly for the influence of the past. As the war continues, she is beginning "to feel that she hated the English" and their sterile life, and almost wishes she had married Tony (who, incidentally, is now a very successful interior decorator in Melbourne). By the 1920s, when hefty, horsy Lydia comes to visit her, things are different again, because of her knowledge of the world, a world so much bigger than Australia. "With Marian, and particularly with Susannah, she still felt herself sometimes to be an Australian, but with Lydia she felt herself absolutely an Englishwoman."

In the end Lucinda is left with "her cool wit, and her good taste which did not entirely depend on wealth". These are inadequate for Stephen. He goes up to Cambridge, plays the flute, and falls platonically in love with a chorister in the King's College choir, whom he later drags out of the water, dying, in the evacuation of Dunkirk. Stephen then falls all-too-conventionally in love with an Australian girl, Heather Vane, who is obviously unsuitable, not only because she is his first cousin but because, as Lucinda sees it, she is a social climber who shares none of his interests. They marry, and she leaves him for a rich stockbroker, one of the "scum" regularly denounced by Paul, a group led by an Australian newspaper tycoon who has bought himself a peerage and the ancient seat of Fitzauncell, neighbouring Crittenden.

In World War II Stephen refuses military service, and is imprisoned and beaten up in the infamous Glasshouse, the military prison at Aldershot. He never fully recovers from his beatings and imprisonment, and dies soon after his release. In King's College chapel, where Lucinda has gone after Stephen's ashes have been scattered on the Cam, she has a kind of revelation which lifts the mood of the book's ending from despair to hope. "For Stephen was a young man of today, and in him was a love of all that was good. He had not been cruel or dishonourable, and he had been a very ordinary young man. There was nothing exceptional about him, except, perhaps, his power of forgiveness." Lucinda has a vision that beauty and good must return to mankind, for "it was as urgent in him as the evil, which at length it must redeem". Paul's denunciations of the modern world are witty and often true, but he has never had a child, and it is youth, at some later time, who will restore the world to health again. The book ends with Lucinda watching and hearing a chorister singing "*Eya, Resurrexit!*"

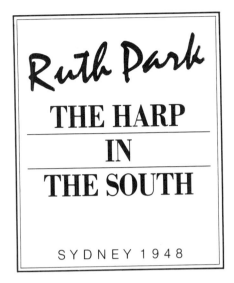

Ruth Park

THE HARP IN THE SOUTH

SYDNEY 1948

Hughie passed Jacky Siciliano's fruit shop, and Bert Drummy's ham and beef, and the second-hand dump and the fish shop. And there was Joseph Mendel's hock joint, with three brass balls swinging like monstrous grapes from the veranda beam. The window was crammed with old jewellery, coarse garnets and peridots and turquoise matrix set in brassy rolled gold; pewter shaving mugs, tarnished silver buckles, cigarette cases with cameos of coursing dogs and girls' profiles; crystal powder bowls with every facet grimy with dust, diamanté inlaid hair slides, gold-rimmed spectacles, naked sets of chipped false teeth, brooches with "Mother" in gold wire, bracelets of square topazes, and little phials full of opal nobbies, like drab pebbles with rainbow veins.

Hughie snorted, and lumbered in through the grille gate. Old Joseph Mendel, his white hair brushed straight back from his sloping forehead, his beak of a nose magnificently jutting, his lips classically curved in the eastern way, looked up from his ledger.

"Good day, sir, what can I show you?" he said automatically, though he instantly noted that Hughie was drunk, that he was truculent, that he had something serious on his mind. Hughie leaned over the counter and blew a gust of wine-sodden breath into Joseph Mendel's face. The old man's expression did not change. He did not even bother to slip his hand along under the counter to reassure himself that the metal-bound cudgel he kept for self-protection was still there.

Hughie exploded into a torrent of filthy abuse. It was filthy mainly because he did not have much vocabulary. He did not have a particularly obscene mind, but the words he used seemed to need adjectival qualification, and so he fitted the expressions he knew into the vacant spaces. With hardly an expression save that of polite interest, Joseph Mendel listened until Hughie, spluttering and scarlet and flaming-eyed, had paused for breath. Then he said, "Be that as it may, what can I do for you?"

Hughie was doubly enraged. The coolness of the man he abused seemed to be a reproach, and to prevent that reproach from being any brake upon his self-confidence, he broke into further abuse.

"That little sneaking swine of a nephew of yours has ruined my girl," he said thickly. Joseph Mendel inclined his head.

"I would not be at all surprised," he replied courteously.

Hughie bellowed, "You mean he's done it to other sheilas?"

"Not that I know about," answered the old man amiably. "But he is twenty, I believe, and most young men of twenty are seducing young women, either in fact, fancy, or desire."

Hughie did not comprehend, so he bellowed even louder. "What you going to do about it?"

Joseph Mendel registered polite surprise. "What can I do about it? What is done is done. It is nothing to do with me. Tommy is not even one of my employees any longer. If you wish anything done you had better see him."

"I'll break his stinking little yid neck," roared Hughie.

"Perhaps that would be the best plan," remarked the old man placidly. Hughie, baffled, tried another tack.

"I'll take it to court."

Joseph Mendel smiled. "Paternity cases cost money, and you will need considerable proof that Tommy is really the culprit. You forget that you come from a street with a very bad name, where the general standard of morality is low."

Hughie's eyes flashed. "You insinerating that my girl is on the town?"

"I am insinuating nothing, my dear sir. I am merely stating public opinion. You are perhaps aware that a Surry Hills girl finds it difficult to obtain a position in the city. She may be educated; she may be more highly moral than similar young ladies in more prosperous suburbs, but her address is against her. Most Sydney people persist, somewhat biasedly, perhaps, in thinking of Surry Hills in terms of brothels, razor-gangs, tenements, and fried fish shops."

Hughie, abashed, said, "Swallered the dictionary, ain't yer?"

Joseph Mendel straightened his shoulders. His black eyes gleamed as opaque and stony as jet.

"I am well aware that you came to me this morning hoping that I would, on behalf of Tommy, attempt to buy you off, so that your daughter's questionable honour might be salved. But you might as well know that I do not care the price of one of those leaden trinkets whether my nephew Tommy fathers a dozen come-by-chances."

"I don't want any of your stinking Jew money," yelled Hughie, defeated and enraged. He flung the remainder of the fifteen pounds on the counter, and gathered it up again quickly in case Joseph Mendel should pounce on it.

The slums of Sydney, and in particular the area around Surry Hills, have been both the inspiration and the locale of three notable Australian novels: Louis Stone's *Jonah* (1911); Kylie Tennant's *Foveaux* (1939); and Ruth Park's *The Harp in the South* (1948).

The harshness of slum life is not mitigated in any of these books, especially *Jonah*, but there is a compensating richness of humanity in all of them which is easy to misinterpret as

187

sentimentality. There are two problems to be faced here. One is that the author may be sentimental. The other is that the people themselves, the originals who bit by bit made up the characters, may have been sentimental themselves. Criticisms such as Marjorie Barnard's of *The Harp in the South* when it first appeared – "hearts of gold and a happy ending" – may be too harsh, and perhaps may not take into account the need of the novelist to be true to his or her subject. Few novelists have succeeded in writing about the urban poor without being sentimental – Balzac and Zola did not, for example, and certainly neither did Dickens. If Ruth Park does veer rather close to sentimentality, she is in good company.

Hughie passed Jacky Siciliano's fruit shop, and Bert Drummy's ham and beef, and the second-hand dump and the fish shop. And there was Joseph Mendel's hock joint, with three brass balls swinging like monstrous grapes from the veranda beam.

It should also be remembered that Ruth Park and her husband, D'Arcy Niland, lived in Surry Hills themselves and had plenty of time to test their literary ideas against the reality around them.

There can be no argument over the accuracy of Ruth Park's observations of the disadvantages of living in Surry Hills. The bug-hunt, when the whole family goes upstairs, armed with kerosene and lighted twists of newspaper, is a desperate and ultimately futile affair:

> Hughie turned over the bed, and they pulled it to pieces.
> "Ah, look at the cows!" he ejaculated. He held his nose, and his blue eyes looked over the knot of his fingers with a disgusted horror. For there were more bugs than could be believed. In every pit and screw-hole, every joint and crack they clustered, so thickly that sometimes there were whole marshalled lines of them, hidden cunningly in a twist of the wire or a crevice in the iron. A faint filthy smell arose from them alive. Dead, they would smell overpoweringly, of mingled musk and ammonia.

And when Roie, the elder daughter, asks querulously whether a fumigator could not be got in to rid the house of them, the authentic voice of the trapped slum-dweller comes from Mumma: "Well, it stands to reason you won't never have *no* bugs . . . Everyone's got bugs around here."

For Grandma, Hughie Darcy and Mumma, there is no thought or possibility of living anywhere else, unless one of them wins the lottery, as Hughie thinks he has when he sees in the paper that 'H. Darcy, Surry Hills' has won £5000. His euphoria collapses when he finds that it is an old lady, Helen Darcy, who is the winner.

For the young it is different. "You're not a rat just because you live in a hole," says Roie with some asperity. By the end of the book it seems certain that she and her husband Charlie, and possibly her young sister Dolour, will rise in the world.

The Darcys are, of course, Irish and Catholic. When they blow off steam they do it, typically, without inhibition until, albeit temporarily, they remember what constitutes sin. When they go wrong, as Roie does, the torment is worse because they have a strong basic morality. And they also possess some knowledge of mercy, and can therefore forgive. When, at the end of the book, in the "happy ending", Mumma forgives Hughie for being a crude, unreliable drinker, it could be argued that this is not sentimentality but an application of Christian principles.

Humour and few illusions make sentimentality difficult. Ruth Park has Hughie's measure exactly. Dropping into church for the first time in six years to give thanks that Roie has recovered from her "disaster", he has a rough and manly chat with God. And then, "Instantly and mysteriously, there shot into his mind the idea: 'Why not buy a lottery ticket?'"

Roie's trouble is an unwanted pregnancy. She is nineteen and longing to fall in love. Pathetic, lame Jewish Tommy Mendel provides an outlet for a love that is hopelessly muddled between pity and desire. He is dishonest enough to make use of her love by a deliberate mixture of helplessness and frustrated maleness. She finally gives in to him out of "a blinding love and desire to please".

Tommy conveniently takes a job in Leichhardt and is seen no more. Ruth Park carefully understates this, but Leichhardt for Roie and the Darcys is in another country, although not three suburbs away from Surry Hills.

Forgetting her religion, Roie manages to scrape together £10 for an abortion, but at the last minute her nerve breaks and she runs from the surgery, only to be beaten up by drunken Dutch sailors on a rampage after one of their crewmates has been murdered. As a result she nearly dies, and loses the baby.

Roie has quite changed by the time she falls in love again, this time with a steady young man in a good job. "Tommy had brought out her maternal instincts; she had wanted to shelter him, to do things for him. Charlie brought out the lover in her; she wanted to be sheltered by him."

Roie is an impulsive but admirable character. There is no prejudice in her. Hughie may be a boozer, but he has a harsh, sceptical eye. After meeting Charlie, he says to Mumma that Charlie has "a bit of tar in him . . . A bit of Aboriginal, that's what. Couldn't you see it looking out of them eyes? And them long strangler hands?" When Charlie tells Roie this is true, she does not mind. "Charlie realised that there was no black-white problem with Roie. Either people were nice, or they were not."

Roie and Dolour, Hughie and Mumma, and the memory of poor little Thady who, when he was six, just disappeared and was never found, are at the heart of the book, but there is a lusty collection of minor characters. The tenants upstairs are Mr Diamond, a fellow-Irishman but an Orangeman, and

WOOLLOOMOOLOO *Sali Herman*

RUTH PARK

Ruth Park was born in New Zealand, and as a child lived in the country with her parents, where she was in close contact with the Maoris. She later trained as a school teacher. In the late 1930s she worked as children's editor on the Auckland *Star*.

In 1940 she took a holiday in Sydney, where she met D'Arcy Niland, with whom she had been corresponding. She was promised a newspaper job in Sydney, so returned there in 1942 with a capital of £10. Instead, she married D'Arcy Niland, and travelled with him in country areas, while he worked as a shedhand in shearing sheds, as well as doing many other jobs. During these years Ruth worked as a fruit picker, a secretary and other things. They also both worked on the opal fields. They were already writing whenever they could. Ruth achieved a number of publications in overseas magazines, and was writing regular stories for *St Nicholas*, the prestigious American children's magazine.

Moving to Sydney in 1943, the only accommodation they could find was in Surry Hills, and there, expecting their first child, they lived in a room over a barber's shop in Devonshire Street. In Sydney Ruth worked for the ABC children's sessions, and also wrote radio plays for the ABC.

The time spent in Surry Hills gave Ruth the material for her two novels about the Darcy family, *The Harp in the South* (1948) and *Poor Man's Orange* (1949); a third novel, *Missus*, was published in 1985.

The Harp in the South, which won the *Sydney Morning Herald*

prize in 1948, and was then published in England and the United States, and translated into several languages, was the beginning of their success and also led to their financial independence. Ruth Park's novel *The Witch's Thorn* sold half a million copies in the USA alone.

Ruth Park began writing children's stories when she was at college; her first children's book was published in 1961. Since then her work has also appeared on radio and television. *The Muddle-headed Wombat* series, first on radio and then as a series of books, has been particularly successful.

Ruth Park writes:

I have never regarded myself either as a novelist or specifically a children's writer. Among the 50-odd titles published only nine are adult novels. The rest are children's books, non-fiction or educational.

I really regard myself as a *writer*. This is because of the diversity of my interests. From 1960 when it became obvious that my husband was seriously ill, I worked intermittently as a film script editor for an American company based in the UK. I also wrote for television, as did D'Arcy. In fact our play *No Decision* won the first British Commonwealth-wide television competition conducted by the Lew Grade organisation.

From 1960 I also worked on journalistic assignments, specials, and I still do this when an interesting job offers itself. I have coached in Australian Literature in Japan, and also worked for the Egyptian Government's English language publicity department.

Playing Beatie Bow (also to appear as a film) won 11 major awards in the United States, including the Boston Globe Horn Book.

I lived for 10 years on Norfolk Island and am in fact still an official resident, though I have found it convenient to live for longish periods in Sydney.

Miss Sheily, a bitter little woman who has come down in the world and has an idiot illegitimate child. Then Grandma comes to stay with the family, bringing old Ireland with her. Next door is a Chinese fruiterer, Lick Jimmy.

One particularly well-realised character is the prostitute and madam Delie Stock, whose offer of £130 to give the schoolchildren a picnic is indignantly refused by Father Cooley, which provokes some splendid invective from Delie. Father Cooley accepts the money when Delie tells him she won it in a lottery.

*H*ughie *exploded into a torrent of filthy abuse. It was filthy mainly because he did not have much vocabulary. He did not have a particularly obscene mind, but the words he used seemed to need adjectival qualification, and so he fitted the expressions he knew into the vacant spaces.*

Roie's marriage to Charlie is of both body and soul. In the rather prudish and anti-sensual gallery of Australian fictional characters, Roie and Charlie stand out as ones who enjoy a triumphant and mutual sexuality. Writing in 1948, Ruth Park could not have risked being too erotic even if she had wished to, but she does manage to convey the truth of

her observation: "Everything in the lives of Roie and Charlie was bound up in sex." Theirs is one of those marriages "springing out of sex and bearing fruit in the spirit itself".

They have a fortnight for their honeymoon, spent idyllically in a pink cottage by the sea at Narrabeen. When they arrive Roie jumps up and down on the bed and sings out, "No bugs!" Neither of them can swim, but they passionately enjoy being knocked around by the surf. Without any heaviness, the honeymoon by the sea is symbolic of what life can be outside Surry Hills, and they are not afraid to embrace it.

Ruth Park has been most successful in *The Harp in the South* at conveying the sturdiness of spirit of her slum-dwellers. This provides the dimension beyond reality that is necessary if a realistic novel is going to be more than reportage. Despite Hughie's failings, there are intense loyalties within the Darcy family. Despite fights, drunkenness, prostitution and murder, there is still a code of behaviour in Surry Hills that unites the people who live there.

Ruth Park expressed this well herself: "*The Harp* wasn't fiction, but a literal report of what I saw. Living there, I learned what loving, and lovable, people there are in the slums. Although they mightn't worry about some of the Commandments, their code is based on charity. I'd rather be broke any time in Surry Hills than Potts Point."

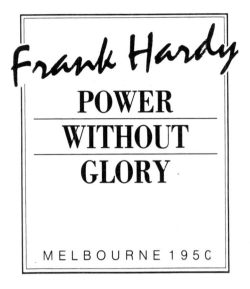

POWER

WITHOUT

GLORY

MELBOURNE 1950

Presently the chilly air was shattered as the back gate of the wood-yard was assailed with axes, picks and crowbars. In an instant it burst open and Dave O'Flaherty dashed through, an axe in one hand and a revolver in the other, followed by several other armed men.

One-eyed-Tommy roused himself, straightened up and rubbed his sleepy eye. The Ape and Cauliflower Dick stirred slowly, but Piggy continued to snore.

When the import of the hubbub penetrated his sleepy brain, One-eyed-Tommy got to his feet. As he did so The Ape and Cauliflower Dick sat up sleepily. They heard the gate of the tote yard itself being attacked. It crashed open and they saw gloomy figures rushing at them.

One-eyed-Tommy was at a disadvantage: not only was he half asleep, but he could not see into the darkness beyond the fire. The Ape and Cauliflower Dick stood up sleepily, and Piggy, finally aroused, sat up rubbing his eyes. One-eyed-Tommy drew his revolver, but before he could use it he was overpowered by several policemen. The other guards climbed awkwardly between the bars of the platform into the arms of their captors.

Then came sounds of axe and crowbar blows on the front door of the shop. But it was not until some of the policemen in the yard smashed their way through into the shop and attacked the bars, chains and padlocks from inside that the entrance to John West's office gave way.

That task completed, the four tote guards were hustled violently into the back lane. The Jackson Street fortress had fallen.

Half an hour later, a noise penetrated the slumber of John West. Beside him, Nellie stirred and groaned softly in her sleep. She was heavy with child again, and had been tossing restlessly. John West, insisting on the need for fresh air, had had the walls of the room removed from the two outer sides to make an open-air bedroom.

He sat bolt upright, drew a revolver from under the pillow, and leapt out of bed. He pulled on his shoes, threw a coat over his shoulders and walked slowly, picking his way in the darkness, out of the door through the dressing-room adjoining, and so to the top of the stairs. There was someone knocking impatiently at the front door. His heart was pounding. He was gripped by a tension of fear and excitement. Who could it be? The police? Some enemy? He descended the stairs slowly one by one. He should have a guard here at the house as well as elsewhere, he thought.

As he neared the bottom of the stairs, the knocking came again—loud and menacing.

He approached the front door hesitantly, crouched with the gun pointed unsteadily in front of him. He hoped the servants would not hear from their quarters at the back of the house. He stood in front of the ornate front door waiting for the knocking to come again. After what seemed an eternity it came. His hair was tingling at the roots. He had difficulty in speaking. When his voice came it seemed as loud as the crack of a stock-whip splitting the air.

"Who's there?"

"Me, Tommy. The traps have taken over the tote. They're there now, dozens of 'em. Come down, for crissake!"

At first the news did not fully register on John West's brain because of his relief that no physical danger lurked outside. His whole body relaxed and the gun slumped to his side. He noticed that he was shivering.

"All right," he said, "I'll come down. Wait there."

"For gawd's sake hurry," One-eyed-Tommy answered.

John West walked back towards the stairs.

"Where are you, John? Where are you? What's the matter?" It was Nellie's voice at the top of the stairs.

"It's all right. Just someone wants to see me."

She began to cry hysterically. As he entered the room, she clambered back into the bed-clothes and lay there shuddering. "What do people want calling at this hour?" she queried, terrified. "And why have you got that gun? Why do you keep it under the pillow? Why did you take it downstairs?"

Frank Hardy set himself the almost impossible task in *Power Without Glory* of disguising truth as fiction in order to focus attention on the truth. A story usually needs strong elements of narrative, character and motivation, as well as of style, imagination and perhaps humour, to qualify as fiction. Unlike many of Hardy's other writings, *Power Without Glory* contains almost no humour. The style is often crude, and imagination is irrelevant. What makes *Power Without Glory* a most remarkable novel is the evil strength of the character of its hero, John West, and the sheer narrative vigour of his rise from poverty to riches, from bribing a policeman with a sovereign to paying off police commissioners, judges, premiers, and, at least in West's point of view, the Roman Catholic church.

The truth is now only of historical interest. It really does not matter after all these years that John West is John Wren, Ted Thurgood is Ted Theodore, and Archbishop Malone is Archbishop Mannix. *Power Without Glory* has to stand or fall by its quality as fiction; we must believe in it as a novel. It is interesting, incidentally, given the danger of prosecution for libel, that Hardy felt compelled to give so many of his characters names that closely approximate to those of their originals.

John West's Irish mother, bringing up her three boys among the poorest in the squalid suburb of Carringbush (Collingwood) in Melbourne, is one of the few sympathetic characters of the book. The three boys, John, Joe and Arthur, are always in minor trouble with the police as members of larrikin pushes. Then Arthur is sentenced to death for rape, the sentence being commuted to 12 years and 50 lashes. Arty's soul is scarred as deeply as his back. His is a Balzacian portrait of implacable hate and loyalty to a fellow-criminal.

Then came sounds of axe and crowbar blows on the front door of the shop. But it was not until some of the policemen in the yard smashed their way through into the shop and attacked the bars, chains and padlocks from inside that the entrance to John West's office gave way.

Hardy obviously studied Balzac closely before writing *Power Without Glory*, and, of all Australian writers, he most nearly resembles the French master in his portrayal of a crowded world dominated by evil and greed and fuelled with energy. But Hardy lacks the breadth of Balzac's social vision; he is incapable of portraying the conservative rich and his love scenes are unconvincing.

The action centres around John West. Bandy-legged from rickets, cold-eyed from want and ambition, and as neatly dressed as the Devil, his evil energy makes *Power Without Glory* immensely readable. Early in the winter of 1893, determined to break out of his family poverty, West begins with a rigged pigeon race and follows on with a tote shop disguised as a tea shop at 136 Jackson Street, Carringbush. This expanded into innumerable businesses later in life, but the tote was the basis of his fortune.

It is fortunate for Hardy that, although as a Communist he is writing *Power Without Glory* to expose the evils of Capitalist society, he is also able to draw sympathy for West as the man who knows that "the worker likes to have a bet" and gives him one, legal or not. Hardy obviously agrees that it is not right that gambling on horses, the great democratic sport, should only be allowed to the rich members of the Victoria Racing Club. Besides, when West has money he

gives a lot of it away. Not only in bribes but to people down on their luck. There is a sporadic generosity in the man. The other redeeming feature of West's life is that the wowsers hate him. Australians may have suffered from the rapacity of men like John West, but Hardy is on popular ground when he also shows them suffering from the wowsers who would interfere with the workers' pleasures in gambling, drinking and sex.

West soon gathers round him a gang of varied supporters. One of Hardy's great successes in *Power Without Glory* is the way he traces the fortunes of these men who range in depravity from the amiable Barney Robinson who "like the others, was semi-illiterate but possessed a thirst for knowledge which led him to read avidly but indiscriminately", the reckless Mick O'Connell, and the crooked eyed, bullet headed Sugar Renfrey, to such hardened criminals as Piggy and Cauliflower Dick. West never forgets a grudge. In 1893 Piggy insults him and would have beaten him up but for the intervention of the saintly Leftist, Eddie Corrigan. After Piggy has worked for West for 23 years, West arranges a double cross, and Piggy is hanged for the murder committed by Arty's prison friend, Bradley.

West's tote business flourishes, and the brilliant lawyer David Garside gets him acquitted of any prosecutions following raids by the police. The most successful of these raids occurs when the police arrive in a cart, hidden under a load of hay. By the early 1900s West is worth £50,000, and Garside teaches him how to invest his money. He is popular among the people: "His gambling establishment was fairly conducted; you got a fair go from Jack West, he was a man of his word and would always help a lame dog over a stile."

Hardy does not spare West's faults. He is a sentimentalist about women but is cruel to his wife Nellie, locking her up in his mansion when she takes a lover (a bricklayer who is working on the house) and has his illegitimate child. He alienates all his children. He disowns his daughter Margery (a musician) when she marries a German. (West is a warmonger and jingoist during both World Wars.) She later dies in a concentration camp in Germany in World War II. His beloved (by his standards) daughter Mary becomes a Communist and dies of cancer in England.

West has no compunction in ordering one of his thugs to beat up anyone who defies or swindles him, but he is a physical coward himself. He has interests in football and horse racing but he has neither culture nor friends. "He did not dance, smoke or drink or play billiards; he rarely went to concerts or variety shows. The only two books he had read in his life were his mother's medical book and a grammar he had borrowed from Barney Robinson."

It is West's energy that is compelling, and his expanding audacity. Having bribed police from constables to the Commissioner, he finds more important people to add to his payroll. By the time he is making £5000 a week he has suborned eight of 14 Labor MPs, the Premier of Victoria, and the Federal Treasurer.

As his interests expand from the tote to organised sport, cycling, trotting, boxing and other activities including mining, country properties, hotels, shops and factories, he needs more and more people to work for him, legally or illegally. Hardy makes clear that West does not exist apart

THE LOBBY, PARLIAMENT HOUSE *Noel Counihan*

FRANK HARDY
1917-

Frank Hardy was born in Southern Cross, Victoria, in 1917, one of eight children of an impoverished Catholic family. They later moved to Bacchus Marsh, Victoria, which Hardy later wrote about as Benson's Valley.

Hardy left school at 13 and worked at a variety of jobs for the next seven years, in the classic tradition of the Australian battler. In 1937 his family moved to Melbourne. Hardy wanted to be a sketcher and cartoonist, and his father managed to get together enough money to help him enrol in a correspondence course in drawing. Some of his cartoons were published in the *Radio Times* in 1937.

The Depression years left Hardy with no faith in capitalism, and he joined the Communist Party in 1940. In 1942 he joined the Army and was posted to Mataranka in the Northern Territory. There he set up and edited a camp newspaper called the *Troppo Tribune*, most of which he wrote himself. He was already an expert yarn-teller during beer sessions. After one of these a friend, Sergeant Frank Fyland, said he ought to write down some of his stories. Hardy replied that he lacked the education, but he had a go, fortified, in his own words, by a "strong hint from fact, a yarn-spinner's flair for apt exaggeration and a desire to use writing as a political weapon". To which one might add a sense of humour and a good ear for Australian idiom.

He sold some stories and won some prizes. By 1950, the year of the publication of *Power Without Glory*, he was established in a writing career which branched out later into radio, television and film.

He had spent five years in researching *Power Without Glory*, which was based on the career of a Melbourne multi-millionaire John Wren. Hardy and some friends distributed the book themselves. It got off to a slow start until Hardy was tried for criminal libel; the court hearings lasted from October 1950 to June 1951. Wren's wife Ellen (Nell in the book) was alleged to be libelled by sections of the book in which she was portrayed as having a love affair with a bricklayer, and then having his illegitimate child. A "Defend Hardy" committee conducted a spirited campaign in his defence, and writers' groups rallied around him. He was acquitted in June 1951. *Power Without Glory* has subsequently sold over a million copies around the world, and the ABC made a two-million-dollar television series based on it which has been screened in many countries.

Hardy's later books include *The Yarns of Billy Borker* (Sydney, 1965), *Legends of Benson's Valley* (Melbourne 1963), and the hilarious satire *The Outcasts of Foolgarah* (Sydney 1971).

Hardy broke with the Communist Party. Some articles, "The Heirs of Stalin", which appeared in the London *Sunday Times*, and the novel *But the Dead are Many* (1975) fill in the background to his decision.

Hardy's great strength is that he writes about what he knows. He has always been a gambler, especially on the horses, he has spent years working with people like the labourers of Benson's Valley or the garbos of *The Outcasts of Foolgarah*. He will never be a great stylist but he has worked hard to become a competent writer able to handle the richness of his material.

---

from society, by simply robbing it like a burglar or a forger. West in fact makes himself a millionaire many times over by working with society; understanding its rules and using them.

He loses the least villainous and the most congenial of his henchmen, Barney Robinson, when he launches a vicious persecution against the great boxer Lou Darby (Les Darcy) because he will not do what West wants. Barney, a friend and admirer of Lou's, is disgusted at West's tactics which even include undermining Darby's career in the USA, which leads to his suicide. Sometime later Barney, now broke, goes back on West's payroll. He is sent to Western Australia on West's business and is shot dead on arrival by a hostile group.

West's most indomitable enemy is Sergeant O'Flaherty who closes down West's tote shop as a prelude to further legislation restricting West's gambling activities. A bomb is thrown into O'Flaherty's house. To West's fury it fails to kill him, but from lack of evidence O'Flaherty is unable to charge West with the crime.

The strangest relationship in the book is that between West and Archbishop Malone. Hardy manages to restrain what must have been a powerful temptation to caricature Mannix and the Catholic Church. West wants to win Irish support in the Labor Party, his political centre of power. There are genuine feelings of warmth between West and Malone. It is particularly Malone's Irishness that forms a bond between West and Malone, for the only guilt West ever feels in his life is for his Irish mother, given such a hard life by her sons, although of course he has helped her financially. West promises Malone he will help finance and organise the great procession through Melbourne on St Patrick's Day, which is threatened with interference from the Lord Mayor and the police. By a brilliant stroke of cunning, West invites (at his expense) every VC winner in Australia to lead the procession, mounted on white chargers. The occasion is an enormous success.

The last 250 pages of the book are much concerned with State, Federal and world politics. West is not the same dynamic central character that he was in the earlier part of the novel, although the intensification of his family's misfortunes is clearly intended to restore the personal balance.

Although West does well out of World War II his confidence is undermined by his ill health. Heart trouble brings him in fear to the Catholic faith; he even reads some books lent him by the Archbishop. At 77 he is looking his age and feeling tired. Only Sugar Renfrey, who had made a lot of money for himself as Mayor of Carringbush, stands by him.

By 1949 West is fervently religious and absurdly neurotic. He has a goat which he milks himself in case he should get polio from cow's milk. He carries his revolver with him everywhere and sleeps with it under this pillow. Finally, in 1950, after another heart attack, he confesses to Almighty God "I have sinned exceedingly in thought, word and deed", and he prepares to die.

Only God could have aroused West's conscience. Hardy, the Communist atheist, was brought up a Catholic. It is ironic that religion adds a badly needed further dimension to the evil doings chronicled so faithfully in *Power Without Glory*.

Dymphna Cusack & Florence James

COME IN SPINNER

LONDON 1951

The sight of a pair of sheer silk stockings sent Guinea's eyes flying to the face of a pretty redhead. Any girl who had real sheers these days must have what it takes. Once, a ferry pilot had brought her two pairs of nylons. Ah, but that was in the great days of '42 when the American Forces first spread over the country in a wave of superbly tailored beige-pinks, olive-drabs and light khakis; a wave that bore on its crest orchids, nylons, exquisite courtesy, Hollywood love-making and a standard of luxury that had never before penetrated below the privileged ranks of the socialites whose fathers and husbands really had the dough.

Guinea paused at the top of the stairs and looked down on the vestibule. She knew every detail of it by heart from the days when she was the decoy at the Bouquet Boutique. Gilt-framed mirrors gave it a deceptive spaciousness and the restless figures were repeated like some fantastic moving mural along the mirrored walls. The air hummed with the incessant clamour of the crowd. Khaki was the major note in the colour scheme; khaki in all its tones from beige to olive, in all cuts from the lounging GIs to the perfectly tailored higher ranks. The dark blue of the RAAF was almost black under the electric lights, the grey-blue of the New Zealand airmen and a group of RAF officers showed up soberly against the bright florals of the girls.

Guinea stiffened and turned sharply as a voice spoke in her ear. "What are you doing here, Miss Malone?"

She looked into a mocking face with prominent brown eyes. "Jeepers, Mrs Cavendish! You did give me a fright. I thought for a moment you were Mrs Molesworth."

Mrs Cavendish drew her lips back in a thin smile. "If you want to know where she is, I just saw her escorting Mrs Ainslie along to her office—you know, the one whose daughter's landed that American fellow whose father's such a big bug. That's the girl along there, isn't it?" She glanced along the corridor to where a laughing girl stood gazing up at a young American officer.

"Yes, the fair one's Constance Ainslie and that's the hero. Real young love, they tell me." Guinea gazed with pleasure at the young couple so completely absorbed in each other. "They are sweet, aren't they?"

Mrs Cavendish raised her brows critically. "Well, if you like that style . . . Who is that dowdy-looking girl beside her?"

"That's Helen McFarland—you know, the Ian McFarlands. They're just down from the country."

"Oh, them! My dear, wouldn't you think with all their money they'd do something about her? Or maybe they'll be able to buy someone for her." She gave a throaty gurgle of amusement at her own wit.

Guinea frowned. "She's a nice kid. She comes into the Marie-Antoinette and you couldn't wish for anyone nicer. Not a bit of nonsense about her."

"Isn't there? What a pity!" she said without interest and peered over the railing. "All these young things look the same to me. I can hardly tell one from the other, what with their peroxided curls bobbing around their shoulders and the terribly healthy look they all have nowadays."

Guinea's eye slid up and down Mrs Cavendish's slender black crêpe elegance. Skinny hag, she said to herself, she looks like one of those walking skeletons out of Vogue. She ought to talk. To hear her you'd think she'd never had her hair touched up in her life.

It is not often that one can disregard the style of a novel for the sake of its content, but this is true of *Come In Spinner*. If there is often a breathless banality in the writing, and the men, in particular, sometimes speak like characters in a bad film, there is also a genuine quality in the book that comes from a feeling of humanity, humour and a wide knowledge of how different sorts of women lived in Australia towards the end of World War II.

Come In Spinner is also important because, apart from the rather too individualistic examples of *My Brilliant Career* and some of the novels of Kylie Tennant, it is Australia's first major feminist novel. Women's lives, jobs and relationships with men and each other are not only realistically described but examined, sometimes directly, sometimes indirectly, through the eyes of other characters.

One of the most original and almost alarmingly convincing of these is Dr Dallas MacIntyre, a successful professional woman who has kept the style and looks of an elegant woman of the world, while at the same time attaining professional and intellectual distinction. Her talk with Deb in the middle of the book is a sharp comment on much of the behaviour of the women in the book.

Wartime makes everything more hectic, more frantic. Time does not have a chance to flow. Everything must happen at once, sometimes too soon. Two abortions and the induction of a 16-year-old girl into a brothel are symbolic of the abnegation of human responsibilities and frenzied tempo of wartime life.

The setting of the novel is very much Sydney. At a time when most Australian fiction was still set in the country,

Cusack and James homed in on Kings Cross, Macquarie Street, the Harbour and above all the Hotel South Pacific, the SP, where the pick-up girls and the servicemen, particularly American, meet in the vestibule by the freshly gilded figurehead of the Bouncing Belle.

"*Yes, the fair one's Constance Ainslie and that's the hero. Real young love, they tell me.*" *Guinea gazed with pleasure at the young couple so completely absorbed in each other. "They are sweet, aren't they?"*

The Marie-Antoinette Salon for ladies in the hotel is where most of the main characters of the novel work: Claire the manageress of the salon, Deborah the masseuse, Guinea and Alice, hairdressers, Val the manicurist and the detested Ursula at the desk. Even more unpopular with the women, and ever-sycophantic to owners, is the manageress of the hotel, Mrs Molesworth. One of the best-drawn characters in the book is Elvira, the ancient room-maid from the sixth floor, full of gossip and bearing silk stockings and underwear pilfered from rich guests to sell on the black market. Other important characters in the hotel are the housekeeper Bessie and the lift-driver Blue, married to Doss the barmaid. One of the best scenes in the book is where the unrepentant Blue plays two-up in a jammed lift with some American soldiers, while the appalled manager and the anxious guests in the vestibule hear the shouts of "Come in Spinner", and "A quid in the guts to see her away".

The SP is an admirable focal point for the tumultuous action of the book, which might have got out of hand were it not for this central base. The Marie-Antoinette Salon also allows Cusack and James the opportunity of satirising the *nouveaux riches* and the snobs of Sydney. There is an ironic contrast between the fat, middle-aged clients and the elegant and often beautiful girls and women whose job it is to beautify them. The most intolerable of all are the young socialites like DDT, Denise D'Arcy-Twyning, who are too superior to come down to the salon, and insist on the girls coming up to their suites. Poor Denny, she is busy extricating herself from an engagement to an American lieutenant-colonel so she can marry a Royal Navy commander.

The girls in the salon detest guests like the D'Arcy-Twynings but are well disposed to the McFarlands, who are the genuine squattocracy, simple, straightforward and used to hard work, quite different from the *parvenus*.

However, the corruptions of wealth are also apparent in the McFarland family. Rich Angus, who lives in Sydney, does not get on all that well with his country relations. He has lost their basic honesty, and is a reactionary, a cultural-cringer and an unashamed manipulator of his power and wealth to get what he wants in a wartime economy. In his possessive and limited way, he is in love with Deb, who is married to a soldier, Jack, fighting overseas, and has a daughter, Luen.

Deb is an attractive and intelligent girl, but her morality is under siege to Angus's money, power and confidence. Interestingly enough, there is no collapse of her sexual morality, and no attempt by Angus to force the issue. Any mention of her being married and having a child "puts a damper on Angus".

Well, he'd just have to be jealous. Men, as Claire said, were the devil. They wanted your company and anything else they could get, and they were damn clever at not being compromised themselves, but jealous of any suggestion that you might have other attachments. It was all take and no give. Not that she could honestly say that of Angus; he'd never made a pass at her. All the times he'd taken her out he had behaved with a flattering deference. And that, judging by the stories the other girls told, was almost a miracle.

For a book written about the relationships between men and women in wartime, there is, outside Kings Cross, extraordinarily little sexual activity. There is any amount of sexual display: bodies, clothes, flowers; but doors are always being closed in men's faces, or else, as in the case of the older lovers, Deb's Angus McFarland and Guinea's American Colonel Maddocks, no attempt is made on the lady's virtue. Marriage is offered instead.

While Deb is inclined to be genteel and buttoned-up and to parrot Angus's opinions, Guinea is very much more uninhibited and does not give a damn about anybody's opinions. Deb is the classic victim who will sometimes raise her voice to protest, but will always retreat before the "Don't bother your pretty little head with this" technique. Guinea would never accept this sort of treatment.

Claire is another victim, a handsome woman of 38 (Deb is 32, Guinea younger), who is extremely efficient at running the salon (if a little too fond of the occasional nip of brandy), but is besotted by a feeble would-be movie actor, the handsome and well-dressed Nigel. Nigel is a gambler, and Claire's dream is that they will win £1000 at baccarat so they can get married and she can open her own salon. In an exciting scene they do indeed win, but later Nigel is easily persuaded by the crooks who run the school to go back and lose it all. Claire says she will have no more of him, but to Deb's disgust he talks her into coming back to him.

On a lower social level than that of the SP there is the tragic story of Guinea's 16-year-old sister, Monnie Malone, who, running away from her implacable mother, gets in touch with a friend, not knowing she is a whore in Kings Cross. An American doctors her drink and rapes her when she is drunk; then Grace, the madam of the brothel, drugs her, and after she is found in bed with a man by the Vice Squad she eventually appears in the Juvenile Court.

Not all the men in the book are monsters who get off scot-free while the under-age girls they have slept with go to court, but they are, on the whole, not impressive. Deb's husband, Jack, is a selfish man, with whom she is no longer in love. She is offered marriage (and the money and legal facilities for a divorce) by Angus. She neglects her child, whom she pays her sister to rear, while disliking her worthy but patronising brother-in-law, Tom. (The honesty with which Deb's faults are exposed is one of the many indications that *Come In Spinner* is no biased feminist novel.) For all their strength, these three men are limited and bullying in their own fashion. Guinea's Colonel Maddocks is charming but shallow, and she eventually goes back to the fairly simple but jolly, self-critical Kim. There are also a few dinkum Aussies like Blue, Lofty and Billo, who are decent enough.

TWO DAYS' LEAVE *Lorraine Hannay*

DYMPHNA CUSACK
1902-1981
FLORENCE JAMES

Florence James writes:
"Dymphna's and my collaboration was a result of the unlikely coincidence of the time (February 1945 to July 1947), the place (a rented cottage in the Blue Mountains) and the loved ones (Dymphna and myself and three small girls) setting up temporary housekeeping together.

"Dymphna had recently been invalided out of the Education Department and I had just given up my wartime job in Sydney to be ready with my two children to leap aboard the first available ship and follow my RAAF husband to England. When his posting was indefinitely delayed, the children started at the local school and, as Dymphna's health was responding marvellously to the mountain air, we decided to write a children's book. It was a fun occupation. We each wrote half the chapters, did some editing patchwork, decided our writing matched well enough, and *Four Winds and a Family* had no trouble in finding a publisher.

"Dymphna was eager to start writing again. Why not another collaboration? We were both pretty steamed up about the problems of women on the home front. So what about pooling our wartime experience and telling the truth about what war had done to Sydney? How it had thrown decent people off-balance and exploitation had become the name of the game. We would write absolutely honestly, pulling no punches . . . The characters began to emerge, the plot took shape and the climate of wartime Sydney became more real than the bush around us as we worked a pattern for the stories of our women and their men.

"Dymphna was indefatigable. As soon as she could hold her head up from the neuralgia which laid her low for days at a time, she would dictate to my typing. In the afternoons while she rested, I edited and wrote. Journalism had been my job and novel writing was a new experience, but it was amazing how I took fire from working with Dymphna.

"In her teaching days, in addition to numerous articles and short stories, she had written several plays and had had her first novel published. She had also collaborated with Miles Franklin in *Pioneers on Parade*, a satire on social pretensions. When Miles visited us, she would insist on reading the latest episode of *Come In Spinner*, and her perceptive comments were invaluable. She cared ardently about Australian writing.

"Dymphna and I came from widely different backgrounds. She was a country girl from the western plains of New South Wales, born of Catholic Irish emigrant forebears who came out in the 1840s and 1850s. She finished her schooldays at St Ursula's Convent, Armidale. I was born in New Zealand of English, Scots and Welsh pioneering families and my last school before joining my parents, who had moved to Sydney, was St Cuthbert's Presbyterian Ladies College in Auckland.

"Our friendship began at Sydney University, where we discovered the appalling deficiencies in our education. Little history of our own countries was taught either of us at school and little enough at Sydney University, where English courses taught only appreciation of traditional English literature and ignored the Australian writers who had been discovering their own land and its people since the 1890s.

"Our writing pattern continued for most of the first draft of *Come In Spinner*, until Dymphna got her dictaphone, which speeded up production wonderfully. We now decided to enter for the *Daily Telegraph* Australian novel competition and started cutting and shaping our huge manuscript. It had taken two years to write, but it was to take another four before it was published. This could have happened only in the bad old days before 1963 when the Australian Society of Authors was founded and we both joined up.

"We submitted our manuscript under a pen name by the closing date of 30 October 1946. It was August 1947 before we heard that it was the prize winner; Dymphna disclosed our identity to the *Daily Telegraph*, and Brian Penton (the paper's editor) described the novel as a 'damn fine piece of work'.

"Then there was a protracted period of delays and demands for significant cuts. We had revised and cut the manuscript to 120,000 words, but the *Telegraph* was asking for a further 50,000-word cut! Strange treatment for a 'damn fine piece of work'. This was unacceptable to us. Three years after the competition closed, the manuscript was released to us by the *Telegraph*.

"In December 1949 we offered it to William Heinemann in London who snapped it up. It was then immediately accepted by William Morrow for US publication. Neither asked for cuts or alterations.

"*Come In Spinner* was published in January 1951, in a first edition of 24,000. It reprinted four times in the first year and sold over 100,000 copies in the original edition. The book has appeared in eight translations and half a dozen paperback editions. It has never been out of print.

"Wherever Dymphna lived, she would have gone on writing, but it was her half of the *Come In Spinner* prize money that paid for her first visit to London and this opened up undreamed-of opportunities of foreign publication. Owing to her Soviet bloc royalty earnings being untransferrable before Communist countries recognised international copyright, Dymphna was able to travel extensively in Eastern Europe. Her books and plays have been published in 34 different countries and have sold eight and a half million copies in the Soviet Union alone.

"*Come In Spinner* has now come full circle with a request for publication of the original story. Dymphna had to do much condensing and reorganising in cutting the original manuscript down to an acceptable shape and size. Now it has been my job to edit in reverse, expanding, organising and weaving the original manuscript and the published book into a comfortable whole. The contract with Angus & Robertson for publication in early 1986 has just been signed.

"How Dymphna would have enjoyed this final irony. But it is not the end of the *Come In Spinner* story. I have just signed a two-year option with a production company for a mini-television series."

The moral concepts of the book are set out in two key scenes, one between Dr Dallas and Deb, the other between Deb and her sister and her sister's family. Deb's idea of "civilized living" — of living well without caring what happens to other people — is contrasted with Tom's idea of a decent world which would "give my kids a chance to be civilized human beings". Deb's ideas of sexual morality are contrasted with Dr Dallas's insistence that what really matters is that men and women should take each other seriously.

In the end it all comes back to the Marie-Antoinette Salon, a satisfying symbol, a place where women work to disguise the true selves of other women.

Russell Braddon

THE NAKED ISLAND

LONDON 1952

It became fairly obvious after two days in which they had been allowed no food, no water and no latrine facilities, that the Japanese were evilly disposed towards our escape party. Van Rennan himself sensed this and managed to throw a note into the main triangular courtyard urging us to ask for clemency towards Bell and Jan, both of whom were only in their very early twenties. This was done and the Japanese seemed agreeably inclined towards the request, nodding their heads and saying, "Baby-ka" many times.

But, in spite of their head-noddings, the next morning we saw the whole party suddenly appear in the gaol's entrance just outside the guard-house. All their gear had been dumped near them—haversacks and clothing—but they themselves were still fiercely shackled and were filthy dirty. They looked very weak.

The Japanese motioned them towards the gaol gate. Enquiringly, Van Rennan gestured with his foot towards the pile of kit-bags. The Japanese nodded negatively, emphatically. It could mean only one thing. They knew it: and we knew it.

They were brave men, those eight. Their heads went up, and while we shouted cheerful remarks at them, trying not to let them know what we sensed, they grinned back at us so that we shouldn't sense what they knew. They went through the big gate. Whenever one of them turned our way, a mass smile would appear on all the strained faces that watched their departure. As soon as their backs were turned, the smile vanished. They were prodded and shoved, clumsy with their arms and legs bound, into a truck. They turned to face us; we smiled. The guard spoke to them: they looked down at him: our smiles vanished. The guard stopped speaking: they looked up: we smiled. Then the truck lurched off and the big gates shut. They were gone. "There", I thought with a lump in my throat, "but for the grace of a mop of sun-bleached hair, goes Braddon."

The Indian who drove the truck told us later that they were taken to K.L. cemetery, there made to dig their own graves and then shot down into them. So ended the first, most promising and last escape plot of Pudu.

A month later, as if to compensate us for the loss of eight of our best men, two more Argylls were brought in. Theirs was a proud but sad tale. Cut off at Slim River, forty Argylls had fought a private war for weeks in the jungle until their ammunition vanished. Undaunted, they built themselves a palm-frond shelter and settled down to live a life of freedom in occupied Malaya until the British re-invaded.

Malaria attacked them. One after the other died. Carefully each was buried and a cross with his name and number placed on his grave. By July only four remained. One day all four fell ill and two died. The remaining two buried them and then—realizing that they had not long to go and yearning for the company they had heard was to be found in Pudu Gaol—they handed themselves up to the Japanese.

They came to us emaciated and dying. But for their last few days they had plenty of company, comrades who talked their own almost unintelligible dialect, and as much comfort as we could bestow. When they died they seemed happy enough.

After reading *The Naked Island* one could easily argue that it was far worse to be a prisoner of the Japanese in World War II than to be fighting as a front-line soldier. The terrible humiliations and cruelties inflicted by Japanese guards on Allied soldiers, the diseases which had to be overcome (when they were not fatal) without the benefit of medicines or drugs, the constant malnutrition, would in combination have been enough to deprive most men of their humanity and turn them into something resembling sick animals. The splendid result of Braddon's account of the experience, however, is that in the end he finds that the war has taught him to like his fellow men.

One should, on the other hand, point out that this liking and respect are confined to other Australian and British prisoners. For Braddon these are his fellow men, not the Japanese; and not all of the Dutch or Italians or Indians or Malays manage to qualify either.

Braddon has never denied that the perilous edifice of survival in Changi or on the Thailand Railway was built on a solid foundation of hate. Hatred of the Japanese and contempt for their philosophy sustained the prisoners on a number of levels, bringing them closer together and also helping them to insulate their minds with a "conscious barrier of 'It doesn't matter—nothing matters.'"

The Naked Island demonstrates also what a powerful role chance plays in the lives of human beings. If the recruiting sergeant in Sydney had not gone outside to have a smoke and told young Braddon to come back after lunch, and if young Braddon had not then called on a family friend who said he would pull strings to get him into his father's old unit, Russell Braddon would not have been in the Eighth Division of the AIF and taken prisoner in Malaya.

If he had not, at the last minute, volunteered to go from Changi to Thailand (where they were told there would be comfortable camps with plenty of rations), Braddon would have remained in relative peace, working on the new

Singapore aerodrome, rather than going through the lower circles of hell building the Burma–Thailand railway. It was part miracle, part the drawing on unimaginable reserves of endurance, that any of the prisoners survived the railway.

The first part of *The Naked Island* can be read as a record of both the futility of war in general, and the unpardonable mishandling by the British of the Malayan campaign in particular. As always, the mistakes of the generals and the politicians are left to be borne by the fighting soldiers. In Malaya they have hardly any weapons to fight with, and no air cover. The only time Braddon and his company see an RAF aircraft is when an ancient biplane, flown with superlative courage, drops supplies on the enemy and bombs on the Allies.

They were brave men, those eight. Their heads went up, and while we shouted cheerful remarks at them, trying not to let them know what we sensed, they grinned back at us so that we shouldn't sense what they knew. They went through the big gate.

One of the happiest achievements of Braddon in *The Naked Island* is his portrait of the Australian soldiers. This he manages without ever losing sight of the individual, and by avoiding easy generalisations. There is a tragic irony in his celebration of the outstanding health and fitness of the Australians when they are first in Malaya, both as a result of their physique and healthy upbringing, and of the hygiene enforced by the authorities. Initially at least, "the dreaded tropical diseases . . . remained . . . unknown to us". How familiar they are to become with them, in the captivity ahead.

Again and again Braddon supplies instances of the Australian soldiers' humour, their irreverence for the rules imposed by British officers, their refusal to humble themselves before the Japanese, their ability to thieve and scrounge and improvise, their commitment to looking after each other in trouble. Braddon's attitudes and sense of

Fit Parade for Work on the Railway *Ronald Searle* (*The Naked Island*) (*above*)

humour are characteristically Australian, and yet some of his warmest praise goes to British fellow-prisoners, in particular to the Scots of the Argyle Regiment.

Whereas in Singapore, during the phoney war before the Japanese invaded Malaya, there were frequent fights between the Australian and British soldiers, there is nothing but friendship (between ordinary ranks, officers are another matter) in the prison camps. Braddon writes, "The prisoner-of-war life of those four years was an object lesson in living together." He goes on, later, to say:

> Strangely enough, our life was almost totally devoid of friction. It is remarkable to record that in the Pudu community of 1,000 and the Changi community which fluctuated between 7,000 and 17,000, and all the camps in Thailand, over a period of four years, there were no cases of murder, remarkably few of theft (from our own men, that is—the Nips, of course, were fair game) and only three suicides. Very few other such large communities over such a long period could boast similarly.

If this is right, it is indeed above the ordinary. Accounts of life in the concentration camps of Hitler or Stalin are full of violence and mistrust between prisoners. Braddon notes that in the Dutch and Italian camps there were incessant brawls.

After the disastrous battle of the Muar River, Braddon was ordered by an officer to surrender. He later maintained that he should have kept running into the jungle. He and the other 500 survivors of the initial 1500 men were taken, in a terrible march, to Pudu Gaol. There a total of 700 men were eventually locked up in a gaol built for 30 women.

Braddon goes on to describe the attitude of the men after the Japanese had told them they were not regarded as official prisoners of war but as slave labour, and that they would be shot when their term of usefulness expired:

> This lent a certain doubtful quality to the average man's expectation of life and resulted eventually—in most cases—in a rather delightful air of detachment. The philosophy of "It doesn't matter" had its birth in those days.

Understatement and ironic humour give Braddon the means of coping with events. In the depths of horror in Thailand he still manages to maintain a sardonic, typically Australian style, though in writing of the worst happenings he falls back on utter simplicity of description.

One of the strangest relationships to emerge from Changi and Thailand is that between the Japanese interpreter, Terai, and Braddon himself. In the comparative luxury of Changi, where Japanese guards were seldom seen and the Allies kept their own discipline, Terai, a former Professor of English in a Japanese university, was generally thought to be pro-British and anti-war. Young and good-looking, he was very helpful to the remarkably talented members of the Australian Concert Party, to the extent of performing favours, such as finding violin strings for them in Singapore.

Terai also went to Thailand. On arrival there he examined Braddon's three books, confiscated the two most precious, G. B. Shaw's works and the *Oxford Book of English Verse*, and left him with *Mein Kampf*. "Thenceforth my

DIGGING BORE-HOLE LATRINES, CHANGI CAMP *Murray Griffin*

RUSSELL BRADDON
1921-

Russell Braddon was born in Sydney on 25 January 1921. His grandfather was Sir Henry Braddon, MLC; his father was a solicitor who died, when Russell was 11, of injuries received in World War I. Russell was educated at Sydney CEGS, where he played Rugby and represented the school at tennis. He enrolled in an Arts-Law course at Sydney University, and then enlisted in the AIF at the age of 20.

Braddon went overseas with the Eighth Division and fought in Malaya before being captured by the Japanese. He spent four years in Pudu and Changi jails, and in camps on the Burma-Thailand Railway.

After the war he returned to Sydney. He became very depressed about the way he considered Australia had changed since before the war, and spent some time in a psychiatric hospital after an attempted suicide.

In 1949 he went to live in England and has remained a resident there ever since. An old prisoner-of-war friend, Sydney Piddington, with whom he had performed mind-reading acts at camp entertainments, asked him to tour the English music halls with him and his wife Lesley. Braddon spent three years with the Piddingtons as business manager, publicity agent and comic relief. He was also at this time writing scripts for the BBC.

The Naked Island was published in 1952 and has never gone out of print. It has sold more than a million copies in English and in translations. Braddon has been inclined to make odd remarks about the book, as on the occasion when he was presented with a gold statuette to mark its millionth sale in paperback. "*The Naked Island* is irrelevant rubbish," he said, "it's about a war and a time that's irrelevant." This can hardly be the conclusion of anybody reading the book, then or now.

The Naked Island was adapted by Braddon for the stage as *You'll Never Get Off The Island*, and it was performed in London in 1960 and successfully produced in Australia by the Elizabethan Theatre Trust in 1962.

Braddon has continued to make controversial statements, as when he returned to Sydney during the Whitlam era and said that Australia was on the way to becoming a banana republic. Nor has he spared the British. In a BBC television programme, *Epitaph to Friendship*, he maintained that Britain was mostly to blame for the fact that British-Australian friendship was now dead.

Braddon has published some 26 books, including a number of novels as well as biographies of Lord Thomson, Group-Captain Cheshire, VC, and Dame Joan Sutherland. He has commented that, "In non-fiction there's very little pleasure at all."

In 1982 he made a television documentary for the ABC on the Burma-Thailand Railway.

Braddon writes, "I love Australia with a passion, but I can't work there. I'm lazy like most writers, and Australia makes me lazier than ever – tennis and swimming and that sort of thing." Thus he continues to live in London.

---

mental companion for however long we remained in Thailand was to be none other than Adolf Hitler." On the railway, Terai used to visit Braddon from headquarters to give him news (mostly bad) of his friends. He asked if there was anything that Braddon wanted, and was told "Quinine". He replied apologetically that quinine was difficult to obtain, and left Braddon a book on Japanese flower arrangement. On the next visit he apologised for the brutal behaviour of the guards – "They are only coolies," he said – and left Braddon another book, *Bushido or Japanese Chivalry*.

On the next visit he came with a list of 30 men who had died in the last few days. " 'There are so many,' he said softly . . . then he went on, 'Mr Braddon, why are you so yellow and thin?' " By this stage Braddon had nearly died of beri-beri.

Finally, after the surrender of Italy, Terai tried to trick Braddon into admitting that he had heard the news on an illicit radio, at the same time giving him to read a play he had written. Again he commented, "But you are still so yellow and thin." Braddon, by this time, had barely survived the malignant tertian malaria by stealing and swallowing a bottle of vitamin B tablets.

Braddon told him the play was "lousy", adding, "Nothing personal, of course." Terai took the typescript back in fury. It was the last time Braddon saw him; he later heard that at the end of the war Terai had attempted hara-kiri – "an odd thing for a man who was pro-British and anti-war to do".

Somehow Braddon survived Thailand, although he had to work without boots and had sores making holes right through his feet. He also suffered from ulcers and "rice balls" (his scrotum was raw from a skin disease) but was grateful for having escaped cholera. The railway had cost a human life for every sleeper in 640 kilometres.

Back at Changi, working on the aerodrome, life had been hard but comparatively secure and hygienic, and the pool of prodigious intellectual, artistic and dramatic talent present in the camp provided opportunities for keeping the mind occupied. In the New Year of 1945 Braddon celebrated his twenty-fourth birthday; in February he passed his one-thousandth day in captivity. Then the war ended. Food and drugs, always said to be unprocurable, appeared in vast quantities. The British paratroopers arrived. Braddon was one of the few that walked the 27 kilometres into Singapore to watch Mountbatten accept Itagaki's surrender.

The Japanese phrase, "War finish one hundred years", haunted Braddon. He later wrote a book, *The Other Hundred Years War – Japan's Bid for Supremacy 1941-2041*, the theme of which is that Japanese industry will conquer the world. But he has said that he no longer feels any hatred for the Japanese.

Hatred for the Japanese is the basis of *The Naked Island*, but it does not control the book. What emerges, from this account of bodies and spirits in torment, is a communion of affection and pride shared between ordinary men.

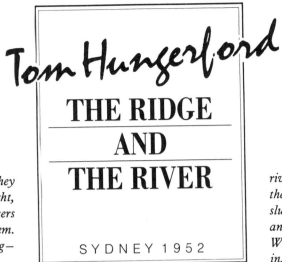

Tom Hungerford

THE RIDGE AND THE RIVER

SYDNEY 1952

"Shh!" Malise held up his finger. They stood still in the greenly golden light, listening, their green shirts and trousers melting them into the foliage round them. "Hear that? Some bastard shouting— down the river, it sounded like!"

As he finished speaking it came again, a faint, high cry, but in a voice unmistakably human.

"Kanakas?" Evans queried softly. Malise shook his head slowly, pointing to the base of the palm. He raised his eyebrows in silence and nodded in the direction of the river. Together they crept through the trees to investigate.

The cover thinned out rapidly. The last was on top of a low ridge of loose gravel at the edge of a narrow open space. On the far side of it a gentle slope descended about ten feet to the water. Crawling softly up the ridge and gently separating enough of the low cover in front of them to afford a view, the Australians looked down on a strip of hard, greyish sand.

On it, about a dozen Japanese crowded round one who carried a bunch of ripe bananas. Three or four more still loitered in the knee-deep green water of the river, idly splashing each other and hurling small stones downstream with the over-arm motion of grenade-throwing. Their cries, and the rapid, gabbling conversation of the group on the sand, came faintly up to the Australians. Evans drew a hissing breath.

"Holy mackerel, that must have been close!" he muttered. "We must've walked into the garden as he walked out!"

Malise grinned sideways in silence, and they watched the Japanese from the cover of the thick creeper behind which they crouched. The Japs were all naked, and the westering sun gilded their bodies strangely, even beautifully, as they skylarked on the sand. While the Australians watched, four of them pounced on a fifth and, swinging him by his arms and legs, hurled him out into a deep pool. He came up spluttering and shouted something at the group on the bank. They shouted back in mirthful derision, pelting him with banana peel, and a couple of them made the same lewd and unmistakable gesture that both Evans and Malise had made a thousand times in similar circumstances.

Pinkie Evans thought, with an unbidden and unaccountable start, of the number of times he and others of the section had frolicked in the waters of just such a swift, green jungle river, exactly as these men were doing. It was always the shot—coming in from a long patrol, they would stop at the last decent-sized river outside the camp and pile in, leaving their clothes on, to beat and scrub and sluice out of them the accumulated stink and sweat of three or four or more days. What if a Jap patrol had followed them in, ever? Or if a party on a walkabout, just as they were now, had heard the shouting and splashing, as they had, and had crept down close to the bank and poked their rifles and machine-guns through the foliage?

It was the first time he had seen a Japanese unarmed, undressed, helpless, playing, and he was afraid with a strange new fear. The Jap he had been used to seeing was always cruel, foreign—a remote face and a shapeless figure half screened by the cover of an ambush position, or a waddling, armed ape who might have raped European women in Hong Kong and would like to do the same in Perth or Sydney. A stinking thing sprawled beside a track, unhuman offal for jungle insects to swarm in. But these men in the creek, playing unaware, stripped the same as any other man.

There was one, short and thickly built, with glossy black hair. Evans could not see his face and for a paralysed moment had the feeling that it was Manetta. And then amongst the others he saw the familiar lines of nearly everyone in the section, even of his own hard, stringy frame. They were men, men!

The setting of *The Ridge and the River*, although it is never specified in the novel, is the island of Bougainville, and the time near the end of World War II. The action is basically very simple, involving a patrol to find a concentration of Japanese, an attack and the return to the forward base. Even to find this base, where Major Lovatt is waiting, is difficult enough in the rain and the jungle.

The rain dissolves time, the jungle obscures place and the tired soldiers are detached from what they are doing, fulfilling the functions of war far from their real life, occasionally and poignantly remembered, in Australia. War is about death, and they also detach themselves from that.

Corporal Alec Shearwood, the leader of the patrol until the arrival of the new officer, often views himself, with a "curious half-panic uncertainty", as through a pane of thick glass, so detached that "somewhere he might have been killed, and that this was the awakening after death, this separate silent awareness on the other side of a glass wall". On such occasions the only assurance he knows is to think of his wife and their life together.

A similar detachment takes the men past the presence of death and the endurance of rain, discomfort and tiredness to "that belief in their own indestructibility without which no soldier could face the daily strain of his living". Hardened by experience, they can view strange corpses as dead meat and not become involved. But when one of their own group is badly wounded or killed, there is a momentary "crack in the walls of their own vulnerability", caused by the collapse of "the wall of impenetrability" about the wounded man.

Death or wounds make a soldier an individual again. Yet it is strange that these soldiers, anonymous in jungle greens and sweat and mud, a net over their faces, are briefly so individual in moments when they talk. One of Hungerford's achievements in *The Ridge and the River* is to handle with great delicacy this elusive evidence of humanity in the dehumanising atmosphere of war; each individual is different.

"*Shh!*" *Malise held up his finger. They stood still in the greenly golden light, listening, their green shirts and trousers melting them into the foliage round them. "Hear that? Some bastard shouting—down the river, it sounded like!"*

The men talk toughly to disguise their vulnerability. Sleep and exhaustion can betray them. There is one moving passage when Alec, the corporal who is effectively in charge of the patrol, looks at the Sydney larrikin Oscar White, the youngest on the patrol, asleep, tired beyond control by the rigours of the forced march when the patrol is returning.

The boy had rolled away from the support of the wall and lay sprawled on the dirt floor. Damp and filth plastered his dark hair down on his forehead, and in the sickly light his skin seemed transparent, with bluish troughs below the deep-set eyes and with unboyish lines about the young, hard mouth. Sleep and exhaustion had stripped him of his daytime armour of toughness—stripped him of decency and humanity, almost.

There was nothing beautiful about his nakedness, nothing appealing, pale and streaked with filth; the thin boy's chest and narrow boy's loins, the long skinny boy's legs and crinkled, mud-caked feet were obscene, somehow, a terrible travesty of what they might and should have been.

The patrol exposes character as well as the body. A deep hostility is revealed immediately the book opens between Alec Shearwood and the other corporal, Malise. Alec is accustomed to being in charge, but Malise, bitter against everyone, is always questioning authority.

Before the patrol begins, the men discover an ambush. An hysterical young soldier who has lost his rifle rushes out of the jungle into their protection, leaving his shot companion behind. The men find his panic embarrassing, doubly so when he is revealed to be their new officer, Wilder. An arrogant and ignorant young product of the Officers' Training College, Wilder is taken in hand by Shearwood, who has the men's deep respect. Alec has to teach the young officer how to command both his white troops and the black carriers and scouts, especially Womai, a proud, fierce man who admits having worked for the Japanese before he came to the Australians.

"Boongs, coons, Kanakas"—the Australians use them and are occasionally grateful to them, but regard them as hardly human. Malise is hated by them, as he has got several of the girls with child, in an ambivalent contact with the natives that is almost unthinkable to the other Australians. There are reasons for this, which emerge later.

Alec understands the natives and respects them. Wilder, thinking the guide Womai is lost, blunders up and asks, "Does this boong know where he is, or what he's doing?" Shearwood angrily answers, "Don't call the guides boongs in their hearing! . . . They're Kanakas, and like to be called that, and nothing else." It is a typically disillusioned Australian response; Alec is well aware that when the natives are not present everyone will call them "boongs" or "coons".

At one stage he has to strike one of the Kanaka carriers to assert his authority. He hates doing it, and rebukes White for saying, "That's the stuff to give 'em!" "Shearwood had always liked the Kanakas. They were good people, kind and humorous and loyal, but no fools." He disapproves of their exploitation by the planters and the government before the war, and sympathises with their present situation, forced to help the Australians in a war not of their making. But he knows they have no time for the Japanese, who have treated them badly.

The presence of the natives, for whom the island and the jungle are home, gives further depth to the novel. As for deeper spiritual levels, the men can do without them except for the Catholic Manetta, son of an Italian migrant. He and Shearwood argue about God, with mutual respect. The minds of the others are uninformed, although at the end of it all some of them will be capable of deeper insights.

The exception is Malise. His bitterness and hostility have been shaped by his birth. Although there is a vague rumour, no one really suspects that he is part Aboriginal in descent. In fact his father is a wealthy station owner and his mother a half-caste lubra working in a country pub. Badly wounded in the patrol, he later confesses to Wilder: "I'm a nigger, Wilder. . . . You didn't know that, did you? . . . My own father never called me anything but 'you black bastard'. *You black bastard*, from your own dad!"

Malise's black blood gives him an ambivalent relationship to the Kanakas. On the one hand he can take out some of his humiliations on them, men who in pidgin call him "white master"; on the other he has not the ordinary Australians' physical revulsion to them. Consequently he commits the dangerous folly of sleeping with their young women.

Malise is not softened by the kindness of his companions, who have performed miracles by carrying him on a stretcher through the jungle along the ridge and across a great river.

LIFE ON SLATER'S KNOLL *Harold Abbott*

TOM HUNGERFORD
1915-

Tom Hungerford was born at Perth in 1915 and educated at South Perth State School, Perth Boys School and Perth Senior Technical College.

In 1932 he joined the printing staff of the Perth evening newspaper, the *Daily News*, and was sporadically involved with journalism for the next 46 years.

The longest "off" period was in the Army during and after World War II. He served five years with the 2/8th Australian Commando Squadron, and saw active service in New Guinea, New Britain and Bougainville. He was a sergeant, and was mentioned in despatches. After the war he joined the British Commonwealth Occupation Force in Japan, and remained with it from 1945 to 1947.

After his discharge he wandered around Australia working at various jobs until in 1948 he was appointed Editor of Publications at the Australian War Memorial in Canberra.

Between 1947 and 1949 he wrote his first two novels, *Sowers of the Wind* and *The Ridge and the River*, which respectively won and shared second prize in the *Sydney Morning Herald* Literary Competition.

He writes of *The Ridge and the River*, "I wanted to record what it was like to be a soldier in the Australian army in the Islands at that time; I wanted also to express the immense admiration I had then for the Australian fighting man. What really started me was in about 1948 when I was told that our CO, a magnificent bushranger by the name of Norman Winning, had been gunned down by Communist insurgents on his plantation in Malaya. He had been a planter before the war, as far as anyone could pin him down. I thought the novel might be a bit of a memorial to him. Winning was the Major Lovatt of the book."

In 1948 Hungerford took a job with the Hon. W. M. ("Billy") Hughes, expecting to work on his biography. He says he left "very smartly". He then went to work as a kitchen hand in a Canberra migrant hostel to get material for his third novel, *Riverslake*.

In February 1951 he was asked to join the staff of the Australian News and Information Bureau in Canberra, and he spent the next 15 years with the Bureau. He represented it in the Antarctic in 1954-55 and in New York from 1957 to 1961. During his time in New York, he wrote his fourth novel, *Shake the Golden Bough*.

Retiring from the Bureau in 1957, he spent four years freelancing, living for a year in Macao. In the 1970s he was public relations officer for, successively, the Tonkin and Court governments in Western Australia, retiring in 1978.

He subsequently continued to travel, including two trips to both Russia and China. During this time he wrote a travel book, *A Million Square*, and three books of short stories — *Wong Chu and the Queen's Letterbox, Stories from Suburban Road* (which won the 1984 Western Australian Literary Award) and most recently *A Knockabout with a Slouch Hat*. He lives on 1.6 hectares of bush 13 kilometres south of Perth.

If they at last like him, it is only temporary. After the war, if he survives, he will be only another quarter-caste again, looking for a job in an outback town. It is ironic that Malise is shot in the shoulder by a dum-dum bullet, after being rebuked by Wilder ("it's against international law") for making his own dum-dums for his sniper's rifle by filing off the tip of his bullets.

Malise grinned sideways in silence, and they watched the Japanese from the cover of the thick creeper behind which they crouched. The Japs were all naked, and the westering sun gilded their bodies strangely, even beautifully, as they skylarked on the sand.

The patrol, the fight with the Japanese, and the incredibly difficult return by the ridge and the river make the novel a very exciting one to read. At the level of action it is highly competent. But Hungerford is concerned with several levels, especially of humanity. Every soldier has to regard his enemy as less than human, even if he cannot hate him, if he is to be able to shoot him. The Japanese are normally several times removed from the Australian soldiers; they are yellow, ugly, members of a cruel society, capable of any atrocity.

Out scouting beyond the patrol, Malise and Pinkie Evans come upon a group of Japanese bathing in the river. Their bodies are beautiful in the afternoon sun, they skylark around and play games just like the Australians. Pinkie realises they are "men, *men*!" "It was the first time he had seen a Japanese unarmed, undressed, helpless, playing, and he was afraid with a strange new fear." He is afraid that "in the future he might see human beings in the sights of his snub-nosed Owen, and not the curious Japanese *things* that he had been taught to kill on sight". Not so Malise, who would like to shoot the most handsome of the bathers right away.

At that moment a Japanese sniper wounds both Malise and Evans. The battle to rescue them, in which some 20 Japanese are killed, makes a man of Wilder, who at last wins the respect of his men, and keeps it on the terrible return march, with the unconscious Malise carried on a stretcher and Evans determinedly stumbling along. As they are crossing the fast-flowing river Evans is swept away and drowned. Thanks to Wilder's skilful nursing, Malise is kept alive.

In the final reunion with their remarkable commanding officer, Major Lovatt, Wilder's seal of approval by his men is stamped by Lovatt who, in a clever exercise in psychology, rebukes Wilder for losing one man and bringing another back badly wounded. The men sympathise with Wilder, which is what Lovatt wanted them to do. Lonely at the top, he does not mind if they disapprove of him.

The book ends with Shearwood's commission coming through. Shearwood is the ordinary decent Australian, a born leader, but several times in the past he had managed to avoid "the dreadful responsibility . . . of having jurisdiction over the lives of the men about him". But the men all approve, even cranky old Beetle, the cook. "You'll be the best of a bad bunch, anyway. Good luck to you."

Hungerford understands the humour, the laconic understatement and the guarded mateship of the Australian soldiers. He also understands and conveys the essence of the terrible environment of the Bougainville jungle, which, with war itself, is a further distancing of these men from normality. The survival of humanity in wartime is the deep, sad subject of *The Ridge and the River*, indicated in the end by stoicism rather than heroism.

ALIEN SON

SYDNEY 1952

From the high picket fence we watched him unload his cart, stacking bottles in pyramids according to their size and shape. Then he carried a great bundle of bags piled high on his strong shoulders into a shed, where dark doors opened like the mouth of a cave. He curried and brushed his horse and carefully mixed chaff and bran into a bin, gently pushing its soft nose aside. Then he disappeared into the shed and closed the door.

When I returned home Mother complained bitterly that I had run away twice in one day; that I had thrown my shoes and socks away and would catch cold. I would get lost; all her gloomiest premonitions would come true. Father was always blunt-spoken and he said that if I disobeyed Mother again he would take to me in no uncertain way.

It was at that stage that I judged it wise to bring out my bit of news. I said that in the afternoon I had only gone to the shed to find out if the old man was really a Jew. Mother was overwhelmed.

"There you are, you find our people in the farthest corners of the world. Perhaps this place is after all not the end of everything. We might have a community here yet."

All my misdeeds were forgotten and even Father smiled.

"Bring him home," he said, cheeerfully. "Let's have a look at him."

It was not until sundown the next day that I saw the old man again. I was in the street with the neighbour's boy looking into shop windows and watching the men go into the hotel, when I saw the old man pacing up and down on the opposite side of the street outside the railway station. The train had just gone and was climbing into the hills that rose beyond the township. Escaping smoke still hung in grey masses against a purple sky, blotting out the stars which had just appeared.

When he caught sight of me the old man hurried towards me. Spacing his words slowly he asked me in a wheedling, high-pitched, sing-song voice if I was a Jewish boy. Immediately I spoke in Yiddish his voice changed; every trace of hesitancy disappeared. He pinched my cheeks and rumpled my hair with his strong, calloused palms.

"Why haven't I seen your father and mother? Where are they hiding? I'll have someone to talk to at last. I'll be able to free my heart."

Then his voice changed and in a wheedling tone, his half-closed eyes blinking innocently, he asked, "And for instance, what does your father do?"

He seemed relieved when I answered that he was a draper.

From that day old Hirsh was a regular visitor to our house. Mother's hope had been realized and we had the beginnings of a community. Every day at six we would see the old man hastening towards the house, his short body erect and his quick stride soldierly. His appearance never altered except on wet days when he wore a long shabby overcoat over his faded blue waistcoat and the bulging leather bag that he never parted from. He no longer lingered over his horse of an evening; he made the horse comfortable and left without even an affectionate glance.

Even after we had sat down to our meal he remained standing with his back to the fire, often without speaking, his hat still on his head, his eyes almost closed.

Father, drinking his soup noisily, would grunt, "And how is business, Hirsh?"

And Hirsh invariably answered with the same words, "No good."

Long before the word "ethnic" became widely used in Australia, and the huge effects of the post-war immigrants began to be assessed, Judah Waten's *Alien Son* gave the first and still the best account of a European family's settlement in Australia. Waten is also the first immigrant from Eastern Europe to make a name as an Australian writer.

Alien Son is a discontinuous narrative, told in 13 short stories, of a Russian-Jewish couple and their two children, a boy (the narrator) and a girl, who settle in Australia in the 1910s. Apart from one story which specifies World War I, both time and place are left deliberately vague. In part this gives *Alien Son* its eternal, universal quality, despite the vivid detail it also contains.

Shortly after their arrival in Australia, Father is 27 and Mother somewhat older. The family simply exists, both in and out of time. They don't even celebrate birthdays. Such celebrations, Mother says, are "only a foolish and eccentric form of self-worship . . . Nothing but deception. As though life can be chopped into neat twelve-month parcels!" The boy once dares to ask his mother when she was born. " 'I was born. I'm alive as you can see, so what more do you want to know?' she replied, so sharply that I never asked her about her age again."

Father is cheerful, handsome, convivial, feckless, born to failure. "Father was a trader in air, as the saying went." Mother is taciturn, pessimistic, looking for "further reason to justify her hostility to the life around us", asking, "Where are the people with ideals like those back home, who aspire to something better?"

She cannot allow herself to be anything but a stranger in the new land, refusing to learn the language, clinging to her Russian-Jewish possessions and customs. The irony is that it was she who persuaded Father to emigrate. She decided on Australia partly because there were distant relations there and partly because, "She was sure that Australia was so different from any other country that Father was bound to acquire a new and more solid way of earning a living there."

But Father, with his gay straw hats and smart suits, is happy where he is. "The idea of leaving his native land seemed so fantastic to him that he refused to regard it seriously." And even when he was told what Mother wanted, even on the journey, "He positively shouted words of indecision."

As soon as they reach Australia the roles are reversed. Father immediately becomes enthusiastic, meets some fellow-merchants, assures Mother there are fortunes to be made here. "It was different with Mother. Before she was one day off the ship she wanted to go back." She cannot bear the good-natured tolerance of Australians; she thinks they are being condescending. To her fellow-Jews who come to meet her she sharply says, "If there are no oppressors here, as you say, why do you frisk about like house dogs? Whom do you have to please?"

It is only when the children go to school that her interest in the world is reawakened. "She handled our primers and readers as if they were sacred texts." She reads them Tolstoy and Gorki and tells them of the ideals of those she worked with in the medical missions to the cholera-stricken provinces of Russia. Such ideals "would save us from the soulless influences of this barren land".

When I returned home Mother complained bitterly that I had run away twice in one day; that I had thrown my shoes and socks away and would catch cold. I would get lost; all her gloomiest premonitions would come true.

The title, *Alien Son*, carries a double meaning. The boy, when he first arrives in Australia, is an alien. He runs into the street to play with the other children, even though he cannot understand a word they are saying, but "as soon as they saw me they burst out laughing and pointed to my buttoned-up shoes and white silk socks". He runs back into the house and tears them off so he can play barefooted like the other children, even though he finds the hot gravel and sand and the short, dry grass of the paddock very painful to his feet.

But very soon the boy is learning the language, mingling happily in Australian life, even going into a Christian church hall and standing under the cross. He has gone there with two friends, Jewish Benny and Australian Martin, and some other boys. When Benny's father, Mr Smutkevich walks past and sees Benny he beckons him to come home, "with one broad, heavy finger. Suddenly Martin and his friends began to mimic Mr. Smutkevich, with their fingers. They shouted at him in their strange gibberish." He looks bewildered, Benny winces, and finally Mr Smutkevich turns away, "his shoulders momentarily hunched as if he had suddenly become an old man". The story ends with Benny and the boy looking at each other, baffled children. "Neither of us knew that there could be no reconciliation with the ways of our fathers."

So the boy grows up an alien son in his own family. The more he accepts Australian life the further he leaves his family behind. Only Father, in his limited way, understands. He says to his friend Mr Sussman, who has enlisted in the AIF, "You're just running away . . . You'll have to come back after the war . . . We belong to this new earth. It has sucked us in whether we know it or not."

Horses feature prominently in the stories in *Alien Son*. Father is an itinerant merchant, with two horses pulling a covered wagon. Later, he is a bottle-oh, an occupation the boy enjoys as he accompanies his father. Father's friend, Mr Frumkin, takes him to the horse bazaar to advise him which horse to buy. Horse after horse comes up for sale but Mr Frumkin finds fault with them all. Finally Mr Frumkin finds Father an old grey in a stall. Mr Sussman examines it, notes its faults and tells Father it is one of Mr Frumkin's own horses he is palming off on him. As they go home Father whispers to the boy that he is to say nothing to Mother about how Mr Frumkin has sold him one of his horses. The boy suspects that Mr Frumkin has lent Father the money.

There are other horses of character. Prince is an ex-racehorse. Father boasts of his past and his beauty but curses him when he canters off with the bottle-oh cart and will not stop when told to. One day when Prince has been particularly exasperating Father strikes him on the face with his fist.

> Father looked round at me, his face twisted sheepishly.
> "What did I have to do that for?" he asked in a regretful voice, more to himself than to me. "He's just like a human being, only he's dumb. Why should he know what to do in a bottle-oh's cart? Did I know what to do when I started? He's a gentleman come down in the world. He's not used to earning his living the hard way."

This hint of Father's world being reflected in that of the horse is typical of Waten's delicacy of approach. The reader is free to make the connections, nothing is forced upon him.

On another occasion Father beats the boy for whipping another of his horses, Ginger, crying, "This'll teach you to respect horses that work for their living, you rascal."

The stories of *Alien Son* gently create the world in which Father works, somewhat unsuccessfully, for a living, and the more discreet and stressful world of Jewish life in Australia. There are beautiful sketches of the jollity of dancing and singing, the pathos of alienation, and the tensions between families, both Australian and Jewish. There is also one fine story about an Aboriginal family who live in the

BOY IN STREET *Robert Dickerson*

JUDAH WATEN
1911-

Judah Leon Waten was born of Jewish parents at Odessa, Russia, on 29 July 1911. To escape the persecution of Jews in Czarist Russia the family moved to Palestine when Judah was only a few weeks old. The family emigrated to Western Australia in 1914, and lived for several years in Midland Junction, about 20 kilometres from Perth. Judah was educated at the Christian Brothers College in Perth, and later, when the family moved to Melbourne, at the University High School. Despite his Jewish and Communist affiliations, Waten still speaks well of the Christian Brothers.

Probably his most useful education as a writer came from being read to, as a child, from the great Yiddish writers, Sholem Aleichem and Bialik, and from his mother's favourites, Tolstoy and Gorki and Chekhov. As he recalls in *Alien Son*, "Never did she stop to enquire whether we understood what she was reading; she said we should understand later if not now." At an early age he discovered the Carnegie Free Library in Midland Junction, and as he grew away from his Russian-Jewish background he immersed himself in his life-long favourites, Balzac, Flaubert, Thackeray and D. H. Lawrence.

Waten began to write short stories at the age of 13, and wrote his first novel when he was 19, but he says his characters were "not flesh and blood people". When overseas in the early 1930s he had stories published in avant-garde magazines in London and Paris. He recalls that one appeared alongside work by Ezra Pound, John dos Passos and Paul Bowles—"However, the combined glow of these contributions could not light up my story."

Waten worked in Australia and England at a number of jobs: junior state school teacher, shop assistant, taxation clerk, postal clerk, postal employee. He was active in radical politics. In November 1932, at a rally of the unemployed in London, he was arrested for urging the police not to use their batons on the workers. He was sentenced to three months' imprisonment, which he served in Wormwood Scrubs.

Waten returned to Australia and worked in Melbourne. The first of the *Alien Son* stories, "To a Country Town", appeared in 1946 in the annual *Coast to Coast* anthology. The complete book was first published in 1952. It was published as a Sun paperback in 1965 and since then has gone into many editions. Waten has written several novels, books of history and travel, and has also edited anthologies.

His books have been translated into Russian, German, Czech and Chinese, and with the accumulated royalties he has travelled extensively in the Communist countries.

For some years he served on the Literature Board of the Australia Council. He has held three fellowships from the Commonwealth Literary Fund and the Literature Board.

Waten's wife Hyrell is a leading educationalist and his daughter Alice is a musician. Waten shares their interests. His writing reflects his Marxist beliefs, but it has never been a narrow product of social-realism. Rather, it conforms more strictly to Tolstoy's belief, "Simplicity is a necessary condition of the beautiful."

---

neighbourhood, of whom 15-year-old Lily is left to look after a wild brood of children while the parents work. As the boy guiltily witnesses the attempt of a group of white boys to rape Lily, sex for the first time enters the life of *Alien Son*. The boy is moving both outside and beyond the world of Mother and Father.

Alien Son is a classic; spare and clean, devoid of ornament, always under control. Deceptively unpretentious, it reveals more of life than many books three times its length. The delicacy of Waten's perception illuminates both the hesitancy and the acceptance involved in the emigrant experience.

Monday morning in the bar was always quiet with very little to do except pull an occasional beer and stand around trying to look indispensable whenever the Missus came into the bar. After lunch, business would pick up, and by four o'clock we were usually too busy to look at the clock. Although the saloon bar was supposed to be more genteel than the public bar, the crowd was just as thick, and just as insistent and, nearing six o'clock, just as noisy.

Most of my customers were business and professional men about the city. A few workers chose to pay a little more to drink the same beer and spirits under almost the same conditions as those found in the public bar.

They were mostly decent fellows, but now and then I would meet a snag. One fellow in particular was a real pain in the neck. A big, jovial, fellow-me-lad this one, as big a nuisance to his drinking mates as he was to me. He was some kind of minor boss and usually drank with several of his employees, which explains why they put up with his habit of having a joke at someone else's expense.

One Friday night he was standing at the bar surrounded by his usual audience of back-slappers. He called for half a dozen beers, and a whisky and soda for himself. I placed the order before him and as I did he leant over the counter and in

CADDIE
THE AUTOBIOGRAPHY OF A SYDNEY BARMAID

LONDON 1953

a whisper which could be heard by all nearby, said: "Listen, baby, what would you charge to do the night with me?"

I was flabbergasted – but only for a second. I knew that every eye was on me. Leaning over the counter, I said in an equally loud whisper: "You go home and find out what your wife charges – or better still, your daughters. I'll charge the same."

There was a burst of laughter and one little fellow said: "Well, you did ask for it."

The look he got from his boss must have made him regret speaking. I don't think that smart alec meant what he said, but that's just the trouble.

Some men think it awfully smart to insult a woman behind a bar. I've often heard it said – particularly by those who have an interest in the liquor racket – that if a customer says anything out of place to a girl behind the bar, she must have encouraged it. That is a lot of hooey. When a man is three sheets in the wind he would be capable of insulting anyone. It depends entirely on the temperament of the drunk.

I became good at my job. I had to be. I was there to make money and I made it. If an inch off the bottom of my skirts meant an extra 5s. a week in tips, I was prepared to put up with the boss's idea of "Art".

Barmaids generally have a bad name. Some of them are not too nice, but most of them are decent, hard-working women, and there are plenty like me who slaved to keep their children. Some of the more fortunate ones lived with relatives, while others fared much the same as I did.

I learned to put the boss before sentiment, with a complete realization of what I was doing. It was my living. I was popular with the customers generally, with always a smile for anybody who breasted the bar. I took an interest in them, knew what they liked to drink. I treated them all the same, unlike some barmaids who rush to serve a good-looking man and pretend not to notice a working man in dirty clothes.

Above all, I never took my troubles to work. A good listener, I avoided voicing an opinion wherever possible. Some customers will tell you their troubles at the drop of a hat. Some of them tell of their domestic life – whatever happens to be troubling them. Quite seriously they asked you for your advice on all sorts of matters.

The flood of books published in recent years on the status and circumstances of women was in some way anticipated by *Caddie*, and none of them has greater integrity. It is the direct story of a real person, and was intended to be neither a manifesto nor a literary exercise.

"Caddie" was born with the twentieth century, and began work in a Sydney bar at the age of 24. Having been deserted by her husband, who had run off with her best friend, she was left with two children to support. She was initially christened Caddie by one of her customers in the pub, "a fine-looking man . . . dressed much better than the majority of our customers". When she asked him why he called her Caddie, he pointed to a very big car standing in the street. "Well, that's a Cadillac, and she's mine . . . You're like her –

an eight cylinder job, and a beauty." The man was the local SP bookie, "a nice chap", according to the landlady. And Caddie she was, from then on.

The book begins with a sensitive, and discomforting, account of Caddie's first day at work as a barmaid. It is the first time in her life that she has set foot in a bar. She has immediately to get used to the bad language and the dirty stories; men who would not talk like that in front of other women have no compunction in doing so in front of barmaids – they are regarded as a special species.

As for Caddie, she is "like a kid at a new school". Her mother came down in the world, but preserved her dignity as best she could against a drunken oaf of a husband. Caddie and her brother, Timothy, often had to sleep in the paddock

211

with their mother when their father came home fighting drunk. Then her mother died, soon after having given birth to a still-born child. At 15 Caddie had to become housekeeper and drudge in the stringybark hut and tents at Glenbrook, in the Blue Mountains, where her father worked as a timber-cutter.

Timothy joined the army in World War I and was killed at Gallipoli. Her father was killed in a railway accident: "I couldn't honestly pretend to grieve for him." And then at her first job, waitressing in Hillier's cafe in Pitt Street, Sydney, a position secured for her by her Glenbrook friend, Esther, she met the handsome John Marsh. They married in 1918, when he was 25 and she was 18. Ominously, his mother, to whom he was slavishly devoted, was a comfortably off bourgeois snob who looked down on Caddie.

I was flabbergasted—but only for a second. I knew that every eye was on me. Leaning over the counter, I said in an equally loud whisper: "You go home and find out what your wife charges—or better still, your daughters. I'll charge the same."

Caddie, with considerable art, presents herself as an artless country girl. She has two children, Terry and Ann, and the family is constantly short of money as John does not seem to be able to hold down a job. In a period of increasing quarrels between Caddie and John, Esther is her only confidante. In a violent scene when he throws her against the china cabinet, John tells her that he and Esther have been in love for six months, and that they are going away together. John suggests that Terry be left with his own mother and that Caddie take Ann with her. But Caddie has no intention of parting with either of her children.

Caddie is possessed of the classic armour of innocence. She goes into the city with almost no money, taking the children with her, "and at the time that was all I thought of". She takes appallingly dirty, bug-infested rooms for 30 shillings a week, and finds a woman, Mrs Platt, "with arms like legs of mutton", to look after the children so she can go out to work.

She gets a job as a barmaid at "two pounds ten to start with and a rise of ten shillings when you become experienced". As if it were not enough to have to come to terms with the subtleties and survival-mechanisms of being a barmaid, Caddie has to cope with all the problems of being a single mother with not enough money. Moreover, Mrs

Platt turns out to be a horror. As fate always seems to kick anyone who is already down, so Ann falls sick and almost dies. It would be hard to find a more distressing picture of the loneliness and powerlessness of an essentially good woman attempting to survive on her own. "Oh, how I needed a strong arm to lean on! But there was no one I could turn to. No rich uncle or aunt. I was on the outer."

Caddie is a portrait of endless resilience. The narrator never gets bitter, never lets despair render her impotent. She learns how to be very good at her job, how to cope both with the men out front and the landlady behind the scenes. These are still the days of the dreadful "six o'clock swill" at closing time, and a barmaid has to combine the nimbleness and strength of a ballet dancer with the repartee of a woman of the world. She has to be a dual personality, to learn "how to be popular with the customers while keeping them at a distance". The country girl soon develops a shell of city toughness.

Caddie, in her description, does not shrink from the brutality and crudity of life on the other side of the bar: the fights; the men vomiting where they stand and then drinking still more beers; the men urinating in the bar rather than lose their place in the queue to have their glasses refilled.

She can cope with all this, but far worse is having to put her two children into homes, one for boys and one for girls. She is allowed one hour each with them every Sunday. Some of the most poignant scenes in the book, told austerely and without sentimentality, are of Caddie saying goodbye to the children from whom she is separated all the week.

Caddie moves to a city hotel and becomes acquainted with two fellow-barmaids, Vicky and Leslie, who are "really good sports". Caddie is deservedly popular with the clients, many of the original ones following her to the city hotel, but she has no close friends since the departure of her best friend Esther with her husband. She will have nothing to do with men, and still, in some ways, hankers after John. But the reader senses that she is longing for a male friend whom she can trust and respect, not the "champagne-Charlies" who take Vicky and Leslie out.

Interestingly enough, this being the period before the great post-1945 migrant influx to Australia, she falls in love with a Greek, Peter. One technical aspect that is handled very well in *Caddie* is the sense of time. There is a slow rhythm to her inner life, however fast she may be at filling the glasses and slapping down the change. Although it is clear that she and Peter love each other, it is several months before they go to bed together, and it will obviously be many years before they can both be divorced and marry. Peter goes back to Greece in order to help out in the family business, his wife still refuses to divorce him, and Caddie lives with the fear that John may try to claim custody of the children.

But she survives. One of the achievements of *Caddie* is to convey the gritty vitality of Sydney life, the humour and the quick tongues of Caddie and her friends, who come out with such effortless remarks as (about a hated landlady): "If ever there was a bitch, it's that old cow"; or Caddie's own remark about the little cottage she moves to: "it was weatherboard and weather-beaten."

Despite the ravages of the Depression, Caddie, at the cottage, is at least able to bring her children back to a true home. Supperless nights and no school lunches there may

UNTITLED *Herbert Badham*

CADDIE
1900-1960

It was thanks to Dymphna Cusack and Florence James that *Caddie* came to be written. The two authors had taken a large, ramshackle cottage in the Blue Mountains, where they intended to settle down together and write *Come In Spinner*. They needed some household help so they could devote all their time to writing, and eventually a woman from the village agreed to do the job. She turned out to be a handsome, well-dressed woman in her forties, who said she wanted to write a book herself, but had "never had the education". She later told them:

You know, I really came to work for you out of curiosity. I'd never before seen an author in the flesh . . . And my son was fighting in the jungle and had at one time been reported missing. I thought I'd have less time to worry.

As she told them her story the two writers realised that the new 'help' "had the gift for a phrase that no education can give . . . She had in some curious fashion the capacity to get outside herself and her own problems." Over many months she told them about the struggles of her life.

One day she gave them the plot of a play, based on an incident from her own life. They urged her to write it herself. She later said: "It was on the strength of your faith in me, and the influence you had come to exert over me that I finally decided to give it a go."

She finished the play, and Dymphna Cusack and Florence James then urged her to go on and write her biography, giving her a large, empty book inscribed, "To Caddie. Now go to it. Dymphna Cusack, 16/1/47" to write in.

After five drafts, the final typescript arrived in London when Dymphna Cusack was living there in 1951. The writer and critic Michael Sadleir loved it. Dymphna Cusack did the final editing in the South of France, and in 1953 Constable and Co. published *Caddie*, to rave reviews. By September of that year it had been reprinted three times.

Caddie clung to her anonymity, even when, in 1958, Dymphna Cusack introduced her to the public at a Fellowship of Writers reception. It was not until the film of the book was released in 1976 (starring Helen Morse and Jack Thompson), that her daughter, Mrs Cathie Wright, released her name.

It was Catherine Elliott-Mackay. She was born in 1900 and died in 1960. Her daughter, one of the children of *Caddie*, has said: "Mum was terrific, and you could always trust her. As a child, I don't remember ever seeing my mother cry." She added that there was no question of Dymphna Cusack or Florence James having ghost-written the book; their role had been to supply constant encouragement and help with editing.

---

be, but it is worth it. Caddie has to go on the dole. Her friends pass the hat around in the bar and raise £9 for her and the children; she has to battle with her pride before she accepts it. But accepting charity is better than her recent experience of fainting from malnutrition.

The Child Welfare Department will not officially allow

Barmaids generally have a bad name. Some of them are not too nice, but most of them are decent, hard-working women, and there are plenty like me who slaved to keep their children. Some of the more fortunate ones lived with relatives, while others fared much the same as I did.

her to take a job, so she becomes an SP bookie. As she remarks, there is money in those sorts of activities where there is little in honest toil.

Three years go by. She continues to get letters from Peter in Greece, but there seems little hope of anything eventuating there, and it is two more years till her own divorce will go through.

And then Peter writes from Athens to say his wife has died, and can Caddie come with the children to Athens,

where he is establishing a good business, and marry him?

I was never so tempted in my life. Here was everything I'd ever dreamed of offered to me — a man who not only loved me and my children but who had been faithful to me for all the years of our separation . . . But I couldn't go. I daren't risk it. I talked it over with a solicitor, who warned me of the dangers if John should suddenly come to light and claim custody of the children . . . Was ever woman so torn?

She refuses. "It was the hardest letter I ever wrote in my life."

At least her finances are better, thanks to her activities as an SP bookmaker, in which she is now her own boss.

Some two years go by, and then there is a letter from Peter saying he is coming back to Australia. *Caddie* seems set for a happy ending. There is indeed a rapturous reunion, but the day before they are to be married Peter is killed in a car crash in the Blue Mountains. Caddie is fated never to have an easy life.

The book ends with further bleakness, as Terry enlists in the army in World War II.

However, *Caddie* is anything but a bleak book. The events of her life make compelling reading in themselves, but the skill with which she has ordered them, her fresh, earthy prose and her courageous and humane character, ensure her book a place among the classics of Australian literature.

Tom Ronan

VISION
SPLENDID

MELBOURNE 1954

It was interesting as he rode along to imagine his camp mates in other circumstances. It helped take his mind off the torture of grass seeds spearing through his socks and trouser legs, and those saddle pains which Marty described sympathetically as "being like a toothache in the rump". Clarrie, he thought, could have been a guardsman, a Roman gladiator, a whale harpooner – anything where brawn and not brain was needed. Bryan, aloof, assured, indifferent, could easily be imagined a "Mr. Speaker", or a chief justice whose decisions would stand as precedents for centuries. Too strong to be a follower, he lacked the power to compromise with inferiority, without which no man can achieve any but minor leadership: the man whose way in life must be always alone. Jack Strapper didn't seem to fit anywhere but with stock. What was that bit of Scripture he'd heard a padre quote once? Something about those "Who knew only the goad; whose talk was only of oxen". Maybe, decided Mr. Toppingham, all the overlanders from Father Abraham and Nimrod to the latest of the Australian pioneers won immortality through the work of the Jack Strappers of their day. And Marty? What a man! Singing "Sweet Adeline" around the camp-fire before daylight; discoursing on the tenets of trade unionism or the geological formation of the country, the place of Kipling among English poets and the relative merits of the brothels of Cairo and Le Havre. Martin Boylan, ex-miner, shearer, teamster, fencer, lancejack in the Royal Australian Engineers, and goodness knows what else, was the eternal troubadour, the philosophic jester, the man capable of great things but stayed from achievement by the sardonic, and perhaps not ill-founded belief that the game was not worth the candle.

"You block the mob, Top," said Marty and trotted around to Block Bryan, who had already dismounted. If the packing up in the morning had seemed fast the unpacking now was amazing. No parade-ground movement, no shipboard manœuvre was comparable to this. Bryan gave no orders, but all hands, white and black, worked with speed and a systematic efficiency. Old Jack Strapper collected kindling and lit a fire. Marty unpacked billycans and water cans, filled the tea billy, and washed his hands in a tin dish taken from a second pack which Bryan had unhitched. Clarrie and the two boys caught the other pack animals and tied them to trees, removing the loaded pack-bags and top hamper but leaving on the pack-saddles.

"Let your horse go, Top." Bryan spoke for the first time. And as Mr. Toppingham dragged his saddle-weary body to the fireside he decided that reports of the Australian working man as a loafer and an I.W.W. were, if these chappies could be taken as examples, grossly exaggerated.

He found that the baker's bread and cold boiled beef eaten, like his breakfast, sandwich-fashion, were equal to the tastiest grill or salad ever served by West End chef. There was a tang about the billy-boiled tea unlike anything he had ever drunk. He smoked the last of his cigarettes and wondered when they would strike the first shop. Soon, he presumed, because he heard Marty tell Block that the bread would last only for supper; to which that worthy made the rather cryptic retort that they would be having an "early camp and coolabah firewood that night". This was another of the numerous remarks which were over Mr. Toppingham's head but he never asked for enlightenment. Without trying to disguise his ignorance he did not mean to advertise it. Sooner or later, he supposed, he would learn the local jargon and customs. Sitting on his swag with his cigarette and his mug of tea, he wondered whether, if one of these chaps had been suddenly transported to a London suburb, his mistakes and breaches of local etiquette would be treated as generously as were his own in the bush.

Tom Ronan said he wrote *Vision Splendid* out of exasperation with both the "factual" and fictional accounts of life in his home territory, which was the north of Western Australia and the "Top End" of the Northern Territory. The result is a book of absolute integrity, which is as apparent to anyone familiar with the country as it is convincing to anyone who has never been there.

The title comes from Banjo Paterson's "Clancy of the Overflow": "And he sees the vision splendid of the sunlit plains extended". One finishes the book wondering how ironic Ronan intended the title to be. Clancy was a drover, and Ronan's lyrical descriptions of a drover's life, with all its hardships, comprise some of the most poetic writing in the book. But Ronan also perceives the "sunlit plains" worn thin by bad management, by the needless destruction of natural waterholes, and then by overstocking following the sinking of bores and the consequent more reliable supply of water.

Nor does Ronan see much joy in the life of the cattlemen and the bookkeeper (Mr Toppingham's job) or the Aborigines on the cattle stations, where the temporary freedom of the drover's life is lost. And yet, despite some of the appalling types who drift through the North, there is a core of good men and women, black and white, who not only keep things running but are happy in their way, and who certainly would not want to live anywhere else.

Ronan was clever in taking, in Mr Toppingham, an absolutely atypical hero. Not tall, lean and bronzed, nor a bushman, Mr Toppingham (Top to his friends) is at 50 a tubby, amiable Englishman – honorary Australian, with a black gin in his bed and a bottle (when available) at his elbow, but still in command of himself. The novel is, with flashbacks, constructed around Mr Toppingham's 25 years in the Kimberley area of north-western Australia.

The suggestion of an English accent, a familiarity with the classics and a gentleman's code of conduct seem to set

It was interesting as he rode along to imagine his camp mates in other circumstances. It helped take his mind off the torture of grass seeds spearing through his socks and trouser legs, and those saddle pains which Marty described sympathetically as "being like a toothache in the rump".

Top apart, but in fact he is accepted from the start by Australians as he accepts them. In one respect, *Vision Splendid* is a study of mateship, although there is only one instance of an explicit examination of it.

In April 1922, a few months after Top arrives in Western Australia, he meets Marty, a typical bushman, 20 years older than himself.

At first sight he was rather disappointed in Marty. "Was this," he asked himself, "the typical bushman? Impossible!" This man, big-framed but fleshless and noticeably stooped, with the hook nose, blue eyes, and well-trimmed Imperial beard, could not be the "Overlander" of the poets and novelists. The shapeless felt hat, grey half-sleeved flannel shirt, and belt-less trousers hanging on a pair of angular hips were surely not the costume of a stockrider.

Marty is certainly a bushman, but he has signed on with a boss drover as a cook. The boss drover (who incidentally has just knocked Marty down for making an uncomplimentary remark about his beard) is Block Bryan. Throughout the novel, Top's fortunes are bound up with these two men, one absolutely straight, the other (Marty, of course) a bit of a rogue.

Ronan spent some of the period in which the novel is set working on cattle stations and as a drover in the North,

a life he was born to as the son of a pioneer cattleman. Of his father Ronan wrote, "He was a good mate and, either as man or cattleman, I don't expect ever to look on his like again."

Of Block Bryan, Ronan writes, "He may not have been completely *au fait* with the finer points of etiquette but in the fundamentals Block Bryan was the greatest gentleman Mr Toppingham had ever known." Mr Toppingham is also aware that in the North there is a certain distinction between "gentleman" and "English gentleman".

When at one stage he is broke and Marty is temporarily in the money from handling explosives by day and running a two-up school at night, Marty peels off a few £10 notes from his roll and reminds Top, who is unwilling to take it, of the tenner Top had lent him at the Border Races.

"Oh well, Marty, that was different."

"Top, if you could only forget for a while that you are an English gentleman, you wouldn't be such a bad sort of bloke."

There is an implicit code of conduct amongst such men that is reminiscent of some of Ernest Hemingway's work. There are unspoken tests of courage; standards of expertise with horses, cattle and men; a stoicism and an ability to let go when off duty that set these men apart from the mundane rituals of suburban life. And life in the North takes a man over; Mr Toppingham has not been born there, and is always hankering after life in the South with a female companion, but his holiday journeys there are not a success, and his wild flirtations do not come to anything.

Being a man of his era and upbringing, he is ashamed of his relationships with Aboriginal women; of Lily, who shares his bed for many years, and of September, who is sharing it when he is 50. But he cannot resist them, and he finds their amorality preferable to that of the "good-time girls" in Sydney or Melbourne. "A lubra would, at any rate, bestow her favours before she asked for a reward."

Despite being published at a time when censorship was obtusely strict in Australia, *Vision Splendid* is remarkably frank about the sexual relationship between white men and Aboriginal women. The women are portrayed as happy to make the first offer, their men happy to accept the gifts that follow.

As he rides back towards the station with Marty, for once Mr Toppingham is not listening to his friend's entertaining discourse. His thoughts, "though he hated himself for the desire", are 240 kilometres ahead with Lily.

Yes, he wanted her, and in so doing realised to what extent propinquity and habit had combined to make this physically mature [she is fifteen when she first goes to bed with him], mentally childish savage an integral part of his existence. Not that he had lost his head over her; he never did that over any gin. But her nocturnal visits once or twice a week had developed into part of the routine of his life. With her artlessness, her frank cupidity, her mixture of animal impulsiveness and almost Victorian prudery, Lily had become in fact as well as in repute the "Storekeeper's Stud".

Ronan's account of the life of the whites in the North does not spare them. There is an appalling episode when a no-

ROUNDING UP A STRAGGLER *Frank Mahony*

TOM RONAN
1907-1976

Tom Ronan was born in Perth, Western Australia, on 11 November 1907, and spent his early years with his sister and parents in the bush. His father, Denis James Ronan, a pioneer cattleman, had a station about 160 kilometres out of Broome. One of Tom's earliest memories was of being carried on the pommel of his father's saddle at three years old, down the two-kilometre-long shipping race at Derby behind a mob of cattle. Tom wrote his father's biography in *Deep of the Sky* (1962), which he described as an "essay in ancestor-worship".

His father not only taught him about the bush and cattle but about men, black and white. Despite the toughness of life in the north-west, he inherited an optimistic and positive philosophy from his father. " 'A thing that you'll find out about this world, son,' Dad told me once, 'is that there are more people in it willing to do you a good turn than a bad one.' "

At the station his favourite character was the household maid-of-all-work, Kate. He wrote, "Now, Kate's world was inhabited by two sorts of human beings, people and Protestants."

When his mother died, Tom was sent down to Perth to board at the Christian Brothers College. He left school at 15, and then spent nearly a year wandering in the bush and droving with his father.

Just before his sixteenth birthday he joined the Broome pearling fleet and spent four years pearling, an experience he described in

Packhorse and Pearling Boat (1964). "Physically and perhaps psychologically it was the most disastrous decision I ever made. I was not quite 16 years old . . . I needed hard work and I needed constant discipline, and these were the two things lacking in the pearling fleets." Nevertheless, the effect of the experience was a lasting one, and in his 50s Ronan wrote, "In among the fever germs and the sediment of overproof rum there is still, nearly 40 years later, a bit of salt water in my veins."

Ronan served in the AIF in World War II from 1940 to 1944. In 1947 he married Moya Kearins, with whom he had six sons and two daughters.

In the 1950s the Ronans moved to the Northern Territory, where Tom managed a cattle station, and from 1950 to 1957 was on the staff of the CSIRO research station at Katherine. He was Chairman of the Northern Territory Tourist Board from 1963 to 1965.

Ronan has said (*Twentieth Century*, 1959) that, "The writing disease only afflicted me at about the age at which most people never recover from it . . . The reason that I became a Northern Territory writer instead of a North Shore, North Melbourne or North Perth one was, that here, four miles from Katherine, we found a home for ourselves and our children within our economic reach and which despite its numerous disadvantages has atmosphere, character and a history. What more could a yarn-spinner want?" He also noted that in the Northern Territory he was not tyrannised by time, and had no set routine, and could keep contact with the ordinary reader. Also, "The Territory is probably the best place in Australia in which to be poor."

Vision Splendid was awarded a Commonwealth Jubilee Prize in 1952. Ronan was awarded Commonwealth Literary Fund Fellowships in 1954 and 1963. He died in 1976.

---

hoper drover, Death-Adder Tom, picks a fight with an Aboriginal stockman and shoots him. Block Bryan, who has a lot more time for "useless boongs", as Death-Adder calls them, nevertheless closes ranks with the white man. He puts a bullet through the Aborigine's corpse, and tells Marty to instruct Top why he must do the same. The whites, Block Bryan maintains, have to stay on top in this country where there are 10 blacks to every white; they have to keep faith with the pioneers who "gave up everything that civilization values for the sake of extending a civilized way of life". Block Bryan really believes what he is saying. Marty puts a bullet into the black stockman's body, and then Marty reloads and hands the rifle to Top. Thus they have all shared the guilt. The body is burned.

Vision Splendid has the drifting quality of a drover's yarn, somewhat like those of the bullockies in *Such is Life*, but without Furphy's complex literary construction. *Vision Splendid* is, however, no simple yarn. In its time structure it reveals both the changes in, and the basic verities of, both the Kimberleys and the people who live there within the ironically delineated moral codes of the white men.

There is a further dimension added in that the stations are usually owned by companies which appoint managers and storekeepers and send up the hated pastoral inspectors to check on the men who are doing the work. The absentee owners, some of them in England, may pay the station one

visit, or none at all, in a lifetime. This fact lends a sardonic quality to the motives of the men who live in the North. It is an existential life, yet not at all improvised, for there is a bush tradition, which governs the decisions made.

Diversions are few, apart from drinking and talking, and silence is respected among those who do not wish to talk. There are some great occasions, such as the Border Races of 1923, a hilarious event which justifies the old hands' memories of it as "the greatest race meeting ever staged".

There are opportunities for great jobs that do not materialise, and chances of making a fortune from gold prospecting, which Marty attempts but does not succeed in. There are the everlasting seasons, wet and dry, and the drink, and the gins.

This sounds depressing, but it is not. When old Marty Boylan dies, a character called Wild William Wraxley speaks his obituary over drinks on the evening of the day of his funeral:

"I respected Boylan. He was a rogue, a most damnably mischievous liar and joker, and I'm not altogether sure that he was a gentleman. But he asked neither quarter nor pity from life, and when he could no longer fight the world he laughed at it."

This is not at all a bad code of life, and Ronan does justice to the men who live by it.

D'Arcy Niland

THE SHIRALEE

SYDNEY 1955

He would push out west. If he pushed out west he could put in an appearance at Eucla and try for a job there. If it didn't come off nothing was lost since it was on his way. He knew the ropes better than the fat man in the Grazier's office. A phone call was all right, but not a patch on being on the spot. A voice talking to a voice over a crackling wire was unsatisfactory: often the tones gave a wrong impression of a man and the impression was often enough to make all the difference between success and failure. The idea was to get before a man, let him see all of you, let him size you up.

But how to get to Pokataroo? He glanced at the smooth overcast sky. It looked unpromising. The road would be bad enough already without any more rain. It would take three or four days at least to walk it even in good weather. He'd had enough of black soil to do him for another twelve months. The chances of a lift? It was most unlikely there'd be anything going through, none of the big stuff, anyway, the trucks and freighters, the best choices for a ride. A light car could make it, but the chances of finding one were pretty remote; and when a man did find one it was odds on he'd be knocked back. The only way was the train, south to Narrabri, west to Burren Junction, change there, then north to Pokataroo—a triangle, a helluva roundabout way.

Buster was fumbling at his trouser-pocket.

"What do you want?"

"Hanky."

"Where's the one I gave you?"

She held it aloft. It was a sodden rag.

He told her to put it in her pocket and he gave her his piece of shirt. He took her hand and led her across the street. They went into a chemist's shop. Macauley asked for a bottle of eucalyptus. The chemist was a lanky man with mild blue eyes and golden hair, fluffed out on either side of a centre-parting so that the top of his head was quite flat. He had a sympathetic, affectionate voice and feminine mannerisms. As he delicately reclined the bottle on its mauve wrapping paper Buster gave a volley of sneezes, arresting the chemist's movement. He looked at her feelingly and then at Macauley.

"This for the little girl?" he asked.

"That's right."

"Poor little thing—she doesn't look well at all, does she? So frail, so skinny."

"You should have seen her before I brought her out in the bush," Macauley found himself saying in bridling defence. "Had a cough even. A bad cough. That's gone now." Then he wondered why he had bothered to speak at all.

"I would suspect her of malnutrition, poor little dear. Do you keep the milk up to her?"

Macauley looked into the bravely inquiring eyes.

"She's got her own Jersey," he said, not without some truth.

"Oh, that's splendid. Milk is so nourishing. So much the child's food. And a little cod-liver oil emulsion with it, too, is a good thing. An excellent body-builder. Calcium and malt, too, for good teeth and strong bones. A child must get off to a good start in life. Now we have some very fine patent—"

"Never mind," Macauley interrupted. "Just wrap that up."

The chemist bent to his task. He hesitated. He looked up with his head cocked on one side. "I could give you something very much better than this, you know. To be candid, sir, I would put it right at the bottom of the list. It has practically no medicinal value. It's reputation is a left-over from the old horse-and-buggy days when—"

"Listen," Macauley said, a little heatedly. "I've seen that stuff do things for a man that no chemist or doctor could do. All they could do was take his money and string him a line of heifer dust as long as your arm. You're talking to the wrong man. Wrap it up."

The chemist acquiesced agreeably but looked a little hurt. He recovered his equanimity when Macauley asked for a packet of aspirin. As he handed over the change he exhorted considerately, "She has a very nasty cold, and you must watch it. You must keep her in bed, keep her warm. You must see that she doesn't get a chill. You must ply her with lemon drinks and liquid nourishment. Don't forget now. Good-bye. Good-bye, little girl."

"Hoo-roo," Macauley said. "Keep up the milk."

D'Arcy Niland's first novel, *The Shiralee*, is a highly skilled production by someone who had already written many short stories and who understood the demands of narrative and character. Niland was born with the gift of creating anticipation in the reader.

The Shiralee could be a textbook study in how a clever novelist can sustain the reader's interest in a character who would seem initially to be crude, violent, insensitive, selfish and suspicious. By the end of *The Shiralee*, however, that same reader could claim the obverse adjectives express the truth about Macauley. Macauley is a tough swagman known only by his surname, or as Mac. He has mates, male and female, all over New South Wales—a pointer to the warmth and kindness in his character which he would mostly prefer to disguise. The fact that they are such a varied lot also indicates a breadth in his own character.

However, the touchstone to his character and the chief motivating force of the narrative is Macauley's daughter, four years old when the book opens, who inspires the title of the novel. Most Australians who have not read Niland's book would not know what a shiralee is. Niland has said that he heard the word used by an old swagman and noted it down for future use, as it had such a lovely musical sound. He said the old swagman pronounced it "*Shirr*-a-lee", with a rippling sound. Its earliest recorded use occurs in *Round the Compass in Australia* by Gilbert Parker, in describing the burial of a swagman, when the grave diggers "drop in his shiralee and waterbag beside him". Morris's 1898 *Dictionary of Australian Words* gives the meaning as "Slang term for a swag or bundle of blankets". So Macauley has two swags to carry, and one of them he calls his shiralee—his little daughter, who answers to the name of Buster.

He would push out west. If he pushed out west he could put in an appearance at Eucla and try for a job there. If it didn't come off nothing was lost since it was on his way. He knew the ropes better than the fat man in the Grazier's office. A phone call was all right, but not a patch on being on the spot.

The opening paragraph of *The Shiralee* has an epic ring to it which is quite alien to the highly realistic style of the rest of the book.

There was a man who had a cross and his name was Macauley. He put Australia at his feet, he said, in the only way he knew how. His boots spun the dust from its roads and his body waded its streams. The black lines on the map, and the red, they knew him well. He built his fires in a thousand places and slept on the banks of rivers. The grass grew over his tracks, but he knew where they were when he came again.

Macauley is the legendary figure, the swagman, the nomad, the one who even when he has a home and family cannot stay with them for long. Towards the end of the book Macauley's wife bitterly accuses him of having spent no more than six months with her in five years. She adds, "And you wonder why I went off the rails." Even then he cannot understand, except in terms of guilt for a mistake he has made. "You never let on it was that bad, if it was that bad."

The true swagman has no sense of responsibility except to his mates along the track, with whom all the ties and formalities of mateship are observed. (It is interesting that in Macauley's case this applies to women as well as men, both to those women with whom he has had a sexual relationship and to those who are like sisters or favourite aunts.)

Buster, on the other hand, is an enduring responsibility, accepted initially as a duty, and finally with love. The story of how Macauley has come to have Buster with him only emerges slowly, with the true skill of the storyteller. Buster's mother is introduced merely as someone to whom Buster is not returning. " 'You don't want to see your mother,' he said. 'She's no good to you, never has been.' 'No,' the kid agreed." A portrait of her as a drab drudge follows.

Some 75 pages later we learn, as Macauley talks to his old mate Beauty Kelly, that "There's not much to it. I came home one night and found her in bed with a bloke. I took the kid and left and I never went back . . . Don't get me wrong son. I didn't take the kid for goody-goody reasons. I took it to spite her, to hurt her. But I made a mistake . . . Because she didn't want the kid. I did her a favour."

Some pages later Macauley remembers the brutal events of the night he came back unexpectedly to the lodging-house in Sydney. Walking in to his wife's bedroom, he finds her in bed with a man, and Buster sleeping in the cot in the corner of the room. Macauley thrashes his wife's lover, breaking his jaw and his ribs, and then bundles up his daughter and leaves.

Macauley has been a boxer in country sideshows. He is a powerful man, a born fighter. Niland, a gentle man himself, who had spent several years like Macauley, wandering the tracks, has an obsession with fists in *The Shiralee*.

Macauley fights with two standover men early in the book and beats them both, even when one comes at him with a broken bottle. He has to lay out his old friend Beauty when he comes home drunk and does not recognise Macauley and attacks him. He restrains the station-owner Wigley, who wants to fight him after a row over what Macauley should do about his daughter, who is sick with the flu.

Ironically, in a country town where he goes to seek provisions and a boarding house where he and Buster can stay while he takes a job, he is innocently caught in a tangle of brawling men as he passes the pub and is arrested.

At the very end of the book he is beaten up (in a boots-and-all fight) by two thugs hired by his wife. He leaves them both unconscious, but his face is a wreck.

All this violence is the most puzzling feature of *The Shiralee*. Although, of course, plenty of fights happen in Australia, it is on the whole a relatively non-violent country. Other stories of wandering bagmen, true or fictional, do not contain the violence present in *The Shiralee*. It is as if, for Niland, Macauley's courage and ability with his fists have to redeem him, as jousting does the Knights of King Arthur's Court in Sir Thomas Malory's story. In Malory's story the good knights and the bad knights all fight, and sometimes one side wins, sometimes the other; the difference is that the good knights do not start the fights.

When Macauley hits it is either in self-defence or because his manhood has been provoked and his honour compromised. In the one scene of excessive and deliberate violence, his wife's lover, with "a smirk of bravado", asks him "now he knew how it was, what was he going to do about

GOLDEN SUMMER *Arthur Streeton*

D'ARCY NILAND
1919-1967

D'Arcy Niland was born at Glen Innes, New South Wales, in 1919, the son of an Irish wool-classer. He was named after the famous Australian boxer Les Darcy, whose biography Niland later wrote.

Niland left school at 14 and worked in various jobs — in woolsheds as a rouseabout; as a baker's assistant; as a circus hand; and as an assistant at sideshows, with an occasional turn as a boxer in a travelling tent show.

In 1935 he went to Sydney and got a job as a copy-boy with a newspaper, hoping to further his career as a writer, as he had already been contributing to children's pages in newspapers and magazines. However, after nine months he had had enough of the city and returned to the bush.

On the advice of Sister Mary Fidelis (of the Sisters of St Joseph, a Roman Catholic teaching order in Glen Innes), with whom he discussed his ambition to write, he wrote to a New Zealand girl with similar aims, who had been helped by another Sister of St Joseph in that country. After the opening letters, which were somewhat formal, Niland and the girl, Ruth Park, became penfriends. They met in 1940 when she came to Sydney, where Niland was working as a railway porter, for a holiday. She returned to Sydney in 1942, intending to take a temporary job with a newspaper before going to London. Instead, she and D'Arcy married.

The wartime manpower authorities in 1943 directed D'Arcy into rural work, and Ruth accompanied him as he worked his way around the sheds and stations. When Ruth became pregnant she returned to Sydney to live in Surry Hills while he continued shearing.

About 1944 the Nilands settled together in the room Ruth had taken in Devonshire Street in Surry Hills and, after considering the risks involved, both began a career of full-time writing. In their joint autobiography, *The Drums Go Bang*, they wrote,

> The chief character in our life was the postman, as he is in the lives of most would-be writers. High in our front door was a perpendicular slot through which he pushed the mail to fall on the floor . . . One morning nine manuscripts came through the slot in the door one after the other. They hit the floor with the thud known as dull, while we watched, too horrified to speak.

The Shiralee, Niland's first novel, was written on the strength of a £600 Fellowship the Commonwealth Literary Fund awarded to Niland in 1953. It was the 1955 Book Society Choice in England, and also *Daily Mail* Book of the Month. It has sold more than three quarters of a million copies, and was made into a film with Peter Finch playing Macauley.

Niland died of a heart attack at the age of 48, three days after finishing his novel *Dead Men Running*.

---

it?" Macauley tells him he is going to take him apart.

Although Macauley, the fighter, does not make Macauley, the man, more lovable, this aspect does add tremendously to the dramatic power of the book. In the end, the tough battler is knocked out by the tiny hand of a four-year-old girl.

"*You should have seen her before I brought her out in the bush,*" Macauley found himself saying in bridling defence. "*Had a cough even. A bad cough. That's gone now.*" Then he wondered why he had bothered to speak at all.

It is soon apparent that Buster has prodigious determination. When she loses her pet caterpillar no blandishments or curses will make her forget about it. They have to walk all the way back into town from their camp to the store where she lost it. When it cannot be found she will only reluctantly be consoled by the gift from the storekeeper of a misshapen felt animal. She names it Gooby, and it becomes her constant companion.

Once, when Macauley tries to sneak out and leave her in the care of their mutual friend the huge Bella Sweeney (a wonderful character), Buster follows him down the road at night and refuses to be left behind.

Finally she binds herself irrevocably to him by nearly losing her life when she is knocked down by a hit-and-run driver. As she hovers between life and death, and Macauley sorts out a last challenge from his wife, it is apparent that the tough façade is cracked for ever. The solitary wanderer no longer wants to be alone. The doctor, who tells him that she has come through and is asking for Gooby, "thought he heard him sobbing. 'Poor bastard,' he said."

Those are the last words of the book.

What sort of a poor bastard is Macauley? The truth of his character has been read at the beginning of the book by the old, blind Aborigine, Tommy Goorianawa, who runs his hands over Macauley's face: "You're a man, every inch of you, and there's a lot of good in you, but it's buried deep and it's twisted . . . Try and not smother it."

It is Buster who releases that goodness. Perhaps Niland's greatest success in *The Shiralee* is that there is little sentimentality, where there might have been, between the four-year-old girl and her tough, fighting father.

Arthur W. Upfield

MAN OF
TWO
TRIBES

LONDON 1956

"When we gain our freedom we have to walk two hundred miles to the nearest homestead. We could cover twenty-five miles a day, the journey thus occupying eight days. That is, of course, if all were in training. Can any one of you honestly say he has ever walked twenty-five miles in one day, or even fifteen miles in one day? Can any of you be utterly confident of walking fifteen miles every day for a week after being cooped in these caverns for years? Of course not. If one or more of you didn't crack within a week, I'd turn gangster.

"Still, we could assume that all of us can walk at least ten miles a day, so that our journey will take twenty days, say three weeks. We then have to provision ourselves for those three weeks, also arrange our own water supply, because it's possible that for days on end we won't find any.

"What you must understand is that it won't be any question of the survival of the fittest. If, after I have placed all the cards face up, you are still determined not to wait for transport, then you will obey my orders without further argument, because it is my duty to return all of you to civilisation, not only the fittest, leaving the weak to perish.

"You will also understand that I am the only one among you who can lead you across the Nullarbor Plain, and that if

anything should prevent me, say a blow to the back of the head, all of you will wander in circles until you drop and die. I can assure you that to perish of hunger, and especially of thirst, is the worst death you can suffer."

Bony paused for comment. They watched him: were silent.

"There is a large number of people, who, because they happen to be born in Australia, believe they know everything about this Continent. They travel by car or bus to towns in the farming belts, or by bus and car on the highways spanning this Continent, even encircling it, and believe they can be told nothing. Doctors and university professors, sailors and old maids—they know everything about Australia. And I have no reason to believe you are not of that vast number of know-alls.

"Since I informed you that you are now at the northern extremity of the Nullarbor Plain, have you asked yourselves why you were brought here when there are many such caverns within a few miles of the railway, within

stonethrow of the only tourist road following the southern extremity? No. You have been so occupied with your grievances, imagined and otherwise. Why were you brought here? Because if you ever did manage to get out, the Nullarbor Plain would claim you as surely as though you escaped into a forest of ravening tigers.

"In fact, if you determine to accompany me back to civilisation, you are going to be beset by worse than tigers. Fatigue will torment you. Your tortured imagination will create monsters to stalk you. And Fear will snap at your heels."

Bony paused for emphasis.

"Remember, I shall be with you. You won't lie down when you are tired, because I shall boot you to your feet. You won't moan about being utterly exhausted, because I shall energise you with a burning match under your nose. If you leave here with me, you will arrive with me, even if then you are gibbering idiots.

"You won't bluff me. The Plain won't bluff me. But the wild aborigines might, so that those who accompany me will walk much further than ten miles per day." With studied insolence he added: "I trust I make myself clear enough for your limited understanding."

Again he paused for comments, and again none were offered.

In *Man of Two Tribes* Arthur Upfield has written a thoroughly professional mystery and detective story.

And, since the hero is Detective-Inspector Napoleon Bonaparte, the book immediately takes on an extra interest. "Bony", as he insists on being called by high and low alike, is a half-caste, or, to use the modern term, mixed blood, Aborigine from Queensland. He has Polynesian as well as white and Aboriginal blood in him. There are also, of course, his famous blue eyes. His presence gives a different focus, and deeper insights, into the superficial events of any of his cases. He has a university degree and considerable inborn intelligence and sensibility. Bony's qualifications and qualities enable Upfield to handle his narrative of violence and detection with an unexpected subtlety.

Then too there are Bony's genes. He has the white man's capacity to cope with theory and planning. He has the Polynesian's warmth and human sympathy and capacity to include all types in the human family. Finally he has the Aboriginal knowledge and love of the earth of Australia, and the capacity to listen and respond to the spirits of the country. And he has the traditional Aboriginal skills of tracking and survival.

His presence as a man of mixed blood in a position of authority sets up undercurrents which give a sense of irony to the story. There is an instinctive racist reaction in some people when Bony comes on the scene; none in others. This gives the reader a further understanding of those characters. Many of Upfield's stories are set in the Outback, and one of his great strengths is that he knows his subject well. The reader does not feel that the writer is an armchair detective story writer who has invented or merely read up his background material. In fact, in *Man of Two Tribes*, the setting of the Nullarbor Plain is also very much the foreground. In its own way, *Man of Two Tribes* is close to *Voss*, being a journey of self-discovery in a land that is also a prime agent in that painful exposure. With the exception of Bony who by his Aboriginal blood is a friend to the land, all the other characters undergo that physical and mental torture suffered by the members of Voss's expedition.

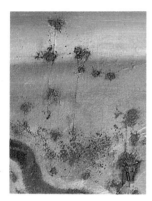

"*You will also understand that I am the only one among you who can lead you across the Nullarbor Plain, and that if anything should prevent me, say a blow to the back of the head, all of you will wander in circles until you drop and die . . .*"

The choice of the Nullarbor Plain for the locale of the story is a brilliant one. The Nullarbor is one of the most extraordinary regions of the world. It consists of some 80,000 square kilometres of treeless plain with an annual rainfall of less than 250 millimetres; the only vegetation is low shrubs, such as saltbush and bluebush, and the flowers that come up after rain. There is no surface water. The Nullarbor was part of the sea in early Tertiary times. Today, the flat expanses and the limestone cliffs give it a quality of the sea. Upfield uses the analogy with the sea several times to give added emphasis to the aloneness and insignificance of man.

But the Nullarbor is more than surface. This not only gives Upfield a vital part of his plot but also gives a symbolic depth to his story. Under the Nullarbor are hundreds of limestone caves, many of them unexplored today. Koonalda Cave, near Eucla, is some 90 metres long by 60 metres wide and the water lying in it is 27 metres deep. Winds, caused by variations in atmospheric pressure, roar and sigh through the small openings of the underground network. The Aborigines think that these underground noises are the stomach-rumblings of Ganba, the Man-eating Snake.

In his crisp and simple style, Upfield moves quickly into the basic elements of the mystery story. Myra Thomas is a woman who has been acquitted of murdering her husband in South Australia. She and her mother decide to leave Adelaide and go to live in Perth. On the 480-kilometre straight of the railway, somewhere between Fisher and

Deakin, Myra disappears in the desert. No trace of her can be found.

Bony is called in to investigate the case, as there are disturbing implications involving national security. Myra has disappeared in proximity to the Woomera rocket range and the Maralinga atomic testing ground.

Bony has the diary of an old dingo-trapper, Patsy Lonergan, who travelled all over the Nullarbor before his recent death. One very odd item recorded in the diary is that he was woken about five one morning by a helicopter going overhead. Bony takes on a different identity as Lonergan's half-caste nephew, playing the part perfectly. He goes to Mount Singular Station where he collects Lonergan's possessions and his two camels, Millie and Curley, and also his dog Lucy, and sets off ostensibly to go around Lonergan's camping spots to collect his traps and the scalps of any dingoes caught in them.

There is something unpleasant and uneasy about the atmosphere at Mount Singular, where the Weatherby families, two brothers and their wives, live and run the station. There is something odd about the younger Mrs Weatherby's eyes, which are large and "mere pools of brown and expressed nothing". No one at the station, neither the Weatherbys nor the Aboriginal stockmen, is pleased that Bony is going round Lonergan's camps, and they try to mislead him into going west instead of north.

Interesting and authentic detail, such as the way Bony catches and loads the camels, Millie and Curley, assisted by Lucy, gives an added vivacity to Upfield's novels.

As Bony makes the journey around the camps, like a lonely boat on the sea of the Nullarbor, the white man's blood in him gives way to the Aboriginal.

> When at Mount Singular, he had acted the character of the half-caste to perfection. Now he acted, without conscious effort, the character of the full-blood aborigine, for his maternal instincts were in the ascendant.

However, Bony is at times fallible. He has a touch of vanity, sometimes humorously exposed, which makes him vulnerable. He finds a white silk scarf above a hole leading to a cave, balanced on "an uprush of air from a blow-hole precisely like a ball on a water-jet in a shooting gallery". He has just secured it and, off his guard, is about to investigate the area when Lucy's bark makes him turn around. He is facing the spears of four wild Aborigines.

They take away his rifle, set the camels free, tie him and Lucy up and drop them on ropes, with his camel bags, some six metres down the hole. There Bony finds five men and a woman, some of them having been living there for many months. The woman is Myra Thomas.

One by one the inhabitants of the cave are revealed to be released convicted murderers, or, in Myra's case, an acquitted but clearly guilty murderer. Kept in bizarre captivity, they are guarded by the wild Aborigines and regularly supplied with food. They are an extraordinary lot, ranging from the elegant psychiatrist Dr Carl Havant to the brutal giant Joe Riddell.

Bony is admitted to their club as a Fellow of the Released Murderers' Institute, but he makes it clear that he is in charge of the little community, and that his duty is to find and arrest the person responsible for the recent murder of one of the

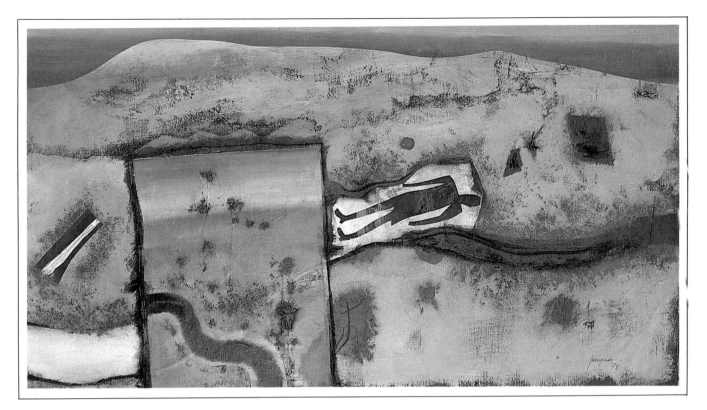

RESTING FIGURE *Robert Juniper*

ARTHUR W. UPFIELD
1888-1964

Arthur William Upfield was born in 1888 at Gosport, Hampshire, in England. His father was a draper. Arthur was educated locally, and encouraged to read widely by his grandparents. Aged 14-15 he wrote a 120,000-word novel about a voyage to Mars which has remained unpublished.

On leaving school he was articled to a firm of estate agents, but was not a great success, and so in 1910 his father sent him to Australia to "try farming". At first he worked in a hotel in Adelaide. Then he got a job as a station hand near Wilcannia, graduating to mule driver's offsider and boundary rider (with camels) along the vermin fence. Over the years he rode his bicycle, taking odd jobs as a drover, through New South Wales, Queensland and the Northern Territory.

He joined the AIF on 23 August 1914 and spent five years in the army, serving at Gallipoli and in France. After the war he returned to boundary riding, and at one stage travelled for three months with a fully initiated half-caste, Tracker Leon. In 1924 when working as a station cook at Wheeler's Well near the River Darling he began to write his first detective story. The second story had a half-caste hero, loosely based on Tracker Leon. At this time his friend Tracker Leon arrived and exchanged some books with

Upfield, one of which was Abbott's *Life of Napoleon Bonaparte*. Upfield decided to give Napoleon's name to his half-caste detective.

In 1926 he answered an advertisement in *The Times* by George Frankland, an editor and literary agent. With his help, Upfield's first novel, *The House of Cain*, was published by Hutchinson. It was followed by *The Barrakee Mystery* in which Detective-Inspector Napoleon Bonaparte, Queensland Police Department, made his first appearance in print.

Upfield continued his wandering life, being in Perth in 1931, and then taking a job with the Melbourne *Herald* in 1932. His books sold well in Australia and overseas, especially in the United States. They received high acclaim from the London critics.

Jessica Hawke's biography of Upfield, *Follow My Dust!* (London 1957), has an introduction by Detective-Inspector Napoleon Bonaparte.

In this Bony says:

> . . . my mother was an aborigine and my father was a white Australian. I knew neither parent, and, when a small baby, had been found with my dead mother beneath a sandalwood tree, and was cared for and reared by the Mission Matron. To her I owe a first-class education, and the eradication of an inferiority complex threatened by duality of race.

The rest of the Preface goes on to speak of Bony's years of friendship and travels with Upfield. Over the years Bony has attained such a convincing reality that this Preface seems perfectly genuine.

Upfield died in 1964.

---

original group, the singer, Igor Mitski. Thus Mitski's death provides a detective story in the midst of a mystery story.

There are two very interesting passages in Chapter 16, "Bony addresses the R.M.I." In one he tells the group what awaits them should they succeed in escaping from the cavern. Only he can lead them to safety, for he is one of the few who know the real Australia of the deserts, and they would die without him. In phrases which are in sentiment remarkably akin to those used by Voss in addressing the members of his expedition leaving civilisation (*Voss* was published a year after Upfield's novel), Bony says:

> "In fact, if you determine to accompany me back to civilisation, you are going to be beset by worse than tigers. Fatigue will torment you. Your tortured imagination will create monsters to stalk you. And Fear will snap at your heels."

The second occurs shortly after this speech, as Bony meditates on his group of murderers. He hates murderers and is nauseated by public sympathy for them and the cold indifference to the murdered. He asks himself now, living amongst these murderers, whether he can any longer hate them. He concludes that now he knows them personally, "There was not among them a human tiger beyond reformation, save only, perhaps, that one who had killed Mitski."

Lucy, the dog, eventually finds a passage up to the open air. By using cordite from cartridges from his pack-saddle,

Bony blasts a way to freedom. He sends one of the company, Maddoch, up to reconnoitre. He comes back beaming with joy. He says he has felt the sunshine on his hand. He has picked a spray of saltbush.

> . . . they surrounded him, to touch the velvety succulent leaves. The girl held a leaf against her cheek, and to Bony came the thought that this was the woman, natural for once.

They all escape by night, except Havant, who is not strong enough for the journey. As the first dawn rises over the Nullarbor, Bony watches their faces, "to measure their first resistance to the Plain". He has to drive them on, to give them no time to think.

It would be giving away the denouements, both of the mystery and of the murder of Mitski, to disclose what happens after Bony leads the party safely to Mount Singular station, again meeting the younger Mrs Weatherby with her expressionless eyes. Suffice to say that the imprisonment of the murderers has been brought about by people who sympathise with their victims, and cannot tolerate the early release of the killers or their acquittal. The ethics of the situation are subtle, and left open to the reader.

Upfield's novels are frequently dismissed as mere thrillers. Such a book as *Man of Two Tribes* is far more and has a secure place as a work of art. Upfield's simple style leads the reader below the surface of both man and nature.

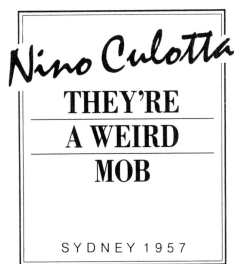

SYDNEY 1957

The driver said, "Where der yer want ut?"

Dennis said, "In me hat, where der yer bloody think?"

The man grinned and said to me, "Ut's the heat, gets a lot of 'em that way."

He backed his truck up to the bay for mud, and tipped out a load of evil looking black stuff. It splashed everywhere. I said to Dennis, "What's that?"

"Bloody black mortar. She's a bastard."

He signed another receipt.

The man said, "Hot, ain't it?"

"Yeah."

The man winked at me and drove away.

Dennis said, "No doubt about old Joe. He's a good organiser."

I was silent. He said, "Wot's wrong with you?"

"Dennis it was not necessary, the fighting. I was not insulted. If I am insulted I fight for myself."

"Know that mate. Just needed an excuse." He started to laugh. "Gees, did yer see his face? He thought I was gunna kill him."

"I thought so too."

"Wouldn've touched 'im. Just lettin' orf steam. Now we'll clean up an' hang around 'til the loam turns up." He was whistling cheerfully as we gathered up the tools and put them in his bag. Joe had said he was a moody bastard. Joe had said the same thing about Jimmy. I reflected that Dennis and Jimmy were the two I liked best. Perhaps I was a moody bastard also.

"Do you think I am a moody bastard?" I said.

"Wouldn't say that. Yer don't laugh much, but y'ain't moody. Why?"

"Joe said you were a moody bastard."

He laughed, "That's Joe. Not a thing in 'is head except buildin'. Says the same about anybody who thinks about somethin' else now an' again. He'd reckon you were if he heard us talkin' at lunchtime."

"What is loam?"

"Gees you're hard ter foller. Yer jump about all over the place. Loam's just dirt. They get ut out along the river. Mix ut with cement, an' ut sets like a bloody rock. We use ut up ter the dampcourse. Joe'll probably only use ut fer backin' up on this job. He'll put black mortar in front. Looks better."

I understood some of this, but did not ask any more questions. "Hope ut doesn't rain. Bill'll get a nice wet wall if ut rains."

"That will be bad?"

"Yeah, soak right through an' wet all 'is plaster."

"I do not think it will rain."

"Neither do I. Wot's the time?"

"Half-past three."

"We'll give ut till four an' then shoot through. Round the back in the shade."

We were about to sit down when there was another shout from the front.

"There she is," said Dennis.

It was Joe, "'Owyergoin'mate, orright?"

"Orrightmate."

"'Owyougoin' Nino—orright?"

"Orright Joe."

"That's the ticket, got 'er all down?"

"No," said Dennis. "Haven't started yet."

"Time yez did. Well, how was she down the bottom?"

"Easy day, he says. Hate ter see ut tough."

Although a very funny book which has deservedly been a best seller for many years, *They're a Weird Mob* operates on two levels. On the surface it is a novel about the mishaps and the gradual but happy assimilation of an Italian migrant in Sydney; on a deeper level it is a shrewd and entertaining study of the importance of idiomatic language to the Australian people.

The book appeared in 1957 under the pseudonym of Nino Culotta, its narrator from Northern Italy, but the secret was soon out that it was written by an Australian. John O'Grady's plot was a brilliant one. By using an intelligent and well-educated hero who is also a journalist, and who can therefore legitimately display verbal skills, he is able to maintain a highly sophisticated narrative. At the same time he throws this Italian journalist-migrant straight into Australian working-class life. Nino has been sent to Australia by his Italian editor to write articles on life in Australia. Nino considers that the best way of filling the assignment is to take a job as a builder's labourer, and thus find out for himself how ordinary people live in Australia.

What he has not allowed for is how ordinary people *speak* in Australia, or at least how they speak in working-class Sydney. He is in trouble from the moment he leaves the ship in a taxi and is dropped in what he understands is called Kings Bloody Cross. Speaking excellent English, of a rather deliberate and courtly style, he is completely baffled by the Australian idiom. As Nino explains at the beginning of the book, "Most Australians speak English like I speak Hindustani, which I don't. In general, they use English words, but in a way that makes no sense to anyone else. And they don't use our European vowel sounds, so that if they do construct a normal sentence, it doesn't sound like one. This made it necessary for me, until I became accustomed to it, to translate everything that was said to me twice, first into English and then into Italian."

His failures to connect multiply rapidly. First the taxi driver says in exasperation, "I 'ave ter get landed with a bloody ning nong who doesn't know where he's bloody goin! Will the Cross do yer?" Then Nino buys a paper to look for job advertisements and hands the paper boy a bronze penny instead of a silver two bob. "Bit sunburned sport!" says the paper boy, going on to explain, "Right size, wrong colour."

One of Nino's most engaging characteristics is that he is determined to learn. Being a big fair man, unlike the small darker Southern Italians whom he despises, and also well dressed, Nino starts off with natural advantages which are increased by his amicability. Though he can be tough when aroused (when he is likely to give his antagonist "a bump on the head"), he is both affable and quick to catch on to the local rituals and idiom. He goes into a pub and talks to a bloke who eventually tells him, "Yer not a bad sorta bloke, either, fer an Itie", after Nino has successfully initiated his query, "Wodda yer do fer a crust?"

"*Gees you're hard ter foller. Yer jump about all over the place. Loam's just dirt. They get ut out along the river. Mix ut with cement, an' ut sets like a bloody rock. We use ut up ter the dampcourse.*"

He gets on well with his employer Joe, a contractor who puts Nino to work digging trenches for foundations, with a man called Pat. After work Joe takes Nino home and introduces him to his wife, Edie: "He's an Italian. He's orright, though." The reasons Nino is "orright" are that he is not stand-offish, he works hard (a bit too hard, Pat points out), he drinks beer, and he genuinely likes "the mob"—Joe, his brother and partner Jimmy, Pat, Dennis, and of course Edie. But perhaps most of all he is accepted because he enjoys the Australian idiom and tries to use it himself. "I said carefully, 'I reckon I could knock over a schooner.' They all laughed very much. I felt pleased. I also felt proud that I was accepted into their company."

Once that has happened the story unfolds naturally, with Nino happily attempting to fit into Australian life, if not

always successfully. For example, there is the time when, with Italian pride, he refuses to swim between the flags at Bondi and has to be forcibly carried ashore by four lifesavers. To his astonishment, he also finds that the police are amiable; one of them even shows him where to get the bus.

But he can still be baffled. O'Grady brilliantly reproduces the horse-racing talk of three table companions in a Greek cafe, at the end of which Nino admits, "It was very depressing. I understood nothing. Yet my boss had said Australians spoke English, and he was a knowledgeable man." Nino has to learn, slowly, how words in the Australian idiom detach themselves from reality and move into metaphor.

For instance, take the word "drum". Nino recounts:

I said, "Pat, what does it mean when somebody says 'e never run a drum'?"

"Means 'e wasn't in the hunt . . . If 'e's with the tail-enders, 'e never run a drum."

But a few minutes later Pat is showing Nino how to cut and bend the reinforcing rods for concrete. He says, "Come over 'ere an' I'll give yer the drum." And the next day, when the concrete is going to be poured, Joe shows him how to shovel gravel into the revolving drum:

"That thing is also called a drum?"

"Yeah mate. 'Ave a go. Bung in another three shovels."

Gradually, and especially during the buck's party for Jimmy's wedding, when the kegs are set up and an enormous quantity of alcohol is consumed, Nino finds, to his joy, that he is beginning to think in Australian—helped by a number of whiskies and jugs of beer. He is also helped by his religious training, he feels, not only in having a familiar institution and ritual to succour him, but by remembering that "In the beginning was the Word." He doesn't quite know what the word was, but he is certainly beginning to know what Australian words are.

They're a Weird Mob reveals as much about Australians as about the assimilation of Nino Culotta. In two key passages in the book, at Jimmy's wedding and when Nino takes his fiancée Kay out to Punchbowl to meet the mob, conventions interfere with natural behaviour. The normally fluent Jimmy is unable to say more than a very few words at his wedding. At Joe and Edie's gathering to meet Kay, everyone is in their best suits, with collars and ties. There is afternoon tea with cake forks. There is no conversation at all, until Nino in exasperation yells out, "Bring out the bloody beer", and the ice cracks.

Looking back years later on the "strange language" of Australians, Nino speculates that:

Good English, used in conversation, now appears stilted and insincere. My Australian friends say that a man who uses it is not fair dinkum. They say he is "bungin' ut on." It is not so much the choice of words that is offensive to the Australian's ear, but the pronunciation and inflexion.

And he notes that on a formal occasion the Australian dries up. "When an Australian is asked to speak for a specific purpose, everything that makes the conversations the delight they are, disappears. . . . He becomes almost inarticulate.

From THEY'RE A WEIRD MOB *an original illustration by* WEP

NINO CULOTTA
1907-1981

There is something schizophrenic in a genuine Australian, John O'Grady, not being able to sell as many books under his own name as under the pseudonym of the Italian Nino Culotta. Yet O'Grady lived with this situation happily for some 25 years. Of course the essence of it all was that the Italian was only a device to get at the heart of the Australian. In this O'Grady certainly succeeded, as *They're a Weird Mob* has sold more than any other Australian novel; sales are now around a quarter of a million copies in Australia alone.

John O'Grady was born at Bondi, New South Wales, on 9 October 1907. He was the oldest of eight children. His father was editor of the NSW *Agricultural Gazette*, but soon after John's birth he moved with his family to a farm in New England, near Tamworth. John had no formal schooling until he was 12. Later he was a boarder at St Stanislaus College at Bathurst.

O'Grady wanted to become a doctor, but there was not enough money available as his father had been forced off the farm by drought. So O'Grady did a course in pharmacy at the University of Sydney. He worked as a pharmaceutical chemist from 1929 to 1936, and for some time lived with his wife and children at Ballina, on the New South Wales north coast.

Bored with the life of a pharmacist, O'Grady sold out and became a commercial traveller selling medical goods throughout Western Australia, South Australia and the Northern Territory. His adventures, often in very remote country, are entertainingly recounted in the *Bulletin* Literary Supplement for 1981.

In 1942 O'Grady joined the AIF and saw service in New Guinea and Borneo as a medical corps pharmacist, staying on after the war until 1950 for a tour of duty in Japan with the rank of Captain.

He returned to pharmacy for four years, but resigned in order to become a bricklayer's labourer, fulfilling an old desire to see if he could be a success at working with his hands. He was, within a week being raised to first-class labourer's rate of £16 10s a week.

In 1955 he decided to take his second wife and family to Western Samoa. At that time Western Samoa was a New Zealand protectorate, and O'Grady was forced to wait in Auckland for some time while the New Zealand Government made up its mind whether it would allow O'Grady to work in Samoa as a pharmacist. Anxious about money, O'Grady began to write a novel, *They're a Weird Mob*. When he moved to Samoa in 1956 the book was half finished.

O'Grady stayed in Samoa until 1958, training students in pharmacy and gathering material for a book on Samoa.

They're a Weird Mob was published in 1957 by Ure Smith, having been rejected by Angus and Robertson. It was followed by a sequel, *Cop This Lot*, when Nino returns to Italy. O'Grady's Samoan novel, *No Kava for Johnny*, was published under his own name in 1961. Between then and his death O'Grady published some 15 books.

He later lived at Oatley, a Sydney suburb, in a house on a ridge high above the George's River. He died in January 1981.

His whole speech changes, his phrasing becomes stilted."

Nino also develops a good understanding of the apparent truculence of Australians, that the interchange of insults and the use of ridicule are signs of friendship, and never to be used to strangers. You *can* call your mate a bastard—it is part of the informality that Australians enjoy. The restrictions of etiquette would interfere with that. At the same time it is notable that the women in *They're a Weird Mob*, particularly Edie and Kay, do not use the idiom of insults. It is as though the women are the sheet-anchor which keeps the Australian male from drifting off into anarchy. This imposes some hardships on women. Nino asks himself, "Would an Italian wife permit her husband to leave her in the middle of the night (to go rabbit-shooting with his mates) as Joe has left his wife?" Nino still has much to learn about courting and marriage, sex and friendship in Australian society. But a certain delicacy in approaching these subjects is in itself typically Australian.

The book ends with the fulfilment of the Australian dream: Nino and Kay have one child, another on the way; they are on their own block of land in their own house which Nino has built himself. Looked at from one angle, the sophisticated Italian journalist has come down to a cruder, uncultured, domestic existence. But, from another angle, he has discovered friendship, humanity, kindness, and independence, and learned to trade in an entirely new sort of humour.

Linking these themes is the Australian language. The book ends with the more-or-less devout Nino ruminating that if ever he reaches heaven, "I will know I am there when I hear Him say, 'Howyergoin'mate orright?'"

Ray Lawler's play, *The Summer of the Seventeenth Doll* (1955) and *They're a Weird Mob* (1957) gave Australians the first opportunities to hear their own contemporary idiom on the stage and in fiction. The recognition was tremendously enthusiastic. The idiom may in some respects be limiting. But the bond it creates is not.

Patrick White

VOSS

LONDON 1957

"Everyone is offended by the truth, and you will not be an exception."

That it would take place, they both knew now.

Consequently, when she did speak, the sense of inevitability that they shared made her sound as if she were reading from a notebook, only this one was her head, in which her memorandum had been written, in invisible ink, that the night had breathed upon; and as she read, or spoke, it became obvious to both that she had begun to compile her record from the first moment of their becoming acquainted.

"You are so vast and ugly," Laura Trevelyan was repeating the words; "I can imagine some desert, with rocks, rocks of prejudice, and, yes, even hatred. You are so isolated. That is why you are fascinated by the prospect of desert places, in which you will find your own situation taken for granted, or more than that, exalted. You sometimes scatter kind words or bits of poetry to people, who soon realise the extent of their illusion. Everything is for yourself. Human emotions, when you have them, are quite flattering to you. If those emotions strike sparks from others, that also is flattering. But most flattering, I think, when you experience it, is the hatred, or even the mere irritation of weaker characters."

"Do you hate me, perhaps?" asked Voss, in darkness.

"I am fascinated by you," laughed Laura Trevelyan, with such candour that her admission did not seem immodest. "You are my desert!"

Once or twice their arms brushed, and he was conscious of some extreme agitation or exhilaration in her.

"I am glad that I do not need your good opinion," he said.

"No," she said. "Nobody's opinion!"

He was surprised at the vehemence of feeling in this young girl. In such circumstances, repentance, he felt, might have been a luxury. But he did not propose to enjoy any such softness. Besides, faith in his own stature had not been destroyed.

He began to bite his nails in the darkness.

"You are upset," he said, "because you would like to pity me, and you cannot."

"If that were the case, I would certainly have cause to be upset," she blurted most wildly.

"You would like to mention me in your prayers."

By this time Laura Trevelyan had become lost somewhere in the dark of the garden. But I, too, am self-sufficient, she remembered, with some lingering repugnance for her dead prayers.

"I do not pray," she answered, miserably.

"Ach," he pounced, "you are not atheistisch?"

"I do not know," she said.

She had begun to tear a cluster of the white camellias from that biggest bush. In passing, she had snapped the hot flowers, which were now poor lumps of things. She was tearing them across, as if they had not been flesh, but some passive stuff, like blotting-paper.

"Atheists are atheists usually for mean reasons," Voss was saying. "The meanest of these is that they themselves are so lacking in magnificence they cannot conceive the idea of a Divine Power."

He was glittering coldly. The wind that the young woman had promised had sprung up, she realised dully. The stars were trembling. Leaves were slashing at one another.

"Their reasons," said Laura, "are simple, honest, personal ones. As far as I can tell. For such steps are usually taken in privacy. Certainly after considerable anguish of thought."

The darkness was becoming furious.

"But the God they have abandoned is of mean conception," Voss pursued. "Easily destroyed, because in their own image. Pitiful because such destruction does not prove the destroyer's power. Atheismus is self-murder. Do you not understand?"

Voss is a novel about exploration, both of the country of Australia and of the mind. In subject and technique it had a revolutionary impact on Australian writing, bringing in new areas of the imagination, and creating new concepts of the constant modification of reality by illusion. As White said of his own purpose in writing *Voss*, "Above all I was determined to prove that the Australian novel is not necessarily the dreary, dun-coloured offspring of journalistic realism."

There are certain similarities between Johann Ulrich Voss and Ludwig Leichhardt: both are German intellectuals, both are proud, highly idiosyncratic, and unskilful in their dealings with other human beings, and both perish in the desert. However, *Voss* is not to be read as an historical novel.

Voss arrives in Sydney, in the middle of the nineteenth century, and secures the backing of Mr Bonner and other Sydney businessmen to lead an expedition across the continent. With him, Voss intends taking Robarts, a good, simple English lad; Frank Le Mesurier, with whom he has already made a journey; Palfreyman, an ornithologist and a Christian; and Turner, a labourer.

However, the book does not open with the arrangements for the expedition (which follow some 20 pages later), but with a meeting between Voss and Laura Trevelyan, Mrs

Bonner's niece. She is a beautiful girl with an active enquiring mind who is starved of companionship. She has lost her belief in God and thinks she may have become a rationalist. She is struggling for self-sufficiency. Voss, however, thinks he has already reached it, and that "Such beautiful women were in no way necessary to him, he considered."

After Voss has gone and the family is discussing him, Laura says, "He is obsessed by this country. . . . But he is not afraid. . . . Everyone is still afraid, or most of us, of this country, and will not say it. We are not yet possessed of understanding."

"*Atheists are atheists usually for mean reasons,*" Voss was saying. "*The meanest of these is that they themselves are so lacking in magnificence they cannot conceive the idea of a Divine Power.*"

Shortly after this, in a key discussion with Le Mesurier, Voss says, "To make yourself, it is also necessary to destroy yourself." He continues:

In this disturbing country . . . it is possible more easily to discard the inessential and to attempt the infinite. You will be burnt up most likely, you will have the flesh torn from your bones, you will be tortured probably in many horrible and primitive ways, but you will realise that genius of which you sometimes suspect you are possessed, and of which you will not tell me you are afraid.

Of the several different worlds in the book, from the outback to Sydney, the most delicately handled is that of Sydney society. White's precise, almost Jane Austenish, social satire is an essential part of the book.

One of the great achievements of White's style and narrative technique is his ability to sustain this delicacy of touch when he is dealing with tougher people and situations. For instance, when the expedition reaches Brendan Boyle's station, and Voss and Palfreyman stay the night in his hut, the discrepancy between appearance and reality is revealed in a few sentences as subtle as those revealing Sydney society. The theme of Brian Penton's *Landtakers*, of the brutalising process of pioneering, is given out in a few words. "Mr Brendan Boyle was of that order of males who will destroy any distinction with which they have been born, because it accuses them, they feel, and they cannot bear the shame of it." But Mr Boyle is, surprisingly, akin to Voss when he says,

"To explore the depths of one's own repulsive nature is more than irresistible—it is necessary."

In Voss's case this process has to be forced on to him. It calls for humility, but, as he says to Laura, "I worship with pride. Ah, the humility, the humility! This is what I find so particularly loathsome."

The expedition is enlarged by another member, the ex-convict Judd, when it reaches Mr Sanderson's Rhine Towers Station. He proves to be the only member of the party not weaker than Voss. Voss, like Milton's Satan, is carrying the hell of his pride within him. But Judd's scarred back is evidence that "The convict had been tempered in hell."

The other character who is not weaker than Voss is, of course, Laura, who in some strange way is also on the expedition. She and Voss are not lovers, but they share a marriage of souls and, at the same time, a war, a fruitful conflict between his God of pride and her rational humility. They have, in Voss's words, "flounder[ed] into each other's private beings". And Laura says to her maid, the exuberant and earthy (and pregnant) Rose Portion, "I can understand him . . . if not with my reason."

Laura, who thinks and reads, feels isolated in the cheerfully social Bonner household. A letter from Voss, from Rhine Towers, is an extension of her being. After this, letters are not necessary. She and Voss become part of each other's dreams, not as fantasy, let alone sexual fantasy, but as a further extension and synthesis of the reality that lies beyond the sticks and stones of the expedition's progress.

Rose Portion has her baby and dies, and Laura adopts the baby named Mercy. It is a "visible token of the love with which she was filled". Mercy is also an embarrassment to the good Mrs Bonner, who is well aware that the gossips are saying that the baby is Laura's. Further gossip will go on to say that the father is Voss. Mercy is one of the flaws of the novel—a symbol too heavy and obvious for the delicate but convincing fabric connecting Laura and Voss.

The expedition itself is totally convincing. It is burdened with the classic afflictions of Australian exploring: heat, dust and flies; the harshness of the terrain; hostile Aborigines; and sickness and distance. But it is also a journey of self-discovery for each of the members of the expedition. Only two of the late arrivals, Judd and the Aboriginal boy Jackie, have no need of this further journey, being devoid of false pride and already totally aware both of themselves and the strange world around them. In a letter to Laura, Voss writes, "Judd's what people call a *good man*. He is not a professional saint, as is Mr Palfreyman . . . It is tempting to love such a man."

Voss, absorbed in his solitary purgatory on the path to learning that he is not God, holds himself back from such love. He is a bad leader. The expedition is stumbling into nothingness when Palfreyman is speared by the blacks and Judd announces that he is turning back. Voss tries to taunt him with cowardice, although Judd knows that that is not the case.

"It is not cowardice, if there is hell before and hell behind, and nothing to choose between them," Judd protested. "I will go home. Even if I come to grief on the way, I am going home."

Ralph Angus (the young squatter) and Turner join him and

TREE OF MAN, SKETCH II *Jon Molvig*

PATRICK WHITE
1912-

Although of a pioneering Australian family, Patrick White was born in London on 28 May 1912. He was brought up in Sydney and educated at Moss Vale until he was sent, unhappily, to Cheltenham College in England. After finishing his schooling he spent two years in the country in New South Wales, working on stations as a jackeroo.

He writes of his early life:

Brought up to believe in the maxim: Only the British can be right, I did accept this during the early part of my life. Ironed out in an English public school, and finished off at Kings, Cambridge, it was not until 1939, after wandering by myself through most of Western Europe, and finally most of the United States, that I began to grow up and think my own thoughts. The War did the rest.

After taking his degree in modern languages in 1935 White was involved with the theatre in London, writing sketches and plays.

White's first novel, *Happy Valley*, a Joycean evocation of the world of the Monaro where he had jackerooed, was published in 1939 and secured some critical acclaim, as did his next novel, *The Living and the Dead*, which appeared in 1941.

By this time White was serving as an intelligence officer in the RAAF. He was posted to Africa, the Middle East and the Western Desert, and finally served a year in Greece. After the war he was tempted to remain in Greece, but decided against it, aware of the dangers of becoming an expatriate. He faced

the alternative of remaining in what I felt to be an actual and

spiritual graveyard, with the prospect of ceasing to be an artist and turning instead into the most sterile of beings, a London intellectual, or of returning home, to the stimulus of time remembered.

So he, with a Greek partner, Manoly Lascaris, bought a farm near Castle Hill, 40 kilometres out of Sydney. Here they bred goats and dogs and raised flowers and vegetables.

His year at Castle Hill gave him some of the experience for *The Tree of Man* and for the Sarsaparilla of his fiction and plays. *The Tree of Man*, published in the USA in 1955 and in London in 1956, was received with tremendous critical acclaim in those countries, if not so well in Australia.

Voss followed in 1957. The initial idea for a novel about an Australian explorer had come to White in the Western Desert while reading Edward John Eyre's *Journals of Expeditions of Discovery in Central Australia and Overland from Adelaide to King George's Sound*; when he came to write the book the parallel, of course, was with Ludwig Leichhardt rather than with Eyre.

White was awarded the 1959 £1000 W. H. Smith prize for *Voss*, and the 1959 £500 Miles Franklin prize for the same novel. In 1973 he was awarded the Nobel Prize for Literature.

White's other novels include *Riders in the Chariot* (1961), *The Solid Mandala* (1966), *The Vivisector* (1970), *The Eye of the Storm* (1973), *A Fringe of Leaves* (1973) and *The Twyborn Affair* (1976). He has also written two collections of short stories.

White has always been keenly interested in the theatre, and three plays were produced in the early 1960s, followed by three more from 1977 onwards. He has also written screen-plays, including *The Night The Prowler* (1978).

Since the 1960s White and Lascaris have lived in Sydney, in a house overlooking Centennial Park. On some occasions in recent years White has spoken out publicly in support of some political and social issues on which he feels strongly.

Voss is left only with Robarts and Le Mesurier, who love him, and the black boy Jackie. As the expedition continues it is ghosted by two columns of Aborigines, shadowy black figures who are not hostile, but simply waiting.

As they ride on, Voss does not write letters but talks to Laura, and she answers him, "I shall not fail you."

The blacks come closer, right alongside the men on their horses, and Jackie tells Voss he must go back to his own people. The pretence of friendship between black and white is meaningless. At the same time Laura goes through a severe illness and her hair is cut off. She feels a sacrifice is needed and so she tells Mrs Bonner to send Mercy out for adoption, "You see, I am willing to give up so much to prove that human truths are also divine. This is the true meaning of Christ." Unexpected depths in Mrs Bonner's character are revealed when she refuses to hand the baby over. Laura's fever grows worse.

As Voss's expedition fails in terms of geographical or scientific discovery it reaches its climax of spiritual discovery. The blacks are now more or less living with Voss's party. Le Mesurier, a wreck, commits suicide. Voss is left with the boy Robarts. "Voss believed that he loved this boy, and with him all men, even those he had hated, which is the most difficult act of love to accomplish, because of one's own fault." Voss has at last learned humility.

Robarts dies, and the blackfellows remove his body, as Voss is too weak to do so, being more at home now with his mind and soul than with his body. That night the blacks kill and eat the horses and mules. In the morning Jackie, ordered by the old men, cuts off Voss's head to rid himself of the white man's magic.

At the same moment Laura's fever breaks, and she cries, "It is over. It is over."

Some time later, Laura, now a plain woman, has become a schoolmistress. One day she meets Colonel Hebden, "a tall, copper-coloured gentleman of a distinguished ugliness", who had led the search party after Voss. Nothing is known of the fate of the expedition, despite Colonel Hebden's returning to search again, and having camped one night, in ignorance, only a stone's throw from the skeletons of Angus and Turner, who had died of thirst.

Near the end of the book, Laura, now the headmistress, Miss Trevelyan, says, in a general conversation, "Knowledge was never a matter of geography. Quite the reverse, it overflows all maps that exist. Perhaps true knowledge only comes of death by torture in the country of the mind."

As that last sentence indicates, Voss and his travels are a mystery which remains impenetrable. Laura is still alive; she alone has shared true knowledge with Voss.

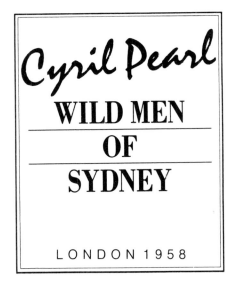

Cyril Pearl

WILD MEN
OF
SYDNEY

LONDON 1958

In 1904, when Norton took his anti-Semitism to New Zealand, he described himself to big audiences as "a self-appointed messenger" from the people of Sydney. On the next visit to New Zealand, he told his public how his 25 years of crusading against "capitalistic corruption, industrial oppression, and social snobbery and salacity", had cost him "over £25,000" and kept him a "poor man".

Not long after, when the "poor man" went to England in his de luxe suite, he took with him, apparently to annoy his wife, his two luxurious motor-cars.

Sometimes, he dramatised his demagogy. In one Melbourne Eight Hours Day procession, Truth was represented by a buxom girl in white Grecian robes, seated on the cage of a cardboard well, holding aloft a mirror. Behind her crouched two sinister masked figures in black, labelled respectively LIES and CORRUPTION. The tableau was mounted on a lorry drawn by two sturdy Percherons, with the legend: "TRUTH Fights the Worker's Cause."

No detail of Norton's personal life was too trivial to be related in the pages of Truth. He would mention, in a signed leader, the "three kidneys en broche and Wiltshire bacon" he had for breakfast on an interstate liner, the excellent grilled flounders served him in a Sydney restaurant, the grit he swallowed when he encountered a North wind on the dummy of a Melbourne cable-tram. He would begin a passionate article on Napoleon with the information that "after returning to my hotel room with my little daughter Joan, from witnessing the famous Cabiria picture, I heard her say her prayers, put her through her deep-breathing exercises, and had some supper (shallots, lettuce, cheese, and an old crust of well-baked bread)", and finish an erudite article on Democracy and Plutocracy with: "I must pause here, as I hear my niece calling me to take afternoon tea with her out on the lawn and under the shady trees after which I shall go for a swim in the sea."

In one of his last signed leaders, a reiterated denunciation of "Reid the Wriggler", as he always labelled George Reid, Norton told the public more about his niece: "Eva, who as a child was brought up at my birthplace, Brighton, in Sussex, the 'Queen of the English Seaside Resorts', was always a strong and graceful swimmer, like her mother." Then he asked an apposite question: " 'What do Truth's readers—a million a week at least . . . want to know about your niece and her natatory aptitudes? It is very amusing to see her and her Yorkshire terrier, Tiny Tim, in the water, the cynosure of all eyes,' I think I hear certain captious, cattish, critics cry. Well, I think there are thousands of Truth's readers who will be pleased to hear news of my niece and her welfare and happiness . . ."

This niece—who was not able to produce legal proof of her relationship—was an intervener in a complex action between John Norton and his wife that was heard in 1915, Mrs. Norton applying for a judicial separation on the grounds of her husband's adultery and cruelty, Norton seeking a divorce on the grounds of his wife's adultery. Mr. Richard Windeyer, opening for Mrs. Norton, said that it was "the most remarkable story of cruelty and wickedness that has ever been put before a jury". He described Norton as "a fiend in human shape", and said that the jury would be satisfied, after hearing him cross-examined, that he had been guilty of murder. Unfortunately, the cross-examination did not take place. Norton collapsed on the third day and the hearing went on for eight more days without him giving evidence. Witness after witness told, in horrifying detail, of Norton's brutal and bestial conduct, and Truth published their evidence verbatim. In one issue, the report occupied four and a half big broadsheet pages of small type. The verdict was for Mrs Norton, notwithstanding the conscientious efforts of four or five of Norton's witnesses, who, in the opinion of the jury of twelve, committed "wilful perjury".

The credulity of the human race underlies every story of villainy. In Sydney, as well as Denmark, "one may smile, and smile, and be a villain" and get away with it. The rogue who is also a demagogue depends for his success on the public's enthusiasm, where the voice of individual scepticism is lost.

Cyril Pearl is a brilliant, sceptical journalist. He has a great story in Wild Men of Sydney, an account of "three remarkable rogues, John Norton, William Patrick Crick and William Nicholas Willis, all of whom sat for many years as honourable members of the New South Wales Parliament".

But he also takes time, which the journalist rarely can, and has the ability to write a profound book on the simultaneous presence of good and evil in mankind. Pearl does not spare his three rogues; their crimes and follies are laid bare. But he allows them their qualities, about which they themselves were often confused, for the champion of the people needs to believe in himself even when he knows he is playing the hypocrite. A politician will always invoke the name of the people. A writer of the quality of Cyril Pearl has no illusions about the people. Pearl also has a sharp eye for national characteristics, for the people have to have a home, and he detects in Australians a disquieting "sort of perverse hero-worship of the fellow who has flouted the law, exploited the community, and defiantly 'got away with it'."

The best summary of *Wild Men of Sydney* is given in Pearl's own words. The sentiments expressed apply to Crick and Willis as well as to Norton.

Norton's story is interesting from many aspects; politically, as a study of triumphant demagogy; psychologically, as the record of a man's malignant struggle to avenge the harshness of his childhood and the humiliation of his physical smallness; and pathologically, as the terrible case-history of an exceptional but unbalanced mind. It is also the mirror to a forgotten town—the dirty, tough, intimate, turbulent, crooked, hard-drinking, politically immature Sydney of the late 19th century.

A Sydney, Pearl goes on to explain, which in the early 1880s contained 288,000 people and 3167 pubs, with the shadow of convictism still hanging over it.

No detail of Norton's personal life was too trivial to be related in the pages of Truth. *He would mention, in a signed leader, the "three kidneys en broche and Wiltshire bacon" he had for breakfast on an interstate liner, the excellent grilled flounders served him in a Sydney restaurant . . .*

Norton was born at Brighton, England, on 25 January 1858. It is not clear who his parents were, though it seems certain they were not married. He was brought up by a stepfather, a sadistic clergyman, from whom he acquired a profound knowledge of the Bible and of the hymns. He had some experience as a journalist and spoke good French, when he emigrated to Australia in 1884.

He got a reporting job on Australia's first afternoon paper, the *Evening News*, which owed its success to its skilful presentation of sensational stories. Norton made his name by his investigation of a petty charge of indecency for which a Norwegian sailor was imprisoned and flogged. He was also involved in the Republican Union and the newly formed Intercontinental Trade Union Congress, for the first meeting of which he edited the official report. In 1886 he was sent by the Trades and Labour Council to Europe to tell the working class about conditions in Australia. Norton, the apostle of protection, carried letters of introduction from Sir Henry Parkes, the high priest of free trade; as Pearl observes, he had "already acquired a comfortable flexibility of political philosophy".

Returning from Europe, this "David of the plebs", as the *Bulletin* called him, already had the reputation of supporting the people against the Goliath of capitalism. He got a job with *Truth*, a "radical and irresponsible paper", and by September 1890 was Associate Editor. The owner was William Nicholas Willis, an actor turned storekeeper and journalist, who was MP for Bourke. (Willis was a friend and partner of William Patrick Crick, a lawyer and MP.)

Pearl gives entertaining accounts of several of the famous *Truth* stories, such as that of the spurious clergyman Dr Keating, who appeared before Mr Justice Windeyer on a criminal charge of assault on a 12-year-old girl. *Truth* thrived on libel, as in the case of George Black, republican, subeditor of the *Bulletin* and parliamentarian who also wrote articles for *Truth* until he fell out with Crick and Norton and in 1892 sued Norton for £5000 for libel. *Truth* won a great victory in the case, which the *Daily Telegraph* declared was a "dismal commentary on the public morals of this country", and went on to thunder about "the prostitution of the public press" and the evil of journals catering to "the prurient-minded".

Norton, now editor of *Truth*, went on the booze for several weeks in triumph. He was an alcoholic for the rest of his life. Crick was finally forced by Norton's behaviour to sack him, which Norton admitted, when sober, was fair enough. What Crick had forgotten was that, in the chicanery of *Truth*'s business organisation, Norton was the registered proprietor. So Norton reappointed himself editor. With the aid of a policeman and a torrent of abuse, Crick ejected Norton, who then charged him at the Central Police Court with threatening language. The Crick-Norton litigation lasted for three years. The feud was continued in and out of court, culminating in a magnificent brawl outside the Metropolitan Hotel in Castlereagh Street. Norton, drunk and in tears in court, lost the final case, and went back to reporting for the *Evening News*.

In 1895 Crick and his partner Richard Meagher, a brilliant young lawyer, were heavily involved in the Dean case. A popular hero, a ferry captain who had rescued drowning people on several occasions, was accused of attempting to poison his wife. Pearl gives a masterly summary of the convolutions of this case, in which Crick, Meagher, Dean and others were charged with conspiracy, as a result of which Meagher was struck off the roll by the Law Institute. Meagher went on to become a very popular Speaker of the House, President of the Labour Party, and first Labour Lord Mayor of Sydney.

By 1896 Norton was once again editor of *Truth*, attacking royalty, Anglican bishops, puritans and the police, a nice mixture and much appreciated by his readers. To Norton's credit is the invention of the word "wowser", something he modestly described as "a stroke of genius".

To my humble self—to me, John Norton, alone belongs the sole undivided glory and renown of inventing a word, a single, simple word, that does at once describe, deride and denounce that numerous, noxious, pestilent, puritanical, kill-joy push—the whole blasphemous, wire-whiskered brood.

Pearl has some interesting remarks to make about Norton's alliterative style. He says "Norton's degree of drunkenness at any time can be measured with remarkable accuracy by the amount of alliteration in his prose." Amazingly enough, amidst the muck-racking, Norton also wrote remarkably erudite essays in *Truth* on such subjects as Nietzsche, de Tocqueville, and "Democracy and Plutocracy".

Certainly the democrat Norton became a plutocrat after he took control of *Truth*, the obvious visible sign of this being his enormous mansion, St Helena, at Maroubra Bay. In this he housed, as well as his daughter and a "niece" from

CYRIL PEARL
1906-

Cyril Pearl was born on 11 April 1906 at Fitzroy in Melbourne. He says he received little education at his numerous schools: Carlton State School, Carlton Roman Catholic Primary School, Scotch College, Melbourne, and Hale College, Perth. However, he did discover the Melbourne Public Library and he educated himself there.

He studied an extraordinary mixture of subjects at the University of Melbourne: Russian, the history of philosophy, metaphysics and neurology. More significantly, he was editor of the students' newspaper, *Farrago*, and some of his caustic editorials drew reproof from the Melbourne Establishment. With some friends he also launched an avant-garde monthly literary magazine, *Stream*, which lasted three issues on a capital of £40.

He joined the new Melbourne evening newspaper, the *Star*, when it opened in 1933 and wrote for it until it ceased publication in 1936. In 1939 he became first editor of the Sydney *Sunday Telegraph* and stayed there for 10 years, moving to *A.M.* from 1949 to 1954 and to the *Sunday Mirror* from 1960 to 1961. In 1954 he published, with his then wife Irma, *Our Yesterdays*, a social history of Australia in photographs, with explanatory captions. It covers the period from 1853 to 1919.

His career as a social historian really began with *The Girl with the Swansdown Seat* in 1955 which, as he says, "broke a lot of ground about Victorian morals". He defines a social historian as "a bloke who believes that how a lot of people lived is more important than how a few people reigned or ruled". He considered in the 1950s that too much had been written about the bush and not enough about the cities. "The enormous overlay of humbug, conformity, hypocrisy, obscurantism, backslapping and stupidity that stifles Australia today surely needs blasting away."

He proceeded to do just that, modelling his style on Bertrand Russell, his social history approach on the American historian Herbert Asbury, and his satire on the American critic of language and words H. L. Mencken.

Wild Men of Sydney was so successful in reaching its targets that Ezra Norton, son of John, one of the rogues of the book, steamrollered a provision under the defamation law of New South Wales through the state Parliament whereby authors could be prosecuted for "defaming the dead". The book was published in London before the bill went through, but booksellers were nervous of the legislation and sales were affected. The "defaming the dead" provision was subsequently repealed.

Pearl has written a wide variety of books, but they all possess his characteristic qualities of attack, verve and wit, not to mention scholarship and attention to detail. There are four fine biographies: of the nineteenth-century poet "Orion" Horne; of the nineteenth-century Chief Justice of Australia, Sir Frank Gavan Duffy; of the legendary newspaper man in China, Morrison of Peking; and of brilliant Dan Deniehy, a tragic nineteenth-century Australian parliamentarian and writer. It was he who in 1854 invented the phrase "bunyip aristocracy" in attacking W. C. Wentworth's attempt to found a hereditary Australian aristocracy.

Pearl also had considerable success with two satirical books, *So You Want to be an Australian!* (1959) and *So You Want to Buy a House* (1961). His most recent major book has been *The Dunera Scandal* (1983) which is about the transport ship which brought 2562 internees to Australia in 1940, amongst them people who are now prominent academics, scientists, artists and professional men.

Pearl recently lived in France where he was no doubt able to continue studies in two of his favourite subjects, wine and cooking. He now lives in Paddington, Sydney.

England, a large collection of statues, busts and paintings of his hero, Napoleon (another little man), and a huge Napoleonic library.

In Chapter IX, "Interlude: Cricketer versus Priest", Pearl gives the story of the extraordinary proceedings when the cricketer Coningham sought a divorce on the grounds that his wife had repeatedly committed adultery with the Reverend Denis Francis O'Haran in St Mary's Cathedral and adjacent buildings. The immortal words allegedly used by O'Haran when he asked her to commit adultery in the Cathedral were: "Now you are here we may as well indulge." As Pearl says, "These three people . . . were the centre of as bitter and shameful a sectarian conflict as ever inflamed Australia, and the principals in a drama of unexampled conspiracies."

W. P. Crick, as Postmaster-General, was involved in the case, but this was mild compared with his and Willis's exposure by the Royal Commission of 1905 into land dealings. Willis, an MP and land agent, had made huge sums of money in crooked deals, while Crick, as Minister for Lands, had practised extortion and blackmail. Crick died shortly afterwards, farewelled by such comments as that he was still "popular in his personal liberality and his hilarious nature". Willis fled to South Africa.

There is not space to mention such gems as Pearl's deft accounts of Norton's attack on Melba for her alleged drunkenness or his relations with John Wren and the queen of Melbourne prostitution, Madame Brussells, or the confrontations between Norton and Meagher and Barton, Australia's first Prime Minister, or Norton's appalling denunciations of his wife in *Truth*.

Norton was a bad man, as were Willis and Crick, but on Norton's death the NSW Labour Premier Holman, "whom Norton had persistently and wickedly traduced" said, "He was a generous man, he was a patriot, he was a fearless democrat."

In the end, credulity may only be an unconscious admission that the flesh is weak. Pearl is a master analyst of human frailty.

NAKED UNDER CAPRICORN

LONDON 1958

Once or twice, sitting on the sand in the evenings, Marriner tried to teach the lad to read and write, drawing the letters with a twig; and Henry would listen and imitate with a serious face.

And then at the other fire there would be a clapping together of the song-sticks, a chanting of wild words, and one after another of the men would join in the song, and the song would gather tempo, and they would fling their clothes to the night and dance in the ancient rhythms; playing out the long-established dramas, running into the night from the mock vengeance, or stamping out the enactment of the kangaroo-dreamings. Young Henry would look pleadingly at them, his attention would wander, and finally Marriner would give him the sign that he awaited and he would join the men, a little mimic, loud in his clearly remembered responses; and by the next night his European lessons were to learn all over again.

Marriner was not a very good teacher, and his son no pupil. Henry could see no use in the ink-tracks cluttered so meanly in the pages of a book, though he proved sharp enough with figures.

But with the other lessons of his life his application was excellent; he was expert in the hunting lessons he had from the tribe, and the newer lessons that developed the herdsman. There is a moment in the mustering of cattle which calls for a precision of judgment and understanding. The cattle are at ease, grazing on the wide plain where they have remained undisturbed for months, perhaps for years. The rider appears, the cattle take fright, galloping with speed and determination to some known place of safety.

The rider joins in the pursuit. After a while his course parallels the course of the cattle, and there is a bovine mental process which, if the rider plays his part well, will induce the beasts before long to believe that they and the mounted man are all fleeing a common danger. At this point—neither before nor after—the man may ride to the lead; and the cattle will follow him. When he turns they will swing in behind him so that he brings them

sweetly to his own destination; and by the time they realize that they are, in fact, under duress, the run is taken out of them. Exertion is saved for both man and horse.

There is, of course, always an old cow who, for the protection of her calf, will turn away from her fellows to strike out for herself. The rider must catch this movement in time and change his plans accordingly. His whole judgment is based upon the external signs—a fractional mitigation of the desperation of speed, a turning of the head that indicates awareness.

Intelligence marks the good stockman. And some other intangibles. A rider who is attuned to the beasts he works can save much effort; and Henry could handle these situations like a veteran. He had no need to be told. The sound of his whip never intruded upon a delicate manœuvring to cause confusion; it was ready enough when its use was justified. And he was friendly with his horses, and with the young, half-broken horses of the plant. He would commune with them by the hour, after the manner and the delight of all young animals. Marriner had a great deal of pleasure in his company.

A deceptively simple novel, *Naked Under Capricorn* is on the surface a highly readable account of the establishment of a cattle station in the Northern Territory, and a man's rise from destitution to being a cattle king. Davis Marriner's success is like much of Australia's history; it occurs casually, in an unpremeditated way. No invading people with a plan for settlement colonised Australia. People just went off on their own and did it their own way.

There is always a dark shadow behind any success story in the Australian bush. "Yes, but what happened to the Aborigines?" an observer might ask. What makes Davis Marriner's story so moving and deeply interesting is that he asks that question himself.

Marriner is found naked near a river pool by a drover. He has been robbed and left there and, after four days without food, will die unless help arrives. It is around 1900, and the young Marriner has previously decided to sell his Brisbane shop and look for adventure. A likable fellow in Darwin, Bob Simmons, has let him join his party to fossick for rubies. Simmons and his gang have robbed him of his £400 and left him to die.

Thanks to the drover, a laconic bushman called Edrington, Marriner lives. Edrington clothes and feeds him. Some hundreds of kilometres further south, they meet a tribe of naked Aborigines. Edrington explains to Marriner that it is the whites who cause all the trouble between Aborigines and themselves. The desert people are wary but not unfriendly.

Then there is a disaster. Edrington is badly injured when his horse falls in a gallop after an emu he wants to kill for food. Dying, he asks Marriner to write his will with a bullet in his only book, Thomas More's *Utopia*, leaving 36 horses, saddles, packs—everything—to the young man.

Marriner is on his own, with only the few things he has learned from Edrington to alleviate his ignorance of this arid country with its hidden waterholes. He must watch birds, look at the lie of hills, keep friends with the blacks. It is the second time he has been left on his own. At least this time he is not naked. He goes on into the waterless desert. His horses begin to drop dead in the heat and from lack of water and feed. It seems that he has been saved by Edrington only to die in the sand.

He wakes from unconsciousness to find he is lying under a bough shelter. He has been rescued by a tribe of about 80 Aborigines, among them an English-speaking man wearing trousers, who has the odd name of Activity. A white man who had run some cattle in this place, Bloodwood Plain, had christened Activity and taught him how to work cattle, before moving on.

Intelligence marks the good stockman. And some other intangibles. A rider who is attuned to the beasts he works can save much effort; and Henry could handle these situations like a veteran. He had no need to be told.

The cattle man had set up a whip-pole to lift water from a well in the creek, and from it the Aborigines have filled a trough for the horses. All Marriner's gear is safe and sound. He is in idyllic country with plenty of grass for the horses and a large waterhole called Argadala a short ride away. Activity takes Marriner to it, and another man and two pretty young lubras come with them.

They ride three days east and come to some red hills. In the summit of the rocks is a chasm with "a placid pool perhaps thirty feet below the lip". Marriner watches while the girls put some sticky substance on their hands and feet and let themselves lightly down over the lip of the crater-like flue, each carrying a canvas bucket, which they fill, and climb up again. Enchanted by the beauty and skill of the girls, he accepts Activity's suggestion that he give them names, and calls them Mary and Rosie. They are delighted. "When they rode out they rode as a company, unified in their intent and their feelings."

Back at Bloodwood Plains Marriner finds Mary more and more beautiful. Activity notices that "he wanted her for his bed. Perhaps, as much as anything else, it was a sign of his assimilation into the country." That night he is awakened from sleep "to the touch of a skin amazingly soft and satiny; with a musky fragrance of flesh in his nostrils, with the sound of a girl's muted giggling and incomprehensible words".

He wakes at dawn, thinking Mary is lying beside him. But there are giggles coming from the face in the blanket.

He turns the girl over. It is Rosie. The old man has said that Mary is the wrong skin for him, and has sent Rosie instead. "Your name's not Rosie. Your name's trouble," Marriner says. So she becomes Terrubiddy or Trubiddy, and she now lives with him and looks after him.

Ruhen precisely conveys the balance of Marriner's character. For a more intellectual man, life with the blacks at Bloodwood Plains might have proved intolerably monotonous. Marriner really intends to push on, but Activity has warned him of the dangers of the desert to the south, and when he does venture forth, he is always happy to turn back. "On the other hand, a man less intelligent, less sensitive, might have been unhappier than he. For Marriner learned to identify himself with the black people, to appreciate their feelings."

He is excited by their singing and dancing, learns some of the skills of their bushcraft and learns "to accept the philosophy of the unburdened man".

Slowly, without even intending to, Marriner begins to accumulate a herd of cattle from those abandoned by passing drovers. Before long he has built a hut for Trubiddy and himself, and his herd has grown to nearly 100. The few white men he meets are itinerants; the first one who wants to stay in this country is a brutal, red-headed man called Blue Dallas, who settles to the north-west with a small herd of 80 cattle and a dozen horses. He also has a black woman with him, Maudie, dressed in a faded blue shirt and blue denims.

Marriner has never used the words "nigger" or "coon", words that Bluey Dallas uses all the time. Trubiddy is pregnant and Dallas says to Marriner, "You got your gin pregnant . . . You want to get rid of her. By God, it looks like I got to get rid of that one of mine too. It looks like she's got herself filled in as well . . . No yellow bastard of mine is going to roam this country."

Five days later Dallas comes back from the country he has selected without Maudie. A few days later he leaves, with another girl in a faded blue shirt and denims. This time it is Mary.

Not long afterwards, Marriner, riding with Activity and Trubiddy on Dallas's trail to see where he has camped, finds the body of Maudie. She has been shot in the back and the head and stripped of her clothes, which Mary is now wearing. So appalled that he is physically sick, Marriner does not know what to do. He decides not to interfere. "He had come to a hard country."

As the years go by, Marriner, to his surprise, finds himself growing to be a rich man. When he takes a mob of cattle south to Adelaide, he is lionised by the pastoral firm that handles his account, and the manager persuades him to take up a crown lease on his property, establishing it at almost 8700 square kilometres. The wolfram he has found on his property becomes valuable on the outbreak of World War I. More buildings go up. He opens a store. An intelligent young man who has dropped out of society, Creswell Cummings, joins him as bookkeeper and storekeeper. He has so many cattle now it takes his men three months to muster. He has not planned the developments; everything just grows.

So it is with his marriage to Monica. She is not prepared for what she finds at Bloodwood Plains, and he has not fully considered what a narrow-minded elegant woman like her

PALMER RIVER STUDY *Ray Crooke*

OLAF RUHEN
1911-

Olaf Ruhen is a New Zealander who has made his home in Australia since 1947. His first short stories were published in the *Bulletin* in the 1930s.

He was born in Dunedin, New Zealand, on 24 August 1911, and went to Otago Boys High School from 1925 to 1928. He writes: "Until 1937 I engaged in outdoor pursuits, primarily to strengthen a body weakened by TB – I could play no sports." The treatment was certainly successful; Ruhen grew into a big man with a fine physique and has spent much of his subsequent life outdoors.

Ruhen spent a few years as a farm worker, and then worked as a deckhand with the Port Chalmers fishing fleet. He later set up by himself and owned fishing boats during the 1930s, including the 9.7-metre schooner *Alice* which he worked single-handed for two years. In the end the *Alice* was wrecked and he went to work in a Dunedin timber yard. Later he worked for a Dunedin newspaper which offered him a job after publishing some of his articles. He had married Claire Strickland from Toowong, Queensland, in 1936 and they had one son.

When World War II broke out Ruhen joined the RNZAF, but his enrolment was delayed because his father had been German. He served as a pilot from 1941 to 1945, and finished the war flying Lancasters for 12 Squadron, RAF.

In January 1947 he came to Sydney and worked for the *Daily Telegraph* until 1949, for Associated Newspapers from 1949 to 1953, and for the *Sydney Morning Herald* from 1953 to 1955. He had been publishing short stories in the *Bulletin* and elsewhere for some time; and as a result of being sent by his newspaper to New Guinea in 1949 he wrote some stories which were published in the US *Saturday Evening Post*. The *Post* was eventually paying him $2250 a story, which was very good money in those days and certainly beyond the reach of many Australian magazines even now.

His wife accompanied him on several visits to the Pacific and the United States. On one of these they spent six months in the Trobriand Islands. She died suddenly, and the following year he married Madelaine Elizabeth Thompson.

His first books were published by the J. B. Lippincott Company in New York. Since 1957 he has had 32 books published, and has been translated into many languages.

Naked Under Capricorn (1958) was published in New York, London, Germany, Holland, Sweden and Denmark, and has since been reissued in Australia in 1982. Film options have been taken on it for 14 years in Hollywood and eight years in Australia, but no film has yet been made. It has a theme of racial tolerance and understanding which is common to many of Olaf Ruhen's books and stories. In an interview with John Hetherington he said that he once joined an expedition that sailed 1125 kilometres up the Sepik River in New Guinea and met tribes, including head-hunters, who had never seen a white man. He found them "ethically ahead of most white men".

When he is not travelling, Olaf Ruhen lives in Mosman, Sydney.

---

will do to his easy-going, semi-native lifestyle. Trubiddy is the first to go. She and Marriner's half-caste children, including the fine young stockman Henry whom Marriner loves, are driven out of the house. A new house has to be built and a garden must be made. The Aborigines have also changed. "They had acquired both clothes and dependence." Many of them are grossly fat. "The balance of nutrition, developed over the ages, has been overthrown."

Dallas is murdered by three men from Marriner's Aboriginal camp in vengeance for the women (including Mary) whom he has killed. The new policeman gets together a posse of miners and, in pursuing Marriner's tribe who have fled, they massacre 18 of them, including women and children. (This episode is based on fact – a similar massacre occurred at Coniston, in the Northern Territory, in 1928.) In a confrontation with Perrin, the policeman, Marriner tells him he is a murderer. His son Henry was among those who were shot.

The policeman is moved on elsewhere and no action is taken. The hard country has become even harder. The wealthier Marriner grows, the further he and Monica drift apart. When he comes back from several months away he finds she has moved the whole Aboriginal camp to Argadala because she cannot stand the blacks' presence. Even the old whip-pole, squeaking as it lifts its bucket of water, is gone.

Riding out after a whirlwind to the windmill near the rocks where the deep pool is, where Mary and Rosie had once gone down the rock flue on sticky hands and feet, Marriner finds three dead bodies in the pool. Three women on walkabout from Argadala have drowned there. Perhaps, he thinks, they did not mix the adhesive well.

> Or perhaps they had the wrong ingredients. And certainly they had not scampered up and down that place as children, and learned the poise and balance that supplemented the material recipe . . . these people had become alien to their own lands.

Riding back through the night, Marriner makes "the first decision of any moment he had ever made in this country. 'I'm going away', he told Activity." The black man goes with him, taking his camels. They go far out, past the last goldmine, past the Pintubi people, and disappear into the desert.

It is a puzzling ending. The combination of a dream and Marriner's first conscious decision destroys him, and Activity is also destroyed by being divorced from his inheritance. Yet Marriner, as he bitterly reproaches himself at the time of the massacre, realises he has himself unwittingly been an agent of destruction, by not denouncing Dallas at the time of the first murder, by not sticking up for his own tribe. Both blacks and whites are victims in *Naked Under Capricorn*; the blacks have lost peace and wisdom and are thus the greater losers.

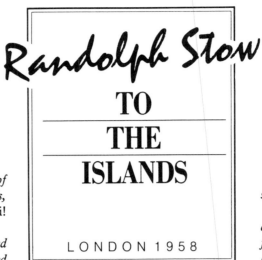

Randolph Stow

TO THE ISLANDS

LONDON 1958

At the sound of wind and at the fall of the branch the girls screamed like birds, clutched one another, trembled. "Ali! Mummy Dido!"

But Dido, huge as a round boulder and in no mood to encourage them, looked placidly over her flock of orphans and growled. "You girls, you think a bit of wind hurt you? Nothing going to hurt you in this dormitory. Real strong, these walls. You stop you shouting and stay on you own beds."

Nothing could move her. She took the hand of a small child who was crying. "What all you girls doing, just sitting there?" she demanded. "You better sing some songs."

They shivered as a bough scraped down the roof.

"Ruth," demanded Dido, "what wrong with you? You start singing, go on now."

"What you want us singing, Mummy Dido?"

"You know plenty songs," Dido said impatiently. "Ah, you girls, you no good! I going to sing myself." And the rich voice crooned, "God that madest earth and heaven, darkness and light—"

At the sound of her voice they took courage, and around Ruth's bed rose a murmur of singing, growing to a raucous shout.

> *From this valley they say you are going,*
> *We will miss your bright eyes and*
> *sweet smile—*

Under this opposition Dido faded slowly into silence and sat still, looking out towards the anguish of wind in leaves and branches. She was a Buddha, a round rock, vast and warm and immovable in the knowledge of her responsibilities.

In the swirling dust; at midday and at the height of the wind, Heriot plodded through the village, his clothes flapping, his wild white hair on end like the crest of a crane.

The village was indoors, sheltering behind its mud walls and threatened roofs from the possible violence about to come. The road was deserted, dotted with small fallen boughs.

Being so alone and in such chaos of air he could have shouted out to the wind that he loved it and worshipped it, that overnight he had become its convert, forestalling ruin by embracing ruin. The wind at least, which knew how to tug and tease a weak branch until it slackened and cracked and fell, would understand him, who had been for a quarter of a century the sheltering tree of this small kingdom and was now, by modern ideals and modern discontent, to be brought down.

Broken. Broken. Broken. On the far shore of the world.

In the breaking of the crucifix he had confessed, at last and forever, the failed faith, so long a swag on his back to be humped by night over the hard countries of his privacy. Now he could admit to himself that what was once the bright fruit of a young tree had shrivelled and dried and sifted away in the late years of loneliness, and was not to be found again on the ant-bed floor of a church; and could admit the idolatry of death, the god least despised in this country of suicides. He cried to himself under the thrashing trees to be taken and broken on the wheel of the wind.

All his age and all his frustrations had come suddenly upon him, he was an old, tired man, though he walked straighter than trees in the dust.

He would take this last walk around his domain, wait for the wind to die, then with all the whites assembled in Way's living room, announce his departure. He had already, soon after Way left him, transmitted his telegram of resignation to the far city. This walk in the wind was his farewell; afterwards there would only be waiting and going.

By the time Randolph Stow had turned 22, he had already completed *To the Islands*; it was published in 1958. In 1982 it was reissued in a slightly abridged version, the excised passages mainly dealing with a rather tepid love-story. "Understandably," Stow writes in the Preface to the Revised Edition, "it contains many faults, due partly to immaturity, but more to the fact that my technical competence was not equal to my ambition." The Revised Edition is certainly superior, but in either form *To the Islands* is an extraordinary achievement for such a young writer.

The islands of the title are the Aboriginal islands of the dead. The novel is a journey towards death, but in the religious terms within which the hero (an old missionary called Heriot) operates, it is also a journey of physical and mental pain, and spiritual discovery and healing.

Stow had the experience, physical and spiritual again, but also practical, to write the novel. He worked as a ration-storeman on Forrest River Mission, run by the Church of England in the wild North Kimberley region of Western Australia. As Stow mildly puts it:

Australian writers before me had generally given missions and missionaries a bad press, and in earlier days some had deserved their low opinion. By 1957, however, the year in which the novel is set, it seemed to me that at least one of them was performing a valuable service to the Aboriginal community which it housed and employed, and which, indeed, it could be said to have created.

All this necessary preamble may give a false impression of *To the Islands*, which is not a strictly factual, let alone a journalistic, book. In his Author's Note to the First Edition, Stow specifically stated, "This is not, by intention, a realistic novel." Nevertheless, Stow's intensely direct evocation of the landscape and its people, black and white, cannot be ignored in the reader's attempt to follow Heriot's, in some ways, cantankerous search for salvation.

Now he could admit to himself that what was once the bright fruit of a young tree had shrivelled and dried and sifted away in the late years of loneliness, and was not to be found again on the ant-bed floor of a church . . .

When the book opens Heriot, the 66-year-old priest and Superintendent of the Mission, is waiting to hear whether his resignation has been accepted and his successor chosen. Stow portrays the man and the setting with the focus of light and the concentration of detail characteristic of a good painting. It is so vivid one almost wonders whether one has actually seen it—a Drysdale, an early Ray Crooke?

The impermanence of the Mission buildings, the tiredness of Heriot, speak already of the need for some resting place. Yet it is clear that although Heriot's life belongs in the far north-west of Australia, in one of the most remarkable regions in the world—the Kimberley Range—he is not at peace there. Image after image of ruin and despair follows, particularly meaningful to Heriot, a great lover of poetry. Like all lonely people, he cherishes the company of hidden things, but at the same time he is haunted by uneasy memories. (It is worth remembering that Stow's first novel was called *A Haunted Land*.)

The memories are introduced obliquely in a conversation between the young schoolteacher Gunn and Heriot's second-in-command, Father Way. Heriot loves the Aborigines, but the old punishment books make it clear that he used to thrash offenders with a stockwhip. Two ghosts from the past return: Stephen, 22, his godson who has been in gaol for stealing and of whom he is still fond, and Rex, whom he hates and who made his goddaughter (Stephen's sister Esther) pregnant. Heriot believes Rex killed the girl after he was expelled from the Mission. In a violent scene, with Heriot calling Rex Esther's murderer, Rex is ordered to leave the

Mission. He refuses. Heriot objects not only to Rex himself; but he also fears his bad influence on the Aborigines.

The Aborigines are in their own country, but their existence there is a fragile one, held together economically and socially by the Mission. The one who has the finest qualities of his race, and a confidence neither shaken nor (like Rex) aggrieved, is Justin, "a man of forty with the quiet dignity belonging to that age among his race". Stow has revealed that his friend Daniel Evans was the original of Justin. It is Justin who tells Gunn, the schoolteacher, and Dixon, one of the brothers, the true story of the Umbali massacre of 1926 (it is called Onmalmeri in the book, and the date is changed). This terrible story, from which amongst the whites only the missionaries emerge well, is the sombre background to the whole book. Even Father Walton, who courageously prevented further massacre and uncovered what had already happened, is also scarred—by the use of the stockwhip, not its cut. The original of Father Walton, Father Gribble, was in fact a subject of a Government report which revealed various atrocities at Forrest River Mission.

Heriot describes himself to Way as "a wicked man who wants to be dead. . . . For years I set myself up as a philanthropist and was really a misanthrope all the time." In a typical display of violence and petulance (Heriot is very much a Lear-figure), Heriot smashes Walton's ivory crucifix and throws the pieces at Way, and then says softly, "I believe in nothing."

Symbolic of this loss of faith and idolatry of death is his meeting with Rex in a storm. They quarrel again, although Heriot now has a strange compassion for him. As he walks away, Rex throws a stone which hits him on the leg. Heriot turns and throws the stone back at Rex. It hits him on the head and Heriot thinks he has killed him. Taking his rifle and some cartridges, Heriot saddles a quiet old horse and rides away. Justin sees him and stops him, asking, "Where you blanket, eh? Where you billy and you tucker?"

He is riding across the plain, heading for the hills, when Justin on another horse, with "the blanket roll, the old flour bag, the billy and two spears", catches up with him and will not be shaken in his determination to accompany and guide him. Heriot eventually gives in, and with Justin's words, "If you go along with me, I go with you, always" Heriot weeps "for very sweetness of love", making the connection (of which Justin of course is unconscious) with the fifteenth-century morality play *Everyman*, and whispers, "Welcome, my Good Deeds." It is Justin who, like Kent and Cordelia with Lear, restores the foolish, fond old man's humanity to him.

Heriot's journey across the fierce Kimberley landscape of rocky hills and tablelands under the harsh cry of crows leads him to other outcasts. Rusty, a murderer, talks to him apprehensively over the campfire and gives him the makings of a cigarette. In a beautifully observed episode, "as he watched the old man's fingers fumbling with the paper his thick mouth was touched with compassion". To Rusty's query as to why he is "exploring" such difficult country, Heriot makes the unexpectedly positive reply: "Found weakness I didn't know of. And despair. And worse than that. But I'm beginning to come out of it, it's like waking."

Meanwhile, back at the Mission, a parallel waking has occurred. Rex has survived, and listens to Helen, the nursing sister, telling him he must forgive Heriot. Rex implies Heriot

NORTH QUEENSLAND STOCKMAN *Ray Crooke*

RANDOLPH STOW
1935-

Randolph Stow was born in 1935 at Geraldton, Western Australia. His family had early connections with the law and the land in both South and Western Australia; and his father was a country lawyer.

He was educated at a state school in Geraldton and then went to Guildford Grammar School as a boarder. Literature of imaginative verbal richness always attracted him, and by the time he went to the University of Western Australia he was deeply read in the Scottish and Border ballads, in Jacobean drama and in the Romantics. At the university, where he began in Law but switched to Arts, he majored in French and English. Like Heriot in *To the Islands*, he has always been interested in languages, beginning with French, Spanish and German, an interest later followed up in New Guinea. He says:

I became a writer for two reasons. One was that in National Service I first collided with the facts of life in the atomic age. The other was the death of a friend. He was not a particularly close friend, but we were at school and college and Law School together, and to me his death, coming at that time of life, was a pretty world-shaking experience. I felt it was terribly necessary for me to do something creative and do it quickly.

He certainly acted quickly, publishing two novels, *A Haunted Land* (1956) and *The Bystander* (1957), and a collection of poems, *Act One* (1957), by the time he was 22. By then he had already finished the manuscript of *To the Islands*. It is rather a sad reflection on the state of publishing in Australia at the time that all of these books were published in England by Macdonald.

Stow has at various times taught in the English Departments of universities (Adelaide 1957, Leeds 1962 and 1968-69, Western Australia 1963-64). He has also been much involved in writing for music theatre with Peter Maxwell Davies; including *Eight Songs*

for a Mad King (1969) and *Miss Donnithorne's Maggot* (1974). Through the quarterly *Australian Letters*, he made contact with Sidney Nolan. *Outrider*, a volume of poems with paintings by Nolan, was published in 1962.

Stow has a wide range of interests. In *Australian Letters* he published articles on Coles' book shops and *Funny Picture Book*, and on hillbilly music. He has also written one of the most attractive and original of all Australian children's books, *Midnite* (1967). After the autobiographical novel *The Merry-Go-Round in the Sea* (1965), there was a long gap until suddenly in 1979-80 he published two new novels, *The Girl Green as Elderflower* and *Visitants*. His latest novel is an analysis of a murder, set in the east of England, *The Suburbs of Hell* (1984).

Visitants, set in the Trobriand Islands of Papua New Guinea, stemmed from a much earlier experience which also gave rise to some of his best poems. In 1959 Stow made a decision to abandon writing novels and, in his words, "to settle down to a non-literary career". He then went to New Guinea to work as an assistant to the Government Anthropologist, where his interest was mainly linguistic. However, he had a breakdown in health, returned to Australia after 11 months and in 1960 went to England. Although he has returned to Australia on several occasions he has lived since then mainly in Essex, in Constable country.

Stow has suffered because of what he calls "a misapprehension about *To the Islands*, which many academics (who have rather innocent ideas about the speed with which writers and printers work) took to have been written under the influence of *Voss*". In fact, as he points out, the novel was in the publisher's hands well before *Voss* was available in Australia, and of course had been begun much earlier.

Although strictly speaking nothing to do with the novel, since 1957 there have been drastic changes to the Forrest River Mission which was the source for *To the Islands*. It was abandoned in 1968 and the Aborigines were removed from their "country" to the outskirts of Wyndham, with disastrous results. In 1973 a group of white men and Aborigines, amongst them Stow's friend Daniel Evans, managed to obtain a Government grant and move back to the Mission lands. Their re-establishment there has not been without difficulties.

---

has wronged him in believing that he killed Esther. Later, in spite of medical advice to the contrary, Rex joins the search party for Heriot.

Heriot meets another mad old man, Sam, living with a mob of goats. Sam asks Heriot why he became a missionary:

"Expiation," said Heriot. "Yes. This is my third life. My third expiation."

"What was the others?" asked Sam incuriously.

"I suppose it was my birth, as a human being, that drove me to charity. Yes, that was the first. And then there was the massacre, done by my race at Onmalmeri."

"I heard of it," said Sam.

"That was the second. It drove me to the mission. And then at the end there was my—my hatred."

"What'd that drive you to?" murmured Sam.

"That?" said Heriot pensively. "That has made a lost man of me."

The object of that hatred, Rex, is the one who will not give

up when the search party begin to despair of finding Heriot. And when Heriot and Justin finally reach the Aboriginal burial caves, full of bones and skulls, beyond which are the sea and the islands of death, he hands over his possessions, knife, watch, rifle, to Justin to give to Rex.

Justin leaves Heriot and meets Rex. In a scene of great dignity and beauty he hands Heriot's gifts over to Rex. The forgiveness is complete and mutual, not only between individuals but races, and even with the land itself. For Heriot's last words are, "My soul is a strange country."

Although a story about an odd old man in a remote region, *To the Islands* transcends both time and place. Stow himself may be allowed the last, and very modest, word.

If the novel retains any interest, other than as an historical sociological document, it may be because this story of an old man is really about a certain stage in the life of a sort of young man who has always been with us, and always will be.

THE
AUSTRALIAN
LEGEND

MELBOURNE 1958

Behind the politics of the Bulletin, the aspirations of the new writers and the spirit of the new trade unionism was the concept of the "noble bushman" whose evolution has been the subject of this book. His was the symbolic figure giving some kind of psychological cohesion to the dominant but disparate social forces of the time: Protection and Utopian idealism, industrial trade unionism and chauvinistic nationalism, Labour Party politics and federalism, secularism and belief in material "progress". Randolph Bedford records that, some time before the great strikes of 1890-4, he saw in Bourke:

. . . a literary and economic enthusiast of the bush, rehearsing men in a play wherein the shearer met the squatter, and talked to him temperately but straightly. If I had known it, I was looking at the birth of that political force which has had more effect on Australian life and progress than any of the regularised parties of High Tariff and No Tariff, Low Tariff and Low Wages; which is the one party under a score of aliases. The great force behind the Australian Labour Party, was the western bush worker; not the craft-union of the factory. The Australian Workers' Union, which is the father of the Australian Labour Party, was born in the bush.

To-day we may query Bedford's estimate of the Labour Party's achievement, but there is less to quarrel with in his account of its genesis. In the final analysis it is not so much the bushman's actual nature that matters, as the nature attributed to him by so many men of the day. The romantic notion that the bushman of the interior was the guardian of "truly Australian" values had

been foreshadowed by the first native-born white man to see the plains extending westward from the Blue Mountains summits. In 1820 the youthful W. C. Wentworth had written:

To those who are acquainted with the local situation of the colony, – who have traversed the formidable chain of mountains by which it is bounded from north to south – . . . the independence of this colony, should it be goaded into rebellion, appears neither so problematical nor remote, as might otherwise be imagined . . . If the colonists should prudently abandon the defence of the sea-coast, and remove with their flocks and herds into the fertile country behind these impregnable passes, what would the force of England, gigantic as it is, profit her?

In 1892 a poem of Lawson's bodied forth the myth in its most exaggerated form. The first stanza reads:

Ye landlords of the cities that are builded by the sea –
You toady "Representative", you careless absentee –
I come, a scout from Borderland, to warn you of a change,
To tell you of the spirit that is roused beyond the range;
I come from where on western plains the lonely homesteads stand,
To tell you of the coming of the

Natives of the Land!
Of the Land we're living in,
The Natives of the Land.
For Australian men are gathering –
they are joining hand in hand
Don't you hear the battle cooey of the Natives of the Land?

The national "dreaming" of the 'nineties had, of course, a sufficiently humdrum issue. The Aborigines used to believe that conception was caused not by sexual intercourse, which these simple people regarded as an enjoyable pastime, but by the parents' dreaming of the child's spirit. Slight doubts began to arise with large numbers of half-caste babies. Wiser in our own conceit we tend to explain historical events largely in terms of material causation, heavily discounting the role of dreaming; and no doubt we are in the main right. The dreaming of the 'nineties resulted, not in a republic embodying such noble practices as would have stupefied the actual bushman, but in much hard political horse-trading and in federation. The discovery of silver at Broken Hill in 1883, and the vast industrial growth that sprang therefrom, has probably had more effect on Australian history than the publication of "Sam Holt" in 1881 and of all the reams of prose and verse of which it was the prototype. Certainly the results of Broken Hill silver-lead mining are easier to measure and to demonstrate. Yet while economic and other material factors are, at least in a gross sense, the principal determinants of events, it is wrong to dismiss entirely less tangible influences. The dreams of nations, as of individuals, are important, because they not only reflect, as in a distorting mirror, the real world, but may sometimes react upon and influence it.

In *The Australian Legend* Russel Ward put forward his thesis as to the development of the national mystique with such ardent freshness that many people took it as a documented fact rather than as an argument. Ward's thesis was that "a specifically Australian outlook grew up first and most clearly among the bush workers in the Australian pastoral industry, and that this group has had an influence, completely disproportionate to its numerical and economic strength, on the attitudes of the whole Australian community"

Ward has a delightful enthusiasm for the people about whom he writes. He loves their independence, their humour and especially their songs and ballads. *The Australian Legend*, because of this affectionate enthusiasm, is a delight to read. It is good, solid, well-documented history, but at the same time it will give great pleasure to any Australian seeking to understand his own country, and enlightenment to any foreigner curious as to why Australians behave as they do.

In the final analysis it is not so much the bushman's actual nature that matters, as the nature attributed to him by so many men of the day.

At the same time it is most unfair to Ward to attack him, as some academics did, for presenting a one-sided account of the origins of our national mystique. One can only do this by ignoring Ward's warning on the book's first page.

> Nearly all legends have some basis in historical fact. We shall find that the Australian legend has, perhaps, a more solid substratum of fact than most, but this does not mean that it comprises all, or even most, of what we need to know to understand Australia and Australian history. It may be, however, a very important means to this end, if only because we shall certainly be wrong if we either romanticise its influence or deny it.

Some 25 years after the publication of *The Australian Legend*, Australians have attained a measure of that national self-confidence which was burgeoning when Ward was writing, after the setbacks of the Depression, the collapse of the British Empire and the Japanese threat during World War II, with bombs falling for the first time on Australian soil. It is not discrediting Ward's book to admit that most Australians for many years now have lived in cities and on the coast, that a suburban docility characterises them, or that their lives are more influenced by capitalism and advertising than by bushmen or bushrangers.

Towards the end of *The Australian Legend* Ward himself succinctly explains the subject of his book, which is the nation's dream of itself. Like most dreaming, this looks back to childhood, before there was an Australian nation.

> Yet while economic and other material factors are, at least in a gross sense, the principal determinants of events, it is wrong to dismiss entirely less tangible influences. The dreams of nations, as of individuals, are important,

Wool-shearing *(above)*

because they not only reflect, as in a distorting mirror, the real world, but may sometimes react upon and influence it.

This particular Australian dream is basically involved with freedom. Ward is writing about Australia from the beginnings to (roughly) World War I, and there is in those years a double edge to the word "freedom". Most of the early pastoral workers were convicts, either assigned or on ticket of leave. To this lesser or major freedom from the chain gangs of the towns was added the savour of the bush, the freedom of distance and solitude. When allowed to, a man could wander, either as a drover or shearer with some sort of programme, or as an itinerant worker going anywhere he pleased. To some extent the situation still exists. A man could attain the freedom of anonymity. There are many examples of men being known only by nicknames such as "Terrible Tommy", a tradition that extended to literary work, especially in the *Bulletin*, where verses appeared over the name of "Ironbark" or "The Breaker" or "The Banjo".

Both the dream and the reality of freedom took shape in the careers of the more notable bushrangers such as Donahoe or Ben Hall. Ward gives plenty of evidence that flogging and hatred of petty tyrants turned men into bushrangers, and that the public were inclined to forgive them their misdeeds. He also mentions the surprising lack of violence (unless the victims resisted) in the hold-ups. The bushrangers wanted to keep public sympathy.

All through *The Australian Legend* Ward uses ballads and songs to illustrate his arguments. (Readers of *The Australian Legend* will also enjoy Ward's Penguin collection of *Australian Ballads*.) No description better conveys the freedom that was the bushranger's dream than the chorus of "The Wild Colonial Boy".

> Then come, my hearties, we'll roam the mountains high!
> Together we will plunder, together we will die!
> We'll wander over mountains and we'll gallop over plains
> For we scorn to live in slavery, bound down in iron chains.

Ward points out that this chorus "is really irrelevant to the specific needs of Donahoe and his associates", and it is not a national anthem in praise of Australia, but a symbol of an embryonic national feeling in its love of the country and its defiance of tyrants.

The vagaries of the climate and the exigencies of the pastoral life helped develop the nomadic tendency already present in the "old hands", the ex-convicts, who wanted to avoid authority by keeping "on the wander". By the 1830s the author of *Settlers and Convicts* noted that the "*free labouring population of Australia . . . is in a state of constant migration*", and John Sidney declared "You can no more change shepherds and herdsmen into citizens and gardeners, than you can turn wandering Arabs into weavers and drapers."

One of the most interesting chapters of *The Australian Legend*, and one containing ideas that could be developed at length, is "The Gold Rush". The already powerful mateship of the bush nomads flourished in the diggings where you needed a mate to work a claim, and where, as contemporary writers noted, the gold diggers were a very

PUB TALK *Noel Counihan*

RUSSEL WARD
1914-

Russel Ward was born in Adelaide on 9 November 1914. His father was a schoolteacher. When Russel was four the family moved to Queensland, and later to Western Australia where he went to Wesley College, Perth. His father was then appointed Headmaster of Prince Alfred College, Adelaide, and Russel finished his schooling there before going on to read Honours English at the University of Adelaide. During long summer vacations he spent several months in the Northern Territory prospecting and road-mending. He has an MA from Adelaide University, a PhD from the Australian National University, and a DLitt from the University of New England.

He taught at Geelong Grammar School from 1937 to 1939 and at Sydney Grammar School from 1939 to 1941. He served in the AIF from 1942 to 1946. After the war he went back to teaching for a few years, with the NSW Department of Education.

Ward held a post-graduate scholarship at the Australian National University from 1953 to 1955 to work on a PhD thesis, "The ethos and influence of Australian pastoral workers". *The Australian Legend* emerged from this thesis, and was published in 1958. In 20 years it sold 40,000 copies and has since gone into other editions. In 1978 it was the subject of a special issue of *Historical Studies* from Melbourne University, when 11 historians contributed essays on *The Australian Legend Revisited*.

Russel Ward was a member of the Communist Party, from which he resigned in 1949. He made no secret of this when in 1956 he applied for the post of Lecturer in History at the University of New South Wales. He was chosen by the selection committee but his appointment was cancelled by the Vice-Chancellor, Professor Baxter, because of a Commonwealth security report. Baxter told the University Council that "Dr Ward was of such character and reputation that no Australian university could possibly appoint him." Professor Hartwell (Dean of the Faculty of Humanities) and Professor A. E. Alexander (who was on the Professorial Board) resigned from the University because of this episode. Ward was appointed Lecturer in History at the University of New England in 1957, and subsequently became Professor and Deputy Chancellor. Now Emeritus Professor, Ward says, "Since I retired I feel much freer to say exactly what I think uninhibitedly."

In his history *Australia Since the Coming of Man* Ward writes: "I am for the weak not the strong, the poor not the rich, the exploited not the select few. I believe reason has done more for mankind than religion, and that reformist and radical political parties have done more for Australia than conservative ones."

---

migratory class. Whereas the Californians on the goldfields were "partners" the Australians were "mates". One piece of evidence, not mentioned by Ward, comes from Raffaello Carboni, an Italian intellectual involved in the Eureka Stockade, who, writing as Carboni Raffaello, in his book about the Stockade frequently refers to "my mate".

Ward points out how the diggers themselves kept order and punished wrongdoers without the assistance of government officials, the worst punishment being expulsion from the goldfield. The Australian goldfields were far more orderly than the Californian. There were many reasons for this, but one was certainly the idea of "rude notions of honour" implicit in the feeling of mateship. Not only did a man not rob his mate, but the independence of individuals meant the abolition of social distinctions. As long as a man did not put on airs, a gentleman could talk on equal terms with a former servant. Ward might also have mentioned that there was an inverted snobbery among bullockies, for instance (see Joseph Furphy's hatred of gentlemen in *Such is Life*), not present on the goldfields or at the meetings which preceded Eureka. Furphy approved of Stewart, the gentleman-squatter who had become a true democratic Australian. Ward does not acknowledge a similar situation in his discussion of the ballad "Flash Jack from Gundagai", where the old shearer recalling all his wandering exploits always comes back in the chorus to his favourite shed, "Shearin' for old Tom Patterson, on the One Tree Plain".

Ward is clear about the virtues and faults of his bushmen; he knows very well they were not all noble. In that same ballad Flash Jack admits to the folly of blowing his cheque in a week at a pub. Drunkenness was a chronic failing. On the other hand there is plenty of evidence, some produced by Ward, that the bushmen were great readers, and were lovers of books and poetry even when they were illiterate. He quotes a touching account, from the early 1840s, of a man beginning to read *Nicholas Nickleby* at night to a hut full of bushmen and being, however, " 'advised that the reading should be stopped, until the men of two or three stations near us, had been invited' to share in the feast".

The prodigious success of the *Bulletin*, the "Bushman's Bible", reflects this appetite. Also, as Ward points out, the increasing literacy of its audience is reflected in its high number of sales, and also in the success of "Banjo" Paterson's and Lawson's books.

Ward gets below the tough exterior of his bushmen. He touches fairly briefly on their sex life, which, owing to their reticence, remains somewhat mysterious, though it is obvious enough that there was a tremendous amount of fornication with Aboriginal women. Sometimes, as in the case cited by Ward of Mrs Johnston, the cook at Ballangeich, a white woman set up as whore with her husband as pimp. Sometimes, harder to substantiate, there was sodomy. One contemporary wrote, "The sin for which God destroyed 'the doomed cities' prevails among the servants of squatters."

There was, as Ward says, some of the softness of love below the rugged exterior of mateship, sublimated from homosexuality, but still running very deep. In Lawson, as Ward points out, the softness was often embarrassingly near the surface.

Ward was at pains to point out that *The Australian Legend* does not give the full picture of Australian life in the colonial period, nor does he claim that the legend is a dominating one. But his book is a great tribute to the power of that dream.

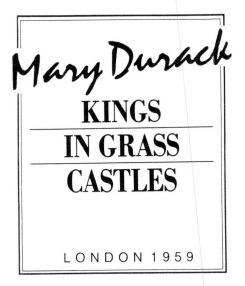

KINGS
IN GRASS
CASTLES

LONDON 1959

The Roper ran west to Red Lily Lagoon, a place of fantastic beauty with its massed water lilies, crimson and blue, green reeds and drooping paperbarks, haunt of wild duck, and judging by the bark canoes floating on the water, wild blacks.

They pushed on to the Overland Telegraph line and the little post office at Elsey Station—symbol of hope and progress in the never-never. Palmer, the manager, welcomed them warmly and filled their depleted tucker bags when they rode in to send wires to their Queensland relatives. Telegrams and letters, advising of the deaths of Urquart and Sherringham and the loss of about three thousand five hundred head of stock all told between Thylungra and the Roper camp, had gone off by the schooner from the depot to Darwin. These had been received when the following telegram reached Thylungra about May '85:

PARTY NOW OVERLAND TELEGRAPH AND TRAVELLING WELL CONDITION REMAINING STOCK REASONABLY GOOD EXPECT REACH ORD FOUR TO FIVE MONTHS TIME REGARDS AND LOVE FAMILY AND FRIENDS DURACK KILFOYLE HAYES MOORE.

A sixty-mile stretch west of the Telegraph was heavy going through rough, heavily timbered but almost waterless country. The long wet was over and the grass quickly turning yellow. The smaller waggon broke down completely and had to be abandoned and around Dry River the cattle began to lag and show symptoms of red water fever. The decision to push on rather than rest the cattle was fortunate as they lost only a few head, whereas later expeditions, lingering in what proved to be a badly infected area, were to lose hundreds.

It would be some ten years before the cause of this dread disease was finally traced to a small bug-like parasite that had come into the Territory with a shipment of cattle from Batavia. The drovers were not then to know the grip that cattle tick was already taking of the north, how the travelling mobs were spreading it across the Territory into Queensland and over to Kimberley. Their deadliest enemies were not after all to be the blacks but two species of insect smaller than a man's fingernail—Ixodes bovis and the Anopheles mosquito.

Hurried down the Dry River for about twenty miles the cattle were again turned due west.

Basalt ridges, swampy flats of tangled cadjibut and Gutapurcha trees, tantalising rivers that turned their tracks to north and south, led on at last to the Victoria. This river around which Nat Buchanan had stocked a vast holding comprising many millions of acres for the city investors Fischer and Lyons in '83 was a major landmark in the journey. "Wait 'til we're eating johnnie cakes on the Victoria," they had said to cheer themselves back on the Georgina.

"Call this a river?" said a returning drover they had met on the McArthur. "Wait 'til you see the Victoria!"

And here she was—Queen of the north, sweeping majestically between the bending ranks of river trees with exultant escorts of wild birds.

Mary Durack's account of her pioneering family, their great treks with cattle from Goulburn to the Cooper in south-west Queensland, and from there to the Kimberley Range in the far north of Western Australia, is in itself a pioneering work. She was lucky in having access to copious family records, but she also interviewed old drovers and Aborigines who had worked for the Duracks, talked to relatives and travelled over much of the country. She also had the advantage of having lived for some years at Ivanhoe station on the Ord River with her sister, the artist Elizabeth Durack, as a cook-housekeeper.

Kings in Grass Castles owes its title to a comment of Mary's grandfather Patrick (Patsy) in 1878, in answer to a journalist who had called him and his like "cattle kings". "'Cattle Kings' you call us. Then we are kings in grass castles that may be blown away upon a puff of wind." It is a thought poetically expressed, and the Duracks were of that Irish breed that loves poetry. Patsy Durack made up many ballads, and his son Michael (Mary's father) carried the works of the classic poets and novelists with him in his saddlebags. It was little wonder that Mary became a writer.

This quality of imagination, of sympathy with something beyond the harsh world of hoofs and horns and money, lent a certain stature to the Duracks. There was a real Irish zest about them. When they got together, no matter how far out in the wilderness, they loved to sing, play musical instruments, dance and of course race horses. And the Durack and Costello (Mary's grandmother's family) women were extraordinary; tough but always feminine, committed to keeping up standards and respected by both white and black stockmen. One of the Durack women gave birth to her baby while floodwaters were rising in the room and her husband was urging her to hurry; he had to wrap the new-born baby in a blanket and swim with mother and baby to safety. These women did not necessarily approve of the family restlessness, but they did what they were called upon to do. Grandmother Mary, when praised by a city friend for her courageous spirit, replied, "I had nothing of the sort, my dear, but when Patsy said we must go pioneering what else was I to do?"

This urge to "go pioneering", to take up more and more land further and further out, was powerful beyond reason, and based on some yearning of the unsatisfied imagination rather than on the simple desire to be rich. In fact, for various reasons, both Patsy and Michael's lives swung violently between riches and poverty, and more than droughts conspired to lay their grass castles low.

Patsy arrived in Australia in 1853 and went to work with his father near Goulburn. He was 18. A few months after the family's arrival Patsy was directing the moving of a dray load of wood while his father held a gate open. The horse was startled by a kangaroo and pulled the dray over his father, crushing him to death. "I had no boyhood," Patsy once told his children. Over the next couple of years, he worked at the Ovens gold diggings, made £1000, and with the help of the Emanuel family, lifelong friends of the Duracks and fellow-pioneers in the Kimberleys, he bought land in the Goulburn area. He raised cattle, made a success of it, married Mary Costello, but was frustrated by the complexities and restrictions of Robertson's Free Selection Act in his efforts to get more land. He decided to "poke along up north" into the new colony of Queensland and look for land.

So off he went in 1863, at the age of 27, with his brother Stumpy Michael, brother-in-law John Costello, Jim Scanlan (whose sister Mary later married John Costello), Tom Kilfoyle (Patsy's uncle Darby Durack's brother-in-law), stockman Jack Horrigan and a German cook known as "Vild Villy"; along with 100 horses and 400 cattle, he set off to Queensland. It took them two and a half months to get as far as Bourke. They went on through worsening drought into Queensland, to the diminishing waters of the Bulloo where the thirsty cattle stampeded and trampled each other to death in the mud. The men and their horses were saved by the blacks, who showed them hidden waterholes.

After such major losses of stock and equipment, it is amazing that Patsy should have tried again, and this time talked his wife into coming with him. They followed the Costellos who in 1865 had obtained title to a lease of 32,000 acres (12,960 hectares) between the Warrego and Paroo Rivers. In 1867, after the death of his daughter, Patsy sold his Goulburn properties and left on a 1600-kilometre trek, deep in debt, with six horse wagons, 150 head of breeding cattle, 27 team and stock horses, equipment and assorted stores, including their fine Irish linen and lace and their silver.

There were 100 cattle left by the time Patsy settled in "a land loved by birds", by a permanent waterhole, at a place the Aborigines called Thillung-gurra and Patsy mispronounced Thylungra. Here he took on as station workers some young blacks from the Boontamurra tribe and, unable to pronounce the liquid Aboriginal names, he called them Pumpkin, Melon-Head, Kangaroo and other names. The Aborigines seem to have thought these names a great joke and never resented them. Pumpkin remained with Patsy and then his son Michael from 1868 until 1908, when he died on Argyle station in the Kimberley.

The original Thylungra holding comprised 4800 square kilometres leasehold, registered between 1871 and 1874, and later expanded to over 6100 square kilometres. The Costellos took up 21,240 square kilometres. Somehow or another they got through the next drought. Supplies were low. It took Stumpy Michael and a native boy, Willie, six months to travel to Bourke and back for stores. No one passed by. Their nearest neighbours were 240 kilometres to the south, and 320 kilometres to the north. To the west there was 560 kilometres of unnamed emptiness and then the Simpson Desert.

The Duracks maintained good relations with the Aborigines, but others, opal prospectors in particular, tended to cause trouble. Finally the notorious native police were used to shoot their own race in a series of massacres. Conflict with the Aborigines came later, but the Duracks treated them with respect and genuine liking. Patsy never carried a weapon on his long solitary rides around his run. His patriarchal attitude to the Aborigines never changed. Mary Durack writes," 'It is the blessing of Almighty God they are kindly and childlike savages,' Grandfather said and would never alter his estimate even when the simple people had turned fiends at last in blind thrusts of bewildered rage."

Patsy would not speak pidgin to the Aborigines who worked for him. He taught them "proper" (Irish) English, good manners and, of course, good stockmanship. And there were no half-castes on his properties. It was to be different in the Kimberleys.

Thylungra prospered and by 1879 the herds had increased from the original 100 to 12,000. Great feats of droving were accomplished in getting them the vast distances to market in South Australia or New South Wales. The boys were sent 1600 kilometres to college in Goulburn. There was money to pay for their education. In 1879, from cattle, horses, land rights and incidental businesses such as hotels, a butchery and houses, the Duracks netted £27,000.

In 1881 Patsy read Alexander Forrest's report of his explorations in the Kimberley area. Forrest wrote of "a land of splendid rivers, fine pastures and reliable rainfall". Patsy and Stumpy Michael, with the support of Solomon Emanuel, went to Perth to interview Forrest. From the map, they secured tentative holdings on the conjectured course of the Ord River. An exploratory expedition started out by sea under the direction of Stumpy Michael. It was shipwrecked and lost half the horses and most of the supplies, but started again. In the magnificent country of the Kimberley Range they discovered the true course of the Ord River, and land that was "the pioneer land-seeker's dream come true". Nobody was dismayed by the difficulties that they would face in getting the stock to market.

After an epic journey to Beagle Bay, the party waited until a ship arrived, to take them to Fremantle. As soon as they returned to Thylungra, Patsy began organising the 4020-kilometre trek, with cattle, to take up the Ord River land. The trek was originally reckoned as 2500 miles — and these were "drover's miles"; they were in fact longer than the distances actually marked on the map.

Mary Durack's account of this great droving journey is enthralling. There were four parties, under Big Johnnie Durack (Darby Durack's eldest); Jerry; Long Michael and Black Pat Durack; and Tom Kilfoyle and Tom Hayes; with a total of 7520 cattle and 200 horses and 60 working bullocks. They left in May 1883. Others such as the MacDonalds and

DROVING *S. T. Gill*

MARY DURACK
1913-

Dame Mary Durack was born in Adelaide in 1913 and spent her early years on the various stations owned by her family in Western Australia and the Northern Territory: Argyle and Ivanhoe on the Ord River, Newry and Auvergne in the Territory. One of her first memories is of holding her father's hand as he counted the cattle running down the race into the boat at Wyndham, from where they would be freighted to the Philippines. Sometimes Mary and her brother Reg accompanied their parents to Manila where the cattle were sold.

Schooling in Perth meant absence from the stations, as the long journey by ship made it impossible to return for the shorter holidays, and in the Christmas holidays the inland tracks were made impassable by the Wet. At 17 she left school and returned to the North where she drove around with her father in the old Dodge between their company properties.

In 1933 Mary and her sister Elizabeth were living at Ivanhoe. She writes: "We were cooks, overseers and housekeepers with a staff of Aborigines with whom we formed a close association, and through whose eyes we got to know and love the country."

During this time Mary wrote sketches and stories of the Kimberley region, illustrated by Elizabeth, which were published in the *Bulletin* and the *West Australian* and which later appeared in book form under the titles *All-About, Chunuma* and *Son of Djaro*.

In 1936 Mary and Elizabeth went to the British Isles and visited their uncle Dermot, a retired professor, in Ireland. Later they travelled in Europe and North Africa.

On their return to Perth in 1937, Mary joined the staff of the *West Australian* as "Virgilia", editor of the country correspondence section, and as "Aunt Mary" she edited the children's section of the *Western Mail*.

In 1938 she married Captain Horrie Miller, a pioneer aviator who had established MacRobertson-Miller Airlines in 1934. They settled at Nedlands in Perth, where she still lives, and reared a family of six children, keeping in close touch with the northwest meanwhile.

Throughout these domestic years she kept writing, and in 1955 published *Keep Him My Country*, a story of station life in the Kimberley district. This novel was a Book Society recommendation in England.

The family saga *Kings in Grass Castles*, published in 1959, was the result of many years of research into family documents and also involved covering the tracks of her family from their early days in Goulburn to Western Queensland, the Territory and the Kimberley. The sequel, *Sons in the Saddle*, was published in 1983.

Mary Durack has written radio features, plays and short stories; the libretti for the opera *Dalgerie* and a children's musical, *The Ship of Dreams*. She has also written *The Rock and the Sand* (1969), a history of the Catholic missions north of Broome, and *To Be Heirs Forever* (1976), the story of the Shaw family, early pioneers of the Swan River Settlement.

She has kept up her close relationship with the Aborigines and has recorded their reactions to the changing world in which they live in "Lament for the Drowned Country", a poem about the country which now lies under the waters of the Ord River Dam.

MacKenzies were already on their way to their destination 5000 kilometres away at the junction of the Fitzroy and Margaret Rivers, where the MacDonalds established Fossil Downs.

The Durack parties went north to the Gulf, then west across no-man's-land; 1300 newborn calves had to be destroyed en route. They ran into drought and had to sit out months by a permanent waterhole. They lost an additional 1000 cattle, and then more through an outbreak of the cattle disease, pleuro. By the time they reached Elsey Station and the Roper River they had lost 3500 head. They went on across great, crocodile-infested rivers and through sheer gorges until, on 25 September 1885, they reached the Ord with about half the original herd.

In the meantime Patsy had decided to sell part of his interest to a syndicate which would take over the management of Thylungra and its herd of 30,987 cattle (from the original 100, 16 years before). The Queensland Co-operative Pastoral Company was to pay him and Stumpy Michael £160,000.

The boys, 21-year-old Michael, and John, who was even younger, were in the process of establishing the homestead at Argyle in the Kimberley when to their astonishment their father arrived with Pumpkin—*and* in the Wet. He began immediately to help them build the homestead on the Behn River. Patsy was soon riding down to the goldfields at Hall's Creek and setting up machinery for his unsuccessful Ruby Queen mine.

But land values collapsed in Queensland, the Queensland Co-operative Pastoral Company did not pay up and went out of business, Stumpy Michael's speculations with his and Patsy's money proved disastrous and Patsy's goldmine did not pay. Patsy returned to Brisbane to find his and his brothers' estate, reckoned at its height to be worth £750,000, had evaporated. Patsy was broke.

Fortunately he could return to the Kimberley, where to his sons' acute embarrassment he took a job, making a road to Argyle, with the Roads Board. Towards the end of his life he visited Ireland for the first time in 44 years.

There were ceaseless difficulties in the Kimberleys, particularly in finding markets for the cattle. Big Johnnie was speared to death by the blacks in 1886. But Mary's father Michael was disgusted by the way in which the police in the Kimberley treated the blacks, and by seeing them working in chains by the road.

In the years that followed there was prosperity of a sort, but there were many years when the sale of cattle on a run of 16,000 square kilometres could hardly pay wages.

Patsy died at Fremantle in 1898. Almost his last words were that the watch his wife Mary gave him on their wedding day should be given to Pumpkin, as "He was the best friend I ever had."

In 1950, at the age of 85, Michael signed away his company's rights to the Kimberley land and stock. Argyle is now under the waters of the Ord River dam.

The Duracks would have been far better off financially if they had stayed at Thylungra and gone in for sheep. But they were wanderers and cattle men, and Mary Durack has told a grand chronicle of their lives.

Robin Boyd
THE AUSTRALIAN UGLINESS

MELBOURNE 1960

The ordinary Sydney male drinking bars are not very different from those of any other Australian city. Late on any long summer afternoon, with the temperature and relative humidity both in the high eighties, hundreds of cream-tiled and stainless-steel-trimmed bars roar behind their street doors with the combined racket of glassware, beer dispensers, electric apparatus, and amiable oaths. Below the solid jam of red male faces there is a jungle of brown arms, white shirt-sleeves rolled to the armpits, and slathers of beer held in enormous glasses; above face level are shelves of seldom-opened spirits and never-opened exotic liqueurs and a grey mist of cigarette smoke swirled by a mammoth chromium-plated fan past an inaudibly mouthing television screen.

This is the bar pattern throughout Australia, with minor regional variations. The new arrangements in the newest hotels of Sydney make a first attempt to civilize the beast. They start with the revolutionary concepts of providing for both sexes and for fresh air. The space set aside in the hotel is usually a very big room, the size of a nineteenth century ballroom but with no more than a few square feet of free floor area. All the rest is occupied by small, square, metal-legged, plastic-topped tables and a great number of oddly-proportioned metal chairs: of normal height but with plastic seats hardly wider than a hand's span. The big room usually opens through a glass wall on one side to a terrace, perhaps twice as expansive as the room, which is similarly packed with little tables and midget chairs. A muffled Dixieland rhythm from a four-piece band in one corner of the big room manages to rise at times a decibel or two above the level of the conversation of the brilliantly-coloured throng perched on the pin-head chairs round the tables of beer glasses. Always there is a television set in view and in some cases, as at the hotel in Sylvania, a southern suburb, the bar terrace extends to take in also a view of a swimming pool.

The total facility is not exactly describable, in international parlance, as a beer garden, and it is certainly not a night-club. But it is somewhere between the two and the unvarying decorative style heightens the ambivalent atmosphere. The usual colouring is in saturated primaries. The usual materials are split stone veneer, chromium-plated steel, anodised aluminium, sprayed vermiculite plaster, crocodile-patterned hardboard, and striated plywood, not to mention the customary plastics. Every element is separated from the next by a dramatic change in tone and texture and is divided within itself by violent contrasts of colour introduced in stripes, wiggles, or random squares.

Sydney is a summer city, tensed for action round an outdoor life. Every year, when the thermometer drops, winter comes as a bitter unexpected turn of fate. Now the wind thrashes rain among the pin-head chairs on the terraces and against the window-walls, and the drinkers in the unheated ballrooms huddle closer in their woollens around the icy beer glasses on the plastic tables. Somehow it is a part of the architectural style to put two-tone crocodiled surfacing on the wallboards before comfort in the unseen air.

Sydney is the unconstituted capital of Australian popular culture. It is larger than Melbourne, older than Hobart and prettier than Perth, and it has by nature and by acquisition most of the things that visitors remark as typically Australian. Sydney is indeed the most proudly Australian of all cities, and the frankest admirer of American ideas. Sydney is alive, impatient to be even bigger and to short-cut ways to be smarter. It is a shop window city. It has more new houses and television sets with fewer new sewerage mains. It has more illustrated advertising painted on higher walls, more moving neon signs, the oldest rows of narrow terrace houses curving over twisting hills in the most picturesque slums. And in such modern palaces of amusement as the musical bar lounges, Sydney carries the contemporary style of the country to its highest intensity.

Although ostensibly a book about what man has done to the face of Australia, especially in the cities, *The Australian Ugliness* really asks the question, as Boyd himself puts it, "Is it what the Australian really wants?" And as he says elsewhere in the book, "There can be few other nations which are less certain than Australia as to what they are and where they are."

The Australian Ugliness can be read both as history and as a still relevant tract for the times. Many of Boyd's strictures about the destruction of Australia's architectural and civic heritage, and vandalism in respect of the environment, are less relevant than they were, except perhaps in Queensland. Anybody who read the book when it first came out and who rereads it today will be able to derive some satisfaction from the tremendous growth of the various conservation movements since the 1960s. It is thanks to people like Robin Boyd that such growth occurred.

Boyd was, of course, primarily an architect, but he is also one of Australia's most lucid, passionate and witty writers. He has that classic balance of mind that enables his writing to stay cool, even when his subject moves him most strongly to indignation and despair. He also has a subtle edge of confidence that came from being a member of one of the most remarkable Australian families, distinguished on both sides in art, literature and the law.

The Australian Ugliness begins with "The Descent into Chaos", a brilliantly evoked picture of flying across the vastness of outback Australia and landing at Darwin and having the visual sense assaulted by the primary colours, the plastic and bric-a-brac of the reception lounge. It is, Boyd says, "a cheerful and compact example of the visual style which rules everywhere that man has made his mark on this continent: the style of Featurism".

Most of *The Australian Ugliness* is an attack on various aspects of Featurism and a constructive attempt to show how this debilitating process might be avoided. Boyd coined the word, and he gives a definition: "Featurism is not simply a decorative technique, it starts in concepts and extends upwards through the parts to the numerous trimmings. It may be defined as the subordination of the essential whole and the accentuation of selected separate features. Featurism is by no means confined to Australia or to the twentieth century, but it flourishes more than ever at this place and time."

Boyd goes on to speculate why this should be. Perhaps, he suggests, it is because of the vastness of the landscape, which forces man to petty surroundings, to avoid anything that may be construed as a challenge to nature. Although Boyd does not mention this, what he is saying may be linked to the sardonic humour so typical of Australians, in the exercise of which deeper affections or anxieties may be disguised in mockery.

Boyd sees the isolation of Australia from the rest of the world, and the isolation of the cities from the outback, as related to the individualistic isolation of houses and buildings. "Isolated is the operative word. Absurdly proud, alone in a vacuum, each new Australian building sets out to create an isolated, competitive grain of beauty, like a rose carried on the wind, unconnected with the living bush, like a bank of seaweed drifting in the tide of fashion."

He mentions the development of Canberra and the buildings of the Australian National University as corruptions of original unifying plans into separate isolated

"Visual chaos of advertising"

items. This betrayal of some higher discipline is also behind the excesses of Featurism.

Boyd makes his point with some piercingly accurate descriptions. Consider, he says, the stone towers at each end of the Sydney Harbour Bridge, a "spectacular example of Featurist irrationality", existing only to camouflage and make presentable the giant framework of steel. "The pylon features thus successfully destroyed the visual reality of the steel bridge, while relieving Sydney of the expense of covering the whole arch with stone veneer. They were a triumph of disruptive patterning."

The unvarying decorative style heightens the ambivalent atmosphere. The usual colouring is in saturated primaries. The usual materials are split stone veneer, chromium-plated steel, anodised aluminium, sprayed vermiculite plaster, crocodile-patterned hardboard, and striated plywood, not to mention the customary plastics.

Boyd continues with his guided tour of Sydney Featurism. He begins with the hotel bars and "beer gardens" (where there are no flowers or trees, only plastic chairs and laminex tables). He continues past the shrieking visual chaos of advertising, saying that Australians are "the most vigorous and undisciplined advertisers in the world". Finally, in one of the wittiest passages in the book, Boyd looks in at the successful Featurist going home to have tea in the feature room, "the room he calls the sunroom".

Looking back at the history of architecture in Melbourne, he speculates that the origins of Featurism may lie in the desire to show off good luck and fortunes after the gold rush, but they are also connected with "a slightly neurotic condition brought about by loneliness". Boyd gives a penetrating analysis of the besotted obsession of Australians with the Mother Country, and goes on to coin the word "Austerica", to indicate the nature of the later swing to imitate all things American. This usually tends to mean picking the wrong things two years later than they were fashionable in the United States, such as the fins and colour combinations of the 1960 Holden, "Australia's Own Car" and "the best example of Australia's happy acceptance of second-hand Americana".

Looking towards either England or America leaves Australians unable to live with what is most distinctive and different in the Australian environment. Australian gum trees and wattles are untidy and sprawling, not like neat beeches or pines. Wildflowers are fugitive and delicate, not like marigolds and mown lawns. The new pioneer removes all traces of everything Australian, whether natural or man-made, with a bulldozer, so that Featurist buildings may go up and exotic flowers and shrubs can be planted. The arboraphobes or tree-haters are performing a public duty. Are not Australian trees a menace to drains, gutters and the European image? Alas, the attitudes of the new pioneer still exist; witness all those shopping centre car parks with not a tree to shade the roasting cars!

If Boyd were alive, he would be very pleased to see that

THE BRIDGE FROM POTTS POINT *Sydney Ure Smith*

ROBIN BOYD
1919-1971

Robin Boyd was one of the most talented of the famous Boyd family of artists and writers, being both architect and writer, although he always liked to say that he was an architect first and a writer second. In fact the two were always intimately linked. As Professor Sir Zelman Cowen said in a lecture after Boyd's death, "It was rightly said that when he began to practise shortly after the war, the role of the architect – in any other than a shallow sense – was virtually unknown to the public . . . In a tribute from his fellow architects in Victoria it was fittingly said, 'Almost single-handed, Robin Boyd brought about this change.'"

He was born at Melbourne on 3 January 1919, the second son of the landscape painter Penleigh Boyd who was killed in a car accident in 1923. Robin was educated at Malvern College, Melbourne, and studied architecture at Melbourne University. During World War II, he served in the Army in New Guinea.

He was appointed inaugural Director of the Small Homes Service of the Institute of Architects in 1947. All his working life as an architect and writer about architecture, he was as much interested in domestic architecture as in large buildings, and he wrote the classic study of the subject in *Australia's Home* (1952). He called Australian housing "a material triumph and an aesthetic calamity". He considered the early traditional Australian colonial homestead "the first and loveliest image of Australian building", and chronicled with dismay the collapse of this image into the ugliness of suburbia. He deplored the fact that architects had shied away from houses in favour of the large buildings that would bring them higher fees; as a consequence most Australian homes were designed by the builders or by the owners. He wrote of the Australian suburbanite and his home: "Anything but humble, his home was made a pillar of the strange society of suburbia, a monument to suburbia. This house was never loved by its occupants . . . In the land of the free, the houses of the free were straitlaced, smug."

Boyd's uninhibited strictures on bad planning and bad architecture went back to his student days, and then to the newsletter *Smudges* which he edited in 1939. A sample blast could be his comments on the fake-Jacobean Toorak Village in Melbourne, which began with the words "This hot-bed of architectural corruption called Toorak Village".

His stern functional principles never lost their strength. When he died he was working on a book about the Sydney Opera House, the outrageous featurism of which, for example, left an enormous and useless space between the sails and the theatre roofs, viewed only by the maintenance crew.

Boyd always maintained close connections with overseas architects. In 1956-57 he was Visiting Professor of Architecture at the Massachusetts Institute of Technology. He was a member of the judging panel for the new Houses of Parliament at Westminster in 1971. In 1973 he was posthumously awarded the American Institute of Architects' Critic's Medal for his distinguished career of architectural criticism.

Robin Boyd died in October 1971.

---

in many areas, in median strips or in plantings by roads and especially in home gardens, there has been the most enormous increase in the planting of native shrubs and trees.

In an attempt to find out what Australians really want, Boyd takes suburbia as the crux of Australian ugliness. He finds the government-sponsored town of Elizabeth in South Australia especially depressing because the care taken with

Sydney is the unconstituted capital of Australian popular culture. It is larger than Melbourne, older than Hobart and prettier than Perth, and it has by nature and by acquisition most of the things that visitors remark as typically Australian.

it led only to mediocrity. (One complaint of Boyd's is unjustified; today there is a tremendous growth of trees in Elizabeth.) But when he compares Elizabeth with the Hansa development in West Berlin, where a number of world-famous architects contributed one design each to a park containing multi-storey flats, Boyd reveals some traces of a dictatorial puritanism that is one of the faults of *The Australian Ugliness*.

There appears to be a contradiction in his defence of functionalism against beauty. "'Honesty' in expression of functions, 'truth' in construction, and 'integrity' in the whole" were the demands of the early Moderns whom Boyd admires. But houses surely exist only to help make human beings happy, and this is easier to achieve in Australian Featurist suburbia than in award-winning blocks of multi-storey flats. It is manifestly unfair to say "the essence of Australian suburban life is unreality". And there are puritan dangers in the attitudes behind declarations such as: "To be free from the sirens of beauty, pleasingness, delight, is to be free to create and to appreciate the real thing, the whole thing."

Yet it would be unfair to Boyd not to admit that he has positive suggestions to make for improving suburbia, especially in his scenario of a good and a bad development of a hypothetical suburb beginning from a hillside occupied originally only by a cottage, an orchard and scrub. Boyd makes his point here succinctly and well.

The last section of the book is more theoretical, a stimulating discussion of architectural theory from Ruskin to Frank Lloyd Wright and of the harmony underlying the realities of good design.

The Australian ugliness still exists, but the changes in attitude which have purged some of its excesses are partly due to the impact of Boyd's clear writing and incisive thinking.

Kenneth Cook

WAKE
IN
FRIGHT

LONDON 1961

The kangaroos watched it impassively until it was about two hundred yards from them. Then they turned and leaped away, stiffly erect, propelling themselves with thrusts of their giant hind legs so that they looked like so many mechanical toys except that at the height of their leap their tails streamed out behind them and their bodies leaned forward so that they speared through the air like abstractions of flight.

Grant forgot even his hangover as he watched the hunter springing after the kangaroos as they crossed the plain like the shadows of aircraft.

The mob rose in a wave over one of the occasional fences that appear inexplicably in the plain country, but two baulked and turned along the fence towards the road.

Immediately the motor of the car roared, the gear slammed in and Dick drove diagonally off the road, cutting across the flight of the two kangaroos.

There was not much difference between the road and the open country, but there were boulders on the plain and Dick performed mighty deeds with the car, keeping it at fifty miles an hour, swerving hard when he reached the fence and driving straight down to the kangaroos.

The dog anticipated the manoeuvre and turned diagonally out from the fence.

The kangaroos sighted the car and they too turned out from the fence, heading back to the patch of scrub. And now the kangaroos and the dog were travelling in two lines which would soon meet.

Tydon had his rifle out now and was firing through the window. Joe was trying to aim across Grant's shoulder, and still the car bounced over the ground at fifty miles an hour.

The men were shouting, the motor was roaring, the sharp smell of gunpowder drowned all the other smells in the car.

The dog pulled down one of the kangaroos in a tangled heap about fifty yards from the fence. The other kangaroo paused for a moment when its mate fell and Grant could see it watching the slaughter, immobile, expressionless. Then it streaked back towards the fence again.

But the car was between it and the fence.

Dick, yelling madly now, drove straight at the kangaroo, pressing down the accelerator, driving as no sane man would do, crashing over stones, through low scrub, wrecking the mudguards on the remnants of trees, and still the kangaroo came on, unharmed by the fusillade of bullets which Tydon was pumping out the window.

Grant clung to the seat, fascinated, watching through the windscreen the fluctuating approach of the kangaroo. Up it went and down, then up, up, and down, a wild grey figure bearing down on them as though in passionless attack.

It turned ten yards from the car, but Dick, quite mad now, pulled the car around and ran the animal down.

It disappeared quite suddenly under the bonnet.

A thud, the car lifted, skidded, rocketed almost over on to its side, righted itself and stopped.

Grant looked out of the rear window as the others tumbled out. A grey bundle was flopping about in the dust behind the car.

Following the others over to the broken mess, Grant saw Dick draw a long-bladed knife from a sheath at his side, kneel down, and cut the animal's throat. It died then.

"It's not worth cutting up," said Dick. The kangaroo had split open and trailed entrails for a dozen yards. Its body was so shattered that bones stood out from the skin every few inches, white and glistening.

Joe and Dick started off to look at the damage to the car, but Tydon lingered, took out his own knife and neatly castrated the carcass.

On the last page of *Wake in Fright* the unheroic hero of the book, John Grant, thinks to himself, "almost aloud":

I can see quite clearly the ingenuity whereby a man may be made mean or great by exactly the same circumstances.

I can see quite clearly that even if he chooses meanness the things he brings about can even then be welded into a pattern of sanity for him to take advantage of if he wishes.

As the events of the novel take place, they seem more like a pattern of madness. Although the meanness of Grant's responses soon becomes obvious, the word "ingenuity" remains puzzling. The novelist later confirmed that what he meant by the term was the ingenuity of God. However the word "ingenuity" also has overtones of a much older meaning: "generosity". At certain crucial stages of his life a man is given choices. John Grant makes all the wrong ones.

He seems a harmless enough fellow to begin with, if a bit weak and ineffectual. He is a schoolteacher, bonded for two years to the Education Department (for nearly £400) to teach wherever he is sent. He regards it as very bad luck that he is sent to the far west of New South Wales, to a township of three buildings, riddled with white ants, called Tiboonda. It is also a railway siding, with the railway leading into Bundanyabba (clearly Broken Hill), always known as "the Yabba".

KENNETH COOK

It is the beginning of the summer holidays. Grant has six weeks of freedom, which he intends to spend in Sydney lying on the beach. After he has paid his airfare he will have £140 to last him out. He has a girl in Sydney, Robyn, whom he hopes will do more than remember him, though there is nothing definite between them.

There is almost nothing but rejection in the beginning of the novel. Grant hates the school (if not all his 28 pupils), the pub where he lives, the publican and his half-caste mistress and her greasy meals, the heat, the dust. As for the Yabba, "it was just a larger variation of Tiboonda, and Tiboonda was a variation of hell".

The dog pulled down one of the kangaroos in a tangled heap about fifty yards from the fence. The other kangaroo paused for a moment when its mate fell and Grant could see it watching the slaughter, immobile, expressionless. Then it streaked back towards the fence again.

Even the friendliness of the inhabitants of the Yabba repels him. They all say the same thing. "New to the Yabba?", "Best place in Australia", and "Best little town in the world." He finds their "friendly habits . . . crude and embarrassing".

He has to spend a night in the Yabba, so he books a room and goes to have a couple of drinks. The pubs are officially closed as it is after 10 o'clock at night, but Grant knows the door of the bar is always ajar. There is a dense crowd in the bar he enters, including the local policeman, Jock Crawford. Sceptically he allows Jock to befriend him and call him John. "It distressed him a little when people, upon being introduced to him, immediately called him by his first name. Yet everybody he had ever met in the west did just that."

John has several drinks with Jock, and then asks where is the best place to have a meal. "The two-up school's pretty good if you want a good steak," says Jock, and takes him there, where everyone amiably greets him, "How goes it, Jock?" and "G'night, Jock." There is no sly grog problem in the Yabba, and no furtive gambling. Everything is out in the open.

John has "the best six bob's worth of steak you ever had" and does not think much of it. His several beers with Jock have relaxed him; he has 12 hours to fill in until his plane goes. He tells himself it would not matter if he lost the

£17-odd he has in cash—and he might win.

Cook cleverly charts the new-chum gambler's downward path. Firstly, "he might as well have a go". Then a small win, and gambler's remorse that he had not put all his money on that winning throw. Next, a bigger win. Finally, gambler's mysticism. "He knew that as surely as he knew that he existed" that it would be tails again. It is.

Feeling faint, he has won £200 from £17 10s, and not touched his wages cheque. He goes back to his hotel room and puts the money out on the floor. Then he is back to gambler's remorse. If he had put the £200 on again, and won, he would have had more than enough to pay off his bond.

He goes back. He loses his £200. He cashes his wages cheque and three minutes later he has lost that, too.

In the morning his situation is all too clear. He is broke. He has not even enough money to pay for the train ticket to Sydney. He tramps the town with his suitcases and finally goes into a hotel where he has just enough money to buy some cigarettes and the smallest glass of beer available.

At this stage the reader begins to realise that the worst thing about Grant is that not only does he make the wrong choices, but having done so he cannot extricate himself. His character is a mixture of pride and self-pity. He thinks himself better than the miners and policemen and publicans and barmaids of the Yabba. After all, *he* is a schoolteacher. He could go for help to Jock, but he does not even think of it.

When the little Irishman next to him in the bar offers him a drink he refuses. This is very bad form in the Yabba, and he has also just disgraced himself by telling the Irishman that he thinks that the Yabba is "bloody awful". Even so, the little Irishman again offers him a drink, and when he again refuses, saying this time that he is flat broke, the little man says, "What's that got to do with it, man? I said I'd buy you a drink, I don't want you to buy me one." So John starts drinking with Tim Hynes. Tim is amazed to hear that John is not a Mason, or in the Buffs (Buffaloes) or even a Catholic. There is nothing for it but to buy him another beer. They drink through the whole morning, and then Tim asks John home to dinner, and they drink more.

Cook is a master at describing the stages of drunkenness. "Hynes was very drunk, and Grant could feel himself following down the pastel sprung corridors of inebriation; his voice echoing splendidly in his own ears; his frame larger than life, expanded and buoyant; and, he was sure, an ironic smile on his lips as he mocked life and his own predicament."

He goes for a walk in the night with Hynes' beautiful daughter Janette, ignoring dirty looks from one of the two big miners who have joined the party. Janette is accommodatingly unbuttoning her dress when Grant can take it no longer and rushes into the bushes and vomits. He wakes up in the shack of an alcoholic doctor, with a terrible hangover, and before he knows what is happening, after endless beers and whisky chasers, he is roaring off on a kangaroo shoot with the two big miners who want meat for their greyhounds.

The kangaroo shoot, by spotlight in the dark, is one of the most powerful pieces of writing in Australian fiction. What makes it both terrible and convincing is that, through the haze of beer and whisky and blood and gunpowder, Grant is quite enjoying it all. John Grant, schoolteacher, is tackling wounded kangaroos with a knife and cutting their throats.

ROAD WITH ROCKS *Russell Drysdale*

KENNETH COOK
1929-

Everything that happens in *Wake in Fright* is so intensely believable that one feels sure than Kenneth Cook has at some time been a schoolteacher in a one-teacher school near Broken Hill. In fact, *Wake in Fright* came from a period he spent with the ABC at Broken Hill.

Kenneth Cook was born in Sydney in 1929. After leaving school, he turned to journalism in 1948, a career that gave him the material for his first three novels: *Vantage to the Gale*, dealing with local politics in North Queensland; *Wake in Fright* (1961); and *Chain of Darkness* (1962), which came from his experience covering a manhunt for ABC television news around Sydney.

In 1960 he bought a commercial boatshed, which led to *Stormalong*. In 1962 he left the boatshed and took his wife and four children on an extended world tour, which resulted in the comic novel, *Blood Red Roses*.

On his return to Australia he went into independent film production (Patrician Films) and, over the next few years, produced,

wrote, directed and appeared in hundreds of documentary and dramatic television films.

He became deeply involved in the debate in Australia over the morality of the Vietnam war, which caused him to write *The Wine of God's Anger*, the television drama *I'm Damned if I Know* (ABC), and the stage musical *Stockade*.

Extensive travels within Australia gave him the background for four further adventure novels. The continuing controversy surrounding abortion produced the novels *Piper in the Market Place* and *Play Little Victims*.

In the 1970s he decided to create the Butterfly Farm, an ambitious natural history park, concentrating on insects, on the banks of the Hawkesbury River. A succession of floods washed out the park, but the project resulted in the publication of *The Man Underground* and *Bloodhouse*.

In somewhat lighter mood he wrote *Eliza Fraser*, a novel based on the screenplay by David Williamson for the film of that name. His long involvement with the film industry led to the writing of *Film-Makers* in collaboration with his daughter Kerry.

His books have been translated into several languages, and he has held a number of Fellowships from the Literature Board of the Australia Council.

He lives at Manly in Sydney.

He is undeterred when the men rip open the bellies of the dead kangaroos, cut off the hindquarters and tails and stuff them in a box in the back of the car, while a great killer of a greyhound slobbers all over him in the back seat. If John were indignant it would not all be nearly so horrible. The only thing he cannot take is the Doc cutting off all the testicles. They are his favourite food, and John has had a meal with him. . . .

Following the others over to the broken mess, Grant saw Dick draw a long-bladed knife from a sheath at his side, kneel down, and cut the animal's throat. It died then.

Next day, filthy, blood-stained and hung over, he meets Jock, who buys him a few beers and arranges with the barmaid for him to have a shower. His suitcases are still in the corner of the bar where he had left them two days ago.

He gets a lift out to Yelonda. A Sydney truck driver agrees to give him a lift to the city. He goes to sleep in the back of the truck and wakes up in Bundanyabba. "I never said

anything about Sydney," says the driver. "You said you wanted to go through to the city—well, this is a city isn't it, mate?"

Cook has taken Grant through every degradation. Now he offers him the option of suicide with the rifle the kangaroo shooters have given him. He spends a last moment thinking of Robyn and the sea and "that he might have been a little more like the man he once thought he was". He pulls the trigger.

He wakes up in hospital. The bullet has nicked his skull and concussed him, severely enough for him to have to spend a month in hospital. Divine magnanimity has allowed him a chance to expiate meanness. He is given some money by the almoner at the hospital, and goes back to Tiboonda to wait for the new school term.

Grant's enlightenment follows a terrible purgatory. He now sees a sadness behind the stoicism of the Yabba. Perhaps later he will also see the kindness and the honesty and the refusal to condemn anyone, except for the minor sin of not having a drink with a man. The brutality of the kangaroo hunt is harder to deal with. There may be many nights to come when John Grant will wake in fright.

Nene Gare

THE FRINGE DWELLERS

LONDON 1961

The girls were walking along the less frequented part of the beach. The tide had climbed high in a curving line, leaving the sand wet and firm. Where the girls walked, their footsteps followed after them, delicately perfect. Between the beach and the road grew thickets of grey-green salt-bush, scored through with a hundred paths leading down to the sea. The noise of traffic was muted with distance, no more disturbing than the wash of the waves or the soft chatter of the girls. Unheard in their ears, the deep strong pull of the ocean went on for ever.

"School for you soon," Audrena said, looking pityingly at Trilby.

Trilby gave her cousin a long look. "I can always get a headache."

Audrena laughed.

"Wasn't you gunna get a job?" Blanchie asked. "Serving or something?"

Trilby looked sullenly ahead. At one time or another she had been into every shop in the town. Foreigners she had found, some golden-skinned, some dark, a few of them hardly able to make themselves understood, but there had been none like herself. Trilby bit her bottom lip savagely. On one point her mind was firmly made up. There would be no housework for her, nor minding of kids. For another year she would go back to school. By that time she would know more about this town and then she would see.

She forced a casual air. "I'm going to get my Junior first," she told her cousins. "So I can get a better job. In an office or somewhere."

Blanchie stared admiringly at her not doubting for a moment Trilby would get what she wanted. Blanchie did not mind taking second place to her glamorous cousin. She found it exciting to be with her, swimming when Trilby decided to swim, looking in shop windows, sitting at the far end of the Esplanade at night with a crowd of young ones, laughing, gossiping, wandering home late at night with a few fellers to keep them company.

Audrena fell in with most of Trilby's plans, too, but sour envy made up a good proportion of her feelings towards her cousin. Even Trilby's untouched body was a source of annoyance to Audrena. It was as though she set a price on herself. Audrena had to admit that Trilby had had her opportunities. The fellers hung round her like ants after jam. It beat Audrena to know why, when there was herself with all her experience and none of this stupid hanging back from something that was bound to happen to a girl some time or other.

Audrena was always watching for a chance to get under Trilby's guard. Her tongue shot venom wherever she knew it would sting most.

"Better not set ya heart on no office job," she said now. "You could be the best typewriter in the world an not get a job here."

"Typiste!" Trilby flicked back.

"All I'm saying, ya want one a them jobs you'll have ta go some other place where they don't know ya got colour in ya." Her glance went spitefully to Trilby's dark gold skin.

"That's what I'm going to do," Trilby said proudly. And in that second decided to do just this. Of course! She should have thought of it for herself. What she must do must be to leave everyone behind her; begin a new fresh life of her own. The thought of it excited her. With a sudden uprush of spirits she sprinted up the beach, turned a somersault and landed laughing and breathless in the odoriferous scratchy seaweed where a group of boys waited for them.

One of the most exuberant, and at the same time poignant, Australian novels is Nene Gare's *The Fringe Dwellers*. It is all the more remarkable for being written by a white woman about half-caste Aboriginal people. She not only captures their idiom perfectly, but she has a deep understanding of their humour, their pride and their faults. They are all individuals, but their lives are determined by their status as fringe dwellers. They live on the edge of white society, never accepted, never quite wanting to be accepted. The focus is the stronger for the action taking place in a coastal town which is never named but is, in fact, Geraldton. (Geraldton has been much written about; it is also the locale of Randolph Stow's *The Merry-Go-Round in the Sea*.)

The central characters of *The Fringe Dwellers* are the members of the Comeaway family, particularly Trilby and Noonah the daughters, who are 15 and 17 when the book opens, and their parents. Mrs Comeaway is one of the great characters of Australian fiction—huge, happy, shrewd, uneducated but with a bubbling flow of words, and at times sadly vulnerable. The one who hurts her most is her beautiful daughter Trilby. Nene Gare's portrait of Trilby is one of the most remarkable achievements of *The Fringe Dwellers*. This girl, so attractive and yet so infuriating, so admirable in her courage and yet so destructive in her self-centredness, dominates all the other characters in the book, even her normally indomitable mother.

Nene Gare writes about these people with skill and imagination. She has a profound experience of her subject matter, the fringe dwellers. Nene came to know these people while living at Carnarvon and Geraldton in Western Australia where her husband was with the Native Welfare Department. Her good friend Mrs Forrest provided the material for many of her characters.

In a letter to the present author, Nene Gare wrote:

She visited our house often bringing others and we all sat around my table drinking large cups of "scald" and laughing while she related what was going on around the town. Their tolerance and serenity confounded me; I thought I should never reach to the bottom of it. There never was such tolerance. They all laughed uproariously at things that would have had most white women in tears. I have reflected that it is possible to laugh only if all of one's friends are in the same boat.

These people had become accustomed to injustice and ill-treatment of the most unbelievable kind from childhood on and they had learned that laughter was the best way to deal with it. For their part, our behaviour among ourselves astounded them and was another cause for laughter.

Her comments illuminate *The Fringe Dwellers* more clearly than pages of criticism. The tolerance of the older women, Mrs Comeaway, Mrs Green and Rene, is astonishing and seems to come from deep wells of human kindness and understanding. "Serenity" seems an odd word to use of people at the centre of such a hurly-burly of life—squeezed into humpies or bulging out of a little government house, in the midst of gambling, drink, wild sexual behaviour and brawling—yet that is exactly the right word to use of those formidable women. And behind the serenity is, as Nene Gare says, the consciousness of friends in misfortune, all in the same boat.

"*All I'm saying, ya want one a them jobs you'll have ta go some other place where they don't know ya got colour in ya.*" *Her glance went spitefully to Trilby's dark gold skin.*

The Aboriginal mixed bloods accept certain features of white civilisation and behaviour, but at the same time they retain the basic Aboriginal feeling for family and tribe. They are constantly sharing not only each other's lives but their possessions, borrowing and lending, giving and receiving. And of course when any one of them is known to have some money, everyone else arrives to help in the spending of it.

As Mrs Comeaway says, in all the frankness of her idiom, "It's all in. Ya bite someone one day, ya gotta expect ta be bit back when it's your turn. Ain't that right?" She is talking to her daughter, Noonah, who is training to be a nurse. Mrs Comeaway goes on to tell about "ole Bung Arrer", who is about to receive a large lump sum in back payments for a pension. He tells everybody about it. "And the day e gets it, there they are, all of em. Seventeen! For a bit of fun I counted eads. All waitin outside the post office fa ole Bung Arrer." When Noonah asks her what she was doing there she confesses, unabashed, "Waitin ta bite im, a course."

Noonah giggles and says, "You're awful", but she is full of affection for her mother. "Despite their undercurrent of tragedy, these were the tales she loved to hear when she came home."

Noonah's sister, Trilby, the most complex character in *The Fringe Dwellers*, is at the mercy of that undercurrent of tragedy. Neither tolerance nor serenity appeals to Trilby. She hates her situation as a half-caste, she detests the communal life all her "lations" accept. When the Comeaways move into the government house she demands and gets a room of her own. She wants the style of life and the things essential to it that white people want. She despises white people, who call her people niggers and treat them as inferior, dirty and unreliable, and at the same time she despises her own people for accepting their status as second-class citizens.

Trilby and Noonah have been brought up at a mission and been given a good education. Noonah is serious and quiet and not attractive to men. Trilby is exuberant, independent-minded, determined, and extremely sexy. This last, of course, is a two-edged weapon. She is naturally fastidious and ambitious, and rebuffs all the men who cluster around her. But at the same time she is hot blooded and cannot resist a boy she likes, Phyllix, by whom, to her fury, she has a baby. *She*, who was not going to fall into all the traps of the fringe dweller's life. *She*, who had gone back to school in Geraldton to fit herself for a good job in Perth in the white man's world.

Although *The Fringe Dwellers* is not a tragedy, Trilby is a tragic character, and, like all tragic characters, incapable of compromise. Conflict is born in her, the Aboriginal blood warring with that of her two white grandfathers, and her mission education and fastidiousness making her a misfit in Mrs Comeaway's easygoing world. With the true novelist's eye for detail, Nene Gare shows Trilby coming "home" to the humpy, searching on her first morning for something to wash in.

She found a basin underneath the table. A skinny grey washer hung over its side. Trilby wrinkled her nose and used it to wipe out the inside of the grey-rimmed basin. Then she took her new washer and soap from her flowered sponge-bag.

Trilby is swiftly taught about the fringe dweller's world, of drinking *conto* (cheap wine, at that time still illegal for Aborigines), of the ever-present threat of the "monarch" (the police) and the "partment" (the Department of Aboriginal Affairs), of racism in milk bars ("a voice came from the next table. 'It's to be hoped they use some sort of disinfectant on these glasses.'") Trilby learns about that sort of white woman who under the guise of Christian charity wants to patronise the Aborigines. When such a neighbour gives Mrs Comeaway cast-off clothes for Trilby the girl burns them, singeing Mrs Comeaway in the process.

As for money, as Trilby accompanies her mother into

ABORIGINAL GIRLS AT CUNNAMULLA SHOW *John Rigby*

NENE GARE
1919-

Nene Gare was born Doris V. M. Wadham at Adelaide in 1919. It is odd that her interest in Aborigines stems from the fact that she came, on her father's side, from an "Establishment" family. She writes:

> I grew up with a foot in two camps; the families of both parents arrived in Australia before the 1850s and my father's family

boasted a surveyor-explorer, a brigadier-general and high ranking public servants. One of my uncles was at the head of the State Public Service. My mother's father was a potter. He lived at Magill in a cottage belonging to Penfold's and worked in the vineyard as well. We were the poorest of our relations on both sides and I was always conscious of patronage. We had nothing to give away but were in receipt of surplus fruit and vegetables and outworn clothing from uncles and aunts who regarded our large family as their chief charity. This did not disturb my father because of his upbringing and in any case he was born a philosopher. It did disturb my mother though she could not afford to refuse the largesse. She made comparisons and was hurt or happy depending on her conclusions.

When I grasped that only money and possessions differentiated us from our relations I was amazed and resentful. I thought and still think this absurd. If anyone offended me by treating me, as I thought, differently from the way they treated my cousins, I held it against them and never forgave. Nearly all of my young photographs show me scowling, looking out at the world from beneath bent brows.

It was as natural to me as breathing to slip into what I thought were the feelings of Aborigines. I resented their lot six times as fiercely as they did and when I decided to write *The Fringe Dwellers* I had to keep cutting out great chunks that sounded more like sermons than stories.

On the other hand, Nene Gare was lucky to have grown up in a family where there were many books, and she was taken regularly to two lending libraries. She admits to having been baffled by what she considered the coarse Australianness of the *Bulletin*—an interesting commentary on the South Australia of her background.

In 1941 she married Frank Gare. She was a war bride, and he was away in the AIF until 1945. After the war he worked for two years in the New Guinea Administration. The Gares then moved to Carnarvon where they grew bananas. Frank joined the Western Australian Native Welfare Department, and worked at Carnarvon and Geraldton, eventually becoming Director of Aboriginal Affairs.

Nene's close contact with Aborigines gave her the background for *The Fringe Dwellers*. Her good friend at this time, Mrs Forrest, with "a bit of Afghan in her and a bit of Irish and a lot of Aboriginal Australian", lives in her books as Mrs Comeaway, Rene, Mrs Magdalene and Mrs Yorick.

The Fringe Dwellers began as a long short story and accidentally turned into a novel. Nene Gare was helped in shaping it by Florence James. It was published in 1961 and has been reprinted many times. Nene Gare is the author of several novels and stories. She lives in Perth.

---

town to buy her a longed-for pair of bathers, Mrs Comeaway suddenly says, "Don't tell me! . . . If I didn't clean forget about money. . . . We'll pick up with your dad again and get some money . . . before he spends it all." When Noonah asks where he is getting it from, "'Round about,' Mrs Comeaway said largely. 'Someone'll be owin im some. Or e'll borrow some. E knows I gotta pick up some tucker, anyhow. Can't do that thout money.'"

When the Comeaways finally get their house from the "partment" Mr Comeaway happily invites his brother and sister-in-law and their two children to live in the little house with them, despite his frequent complaints at "the great heap of womans" around the place.

The overt tragedy in *The Fringe Dwellers* is the accidental death of Trilby's baby in hospital. It is not altogether her fault that the baby slips out of the blanket and hits her head on the floor, but the dreadful thing for Trilby is that she had wished the baby dead.

Phyllix, the baby's father, wants to marry her. Her pride not only makes her refuse him, but even makes her tell him that she does not know who the father is, despite the fact that she has had no other lover but him. She tries to run away to Perth. Phyllix finds her and brings her back. She agrees to stay with him—for a while. In the last words of the book, "So long as she had youth and strength and pride, so long would she seek to escape this life."

It is a tragic dilemma. Trilby must escape, yet there is no certainty at all that she will be accepted in the white world for which she yearns.

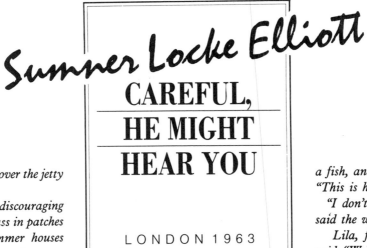

CAREFUL, HE MIGHT HEAR YOU

LONDON 1963

Tin letters slipping sideways over the jetty said: FAIRYLAND.

Beyond the jetty lay a discouraging picnic area, worn bald of grass in patches of gray dirt. Trellised summer houses leaned and sagged under the ancient gum trees. A kiosk, unpainted for many years, bore a sign: HOT WATER. SAVELOYS SARGENT'S MEAT PIES. Tables and benches were scattered throughout the area between the trees. There were seesaws and a row of weary swings drooping into pools of dust. A wooden stage had been erected near the kiosk, and strings of flags and coloured electric lights had been looped between the trees in an amateurish attempt to lend an air of festivity to the weedy, drab tobacco-colored landscape. A pall of sadness hung over the place. It was a playground of dead picnics, stale as old sandwiches, wallowing in its own litter of rusted tin cans, schnapper and whiting bones, brown beer bottles, IXL jam jars and old rubber bathing caps. Staler than the news on the yellow newspapers that blew in the breeze and wrapped themselves around legs of tables. But sadder than the rain of dead gum leaves and dried berries was the sense of mortified fun, the smell of old joy. Where now were the lovers, the dancers, the mandolin players, the children skipping rope, the ring-a-ring-a-rosies, the beery elated aroused moonlight-seekers in the row boats? The dancers were gone, the lovers had choked to death in the spiky lantana vines and blackberry bushes; the skipping children were skeletons flung away into the shrubbery; the secret whisperers in row boats had sunk into the green sludge at the bottom of the river.

What has happened to Fairyland? thought Lila as the ferry blundered toward the rotting jetty. And then, Something happened here. What? Murder? Food poisoning? The razor gang?

She saw a dead dog floating in the water and quickly directed the attention of P.S. to the tattered flags.

"Quick, quick—see how pretty they are?"

(What had happened here?)

They went up the narrow wooden gangplank with a handful of dispirited-looking people as the sun went behind clouds, casting a bilious tarnished light on the rotting summer houses and heightening the illusion that this fairground was a once lavish stage setting left out on a city dump to be burned.

(We shouldn't have come! . . . Too late now!)

Lila smiled at an emaciated woman wearing a bright dirndl who was handing out tickets behind a table from which hung a banner declaring: WELCOME SCRIBES AND DAUBERS 1934.

"Five bob. Children half price," said the woman.

Lila said in her best-manners voice, "I'm Mrs. Baines—I'm Sinden Scott's sister."

The woman stared at her, unmoved as a fish, and Lila flushed slightly, added, "This is her little boy. We're guests."

"I don't know anything about that," said the woman.

Lila, flattened, expecting a fanfare, said, "Well, we were invited—I'm Sinden Scott's sister. Pony Wardrop—"

"Oh, just a minute then." The woman went on selling tickets and giving chits for billy cans, hot water and tea.

Lila found Pony's letter in her bag and thrust it toward the woman. "This letter will explain who we are—Sinden Scott's relatives—Sinden Scott, the late novelist."

"They're all writers here," said the woman.

Really! This was dreadfully insulting. How like them to have some fool of a woman at the gate who was so common and ignorant and terrible-looking into the bargain. And not to know who they were! Poor little Sin. Could they have forgotten her so soon?

"Stand over to the side," said the woman. "You're blocking the line."

They stood to the side. Like poor relatives, Lila thought. Five shillings! Her heart sank. And another two and sixpence for P.S.! She felt in her purse. Seven and sixpence could have been George's new hat. And they had defied Vanessa just to be stood aside at the gate like this.

"Now," said the woman, "I wasn't told anything about free passes. This affair is for charity. For writers."

One of the finest and most subtle of Australian novels is *Careful, He Might Hear You*. This story of a six-year-old boy, whose custody is being fought over by two aunts, with two more involved in the background, is often one of anguish and pathos, but it is always cauterised of sentimentality by Locke Elliott's brilliant sense of comedy.

We do not learn the little boy's name until the very end of the book. He is called P.S., because his mother Sinden, a writer, who died when he was born, referred to him as "my 'P.S.', for that's what he'll be—a postscript to my ridiculous life". Her husband Logan is a charming drifter, hopelessly irresponsible, who is usually away gold-mining in the Northern Territory.

P.S. has been brought up by Lila, the oldest of the sisters, and her husband George, who works in the Trades Hall and is an old Labor supporter. The glamorous sister is Vanessa, who lives in London as companion to rich Cousin Ettie (who has a weakness for the sherry bottle). Vere, a comic character of greater richness, has been around the stage and lives at Kings Cross in a room that P.S. adores "because it was so full of Things". It is also usually full of friends whom P.S. finds immensely entertaining, with "wonderful names like Dodo, Ukulele, Widget and Gussy". Finally there is Agnes, who has religion, and is a prominent disciple of the American Dr Pollack and his Temple of Everlasting Love; she spends her life handing out pamphlets to scoffers and preaching in the Domain. However, Agnes has flashes of intuition, and it is always as well to listen to what she says, as sometimes hidden truths appear.

There are regular expeditions with Lila and George to Sinden's grave, which is known as Dear One's Garden. "Dear One . . . was a saint and an angel and too good to live and so God called her away." We find out about Sinden later.

The book opens with the news, pieced together by P.S. from hints through codes of spelled-out words and schoolgirl French, that Vanessa (Ness) is coming home to Sydney to claim part-time custody of P.S. (P.S. hears it as "custardy", and wonders what desserts have to do with Vanessa.) One of P.S.'s legal guardians, Ernest Huxley, Sinden's publisher and former fiancé, has relinquished his guardianship to Vanessa, with Logan's permission. So it is all legal.

Poor P.S. He not only hears his aunts gossiping about Vanessa, but the little girl next door has heard it from her

*T*in *letters slipping sideways over the jetty said: FAIRYLAND. Beyond the jetty lay a discouraging picnic area, worn bald of grass in patches of gray dirt. Trellised summer houses leaned and sagged under the ancient gum trees.*

mother and tells P.S. that he is going somewhere else to live. "They're comin' in a big car to take you away for good."

Vanessa arrives on the P and O liner with Ettie, met by Lila and George and P.S. and Vere, and the whole party goes to the Carlton where Ettie and Vanessa have a suite. Vanessa is cool, elegant, precise; she does everything slowly, quite unlike Lila who fusses and darts and has asthma which comes on worse at moments of emotion. Though uncertain of her own motives, and with deep fears (as of thunderstorms) hidden under the immaculate facade, Vanessa is honest about other people, unafraid of hurting their feelings. Lila, a thoroughly good person, is always wrapping her thoughts in sentimental tissues and wheezing when they are pulled away.

Lila is offended when Vanessa speaks irreverently of Sinden as she really was—emotionally untidy. "Sinden simply put her own emotions into other people and convinced herself that that was how they felt."

Finally a large house, with servants and gardener, is taken by Vanessa and Ettie at Point Piper, and P.S. unwillingly has to share his life between Vanessa and Lila, the Harbour separating them. Leaving him in this unwanted splendour, Lila says, with her typical well-meaning half-truths:

"Remember, Darling, it's only till Sunday night. Then George will come and get you and bring you home. Now don't forget what I told you, that if you feel a teeny bit lonely, all you have to do is look out the window across the harbour and there we'll be, waving to you."
"Which way?"
"Why, over there."
"But I only see trees and things."
"Well, we're over there anyway and don't you worry."

P.S. is torn between two "homes". Vanessa tries to make him a little English boy—she gives him beautiful clothes and toys, sends him to a private school which he hates, although he has to learn to say he likes everything. He has a sort of ineffectual ally in Ettie, a beautifully drawn study of a weak woman whose money makes her indispensable to Vanessa.

Locke Elliott's narrative method is very subtle and handled with great deftness. Sometimes P.S. is experiencing it all, from the crudities of Lila's neighbours and the cruelties of Miss Pile's school to the shrouded hints in the grown-up conversations he hears. Sometimes one or other of the sisters is at the centre of the action. And all the time there is a slow re-creation, through the memories of the sisters, of Sinden and her rackety life and her infatuation with Logan. The funniest revelations come through P.S.'s and Lila's visit to a Writers' Picnic, to which they are invited in memory of Sinden by Sinden's old friend Pony Wardrop. The picnic is at Fairyland, reached by boat from the Lane Cove River Wharf, and is to raise funds for destitute writers and artists.

On the surface this episode is a great piece of comic writing, as the bewildered P.S. is led through the exhibitionism and verbal rococo of these tatty bohemians and he hears strange words like "poofter", and "bosh and balls". At the same time his sainted mother's true character is being artlessly revealed by tiddly Pony. One of her old lovers is there, Charlie Seay; Lila is horrified to hear that Sinden shared a cottage, which she called "Wild Oats by the Sea", with Charlie while she was engaged to Ernest. Charlie even asked her to marry him, but she said to Pony, "Pony, he's got beautiful hands and beautiful manners but for sheer unadulterated fun I'd sooner be married to the Archbishop of Canterbury."

And then she met Logan. Pony recalls:

"Five days later I get a telegram: 'Married Logan Marriott. Meet us Carlton drinks at once.' . . .
"Oh, Pony—Ernest could have stopped her."
"Ernest couldn't stop a taxi."
"They had so much in common."
"Books."
"Books were her life, Pony."
"She was her own life and she didn't want it edited by Ernest. All he ever *did* was edit her."

But the implications of the Writers' Picnic go deeper still. Vanessa had forbidden P.S. to go to it. Lila, of course, was indignant at such interference and was all the more determined to take him. But she swears him to secrecy.

Vanessa, with her cold skills, quickly breaks down P.S.'s defences and makes him confess. But as he does so, and recounts the awfulness of the picnic, it becomes clear that Vanessa plotted the whole thing, in order to discredit Lila and her friends with P.S. and bring him closer to her. He

MOSMAN BRIDGE *Margaret Preston*

SUMNER LOCKE ELLIOTT
1917-

Sumner Locke Elliott was born in Sydney on 17 October 1917. His mother, Sumner Locke, who died when he was born, was a popular novelist, a sort of female Steele Rudd, who sold many thousands of copies of *Mum Dawson, Boss* and other books. A memorial book published after her death contained appreciation of her and her work by writers such as Vance Palmer, Mary Grant Bruce, Steele Rudd and Randolph Bedford.

Elliott's father was an alcoholic whom he never met. Their only communication was a telegram on Sumner's twenty-first birthday and a letter in reply. The father, Henry Logan Elliott, came from Bacchus Marsh in Victoria.

Sumner was left with two guardians, his mother's elder sister Lily who was married, and a younger unmarried sister Jessie who lived in England. There was a court case over his custody, and he was sent to Cranbrook as a boarder, which he hated, spending alternate holidays with the two aunts. He had to adjust between a large house with servants in Vaucluse and a tiny suburban cottage in Banksia, on the Illawarra line near Arncliffe. Later Sumner met another aunt who lived in Boston, USA (the basis of Agnes in *Careful, He Might Hear You*).

Elliott wanted to be a writer, but not to be a novelist like his mother, so he became a playwright. He based *Rusty Bugles* (1948)

on his experiences in the Army in World War II in the Northern Territory. As Elliott says, the play had the good luck to be banned by the NSW Chief Secretary for "objectionable language", and was a great success when staged by Doris Fitton at the Independent Theatre. It is an important play, as apart from its excellent craftsmanship, it gave Australians the opportunity to hear their own idiom (seven years before *The Summer of the Seventeenth Doll*), and in the bored soldiers' nostalgia for the city and the suburbs it ironically gave an urban emphasis to a play set in the far outback.

In 1948 Elliott went to New York and, apart from brief visits to Australia, has lived there ever since, supporting himself by writing more than 50 television plays.

He had tried unsuccessfully to make the extraordinary events of his upbringing into a play, and abandoned it. Years later he thought he might try to make it into a novel, "and I discovered that, to my great joy, I loved writing prose and that this was really the medium that I should be in, and which I had never been in because my mother was a novelist".

Careful, He Might Hear You was a great success when published in the USA and England in 1963. It was translated into seven languages, and in Australia won the Miles Franklin Award. As Elliott says himself, it is "almost entirely autobiographical", except that he shifted the action from the 1920s to the early 1930s.

Since 1963 Elliott has written a number of successful novels, some set in Australia such as *Edens Lost* (1969) and *Water Under the Bridge* (1977), others in the USA. *Water Under the Bridge* was made into a television series, and *Careful, He Might Hear You* into an award-winning film. Elliott received the Patrick White Award in 1978.

---

bursts into tears and clings to her as he confesses how awful it was.

The undercurrent to the luxury of Point Piper is the Depression. George gets the sack. This is another secret. Lila is terrified that the fact that they are on the "dole" will be used by Vanessa to take P.S. away for good. Once again Vanessa neatly worms the secret out of P.S.

And now Vanessa brings Logan back, a rather run-down, seedy Logan, but with some of the old charm left. As she sees him again she remembers how she loved him, for she met him before Sinden did, and how, at the last abandoned moment, she would not let him make love to her, and how he had called her a fraud. Vanessa knows it herself, that she wept not for Logan, "but for the irretrievable loss of herself".

Logan confesses to Vanessa that the real reason he gave her guardianship of P.S. was that she had access to money. And also, protests Vanessa, because, "I was closest to her." "Balls . . . Cut that out, Vanessa. You didn't even know her . . . None of your family knew her. Vere, a little. Not much, but a little. I knew her absolutely."

The meeting between P.S. and Logan begins very awkwardly. However they both relax and soon P.S. asks Logan all sorts of questions. After a final ferocious row with Vanessa, Logan disappears. Vanessa comes up to P.S.'s room. "He is an awful man. Awful. A beastly man, P.S." Vanessa raves on about the life ahead when she takes P.S. to England. P.S. cries that he won't go. She slaps him. He locks himself in the bathroom and throws all Vanessa's Parisian perfumes and soaps and lotions out the window.

When he returns to Lila's he says he will never go back to Vanessa's. A brilliantly described court case over custody follows. Vanessa wins, her lawyer discrediting Lila and

George and reducing Lila to asthmatic wheezes.

But the P.S. that Vanessa has won, surrounded by expensive presents, is a deadly calm, model child. In a terrible climax, as Vanessa is crouching in mortal fear in the midst of a thunderstorm, she hears P.S. devastatingly mimicking her and her fears to a group of children who have come to a party for him.

It is the end. She gives him up. To her credit, not without dignity, and she gives him excellent parting advice, "And don't just be a P.S. to your mother. Find you. If you can find out who you are and what you are, my dear, then you'll know how to love someone else." Going in a ferry to tell Lila she is giving him up, there is a collision between the ferry and a big ship and Vanessa is drowned.

The book ends in the big, sad house at Point Piper, with Lila and Vere sorting out Vanessa's belongings. With Logan's false gold in his pocket, P.S. walks around, from the kitchen to the garden to Vanessa's room, asking everyone "Who am I?" They think he is joking, and invent new identities – Don Bradman, Kingsford Smith. They eventually tell him that his name is William Scott Marriott but that he'll still be P.S. to them. "No," he cries, "I'm Bill." And he shouts it around the house, and climbs the front fence and shouts it again and again, "I'm Bill." He is himself, and has escaped from being suffocated by possessiveness in the name of love.

The establishment of P.S.'s identity, even to giving himself a name, comes as a climax to the revelations of all those other confused or disguised identities, the four aunts and Logan.

It is astonishing that *Careful, He Might Hear You* is a first novel, it is so technically and stylistically assured. As a novel of character it has few equals.

Alan Moorehead

COOPER'S CREEK

LONDON 1963

Brahe was now beginning to have doubts about Burke. Was it just possible that Burke had come back to the depot on the Cooper? Should he not go back to make sure? Should he not satisfy himself that the blacks had not disturbed the cache? They were still only eighty miles from the creek. Brahe put it to Wright that the two of them should make a visit to the depot while the sick were recuperating at Koorliatto, and Wright, surprisingly, agreed. Probably he wanted to be able to say when he got back that he had actually reached the depot. Taking three horses with them the two men set off on May 3, and after three days' hard riding arrived at the nearest part of the creek. Early in the morning of May 8 — fifteen days after Burke had left it — they rode into the depot.

The place was silent and deserted. They tethered their horses to the trees and went inside the stockade. The cache appeared to be undisturbed, the camel-dung raked over the ground as it had been before. They saw camel tracks about the camp, but Brahe presumed that these had been made by his own animals before he left the depot. It was true that there were the ashes of three fresh campfires on the ground, but the blacks were always making such fires, and no doubt, Brahe decided, some of them had camped here since his departure; indeed, it would have been strange had they not visited the place. Brahe did not notice that the rake had been moved, nor the glass of the broken bottle on the top of the stockade, nor the bits of rag that King had hung there, nor the square that had been cut out of the leather door. He did not see the billy that King had left behind, or at any rate placed no significance upon it. The blazes were there on the trees with nothing added. In other words, Brahe saw what, no doubt, he wanted to see: that nothing had been disturbed, that he had been right to come away from the depot when he did.

They decided not to dig up the cache because the freshly upturned earth might attract the attention of the natives, and they did not think of adding another note to the bottle — what was there to say? Nor did there seem to be any point in adding a fresh blaze to the tree indicating that they had made a return visit to the depot. After fifteen minutes they decided that they had seen enough. They got on their horses and rode away.

It is tempting at this point to pause and consider what they would have done if they had dug up the cache and discovered Burke's letter there, and the rations gone. There is only one answer to this: they would have got on to Burke's tracks and followed them down the creek. Their horses were capable of at least twenty miles a day, while Burke and the others were on foot and very weak, and so there is no reason why they should not have overtaken them. Brahe and Wright did not have much food with them, but Burke's party still had most of the supplies they had got from the cache; and in any case they could have sent back to Koorliatto for more.

As things were, however, Brahe's conscience was clear: Burke's party had now been gone nearly five months, and he went off with Wright feeling that, for the moment, he could do no more.

Alan Moorehead's initial love was journalism, and in his early career he became one of the greatest of war correspondents. In *Cooper's Creek* he approaches the Burke and Wills story with the same lack of bias, grasp of events, and eye for character and detail that are characteristic of the best investigative journalism.

Yet all this technique and ability is only a beginning for Moorehead. In *Cooper's Creek*, as in *The White Nile* and *The Blue Nile*, he wrote works that are amongst the finest examples of their genre, encompassing history, biography, and an imaginative and sympathetic evocation of the natural environment. In the case of Burke and Wills, the environment is more than a background; it is both a destructive element and a potential saving force. The tragedy of Burke and Wills' deaths, and those of other members of the appallingly bungled expedition, was that they died where the Aborigines were able to live. Burke and Wills, in particular, grew weaker and weaker on the banks of a river abounding in fish and visited by birds of many kinds. Others died of scurvy — and this in the 1860s, long after Cook and other navigators had discovered how to control it.

The Aborigines along the Cooper were on the whole friendly. But Burke in particular was incapable of communicating with them. His level of thinking is implicit in his instructions to Brahe concerning them. Brahe told the Royal Commission: "He told me if they annoyed me at all to shoot them at once."

All the prejudice and ignorance of the British in the nineteenth century is expressed in one pathetic anecdote told by the survivor, King, about an incident which occurred a few weeks before the deaths of Burke and Wills. The Aborigines, he said,

came with some cooked fish and called out "White fellow". Mr. Burke went out with his revolver, and found a whole tribe coming down, all painted and with fish in small nets

271

carried by two men. Mr. Burke went to meet them, and they wished to surround him, but he knocked as many of the nets of fish out of their hands as he could, and shouted out to me to fire. I did so, and they ran off. We collected five small nets of cooked fish. The reason he would not accept the fish from them was that he was afraid of being too friendly lest they should always be in our camp.

Moorehead has also vividly chronicled the other utter failure of communication amongst Burke and most of his men—their inability to live with the land or understand the environment.

When, in 1860, the Exploration Committee of the Philosophical Institute of Victoria, with the help of the Government, raised finance for, and appointed members of, a huge expedition to cross the unknown heart of the continent, they simply failed to pay due attention to the country which was to be explored. With one exception, and this was the great botanist, Ferdinand von Mueller, the Committee consisted of typical members of what would now be called the Melbourne Establishment. Mueller had done some exploraton as part of his work and should have understood that this new expedition must have at its head someone familiar with outback Australia. Perhaps Mueller was outvoted, but his strange acquiescence in the choice of Burke as leader is symptomatic of the weird malaise which seems to have afflicted the expedition from the start.

Moorehead gives lively character sketches of some of the members of the expedition. Burke, a charming, impulsive, courageous Irishman, who had managed to get bushed on a well-beaten track between Yackandandah and Beechworth. Wills, a serious, intellectual 26-year-old astronomer. The two Germans, Dr Beckler, botanist and medical officer, and the similarly named and altogether delightful naturalist, Ludwig Becker. (Amongst other accomplishments, Becker had a rare talent for painting and drawing, but at 52, and not in the best of health, he was not really a good choice for the expedition.) William Brahe, of German extraction, an educated man with experience of sheep stations and the goldfields. George James Landells, a vain, greedy and unstable man who had brought the expedition's camels from India, and who was appointed Deputy Leader (Landells was paid £600 and Burke only £500). An American gold-digger, Charles D. Ferguson, who was appointed foreman.

Also there were 27 camels, a number of horses, two huge, specially built wagons and three hired drays, and in all 21 tons of equipment. In the end, the expedition was to cost an incredible £60,000.

Moorehead masterfully outlines the early quarrels and disasters. By Menindie, several men had been fired; Landells, Ferguson and Beckler, after disputes with Burke, had resigned. A lot of equipment had been dumped or auctioned, including eight demi-johns of lime juice especially brought to combat scurvy.

Wills was then appointed deputy and Brahe foreman. At Menindie Burke took on William Wright, formerly manager of a nearby station. Illiterate, but said to be an experienced bushman, he was engaged as guide for the next stage to Cooper's Creek. The advance party for this consisted of Burke, Wills, Brahe, King, Gray, McDonough, Patton and a sepoy, Dost Mahomet.

One of the achievements of *Cooper's Creek* is Moorehead's ability to accurately describe the country, the birds and animals along the expedition's route. Too long to quote here, these descriptive passages are vital to the book, conveying the untouched presence of the Australian landscape and contrasting with it the bumbling progress of the expedition. One of Moorehead's great qualities as a writer is his ability to convey exotic detail without ever losing grip of his clear, uncluttered narrative style. As he himself once wrote, "Rewrite everything until the words are absolutely clear and simple with as few adjectives as possible."

Responding to pressure from Melbourne, Burke changed the objectives of the expedition in order to race the South Australian transcontinental party led by John McDouall Stuart. After treating them like labourers, Burke left the scientists behind at Menindie. He kept no journal or field-book himself, although Wills did. He had no respect for either the country or the Aborigines; fortunately, on the whole, the blacks he did meet were friendly.

From a place Burke called Torowoto Swamp, near the Queensland border, he sent Wright back to Menindie, appointing him third officer of the expedition, subject to the Committee's approval. Wright was to bring the rest of the party to Cooper's Creek to join the advance group. Burke went to Cooper's Creek and established Depot LXV, beside a magnificent stretch of water, on 11 November.

Moorehead points out that the Committee's instructions to Burke were astoundingly vague. He was to go almost anywhere he liked from Cooper's Creek.

While his party made various reconnaissances, Burke stayed at the Depot for over a month, waiting for Wright to arrive. Expecting him in a few days, Burke again split the expedition and decided to make a fast, light run to the Gulf, taking Wills, Gray, King, six camels and his white horse Billy. He told Brahe, and wrote to the Committee, that he expected to be back within three months at latest. When they rode off on 16 December Burke called out to Patton, who was in tears, "You must not fret; I shall be back in a short time. If I am not back in a few months you may go away to the Darling." This is an unbelievably vague instruction from the leader of an expedition.

As Moorehead says, "it was an expedition no longer: it was an endurance test, a race." Travelling into the Wet after they had passed the Tropic of Capricorn, the party finally reached a tidal creek flowing into the Gulf, but never saw the sea. For the 1100 kilometres or more of their return journey they had only one third of their provisions left. They had discovered, however, that they could eat the native portulaca ("portulac"). Also they could shoot birds and catch fish (though they did not have much success at this) to supplement their rations.

On 25 March, after 40 days, they were halfway back. Gray was sick, and Burke had thrashed him for stealing stores. Eleven days later they ate the horse Billy, having already eaten four of the camels. On 17 April Gray died. When they buried him they abandoned the rest of their equipment, keeping only the firearms and Wills's fieldbooks. It was now bitterly cold at night. Burke, Wills and King were very weak.

What happened next is indeed one of the strangest

CROSSING THE TERRICK-TERRICK PLAINS August 29, 1860 *Ludwig Becker*

ALAN MOOREHEAD
1910-1983

Early in the 1960s Alan Moorehead hired the services of a guide, Jeff Findley, and his Land-Rover, and set off to follow the tracks of Burke and Wills in their journey across Australia, from Melbourne in the south almost to the edge of the Gulf of Carpentaria. (It was typical of all the anticlimaxes of that expedition that Burke and Wills never saw the waters of the Gulf.) As well as giving Moorehead invaluable background material for *Cooper's Creek*, the journey was, for him, a profoundly important re-introduction to Australia.

By 1960 Moorehead was one of the most successful writers in the world. He had lived outside Australia since 1936, apart from a visit of six months in 1945 to write a biography of Field-Marshal Montgomery, and another visit in 1952. After this latter visit he said, "I don't think I shall ever live in Australia again, but I am certainly going to return on a trip, and perhaps a book will come of it." *Cooper's Creek* was the book.

Alan Moorehead was born on 22 July 1910, in Melbourne, the son of a journalist, Richard Moorehead. He was educated at Scotch College and the University of Melbourne where he took a BA. He then continued to study for a law degree, but in his final second-year examination walked out and applied for a job as a full-time reporter at the *Herald*. Fortunately, he got the job.

Of his youth in Melbourne, Moorehead says, "somehow it was wrong, it ought to have been different". The same school and city that provided his contemporary Graham McInnes with some 500 pages of autobiography kept Moorehead going for just 19 pages in *A Late Education*.

"At last in May 1936 I got away. I was almost twenty-six." When, some weeks later, he landed on European soil for the first time, at Toulon, he wrote, "This was the crisis for me. As I stood there on the sidewalk I knew that I would never go home again—not at any rate for many years . . . This was it. This was what I had come for."

Yet Moorehead continued to think of himself as an Australian, and was never one of those Australian expatriates who take every opportunity to denigrate their homeland.

Moorehead soon got a job as the Gibraltar correspondent on the *Daily Express*. It was at the time of the Spanish Civil War, and Moorehead had a number of adventures, including sailing to Spain on a blockade-running tanker which was carrying 8000 tonnes of petrol. During World War II he became chief correspondent for the *Daily Express* in the Middle East. His war despatches, from the Western Desert and, later, from Europe, especially those from D-Day to the surrender on Luneberg Heath, made him world famous.

After the war he took the risk of giving up regular journalism and became a writer of books. A trilogy about the war in Africa was followed by *Montgomery*, and *Gallipoli*, which won the 1956 *Sunday Times* Book Prize and the Duff Cooper Memorial Award. *The Blue Nile* and *The White Nile* were two of his most successful books, displaying, like *Cooper's Creek*, the author's particular ability to convey character through a narrative which creates an intense awareness of the environment of the story.

In 1959 Moorehead built himself a house near Porto Ercole in Italy, where he lived with his wife Lucy and, during holidays, his two sons and daughter. In the early 1970s he suffered a stroke which, although it did not totally incapacitate him, prevented him from reading or writing again. He died in 1983.

---

episodes in world exploration. The party arrived at the Depot on 21 April, to find that Brahe had left a mere nine or ten hours earlier. He left a message in a bottle under a fresh blaze on a coolibah: "DIG 3 FT. N.W. APR.21 1861'.

Brahe had left a cache of rations, enough for a month. These should have been sufficient to get them the 240 kilometres to the police station at Mount Hopeless in South Australia. But Brahe had taken with him the supply of spare clothes that they so desperately needed now it had turned cold.

A letter of Burke's explaining their plans was buried, in another bottle, but in the same hole under the DIG tree. No fresh blaze was cut on the tree. On 23 April they set off for Mount Hopeless.

Moorehead devotes more than half of *Cooper's Creek* to the cataclysmic follies and miscalculations that preceded and followed that fateful 21 April. Wright had only recently left Menindie, for reasons that were never to become clear. Becker and two other men had died of scurvy and dysentery. Brahe and Wright now returned to the Depot, but did not dig as they thought the cache had not been disturbed. They too failed to add a fresh blaze to the tree. On the return journey to Menindie Patton died.

Meanwhile Burke's party stumbled down the Cooper, lost both camels, could not face the desert and turned back towards the Depot. Wills went on alone to the Depot, found the cache as they had left it, buried another message and did not cut a fresh blaze. Succoured by the blacks, they decided to sit it out until they were rescued.

There was frightful consternation when news of the disasters reached Melbourne. Alfred William Howitt was sent out with a search party from Melbourne, while McKinley took another from Adelaide, and two parties, under Landsborough and Walker, were sent out from Brisbane.

That Burke and Wills died and King lived must be put down to the fact that King allowed himself to be completely adopted by the Aborigines. Moorehead sees a strange torpor, partly induced by the spirit of the place, and partly by their own foolish exclusiveness, descending and destroying Burke and Wills.

The best practical result to come from the Burke and Wills expedition is probably that, due to the explorations of the four search parties, the centre of Australia was opened up. Howitt's expedition was a model of how such things should be done.

A bewildered and weakened King received a hero's welcome in Melbourne. The remains of Burke and Wills (brought back by a second expedition under Howitt) were taken to the cemetery, through enormous crowds, in a hearse modelled on that used for the funeral of the Duke of Wellington. A Royal Commission castigated Wright and the Committee, and criticised Brahe and Burke.

The tragedy of their useless deaths transformed these ineffectual people into heroes. Without it, as Moorehead says, "they would have remained rather minor figures, but with it they were lifted to another and higher plane, one might even say a state of grace".

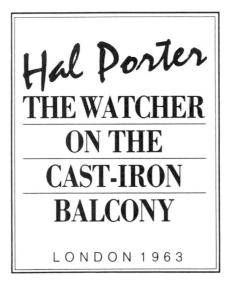

Hal Porter

THE WATCHER ON THE CAST-IRON BALCONY

LONDON 1963

I am, however, gradually aroused into a sort of useless, lopsided and off-again, on-again pity for child-ridden Mother who seems as happy-go-lucky, busy and noisy as ever. I observe for the first time that the gold of her wedding-ring is worn smooth, that the backs of her hands, the texture of her elbows and the skin at the sides of her neck have all changed. Mother is older. Older than what, I am not sure, for she cannot be older than herself (in 1925 she is thirty-six) and yet that is my impression: older than herself. I sense that she has become an engagement of forces within herself, that the "natural" side of her being, with its demands of being maternally omnipresent, has to stand with conscious nobility, as though defiantly excusing its workaday splendour against the sardonic side, the sharp-shooting and self-ridiculing side. It is her outward expression of this inner war, the behaviour and utterances of a younger and gayer person, that make her seem older.

Several things rapidly happen—or seem, at this distance, to happen rapidly.

The baby is no sooner weaned than Mother has her hair bobbed. In early 1926, in that country town, fashions drift slowly into the stream of provincial life, a year or so late and, having drifted in, take at least another year to rise up from the younger and more reckless to the older, more wary women. Not so with Mother. She goes to the barber's, for there are no beauty parlours in Bairnsdale then, in the same month as the young women, the flappers and hussies with their knee-high skirts and jazz garters. This is almost shocking, and is certainly defiant of Mother. The operation does not make her look younger, merely impertinent. Once, an eternity ago it seems, most of her aids to beautification disappeared from the elaborate dressing-table, freeing her once-suburban hands to take up the duties and tools of a country mother. Now, without relinquishing any of these tools, seemingly as many-handed as a Hindu goddess, she takes up once more the pots of Pond's Cold Cream and Vanishing Cream, the dry rouge, the tinted face powders: Peach, Rachel, Flesh. Why? And how does she find the time to lacquer her face with egg-white?

Certainly, she is helped about the house by us older children: there is the washerwoman; there is the old Scotchwoman who milks Dolly the Jersey; but a flock of servants would, I think, have made little difference to the total of work Mother does. A job taken over by someone else only means that she is somewhere else magicking other work, extra exercises in perfection, out of nowhere. This striving, this positive need for everything to be speckless and decorously tied-off is something I have inherited or imitated from Mother. I can jibe at every scrupulous effort I thus make in Mother's manner, every sally at a faultlessness invisible to most others; I can even compel myself to commit momentary slipshoddinesses. It avails nothing. I must turn back and retie the bow, find le mot juste, write the bread-and-butter letter, empty the ash-tray, be absolutely abstemious and sleep eight clear-eyed hours, or drink all night until garnet-eyed drunkenness is perfected.

The first volume of Hal Porter's autobiography, *The Watcher on the Cast-Iron Balcony* begins and ends with his mother's death, and takes his own life from his earliest memories to his presence by her death bed as an 18-year-old man emerging from adolescence.

For all its wonderfully evoked detail (Porter has total recall, perhaps a compensation for the imagination he says he does not possess), *The Watcher* is really a book about innocence. His mother is the innocent one, happy and singing through six children, dying when she is 40 of cancer, a lover of bric-a-brac although compulsively tidy, full of games learned in her country town girlhood. The portrait of her is of a whole and consistent person, with an innocence that gives a perennial freshness to her presence. By comparison with her, Hal's father is a dull fellow who knows it. "Ask your mother," he says in answer to any question that might turn out to be interesting.

The boy Hal is a watcher, both of himself and other people, not to mention the boundless complexities of nature and man's creations. Porter turns the usual ideas of innocence upside down. For him the child, up to 10 or so, is not at all innocent, except of experience. First experiences, he says, "do nothing to innocence, for I have never possessed innocence. They give edges to intelligence, they refresh watching eyes." His first experiences, with his friend Victor, such as comparing their penises, are "essentially a confrontation of primitive and unashamed wariness; it could have been the meeting of sophisticated centenarians with nothing to lose and every hope of gaining". Elsewhere he says,"I am hardly old enough to be unsophisticated: I am still six. I am still sophisticated at seven or eight or nine or ten." At 10 he is being "nudged towards self-consciousness", which is the end of childhood sophistication, the end of "my early poise, . . . the last year of unflawed non-innocence". He is now beginning "that long, tempting and often shocking journey through the experiences of others".

For such a sensitive and aware person, Porter has an extraordinarily happy childhood. He adores his mother and is not in conflict with his father. He enjoys both primary and secondary school and the opportunity to learn, the excitement of getting facts.

When Hal is six the family moves to Bairnsdale in Gippsland, a town and a district of which he was always to remain fond. The city child becomes a country town boy, discovering how sustaining is the rich variety of nature. Bairnsdale is without sewerage, and some of the best descriptions in the book are of the visits of "the night-man", the bucket on his head, his arms and face "enmeshed in a knitting of flies".

Although his upbringing is middle class, there is nothing stultifyingly bourgeois about it, mostly thanks to his uninhibited mother. Of his father, he speculates, "Brought up middle class he *chooses* to become lower middle class", accepting with that class's rough and ready self-respect "its central fear: a fear of the intellect". Hal's father is "an unfurnished man", and Hal is aware of the dangers of his heritage, "a lack of imagination", "bland selfishness". He admits of himself that "having no imagination, I do not understand people . . . What they will *do* is too easily foreseeable; for me it is nearly always impossible to know *why*." He charts the simultaneous growth of knowledge and cunning with the loss of instinctive awareness and sophistication.

I can even compel myself to commit momentary slipshoddinesses. It avails nothing. I must turn back and retie the bow, find le mot juste, *write the bread-and-butter letter, empty the ash-tray, be absolutely abstemious and sleep eight clear-eyed hours, or drink all night until garnet-eyed drunkenness is perfected.*

The portrait of his mother is so good because when he is young he understands her instinctively. She is as real as a tree whose leaves the wind sets shaking. Only after the birth of her sixth child at 37, when she goes and has her hair bobbed, and washes, powders, scents and decorates herself, Hal smells "defiance; there is a faint odour of despair". Perhaps it is money worries; perhaps, without being technically unfaithful, his father is "performing mental adulteries". Hal at "selfish fifteen, mad about myself", in his last year of High School, will never know what was motivating her.

Original illustration by Hal Porter (*Bairnsdale—Portrait of an Australian Country Town*) (*above*)

Hal at 13 played at sex with another boy, Alex. Now at 15 he is in love with Olwen Connor, the female school captain, daughter of a neighbouring grazier, who drives her own jinker every day into school. She does not take much notice of Hal, but she gives him a curl when she has her hair cut off, which he keeps in an envelope for 25 years until he meets her again, "a pretty, little, grey-haired" grandmother. He burns the worn envelope and the curl and wonders at his foolishness "to have persisted for a quarter of a century in being a sort of sentimental boy when I am really a sort of unsentimental man".

When he leaves school he works for a while, in a stupor of trivia, as a cadet reporter with the *Bairnsdale Advertiser*. He gets bored with Bairnsdale, and yearns for the city. Finally his headmaster gets him a job at Williamstown as a schoolteacher—a "Junior Teacher". It is astonishing now to think that a 16-year-old boy with no training should have been teaching children not much younger than himself, but Hal was obviously a success, then and later, as a schoolteacher. He says he would not like to live those 18 months at Williamstown over again, but he would, however, "like to have restored to me the vitality and enthusiasm, the recklessness and piratical impertinence, the perfect unawareness of pitfalls" which he had then.

With consummate delicacy and humour Porter recalls the young Hal's entry into the world's sophistication, sipping port wine like a chicken, aged just over 17, "stealing the lives of others", knowing that "Having frisked myself first, nothing is left for others."

He is accepted as a student of drawing at the Melbourne National Gallery Art School, under Charles Wheeler, and to his surprise wins the prize for the ticket design for the Artists' Ball. However, Hal is too shrewd to have any illusions; he knows that "the famous artist, Porter, is dead".

He has more enduring luck with the theatre, having, to begin with, the great good fortune to be befriended by the actor-manager Gregan McMahon. George Bernard Shaw once remarked that all he knew about Australia was that it produced sheep and Gregan McMahon. Not only did McMahon talk to young Hal and give him parts in his plays; he lent him books, introduced him to famous actresses and actors, and gave him free seats for his productions which most enterprisingly in 1928-29 included plays by Pirandello, Shaw, Ibsen, O'Casey and Chekhov. Porter speculates that Melbourne at that time was offering "the avid young" very much more than Melbourne does today.

Porter is also honest about his own inadequacies. He cannot appreciate music or opera; Bach, Beethoven and Mozart leave him cold.

So does sex, despite some hot flushes. He has an affair with a temporary teacher at the school, Lucy Hart. She is two-and-a-half times his age, and her nudity is a matter of "painful flushed bulges and floppings". She makes use of his young body. Later he walks along the beach under the moon, asking himself, "Was she a woman? I'm no longer a virgin. I'm a man. Am I a man?"

He continues to visit her. A fortnight later, like a gigolo, he borrows £15 from her which he has no intention of returning, and buys himself shoes and clothes, including a black suit. "Black, as Mother has said, breeds black."

There is an avalanche moving that will push Hal "to the

THE VERANDAH *Liz Seymour*

HAL PORTER
1911-1984

In an interview with Graeme Kinross Smith, Hal Porter said: "Posterity will probably see me, I'd say, as a passable novelist, a fair playwright, man, but a pretty *good* short story writer."

It is a fair assessment, except that many critics would consider his autobiography, and especially the first volume, *The Watcher on the Cast-Iron Balcony* (1963), as his finest work. His prose style at its sparkling best and an extraordinary capacity to remember every detail of his life combine to illuminate not only Porter's life but that of an era. Seldom has there been such a perfect fusion of the subjective and the objective.

Hal Porter was born on 16 February 1911 at Albert Park in Melbourne. He was educated at Kensington where the family lived for three years, when he was aged from three to six, and at Bairnsdale, where the family then moved. Porter's life up to the death of his mother, when he was 18, is covered in *The Watcher*; his life up to the 1970s is the subject of *The Paper Chase* (1966) and *The Extra* (1975).

After leaving school at 15 he went to work as a cadet reporter on the *Bairnsdale Advertiser*, a boring job which made him long for the city. His old headmaster found him a post teaching at North Williamstown State School No. 1409. Porter liked teaching and was surprised to find he was a good teacher. "Children," he says, "always know whether or not they are being properly taught. You can't fool them."

While teaching he also attended art classes at the Melbourne National Gallery Art School, and acted with, and generally came under the influence of a remarkable actor-manager, Gregan McMahon.

Some poems and stories had begun to appear in print by 1937 when he resigned from his teaching job and took a flat in Collins Street, writing at night and working by day in a shop furniture factory.

He married in 1939; the marriage was dissolved in 1943. On the day of the outbreak of World War II, 3 September 1939, his hip was smashed when he was run over by a car. He did not walk again for nine months, and his injury prevented him from taking part in the War.

He went back to school teaching, and was English master at Queens School and Prince Alfred College in Adelaide until 1946. He then went to Hutchins School in Hobart; to Knox Grammar in Sydney (where, somewhat out of character, he also taught the Sixth Form Divinity); and to Ballarat College.

In 1949 he went to Japan to teach English to the children of the Occupation Forces; he returned to Japan in 1967. The novel, *A Handful of Pennies* (1958), and the travel book, *The Actors* (illustrated by himself) (1968), were the results of his experiences in Japan.

In 1954 he returned to Bairnsdale to establish a modern municipal library, and in 1958 went to Shepparton as City Librarian, resigning to go to Europe in 1960 to research a novel about the artist-convict Thomas Wainewright in Van Diemen's Land. Published in London in 1961 as *The Tilted Cross*, it was very well received by the critics. His short stories have been, and rightly, widely acclaimed.

After this Porter gave all his time to writing fiction, autobiography, biography, books of travel and history, and poetry. He also received a number of fellowships from the Commonwealth Literary Fund and the Literature Board, and his work won a number of prizes.

In 1983 Porter was badly injured when knocked down by a car at Ballarat. After remaining some time in a coma, he died in 1984.

---

very heart of blackness". It continues to move with the death of one of his boys, Wock, who with two other boys was playing with detonators that exploded. At Wock's funeral, "as though all the lights have been turned on in another dimension", he discovers that awful sophistication which says that tragedies are terribly amusing, "that sex is hilarious, and death too screamingly funny for words". Yet while others can laugh in this style, Porter can only weep, for "I have no sense of humour at all."

He continues to write highly ornamented poetry, and to parade a devastating sophistication at the Café Latin, but in 1928 at the end of the school year he returns to Gippsland, to Bairnsdale, to home, to Mother, and to sexual tussles with Bunty (one of "my four frivolous friends of High School Days") that are more exhilarating "than Miss Hart's struggles with me". He is in love with home.

However, no sooner is he settled in Bairnsdale than his mother tells him she is going to hospital; she has cancer. He has to return to Melbourne, until he is summoned back to Bairnsdale by a telegram saying that "Mother's 'condition' is 'grave'." At the beginning of the book he sees her "locked and denying face through a lens of tears". At the end of the book Hal is taken by the nurse into a room where a woman lies. "This fowl-like creature with the sharp nose and the diminished cheeks and the damp hair and the glittering eyes is Mother." She is dying. A bottle of champagne has been poured into a vessel with a spout, and Hal "feeds the unsteady mouth" with it, and she sings a favourite old music-hall song:

> *"Shahmpeen Chawlie is m'name,*
> *Shahmpeen-drinkin' is m'game."*

When it is over, "Mother is dead, God is dead, love is dead, all that I was is dead." He waits to begin to watch again.

The richness of the material in *The Watcher*, the accumulations of vivid detail which are too long to quote, demand a style that can convey it all. Porter's style is often misunderstood. It is true that at times it is certainly ornate, sometimes even overenthusiastic. But it is always skilfully modulated, sometimes by precise observation, "wild-eyed saints dirty as a potato", at other times by the plainest statements, "He falls in love with ties and silk socks." Porter's style is never a "difficult" style, because he is never trying to say anything "difficult".

The Watcher, for all its apparent complexities, is in fact a very simple and honest book about a child and his parents, and a young man and the world he gives a wary welcome. The metaphysics of joy or despair would call for understanding and imagination, qualities Porter modestly says he does not possess. But the world he presents is so real and rich that it can satisfy any reader with his own capacities for understanding or imagination.

Colin Thiele

STORM BOY

ADELAIDE 1963

When morning came over the world at last they could see the tugboat clearly, lying like a wounded whale, with huge waves leaping and crashing over it, throwing up white hands of spray in a devil-dance.

"They can never swim it or launch a boat," said Hide-Away. "Their only hope is a line to the shore."

"No one get line out," Fingerbone said. "Not today."

"No," said Hide-Away sadly. "And by tomorrow it will be too late." Sometimes in a lull between the waves they could see three or four men clinging to the tugboat, waving their hands for help.

"Look at them," Storm Boy yelled. "We must help them! They'll be drowned."

"How can we help?" said his father. "We can't throw a line, it's too far."

"How far is it?"

"Too far. Two or three hundred yards at least."

"No blackfellow throw spear so far," said Fingerbone. "Not even half so far."

"Especially not with a line attached. We'd need a harpoon gun."

"Then I couldn't throw a stone a quarter of the way," Storm Boy said. He picked up a pebble and hurled it towards the sea. It fell near the shore . . .

Suddenly there was a swish of big wings past them and Mr Percival sailed out over the spot where the pebble had fallen. He looked at the foam of the waves for a minute as if playing the old game of fetch-the-pebble; then he changed his mind, turned, and landed back on the beach.

Storm Boy gave a great shout and ran towards him. "Mr Percival! Mr Percival is the one to do it! He can fly!"

Hide-Away saw what he meant. He raced back to the humpy and found two or three long fishing lines, as thin as thread. He tied them together and coiled them very carefully and lightly on a hard patch of clean sand. Then he took a light sinker, tied it to one end, and gave it to Mr Percival.

"Out to the ship," he said, pointing and flapping. "Take it out to the ship."

Mr Percival looked puzzled and alarmed at the idea of fishing on such a wild day, but he beat his wings and rose up heavily over the sea.

"Out to the boat! Out to the boat!" they all shouted. But Mr Percival didn't understand. He flew too far to one side, dropped the line in the sea, and turned back.

"Missed," said Hide-Away, disappointed.

"But it was a good try," Storm Boy said, as Mr Percival landed. He gave him a piece of fish and scratched his neck. "Good boy," he said. "Good boy, Mr Percival. In a minute we'll have another try."

But they missed again. This time Mr Percival flew straight towards the boat but didn't go out quite far enough. "Never mind," said Storm Boy. "You're a good pelican for trying." He held Mr Percival like a big duck and gave him another piece of fish.

Again and again they tried, and again and again they missed. At first the men on the boat couldn't understand what was going on, but they soon guessed, and watched every try hopefully and breathlessly.

Storm Boy and Hide-Away were disappointed but they didn't give up. Neither did Mr Percival. He flew out and back, out and back, until at last, on the tenth try, he did it. A great gust of wind suddenly lifted him up and flung him sideways. He threw up his big wing and, just as he banked sharply over the tugboat, dropped the line. It fell right across the drowning ship.

"You've done it! You've done it!" Storm Boy, Hide-Away, and Fingerbone shouted together as Mr Percival landed on the beach. "You're a good, brave, clever pelican." And they patted him, and fed him, and danced round him so much that poor Mr Percival! couldn't quite understand what he'd done that was so wonderful. He kept snickering and snackering excitedly, opening his beak in a kind of grin, and eating more fish than he'd ever had before.

This is a children's story that has been very successfully made into a film; and indeed, the visual element of *Storm Boy* is very strong. The setting is, "The long, long snout of sand hill and scrub that curves away south-eastwards from the Murray Mouth. A wild strip it is, windswept and tussocky, with the flat shallow water of the South Australian Coorong on one side and the endless slam of the Southern Ocean on the other. They call it the Ninety Mile Beach."

The odd shape of the Coorong lagoon gives it a unique ecology particularly attractive to fish and birds. There is something primeval about the close proximity of calm water and wild surf, with only the thin line of sandhills holding them apart.

Although a main road runs beside it, there are very few dwellings along its 145 kilometres, so the humpy where Storm Boy and his father live has a simplicity and remoteness akin to its environment. Storm Boy has been brought there by his father after the death of his mother, and he is as wild and free as the sandhills and the sea. After years, he is as familiar with it all as the thousands of birds which also live there. His father Tom is known as Hide-Away, and is regarded as a hermit and a beachcomber. He lives as a fisherman, occasionally taking his little boat across the inlet of the Murray Mouth to the town of Goolwa.

Their only neighbour is an Aborigine, Fingerbone Bill, who lives in another humpy of wood and iron and brush about two kilometres away. He is a friend of Storm Boy's, and teaches him all about the fish and birds, the signs of the weather and the sea. "And he could read all the strange writing on the sandhills and beaches—the scribbly stories made by beetles and mice and bandicoots and ant-eaters and crabs and birds' toes and mysterious sliding bellies in the night."

When morning came over the world at last they could see the tugboat clearly, lying like a wounded whale, with huge waves leaping and crashing over it, throwing up white hands of spray in a devil-dance.

Storm Boy's education is not in books, but it is no less profound for not being conducted in a school. He is perfectly in tune with his environment, he knows all the shells, and his father and Fingerbone tell him about the huge heaps of cracked mussel and cockle shells, ancient Aboriginal middens, where for hundreds of years the tribes used to gather for feasts. The wild place has a long human history, but now it is all gone.

The present is cruel and disruptive. Hide-Away's humpy is just on the edge of the great Coorong sanctuary, and the duck shooters who descend on the peaceful water every year often sneak into the sanctuary chasing wounded birds. Even worse are the men with rifles, "who called themselves *sportsmen*", says Thiele with ironic disgust, who, for bets, shoot an egret or a moor-hen or a heron. And even worse,

From the film *Storm Boy*

if possible, are the vandals who attack the pelican nests, break the eggs and kill the nesting birds.

These great birds are Storm Boy's special friends. When he walks by they "sat in a row, like a lot of important old men with their heavy paunches sagging, and rattled their beaks drily in greeting".

In one of the broken nests Storm Boy finds three baby pelicans still alive. One of them is very weak and sick, and the boy wraps him in one of his father's scarves and brings him with the other two to the humpy. His father and Fingerbone think the sick one will die, but Storm Boy spends three days and nights nursing him back to health. He calls this baby pelican Mr Percival, and the other two Mr Proud and Mr Ponder.

> Before long the three pelicans were big and strong. Their white necks curved up cleanly, their creels grew, and their upper beaks shone like pink pearl-shell. Every morning they spread their great white wings with the bold black edges and flew three or four times round the humpy and the beach near by to make sure that everything was in order for the new day. By then they thought it was time for breakfast, so they landed heavily beside the humpy, took a few dignified steps forward, and lined up at the back door . . . If nothing happened Mr Proud and Mr Ponder began to get impatient after five or ten minutes and started rattling their beaks in disapproval—a snippery-snappery, snickery-snackery sort of sound like dry reeds crackling—until someone woke up.

The fineness of Colin Thiele's observation extends beyond the appearance of the birds to their character, and *Storm Boy* operates at its deepest level on the common bond between man and nature that can only be achieved in man by endless patience and humility. The wildness and timidity of creatures are not based on natural hostility, but on mistrust of man. Sometimes, if they can be taught when young to trust man, they will allow him to share their lives, as long as they preserve that vital area of wildness which is freedom. Mr Percival is one among the very rare ones who will share even that.

Hide-Away, after a while, very reasonably says to Storm Boy that he cannot afford to feed three huge birds. Storm Boy agrees to take them eight kilometres up the sanctuary and let them go, although it is agony for him to part with Mr Percival. After the birds have flown away, Hide-Away and Storm Boy spend a gloomy day fishing. When they return to the humpy in the evening there is a big shape sitting on the Look-Out Post on the sandhill. Mr Percival has come home.

From that day the boy and the bird are inseparable. They even play ball together. Mr Percival loves to retrieve the ball or a stone or an old fishing reel that Storm Boy has thrown out across the water, and he also loves, as reward, to have Storm Boy's fingers rub the back of his neck.

A terrible storm comes up, so bad that even Mr Percival has to come inside the humpy to avoid being blown away. At the height of the storm a tugboat is blown aground, far out in the surf. There is no hope for the crew unless a rope can be got ashore, but there is no apparent way a line can be run out the two or three hundred metres to where they are. Storm Boy throws a stone towards the tugboat in despair;

From S T O R M B O Y an original illustration by Robert Ingpen

COLIN THIELE
1920-

Colin Thiele, AC, author and educator, has published over 60 books in many fields – poetry, history, biography, drama, education, fiction and children's literature.

Thiele was born on 16 November 1920 at Eudunda, South Australia, and was brought up on a nearby farm close to the village of Julia. His family was part of the German community descended from those who had emigrated to South Australia in the early stages of its settlement. As a child, Thiele spoke German.

He went to Julia school from 1925-32. He has written of his education at the little Julia school, which had only one teacher:

A school of that kind was a family of twenty. The big children were like older brothers and sisters. Often they really were brothers and sisters. They heard the younger ones read, helped them with their sums, found their lost pencils, shared a sandwich with the fuddlehead who had forgotten his lunch, or led the kindergarten babies down to the dunny to see that they didn't fall through the hole into the pit below.

Thiele thinks that those little rural schools, "with their friendliness, family spirit and opportunities for individuals to grow and develop self-reliance, were a very useful way of educating children".

He then went to Eudunda Higher Primary School (1933-34) and Kapunda High School (1935-36). At 16 he attended the University of Adelaide, then went to the Teachers' College for two years before joining the RAAF. He married Rhonda Gill, an art teacher, in 1945 and they had two daughters.

Thiele has had a long and distinguished career as an educator, finishing as Principal of Wattle Park Teachers' College from 1965 to 1972. In 1973 he was appointed Director of Murray Park College of Advanced Education, but resigned this position in the same year to become the Director of Wattle Park Teachers' Centre, a position he held until his retirement in 1981. In 1977 he was made a Companion of the Order of Australia for his services to literature and education. After his retirement, he devoted himself to his writing.

His books have been translated into many languages and have been published in England and the USA. *Storm Boy, Blue Fin* and *The Fire in the Stone* have been made into films, and many others dramatised on radio.

Storm Boy, the film, was especially remarkable for the training of the pelican, Mr Percival, which not only played with the boy along the Coorong but actually performed many of the tasks described in the book and required in the film.

Thiele's books have received many Australian and international awards, including the Austrian State Prize in 1979.

Tolerance, balance and kindliness are present in all Thiele's work. Critically, he is a much underrated Australian writer, especially as a poet and author of children's literature. Amazingly enough, though many times commended by the Children's Book Council of Australia, only one of his books has ever won the Children's Book of the Year Award, *The Valley Between*, in 1982.

---

immediately Mr Percival rocks down through the gale to where it lies.

Storm Boy has the solution. Mr Percival can fly out to the sailors with a line. Hide-Away gets out a fine line, attaches a sinker to one end and gives it to Mr Percival, who flies out to the tugboat. But it seems he cannot drop the sinker on the boat in the teeth of the gale, no matter how many times he tries. Then, on the tenth try, he succeeds. The sailors get a thin rope ashore, followed by a heavy one, and the whole crew is rescued.

Suddenly there was a swish of big wings past them and Mr Percival sailed out over the spot where the pebble had fallen. He looked at the foam of the waves for a minute as if playing the old game of fetch-the-pebble; then he changed his mind, turned, and landed back on the beach.

Mr Percival is a hero. In thanks, the captain and the crew offer to pay to send Storm Boy to Adelaide to boarding-school. A 10- or 11-year-old boy ought to be at school, they say. But Storm Boy refuses to go unless Mr Percival goes with him. That is impossible, so Storm Boy stays on the Coorong.

The year goes by, and then the next duck season opens and the air is hideous with shots and the stench of gunpowder. Mr Percival has his own ideas about duck-shooters. He dislikes them and enjoys splashing around them or flying "round and round their hiding places in wide circles like a cumbersome old aeroplane on patrol". The ducks understand Mr Percival's warnings and keep away. The duck-shooters grow angrier and angrier, until one day, to Storm Boy's horror, one of them shoots Mr Percival.

This time, no amount of nursing can save him, and Mr Percival dies while Storm Boy whispers, "Mr Percival . . . you're the best, best friend I ever had." After they have buried Mr Percival at the top of the sandhill, Storm Boy turns calmly to his father and says, "All right . . . I'm ready to go now if you like." So he goes to boarding school in Adelaide.

Storm Boy is a touching and highly believable story in which the reader lives as much with Mr Percival as with Storm Boy. With great delicacy and tact, Colin Thiele conveys his message that to live in balance with nature, man must learn to live with and understand her creatures. He avoids the trap of being too bitter about destructive man. After Mr Percival's death, in answer to the question, "Why did they shoot Mr Percival?", Hide-Away says to the distraught boy, "In the world there will always be men who are cruel, just as there will always be men who are lazy or stupid or wise or kind. Today you've seen what cruel and stupid men can do."

Any reader of *Storm Boy*, young or old, will recognise what a wise and kind man can do, especially if he is also a highly skilled writer with the imagination of a poet.

Donald Horne

THE
LUCKY
COUNTRY

MELBOURNE 1964

In some parts of New Guinea there are people who believe that Heaven is to be found somewhere in the clouds just above Sydney and is connected with Sydney by a ladder. Here, while the Spirits of the Dead loll in their cane chairs and gorge themselves on the canned meat and whisky that is served to them by the angels, God spends his time creating consumer goods, which go down the ladder from Heaven to Sydney and then, as ship's cargo, on to lucky people in New Guinea.

Australians do not have this look-no-hands attitude. They manufacture most of their own consumer goods. But a look-no-brains attitude is endemic among some Australian attitudes to manufacturing. The processes of invention and innovation that are such an essential part of the Western Mind play less domestic part in Australia than in any other prosperous country, apart from Canada. No matter what miracles Australians achieved in the earlier settlement of the continent and however spectacularly successful they can be at improvising when they are pushed to it, Australian businessmen have not

proved to be very good at getting people to think up new things to make. Instructions about how to make new things usually come from the heavens that lie across the U.S.A., Britain, and Europe. Unlike Sweden and Switzerland, Australia has not developed any significant world specialities of its own in manufacture. Not only do Australians not think things up: in their behaviour they often show a remarkable distrust for another essential part of the Western Mind, a practising belief in the efficacy of competition.

Australia is a rich prize in international investment, full of loot. Recently discovered bauxite fields show the largest known resources in the world. Reserves of iron ore are estimated at as much as eight billion tons. Oil is being

discovered in commercial quantities; reserves of coal are huge; production of lead is the largest in the world; production of zinc is the third largest; wool production is a third of the world total. Most of the manufacturing in what can be accurately described in the cliché term as a "land rich in resources" is now under foreign control.

The only major manufacturing industry groups that are not dominated by overseas firms are steel, cement, glass, sugar, and paper. Probably a third of Australian manufacturing industry is owned outright by overseas firms—about two thirds are British and 27 per cent American—but many other companies are controlled with less than full ownership. Of the top hundred Australian firms at least two thirds are overseas controlled. When it is remembered how these firms then dominate their suppliers and clients it would be safe to say that most Australian manufacturing is ultimately dependent on overseas enterprise and decision.

A s soon as it appeared in 1964, *The Lucky Country* was a great success. There had been stimulating books before about the Australian people and their beliefs and habits, but never one so exactly right for the times, and by an author who was not only witty and extremely knowledgeable, but also unalienated from his own country. As Horne himself has pointed out, this last was not the case with most Australian intellectuals.

The Lucky Country is in effect two books in one. It is, and remains, the liveliest and most penetrating of all surveys of Australia in the 1960s. What was then contemporary observation is now social history. This, says Horne, is what it was like to live in urban, suburban and country town Australia in the twilight of the soporific Menzies era. However, although Horne makes some extremely relevant remarks about rural economics, he makes no attempt to give a broad view of life on the land in Australia, nor to describe the quality of its landscape and climate—what D. H. Lawrence called "the spirit of place". His treatment of the Aborigines, though well intentioned, is also perfunctory.

Nevertheless, what might be termed the second book in

The Lucky Country, the delineation of the Australian character, is what makes the book a classic, a work that in its way is as stimulating and re-readable as de Tocqueville's *Democracy in America*. Horne, like de Tocqueville, was in fact writing about human kind in general, taking his subject as a fresh and as yet unexamined case history of what other democratic peoples, given the opportunity, might come to be. In Horne's case, his most important theme is happiness. (He is well aware of the precarious state of this quality in most countries in the world.)

> Why write a book about such a happy country? One reason is that in some ways it is not so happy: one can learn something about happiness by examining Australia—its lingering puritanism, the frustrations and resentments of a triumphant mediocrity, and the sheer dullness of life for many of its ordinary people.

Although the last statement is an arguable one, Horne does not shrink from debating it, and unlike other intellectuals he does not take Australians to task for living in suburbia as most of them do. His own firmly middle-class background is one that he has lovingly and honestly portrayed in *The Education of Young Donald*. There is a strong community feeling in Horne that will not allow him to betray ordinary, decent people. He pays them the respect of taking them seriously. He is well aware (in 1964, perhaps less so now) how rare this is.

Most Australian writers seem to find it impossible to come to grips with their own people. They caricature their fellow countrymen or idealize them for qualities most of them do not possess . . . This failure to take Australian life seriously leads to a hollowness and hesitation in attitudes . . . They feel betrayed by their own people.

Not only do Australians not think things up: in their behaviour they often show a remarkable distrust for another essential part of the Western Mind, a practising belief in the efficacy of competition.

Horne goes on to say that in order to understand Australia one must approach with sympathy the life that most Australians lead and the values that they embrace. He proceeds to consider the following characteristics of that life. Stability, based on owning a home and the philosophy that this entails. Democracy, and the rendering out-of-date of the old "gentility–vulgarity confrontation". A deeply inlaid scepticism, which "may be the most pervasive single influence operating on Australians. It has much to its credit." The "fair go" ethic, which, as Horne says, "is what happened in Australia to the ideals of Liberty, Equality and Fraternity". Sport, in which, as Horne acutely observes, some of life's principal motivations are given play.

The elements of loyalty, fanaticism, pleasure-seeking, competitiveness, ambition and struggle that are not allowed precise expression in non-sporting life (although they exist in disguise) are stated precisely in sport.

Pleasure in itself Horne sees as part of a pagan attitude to life that is conquering the old puritanism. He has not forgotten what it is like to surf and lie on the beach and then in the evening feel "nice and glowy", as he wrote in his schoolboy diary for 8 January 1934 (*The Education of Young Donald*).

In Horne a characteristic intellectual honesty goes with a sense of belonging. He gives his fellow countrymen and their lifestyle their due. But he is only too aware that the

inhabitants of the "Lucky Country" are not living in the ideal state. Their easy-going scepticism, lack of interest in ideas and their indifference to the fiercer demands of ambition make for a peaceful life, but these all lead to a lack of quality in management and political leadership. Horne's account of Menzies, "the great survivor", his government and his style is one of the great pieces of analytical writing in Australian literature. Never losing the coolness of his wit, he delineates Menzies as a great actor, confident in his egoism but regretting the 1960s play that he is in. Horne suggests that Menzies' deepest flaw was that, despite his humble origins, Menzies lacked a true sense of belonging. "Throughout his career Menzies has stressed 'loyalty', by which he does not seem to mean loyalty to Australia but to the British connection, and to the Monarch (when he was not referring to loyalty to himself)."

The most devastating criticisms in *The Lucky Country* are of management, whether in business, education, the trade unions or politics. For Horne, managers all suffer from a lack of intellect, a failure of nerve, and an inability to take Australia seriously. One of his adverse comments on the typical manufacturer can be applied to all those in power: "he is usually not concerned with scientific research, but with taking over other people's ideas." Beneath the amiable laziness of Australians there is, especially in the 1960s, an immense reservoir of untapped ideas and energy. In fact Horne, in this respect, is a little unfair to Australians. His case against those in power would have been stronger if he had taken account of the remarkable number of Australian inventions and discoveries.

Re-reading *The Lucky Country* 20 years after it was written, one is still impressed by the keenness of Horne's observation but also agreeably surprised by the areas where changes in attitude and fact have occurred. The racial modification that Horne saw as Australia's destiny is taking place, and remarkably peacefully. The failure to understand Australia's position in relation to Asia, and the "oblivion to Oceania", is less than it was. Although there is a long way still to go, the conditions of the Aborigines have certainly improved since 1964.

But Australian unionists' apathy and indifference to their unions still continue, as do the arcane workings of the Arbitration Court, which Horne had summed up with the comment: "It is almost as if a medieval ecclesiastical court took over the economic planning of Australia." Also the development of the North, the second half of the nation, is still in ragged confusion.

But a look-no-brains attitude is endemic among some Australian attitudes to manufacturing. The processes of invention and innovation that are such an essential part of the Western Mind play less domestic part in Australia than in any other prosperous country, apart from Canada.

One weakness of *The Lucky Country* was its inadequate handling of the subject of women. It is a tribute to Australian feminism that such an attitude would no longer be possible.

AUSTRALIAN BEACH PATTERN *Charles Meere*

DONALD HORNE
1921-

Donald Horne himself has given the best account of his youth and education in one of the finest of Australian autobiographies, *The Education of Young Donald* (1967). Sceptical but longing to be identified with some worthwhile cause, humorous but willing to be serious, critical of Australia but conscious of the virtues of ordinary Australians – all of these characteristics of the author combine to give a personal as well as an intellectual strength to his earlier work, *The Lucky Country*.

Donald Horne was born in Sydney, New South Wales, on 26 December 1921. His father was a schoolteacher. His mother's family was descended from James Mileham, who arrived in the colony in 1797 as a surgeon. As Horne wryly observes, "I was descended from the 'solitary instance' of an official of the colony who had not made his fortune out of it." Donald was much influenced by his mother's father, "Pa, who was both a member of an old family and a retired sleeping-car conductor".

Another potent source of Australian identity came from Donald's father, David, who served in the Middle East in World War I in the Light Horse. There were photographs: "Dad, in his hat with the emu plumes, rode down a desert wadi." The day of ceremony in the Horne household was Anzac Day.

Donald was educated as Muswellbrook District Rural School. His long familiarity with the country town atmosphere, and with his mother's vivid social life, has given Horne a great advantage in discussing Australian life and character. At the same time there were always strong links with Sydney, where the holidays were spent, and where the Hornes stayed with Mrs Horne's parents at Kogarah. The family then moved to Sydney, and Donald went from Maitland High School, where he had been a weekly boarder, to Parramatta and Canterbury High Schools.

By the time he went to Sydney University, young Donald's head was filled with incongruities and tragi-comedies. His father was in a mental hospital, he was reading Evelyn Waugh and T. S. Eliot's "The Hollow Men", and he felt "Australia was an inadequate country, not written about in good literature".

At university, where, he wrote, "I affected boredom . . . my mind was also jumping with excitement", Horne was editor of the student newspaper, *Honi Soit*, but his future in journalism was to be delayed by World War II, in which he served in the AIF from 1941 to 1944.

After a short period as a Diplomatic Cadet from 1945 to 1946, he joined the Sydney *Daily Telegraph*, and worked there as a reporter and feature writer from 1945 to 1949. After four years working on newspapers in London he returned to Sydney to edit *Weekend* magazine from 1954 to 1961, followed by *Everybody's* from 1961 to 1962. More importantly, he was editing the lively new weekly, *The Observer*, from 1958 to 1961, which, with *Nation*, gave a new impetus to Australian public intellectual life.

Horne was responsible for the completely new-look *Bulletin* which appeared after Frank Packer bought the famous weekly in 1961. He edited it from 1961 to 1962. He then spent three years in advertising, as Creative Director of Jackson Wain Advertising, while at the same time co-editing *Quadrant* and beginning to write his books. The first to be published, *The Lucky Country*, appeared in 1964. This was followed by some 14 books of fiction, biography and social comment.

Horne married Myfanwy Gollan, and has a son and a daughter.

From 1973 he was a member of the staff of the School of Political Science at the University of New South Wales, where in 1984 he was appointed Professor as holder of a personal chair of Politics. In 1985 he became Chairman of the Australia Council.

One particularly acute insight still holds true. "It is Australians' failure to understand the tragic (or the comic) in life that may place them at a disadvantage in a world in which happiness is largely still hard to achieve."

However, in one profoundly important respect things have undoubtedly improved. A few pages from the end of *The Lucky Country* Horne asked, in some anguish,

Why is there no longer any sense of importance in Australia, no feeling that great events (except catastrophe) can still occur? Small nations usually have histories to sustain them or futures to enlighten them. Australia seems to have lost both its sense of a past and its sense of a future.

Books like *The Lucky Country*, which set people thinking about just these ideas, have helped to make this last judgement no longer true.

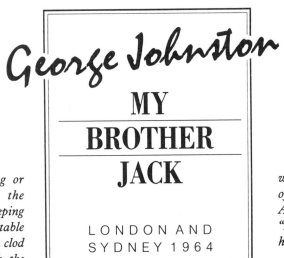

MY BROTHER JACK

LONDON AND
SYDNEY 1964

It was like a great river flooding or changing its course, the way the Depression came—the insidious creeping movement of dark, strong, unpredictable forces, the flow of hidden currents, a clod falling and dissolving, a slide of earth, the cave-in of an entire bank, a sudden eddy swirling around a snag, tilting it over, sweeping it off into a black oblivion.

Even when the disaster had spread everywhere and its destructive menace understood, something unfeasible remained. The work trains, to me, going to my job at the same hour on the same days, seemed just as crowded, the same people pushed at the ticket barriers with the same impatient roughness, the shops were as full as ever of their desperate enticements. It was out in the suburbs mostly that one gradually came to see it.

They brought in the dole, and then the dole became "the sustenance," and around this time they unlocked the Defence Department warehouses and out of the mothballs they took the old surplus greatcoats and tunics and they dyed them a dull black—all that brave khaki of 1914-18—and against the contingency of a Melbourne winter issued them out as a charity to keep the workless warm. So that as the unemployed grew in number the black army coats became a kind of badge of adversity, a stigma of suffering.

One would see the shabby figures shambling along the suburban streets, carrying a loaf of bread and in a cloth bicycle-bag their meagre handout from the Sustenance Depot of tea and sugar and flour and potatoes, and a wisp of tobacco. Or there would be a queue of men the length of a block, most of them in the ill-fitting, shameful black, in apathetic competition for half a dozen casual jobs. As the situation grew worse desperate attempts were made towards alleviation, and the "black coats" moved then in the more regimented bands of the "sustenance-workers" and you would see them with their brooms and picks and shovels and council tip-drays working in slovenly unison on pointless municipal projects. Every now and then one would recognise a familiar figure among them—Dud Bennett, the one-time leader of the Grey Caps gang, driving a council dray laden with gravel, looking small and shrunken now: and Snowy Bretherton in a black greatcoat top-dressing the strip of lawn outside the local town hall. It was a time of a sad and terrible human degradation for which there seemed to be no remedy.

This was the time, too, of the first trickle in from Europe of that other human flotsam, Jews mostly and refugees from a new malignancy, and this, also, was misleading at first for the trickle had become a flood almost before one realised what was happening. Even the language of suffering, of course, had to be Australianised. The refugees became the "Reffos," just as the sustenance-workers had by this time become the "Sussos."

Dad by now was depot foreman so he kept his job at the tramways running-shed, but Bert, who had been "retrenched" from the Repatriation Department, put on his uniform again, although this time the tunic and the greatcoat were dyed a dull black, so he must have had a different feeling about it from the time, fourteen years before, when as a hayseed kid from Corindhap he had gone away with an assumed name and bright badges and a sense of glorious adventure to have his leg blown off in France. He went back to casual snobbing to eke out the sustenance. By this time he had three children to keep.

In our suburb there was a constant, unnerving movement of these pathetic and yet somehow oddly sinister figures in their black tunics and greatcoats. Sometimes they would come to the door asking for an hour's work to cut the hedge or to mow the lawn or to stack firewood or even to run errands ... or sometimes more bluntly just to ask for a handout of food or money. A few of the more resourceful among them had made themselves crude little handtrucks which they would push clatteringly around the streets, collecting old newspapers or scrap-metal or unwanted clothes, or with coal or kindling-wood to sell.

A major part of George Johnston's autobiographical novel *My Brother Jack* deals, from its very humble beginnings, with his career as a journalist. However, *My Brother Jack* is a structurally complex and ironic novel as well as being the good, clear story one would expect a skilled journalist to write.

Johnston appears in the book as Davy Meredith. By writing about Jack, Johnston gives a troubling depth of irony to the portrait of Davy, and Jack's own shortcomings are made poignant by the love and admiration Davy has for his big brother. Both put together, they form one of the most profound essays ever written on the Australian character. Jack would seem to be the mythical Australian hero; quick with his fists, light on his feet, afraid of nothing, good with the girls and the drink, first to volunteer for the AIF when war comes. But poverty and the Depression nearly cripple him, and then an accident keeps him "sitting on his arse" throughout the War.

Davy, the reverse side of the coin, is shy, hopeless at fighting, scared of girls and drink, and does not volunteer for the AIF. Yet Davy is the "success" in worldly terms. He is seduced by a beautiful woman who becomes a showcase

287

wife, and who at the end of the book is clearly going to be succeeded by a girl of even more extraordinary qualities.

Neither Jack nor Davy has had any education to speak of, and Davy's engagement by the *Morning Post* is based on an Intermediate Certificate he does not in fact possess. However, Davy's upward movement into literacy does not make him superior to Jack. Jack remains as a touchstone of integrity and basic honesty to which, even after long absences, Davy always returns.

Similarly, their home and family life is a battleground from which they both escape, yet to which they often return. It is the family that gives solidarity to *My Brother Jack*, even when there are fights between Mother and Dad that shake their existence like an earthquake.

The simple, conservative, and sometimes bigoted, views of Dad and Mother and Jack do not lead to the security they wish to defend. A war hangs over the beginning of the book. Dad is a Gallipoli Anzac who was mildly gassed at Vimy Ridge; Mother is a returned nursing sister with the Army, overseas for more than three years. Jack and Davy grow up among crippled returned soldiers. The myth of the heroic Australian soldier rears up yet again at the outbreak of World War II, but does not survive Jack's injury and Davy's insights into it all as a war correspondent. And Australia, so far away and yet so involved in both those wars (although the Japanese come close in the second), is not immune to economic depression. Ironically, Davy, who has no trade but is apprenticed to an engraver, survives because of his almost illicit talent as a writer for the *Morning Post*, a talent which angers his father and baffles his brother Jack.

The work trains, to me, going to my job at the same hour on the same days, seemed just as crowded, the same people pushed at the ticket barriers with the same impatient roughness, the shops were as full as ever of their desperate enticements.

Davy and Jack, who is three years his senior, grow up under the shadow of World War I in a dreary suburban house in Melbourne. "There was no corner of the house from the time I was seven until I was twelve or thirteen that was not littered with the inanimate props of that vast, dark experience." Dad was a tram mechanic, the eldest boy of 19 children. Mother's father was "rich and mean and puritanical"–and hypocritical, for after his death it was revealed that he had kept a mistress for over 25 years. His widow, Emma, looks after the children while their parents are away at the war. (There are two sisters, Jean and Marjorie, as well as Jack and Davy.)

Davy grows up depressed by "the horrible flatness" of lower class suburban life, in its gentility more soul-destroying than the slums. He is made insecure by the frightful rages of Dad, who regularly beats the children, and who shouts at Mother and has once chased after her round the house with a revolver. "I can hardly recall a night," says Davy later, "when I was not wakened in panic by the stormy violence of my parents' quarrels."

At technical school Davy finds some congenial boys who also like reading. Neither Dad nor Jack approve of all this reading, nor of his "sonky mates". Jack says the boy needs to "go out and pick up a sheila". The only time in his life that Davy ever hates Jack is when he tries to introduce him to sex by showing him his condoms, or buying dirty French postcards to shock him.

Davy at 15 secretly becomes a writer when he sells a story about an old sailing ship to the *Morning Post* under the pseudonym of "Stunsail". He attends the National Gallery Art School as part of his apprenticeship with the lithographers. He becomes friendly with bohemian artists. He buys a typewriter, and is thrown out of the house by Dad when he brings it home. Dad sees it as taking him away from the trade he should be learning.

Davy leaves home and takes his typewriter to his friend Sam Burlington's studio, where he stays, bewildered by the wild life of sex and drink in which he takes no part. He is horrified when Sam and Jack meet; they are from such different worlds he fears that not only will they have nothing in common but that Jack may take it out in aggression. Instead of which, they get along famously.

Jack goes to work as a farm hand in the Wimmera, and Davy gets the job on the *Morning Post*. As so often happens in a relatively unstructured, democratic society, Davy's progress is a mixture of luck, talent and the ability to seize time by the forelock. Jack's lack of progress is based on his philosophy of "give it a go", without ever working out where the go is going.

Johnston does not spare his *alter ego*, David, as Davy is now coming to be known to all except Jack. He is often a moral coward. When Sam Burlington is involved (albeit, in the end, innocently) in the rape and murder of his model and mistress, David shies off, and is terrified when the police come to question him. Jack, on the other hand, writes immediately from the Wimmera to "tell Sam Burlington when you next see him that your brother Jack is on his side". It is not till the following Saturday, when Sam's innocence has been established, that David goes to see him.

Jack comes back from the Wimmera with a "sheila" called Sheila, a very pretty, well-educated and self-possessed girl who causes havoc in the family because she is Catholic. Even though she is sick, and Mother is happily nursing her, Dad wants to drive her out. "We're Protestants in this house. . . This is a decent, God-fearing house. And I want no confounded Roman Catholics under this roof . . ."

Jack and Davy later discuss Dad and what's wrong with him, and come to the conclusion that "He just can't bear that other people should be able to do what they want to do." Davy lends Jack £50 ("*fifty quid!*") so he and Sheila can set up house together.

During the Depression, David resigns the apprenticeship so that he can take up a full-time career as a journalist with the *Morning Post*. Jack, unemployed, refuses to take the dole and disappears, to return, almost dead, after a long absence in South America and elsewhere. David traces Sheila, who now has a baby, and gets Jack a job as a storeman with his old masters, the lithographers. The balance is shifting more and more. Davy, the kid brother, is proving the strong one, and Jack (with no false pride) is grateful for his help.

But David is also pathetically unmanly by Jack's standards. He has never had a girlfriend, let alone been to bed with a girl. Life now presents such delights to him in

STUDY OF A MAN *Russell Drysdale*

GEORGE JOHNSTON
1912-1970

George Johnston's life story is closely interwoven with the events in his three autobiographical novels, *My Brother Jack, Clean Straw for Nothing* and *A Cartload of Clay*, in which he appears as David Meredith. The epigraph to *My Brother Jack* is from Andre Gide: "Fiction there is—and history. Certain critics of no little discernment have considered that fiction is history which *might* have taken place, and history fiction which *has* taken place . . ." Johnston's best books are constructed on these paradoxes of fiction and history.

Johnston was born on 20 July 1912, at Malvern, Victoria. He was educated at Caulfield State School, Brighton Technical School and the National Gallery Art School. He worked at a variety of jobs and then became a journalist.

During World War II he became a war correspondent in New Guinea, 1942-43, and in Italy, Burma and China, 1943-45.

His first marriage, by which there was a daughter, ended in 1945. In the same year he married Charmian Clift, with whom he lived until her death in July 1969.

In 1941 he published *Grey Gladiator*, about HMAS *Sydney*, which was followed by other war books and books of travel. A novel, *High Valley*, written in collaboration with Charmian Clift, won the *Sydney Morning Herald* competition in 1948.

In 1955 the Johnstons went to live on the island of Hydra in the Aegean Sea off Greece. Their life there is the subject of *Clean Straw for Nothing*.

My Brother Jack (1964) won the Miles Franklin Award in 1965, as did *Clean Straw for Nothing* (1969) in 1970.

After 10 years on Hydra the Johnstons returned to Sydney in 1965 with their children. In an interview he said that writing *My Brother Jack* made him homesick. In all he wrote 30 books, three in collaboration with Charmian Clift.

Johnston's character, David Meredith, had already appeared in two novels when *My Brother Jack* was written. *Closer to the Sun* (1960) has a number of parallels with the Johnstons' life at Hydra, and *The Far Road* (1962) is about events in southern China when Meredith was a journalist. The best comment on this *alter ego* in *My Brother Jack* comes from Johnston himself, in a radio interview (ABC Radio 2, 5 April 1974).

I must quickly point out . . . I honestly do not believe that I was quite so treacherous a young man or so gifted for betrayal and self-interest and opportunism, but it was necessary to draw the Davy character in this way to build up the almost tragic irony of the final situation where Davy becomes his brother Jack's hero, and also to point out the contrast with Jack's honesty, guts and in a real sense his uncomplicated nobility.

George Johnston died in 1970, a year after the death of Charmian Clift.

---

the shape of an elegant and beautiful librarian, Helen Midgeley. In a disturbing scene she appears naked in front of David in the back room of the library, where they meet when it is closed. He runs away in blind panic. Undismayed, Helen succeeds on the next evening in divesting him of his virginity.

Helen's character is beautifully drawn. She senses the haphazard nature of David's life, but also its potential security, for he is doing very well at the newspaper. She has decided that he will be her husband. She is David's first experience of "political woman", an ardent Leftist. But at the same time she has pledged herself to what is now called upward mobility. One of the most brilliantly observed episodes of the book is when David takes Helen to Mother's sixtieth birthday party. Her genteel revulsion at the assembled crudity of the Meredith family is symbolised by the row caused when one of the children tips a bowl of trifle and jelly all over her best suit. David is right out of character in supporting her against his family. Nevertheless, the Merediths rally round at the inevitable wedding, for Helen has made David mortgage his life to her and a house in suburbia and a red MG car.

Yet it is apparent, under David's superficial taming, that, in the words of his journalist friend Gavin Turley to Helen, "there is no guarantee to him". He rebels against all the suburban rituals, and even plants a gum tree (a *gum* tree!) in treeless Beverly Park Gardens Estate, to the potential detriment of his neighbours' paths and drains. David finally confesses to himself that he does not love Helen.

The war appears to offer the status of hero to Jack. He longs to be in it and rushes to enlist, under the spell of the same myth that had taken Dad away. "This Australian myth seems to derive from something primal, an earth-challenge . . . [it] was lodged and burning deep inside him." And David sees him as soaring into a new element; "I envied the profound certainty there was about him, when I was so uncertain."

But Jack has his femur broken in an accident, and never gets to the war, whereas David is everywhere in it and on the edges of it, becoming famous as a war correspondent. In the end David (who is not even in the army) pulls strings so that at least Jack is sent to Darwin, a little closer to the war than Melbourne.

A whole new current is set flowing when David meets an AWAS girl, Gunner Morley, reading *Tristram Shandy* in a gunpit at an anti-aircraft training camp. Cressida Morley will obviously take over where David and Helen long ago gave up. She is everything that Helen is not, discomfiting and exciting and real.

The book ends with yet another minor betrayal. Johnston is very hard on David. He has a drink with Jack, and then has to leave because he has a dinner engagement with Cressida. He half-heartedly promises to make it back to Jack, who is soldiering on with his mates. The book ends with David seeming to hear Jack saying to them, "He'll be along. . . . My brother Davy's not the sort of bloke who ever let anyone down, you know. . . ."

They share a basic decency, and a basic sentimentality. David ought never to have said he might be back. Jack ought never to have believed him. As always, David may be left with the images of success, but Jack remains the touchstone by which the ruses that lead to success are ultimately found wanting.

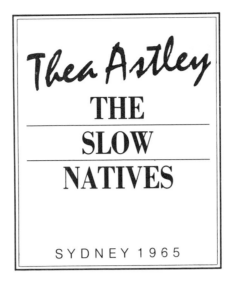

Thea Astley
THE SLOW NATIVES

SYDNEY 1965

"Sorry," Keith mumbled through savoury.

He sidled past them, past the lavatory and round the side of the house into the maze of privet and japonica. All of a sudden his sophistication had gone where? He could not support the flimsy child who began walking groggily to the gate but who still did not look back once at the lighted windows behind which adults talked and corrupted each other, slandered, hated, betrayed, remained pathetically loyal and pretended—above all, that was it—pretended self-containment, assurance, all the adult virtues he had regarded himself as having.

The slopes down to the river were sticky with moonlight that fawned all over the posh houses and the blocks of flats between which he then strode, not looking really, not seeing the wet moonlight or the tiger gardens crouched across the river. Curled tight as a fist he went smashing, punching darkness that syruped out thinly to the ferry hill, below which the river, seen suddenly, its swoop and the deep grooving of it and the boat hulks, was black as lusting Coady, lusting for the sea. It was so still that behind the chug-chug of the ferry dripping drunk across on its cables, drunk as Coady and as purposefully finding the shortest distance from A to B, he could track the rattle of a Queen Street tram.

As he waited in the ferry-shed his thumb smoothed over the impersonal face of his watch and in the half-dark he rested on the sweep of the hands that now, greenly luminous, moved up on midnight. Later, he decided, later he would go home. But some time before that his parents would be anxiously pestering Mr Coady's embarrassed ear, a Martian projection that caught up the delicate sound-waves created by girls' skirts.

Rattling his small change, he stepped aboard the rocking ferry. Ten minutes to walk up town. Another thirty to circumnavigate the shoppers' coasts. Perhaps twenty for a coffee. Ideally absorbed, Keith had watched the minute hand move steadily up the dial. It seemed to become slower, sweeping across the moon's face, bridging craters of sixty seconds deep down which Keith plunged again, again. Soon, he told himself. Soon.

The river quivered. Fish-tail lights flickered. The town's big gold teeth grinned. Soon they would be home.

Prowling downtown, all-absorbing, he slipped into an arcade cellar, where he huddled on a late-night-diner stool, prodding the nerve-spots of the last two hours.

Lay me down baby blues . . ., bawled a crooner, canned, from a corner microphone, moaned loudly and dreadfully above the chairs and tables and the three other patrons. Keith watched the electric wall-clock creep down the next day, sensing his smile brazen as a juke-box, as the machine now whimpering:

Pay me down baby,
Never say maybe,
I've got the want you blues.

There they would be. The old folks at home. They would call "Keith", then "Keith" again, with interest and increasing urgency, and while Bernard looked hopelessly at the smooth bed Iris would pick up the receiver and start dialling.

He kicked the chrome legs of the stool and nodded sadly to the music beat . . .

Lay me down baby,
Pay me down baby,
I've got the want you blues . . .

The title of Thea Astley's novel comes from a popular joke of the 1960s: "What is the black stuff between elephants' toes?" Answer: "Slow natives!"

One is warned, as it were, to expect satire, a toughness of approach, and also a relish of sardonic humour. *The Slow Natives* contains all three of these ingredients, but Thea Astley, in typical Australian style, also uses them to disguise deep feelings of love and tenderness and an exercise of Christian charity. *The Slow Natives* is a mocking, harsh and even cruel book, but one finishes it with a respect for the inherent goodness in weak humanity.

All this means, of course, not that *The Slow Natives* is a sermon, but that it displays the true novelist's ability to sense and portray both good and evil in human beings. "Evil" might be too strong a word; of the catalogue of deadly sins, several of the leading characters in *The Slow Natives* are guilty of the most subtle sin of all, the medieval idea of accidie, somewhat inadequately translated as "sloth" or "torpor". They have lost freshness, sparkle, energy and the capacity to love that inspires all of these virtues.

The opening chapter of *The Slow Natives* is the hardest in the book to read. It is as if Thea Astley, writing about inadequate lives in order to show how they become inadequate and how they may recover vitality, cannot at first overcome her distaste for such foolish and immoral people.

Bernard and Iris Leverson and their son Keith are certainly seen at their worst when the novel opens. Keith, who is 14, has been stealing and getting away with it. It is all a sort of revenge: "his actions were motivated solely by the longing to protest against his home". It is a boring home, where the wife bosses the husband and takes a lover out of boredom, as a reaction to her husband saying to her, "You know, Iris, after twenty years of marriage you feel as if you're the same sex."

Bernard is a Brisbane music teacher and examiner. In his son's words, "He's sloppy and middle-aged and going bald and red and gets full." Iris, according to the same source, is "A nice dull ordinary mum".

A friend of the Leversons, Leo Varga, who gives private tutorials and has homosexual tendencies, casually but deliberately tells Keith about his mother's infidelity. Keith stays away from home one night (at Varga's beach cottage) to punish his parents. He succeeds with Iris, but not too well with Bernard, who sums himself up in "a sudden awareness of emptiness . . . I read. I play the piano—only a little—but still I do perform, if indifferently. I drink more than a little but do not womanise. I smoke to excess. I am punctual on the job. I play a record now and then and I am gentle, calm and completely civilised when my wife deceives me, my son leaves home."

There they would be. The old folks at home. They would call "Keith", then "Keith" again, with interest and increasing urgency, and while Bernard looked hopelessly at the smooth bed Iris would pick up the receiver and start dialling.

A good novelist always has an eye for the trivial occurrence that can trigger an explosion. Keith asks Bernard (he calls his parents by their first names) if he can have a duffle coat. Bernard says no. At dinner the boy asks again, and is refused again. Keith, getting nastier, comments that Iris pushes Bernard around and he is afraid to have an opinion of his own. Bernard speaks more severely to him. Keith responds. " 'You stupid blind cuckold,' he said at last, deliberately and clearly, and stared straight into his father's eyes."

For once Bernard acts. He slaps Keith hard across the face. And as Keith crumples into tears, "he loved his father so much he wanted to die".

Thea Astley is concerned, in *The Slow Natives*, to distinguish between those who are still capable of love and those who are not. All her characters are adrift, but some are capable of steering their way back to humanity. As the circle of the novel widens, this basic pattern does not change.

When Leverson goes to a Catholic school to examine the music students, he talks to Father Lingard about boredom and is surprised to hear that priests suffer from it too. "A kind of spiritual aridity" is what Lingard calls it. It is also

a kind of isolation. Later on, Lingard says, "Perhaps if I committed some whacking great sin I'd regain the sense of communication."

There needs to be an arousal of emotion in people before they can communicate, but of course a failure to control emotion can also destroy communication. One of the most subtle and most touching portraits in *The Slow Natives* is that of Sister Matthew, who is herself a candidate for the music examination. Bernard tells her that she plays well but mechanically, without emotion; losing, in her Bach, the quality of joy. The incident seems little at the time, but is to be a turning point in Sister Matthew's life.

After Bernard's visit as examiner, the Monsignor receives an anonymous letter saying that Bernard has been behaving improperly with the examinees. When Bernard returns a week later, little Sister Matthew asks if she can play him the Bach piece again. She does so, this time with "terrible emotionalism". She breaks down and says, "I'm fit for nothing. Neither in this life nor any other." Bernard is highly embarrassed. Should one pat the hand of a religious? Instead, he confesses his own unhappiness and his inability to get on with his son. A key passage for the whole book follows. "Charity, like cancer, grows slowly until it involves the whole being and he could only regard her through the increased understanding of his own unhappiness."

Later in the book Sister Matthew runs away from the convent, makes her way to the Leversons' house, and confesses to Bernard that she wrote the anonymous letter. Bernard does not know how to help her, except by sending her back to the convent.

One reason for his ineptness is that Keith has also run away, this time apparently for good. Bernard is oblivious of the ironic parallels between Sister Matthew's plight and that of Keith. A basic lack of charity in other people is behind both desperate actions.

Keith has joined up with a disreputable, dangerous young bonehead called Chookie, who has assaulted a little girl and raped (albeit with comic elements of seduction) an old lady. He has also stolen Keith's duffle coat, which in fact Keith himself has stolen in the first place. They are two of a kind, wishing only to get away from the families that have rejected them, though they are not sure of where they want to go or what they want to do. They are both about 15 years old. What is so sad about them is that they have no sense of adventure in running away. Chookie is fleeing what he thinks are two crimes (actually the old lady has forgiven him); Keith is really fleeing the crime of being himself. "We're just the same. Two of a kind," says Chookie, but the seeds of expediency are growing in Keith. He says he cannot see what they have in common. What in fact is happening is that he is feeling "aching, cold, hungry, bored", and feels like "tossing it in and going back".

Chookie has confessed that he raped Miss Trumper. Keith confesses that his mother has a lover, an admission that produces a "so what?" response from Chookie. However, Chookie himself is by no means immune from guilt. He has not emerged unmarked from his Catholic upbringing. When the two boys get a lift to Coffs Harbour, Chookie sends Miss Trumper a card saying he is sorry. Chookie, unlike Keith, has really never had a chance. If there is good in him, no one has ever encouraged it. At school, at confession, when

FAMILY AT TABLE *Tony Tuckson*

THEA ASTLEY
1925-

Thea Astley's novels have probably been given more awards than those of any other Australian writer with the exception of Patrick White. This might seem to indicate that her work is "literary", of the kind that particularly appeals to the judges of literary competitions. Her books are certainly very well written and extremely intelligent, but they are definitely for the general reader. She writes about ordinary people and there is nothing difficult about her style. She belongs to no literary coterie and her originality is not strained. Thea Astley remains one of the most remarkable of Australian novelists.

Thea Astley was born in Brisbane on 25 August 1925 and educated at All Hallows convent and the University of Queensland. She taught English in Queensland schools from 1944 to 1948 and in New South Wales from 1948 to 1967. In 1948 she married Edmund Gregson and they have one son.

In 1968 she left secondary school education and became a lecturer at Macquarie University, from which she retired as Fellow in English in 1979. She was awarded the AM in 1980.

Her novels began to appear in the 1950s, starting with *Girl With A Monkey* (1958). She received Commonwealth Literary Fund Fellowships in 1961 and 1964 and lectured for the Fund on Australian literature at Queensland University in 1969 and 1970.

She has also published a number of short stories and poems.

The Well-Dressed Explorer won the Miles Franklin Award in 1962. *The Slow Natives*, probably her best novel, was also the most successful at winning prizes, being given the Miles Franklin Award, the *Age* Novel of the Year prize and the Moomba Award. Her third Miles Franklin Award came with *The Acolyte* (1974). *A Kindness Cup* (1972), won the *Age* Book of the Year Award in 1972. More recent work includes *Hunting the Wild Pineapple* (1979), short stories, and *An Item from the Late News* (1982), a novel. *Beachmasters*, her latest novel, was published in Australia and New York early in 1985.

The main target of her satire has been middle-class morality and small-town Philistinism. She is a keen conservationist and the growing destruction of the Queensland rain forests has made her think of leaving that State, where she lives at Kuranda, and returning to New South Wales. Her interest in music is apparent in several of her books, notably in *The Slow Natives* and *The Acolyte*.

Writing about herself as novelist (*Southerly*, No. 1, 1970, "The Idiot Questioner"), she said, "A chance phrase about someone I had never met, never did meet, gave me the whole of *The Slow Natives*." She also said that, for her, the key to the book was her "sympathy with the misfits". Scenery is important to her, a sense of place: "I've always been enormously responsive to scenery, landscapes with or without figures; my Dad singing shanties in the sea-rotten houses we used to rent along the Queensland coast when I was a small girl."

She has also said, "Writing is incredibly hard work and I'm naturally lazy. Perhaps that's why, if given a choice of talents, I would plump for a musical one, an ability to play jazz piano. For there is, as you play, instant orgasm."

---

the priest asked him to tell God he was sorry for filling the Monsignor's biretta with ink, Chookie can't. "Well, I'm not really sorry. I mean I thought it was funny," he says. It is a step forward now, spiritually, for Chookie to tell Miss Trumper he is sorry.

The boys accept a lift back to Brisbane from a surfie in a convertible. When the surfie stops in a town and goes off to the pub, the boys have milk shakes with the last of Keith's money. There is an illuminating episode when Keith refers to Bernard; Chookie is now shocked to hear Keith calling his father by his first name. "I never wanted to, Keith stopped himself from admitting." Nor did he want the other proofs of suburban liberalism.

At a nightclub near Varga's cottage, where Chookie is demonstrating an unexpected talent on the mouth organ, playing with the band, Varga comes in and sees Keith. Before he can talk to him, the surfie picks a fight with Varga. Frightened that the police will arrive to quieten the mêlée that follows and pick them up, the boys leave and steal the

surfie's car. Chook assures Keith that he is an expert driver.

The car crashes, Chookie is killed and Keith loses a leg. In an ironic touch the police bring Bernard and Iris to identify Chookie's body, which has been clothed in Keith's duffle coat with a book of Keith's in the pocket. The boys might have been the same, two of a kind. But Keith is still alive.

He is also another person, Bernard realises. "It is too late, Bernard thought, too late to give you the sort of discipline I now know you wanted more than anything in the world." One remembers that slap on the face which made Keith love his father. Now, "Bernard's love shook him with its surprise."

It is a surprising ending, but convincing. It remains that there is little hope for Iris, who is a negative character. Bernard, however, though hardly positive, has shown a consciousness of the desolation of his soul with Father Lingard, and has clung to his capacity to love. It is only the slow natives who are crushed. There are others who get away to live.

D.E. Charlwood

ALL THE GREEN YEAR

SYDNEY 1965

We reached the sheoak where the camel stood dribbling greenly, surveying us with contemptuous eyes. It was a moth-eaten animal and it stank. Squid picked up its nose-line.

"Now we get it to lie down. I saw how to do it at last year's circus. Then we ride it."

"I don't want to ride it," I exclaimed.

"Well, I'm going to—there's nothink to it."

I looked round wildly, hoping for a miracle.

"Hooshta!" cried Squid with authority. He said to me, "That's telling it to lie down in Arab."

The camel roared in our faces with a foul breath, its neck striking like a snake.

"We'd better leave it."

"They always grizzle. The circus man said they're never happy, not even when you're feeding them."

"Hooshta!"

It darted its head at us, baring yellow teeth.

"Listen, let's go home."

"Hooshta!"

The camel dropped reluctantly to its knees. Squid's face was shining triumphantly.

"I'm not going to ride it."

He ignored me. As the camel subsided he climbed into the double saddle. As he sat there, the expression on his face reminded me of Rudolph Valentino.

"See you at school," he said carelessly. The camel was moving to get up. I ran over to it and leapt up behind him.

The affair of Perry's camel was talked of for years round Kananook. I was always named as the main culprit. The truth was that I was only held in the saddle by a kind of paralysis. Squid was full of wild cries. He put his school cap on backwards and had a dirty handkerchief caught under the peak of it as a neck-cloth. Sometimes he clapped his hand up as a shield to his eyes and stared into the distance. There wasn't much doubt about what lay in the distance for it was obvious that the camel intended heading for the town.

I don't know when it was that I realized all wasn't well with Squid. After we had been swinging like a pair of metronomes for ten minutes I said faintly, "It's going to take us through the main street! What are we going to do?"

We were by this time approaching the sign WELCOME TO KANANOOK A GOOD REXONA TOWN.

"I dunno," said Squid in a hollow voice.

"You what?"

"I don't feel well."

He tried to lean on the neck of the camel, but it was too far off to be of comfort to him.

"I thought we'd given up the idea of you being sick?"

"I can't help it—I feel crook in the stummick."

"Well, what do we do?"

"Don't talk," he begged.

At that point in our journey we engaged with our first townsman. The Presbyterian minister appeared in his buggy. The horse was moving with a sort of side-step, its ears twitching and its nostrils agape. For a moment it stopped and shivered all over, then emitting a sound I'd never heard from a horse, it wheeled round and was gone. Behind it the buggy scarcely touched the ground and Mr Wetherby scarcely touched the seat.

I prodded Squid. "We've killed Mr Wetherby."

"I'm glad," he moaned.

"You've got to do something."

"I'm going to jump off."

"You can't leave me."

"Ah, shut up," he wailed.

In the paddock by the local dairy I caught sight of cows performing in an unmatronly dance, hind legs in the air, tails streaming out behind. At that moment Squid half fell, half jumped off. Scarcely pausing in its stride the camel kicked him into the roadside grass.

Any idea I had of following him was cut short when I heard him scream, "I'm dead!"

An unpretentious and simply told story, *All the Green Year* has enjoyed enormous popularity (21 editions between 1965 and 1983), due partly to its extensive use in schools as well as to general sales; such popularity constitutes a firm basis for being regarded as an Australian classic. Charlwood says: "I did not write *All the Green Year* for young people; much less did I write it for use in schools . . . nevertheless . . . the response of young people to it . . . has delighted me."

This is one of those books about childhood which, like *Huckleberry Finn*, can be read by all ages. (Actually Charlwood has said that he often was worried by the sophistication of *Huckleberry Finn* when he was reading it, because it is supposed to be narrated by a boy, and this "limits you in maturity of observation, reflection, awareness".) Charlwood solved this problem by making his narrator a man looking back, mature enough to perceive the fragility of the veneer of toughness of 14-year-old boys.

All the Green Year is so vivid and personal that it reads like autobiography, but Charlwood has on several occasions been at pains to explain that it is a novel; based, like all novels, on both personal experience and invention. However, in one very important aspect the book is autobiographical, for while it contains many lively and sometimes hilarious episodes and characters (of the latter, Grandfather is a notable example), basically it is about the failure of parents to understand teenage children. Charlwood confesses that the writing of *All the Green Year* was therapeutic. As a parent he had found himself over-reacting to the problems of his own teenage daughters, and he declared he would write a book about the generation gap.

> In fact, I knew little about growing up in the sixties—indeed, that was half my problem—nor could I have written about my own family. But outlet I must have. I realized then that my feelings as a father were transferrable; that I could create scenes against the background of my own growing up and enliven them with the pent-up emotions of a 1960s parent—This is exactly what I did . . . In the book I was able to play a dual role: I was Charlie Reeve, the narrator—myself when young—and George Reeve, his exasperated father—myself of the 1960s.

The novel derives a lot of its strength and authenticity from the fact that it is written from these two viewpoints.

The affair of Perry's camel was talked of for years round Kananook. I was always named as the main culprit. The truth was that I was only held in the saddle by a kind of paralysis.

Set on the eastern peninsula of Port Phillip Bay, *All the Green Year* opens with a distinction being made between events that simply happen—like riding to school on Perry Brothers' camel—and events that are linked to subsequent developments in life. The latter begin with injustice and end in disgrace. Charlie and his tall, melancholy friend, Fred Johnston ("Johnno"), feel themselves to be badly misunderstood, both at home and at school. The old headmaster, Moloney, a thin-lipped little bachelor of about 50, does not take Charlie seriously and never misses an opportunity to mock Johnno. "About Johnno himself there was a contradiction I have never forgotten. He had practically no physical fear, yet he was always afraid of his father and of old Moloney." It is noteworthy that Charlie and Johnno do badly in English until Moloney goes to take another class and they come under a new teacher, Miss Beckenstall, who is really interested in teaching them.

Johnno's desperate unhappiness, and the lesser anxieties of Charlie, do not stop them having a great deal of fun together and with the other boys in the group. Johnno, with his extraordinary physique—188 centimetres, with huge hands—gentle and shy but a powerful fighter when aroused, nervous of girls but capable of being seduced, is a notable character in Australian fiction, especially when caught up in the nightmare events at the end of the book.

Another memorable character, totally different, is Grandfather, an old Port Phillip pilot and master in sail. Grandfather lives in a rather ricketty old wooden house perched on a cliff overlooking the sea. As long as Charlie can remember he has been "peculiar", but now he is getting

so odd that the Reeve family—Charlie and his brother, Ian, mother (Grandfather's daughter) and father—move in to look after him. The old man is quite harmless. He has a ship's wheel fastened to the veranda and likes to think that he is steering the house across the bay. He yells instructions at real or imaginary ships, and treats the family or passers-by as crew. He likes to argue about Charles Darwin, and calls himself a Tolstoyan. He is liable to interrupt the dinner conversation with loud challenges, backed with a glare, like "Who made the first monkey? . . . Did the first monkey make itself?", while George Reeve is in the meantime saying unpleasant things about Charlie's friend Johnno, and mother cries in desperation: "All I can say is this: if we don't settle to our dinner like human beings, I'm going to leave this table." No wonder Charlie says to himself: "Life was becoming intolerable."

The chief pest in Charlie's life, outside the family, is the neighbouring widow's boy, Squid. Squid has certain abilities, one of them a mysterious ability to hypnotise hens, but he also has an unpleasant capacity to come out on top by manipulating other people. He is Mr Moloney's pet; we find out why at the end, when Moloney marries Squid's mother. He is a trouble-maker, as in the case of the camel, which he mounts, followed by Charlie. When they reach town, Squid jumps off, leaving Charlie to ride through the town (causing the horses to bolt) and, disastrously and unintentionally, to school. Moloney does not know that Squid has ridden the camel, and Squid has a week off from school because of "a most unfortunate fall". Squid is emphatically not to be trusted.

Although Johnno has a sister, Eileen, both boys are terrified of girls, and are dismayed when Johnno's father orders his son to accompany Eileen to a dance, so that her "honour" can be protected. Johnno persuades Charlie to go too, to provide him with moral support. Eileen has designs on a public-school boy with a Riley car, which leads to a fight between Johnno and the boy, Johnno thinking he is doing the right thing by his sister's "honour", much to her fury.

But then, to Charlie's dismay, Johnno falls for a girl. Without explaining to Charlie, he lures him to an assignation at Coles Bay, a secluded beach, with his girl Noreen and her friend Kitty. Johnno and Noreen go off together, and Charlie, who despises and fears girls, in no time finds himself holding Kitty's hand, her hair brushing his cheek. Then Charlie looks up and finds himself facing Big Simmons, the local larrikin. Fighting dirty, albeit with his nose broken by Charlie's one blow, Big Simmons knocks Charlie unconscious and temporarily blinds him by sticking his fingers in his eyes. Later, Johnno tries to avenge Charlie, and as a result is sent by his father to work at weekends at Digger Hayes's blacksmith's shop.

Charlie and Johnno are both done with girls. "I'll never get married," says Johnno. "Neither will I," says Charlie.

It is the fault of neither of the boys that they get into fights, until the last fight in the book. The major crisis in the lives of the two boys is brought about by chance (how true to life!), when Moloney takes over the class for a day from Miss Beckenstall and sarcastically reads out the composition, both strikingly original and poetic, which Johnston has written for the new teacher. " 'I didn't know

BOYS BATHING, HEIDELBERG *Arthur Streeton*

D. E. CHARLWOOD
1915-

Don Charlwood was born at Hawthorn in Melbourne on 6 September 1915. When he was eight the family moved to his mother's old hometown of Frankston. In those days it was a fishing village and seaside resort, and Don loved the freedom of the sea and the bush.

He attended the local state primary school. It and its headmaster became the models for the school and Mr Moloney in *All the Green Year*. When the boy moved on to the Frankston and District High School he was fortunate in having exceptionally good teachers of English and History. The teacher of the latter set Don a local history project which led to his interviewing many of the Frankston pioneers, friends of his grandparents, and the project was serialised in the local newspaper when he was 13.

Don left school at 17 and took a job with an estate agent, but lost it when he was approaching 18, when his wages would have risen to 22 shillings and sixpence a week.

In 1934 a cousin of his mother's who owned a property near Nareen offered him a job, in which he stayed for seven years. There he began seriously to study the craft of writing, and during this time some of his stories were published.

From 1941 to 1945 he was a navigator in the RAAF, serving in Bomber Command in a Lancaster squadron based in Lincolnshire. He survived the war unscathed, and "to tell the story of those lost men" wrote *No Moon Tonight*, one of the most notable of Australian war books. In editing it he had considerable assistance from the critic A. A. Phillips, with whom he was connected through his marriage to Nell East in 1944. (The couple had one son and three daughters.)

He was also writing short stories, especially about his Nareen days, and many of these were published in *Blackwood's Magazine*. Later they were collected under the title *An Afternoon of Time*.

Charlwood began work as an air traffic controller in 1945, and from 1948 to 1952 was Senior Operations Controller at Melbourne Airport. From 1954 to 1975 he was Senior Supervisor of ATC Personnel, a job that entailed much travelling in Australia and overseas. He has said, of *All the Green Year*:

> Consequently I wrote on planes, in motels, in English pubs, and, when I was at home, in the RACV reading room to which I escaped during many a lunch hour. To me the book reflects my unsettled life of that time.

In 1967 he published a short history of the development of ATC and a description of its function, *Take-off to Touchdown*.

After his retirement in 1975 Charlwood again turned in his writing to the past, drawing in particular upon his interest in wrecks and the sea, first aroused by the fact that his paternal grandmother had been wrecked near Peterborough in the *Schomberg* in 1855. He combined the story of the *Schomberg* and its eccentric commanding officer, Captain 'Bully' Forbes, with the story of Captain Gibb of the *Loch Ard* in *Wrecks and Reputations* (1977).

He then spent four years researching and writing a book based on the shipboard diaries of emigrants coming out to Australia under sail, *The Long Farewell* (1981), which was awarded the New South Wales Premier's Ethnic Award in 1982. At present he is writing about the period of his upbringing and "the conditioning of our generation and the consequences of this conditioning when war came".

Charlwood lives in Templestowe in Victoria.

---

anyone but Miss Beckenstall would read it,' says Johnno in a strained voice." This is said after Johnno has flung an inkwell at Moloney, hitting him in the chest, causing him to drop his glasses, which Charlie deliberately treads on.

Johnno's father (a former welterweight champion of the RAN) hits the boy when Moloney comes to tell him his version of the events. Johnno hits his father back, once. Then his father really beats him up. Johnno clears out, and Eileen comes at night to tell Charlie where he has gone. Charlie fears Moloney arriving at his home to tell his father, and he runs away to find Johnno.

Just after the inkpot incident, when the two boys are walking away from school, the full implication of it all dawning upon them, the narrator says: "To think of it and of the next twenty-four hours is to be a boy again."

It was these words, perhaps, that prompted two distinguished people of letters, A. A. Phillips and Beatrice Davis, to claim: "The first part reads as a book *about* boys; the second part—the flight from home—as a book *for* boys."

Charlwood disagreed, and perhaps most readers would align themselves with him in his comment that "I was writing as an adult repossessed by boyhood and this state of 'repossession' intensified as the book neared its climax, so that, briefly, I shed my age and became in spirit a boy again".

Johnno asks Charlie to row him across the bay to Queenscliff, so that he can escape to the "Otways, Queensland—anywhere". Charlie decides that not only will he row Johnno in the old family dinghy, but also that he, too, will fly from home. At the last moment Gyp, the old family dog, jumps in as well.

The last 30-odd pages of the book are extremely exciting. There is no place here for the humorous, wry or reflective tone of the earlier part of the book. It is all pure action, as the dinghy is very nearly run down by the liner *Maloja*, causing the loss of the oars, and the helpless boys drift out through the perilous Rip (where Gyp is swept overboard) into the open sea. The current eventually brings the boat close enough in for the boys to be able, just, to swim ashore.

It is true to the spirit of the book, and the characters, that in the end Charlie is ruefully reunited with his parents, who arrive with Johnno's father and Eileen with a search party at the beach near which the boys are hiding, but that Johnno goes off into the night, alone. Old man Johnston is "bowed and shrunken-looking". When Charlie incautiously says Johnno has only just left, Eileen says quickly: "We must tell the police." However, Johnno's father has at last learned enough wisdom to say: "No. He's alive and that's all that matters. He'll come back if he wants to come back."

The short sentences and uncluttered style of *All the Green Year* let the light of such understanding shine all the more clearly. As usual with matters of human relationships, it is all a matter of communication.

Colin Johnson

WILD
CAT
FALLING

SYDNEY 1965

I wake with a pounding heart and sit bolt upright, remembering. I've got to face the day and this hole I'm in. Can't stay here and talk to a crazy old nigger with all the cops in the district combing the bush for me. Got to get up and move on. I've killed a cop back there and I'm in for it if I don't think clear and act shrewd. Get my bearings and head East. Pinch another car if I can and get out of the State. I can lose myself over East. Grow a beard. Dress differently. No mercy for a man who kills a cop. I'm not sorry for him. All cops deserve to die, but most people don't see it that way and the world's going to be more against me now than it ever was.

I look around the hut. On an upturned box there is a battered pannikin, a couple of spoons, a butcher's knife and a cracked cup containing a few shillings. I put my head outside and look around, blinking in the white glare of the mid-day sun. No sign of the old man. The old bastard's probably gone to put me in. I was a fool to trust him. Should have remembered you can't trust anyone.

I take the money out of the cup and put it in my pocket. I've got all this other cash from the job at the hardware store, but I'm going to need all I can get, and

more. My hand hovers over the knife. I hear a sound and look outside again. The old codger's coming back alone across the clearing, dangling some rabbits on a stick and droning his dreary blackman's song. It gets on my nerves. I drop the knife and put my hands over my ears.

He walks slowly to the fire, puts down the rabbits and peers into the hut. "Just been to the traps," he says. "Fresh meat for dinner now."

I crawl out and get on my feet.

"I'm on my way."

I think he's going to ask me "Where?" but he just nods and says, "You got a long way to go, son. Better eat while you got the chance."

I look at the limp, furry bodies by the fire. "No time," I say.

He goes to the billy, sniffs it, nods and tips the contents on a plate. I eat standing up while he reaches into the hut for his knife and begins to skin his catch. I put the plate down and he smiles at me again.

"Wait a tick," he says, getting to his feet. "I got a few bob here put by. You might be glad of it."

I stand rooted to the spot until he returns with the empty cup in his hands. He looks at me quietly and I feel he is reading my whole life from my face. Everything, as long back as I can remember, even before. So what? I tell myself. What do I care for an old abo crank in beggar's clothes?

I look him straight in the face with my practised sneer. His eyes are faded like potch opal, but clear and sad. Not judging me, only seeing how I am. I feel the blood flushing up my neck and over my face and I hang my head. No one ever made me feel this way before. No one. Not the magistrate, or the probation officer, or the brothers with all that thunder about the eye of God. Not even my Mum's suffering face.

I take the money from my pocket and drop it back in the cup.

He shakes his head. "You take it, son. I don't have much use for it."

He puts the cup on the ground, then sits cross-legged and goes quietly on with his job. I want to run and hide my shame in the bush, but something holds me here.

This book was the first novel by a writer of Aboriginal blood to be published in Australia. That fact alone would lend it a certain historical interest, but in fact it is a work of distinction in its own right. Thanks to the encouragement of Mary Durack and Criena Rohan (the author of the novel *The Delinquents*), Johnson achieved confidence in himself as a writer and also learned how to revise and pare down his work. As a result, *Wild Cat Falling* is a lean and fast-paced book, with an inner energy that is movingly at odds with the disillusioned inertia of its hero. Although, of course, Johnson has experienced the sort of life he is writing about, he has been at pains to point out that the book is not autobiographical.

Wild Cat Falling is one of an important trio of books that appeared in the 1960s dealing with the delinquent semi-underworld of what were then called bodgies and widgies. These were the boys and girls who, in their "sharp" clothes,

hung around favoured milk bars listening to rock and roll music on the juke box, dancing and committing petty crimes. The first book was Criena Rohan's *The Delinquents* (1962), followed by William Dick's *A Bunch of Ratbags,* and *Wild Cat Falling,* both of which were published in 1965.

The boy who is the hero of *Wild Cat Falling* (we never learn his name) has a part-Aboriginal mother and a white father who is dead. His world is not the cheerful community of Nene Gare's *The Fringe Dwellers* (1961), which is also about the substrata of Australian society. The boy's mother wants him to grow up white, to keep away from the old full-blood rabbiter ("I'm not interested in the old blackfella but I always get a bite if I mention him," says Johnson's hero), and not to play "with those dirty Noongar kids". They are "half-castes", some as light as the boy's mother, some "even as near white as me but most of them are pretty dark skinned". The boy tells his mother that some of the white children play with the Noongars: "That's different. They belong on the white side of the fence. You've got to prove you do, and don't forget it." The threat that always works is that "the welfare will be on to us again", and Mum will lose her pension and her good house and he will be taken away to one of those places ironically called "homes". (This was a threat that perpetually hung over Colin Johnson's own fatherless family. One by one his six sisters and brothers were taken away from his mother by the Child Welfare Department, until finally the turn came for his little sister Shirley and himself.)

Wild Cat Falling opens on the day the boy is released from Fremantle jail. "For me Fremantle jail has been a refuge of a sort. They have accepted me here as I have accepted hopelessness and futility." The difference between the boy and most of the other convicts and the group he hangs around with outside is that he is highly intelligent. In jail he has been reading Dostoyevsky and Tolstoy. When he gets out, the book that most appeals to him is *Waiting for Godot*.

The problem is that he has no mode of life into which he can gear this intelligence. He sums up the desolating experience of his education to a white girl he meets on the beach, a psychology student from the university: " 'I went to an ordinary school for a couple of years,' I tell her. 'There I learnt the art of survival against mob rule. Then I got copped for stealing and I was sent to a home where I was educated in the simple techniques of crime and learnt to survive the harshness of Christian charity. In the Noongar camps I learnt the art of being completely unexploitable and of sabotaging every make-believe effort to improve the native's lot. I also learnt to take raw alcohol and raw sex. In jail I graduated in vice and overcame my last illusions about life. Now I know that hope and despair are equally absurd.' "

I wake with a pounding heart and sit bolt upright, remembering. I've got to face the day and this hole I'm in. Can't stay here and talk to a crazy old nigger with all the cops in the district combing the bush for me. Got to get up and move on.

This bleak history of negative learning excludes love. The boy has a sort of affection for his mother, which later changes to contempt. This inability to love is partly due to an innate sense of rejection, a protective shell that has grown over every area of potential sensitivity, and partly to the bodgie way

of life. Yet even this is not altogether incompatible with love, as witness the deeply moving and tragic love story of the two young delinquents in Criena Rohan's novel.

When the boy gets out of jail, aged 19 yet still a boy, there is nowhere to go, nothing to do. Loneliness is his worst form of anguish, and the songs on the juke boxes are full of it. He goes back to the milk-bar crowd, despising them as morons, because of his loneliness. As for sex, it "is such a bore sometimes". But he is stirred by the body of the white girl on the beach, and realises that "jail has not killed my sex urge". He accepts her invitation to meet him again at the university.

He gets drunk and picks up with an old friend, a semi-prostitute called Denise, and listens to the juke box with her. " 'I've picked a couple of good numbers that'll cheer you up.' She's kidding me. The sad tune makes me ache with loneliness.

*". . . they'll never, oh never come back.
'Cause they're so lonely, oh so lonely,
They're so lonely they could die."*

He takes her to his room and they go to bed. "I want her and hate her for making me want her . . . Hate her. Hate her. Love her. It is finished. . . . why should this girl mean something to me? I want to be unmoved by everything—like a god."

There is indeed a glimpse of love, of meaning, visible again and again to the boy, but when he sees it he slams the door on it. In order to be a god he has to be indifferent, to keep saying "Who cares?", to cling to boredom. Because he must keep that indifference he has to say that questions bore him.

Nervously he goes to meet the psychology student. Arriving two hours early he hangs around the university espresso bar, then has a drink at a pub, wondering if he will be picked up for being under 21 and a half-caste without an exemption ticket. (Aborigines were still not allowed to drink in this period.) He goes back to the campus, wanders into the bookshop, starts to read *Waiting for Godot*. "We wait. We are bored. No, don't protest, we are bored to death, there's no denying it." He recognises the voice of a friend. He buys the book.

The girl he had met on the beach, whose name is June, introduces him to her circle of friends—students and artists. The boy, suspicious of being patronised, as intelligent as those asking him questions, quickly works out a psychological-sociological or artistic jargon suitable for whomever he is talking to. "This art jargon is a pushover once you have the key to the artist's mind."

He is asked to a party at the artist Dorian's loft that night at eight and says he will go. "They're not my crowd, but I suppose they're trying to make me feel at home and they're interesting in a way." As he has a greasy Greek meal in the evening, waiting for eight o'clock (he always seems to be waiting, in relation to the "real, big intellectuals"), he thinks about his bodgie mob.

I don't want to belong to them anymore. They are a pack of morons. Clueless, mindless idiots. What about this other mob? No good pretending I could ever belong with them, even if I imagined life would be any better if I did.

LIMBO *Robert Boynes*

COLIN JOHNSON
1938-

Colin Johnson was born at Narrogin, Western Australia, on 21 August 1938. His father died when he was very young, and Colin was the second youngest of seven children of a part-Aboriginal family. He describes his "first awareness" as of living in a two-room shack in Beverley, a small town in the wheatlands on the Perth-Narrogin road.

The Child Welfare Department took the children away from Beverley to be educated in Perth, where Colin spent eight years at Clontarf Boys Town in Victoria Park. He passed his Junior Certificate and got a job, but left it to hang around with the local "bodgies". He soon got into trouble, but was helped by Mary Durack and the Reverend Stan Davey of the Aboriginal Advancement League in Victoria, where he went to work for his matriculation, which he took (at night school) in 1966.

In Melbourne he joined in the literary and artistic life of the city, and became interested in Buddhism. He also continued to correspond with Mary Durack.

In 1963 the literary magazine *Westerly* held a story competition for writers of Aboriginal blood, and Johnson won it with a sketch of a boy leaving jail, which was part of a novel he was writing called *Wild Cat Falling*. This initial success set him to working hard on the book, and in a series of progress reports to Mary Durack in which he spoke of his character's "faulty perception of the world", he said:

I wanted the book to be a sort of *Pilgrim's Progress* rather than a particular person beset with his own separate problems . . . I am . . . making my character more positive in tone and altering his outlook a little, while keeping his ambiguities, false thinking and contradictions . . . the character I portray is not against the world—he thinks the world is against *him*.

In Melbourne Johnson began to orient himself to the Aboriginal community, and he attended the first National Convention of Aboriginal Advancement Leagues.

After the publication of *Wild Cat Falling* in 1965 (with an introduction by Mary Durack), he left on a trip through Asia to London in 1966. He studied at Buddhist monasteries in Thailand and travelled in Burma and India, where he said he felt more at home than in Australia. As he wrote to Mary Durack, "I feel very detached from what they call 'The Australian Way of Life'."

In 1968 he returned to Melbourne and got a job as library officer in the State Library. After saving up enough money he returned to India and made contact with the Maha Bodhi Society in Calcutta, where he worked in their library and helped edit their English language journal. Johnson became a Buddhist monk in 1970, but re-entered more mundane society in 1974 to resume writing.

He received a Literature Board Grant in 1976 and used it to write a novel about the Aboriginal freedom fighter known as Pigeon. This was *Long Live Sandawarra* (1979). A novel about the Tasmanian Aborigines, *Dr Wooreddy's Prescription for Enduring the End of the World*, was published in 1983.

Johnson visited America in 1976-77 and attended the Commonwealth Literature Conference in Bayreuth, Germany, in 1983. He was writer-in-residence at Murdoch University in 1982, and part-time tutor in Aboriginal Studies at Koorie College in Northcote, Victoria, in 1983. In 1984 he was awarded a Churchill Fellowship.

Maybe they are really as bored in their way as I am in mine . . . If I let up a minute on my mental discipline it creeps in again suggesting there might be something in life besides absurdity—even a hint of meaning. I have to shout it out because it is a liar. It is the most dangerous illusion of all. Except maybe love!

This is the turning point of the book. If the boy had not so carefully constructed this bitter persona, stiffened with absurdity (learned from reading existential writers such as Camus), he could have joined the "big intellectuals", the artists and the bohemians, and done something with his brains. But when June urges him to apply for a scholarship all he can do is retreat to an attitude of "So what?" He thinks, or forces himself to think, that it is too late. (This, incidentally, is the major difference between the boy and Colin Johnson, who did not think it was too late.)

He ends up in bed with one of the students, hating it. There is no refuge anywhere. The last section of the book is called "Return", but it is a despairing notion of return.

The boy and an old jail mate steal a car, and pull a crude job in the boy's home town. He shoots a policeman. Running for shelter he is taken in by the old full-blood Aborigine, the rabbiter, whom his mother had warned him against. He is his great-uncle.

By his dignity and genuine charity the old man at last gives the boy an idea of belonging to his own country, and shames him when he steals his bowl of coins by offering them to him anyway. When the boy gives himself up to the police there is at last a hint of meaning to his life. He says to himself, "Why not stick around and face up to something for a change?"

No one ever made me feel this way before. No one. Not the magistrate, or the probation officer, or the brothers with all that thunder about the eye of God. Not even my Mum's suffering face.

Taken out of context, this might make it appear that the author is delivering a moral lecture to his hero. But after the purgatory of the boy's life, this final decision remains convincing.

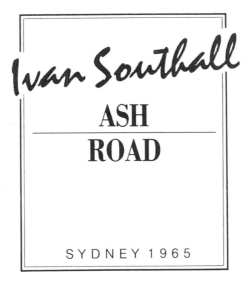

Ivan Southall

ASH
ROAD

SYDNEY 1965

Peter wondered what time it was. It was not something he had to know; it was only part of his restlessness and anxiety. He didn't know whether it was seven o'clock or eight o'clock or later. The summer sun was deceptive. It was so high in the sky so soon in the day.

It was hard to say exactly what thought was uppermost in Peter's mind, for he was unable to concentrate on any one thing long enough. He knew he had to go home to Gramps but the longer he delayed the act the harder the decision to move off became. He feared the consequences of his break with Pippa but was reluctant to try to mend it in case the rift became worse. He knew it was not yet ten-thirty, when the Buckinghams would leave for Deer Sands—if they were to go at all—so the point of urgency when he had to find Pippa had not arrived. He was suspicious of the intentions of the unknown boy hiding somewhere in the bush behind him but didn't have the courage to turn back to face him. Facing people was much harder than following them. And he was frightened of the sky. It was so threatening, so ugly, so unlike anything he had ever seen. It was a hot brown mantle over the earth with pieces breaking off it, little black pieces of ash; an oppressive mantle that did not prevent the penetration of the sun's heat but imprisoned it, added to it, and magnified the hostility of the day.

It was an angry day; not just wild or rough, but savage in itself, actively angry against every living thing. It hated plants and trees and birds and animals, and they wilted from its hatred or withered up and died or panted in distress in shady places. Above all, it hated Peter. It seemed to encompass him with a malevolence that would strike him down if he ventured to defy it. There was a wall around him, an invisible wall that confined him to a few square yards of hot, dusty earth at the bottom of the Georges' carrot paddock. He longed to burst out, to seek the shade like the birds and other creatures, to drink a long draught of cool water, but he couldn't move.

The day was so angry with him that he was frightened to raise a hand against it.

In the house it was dark behind drawn blinds, and less hot, and Lorna said there was a jug of lemon water chilled in the refrigerator. Pippa had difficulty finding it; there was no light inside the refrigerator and everything was so gloomy. When she flicked the switch on the wall the light in the ceiling didn't come on either. Eventually she took a glass of lemon water into Lorna's bedroom and said, "Do you want this, or would you rather have tea?"

Lorna drank the lemon water.

"What about breakfast?" said Pippa. "Have you had any yourself?"

Lorna nodded.

"What about a plate of cornflakes or something?"

"No. But if you cook something I'll eat it with you to keep you company."

"You're to stay where you are—unless you want to take a bath."

Lorna smiled wanly. "You mean I should take a bath?"

"It's bound to help you pull yourself together. Particularly if it's a warm one."

"I suppose so." Lorna lowered her feet from the bed to the floor. "Perhaps I will, and change my clothes."

"Yes," said Pippa. "I'll run it for you."

"It's a kerosene heater, Pippa. It's so slow and makes a dreadful noise. It's not like yours."

"I'll manage."

"I'd rather do it myself. You might blow the place up. And I'd rather you tried to get a message through to John."

"Yes," said Pippa. "I'll do it now."

"Do have your breakfast first."

"Don't be silly. I wouldn't dream of it."

"You're very good, Pippa."

"Don't say that. I don't feel good at all."

Talking wasn't easy. It would have been better not to have tried. They had gone through a raw time together and hadn't got over it. Lorna was nerve-racked and weak. It was too soon to forget the desperation and the pain: much too soon. She felt as if her soul had been stripped in front of Pippa, and she was still embarrassed, still faintly humiliated. For Pippa, though a friend, was not an intimate friend. Lorna had not an intimate friend in the whole world. She needed time to get her dignity back, time for the aches of her heart and head and body to heal a little, to be washed over by fresh events. And Pippa, with unusual intuition, all but guessed the state of Lorna's mind. Indeed, she needed time herself to recover from the bewilderment of confronting, for the first time in her life, a fellow human-being in an hour of cruel crisis. Anguish had never touched Pippa's life before. It shocked her.

"I'll ring the fire brigade first," Pippa said. "And if they don't answer I might try the vicar."

"Oh," said Lorna.

"What is it?"

"I should have thought of the vicar before."

"Goodness. I don't know how you thought of everything that you did think of."

Only someone who has been close to a big bushfire can know what it is like unless he or she has read *Ash Road*.

Fire is the evil genius of the novel. Its presence dominates almost from the first page, but at first it is a monster no one wants to believe in. Having briefly declared itself by accident, it hides itself behind the ranges; only wary old men can scent its coming in the air before the smoke shows.

Even when the smoke rolls over the hills, children believe that grown-ups will take care of the fire, get it under control. But pig-headed old men with a job to do, such as picking the raspberry crop, ignore it. Quite sensible men and women are muddled and then panic. Those faithful servants of technology—telephones, electricity, motor cars—suddenly leave their masters in the lurch. Then, as the danger comes closer, people's true characters are revealed. It takes a fine novelist to convey all this. Although *Ash Road* is classified as a children's book, Ivan Southall's perceptions and dramatic sense and narrative skills are those of a writer for all ages.

Ash Road begins, ironically, with the happiness and exhilaration of three 15-year-old boys off on their own on a camping hike, individuals at last, free from the direction of home and school, flushed with elation, "too excited to speak logically". Graham, the weakest but the most imaginative of the three boys, has for a flowing moment a vision of life as a whole with himself separate but belonging, "one of those rare moments when all the things of heaven and earth are private and personal property".

It is the joyful freedom that lets loose the terrible freedom of fire. It is a fiercely hot and windy day as the boys walk along the road by the foothills where the grass and small trees run up to the wild gullies and great forests of the mountains. They light a fire by the road to boil a billy and grill some sausages. A woman stops her car and rebukes them severely, telling them to put the fire out. The boys do so, but are resentful at having to eat buns and drink cold water.

It was an angry day; not just wild or rough, but savage in itself, actively angry against every living thing. It hated plants and trees and birds and animals, and they wilted from its hatred or withered up and died or panted in distress in shady places. Above all, it hated Peter.

So in the little town of Tinley they buy a tiny stove that burns methylated spirits. That evening they cook their meal and go happily to bed. It is hot in the sleeping bags, and Graham wakes at about one am and boils some water for coffee. Wallace wakes and joins him while Harry sleeps on. Graham reaches for the saucepan lid and in the dark knocks over the uncorked metho bottle. Blue flame runs up to the bottle, Graham instinctively throws it away. The bushfire has started. The boys run for their lives.

On the other side of the ranges, 23 kilometres away by road, 9 or 10 in a straight line, is Ash Road with its straggling houses, little farms and potato paddocks.

Ivan Southall is one of those companionable novelists who lets the reader get to know all his characters, from grandfathers to babies. We care what happens to them, even the tiresome ones. He is a realist with a very clear idea of the results that follow certain actions, and even when the sky is clouded by smoke and falling ash events still take place in the clear light of his style.

The oldest house, dating from the turn of the century, belongs to Grandpa Tanner. The Fairhalls are retired farmers with a secret source of income, living in a house that was built in about 1919. An orchard and a nursery date from the 1920s and 1930s. Then there are the post-war settlers: the Robertsons, the Georges, the Pinkards and the Buckinghams. The Georges grow carrots and raspberries; the old man is a tyrant to his children, John who is a young man, and Lorna who is in her teens.

The Buckinghams, who are going on holidays, have five-year-old Julie, who floods the house and drains the tanks playing boats in the bath, and runs away in guilt to hide. Her brother Stevie is nine, her sister Pippa is in her teens. Peter Fairhall is an only grandchild and too conscious of it, seeing himself as a molly-coddled kid.

Grandpa Tanner "could smell eucalyptus smoke on the wind from a fire burning fifteen or twenty miles away; he could smell it and feel it and see it with his eyes shut, with tingling senses, with an awareness that was electric". *He* knows there is a bad fire somewhere, and it is the worst sort of day for a fire. He remembers the fire that wiped out Prescott in 1913.

The Fairhalls take the fire seriously and tell Peter, to his shame, that he must be sent home. Most of the others begin to take it seriously only when the siren begins to wail. "There was something about a siren that welled up from the inside. It was almost like being sick."

With the threat of fire, all the children want something different. Peter longs to be able to go and fight the fire like John George who is lieutenant of the local emergency fire service. Little Stevie wants to go and look at it. Pippa wants desperately to find her little sister Julie, who has in fact taken refuge with Grandpa Tanner. Lorna wants to help her father pick raspberries. But suddenly he collapses in the heat with a stroke. She cannot get a doctor or an ambulance—they are at the fire.

Huge Gramps Fairhall, slow and ponderous, joins his wife as usual for a large breakfast at six am. They hear on the wireless that this is no ordinary fire, but a fire that is threatening hundreds of homes and several towns.

As Lorna is trying to get help for her father, there is a knock at the door. It is the three boys who had started the fire, looking for the Pinkards with whom they had been going to stay. They are now looking for somewhere to hide, singed, footsore, trembling with guilt. They agree unwillingly to help Lorna. Peter sees their haversacks by the road and in a flash of intuition knows that they are the missing boys of whom the radio announcer had spoken.

Southall brilliantly creates a world within many levels of awareness, especially among the children; awareness of each other and of the as yet unseen menace of the fire. Emotions are aroused, ranging from fear and suspicion to incipient love. Characters are not fixed but tremble like heatwaves in the air, influenced by the fire, and by the mysterious "they" who are putting up road blocks, evacuating towns, making puny efforts to fight the fire. The fire is already too big, even for thousands of volunteers.

THE FIRE *Rosamund Heritage*

IVAN SOUTHALL
1921-

Ivan Southall was born on 8 June 1921 at Canterbury, Victoria, and grew up in Surrey Hills, also in Victoria. He sold newspapers as a boy and was educated at Chatham State and Mont Albert Central School and at Box Hill Grammar. His father, a former Presbyterian Home Missionary, died when he was 14, and Ivan went out to work washing bottles and glassware. He had written stories when living at Surrey Hills, and when he got a job as a copy boy at the Melbourne *Herald* he hoped to become a journalist.

However, he was then apprenticed as a photo engraver and had to be a spare-time writer. He completed four books before he was 20, three of which were published after the war.

During the war he joined the RAAF and became a pilot and flew 57 missions in Sunderland flying boats in the Battle of the Atlantic. He was awarded the DFC in 1944.

He was married in London in 1945, and, returning to Australia in 1947, decided to become a full-time writer. To support his wife and infant son he travelled round East Brighton, Victoria, in his Austin with a lawn mower, cutting lawns. In 1950 he and his family went to live at Monbulk, supplementing his income by delivering produce to Victoria Markets in Melbourne two days a week, rising at 1.30 am and working until 5 pm.

Between 1956 and 1962 he published books on the RAF, the RAAF, and the RN, and one on the Woomera rocket range.

He has now published more than 50 books, about 30 for children; his own four children are now grown up.

Ivan Southall has won the Australian Children's Book of the Year Award four times, with *Ash Road*, *To the Wild Sky*, *Bread and Honey*, and *Fly West*. *Josh* received the Carnegie Medal in Britain. Other books have received honours in Japan, Holland, Austria and the USA. His work has been translated into 22 languages. He was made a Member of the Order of Australia in 1981.

Let the Balloon Go was made into a film by Film Australia.

Southall has travelled extensively and has lectured about children's books in Australia and overseas. He was Poetry and Literature Lecturer at the Library of Congress, Washington, DC in 1973, and lectured for the American Library Association in 1974.

Southall has been a Methodist lay preacher and there is a strong spiritual optimism beneath most of his books. He describes his recreation in *Who's Who* as "daydreaming". He likes to do things with his hands, and is constantly altering the houses he lives in. He enjoys gardening and likes to grow his own food.

Those who try to get away do not succeed. Graham leaves the other boys but has to hide by a creek. Gramps Fairhall's car battery is flat. With the help of Wallace and Harry, Lorna gets her father into his car, but then cannot find the key. But now the sky is full of ash.

Gramps finally gets his car going with the help of the milkman, and after initial complaints agrees to drive Lorna's father to the Miltondale hospital. To Peter, hiding at the bottom of the Georges' carrot paddock, the day is angry, "not just wild or rough, but savage in itself, actively angry against every living thing".

The section of *Ash Road* that follows, Gramps's epic drive in his old car with Wallace and Harry in an attempt to get the stroke-silent Mr George to the Miltondale hospital, is the most exciting in the book. More than that, it is a fine example of the novelist's art, of revealing characters in action. Gramps, hitherto a rather unattractive grumpy old man who has run to fat, takes on a new life and purpose as he charges past astonished policemen at road blocks and draws on 40 years experience of the road to drive, in short-sighted euphoria, at high speed through the smoke-filled forest with headlights blazing. Finally he drives right through the fire.

Gramps's voice intruded suddenly. "Wind up the windows! Jump to it!"

It was the voice of command, and their hands leapt to obey. Then they saw flames to the right, flames at tree-top height exploding like surf on rocks: waves of flame, torrents of flame, flame spraying in fragments, in thousands of pieces, in flaring leaves and twigs that rained on to the road in a storm of fire. It was upon them in seconds, or they had come upon it so swiftly that there was no turning from it: no time to turn, no chance to turn, no place to turn.

Southall's technique in *Ash Road* is to switch from one group to another. This heightens the tension. While Gramps and the boys are walking, carrying old man George, from the abandoned car to Miltondale, Lorna finds Graham, almost unconscious with exhaustion and forces him (for he would have been burned to death where he was on the edge of the forest) to go with her. Something like love grows between them.

Gramps and the boys reach the outskirts of Miltondale and meet Buckingham, who tells them that the town has been burned out and the hospital has been evacuated. Old man George dies. Grandpa Tanner lowers Julie in a chair and the Robertson baby in a basket down the well and covers it over, then wraps himself in a wet blanket. Pippa gets Stevie down to the Georges' where she hopes they will be able to sit under the sprinklers, but the pump has run out of fuel and the sprinklers are not working. Peter grows towards manhood as he searches for and finds his distraught Gran and pulls and pushes her into a pool. The fire goes through, a terrible fire so hot that it "burned minutes before it arrived".

The book ends with an explosion of rain. As Grandpa Tanner pulls the sheets of corrugated iron off the well, Julie yells as instructed, "Here I am everybody. Down the well. Safe and sound."

Ash Road is a subtle chronicle of the slide from safety into terror, and the mental and spiritual adaptations of young and old to the unimaginable calamity that has descended on them. The fire is enjoying its freedom, like a horrible parody of the boys at the beginning of the book; it is up to each individual not to be made a prisoner of fear.

Geoffrey Blainey

THE TYRANNY OF DISTANCE

MELBOURNE 1966

Sailing ships still had the marked advantage of paying nothing for the power that moved them. None of their cargo space was occupied by engine room and coal bunkers. They were cheaper to construct and, on the Australian route, cheaper to operate than steamships. It was true that steamships were slowly becoming more competitive, but one of the steamships' vital technical advances was shared also by sailing ships. In the many shipyards which still built sailing vessels, iron was replacing timber as the main material.

The use of iron helped sailing ships to resist the challenge of steam. An iron sailing ship was cheaper to build than a wooden sailing ship. The framework or skeleton of an iron ship was less bulky, freeing more space for the carrying of cargo. An iron clipper, unlike a wooden clipper, was relatively watertight. Though the iron bottoms of ships became fouled and encrusted, thus increasing the resistance of the water and thereby slowing the speed of the ship, the iron bottom could be periodically scraped clean in a dock.

Iron clippers in the 1860s became the sturdy work-horses of the Europe-Australia route. They were not designed for record passages, nor did they make them, but they were cheap carriers of all kinds of cargo. The rows of Glasgow-built iron clippers which could be seen in Melbourne or Sydney no longer drew crowds of fascinated spectators to the harbour on Sundays, and yet their captains and sailors were probably worthier of hero worship than the crews of any other kind of ship which ever traded with Australia. For the iron clippers were not as buoyant as wooden ships, they did not ride the waves so neatly, and in the wild seas which so often ran between the Cape of Good Hope and Cape Horn they were battered and deluged. Any reader of Australian newspapers in the 1860s would have observed, if he read the long column of daily shipping news, that the so-called "iron clipper ships" were usually pummelled on the last leg of the passage to Australia. The maiden voyage of the iron clipper Melpomene, built at Port Glasgow for the Australian trade, was typical of the ordeal which iron sailing ships faced in the Southern Ocean in winter. Running before the wind in August 1869, she was overtaken by a huge wave which smashed the wheel and broke every spoke. Huge waves washed away the binnacle and compass and hencoops. Several times the sea ran so high that the maindeck was filled with water and the new cabins were flooded, and the men who were exposed at the wheel to the seas breaking on deck were lucky to remain aboard. Even though iron clippers avoided the high latitudes and the old Great Circle route of the 1850s, preferring instead the slightly fairer weather of the zone of latitude from 40° to 45° south, they could not evade punishment.

The subtitle of Professor Blainey's book is "How Distance Shaped Australia's History". His concept of distance includes both exterior distance, in particular Australia's remoteness from Europe and America, and interior distance, which imposed peculiar difficulties on the development of all Australia's industries.

The Tyranny of Distance is of course an invaluable book for students of Australian history, but its wider success is in its quality as literature, the excellence of its prose style being allied to an imaginative use of facts. As well as expounding his theories concerning distance, Blainey positively enjoys telling his readers about winds and engines, about ships and bullock drays, charts and rail gauges. These practical matters were not only problems for the professionals who dealt with them, but they also affected the lives of inland workers who had never seen a ship, or graziers who had to wait three years for a cheque for their wool.

Until the connection of Australia to London by telegraph in 1872 all news had to come by ship. Often decisions were made in London which were quite out of step with what was happening in Australia. Blainey gives the tragi-comic instance of Raffles Bay, north of what is now Darwin. It was established as a fort and trading post to make contact with the fleets of Indonesian proas that visited Australia annually to gather trepang. It was also hoped that Raffles Bay would become a port of refreshment for trading ships on the Torres Strait route from Sydney to India. For months no sail was seen, and the garrison fell sick with scurvy. As a result of a report from Raffles Bay written in October 1827, the British decided to withdraw. This order reached Raffles Bay in August 1829, by which time large fleets of trepang traders had paid visits.

Despite the hazards of the Torres Strait route many ships used it. Blainey gives the incredible story of an Indian shipowner and master William Bampton, who in 1793 brought a large ship into Sydney with a valuable cargo from Bombay. The Governor persuaded Bampton to return to India and bring back cattle, pork or beef, and rice. It took him 72 days to cross the Great Barrier Reef and to negotiate Torres Strait. His contract for the shipment specified 10 months; it was 25 before he returned.

This early example of the colony waiting over two years

for urgently needed supplies is typical of the whole story of Blainey's book. Flockowners waiting up to three years for news of, or the proceeds from, the sale of their wool have already been mentioned.

And during these years of waiting for an income the sheepowner had to pay his shepherds, shearers, the men who carted his wool to port and carried back his supplies, the shipowner who arranged the freight of the wool to England, and an endless variety of agents, storekeepers, contractors, merchants and employees of one sort or another. A sheepowner had to be a small capitalist even if only to borrow the money he needed.

Blainey draws the reasonable conclusion that if Australia had occupied the geographic position of the USA, then the wool industry "would not have been so markedly an industry for wealthy men".

Sailing ships still had the marked advantage of paying nothing for the power that moved them. None of their cargo space was occupied by engine room and coal bunkers. They were cheaper to construct and, on the Australian route, cheaper to operate than steamships.

The constant pressure on ship designers and captains for speeding up communications with London and elsewhere leads Blainey into an area where beauty and practicability coincided, in those American and British clipper ships that made more and more amazing times from London to Melbourne and back. Their names are still exciting: *Lightning, Thermopylae, Cutty Sark.* It also leads him into the wild waters of high latitudes, to previously uninhabited islands, like Kerguelen and Heard Island and the McDonalds, on the Great Circle route that led from London to Tristan da Cunha to Melbourne in the 1850s, when captains used the technology of the Towson chronometer to follow what had long been recognised as the quickest way round the world—the curve of the globe. These ships used the charts of Matthew Fontaine Maury, who constantly collated reports from sailing masters and who regarded the sailing ship as "a floating observatory or a temple of science".

Wool Drays *S. T. Gill*

Some of these ships made amazing runs of more than 640 kilometres in a day. The Roaring Forties must have tried the nerves of many a passenger, not to mention the sailors themselves. Blainey, with that typical mixture of scientific curiosity and the ability to be involved in the spirit of time and place that makes his work so readable, presents the evidence of an extraordinary old man, Dr William Scoresby, on the problems of the clippers on their Australian voyages.

Scoresby was a whaler and explorer in the Arctic who became a clergyman and scientist. In 1856 he embarked at the age of 65 on the iron clipper, *Royal Charter*, for Melbourne. He believed, with reason, that the iron of the new ships affected the compass, and every day he climbed to the mizzen masthead to take readings from his own compass, which up there would be free of the ship's magnetic influence. This "frail thin old clergyman", in Blainey's words, must have been uncommonly tough to have climbed that mast in wild seas. He describes one bad storm as having seas that were bigger than any he had ever seen in the northern hemisphere, and which also rolled from two other quarters into the main line of waves breaking in the gale.

Old Dr Scoresby watched, with alternate feelings of awe and scientific detachment, the four men keeping the ship's wheel in active play, the captain standing a few paces away.

While Blainey shows how Australia's history was affected by the time ships took to cross the world to and from Australia, he also follows the growth and difficulties of inland transport. Owing to the proximity of the Great Dividing Range to the east coast, all the eastern-flowing rivers are short and initially fast-flowing. The Murray and the Darling opened up the interior, but these winding, snag-ridden, sandbank-crowded rivers could never fulfil the functions of the Mississippi. Then the railways came, in the most absurd mix of different gauges. Melbourne's first Professor of Engineering, W. C. Kernot, called them "the most lamentable engineering disaster in Australia". Lord Kitchener observed in 1910 that the broken railway network seemed "more favourable to any enemy invading Australia than to the defence of the country".

Blainey explains how it all happened in terms of access to sea transport. The railways initially existed to link inland areas with the nearest port. At this time there was little call for an Adelaide-Melbourne-Sydney railway. Blainey has a splendid eye for detail. He gives a telling example of the differences between the various States in his description of the governors and dignitaries, 1016 people in all, meeting at a great banquet at Albury in 1883 to celebrate the joining of the two rail systems—the Melbourne guests wore morning dress, the Sydney guests wore evening dress.

Without ever losing sight of his major theme, Blainey again and again picks up this sort of detail. For instance, he notices, when discussing the extremely important development of shipping frozen meat and butter to England in 1879, that in the goldrush days of the 1850s enterprising Americans were exporting ice to Melbourne.

On 14 October 1858, for example, the sailing ship *Alma* reached Melbourne from Boston, U.S.A., with a cargo of lumber, lobsters, four cases of pain-killer, and 531 tons

CLIPPER SHIP *THYATIRA* ENTERING SYDNEY HEADS *Artist unknown*

GEOFFREY BLAINEY
1930-

Geoffrey Blainey was born on 11 March 1930 in Melbourne, his mother having gone there from Terang to have him. Geoffrey's father, the Reverend S. C. Blainey, was the Methodist minister at Terang.

Blainey writes: "All my eight great-grandparents were in Victoria at the time of the 1850s gold rushes, and all the men dug for gold. My father's side of the family stayed in mining, and my grandfather worked underground at Bendigo and then became a mine engine-driver—at Boulder City and Bendigo—and also managed a little mine in the old Straits Settlement for Chinese owners. My father became a Methodist minister, that great Bendigo occupation."

Blainey is one of the most eminent of Australian historians, but he says he read no Australian books until he was 13 or 14, and that there were very few in his parents' house. He writes, "There was no school library in any Government school I went to; the first good library we belonged to was the Ballarat Mechanics Institute. Interestingly we lived four years in Ballarat and one sensed there was history around, and I was interested in history, but I never set eyes on a Ballarat history nor were we taught even a sentence of Ballarat history."

When he was 13 he went on a scholarship to Wesley College. A. A. Phillips was his English master and interested him in Australian literature, and he also learnt a lot of Australian history at Wesley. He took an Arts degree with honours at the University of Melbourne, and edited the university magazine, most of which he wrote himself.

In 1950 he became a freelance writer specialising in Australian history; the only one, he thinks. In that year he went to Tasmania and worked for the Mt Lyell Mining and Railway Company, and wrote a book about the company history, *Peaks of Lyell* (1954).

This was followed by books on Mt Isa and Broken Hill, and a history of Australian mining, *The Rush That Never Ended* (1963) These years of practical experience of mining gave him a unique perspective among Australian historians, and Blainey still occasionally writes articles for the press, or gives interviews, trying to explain some of the realities of, and misconceptions about, mining in Australia.

In 1962 he was appointed Senior Lecturer in Economic History at the University of Melbourne, and was Professor of Economic History there 1968-77, when he became the Ernest Scott Professor of History. He was a member—and the last Chairman—of the Advisory Board of the Commonwealth Literary Fund 1967-73, and Chairman of the Literature Board of the Australia Council 1973-74, and Chairman of the Australia Council 1977-81.

Writing in the *Sydney Morning Herald* (9 July 1977) Lenore Nicklin described him as "honest, unegotistical, an eloquent persuader in argument".

He was Chairman of the Australia China Council from 1979 to 1984.

The Tyranny of Distance was published in 1966. *Triumph of the Nomads*, about the early history of the Aborigines, appeared in 1975, and a further book on Australian history in relation to Australians and their environment, *A Land Half Won*, was published in 1980.

In 1982 he wrote and narrated a television history of Australia, *The Blainey View*. In an interview at the time he said, "It is very satisfying to reach a new audience, one which by and large doesn't read books, and to see the pleasures they get out of something about their history."

In 1984-85 he was both strongly attacked and supported for his views on Asian immigration.

Blainey has never been a narrow academic historian, though there is nothing lacking in his scholarship. His words about writing history are very relevant to his own work: "Your platform of judgement is fragile if your experience is narrow."

Blainey is married, and has a daughter. He gives his recreation in *Who's Who* as "chopping wood". He was awarded the Order of Australia in 1975.

---

of ice that had been cut from the Boston ponds. Though the ship had been at sea more than one hundred days and had passed through the tropics, most of the ice was still ice when it was hustled to city saloons.

Blainey gives fresh perspectives to Australian history by such insights as perceiving the long-range effects of changes in technology. Until 1900 or thereabouts Australia was self-supporting in its energy needs. Sailing ships needed no fuel, river boats used wood and steamships and railways used local coal. Wood fed the steam plants of sawmills and mines, horses and bullocks ate grass. "Virtually the only fuel which Australia had to import was the illuminant, kerosene, a product of United States oil refineries."

The shift to oil meant that Australia lost its self-sufficiency. This was crucial during the war years and in the expansion of the economy that followed. Fortunately the discovery of large oil reserves in the 1960s has saved the day.

Blainey writes in a straightforward, clear style, but he has a pleasant gift for the epigram. For example, early Sydney, that could not feed itself, Blainey describes as being "like a wounded seabird, stranded on a lonely rock". He sees the early development of small industries as intimately related to problems of distance, in the time taken, the expense, and the risk of deterioration in ordering such goods from England: "The ocean was Australia's first tariff wall."

He ends his book by suggesting that one of the dangers of distance is that an intellectual tariff wall still exists, or existed until recently. "Australians' chief blindness to the changing world in which they lived was blindness to what had happened to Britain." Even after the fall of Singapore people did not believe in Britain's decline as a world power. Yet in the last 40 years the decline of British influence has become more obvious; as has Australia's tendency to look towards America in many fields of policy and culture. And Blainey's last finding cannot be challenged. "Distance has been visibly tamed in the last quarter century, but it has not been conquered."

Peter Mathers

TRAP

MELBOURNE 1966

Today Trap had a bad headache. He refused to stay with me. I hurried with him along the street, towards home. For some reason we walked on the eastern side and the sunlight struck at us. Our heels sank in the fresh patches of footpath bitumen. Trap said:

What you bastards don't want is anyone who's not the sun-bronzed digger type. So most of us Abos are out. So are the short, thick Greeks and Italians and Poms. And do you really think there are many of these ideal diggers? My arse. I'll tell you this—there's not many of us, but we're getting the guts of things. And if we can't coax concessions from you we'll try battery and if this doesn't work we'll go all cunning—I know we should try this angle right from the start, but things don't just work out the way you'd expect.

He amazed me.

Do you, I demanded, yourself, love your fellows? The bright and stupid, fat and thin?

He stared morosely at the ground.

He turned right abruptly at the next intersection.

I am not frightened of Trap so much as the awakened consciousness of Trap's kind.

A host of Trapists is awful to imagine.

He has just telephoned:

A couple of Coms tried to get me to join them, once.

I'm not the joining sort, I said.

Your army days, they said, didn't you enjoy the comradeship, the idealism, the adventure?

I wasn't in the Army or the Navy or the Air Force. I was CCC.

Well, they said, it's all the same.

I keep to myself, I said.

That can be dangerous, they said.

I'll think about it, I said.

And I did, I thought a lot about it. They decided that my goal in life was to have a little corner shop, to become a black bourgeois. But at the time, and long after, what I wanted was to be left alone. To wear my skin without fear—and it wasn't fear of physical violence. Sneers, I dreaded. To avoid the casual glance I watched the ground. My method had its reward for I found quite a lot of money.

Without much trouble I could imagine myself in my father's skin.

Fair warning about Trap is given very early in the book that bears his name. "Trap eh. So it's old Jack you're interested in? . . . You go to him a reasonable conservative sort, a defender of established things and you leave fermenting with ideas of—wait for it—anarchism, nihilism, Buddhism, allisms and wild, general revolt." These words come from Nina, "the most outstanding social worker I have ever met". She is talking to the "I" of the book, David David, also a social worker, an earnest yet susceptible young man of 25 on whose diaries and conversations with Trap and others the book is based.

Though the style of *Trap*, however ebullient, is perfectly straightforward, the novel has a complex structure. This is necessary because the novel not only tells the story of Trap himself but also of his strange mixture of ancestors, who in themselves provide an alternative history of Australia. The novel begins and ends with David David's diary for May. (The year is not mentioned, but it would seem to be in the late 1950s.) After the diary entry for 2 May, the entries return to 1 April and continue through April, until the last short diary entry which is for 3 May.

Trap, "about forty and running to fat", was, we learn about 60 pages later, born in Balmain in 1916 of parents who were both part-Aboriginal. Ironically, his father "did not look the slightest bit Aboriginal. This was his shame. He lamented his paleness." Whereas Sarah, Jack's mother, was "a dark sheila" who looked her colour. Jackie obviously has a "touch of the tar brush". "God, Jackie, she'd say. I don't know how I came to have you. You'd never credit it. You're as dark as night."

Although Jack's father Wilson, a militant radical, was in prison at the time of his birth ("Arson, sabotage, anarchy, nihilism—something like that") Jack is given a good education: ". . . there was always someone to say: Well, just listen to the lah-di-dah boong Abo." He leaves school at 14 and is apprenticed to a joinery and metal works, and he is proud of his skills in these trades.

But Trap is more complicated than the label "literate tradesman" would suggest. He is the product of his past, and much of the novel is devoted to re-creating the past, which is as alive as the present and thoroughly subversive of the prosperous, comfortable bourgeois values of Australia in the 1950s. Mathers' originality in *Trap* is to create a hero whose nonconformism seems perfectly natural, outrageous at times but neither capricious nor doctrinaire. Though the theme of racism is integral to the book, Mathers is not crusading for the Aborigines, nor is Trap a champion of the workers. He is, rather, an embodiment of his turbulent past, of the possibilities that are bubbling away beneath the double-breasted, pin-striped stately image of Australia in the age of Menzies.

The diarist and part-narrator, David David, is skilfully

311

integrated into this dangerous history of subversion. He is an amiable young man who would like to get on in the world and be a pillar of society, but exposure to Trap and his origins gradually corrupts him. At the end of the book he commits a violently anti-social act which, ironically, is the sort of thing Trap has warned him against, "unchannelled dissent".

Trap has been called anarchic, but its anarchy gives an injection of life, something like insulin; it is not an aim in itself. It is Trap's word that counts, his example that has to be watched. Long ago he had learned worldly, as well as intellectual, wisdom from his mentor, the Reverend Oswald Potts, later unfrocked, who had sheltered Jack and his mother for the five years his father was in gaol. Early in the book David notes in his diary for 3 April, "Trap, I realise, is an anti-social black racialist bent on destroying the power of civilisation." But David was still very naive when he wrote that.

Before the novel opens, there is a list of major characters which immediately recalls the list that precedes Xavier Herbert's *Capricornia*. The names, with descriptions, are often larger than life but pointing clearly towards certain satirical possibilities. Colonel Sancty-Mony, pioneer pastoralist whose descendants prefer to call themselves Santymony; R. G. Free-Rutt, young businessman; Turnbuckle, Hobart merchant. The name "Trap" itself is fraught with possibilities, several of them suggested within the first few pages of the book:

> Trap. God what a name. Rhymes with crap. American word inelegant but succinct. Equals our demotic bullshit or genteel bulldust. Crap: don't crap me; what a load of c— etc. Crap: a game. All Trap's life has been a bloody clumsy game. Crap is something to be expelled, cast out.

They decided that my goal in life was to have a little corner shop, to become a black *bourgeois. But at the time, and long after, what I wanted was to be left alone. To wear my skin without fear—and it wasn't fear of physical violence.*

Later on a more sinister association becomes apparent when Trap's old partner in a mobile trades business takes on the government contract for making scaffolds, Victoria still being a hanging State. The operation of the trap later gets Trap into trouble. And there are other, unspoken, connotations, such as "Shut your trap," or the trap that is akin to prison, with a variety of which Trap is familiar. And, a comic paradox, the police in the nineteenth century were called traps. Finally, clearly a warning, there is the expression, "a trap for young players". Truly, things in *Trap* are not always what they seem.

The book opens with Trap, the subversive, going north to Naraki Mission on Cape York, where a giant consortium is about to mine an unspecified ore; a motley band of followers is to accompany him. They are going to camp near the mine and make contact with his people, the local Aborigines, who feel they have been betrayed and sold out. But behind the scenes Mrs Nathan, chairman of the immensely powerful Circle Investments which is in control of the Naraki venture, is afraid of Trap's influence but she wants to use him.

> As a gesture of goodwill towards our country's Aborigines my company would like to have him at Naraki. We feel that pioneering would suit him down to the ground.

Trap is on remand for assaulting the manager of a shoe factory, but Mrs Nathan is confident that thanks to the influence of Circle Investments, and the promise of getting him out of the State, Trap will be bound over. She wants to use David as a contact with Trap. David is innocent enough to be flattered; he also finds her attractive, and her wealth irresistible.

One of the many subjects revealed as David meets Trap and talks to people who know him is the city of Melbourne itself. In the 1960s many critics were asking for a novel of the city, that environment where most Australians live. Indirectly, *Trap* answered the need. Through Trap's behaviour the novel is a protest against bourgeois predictability; it is also a plea for unreconstituted, untidy city life; against both bourgeois respectability and bourgeois trendiness, against red-brick veneer and against tarted-up terraces.

David talks to a wide variety of people, white and part-Aboriginal. Nina tells him about Jack's wife Sally, and her niece Maisie and Eb Cruxtwist, the Lothario foreman of the shoe factory. Trap takes over the story of the iniquitous Cruxtwist; at least there is the minor satisfaction that Maisie gave him crabs.

As David reports back to Mrs Nathan he in turn is educated about the sort of society she moves in, with her Toorak house and her paintings bought as investments and her passion for astrology. David finally passes out behind a sofa, having nearly seduced her, or having been nearly seduced. He resigns the next day to work for Mrs Nathan.

David hears more of Trap's history from Adamov, a wineshop proprietor. Throughout these revelations, and those of Trap himself, David tries to maintain "my own hard factual style", that of the social worker, but already his values are being corrupted by what he is hearing about those at the top of the social hierarchy he had believed in. Congratulating himself on his honesty he can feel himself losing it.

He learns about Trap's work in the war in the Civil Construction Corps, and his proud acceptance as "Aboriginal

ABORIGINES IN FITZROY *Josl Bergner*

PETER MATHERS
1931-

Peter Mathers was born in 1931 in the United Kingdom and arrived in Australia in the same year. As a child he lived in Sydney and in South Australia. He attended Randwick and Sydney High Schools, and then went to Sydney Technical College.

He has worked at a variety of jobs in industry, farming, the public service and teaching. While living in London in 1967 with his wife and daughter, he worked as a researcher in the British Museum. It was in London that he heard that *Trap* (1966) had won the Miles Franklin prize.

He then went to the USA to be writer-in-residence at Pittsburgh University ("The Cathedral of Learning"). Often Mathers' life seems to be like his books. He writes of this time at Pittsburgh (*Overland*, No. 39, 1968):

I tried to borrow from the library but couldn't because I didn't have an identification card, and in fact I was ineligible for most things. I couldn't get an identification card because I was neither faculty nor student. The identification office was very firm about it, they didn't want to create a precedent. "Then I'm nobody?" I cried.

"I'm not at liberty to say."

Altogether he remained overseas for five years before returning to Australia, where he now lives in Melbourne. He is divorced, and has two daughters.

Mathers has been writer-in-residence at Salisbury College of Advanced Education, the University of Melbourne, La Trobe University, the Footscray Institute of Technology, and Darwin Community College. For eight weeks in 1984 he shared a community arts job with painter William Kelly in a foundry at Sunshine, Victoria.

As well as *Trap*, he has published *The Wort Papers* (1972), a novel, and a book of short stories in 1984, *A Change for the Better*. He has written a number of plays, radio plays and documentaries. He writes: "*The Wort Papers* is something of a puzzle: big reviews in Australia, Ireland, the UK – for two small, unsuccessful printings" (Cassell and Penguin).

In an autobiographical piece ("Extractions", *Southerly*, Vol. 31 No. 3, 1971) he says: "Whenever I write a fiction I build it round an idea. And the idea is in character and action." Elsewhere he writes (quoted *Meanjin*, Vol. 29, 1970): "As writers we must practise and preach subversion. We must be subversive all the time. Pattern and order can be pleasant. But still, this is it. If we feel that disorder is necessary, it's to be disorder."

Tradesman" by Steelcyl, the Factory of All Nations. Trap, "fundamentally an experimenter", almost at the end of the book, finally welds the foreman inside a cylinder, leaving him a hole for breathing and a hole for excretion. He goes to jail for this. It is in fact a later assault on the manager that sees him on remand – ready to be rescued by Mrs Nathan.

David hears how Trap met his hefty young wife Sally, and how he told her about his grandmother Maria who came from Tierra del Fuego, and Armstrong Irish Trap, who sired Jack's father Wilson on her. Armstrong Irish was a cedar spotter and feller, involved in the indiscriminate milling of this valuable timber in the north of New South Wales. Maria hates the mill and wants Irish Armstrong to move to a farm. She sets fire to the mill, but unfortunately incinerates him. A number of events in *Trap* do not have the expected consequences.

The story of Trap's ancestors continues with the account of Old Peters, of convict heritage, in the cedar country, and his brief fornication with Feed, the daughter of the ex-convict who had saved his life after he had lost his hand, crushed by cedar logs in the river. The whole section centred on the cedar milling adds another harsh but beautiful dimension to the book. Feed's daughter is the great-grandmother of Trap's mother. And through her he got those black genes; often in fury he wishes he looked like his father.

Trap explains nothing, and advocates no programme of reform. It creates a swirling world of contradictions and possibilities, myths and absurdities. Like *Capricornia*, there is laughter and clowning and vistas of immense wrongs.

No one emerges unscathed, least of all Trap. The book ends full circle with Trap's ragged expedition north stopped a mere 320 kilometres from Melbourne by the police. Mrs Nathan is happy. She did it.

According to Nathan the charges are: Shoplifting, resisting arrest, assault, having unroadworthy vehicles, being a common prostitute, living off immoral earnings and, for Trap himself, the crown – attempted murder. He is supposed to have thrown an axe at a traffic inspector.

In the last paragraphs David, almost devoid of shame, throws a brick through the huge aluminium and glass doors of the Megopolis Building. It is the Trap taint. But he can hear Trap's warnings. He must beware.

Trap is an extraordinary novel. It proves nothing but is totally convincing in its portrayal of the chaotic fragments of reality and deception that are gathered from history by the present and only just kept in order by society. Trap himself is a particularly original hero. His network of relations (typically Aboriginal) paradoxically establishes him firmly in white Australian history, but his Aboriginal blood gives him full licence as an outsider.

Joan Lindsay

PICNIC AT HANGING ROCK

MELBOURNE 1967

Miranda was a little ahead as all four girls pushed on through the dogwoods with Edith trudging in the rear. They could see her straight yellow hair swinging loose above her thrusting shoulders, cleaving wave after wave of dusty green. Until at last the bushes began thinning out before the face of a little cliff that held the last light of the sun. So on a million summer evenings would the shadows lengthen upon the crags and pinnacles of the Hanging Rock.

The semi-circular shelf on which they presently came out had much the same conformation as the one lower down, ringed with boulders and loose stones. Clumps of rubbery ferns motionless in the pale light cast no shadows upon the carpet of dry grey moss. The plain below was just visible; infinitely vague and distant. Peering down between the boulders Irma could see the glint of water and tiny figures coming and going through drifts of rosy smoke, or mist. "Whatever can those people be doing down there like a lot of ants?" Marion looked out over her shoulder. "A surprising number of human beings are without purpose. Although it's probable, of course, that they are performing some necessary function unknown to themselves." Irma was in no mood for one of Marion's lectures. The ants and their business were dismissed without further comment. Although Irma was aware, for a little while, of a rather curious sound coming up from the plain.

Like the beating of far-off drums.

Miranda was the first to see the monolith rising up ahead, a single outcrop of pock-marked stone, something like a monstrous egg perched above a precipitous drop to the plain. Marion, who had immediately produced a pencil and notebook, tossed them into the ferns and yawned. Suddenly overcome by an overpowering lassitude, all four girls flung themselves down on the gently sloping rock in the shelter of the monolith, and there fell into a sleep so deep that a horned lizard emerged from a crack to lie without fear in the hollow of Marion's outflung arm.

A procession of queer looking beetles in bronze armour were making a leisurely crossing of Miranda's ankle when she awoke and watched them hurrying to safety under some loose bark. In the colourless twilight every detail stood out, clearly defined and separate. A huge untidy nest wedged in the fork of a stunted tree, its every twig and feather intricately laced and woven by tireless beak and claw. Everything if only you could see it clearly enough, is beautiful and complete—the ragged nest, Marion's torn muslin skirts

fluted like a nautilus shell, Irma's ringlets framing her face in exquisite wiry spirals—even Edith, flushed and childishly vulnerable in sleep. She awoke, whimpering and rubbing red-rimmed eyes. "Where am I? Oh, Miranda, I feel awful!" The others were wide awake now and on their feet. "Miranda," Edith said again, "I feel perfectly awful! When are we going home?" Miranda was looking at her so strangely, almost as if she wasn't seeing her. When Edith repeated the question more loudly, she simply turned her back and began walking away up the rise, the other two following a little way behind. Well, hardly walking—sliding over the stones on their bare feet as if they were on a drawing-room carpet, Edith thought, instead of those nasty old stones. "Miranda," she called again. "Miranda!" In the breathless silence her voice seemed to belong to somebody else, a long way off, a harsh little croak fading out amongst the rocky walls. "Come back, all of you! Don't go up there—come back!" She felt herself choking and tore at her frilled lace collar. "Miranda!" The strangled cry came out as a whisper. To her horror all three girls were fast moving out of sight behind the monolith. "Miranda! Come back!" She took a few unsteady steps towards the rise and saw the last of a white sleeve parting the bushes ahead.

"Miranda . . .!" There was no answering voice.

A highly readable, realistic novel, *Picnic at Hanging Rock* centres upon a mystery that cannot be explained. Hanging Rock does exist; it is a notable landmark near Mt Macedon in Victoria. The three senior schoolgirls who supposedly disappeared together there, and their mathematics teacher, who also vanished on St Valentine's Day, 1900, are Joan Lindsay's creations. The three girls—Miranda, Marion, Irma—are linked by the first four letters of their names. What happened to them at Hanging Rock is never revealed. Irma, who magically returns, has no memory of what has occurred.

The girls are all pupils at Appleyard College, a school

of some pretensions for young ladies. It is run by an Englishwoman who arrived in Victoria in 1894 to look for a suitable large house where she could establish a school. It is never made clear whether she has any qualifications to do so, apart from her looks.

With her high-piled greying pompadour and ample bosom, as rigidly controlled and disciplined as her private ambitions, the cameo portrait of her late husband flat on her respectable chest, the stately stranger looked precisely what the parents expected of an English Headmistress.

The main characters who go on the fateful picnic are

Miranda, Irma, Marion, Edith, Mademoiselle Dianne de Poitiers, and Greta McGraw. Miranda (we are never told her surname) is the most glamorous and admired girl in the school, while Irma Leopold is the richest. Miranda has a "calm oval face and straight corn yellow hair". Mademoiselle de Poitiers, the French and Dancing mistress, says she reminds her of a Botticelli angel. Irma is 17, "radiantly lovely", with "blue-black curls", and despite being an heiress (her mother was a Rothschild), she is "without personal vanity or pride of possession". Marion Quade, also 17, is highly intelligent, thin and quick like a greyhound.

The other girl involved in the disastrous picnic is Edith, "a pasty-faced fourteen-year-old with the contours of an overstuffed bolster". She is the sort of girl who annoys everybody and enjoys it. Mademoiselle is elegant and worldly, in the best French tradition, and is particularly fond of Irma. Greta McCraw, the Mathematics mistress, is a brilliant mathematician, as oblivious of Australian surroundings as she had been of her native Scotland.

Sara Waybourne, aged only 13, is the youngest boarder. She is an orphan, and is constantly tormented by Mrs Appleyard. She has been kept in to learn a poem and so misses the outing to the rock.

Suddenly overcome by an overpowering lassitude, all four girls flung themselves down on the gently sloping rock in the shelter of the monolith, and there fell into a sleep so deep that a horned lizard emerged from a crack to lie without fear in the hollow of Marion's outflung arm.

The novel opens (and the picnic ends) on St Valentine's Day, the fourteenth of February. We are told that Mrs Appleyard is probably the only person at the college who has received no cards that day; this is not surprising, for she neither loves nor is loved. The girls certainly make an enormous fuss of theirs. There is a fluttery atmosphere of virgin emotion. Sara, who has the privilege of sharing the best room in the school with Miranda, adores Miranda, but otherwise there is no specific mention of lover or beloved. Even for 1900, the girls are a sheltered lot.

The departure of the girls and Mademoiselle, with Miss McCraw in charge, in a covered dray from Hussey's Livery Stables is splendidly described. Mr Hussey expertly manages his five bay horses, the girls are all excited and looking pretty in their best clothes and hats. But when they reach the picnic grounds at the Rock there is a suggestion that their clothing sets them apart from nature.

Insulated from natural contacts with earth, air and sunlight, by corsets pressing on the solar plexus, by voluminous petticoats, cotton stockings and kid boots . . . the girls . . . were no more a part of their environment than figures in a photograph album, arbitrarily posed against a background of cork rocks and cardboard trees.

Before the day is out some of the girls are to come to a freer existence among the myriad living creations of the bush and the mysteries of the rock.

Hints of something strange begin to emerge. Mr Hussey's watch has stopped dead at 12 o'clock. Mademoiselle's little French clock is being repaired by "Moosoo Montpelier", as Mr Hussey calls him, at Bendigo. Mademoiselle blushes at the mention of Monsieur Montpelier. Miranda is not wearing her watch—she says, "I can't stand hearing it ticking all day long just above my heart." Finally, Miss McCraw pulls out her old gold repeater and finds it too has stopped at 12. "Never stopped before," she says. Events are being shaped outside the ordinary structure of time.

Miranda, Marion and Irma, inseparable companions, go for what is meant to be a short walk along the creek towards the Rock. Marion wants to make some measurements at the base of the Rock. They have been warned not to climb it. As they are moving off, Edith attaches herself to them, "bumbling along in the rear".

They pass another picnic party: an old gentleman asleep under a tree; his wife seated near him; a young man reading a magazine; and another young man, "as tough and sunburned as the other was tender and pink of cheek", washing champagne glasses in the river. He is the coachman, Albert. The other young man, the Honourable Michael Fitzhubert, is the English nephew of the old couple. Michael does not approve of Albert whistling at the girls. However, the two young men obviously like each other.

Mike walks up the creek after the girls, already in love with Miranda, "the tall pale girl with straight yellow hair, who has gone skimming over the water like one of the white swans on his Uncle's lake". Albert thinks he is after the "little beaut with the black curls". As he walks, Mike is thinking that this is not at all like England, where everything has happened before. It is "Australia, where anything might happen".

The girls, who have decided to climb a little way up the Rock, reach "an almost circular platform enclosed by rocks and boulders", and think they will rest there before returning. There is a discussion of the word "doomed", occasioned by Irma's saying that poor little Sara reminds her of a little deer her father brought home once, and which her mother said was doomed. "What's that mean, Irma?" asks the obtuse Edith. "Doomed to die, of course!"

The three big girls have taken off their stockings and shoes. Irma dances on the rock barefoot. Miranda and Marion climb the next rise. Irma, slinging her shoes and stockings about her waist, follows with the protesting Edith. They come out on another shelf, and see the rest of the party far below, like ants. "A surprising number of human beings are without purpose," says Marion in her lecturing voice. And there is a curious sound coming from the plain, "like the beating of a far-off drum". The girls fall into a deep sleep.

They wake, and Edith wants to go home. But Miranda gets up and walks away up the rise, followed by Irma and Marion. "Well, hardly walking—sliding over the stones on their bare feet as if they were on a drawing-room carpet." Edith calls out to them, but they move on, unheedingly. Terrified, she runs back towards the plain. The three girls have disappeared.

In three brief chapters Joan Lindsay has created the mystery which dominates the book. And in the limited space available, she has skilfully produced a haunting portrait of Miranda.

MORNING IN THE GARDENS *J. J. Hilder*

JOAN LINDSAY
1896-1984

Joan Lindsay was born in November 1896 at St Kilda, Victoria, the daughter of Mr Justice Theyre à Beckett Weigall, and the granddaughter of Sir Rupert Hamilton, Governor of Tasmania. She was educated privately and at Clyde School, Woodend, which was then at East St Kilda. After her father's death her mother married Professor T. G. Tucker, Professor of Classical and Comparative Philology at the University of Melbourne from 1895 to 1920. He was also much involved with Australian literature as a part-time editor for Angus and Robertson.

Through her à Beckett blood Joan Lindsay is related to the Boyd family of artists and writers. When living in London she used often to see her cousin Martin Boyd, the novelist. Through her marriage to Daryl Lindsay, she joined another redoubtable family of artists and writers.

Joan Lindsay first met Daryl when she was studying at the National Gallery Art School under Bernard Hall and Frederick McCubbin. Her paintings are represented in the Ballarat Art Gallery and other Victorian art galleries, and she was for six years President of the Arts and Crafts Society of Victoria.

She married Daryl (later Sir Daryl) in London in 1922 and they returned to live in Melbourne, where Daryl worked as a commercial artist, doing illustrations for magazines and surgical drawings for Dr (later Sir Hugh) Devine. After four years in Melbourne the Lindsays bought Mulberry Hill, a cottage and 12 hectares at Baxter. Lady Lindsay continued to live there alone after Sir Daryl died in 1976.

During the Depression the Lindsays had to let Mulberry Hill. They went to live in a rather battered house called "The Laurels" at Bacchus Marsh. It was sparsely furnished and had no clocks in it. Lady Lindsay was to call her autobiography *Time Without Clocks* (1962). She says of this period, " . . . we were so absurdly happy . . . At 'The Laurels' emptiness was not a negative statement but a positive affirmation of truth and beauty like the holes in a Henry Moore sculpture."

When their finances recovered they returned to Mulberry Hill, and then made a prolonged trip to England and Europe where Daryl studied in museums and galleries. On their travels they made many friends in the art world, in particular the celebrated Professor Tonks of the Slade School. These contacts were invaluable to Daryl in his later career, as Director of the National Gallery of Victoria from 1942 to 1955.

Daryl always had a passion for horses, and secured many commissions to paint them. Joan's own knowledge of horses is evident in *Picnic at Hanging Rock*, in the spirited descriptions given of them.

Joan Lindsay's interests are also reflected in the authenticity of detail of *Picnic at Hanging Rock*, as revealed in her description of the gardens and architecture of the college and the Fitzhuberts' house, the girls' clothes, and the bush. The subtleties of social tone are also exactly right in *Picnic*, as they are in the novels of her cousin Martin Boyd.

We have it on the authority of the columnist Phillip Adams that St Valentine's Day, when the picnic took place, is "a magic day" for Lady Lindsay. She says that *Picnic* " . . . just came to me. I never had to think a moment about what any of the characters were called. They simply sprang to life, ready. I just had to write them down."

In 1976 Peter Weir directed the very successful movie of the book, introducing the book to a wider readership and acclaim.

Lady Lindsay died in December 1984.

There is one important detail that Edith, who is not much good at remembering anything, later recalls when revisiting the picnic ground with the policeman, Constable Bumpher. There was a cloud, of a nasty red colour, just as she passed Miss McCraw. And that reminds her that she saw Miss McCraw, who also disappeared, walking uphill, without her skirt, in her drawers.

The remaining three-quarters of the book follows the lives of those involved in the events of the picnic, and of those who were left behind. Some are happy: Mademoiselle leaves the college to marry M. Montpelier the watchmaker; Tom the handyman at the college and Minnie the maid likewise are to marry, and Tom is to take Albert's job when he goes to Queensland with Michael. Sara is to commit suicide, and, as a result, so is Mrs Appleyard.

Above all, Irma is to return. She is found eight days after the disappearance, initially by Michael, who is afterwards injured and knocked unconscious by a fall. In his notebook he has written, "ALBERT ABOVE BUSH MY FLAGS HURRY RING OF HIGH UP HIGH HURRY FOUN." Albert remembers that during an earlier search Michael had torn some pages out of his notebook and stuck them on bushes to mark how far he had gone. Albert organises a search party and hurries out to the Rock and finds "the little dark one", Irma, in the

ring of stones, still alive. "Her feet, strange to say, were bare and perfectly clean." She is without her corset, but is still a virgin. When she regains consciousness she can remember nothing of the events on the Rock.

After the slow recovery of both Irma and Michael (the expected love affair never materialises), Irma pays a final visit to the college, from which her father has ordered her to be removed. In an extraordinarily powerful scene she is mobbed, almost physically attacked, by all the girls in the gymnasium. Mademoiselle, who attempts to rescue her, remembers the scene of panic all her life. The girls want revenge, and to know the secret of what happened to Miranda and Marion. It is as if Irma had been initiated into another existence.

Picnic at Hanging Rock leaves all questions hanging. Were the girls drawn into another time and world, some sphere of freedom and joy? Were they holy virgins to be sacrificed in some primeval ritual of nature? Whether the answer lies in the supernatural or in science fiction is irrelevant, because an answer is not needed. *Picnic at Hanging Rock* is another fictional representation of Hamlet's words to Horatio:

There are more things in heaven and earth, Horatio,
Than are dreamt of in your philosophy.

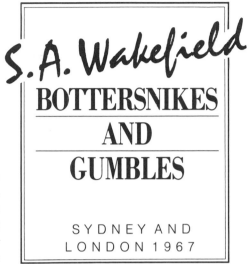

S.A. Wakefield

BOTTERSNIKES
AND
GUMBLES

SYDNEY AND
LONDON 1967

Bottersnikes eat pictures of food in papers and magazines. There are plenty of these in rubbish heaps—that's partly why they are so fat. Also they eat the stuffing out of mattresses. This they like fried. For sweets they are fond of rusty nails, though their favourites are milk bottle tops, which they chew like chewing gum. They will eat earwigs and cardboard too, but only if they are hungry.

So the Gumbles had to go through all the rubbishy papers carefully cutting out the food pictures. They had to search the junk heaps from end to end for bottle tops and rusty nails and, worst of all, they had to carry in the stuffing from four mattresses and pile it ready for frying. The Bottersnikes yelled at them all day long.

By evening everything was nearly ready. The Gumbles had built a large table from sheets of iron propped on bricks, and a stone fireplace too, to do the cooking on.

From the roof of his palace the King bawled: "Light the fire and fry the stuffing!"

Firelighting was the one job the Bottersnikes did themselves. As no one happened to be angry at the time, they grabbed a snoozing 'snike, thrust his head into the fireplace and kicked him and twisted his tail until he was thoroughly enraged. The kindling quickly caught from his red hot ears and the fire blazed in no time.

In great excitement, Smiggles woke from a little nap he happened to be taking. "Look what I done!" he shouted. "Look what I gone and dreamed!"

"You wasn't ordered to dream anything, Smiggles," the King roared. "Sit on his head!"

"But it's tomato soup!" Smiggles protested. It was too, a large tureen of it, rich, red and steaming, fresh from the depths of Smig's sleep. "I dreamed it special," he added craftily. "As a birthday present."

The King could not be angry. Everyone loves tomato soup. Yet care had to be taken lest the present vanished before it could be used; so Smiggles was hung up by his tail to stop him going to sleep. From time to time he was given a kick to make certain of his wakefulness, then a pat on the head to show there were no hard feelings.

Quite pleased with the gift of soup, the King announced, loudly: "I will receive the rest of my birthday presents."

The Bottersnikes blinked.

"Now," the King said. And sat there waiting.

Once more the tired Gumbles had to comb the rubbish heaps, with the Bottersnikes waddling behind, this time for suitable presents for the King. His Majesty received a whistle, a water pistol, a mousetrap and a quantity of fruit, mostly rotten—the best that could be found at short notice.

Presently the King stood atop his car and blew a shrill blast on his new whistle. In the grand manner, the King said: "Bottersnikes! I declare my birthday party open!"

Two of the most original Australian children's books must surely be *The Magic Pudding* and *Bottersnikes and Gumbles*. Entirely different in conception, they share immense high spirits, the comedy of rage and greed, and a refusal to be nonplussed by disaster. Although S. A. Wakefield did not illustrate his own work, Desmond Digby's paintings and drawings are so perfectly in harmony with the text that, as with Norman Lindsay's book, it is impossible to imagine the text with other illustrations.

In *Bottersnikes and Gumbles* Wakefield took for his starting point that entirely characteristic if unsalubrious feature of the Australian countryside, the rubbish dump. Wakefield is a farmer. Like most of us, he is familiar with those sites, usually in an old quarry, where countless empty cans pile up alongside old car bodies, baths, pots and pans, mattresses with the springs popping out of the material, all amid a general atmosphere of dirty and rusty decay.

It was his genius to invent exactly the sort of creature that would live in rubbish dumps, the dirty, bad-tempered, lazy, greedy Bottersnikes. "Best of all they like the rubbish heaps along dusty roadsides in the lonely Australian bush, where they can sleep for weeks, undisturbed." The King of the Bottersnikes emerges from such a rubbish heap.

. . . two long black ears poked out of a watering can. The ears came first because they were twice as long as the head they belonged to. Between the ears appeared an ugly green face with slanted eyes, a nose like a cheese grater and a mean mouth with pointed teeth sticking out. The skin was wrinkly all over and little toadstools grew where the eyebrows should have been . . . The King's ears turned bright red because he was angry—this always happens with Bottersnikes when they get angry. . . .

Bottersnikes are almost always angry about something, usually something trivial and selfish. They get so angry when it rains that the rain just sizzles on their ears.

As soon as the reader has met the King of the Bottersnikes, the Gumbles are introduced:

on their way down the hill to a little stream they knew of, called Earlyfruit Creek, where the water flowed into quiet pools and banks of sand made tiny beaches just right for Gumble paddling.

The reader immediately knows that Gumbles are peaceable, clean, lovers of nature and quiet fun. Not for long. The King has seen an old rusting car propped against a gum tree and, too lazy to open the door, he has roared to his 20 or so subjects to open the door for him. But they are snoring too loudly in the rubbish heap to hear him. So he bawls at the Gumbles to come and help him. The Gumbles are astonished, for they are used to bush creatures who are polite to each other, but being cheerful and friendly themselves they agree to help the King. "By climbing up each others' backs the Gumbles managed to open the car door, and with a one-two-three altogether *shove* they heaved the King into his new palace."

In gratitude, the King thinks they would make good slaves, and orders his subjects to grab them, which they do easily because Gumbles' legs are so short. Having caught them, they discover a peculiar thing about Gumbles, which is that they can be squeezed into any shape without hurting them, "and that if you press them very hard they flatten out like pancakes and cannot pop back to their proper shapes unless helped".

*B*ottersnikes eat pictures of food in papers and magazines. There are plenty of these in rubbish heaps—that's partly why they are so fat. Also they eat the stuffing out of mattresses. This they like fried.

This is very useful. "We can pop 'em into somethink and squash 'em down hard so's they can't get away, and when I want some more work done they'll be ready and waiting to do it," growled the King.

The Bottersnikes are enthusiastic about having servants available forever, but the problem is what to keep them in. "'Jam tins,' roared the King."

The poor Gumbles are squashed down hard, by the horny fists, into the jam tins and left out in the hot sun, when they had been looking forward to paddling in the cool creek. They can't get out of the tins, so their fate seems sealed.

But there is one Gumble who comes up with ideas. He is called Tinkingumble because when he has a Tink, a good idea, you can hear it, "*Tink*! Clear as if you had tapped the

edge of a glass with a spoon." Tinkingumble is under the King's car and the Bottersnikes don't see him. There he finds a tin-opener and he works out how it operates.

Quietly and quickly he cuts the bottoms out of all the tins, so that when the Bottersnikes have finished making the Gumbles work for them, and shove them back in the tins before going to sleep, the Gumbles can escape. At first they don't know how to, because they are jammed in so tight they can't move their legs, but they rock themselves until they fall over and roll down the hill to the creek. They nearly get the giggles, but it is just as well they don't, as Gumbles "are quite hopeless when they go giggly". Released from their prisons by a friendly bandicoot, they put all the tins into a big bin marked "Please Be Tidy". There is more than one moral to this story.

The adventures that follow are inexhaustible, and the seesaw goes up and down with sometimes the Bottersnikes getting their deserts, with much fiery reddening of ears, and sometimes the poor Gumbles being captured again, especially if they are giggly.

Once again, and once too often, the Gumbles went giggly. Rolling about quite hopelessly, quite helplessly, they suddenly found themselves surrounded by a ring of green and wrinkled faces with long red ears, upward slanted eyes, noses like coal scuttles and little toadstools—

"Got You!" shouted the Bottersnikes, and they grabbed those little giggling Gumbles and popped them into jam tins.

However, the Gumbles do have certain advantages. They cannot swim, but love the water, whereas the Bottersnikes, dirty creatures, not only hate the water but shrink if they get wet, and have to be hung up by their tails and dried out.

The natural playfulness of the Gumbles, their capacity to become completely involved in a game, often leads them to disaster. One particularly fat, important Bottersnike called Chank goes to sleep under a tree, while looking for his straw hat which the wind has blown up into a tree. The Gumbles obligingly offer to bring it down lower so that Willy Wagtail can make her nest in it. They can do this because they have the capacity to join themselves together into a Gumblerope. Seeing the solitary Chank asleep, they cannot resist jumping from the tree and bouncing off his fat stomach. But they don't notice the row of Bottersnikes watching, ready with jam tins. They are caught as they jump one by one, and are brought back to slavery to do all the work for the King's birthday party.

The adventures continue, and it seems the Gumbles will be trapped forever as Tinkingumble has lost his Tink and cannot come up with any solution to their troubles. However, little Willigumble, who has escaped, has an idea for liberating his friends. With the aid of a friendly kookaburra he takes all the springs from an old inner-spring mattress and hides them in the bottom of the jam tins. The King roars, "Them Gumbles ain't doing any good!" (Bottersnikes do not speak good English.) "Put 'em in their jam tins and squash 'em down hard!" The Bottersnikes "squashed them down most savagely but instead of flattening out like lumps of dough as they were supposed to, the Gumbles came shooting out of their tins as if on springs . . . They were on springs . . . The Gumbles held on to the springs with their toes and went

From B O T T E R S N I K E S   A N D   G U M B L E S an original illustration by Desmond Digby

S. A. WAKEFIELD
1927-

Sydney Alexander Wakefield was born on 13 May 1927 at Sydney on the day of his parents' arrival from England. The family settled on an orchard near Griffith, but Wakefield's mother died when he was six months old. The rest of the family returned to England in 1930 and Wakefield's father took up a farm in Oxfordshire. He married again when the boy was eight. Of his step-mother he says she "had an enormous influence upon me, mainly good".

Wakefield was educated at small schools in Gloucestershire and then at Burford Grammar School and Cheltenham College. He enlisted in the army in January 1945 and served in India with the 2nd Punjab Regiment. After the war his father, having sold the Oxfordshire farm, returned to New South Wales and bought an orchard near Gosford. Wakefield joined him here after his release from the army. After finishing a social studies course he worked for about two years as a social worker—"adequate though seldom inspired".

After his marriage in 1953 to Betty Wegerif, who wished to live on the land, and after the death of his father, the Wakefields settled on undeveloped land at Kariong, near Gosford. They built a house there and ran a mixed farm. Despite droughts and floods they survived there for 28 years and raised a family of two daughters and a son.

In 1982, the farm having been claimed for residential expansion, the Wakefields began development of a new orchard and farm at Raglan, near Bathurst.

Wakefield has always written, but ineffectually until he had a family to amuse. He writes:

> The *Bottersnikes and Gumbles* stories (of which three volumes have been published) were begun solely for my own children, without the thought of publication at the time. Scribbling has been (and is) strictly a hobby, pursued mainly during the brief winter lull in farm operations.
>
> The main influences are clearly enough family and environment. (Throughout our years at Kariong I tried to serve the latter in a practical way by active participation in the bushfire organisation, being captain of a brigade for 20 years and group captain for three.)

He says that he has abandoned various theories about writing for children, and his primary aim is to entertain, by the means of fantasy and humour. He agrees with Tolkien that fantasy is "not a lower but higher form of art . . . and so (when achieved) the most potent".

Bottersnikes and Gumbles has been successful overseas as well as in Australia. *The Times Literary Supplement* wrote of it:

> Rarely does one have the pleasure of discovering an entirely original creation, but this is what happened when this reviewer met *Bottersnikes and Gumbles* . . . a complete mythology of the rubbish dump . . . one of the most brilliantly funny books to appear for a long time.

---

zoinng! zoinng! over the heads of the startled Bottersnikes like rubber kangaroos."

*O*nce more the tired Gumbles had to comb the rubbish heaps, with the Bottersnikes waddling behind, this time for suitable presents for the King. His Majesty received a whistle, a water pistol, a mousetrap and a quantity of fruit, mostly rotten—the best that could be found at short notice.

This made the Bottersnikes angrier than they had ever been before and they tripped over each other's tails, "and their ears became like crimson bottlebrushes though not as pretty". The King roars "Snonk", the signal for silence, and orders that the Gumbles be caught again. By various stratagems, and not without being discomforted, they succeed. But at last Tinkingumble gets his Tink back, and the Gumbles, jammed all together into a soup tureen, form themselves into one giant Gumble that develops a huge voice and quite intimidates the King and his followers. The Gumbles have discovered that solidarity is strength (though of course they do not say so). However, ominously for their future, they are still liable to get the giggles.

The forces of good and bad are fairly evenly matched in *Bottersnikes and Gumbles*, but beneath its fantasy and humour it is a very moral book. The Bottersnikes are lazy, dirty, bad tempered, greedy and selfish. No child would want to be like a Bottersnike. But the Gumbles are not all goody-goody. They are simply thoroughly likable for their good nature (they even rescue the Bottersnikes from their own Gumbletrap). They are cheerful, convivial and clean, and their giggle leaves them vulnerable. And, on a deeper unspoken level, they live in harmony with the bush and its creatures.

Night noises, of course, puzzle us all at times. There was a bird which came regularly around my homestead at Boggabri at night. We heard it eight or nine times. It made noises like a cat fighting, only its cry was much louder, much deeper and more savage than any cat could make. The first time it came it cried from a tree near the dog-yards and the dogs grew so excited that their barking changed to the horrible high-pitched scream a dog makes when it meets something it cannot understand. The children's ponies raced about so wildly that I feared they would injure themselves. Even the sheep could be heard running together and milling in a tight frightened mob. The animals grew used to the bird and eventually took little notice of it. I tried several times to record the cry on tape, but the bird always flew off before I could get the tape-recorder going.

Of course, though, there are sweet sounds as well. There was no need to import song-birds. As late as 1900 which is a date that seems to bridge the past and the present in Australia, F. R. Godfrey who was the president of the Zoological and Acclimatization Society of Victoria, gave an address to the Australasian Association for the Advancement of Science in which he quoted two verses of Shelley's "Ode to a Skylark" to express his joy that there were still in Victoria descendants of the English skylarks, on the

Eric Rolls
THEY
ALL RAN
WILD

SYDNEY 1969

importation of which his Society had spent so much money. There is an Australian field-lark whose song and habits are remarkably similar to those of the English skylark. The field-lark is a neater, smaller, and fussier bird than the skylark. The latter has a dilapidated jauntiness which is more appealing, but the field-lark's song is as rich and joyous. Both birds are now having a hard time, as are all ground-nesting birds. The fox, the feral cat, and the cultivation of nesting-grounds are more than they can cope with.

The willy-wagtail is a lovable bird and often sings during the night. There are no cries more cheerful than those of the grey-crowned babblers who move about the ground in the very early morning in flocks of a dozen or more, probing under stones and sticks with their curved beaks. They hop up tree-trunks and all round the bigger branches, then hop down again and hop and run to the next tree, and all the while they chatter without ceasing.

The bellbird, the whipbird, the magpie and the striped honeyeater all possess interesting or beautiful voices. The

outlandish but cheering clatter of the kookaburra is more arresting than imported cries, and the brassy trumpeting of channel-billed cuckoos is as exciting as a summer storm. They fly high and grey near the dark clouds and their big bodies and long necks and beaks are stretched like organ pipes as they challenge the thunder. Such volume seems impossible.

Then there is the butcher-bird who has the finest voice of birds the world over—not the grey butcher-bird who flutes melodiously in the manner of the magpie, but the bigger pied butcher-bird who sings at least four distinct airs and is, perhaps, the only bird who can do so. One of the tunes runs through four bars and thirteen notes. He sings better in the winter-time and best of all when there is a heavy frost. He sings solo, in unison, or in parts. As well as his four airs there are grace-notes and churrs and short turns that he adds to a chorus. As many as half a dozen will station themselves in trees half a mile or more apart, so that several hundred acres are boxed-in by singing birds. Then one will begin an air and another take it up—then another farther away. Then one bird will join in with a different air that harmonizes and another adds grace-notes, until all six are singing a chorus which may last for half an hour. It always seems to be a good day after the butcher-birds have sung.

This is, in a way, an alternative history of Australia, although Rolls writes, "The book is intended as literature rather than history." The author says of his remarkable book: "Since I was chiefly concerned with imported animals that became pests on the land in Australia, the rabbits naturally became its principal theme." For four years he worked on finding answers to questions that had troubled him since he was a boy—where did the sparrows come from, the cats, the hares, the foxes?

Rolls is the ideal author for such a book, being a poet and a farmer. These two callings gave him insights and perspectives that took him far beyond the facts he gathered in his research. Australia itself is the tragic victim of his story,

a country with a unique ecology, locked in isolated innocence until the coming of the white man. Australia's geography and climate gave it a delicate balance which was cruelly disturbed by its imported pests which ran wild. Rolls' list is not exhaustive, as he admits. He does not discuss the cane toad, the Argentine ant or any of the weeds except blackberry and prickly pear. As he says, "There is a full book and a good one in weeds."

As well as writing with love and understanding about the ravages caused by imported animals to vegetation, birds, small animals and the soil, Rolls reveals a number of human conflicts, between squatters and farmers and governments, between vested interests and science, between the practical man and the idealist. Moreover, he has a deep sympathy for some of the animals themselves. He is much attracted to the hare and the dingo, he is more than fair to foxes, and, despite being a farmer, he can even see some positive qualities in rabbits.

The rabbit that moved across Australia in untold millions is still an individual to Rolls, and quite different from a hare. Rolls has observed them both on the blacksoil plains of northern New South Wales.

> The base of a rabbit's paws is densely haired. Rabbits loathe getting them matted. A rabbit caught on black soil in the wet looks as uncomfortable as a rooster in a thunderstorm. It runs a few yards, shakes each front paw to fling the mud off, kicks out with hind legs alternately, runs another half dozen yards and repeats the performance. Yet hares have similar paws and are quite at home.

Rolls goes on to say that the black soils, "the only areas that rabbits ignored, were the only soil that the rabbits could not have damaged. The black soils are too flat to wash; their particles are too big and too heavy to blow."

This intimate relation between soil and animal and the revelation of the character of the animal are typical of what might be called the ecology of *They All Ran Wild*. There is never just an accumulation of facts.

Nevertheless, the facts are amazing enough. There were rabbits in the colony from the earliest days, but they were of varieties that remained domesticated. It was Thomas Austin, of Barwon Park, near Geelong in Victoria, who in 1859 imported wild rabbits from England in the beautiful clipper ship *Lightning*. He had done well on the land and he wanted to be able to provide for himself and his friends

Rabbit Auction at the Melbourne Fish Market, 1872
(*Illustrated Australian News*)

the typical sport of the country squire, rough shooting. He imported 72 partridges, 5 hares and 24 wild rabbits, and only 6 partridges and a hare died on the way.

Rolls thinks that other squatters in New South Wales, Victoria and South Australia might also have imported rabbits and let them run wild; although within three years Austin's 24 rabbits had produced progeny of thousands, it still seems extraordinary that rabbits appeared so quickly in places so far apart.

Austin's shoots were well publicised. The English *Field* for 1867 reported: "Last year's shooting on Barwon Park: rabbits 14,253; hawks 448; eaglehawks 23; native cats 622; tame cats 32."

The willy-wagtail is a lovable bird and often sings during the night. There are no cries more cheerful than those of the grey-crowned babblers who move about the ground in the very early morning in flocks of a dozen or more, probing under stones and sticks with their curved beaks.

Two years later William Robertson of Glen Alvie station was employing 100 men to destroy 2,033,000 rabbits. Later, he estimated it would cost £10,000 in wages to trappers before he achieved real success. And Dr Stoddart estimated that 29,000 rabbits infested a 130-hectare paddock on his property. Ironically both men had tried unsuccessfully to breed rabbits.

Until 1870 squatters were still releasing rabbits on their properties for sport, although in the same decade governments were introducing legislation to force run holders to kill rabbits with dogs, traps, guns and fumigants.

By 1880 Peter Waite on Paratoo station in the far north of South Australia found that the rabbits were coming in waves across the saltbush plains. He attributed their spread partly to the activities of the rabbiters, whose harassment forced the rabbits to move into virgin territory all the time, instead of settling down in a stable area.

By 1884 they were nearly to the Queensland border, and were only held back by a drought. By 1886 they were moving down Eyre Peninsula in South Australia. In the first eight months of 1887 10,000,000 rabbits were destroyed in New South Wales. By 1887 the delicate balance of nature in the low rainfall areas had been seriously and permanently disturbed. Near Peterborough in South Australia, in country that receives only 125 millimetres per year, most trees and plants over a radius of 160 kilometres had been destroyed. Rabbits were eating the bark of trees as well as the saltbush and bluebush and *Eremophilas*. "Rabbits crawled like possums in branches several feet off the ground."

Many of the runs had been overstocked with sheep in good seasons, and by 1890 there were 62,000,000 sheep in New South Wales alone, but the rabbits ate roots and bark while the sheep were content with dry feed. Rolls estimates that stations were carrying about 40 rabbits to the hectare so that a western property such as Gunbar of 145,000 hectares was carrying 36,000,000 rabbits. No wonder that "runs about Cobar were now unstocked and barren".

RABBITS CLUBBED TO DEATH IN A BATTUE AT CORACK *(Illustrated Australian News)*

ERIC ROLLS
1923-

Eric Rolls was born on 25 April 1923 on a farm at Grenfell in the central west of New South Wales. He began his education with lessons sent from the Blackfriar's Correspondence School. He writes, "It was good schooling. The teachers fed pupils as much extra work as they wanted. I wanted a lot." He went to school in Sydney at Fort Street High School (like so many other writers) and in 1939 was editor of *The Fortian*, the school magazine, introducing a new flavour of eccentricity to what had been a very intellectual magazine under James McAuley's editorship.

At Fort Street he was fortunate to have as his English teacher John Tierney, who wrote short stories and novels under the name of Brian James. He was already writing poetry, and Douglas Stewart published a poem in the *Bulletin* called "Death Song of a Mad Bush Shepherd", written when Rolls was 15, that aroused a lot of interest and that confirmed in him the importance of writing.

He joined the AIF immediately after high school, and spent four years in the army, two of them "in Papua New Guinea in the interesting New Guinea Air Warning Wireless Company of independent stations reporting on aircraft and troop movements".

Since 1948 Rolls has farmed his own properties, "first at Boggabri on beautiful black flats of the Namoi River. But it's no fun being in the river when it floods ten kilometres wide, so we sold out and bought beautiful red soil at Baradine between the Warrumbungle Mountains and the Pilliga Forest, alive with trees and more birds than we had ever seen. The soil gives a writer a solid foundation to work from, and it keeps life in perspective. It allows nothing to be taken for granted."

Rolls first published a book of poetry, *Sheaf Tosser* (1967), and then began to plan "to tell the story of the rabbits, the hares, the foxes, sparrows, starlings I saw every day". It took between five and six years to write *They All Ran Wild*, while managing the farm. It was published in 1969 and won the Captain Cook Bicentenary Award for non-fiction in 1970.

Rolls wrote, "I found I could write non-fiction with the same discipline and the same imagination as I wrote poetry. Facts do not inhibit the imagination, they challenge it. There is imaginative writing and/pedestrian writing; that's all that matters."

In 1981 Rolls published *A Million Wild Acres* about the Pilliga forest near his farm. It won the *Age* Book of the Year Award, the C. J. Dennis Prize, and the Royal Blind Society's Talking Book of the Year Award. His latest book is *Celebration of the Senses* (1984), of which he says, "The idea is so simple: the experience of five senses."

Rolls is now working on what he describes as a "human history" of the Chinese in Australia. He, his wife Joan and photographer Sinan Leong went to China and Hong Kong to research the book.

Rolls has had in all eight Commonwealth Literary Fund and Literature Board Fellowships. He says, "These grants have been of enormous benefit to me. It would be intolerably difficult for an author to finance six years' work on a book without help."

Rabbits were dug out, shot, trapped and poisoned. An export trade grew from the meat and skins. Rabbiters became interesting new members of the workforce. Rolls gives a beautifully detailed description of how a rabbit trapper works, and, elsewhere, how a skinner goes about his business. As he says, these men are astoundingly skilful; two working together can skin 600 an hour.

All sorts of methods of combating the rabbit plague were put forward, especially when a £25,000 reward was offered for a solution. A New Zealander, Coleman Phillips, gave lectures around the country and canvassed politicians with his theories of controlling rabbits by introduced diseases. By feeding dogs on rabbits diseased by bladder fluke and taking the dogs around properties to excrete tapeworms, more rabbits would get the disease.

W. Rodier took advertisements in the papers to put forward his theory that trapping females only would cause the bucks to fight over the remaining females, which would become infertile. Another man believed that the release of cats in large numbers would seal the fate of the rabbits within three years, when 100 cats initially released among 10,000 rabbits on 40,500 hectares would end up with 900 cats needing to eat 328,500 rabbits.

Enormous sums were spent on netting, at which Rolls looks with a farmer's jaundiced eye. Kangaroos, emus and wombats knock holes through it, floods sweep it away, sandstorms cover it and little rabbits can climb through the mesh.

Fencing dams with runways with doors that only opened inwards yielded 10,000 or more rabbits every night; men wading in with clubs had the sickening job of killing them all. Poisoned grain was set and killed thousands of birds, from plovers to bustards (the beautiful plains turkey).

Then, of course, came myxomatosis. One of the most interesting sections of the book is the story of "myxo"; Rolls tells how it was opposed by those engaged in the rabbit trade and by scientists who, not knowing the disease was carried by mosquitoes, pronounced it useless after seven years of trials, and how a remarkable woman, Dame Jean Macnamara, pushed until further trials were given. By the beginning of 1953 "most of Australia was virtually free of rabbits . . . the annual wool clip increased suddenly by 70,000,000 lb". Rolls goes on to give the subsequent history of myxomatosis and the growth of the rabbits' resistance to it.

Rabbits take up half of *They All Ran Wild*. Using the same techniques, Rolls is equally fascinating about the other pests. He writes particularly well about the hare, an endearing animal that has certainly done damage to trees and crops, but not on the same scale as the rabbit.

Rolls gives a good account of the well-meaning Acclimatisation Societies that introduced English birds for homesick Anglo-Australians to hear their songs again (Australian birds not being considered to sing at all) and sparrows to eat caterpillars. Ostriches, llamas and of course donkeys and goats and many more were all introduced; but fortunately not all ran wild.

Rolls says that a news item that 10,000 wild donkeys were shot on a Western Australian station finally stimulated him to write the book. If this is so, there is something to be said for the wild donkey.

Vincent Serventy

DRYANDRA

SYDNEY 1970

The earth stirs. Days are still warm but change is coming. The chill of evening is a stimulant after the long enervating nights of summer. The whole of Nature seems poised. It is a time of silence, of immobility; not the somnolence of summer but an eager awaiting.

It was a perfect autumn day. Clear blue skies after heavy rain and the air fresh, the first of the winter grass glittering green. The words of Browning's poem, Oh to be in England, now that April's there, *do not sound so strange in the Antipodes.*

Suddenly I saw the urgent brown procession crossing the track. A rippling mass of hairy bodies, snakelike in their progress, busily engaged in finding a good hiding place for pupation. Idly I wondered if the caterpillars went into the pupation in autumn before the return of the cuckoos. To a cuckoo, nothing is more succulent than a hairy grub, to other birds nothing more repulsive. A pallid cuckoo would make short work of even the longest procession. It is no doubt good biological sense to get under cover in April before the cuckoos arrive in June.

I had a hand mirror in the car so tried the effect of reversing the sun by blocking one side with my shadow and shining the mirror on the other. The effect was dramatic. The leader promptly rightwheeled. Behind it all the others followed in the new direction. Before, the group had been moving at right angles to the sun. Now they were heading straight into it.

I had no time to experiment further so gathered the procession into a plastic bag to study later.

The next day was not so perfect. Occasional clouds swept across the face of the sun but the caterpillars seemed active enough when I tipped them into a squirming heap. For a time they milled in a shapeless group, then gradually pattern appeared. First the seventy grubs broke into two masses, one of about thirty, one of about forty individuals. Both groups began to move more regularly, like an eddy in water, the individuals marching around three or four abreast but beginning a circular movement. It was quite dramatic seeing the mass of hairy bodies swirling in a tight circle. Suddenly a leader broke out and headed south-east, still at right angles to the sun. Soon the larger group moved in concert, in the same direction but with about a yard separating the files of caterpillars. Two grubs which had fallen out of the main masses also started off in exactly the same direction. Was it the sight of their fellows that guided them? Was it the sound of pattering feet? Or was it some other sense, smell, shaking of the sand surface, some ultrasonic call? I could not say.

One file I let go unhindered. Soon it

had disappeared under a sheltering blackboy. Hours later I found the huddled mass under a neat nest of dead leaves, all glued together with silk. The longer file I experimented with. Gently I nudged the leader in a wide circle until after some five minutes' work I had joined it on the tail of the procession. It was then that the silken trail laid down by each caterpillar became clear. Sand grains stuck to it as I pushed the leader on to the procession's tail.

Minutes passed and still the caterpillars swept smoothly on, circling contentedly. A half-hour went by. An hour. In the distance a raincloud gathered, so reluctantly I stopped the experiment. I deliberately forced a break in the circle. The grub selected as the new Alexander-Cook-Columbus set off unhesitatingly but this time north-west, still at right angles to the sun but in the opposite direction, the direction in which I had nudged it. This time mirror sunlight did not change the course. Then I broke the procession into four parties. Each settled into a parallel file and marched on. Soon the groups were huddled under the leaves, rapidly spinning shelter against the dangers surrounding them. The rain came and left me unsatisfied, aching to meet another procession and try once more.

How long would they have circled? All day, or would some less facile follower have broken ranks and led its people to a real destination, instead of round and round the futile circle I had forced on them?

The best introduction to Vincent Serventy's *Dryandra*, the story of a year in the life of a Western Australian forest, could come from the *Journal* for 23 January 1858 of the great American observer of Nature, Henry Thoreau:

> To insure health, a man's relation to Nature must come very near to a personal one: he must be conscious of a friendliness in her; when human friends fail or die, she must stand in the gap to him. I cannot conceive of any life which deserves the name, unless there is a certain tender relation to Nature. This it is which makes winter warm, and supplied society in the desert and wilderness. Unless Nature sympathises with and speaks to us, as it were, the most fertile and blooming regions are barren and dreary.

Serventy is an energetic, practical naturalist who has written many books and has a deep involvement with the conservation movement. *Dryandra* is his finest work, as it is the one in which he has most allowed the philosopher to emerge as well as the scientist, and in it he has not been afraid of showing that "certain tender relation to Nature" described by Thoreau.

Dryandra is also a book with a clear message: that the conversation with Nature must be a two-way one. In order for Nature to "sympathise with and speak to us" we must sympathise with and speak to her. Serventy's relation to Nature is that declared healthy by Thoreau, it is "very near to a personal one".

Although *Dryandra* is a month-by-month account of the life in the forest, it is the result of years spent as an observer, of many long and patient visits at all times of the year and all hours of day and night.

Dryandra is a Forest Reserve of 15,968 hectares, consolidated in 1934-35, which lies about 210 kilometres south-east of Perth, near Narrogin. It has an annual rainfall of about 508 centimetres, with a cool, wet winter and a hot, dry summer. The dryandra, with its beautiful golden flowers, flourishes on the rocky slopes, and there are fine stands of wandoo and mallet. In his visits to Dryandra Serventy set himself the task, "to probe deeply into the interweavings of this life of the forest", a life involving birds, ground animals, insects, flowers, trees, shrubs, grasses, rocks and soils. A humble man, Serventy thinks of his book as at least contributing something to the job of conserving the bush, and as an indication "that here is work for naturalists for hundreds of years to come". And he mentions that Dryandra was then only a State Forest, and not a National Park. (And indeed this is still the case.)

The earth stirs. Days are still warm but change is coming. The chill of evening is a stimulant after the long enervating nights of summer. The whole of Nature seems poised. It is a time of silence, of immobility; not the somnolence of summer but an eager awaiting.

Serventy does not only describe what he sees, but continually places the reader in historical perspective, which reaches back to the coming of the Aborigines, who hunted the animals and, in the course of hunting, lit fires which certainly altered the original forest. Then the white man came, "armed with more efficient hunting weapons and bringing more deadly foes still—new plants, new animals; and the plough, most deadly of all". But the undisturbed forest, hemmed in though it was, defeated the intruders. "So the forest lives on today. The web of life remains secure so long as the forest remains."

Serventy has arranged the book in 12 chapters, under the months, and breaks these up into shorter sections named after particular features of the forest. Some of these, for example "Magpie", recur during the book, so the reader could make a mini-anthology of various observations for a specific subject.

Serventy's eclectic method is apparent in an early section simply labelled "Granite". As a geologist, he has a particular respect for this part of the ancient shield of Western Australia that has been above the sea for hundreds of millions of years: "Like grey elephants granite domes heave their way out of

the soil of the Dryandra forest." In his wanderings he has traced granite outcrops up to the Pilbara and across to the desert, where their deep rockholes became reservoirs of water enabling man and other animals to survive in those arid regions. Here in Dryandra, Serventy outlines the slow cycle of plant life that grows from the exfoliation of the granite, and, observing by day and night, he becames familiar with the animal life that shelters in the granite. His favourite among the smaller lizards which abound is the barking gecko:

> Most people refuse to believe that it can bark but it does. When one of these lizards is disturbed by turning over a slab of granite, rather than scuttling away to safety it rises stiffly on stiltlike legs, arches both back and tail upwards, and barks. The sound is quite distinct though muted in terms of body size.

Serventy goes on to say that the gecko has a relatively large tail, which, like other lizards, it discards when in danger, so that the predator will eat the tail and the lizard can escape alive. With typical humour, Serventy observes: "So, no doubt as philosophically as humans after the visit of the tax collector, the gecko begins to gather more food and grow a new tail."

The great naturalist-observers, White of Selborne, Richard Jefferies, Henry Thoreau, E. J. Banfield, were all devoid of human arrogance in the face of Nature. Not only were they humbled by the infinite power, complexity and hidden balance of Nature, but they also realised the limitations of man. Serventy is emphatically in this tradition. Take, for instance, the beautiful passage towards the end of the chapter of "January" about exploring the forest at night.

> So as I wander through the forest at night and hear the click of the insect-eating bats as they circle high overhead I think how full the night air must be with those other cries, so high pitched that human ears fail to hear them, the bat's radar. Who knows what calls fill the air? Perhaps the owls and frogmouths, and the owlet nightjars also have supersonic calls. Certainly many insects whose shrill creaking makes the summer forest echo have their own unheard calls. The mammals have an orchestration of sound we can never hear, they also have an orchestration of smells our noses are too coarse to distinguish. Even in the field of sight where humans stand high, there are wavelengths in the infra-red and ultra-violet we cannot see but other animals can. Some snakes see the infra-red. Bees can see the ultra-violet.

Throughout the whole book Serventy delicately conveys this sense of both privilege and humility in the human presence in the forest. In Thoreau's sense of the words, his relation with the life around him continues to be a personal one.

In "April" he is watching a procession of caterpillars, but he sees much more than that weird snake of hairy bodies joined together. As well as being a scientist, he is a keen reader of poetry, and, paradoxically, the clear autumn day makes him think of Browning, "*Oh to be in England, now that April's there,*" words which "do not sound so strange in the Antipodes" with "Clear blue skies after heavy rain and the air fresh, the first of the winter grass glittering green." It was a long time before the early settlers could

DRYANDRA FOREST *Vincent Serventy*

VINCENT SERVENTY

Vincent Serventy was born on a farm near Bickley in the Darling Ranges, Western Australia. His father was a Yugoslav migrant, and Vincent was one of eight children. In a memoir written especially for this book, he writes: "My first memories are of the hills beyond our farm. Here we ran barefoot like so many brumbies, exploring rock tumbles, climbing trees and picking flowers. At regular intervals we were dragged reluctantly back to an adult world; picking grapes and other fruit in the never-ending tasks of a small farm and orchard. . . . Dominating my life was my father, Victorian in spirit although coming from Yugoslavia. . . . He had torn himself, and my mother, away from Australian Slav enclaves, psychologically bleeding, by strength of will. He remained a loner but bearing the pain with the bold command, 'You're an Australian. Why live with those who cling to the past? Europe has only a past. No future!' . . . He dinned into the willing ears of his eight children that there was no future on the land. Our only future lay with education."

Serventy went to the famous Perth Modern School, but did not think highly of it: "Intellectually I was stunted." By this time the family lived in Subiaco, close to the bush of King's Park. Serventy wryly notes that "Schools in those days did not encourage boys to study natural history of any kind—that was for girls."

After school, "Then came the boredom of university where I learned how to regurgitate facts poured into my mind." He took a science degree and then a second degree in education. Outside the university he met a wider circle of artists, radicals and open-sea yachtsmen: "From these men and women I learned about music, film, modern books (an eye-opener to me) and above all life and love."

He had been writing for many years, and achieved publication with some essays as he began a career as a science teacher. He was much involved with naturalists' clubs.

> Then, angered by the education bureaucrats, I threw it all up and went awandering. I became a scientific beachcomber, professional zoologist, a wanderer in Australia and abroad. It was then I fell in love with the woodlands of Dryandra. . . .
>
> Then came marriage and a new start in science education. In any spare time I organised expeditions and wrote books. I also found a new love—movie photography. . . . Then I threw it all up once more and began a new career.

He wandered with his wife Carol and children, made some very successful television films, and finally settled in Sydney. "I began a new exploration of the bush. I crossed the Simpson Desert, was the first and probably the only person to be shipwrecked twice in Lake Eyre, and went camping with the painter John Olsen."

He spent nine years with the committee which drew up plans for the Australian Heritage Commission and became one of the first commissioners. He has written more than 40 books and been involved in the preparation of 50 documentary films. He has also lectured extensively around the world.

He writes of *Dryandra* that it is his favourite amongst his books.

> Carol and I spent many happy hours camping in Dryandra Forest. With good friends owning a farm close by it also became a holiday home for our children. This is a book that was woven together over many years of living in and loving the Australian wild.
>
> For my life today and perhaps my own sanity is guided by that Thoreau injunction, "In wildness is the preservation of the world."

---

accept the fact that autumn in Australia is not the melancholy season it is in Europe, but a hopeful one, when after the long, hot, dry summer the first rains turn the red earth green again.

As for the caterpillars, the description is one of the most fascinating in the book. Serventy watches them, and then reverses the sun by using his shadow and a hand-mirror. Immediately the leader right-wheels and all the others follow, so now they are heading at right angles to their original course, straight into the sun. He gathers the 70-odd caterpillars into a plastic bag and releases them on the next day. They swirl into circles, until a leader breaks off and heads south-east, again at right angles to the sun, to be followed by another group. One group hides under a nest of dead leaves, glued together with silk. Then he takes the leader of the other procession and joins it to the tail. "Minutes passed and still the caterpillars swept smoothly on, circling contentedly. A half-hour went by. An hour." Rain then forces Serventy to abandon the experiment and set the caterpillars free to form their nests. But, he asks, "How long would they have circled? All day, or would some less facile follower have broken ranks and led its people to a real destination, instead of round and round the futile circle I had forced on them?"

Serventy is human enough, and humorist enough, just occasionally to drop his humility and play Gulliver to the Lilliputians of Nature.

Of all the animals and birds whose habits he follows throughout the year, perhaps he writes best about the magpies. He introduces the familiar bird with a bizarre observation in "January", when he finds one lying on its back in soft soil with its wings outspread. He thinks it is dead. But "As I got nearer the corpse came to life, glared at me, and with ruffled feathers flew off. My dead bird was only sunbathing."

Serventy follows this observation with a generous tribute to a friend, Angus Robinson, a Western Australian farmer-naturalist, who explained to him that this habit was common with moulting birds. Throughout the book Serventy follows up what he says here of the "importance of a good friend or a good book in natural history".

The observations of magpies are varied: finding them at their dawn chorus (one of the most joyful passages in the book); defending their territory, a harsh episode; egg-guarding; and watching over the first flights of their young, when they will dive-bomb anyone who interferes.

One could happily trace similar revealing episodes with mallee fowl, the grey kangaroo, or the wagtail, but there are also fine, more or less isolated observations such as that of the Christmas tree, a strange member of the mistletoe family, which Serventy is prepared to call "the most beautiful tree on earth".

The book ends with a plea for human beings to strive, like Nature itself, "for ever growing sensitivity to the environment, a greater richness of living". The book itself has justified that plea.

IDEAS FOR AUSTRALIAN CITIES

ADELAIDE 1970

Organic theories have taken such thrashings from modern political philosophers as to be scarcely worth another attack; but they do appeal to a few planners, and for all their faults they do pose interesting questions about urban growth and change, and about some qualities of city life.

Organic language *need not be* metaphorical at all. People are a species of organic life. Their health depends on their environment. They need fresh food and air and water, sunlight and regular darkness. Their nervous systems can suffer from too many quick-changing stimuli, from buffetings and confusions and anxieties. They may be wise to keep some touch with plant and animal life, with wind and rain and seasons. Cities should meet these needs of their organic inhabitants; but that doesn't make the cities organisms too.

Even as a metaphor, "organism" has some harmless uses. A city is complex and many of its people's activities are interdependent. One way of emphasizing this is to compare a city to a person. Like a person it has physical structure and functions, cellular decay and replacement, and mental life. The health of the whole depends on the efficient working of transport "arteries", administrative "brains", rubbish and drainage "bowels". If you remove any essential organ from the city, the whole may suffer like a body that loses an essential organ. The whole may adjust to changes in particular parts of it, as a living body does.

It is in these two senses that urban philosophers like Lewis Mumford make liberal use of organic language. Mumford seems also to include in his thought an idea sometimes called "the human fallacy". Small towns are built "on human scale" and house "human" relations. Big cities have "inhuman scale" and their complex organization makes their people's relations "inhuman". In fact of course Manhattan—and rockets to the moon—are artifacts as human as any grass hut. Complex organizations are built and run by people as human as the village squire and parson ever were. Loneliness, anonymity and alienation are qualities of relations between humans, just as love is.

Those who say human and inhuman when they mean good and bad are assuming that goodness is natural to humans but evil is not. All the cruelties of the big cities are done by humans, most of them deliberately enough. Plenty of face-to-face relations in smaller communities are also selfish and unloving. Personally I agree with Mumford that on balance, in societies like ours, direct relations probably do allow more good relations, while the indirect relations and manipulations characteristic of complex organizations do tend to make selfishness easier to commit and harder to combat: stand-off bombing is easier on the conscience than face-to-face bayoneting. But all the parties are equally human. Even when complex machinery makes for impersonal mistakes, and for effects beyond the mechanics' intentions, those errors are as human as any others.

These various uses of organic language—to emphasize man's organic nature, or the complexity of cities, or the value of small groups and face-to-face relations—are common usages in everybody's language. They have scarcely any connection with formal theories of organic society.

Most Australians live in or around large cities but few take, or perhaps are not even given, the opportunity to think what is happening to them. There are planners in all the capital cities, but few people know what they are doing. When Hugh Stretton was writing *Ideas for Australian Cities*, "of the six mainland capitals, every one at the moment has an immigrant chief planner . . . In the four south-eastern capitals there are five planners with effective opportunities to design whole neighbourhoods; only one of them was born or trained in Australia."

As for suburbia, Australians are the most suburbanised people on earth, but most intellectual attitudes to suburbia are as full of clichés as of hypocrisy.

Hugh Stretton's *Ideas for Australian Cities*, written in 1969, contains a certain amount of specific discussion of planning details of that time but those sections that are out of date may now profitably be read as history. *Ideas for Australian Cities* is what it says, a book of ideas. It is also a profound essay on the Australian character, or indeed on humanity in general. Some of the deadliest prose has been poured like concrete on the subject of urban planning. Stretton has a witty style and a courteous mind; besides he is a modest man who does not want to ram any system down the reader's throat. He says he is an amateur. So he is, in the best old sense of that word, "one who loves, is fond of, or has a taste for, anything". Thus his enthusiasm for the possibilities of urban life is associated with, to exceed the dictionary, what could be called a passion for justice and decency for women and children and the poor, for good company and the arts, for simple and complex pleasures. Stretton is a historian who has been Deputy Chairman of the South Australian Housing Trust since 1971. He is a very informed amateur.

It is a pleasure to illustrate the qualities of Stretton's style.

Of Sir Thomas Playford, who ruled South Australia for more years than Sir Robert Walpole was Prime Minister of England, Stretton writes: "In everything except politics he had very simple tastes. He was a total abstainer from alcohol, education and tobacco." Despite Stretton's sensitivity and imagination he is a realist: "Entrenched mediocrity need not be bad for every branch of government." He is also very wary of "realists", like people who say that cities should be segregated into rich and poor suburbs: "When it isn't 'freedom', the segregationist philosophy is usually a racket called 'realism'." He admires and advocates sensible and humane planning, but abhors the rigorous and boring application of theories, such as that which rules that Canberra's suburban gardens should not have fences or hedges between the houses and the road: "This merciless publication of everybody's gardening, to widen already-wide streets, is not always good landscaping, and it makes one more monotony where the design of the streets themselves invites, instead, an entirely wholesome diversification."

Although an intellectual of formidable ability, Stretton is a staunch defender of suburbia, an attitude he shares with Donald Horne in *The Lucky Country*. He likes the freedom and privacy of suburbia, and is prepared to answer his own question, "Why *do* so many Australians choose to live in a way so unfashionable with intellectual urbanists?" While being conscious of the difficulties and dangers of suburban life he stoutly maintains "You don't have to be a mindless conformist to choose suburban life."

> People need city centres, crowded with opportunities for fun and profit; but as long as they are there within forty minutes' travel, people will be freer and happier in proportion as they also have a generous tract of privacy at home, and steady friends at work.

These remarks come from an introductory chapter, "Australia as a suburb". This is followed by a section called "New Directions", which consists of four chapters in which he discusses Canberra in terms of "some of its real novelties, if only as a measure of what the bigger cities are *not* so far achieving".

A city is complex and many of its people's activities are interdependent. One way of emphasizing this is to compare a city to a person. Like a person it has physical structure and functions, cellular decay and replacement, and mental life.

Stretton's humanism leads him to see beyond the easily scorned dreariness of Canberra as unadventurous suburbia. In a few brilliant paragraphs he demolishes the "soaring brilliance" of that other planned city, Brasilia, coming down in favour of Canberra's preference for the rights of man. In more technical terms he then criticises the planners for the cluster development of Canberra, with its transport problems that are so hard on women and children, and, as elsewhere in the book, puts forward the advantages of linear development. He begs patience of the reader, to control an immediate repulsion to "the image of this snake-shaped conurbation", and then gives some of its advantages.

Stretton is a patient writer who explains, not a domineering one who insists. He is also an ironist, quick to appreciate the paradox of free-enterprise Liberal governments supporting the public control of land sales and development in Canberra. In the final chapter on the nation's capital, "Canberra as an experiment", he finds more to approve than condemn, before turning to three of the older cities, Adelaide, Melbourne and Sydney to imagine "what we will probably make of *them* if we continue to let them monopolise our urban resources".

Adelaide he approves of. (Born in Melbourne, he lives in an old stone house in North Adelaide, an area which has the mixed, unsegregated population which he sees as giving the most opportunities for urban living.) The historian in Stretton is allowed full rein as he covers Adelaide's history, an odd mixture of radical and conservative not often understood outside South Australia. He is particularly enlightening when discussing the industrialisation, and in some ways socialisation, of South Australia by the allegedly conservative Playford and his talented and un-Establishment administrators. Stretton then goes on to explain why the South Australian Housing Trust has been such a success, and why the satellite town of Elizabeth (with all its faults) is so preferable to the New South Wales equivalents of Green Valley and Mount Druitt.

In such matters Stretton has the advantage of being, as he confesses at the beginning of the book, in favour of a programme that could be labelled "moderate socialism or radical conservatism". Once again, it is the mix that he favours, of old and new, established and radical. For instance, he is caustically against all commercial "developers" or government planners who would, whether for freeways or large buildings, pull down smaller or older buildings where people can and do live pleasantly and relatively cheaply. The Adelaide City Council's attempt to drive a great road through the houses and squares of North Adelaide is exposed as urban outrage.

Ideas for Australian Cities can be read on one level as an essay on Australian egalitarianism, and how constantly it is under attack in the cities. A watchdog for the poor, Stretton is amused at the attitudes of the rich.

> The lady wife of one Lord Mayor (knighted or not, Melbourne mayors are wed to good ladies, never to women) once appeared on television to defend Toorak. "People think Toorak is full of millionaires with Bentleys and Rolls-Royces," she said. "This is quite wrong, not true. I have lots of very good friends with Bentleys and Rolls-Royces who *don't live in Toorak at all*."

On a more sober level, he is aware that there is no possible way in which a freeway, however desirable, could have been driven through Toorak.

He writes of Melbourne with the authority and fondness of one who grew up there, but also with an acute consciousness of (to use his chapter heading) "Melbourne as a private enterprise". Melbourne, at least up to the 1970s, has been under rigid conservative control. This is as much a matter of bureaucracy as politics. Stretton's sharp eye and sense of humour pick up details such as this in a report by the Victorian Housing Commission:

> Only in Melbourne can you find a public authority's

BACKDROP FOR *ROUNDELAY* *John Brack*

HUGH STRETTON
1924-

Hugh Stretton was born in Melbourne on 15 July 1924, son of Judge L. E. B. Stretton. He has made the following notes for the present book:

My father was a good writer. My mother was a teacher and a good gardener. I spent the first 11 years, mostly barefoot, in Beaumaris when it was a sandy seaside hamlet surrounded by miles of tea-tree scrub and open heath. We then moved to town where we lived across the Yarra from Ruwolt's steelworks.

I went to school at Beaumaris State and Mentone Grammar when its owner/head was an excellent English teacher.

He has amplified this information in a description of the two headmasters in *Ideas for Australian Cities*.

Public and private were symbolized more personally by two tiny, two-teacher schools. In the state school, society paid its debt to a wounded soldier with a damaged skull, terrible headaches and a laminated strap from which one side had been peeled to leave its rivets projecting slightly. The other school was the private property of C. A. Thorold, M.A. Oxon., a gentle, intelligent, civilised man who charged nine pounds a term for principles of self-expression and individual progression which are still beyond the state schools' means in 1969.

His next school was Scotch College "when it had excellent music and drama teachers, a Christian Socialist chaplain, and newspapers and magazines which gave their boy editors exceptional freedom and editorial training".

For some years Stretton travelled once or twice a week through Port Melbourne to Fishermans Bend to help run a Boy's Club in the Victorian Housing Commission's first estate; it was the beginning of a long association with Housing Commissions. Stretton continues:

I spent 1942 at Melbourne University, and from 1943 to 1945 as a rating in the Royal Australian Navy. I spent a year in corvettes, and a year in Darwin when I ran a naval grocer's shop on Darwin wharf, and also a free-enterprise laundry.

From 1946 to 1948 and from 1949 to 1954 I was at Balliol College, Oxford, first as a student, and then as a don teaching history, fraternising with left-Keynesian economists and economic philosophers.

In 1948-49 at Princeton Graduate School, USA, I sampled courses in sociology, political science and other social sciences. I concluded the modern social sciences were (1) about half intellectual frauds, (2) spreading like wildfire, and (3) fit subjects for study by a young historian.

From 1954 to the present day Stretton has taught history at the University of Adelaide, where he was appointed Professor of History in 1954. In 1968, to gain more time for writing, he resigned his chair and was appointed Reader. His book *The Political Sciences* was published in 1969.

He has been married twice, and has four children. With Patricia, who is a research worker, and the children he has spent his study leaves, mostly writing books, in London (three years) and for one year each in Canberra, York and Northampton (Massachusetts). He writes: "I am very fond of all these places, except when compelled to live in an upstairs landless flat with four children." He adds a comment very relevant to *Ideas for Australian Cities*: "The nearby resources of two or three famous London parks were less helpful to domestic peace and order than one 40-foot back yard would have been."

Stretton has for many years been associated with the South Australian Housing Trust, and since 1971 has been Deputy Chairman. He lives in North Adelaide.

---

routine report which gives four of its first five pages (the fifth is the table of contents) to full page displays with photographs and facsimile signatures and lists in hierarchic type of its own Directors.

The last of the three "Old Investments" to be discussed is "Sydney as the magic place". Some aspects of Sydney, however, have already been explored, as in the comparisons between Elizabeth and Green Valley, and also in the depressing dilemma that 75 per cent of those who have lived in those appalling Melbourne 40-storey high-rise flats say they would prefer to live in cottages, while 75 per cent of those who live in the cottages of Green Valley would like to leave them.

Stretton writes with love of the beauties of Sydney, the Harbour, the zest and magic of the inner city. Hence, when he looks at what has been done to it since he wandered the Cross as a sailor in wartime, his protest is "a lover's howl of pain as big Sydney's heart grows more heartless and remote, too full of glossy spenders, less and less accessible to lovers".

But in Sydney he has also taken the trouble to experience something of what the western suburbs are like to the poor, to spend three hours on public transport getting to Green Valley, buying "grapes, a Mars bar and a fizzy drink" and "For the neighbourhood's only public shade, I made for the well-designed pedestrian tunnel under the main road."

The most concentrated thinking in *Ideas for Australian Cities* is packed into the last three chapters, "Ideologies", "Interests" and "Policies", under the section heading, "What Next?" Perhaps the most basic themes here are conservation and change, and their interrelation. Stretton maintains that people who are concerned about cities have to be aware of more than "the traditional objects" of conservation; social structures are involved. A similar sharp-eyed attitude to change is necessary, for there is no such thing as general change. Cities are organic (elsewhere Stretton has some fun with those idealists who think only in organic terms), and therefore alternatives are involved as "one can't even recognise change in a *purely* factual way. It requires value judgements as well."

Stretton has a powerful ability to exercise convincing value judgements throughout the whole book; he is a many sided man and these judgements are made on human, aesthetic, economic and historical evidence. *Ideas for Australian Cities* is a profound and important book, both for planning the future and understanding the past of Australians as well as their cities.

THE UNKNOWN INDUSTRIAL PRISONER

SYDNEY 1971

GOING HOME IN THE DARK

Going out of the refinery at night, hanging their heads, straggling like convicts loosely chained, the lowest grade of prisoners looked in on the occasional parties held in the dining-room where staff men and girls ate from buffet tables lobsters, roast beef and soft pink hams, stood around drinking from dainty glasses and talking of Puroil and its concerns and the details of their lives daily given for the company in return for monthly bank deposits.

The men passing by in the dark were conscious of their own badges. Their red necks, heavy hands and every word that proceeded out of their mouths, their lack of interest in office affairs, their partial interest in the actual messy business of refining—these were inseparable from them and an insuperable barrier to intercourse with the elegant creatures from the Termitary. It was another world in there. Office people didn't care what the process was on which they and the prisoners depended: their skills could be transferred to the refining of toffee or the manufacture of hearing aids with no significant difference. The less they knew about oil the cleaner they felt. The men down on the job never understood this— they sneered at accounting people for not knowing refining processes, never realizing that business people didn't need to know and certainly didn't want to know anything but through-put and production figures, sales and stocks on hand, costs and revenue, payroll-tax and salary. If there can be said to be a literary culture and a scientific, there must certainly be a business culture in which it is necessary to be able to define money, recite a selected passage of company law and to be inward with the Banking Act of '45. The men going home in the dark belonged to none of these cultures.

A GRIN IN EVERY GRAVE

At the water's edge, waves muttered little asides and slapped the stone slabs in irritation. Out on the bay, the hop and splash of mullet swimming for their lives. At night the money plants of the refinery were covered in lights; for miles they were Christmas trees on the dark plains of industry. From cars and house windows people admired their fairy grace and pointed happily to them as sights to be seen.

Coming out of the dark it was heartening to see the light in the mangroves. At the Home Beautiful, Blue Hills came on the Great White Father talking to the Glass Canoe. He went past them to get a can of beer and the Glass Canoe dated him savagely, making him jump. He knew the man did this in order to interrupt the Great White Father so that a third person wouldn't hear him giving advice to the Glass Canoe. Blue Hills had left this sort of pride behind him; he waited frankly for the Great White Father to finish so that he could tell his own troubles.

The Glass Canoe's manoeuvre did not silence the Great White Father. "You want me to continue this some other time?"

"No, no! There's no privacy about it. I have nothing to hide." The doctors impressed on him that he must never again seek privacy, he must confess and be open about everything. With everyone. Privacy was unhealthy.

"Good," said the Great White Father in his deep, dry, crackling voice. "So you've got high blood pressure now. OK. Don't fight it. It is you."

"Don't fight it? You mean let it kill me?"

"It is you. It's like Puroil. Take the kicks as they come. If Puroil toes you up one buttock, turn the other cheek. Same with life. You are a person with high blood pressure. Don't fight it. Be yourself, not a half-dead ninny trying to side-step death."

The sting in the tail of the speech fought with the public nature of the advice, given in front of Blue Hills, to decide whether the blood should recede from the Glass Canoe's face or flood it with a shaming blush. Blue Hills won and the red started to glow behind the greasy brown of his cheeks.

"Whatever you are, you are you. Live with yourself and try to like it or lump it." The Great White Father turned to Blue Hills. "How are your tomato plants, Blue?"

This is a novel that dispenses with the usual fictional framework of sequential narrative and development of character. It is typical that the author's preface occurs five pages from the end of a book nearly 400 pages long. It speaks of the book as an unassembled mosaic, and echoes an early passage, "There is no me," by stating, "And I myself am missing, but this lack is essential." In many ways it resembles that great English classic, Laurence Sterne's *Tristram Shandy*, in demonstrating that life and fiction are fragments of a whole that is never revealed, incidents in a progression that is never logical or foreseeable.

Although *The Unknown Industrial Prisoner* carries a contents page that appears to reveal the names of a number of chapters, these names are usually little more than ironical comments on the fragments, each carrying its own label, of which they are composed.

Prisoner (to abbreviate the title for convenience's sake) is as full of paradoxes as *Tristram Shandy*. It has no plot or story, yet it is a perpetual narrative, things are happening all the time. There is no shortage of drama, comedy or bawdry. It is a profoundly pessimistic book, which means that it lacks the transcendant good humour of *Tristram Shandy*, but the character who is nearest to being its hero, the Great White Father, is a humane and humorous lover of life, and especially of beer and women. It is a harsh book, but full of sympathy for anyone displaying some ability to rebel against fate.

That fate is the predicament of Western industrial man, imprisoned not only by international capitalism but by the acceptance of imprisonment. Ireland is bringing Rousseau up to date; instead of man being born free, and everywhere in chains, man is born in chains and incapable of achieving freedom. The workers in the Puroil refinery, which is the specific prison of the novel, have the hereditary scars of chains on their ankles but they have only one alternative to work. "There was an infinite freedom of choice: they could starve sitting, standing, asleep or awake; they could starve on a meat or a vegetarian diet. Anyway they liked as long as they didn't bother anyone."

Ireland is deliberately forcing the issue to extremes by immediately introducing obvious parallels to Russian literature. The first chapter is called "One Day in a Penal Colony", which at once evokes Solzhenitsyn's novel of the Gulag, *One Day in the Life of Ivan Denisovich*. As if this were not enough of a hint, the first section, "Lower Depths", carries the same title as Maxim Gorky's famous play about the dregs of Russia in 1902. The Puroil workers are certainly the dregs; they are frequently referred to as "crap".

"*No, no! There's no privacy about it. I have nothing to hide.*" *The doctors impressed on him that he must never again seek privacy, he must confess and be open about everything. With everyone. Privacy was unhealthy.*

He is of course aware that workers in a refinery in Sydney in the late 1960s do not suffer as Gorky's down-and-outs or Solzhenitsyn's Gulag prisoners did. Ireland wants to shock his readers into awareness, and throughout all his work he is prepared to outrage actuality by hyperbole or burlesque or even by complete surrealist dislocations of reality. It is also, within a very different style, the method of Swift in *Gulliver's Travels*: of course such things do not happen, but if they could, they would be just like that. The alienation from ordinary life is conveyed by the nicknames of the characters, whose real names (but how *real* are given and surnames?) are never mentioned. The nicknames also reveal what is really going on. Ireland's names give more hints than would Smith or Jones: the Great White Father, the Samurai, the Sumpsucker, the Python, the Glass Canoe, Far Away Places, Blue Hills, the Wandering Jew.

Ireland is an anxious writer, filled with a hatred of modern society but, also like Swift, with a love of individuals. Ireland, through his characters or through the author's own voice, starts asking questions from the beginning of the book. "Why imprison these men? Why not free them?"

The Great White Father broods on his fellow-workers.

Poor sods – thinking of the men herded inside the high cyclone wire fence topped with tight barbed wire – they have to be told they're human. Where had they all got off the track? . . . Sooner or later someone has to teach them freedom.

His exemplar of freedom is the Home Beautiful, hidden in the mangrove swamps, where booze and women await the workers ferried there by Volga.

"What we have to do is make our little hole in the barbed wire and creep out now and again to our hidey hole where we can forget we are born prisoners and will die prisoners. . . . Beware the evils of temperance and sobriety and embrace the worship of the bottle!"

While the Great White Father addresses the workers the whore Cinderella is working away at the other embrace which liberates, hooting like an owl when excited.

The Samurai is more solemn in his pursuit of solutions. He too is filled with pity for his fellow-prisoners, "kept ignorant of the fact that they were slaves". He has a prayer on his wall, written on a piece of cardboard, "Help, Care, Listen". He has seen at first hand the gulf between white- and blue-collar workers, and the addictive passion among all of them for the extra perks at Puroil which in fact seal their slavery. He knows there is no such thing as mateship in industrial society. As for the union, it has "the same pyramidal hierarchy as Puroil's". The Federal Secretary of the Union, addressing the men over a projected 24-hour stoppage, assures them, " 'You have the Union behind you.' He didn't say which way it would be facing."

The Samurai would like to see beyond all this hopelessness, he has a notion of "a shining idea" that would set all this vast complex of machinery working for a purpose. But the purpose eludes him.

Ironically, the Samurai is the only one whose life is seen outside the shadow of Puroil, and it is not in the light of "a shining idea", but in frenzied adultery with Mrs Blue Hills. In a slapstick scene, the sickly Blue Hills, who has found out about the Samurai and his wife, invites the Samurai to his house and like a procurer offers him his wife. Disgusted, the Samurai bolts; Blue Hills follows, on his way to the Home Beautiful, where, in the afternoon, after a bout with a whore, he dies. The Samurai lugs his body to some unfinished concrete work and hides it. At seven in the morning fresh concrete would be poured. "After that the steel tower would go up. Blue Hills would be part of the enterprise." That is the end of "a shining idea": only a corpse could be truly integrated with industry.

In the end the Samurai puts his energies into writing a book about the company, saying to the Sumpsucker, who is suspicious of this literary activity, "I'm an industrial man And yes, I want the filthy place to work. I want the whole army of industry to work." The Samurai has no "residual shackle scars" itching his ankles. He wants to wake the pitiful toilers. "Australia was dreaming off to death." Only terror and hate could wake it, and this could come only through the work of individuals, of martyrs and agitators.

But the Great White Father has already foreseen this scenario, as his reply shows, when the Glass Canoe with his

INDUSTRIAL LANDSCAPE *Russell Drysdale*

DAVID IRELAND
1927-

David Ireland was born on 24 August 1927 at Lakemba, a southern suburb of Sydney. His father was a member of the Plymouth Brethren, and so there were no radios or newspapers in the house, and of course no alcohol; he was an insurance salesman who lost his job during the Depression. The family's consequent poverty led to frequent moves, and David attended four different primary schools. He then went to Sydney Technical High School, leaving school soon after his sixteenth birthday. By this time he had decided to become a writer.

He constantly wrote poetry. Then, in 1958, prompted by an advertisement for a play competition, he wrote a play about an Aboriginal family living by the Murrumbidgee where he had been working as a timber-cutter; *Image in the Clay* was published in 1964.

Ireland has worked at many different jobs, including an 11-year stint at a Shell oil refinery. Here he was employed both as a white-collar and a blue-collar worker, which gave him some of the background for *The Unknown Industrial Prisoner*. On shift work there in 1962 he began to write his first novel, *The Chantic Bird*.

He married in the 1950s and lived on the outskirts of Sydney at Winston Hills until 1973; the Irelands have four children. In 1973 Ireland moved into the city alone and lived for four years in what he describes as "a sunless cave" in Elizabeth Street. "It depressed me profoundly at times," he says, "but at other times it was wonderful because I had nothing to do but write." In 1977 he moved to a flat above Beppi's Restaurant in East Sydney, described in *City of Women*; in 1984 he moved again, out of the central city.

David Ireland has received many literary awards. In 1966 *The Chantic Bird* won the Adelaide *Advertiser* prize, and he has won the Miles Franklin Award three times, with *The Unknown Industrial Prisoner* in 1972, *The Glass Canoe* in 1976 and *A Woman of the Future* in 1979.

In 1977 arrangements were made by Film Australia to make a film of *The Unknown Industrial Prisoner*, produced by Richard Mason, with a script by Alan Seymour, and to be shot at the Total oil refinery which was shut down for six months. However, on 24 April 1978 Mr R. J. Ellicott, as Minister for Home Affairs, used his powers under the Australian Film Commission Act to veto investment in *The Unknown Industrial Prisoner*, allegedly because it "would not be commercially viable". Despite a storm of protest, Ellicott held to his veto and the film was abandoned.

Ireland also struck trouble in New South Wales in 1982 when *The Glass Canoe*, a Rabelaisian novel based on the drinking habits of Australians, was removed from the recommended reading list for the NSW Higher School Certificate by the NSW Board of Senior School Studies. The Board claimed the book was "unsuitable" and "pornographic". The absurdity of the ban was demonstrated by the *Sydney Morning Herald* which printed the offending passage on the front page.

A critic, Ken Gelder, in *Australian Literary Studies* (Vol. 9, p. 535) noted some parallels between the American novelist Nathanael West's *Miss Lonelyhearts* (1933) and *The Unknown Industrial Prisoner*. These are not important as possible plagiarism but as a reflection of West's and Ireland's common concern with the eternal issues between God and man, with phrases like "overwhelmed by the desire to help his fellow men", and "If only he believed in God or something . . . He would be a trumpet to blaze forth to the world its failings and its ills." Ireland's childhood with a Plymouth Brethren father has left in him a strange mixture of sympathy with humanity, abhorrence for its evils and a wish to proselytise that has no basis of coherent belief.

---

great, powerful body and his unstable mind, previously said, "It's better to die standing than live on your knees."

"I know how it feels," said the Great White Father. "Sometimes the worker feels like a big gun, loaded and primed, ready to go off. But there's only one target . . . only one enemy! Who is the enemy? . . . Your own brother is your enemy! The only target is your fellow man."

And so the Great White Father accepts the shame of the rabble, "the arse of the pile. . . . The undiluted, eternal crap." The only way is the way of the Home Beautiful, women and drink.

Ireland has worked in an oil refinery and the technical superstructure of the book is skilfully assembled. The Puroil plant is extremely inefficient, and is always breaking down. Even so it has a kind of beauty at night, after the white-collar workers have scuttled off. Yet it is cruel that this other world, with its glimpse of beauty, is also the prison—the refinery.

The farce of company and union negotiation goes on, and the chain of responsibility remains hidden, disappearing into overseas headquarters and anonymous shareholders, so that Puroil is an image of the whole world. "We know man is alienated from his true function, but what is he? What is his true function?"

This question, asked at the beginning of the book, is answered by the Samurai with a religion of hate. "Sabotage, destruction, hardship, violence, blood."

But a cruelly humorous fate, outrageously slapstick, has the Samurai kidnapped by Mrs Blue Hills's four brothers and tied to her bed for her pleasure, while in fact Puroil is sabotaged and the plant blows up. The Samurai, the man "in love with the industry", had pinched in an air-pipe he thought was not in service but in fact was, and disaster has followed many further deliberate or accidental malfunctions.

So much for the Samurai. As for the Great White Father, he has been rechristened the Great White Feather, a name that amuses him. But those who know, know that "the Home Beautiful wasn't a spontaneous movement of men: it was one man. One good man."

The Unknown Industrial Prisoner would seem to be an unbearably nihilistic and despairing book were it not for the comedy of the Great White Father/Feather, whose death is celebrated by six whores kneeling around his body and singing their favourite sentimental pop songs, and Dial-a-Prayer offering consolation. Like the refinery at night, the scene of the death is a glimpse of unsentimentalised beauty and goodness. But the Great White Father/Feather is not dead, only drunk. The parody of death and religion is complete. "A third time the Great White Feather struggled to rise and a third time the weight of their devotion kept him under."

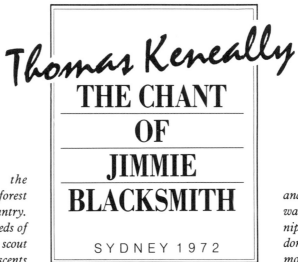

Thomas Keneally

THE CHANT OF JIMMIE BLACKSMITH

SYDNEY 1972

Twelve days after Healy's, the Blacksmith brothers were still in forest and had tired of it. It was tricky country. One kept coming on drops of hundreds of feet, perhaps a thousand, and had to scout about for a way down. The descents themselves seemed profitless and unreal. The Blacksmiths had the tedium of ceaselessly outdistancing their pursuit.

They needed the heady sight of hunters; to be made to flee at high speed and in the route of armies.

Fires and long meals soothed them. Sometimes they overslept. Mort spoke, the little he did, of visiting women.

Jimmie believed it was wise of Mort to think of women, and to find Pilbarra camp one night after dark, where he knew a girl called Nancy. Certainly they were reckless, but had come to a point where they needed to be assured of the tangible world of search-parties and towns aghast by the dozen.

So they heedlessly knocked on Nancy's door in Pilbarra. It happened that Nancy's husband was away, but he was a hospitable man anyhow, or if not hospitable, easily frightened.

Both her children were there, a half-caste called Simon and a full-blood called Peter. Nancy took them aside. She had a flat solemn pleasant face. The Blacksmith brothers could hear what she told them.

"These two fellers pretty bloody tough, cut yer water off or bloody throat like as not. You git off with yer into bush and catch possum a few hours. Orright? Yer go quiet and if yer go near Constable Harrogate they'll shoot the two of yer and him as well. Off yer go."

Unbuttoning, Mort said, "Who's this Constable Harrogate?"

"All the blacks' camps got a constable, pertect 'em against angry whitefellers. There lot of whites with rifles ridin' up and down the countryside."

Nancy herself was undressing, in a random way. Her kindness to killers—it looked like kindness, anyhow, not fear, made Jimmie's throat stick and caused him to colour and brought tears to his eyes. Her off-hand mercy.

Without warning, Mort fell on her and wept with an alarming loudness, and was soothed into sucking at one of her nipples like a child. "Yer know what we done?" he asked her, half-choking, his mouth champing at her.

"Yair, yer ripped up some people, didn't yer? Yer ain't goin' t' rip me up though, are yer, Mort?"

Mort howled. Nancy made hushing noises.

Jimmie as well wanted his turn to weep on her, but could not delay the spasm of grief. He fell onto his knees shuddering. It was beyond him to hate the Newbys any more. It was far less than that he felt no victory over them. Their judgments seemed to hang over him still, of their own strength.

So Jimmie was still the victim. The obviousness of the fact bent him to the ground abjectly, as Healy himself had been bent.

Then, as Mort still sweated towards satisfying his mothering Nancy, Jimmie lay inert, his mouth open. He could neither move nor imagine himself ever moving again. It would take someone to come armed and demanding surrender to undo his paralysis.

The good Mr Neville, the Reverend H. J. Neville, BA, Methodist Minister, had hoped that he just might be able to imbue *one* Aborigine with "decent ambitions". Neville thinks mixed-blood Jimmie Blacksmith might be such a one, but Jimmie goes away with his black people without telling Mr Neville, into the bush for his initiation and circumcision ceremony. And later Jimmie murders three women with an axe, the beginning of his war against certain whites.

The Chant of Jimmie Blacksmith is a book where evil begets evil, and good is only at best marginal. Yet Keneally's artistry and capacity for human sympathy clearly establish the presence of some goodness in Jimmie and his two assistants in murder, his full-blood half-brother Mort and his Uncle Tabidgi Jackie Smolders. Although the book is based on the story of Jimmy Governor and his brother and the murders they committed in 1900 in New South Wales, the tale of Jimmie Blacksmith is not a journalistic account written from the outside. It is a major novel.

Jimmie's black core is "eroded by the Nevilles' ceaseless European pride". He leaves the Nevilles' to look for a job, to get on in the world, and even, maybe, to take a white girl to wife. He will stay sober for the final test. "I gotter start working so I kin git property."

It was not at all easy in the 1890s for an Aborigine to start working. At last a harsh Irish farmer gives him a job making a post-and-rail fence, for £2 12s. 2d. He makes a fine fence, but the farmer pays him only £2 and will not give him a ride with his gear into town when he leaves. In incidents such as these the generalised role inflicted by whites on Aborigines becomes personal injustice.

Jimmie is also puzzled by sex, lust and love. In the black man's world of religion there is, or should be, order and ritual that extends from these to nature itself. In the white man's world of religion there is the love about which Mr Neville had spoken, coming down from God, and sanctified between one man and one woman. Jimmie has plenty of time to observe the result of the white man's lust in the blacks' camp, even to the murder and burial by the blacks of one young white man. It is a harsh counter theme running through the book that, as an old Aborigine says to Jimmie, white women don't make white men happy. "Why else he come after black girls?"

Desperate for a job, Jimmie goes to work for the police and is dressed up in an ill-fitting uniform and in this way becomes a "comic abo" stock figure. The clothes are symbolic of Jimmie's life, his identity fluctuating between white and black. Having suffered further employers of the likes of Healy the Irishman, he is now working for a sadist and a pervert, Senior Constable Farrell. He is instrumental in bringing one of his own people, the murderer of the young man who had been sleeping with a black girl, not only to gaol but to his death at Farrell's hands. In some painful way, Jimmie despises the vulnerability of his race.

Jimmie throws away his uniform and goes to work for a farmer called Hayes and marries the 17-year-old kitchen maid, Gilda, after she tells him she is pregnant by him. He takes her to live on another station, of about 2800 hectares near Wallah, owned by a man called Newby. Here Jimmie has a fencing contract. There are some "terse kindnesses" in Mr Newby, who lends Jimmie a horse to bring his bride back from Gilgandra. He leads her back to the one roomed house with an earth floor, "A slowly descending white was wedded to a black in the ascendant. That was what Jimmie hoped had happened." But Jimmie remains cagey with a Newby in whose eyes there is always mockery.

Nancy herself was undressing, in a random way. Her kindness to killers—it looked like kindness, anyhow, not fear, made Jimmie's throat stick and caused him to colour and brought tears to his eyes. Her off-hand mercy.

The schoolmistress from Wallah, Petra Graf ("finer in texture than the Newby girls" and engaged), and Newby's wife and daughters take Gilda from Jimmie and superintend her confinement. Excluded as a man, Jimmie is excluded as a father when the child is born—white. It is not his baby. Gilda had trapped him into marriage.

At this moment, as it were with a promise of black solidarity, Tabidgi Jackie Smolders and Jimmie's laughing half-brother Mort and a boy, Peter, arrive with Jimmie's

tooth that had been knocked out at initiation, to keep him safe after marrying a white girl. Jimmie does not want such "high tribal seriousness", any more than he wants them to stay. But they do, constructing a lean-to by his hut.

Jimmie is again in a vicious circle regarding work. Newby owes him £15. He neither wants to pay it nor wants Jimmie's tribal relations on his property. Newby determines to starve them out, by refusing to take Gilda's weekly order to Wallah.

On the surface, it is money—yet another example of white man cheating black—that precipitates violence in Jimmie. But on a deeper level it is something sexual; the challenge of the smooth, sleek Miss Graf who lends tone to the Newby household, who is listening at the door when Jimmie goes at night to demand his due wages. He has "A desire for her blood . . . to scare the schoolmistress apart with his authority". Thus he does not kill Newby, although he prods his belly with his Enfield rifle when Newby refuses him his wages. "Newby was not what he wanted. He was in a fever for some definite release." He returns to the house, exchanges the rifle for an axe, and gives Tabidgi a tomahawk. In a few minutes he and Tabidgi have mortally injured four women, Mrs Newby, Miss Graf and two of the daughters.

Jimmie has chosen to feel "large with a royal fever, with rebirth", "The first necessary qualities of a war regally undertaken". He says later to Gilda, when he intends to leave her with the baby along the Dubbo Road, "Tell the p'lice I said I declared war." There were earlier hints, when "He had even begun remotely to wonder if a man's only means of treating with them [i.e., whites] was to 'declare war'. It was a phrase he had picked up on the shearing floor the previous year. It connoted for him a sweet wide freedom— to hate, . . . debase as an equal." By murdering the women, Jimmie has become "an equal".

Jimmie, Mort and Tabidgi and Peter take to the bush. Tabidgi and Peter are soon left behind, and the half-brothers are on their own. Miss Graf's fiancé, Dowie Stead, rides up to the Newby homestead with five farmer friends, a posse to track down the murderers. It seems an act of noble revenge, the wronged lover hunting the killer of his beloved. But, in common with almost every white man in this novel, Stead is not at peace with himself; his soul is uneasy with lust and guilt and something more. He in particular is carrying a horrible image. Riding drunk one night to the blacks' camp to his favourite black girl Tessie, thin, consumptive (how unlike Miss Graf!), he pushes into her humpy and finds his own father in his shirt tails sitting on the mattress. The blacks represent some elemental passion the whites can neither ignore nor avoid.

To Jimmie the whites represent "pretensions of permanence" that must be chopped down. He is after his cherished enemies. After Mort has shot the Healys' mother's aide, Jimmie shoots Mrs Healy and her baby. Mort is appalled. "'Healy deserve all this?' Mort asked thickly. There was no irony in him. He was silly with shock." The returning Healy is shot by Jimmie as he tries to shoot Mort. Jimmie regrets that Healy died outside the home: "I wanted him to see what he bloody caused."

Jimmie now promises Mort, "No more women."

Alone amongst the outraged whites of New South Wales the Reverend Neville has some understanding of what is going on in Jimmie's mind, for he has sown some of the seeds

REFLECTED BRIDE *Arthur Boyd*

THOMAS KENEALLY
1935-

Thomas Keneally was born of a Catholic family in 1935 in Sydney and educated at St Patrick's College, Strathfield. He began studies for the priesthood and the law, but did not complete either.

He was a high school teacher in Sydney from 1960 to 1964, when he also began writing. His first novel, *The Place at Whitton* (1964), was a sort of Gothic romantic thriller based on his time in the seminary. His next novel was *The Fear* (1965). He has said, "I would like to be able to have disowned my first two novels." This is a pity, as there is much of merit in both of them, and they certainly indicated the arrival of a new talent in Australian fiction. This was confirmed by *Bring Larks and Heroes* (1967), which he himself described as "An attempt to follow an epic theme in terms of a young soldier's exile to Australia."

Keneally was lecturer in Drama at the University of New England from 1968 to 1970, after which he became a professional writer. He married Judith Martin in 1965 and they have two daughters.

Keneally was given support over a number of years by the Commonwealth Literary Fund and then by the Literature Board, and his career makes a very good case for such support, as it is probable that he could not have written so many, and such good, novels and plays if he had not been able to devote his energies to writing full-time.

Keneally is one of those writers who stay at home but roam far abroad in their books. In the last 10 years his novels have been set in locations outside Australia, such as France, Yugoslavia, the USA, Poland and Antarctica. He has realised that until perhaps very recently, the outside world has not been very interested in Australia, and books about it are not going to sell widely overseas. Like Graham Greene and Morris West, he has taken his stories from all over the world, and most of them from historical sources. Unlike Greene, he has not been much of a traveller. In fact, he has followed the Shakespearian tradition of letting his imagination work on the facts provided for him by others. The exceptions are his fables such as *A Dutiful Daughter* and *Passenger*.

Keneally has found that all this has exposed him to a certain amount of criticism from nationalistic Australian critics. He has had some sharp words to say about them: "Certainly I have moved outside Australian subject matter which is something very frowned on by the cognoscenti here. There is a cultural KGB here which says what you can write about." Nevertheless, many Australian critics have agreed with their colleagues in London and New York and praised Keneally's novels about such subjects as Joan of Arc, the meeting of the allied and German leaders in the railway carriage at Compiègne after the end of World War II, the American Civil War, and the protecting of Jews by a German in World War II— this being the subject of *Schindler's Ark* which won Keneally the internationally prestigious Booker Prize in 1983.

Although the narrative techniques in his novels vary, Keneally does not use his assured technique to experiment radically with form. His doubts are not of his craft but of human motives. His early religious training still leads him to forgive all sinners except those who damage the human spirit.

---

that have borne such deadly fruit. "He knew what sickness Jimmie was suffering. Having a true talent for religion, he understood the obsessive spirit, and understood that he himself might have been sent racketing around if ever he had touched a black woman." And he remembers, "with nausea that he had recommended this sort of marriage to Jimmie, this stupid, cunning and insipid girl".

Twelve days after the Healy murders, Mort shoots a young white called Toban, an armed member of a posse. To Mort, the killing is something from "an antique code", from "tribal face-to-face warring. Besides, Toban was a man."

After this shooting Mort goes back more and more into his race, speaking his native language at times, talking of himself as a warrior, painting his face with white clay. "It made Jimmie peevish . . . 'What's this bullshit?' " Mort calls Jimmie "devil-man". They are reunited by being outcast, and go off again together, until finally they take an asthmatic teacher with them as hostage. This teacher, McCreadie, is the only wholly sympathetic white character in the book, and this is one reason Jimmie takes him along, "in the hope of finding a genial self-reflection in McCreadie. But people are never passive mirrors."

Jimmie develops a love-hate relationship with McCreadie, while Mort defends him, but both begin to need him. He can understand their anger. He knows how the whites have massacred the blacks. "Jimmie secretly loved to hear these admissions. They were the luxuries he kept McCreadie for." McCreadie has studied folklore, he knows of some of the secret ceremonial places of the Aborigines, and he leads the

brothers to one on a mountain above the coast. Mort sings a chant to the place and its spirits. "Jimmie sang nothing and was afraid." This is the climax of the book, a non-violent moment in a story of terrible violence. McCreadie can see the fear and the confusion: "Mr. Jimmie Blacksmith, mighty terroriser, lost beyond repair somewhere between the Lord God of Hosts and the shrunken cosmogony of his people."

The ending is inevitable. Through McCreadie's sickness, and their wanting to carry him to help, the brothers more or less give themselves up. Mort is shot dead. Jimmie has escaped, but he is wounded in a magnificent swim across the Manning River. He is finally captured, in a fitting irony, in a convent where he has been hiding in the guest room, suffering from his infected wound.

As Jimmie waits in prison to be hanged, the Reverend Neville writes a letter to the Methodist Church *Times*, admitting some responsibility for Jimmie's career, for encouraging ambitions in him in a society not "yet ready to accept the ambitious Aborigine". He has no answer, except prayer.

Nor should a novel provide answers. Instead, Keneally, having evoked the spiritual, returns to the political, the fact of Australia's Federation, first hinted at about 50 pages into the novel, by Jimmie in an attempt to "open up responsible subjects of conversation", asking Mr Newby if he is looking forward to Federation. So, in 1901, "the rape of primitives" forgotten, after a decent pause Tabidgi Jackie Smolders and Jimmie are hanged.

THE AMERICANS, BABY

SYDNEY 1972

"Life is not a continually pleasant thing," he said, "but it has things to offer—love, the mastering of something. Making beautiful things. And, if you like, fast cars."

"But take the idea of mastering something—you only get really good at it when you're old and ready to die."

"They say the mastering is the best part," he said. But this drummed hollow. "I mean that there are stages which give the pleasure." This drummed less hollow but still sounded empty. He thought how fleeting these pleasures were compared with some of the groaning hours.

He was nervously agitated in the stomach. It was caused by the girl being stronger in her arguments than he was. She was bringing home to him things he had not thought for some time. In her mouth they seemed freshly and cruelly correct. And too many of the things he was saying seemed downright untrue. He needed to prove his wisdom. For his vanity as well as for the girl. But why was he finding it so bloody difficult?

"Love's a good thing," he said, "and the making of beautiful things."

"I've never been in love," she said. "Perhaps love is dead."

"Come, now, you're only twenty."

He was thinking though of the doubts you suffered both in love and in the making of beautiful things. You doubted whether the things you made or did were beautiful and you doubted whether you were loved and whether you really loved.

He told her that, "But there are short periods when you do. It's pretty good then." He was thinking, strangely, about his cooking, which was about the only time he made anything that could be called beautiful.

"But what if we're incapable of either," she persisted.

"You don't know yet."

She took his hand and kissed it, then sighed, "No . . . love is dead. Art is dead. Everything an artist spent a lifetime striving for any old hippie can do with two hundred milligrammes of LSD."

"Then there is LSD," he said, smiling. Glad of even the simple response of a kiss on the hand. He wanted now to pull out of the conversation and its disturbance. "The pleasures of drugs and grog," he laughed, drinking a toast. Although he had never tried drugs.

"Alcohol is a bore and pot and LSD are affectations," she said: she could have been serious.

"The new sophistication. The unhappy princess of the mid-twentieth century," he said tightly.

She looked at him, a little surprised by his tone.

"I guess that was a little sarcastic," he said.

In a sudden change of mood unrelated to anything he'd said, she said, "I'm ready to go to the party now."

She pulled him into a run across the lawn.

As they entered the party she said, "You're a very attractive man for your age," and laughed.

"Wait until I'm fifty—and I'll really have a distinguished sexuality," he said, grinning artificially, conscious of the sham humour groaning under sham optimism.

He went over to his wife.

"I've just saved a young woman from despair and futility." And he made this and another genial remark and as he did he felt sick to the stomach.

"Must try your line on me some time," she said.

It is difficult for a writer of fiction who succeeds in conveying the flavour of contemporaneity to avoid the risk that it will fade. The most dangerous period for such a book is about 10 years after publication; a generation later, it may begin to achieve permanent status as a period piece, the essence of its time. This is especially true when the book deals with characters who are not sustained by any tradition, who need a new dawn as a drug addict needs a fix.

Frank Moorhouse runs this risk in *The Americans, Baby*, which he calls "a discontinuous narrative of stories and fragments". Its characters are completely of their time, the late 1960s and early 1970s. He succeeds because he creates living intensity of detail of event and character, which is saved from transience by the permanence of irony. It is the same method used by the great Impressionist painters, by Manet in "Le déjeuner sur l'herbe" or "Le bar aux Folies-bergères", in which a naked woman with the clothed men or the abstracted expression on a barmaid's face set up disturbing ironic vibrations under the apparently calm surface of contemporary reality.

Moorhouse deals with the misapplication of theories of revolutionary politics and sex, with the chastening of those whose attitudes are clichés, with the gulf between small-town and big-city mores, with the web of suspicion and acceptance that makes up American–Australian personal relations. His characters are most at sea when they are most theory ridden, heading off with fixed ideas about navigation but without a compass or sextant. Often a rather rueful narrator is involved in the story, the comedy of his situation bumping up against the theory-directed, solemn lifestyle of his companions. There is a good example of this, and of Moorhouse's honesty of approach, in the story "The Girl from the Family of Man", the girl being an American in Sydney, who is into non-violence, eating honey and peace marches.

> She looked into my eyes. "I worry," she said. "I worry that people like us treat sex too carelessly – just because we're the full anti-convention bit – we tend – I don't know . . . I suppose we tend to *undervalue* sex."
>
> Not me, I thought, I don't undervalue it.

Moorhouse's discontinuous narrative technique is part of a long tradition. In Australia it belongs with Henry Lawson and *Joe Wilson's Mates*; further back, with Chaucer's *Canterbury Tales*. Sometimes the characters are the same in various stories, and they also appear in other books by Moorhouse. (Cindy in "The Story of Nature" appears in an earlier book, *Futility and Other Animals*.) Sometimes contemporary follies and would-be wisdoms, the acting out and repression of desires, give the book a kind of unity.

She took his hand and kissed it, then sighed, "No . . . love is dead. Art is dead. Everything an artist spent a lifetime striving for any old hippie can do with two hundred milligrammes of LSD."

The book also has subtler parallels between big, sophisticated America and small, imitative Australia on the one hand, and, on the other, uninhibited Sydney and conventional Coolamon (or whatever name Moorhouse gives a country town). But Moorhouse's irony makes more of these parallels than simply geometry; they illuminate each other. The most interesting character in the book, Becker, the Coca-Cola salesman, is always looking back from Sydney to America, where the wealth exists, "piled high in bags, . . . not in this godforsaken country". When Becker's boss asks him "You OK?", the conversation goes, " 'Sure Sam, just pooped.' 'Too much action?' 'In this city!' "

The inference is that Sydney is so boring and provincial that no full-blooded American could become exhausted by it. Becker is always remembering that he is "a long way from old Atlanta, Georgia, and the action". Moorhouse does not labour the point at all, but of course it is there in the home town Becker longs for. *Atlanta*, Georgia! That is where the action is! So much for sophistication and provincialism!

Similarly, in another discussion, in the opening story "Dell Goes into Politics", Dell comes back to her home town, Coolamon, from the big city of Sydney. She is immediately asked by her mother if she has a young man yet. " 'No', replies Dell, '– at least not one.' " She has lived for a while with Kim, a Trotskyist schoolteacher full of theories about politics and sex. When she says to her mother that Kim was a bit odd, " 'What you mean odd?' her mother said, fearfully, knowing the word had something to do with sex or madness."

Once more the tensions are set up with a delicate irony that waits its moment to question the apparent truth of what is happening on the surface. Dell is the city girl now, as her father says mockingly, and she has come home to what she does not want as home, "to sleep in that rotten narrow bed, in that room in that shack of a house with a chip heater", where even though it is early morning Dad is already "drinking beer from a hotel glass, sitting there, King of the Kitchen Table". Her crude father wants to know about her sex life, asking her, "You're not in trouble, are you?"

Dell looks up an old boyfriend, Harry, a mechanic, and goes to the pub with him where the local MP is buying drinks. Dell, who has been deep into the theory of politics with Kim, is disgusted that Harry does not even know whether the MP is State or Federal. " 'He's in Sydney I guess,' flounders Harry, 'no, it's Canberra.' "

When Dell, the city activist, yells out to the MP, "Why don't you bring the boys back from Vietnam!", someone at the bar says, "Aren't there enough around, Dell?" Caught off guard, she blushes, but continues to heckle, to Harry's intense embarrassment. Yet Dell is honest enough to realise that "she'd been mouthing a few of the things she'd heard with Kim and the others at meetings she'd been dragged along to".

When she is eating spaghetti on toast for tea at home, her father and mother tackle her about drinking at the pub on a Sunday morning and talking politics. " 'I think I'll go into politics,' she said, quite without thought, just for the fun of saying it." Her father is amused and her mother horrified.

The story ends with Dell reflecting "What else was there to do in this stinking world?", and remembering "she hadn't had her periods for two months and she was putting on weight". Perhaps Dad is right; she may be in trouble after all.

One can see why the judges awarded this story the State of Victoria short story prize for 1970. The lights of its ironies play around city and country town, parental relationships, sex, but most of all around politics, which is both the arena where something can be done and a stage for frauds. Fuller, the local Member, is bringing a bunch of folk singers to town as his contribution to the seriousness of politics. (A variant of this occurs in another story, "Becker and the Boys from the Band"). Kim the schoolteacher, with his politics and sex, it is hinted, is also more involved for the sake of his ego than that of the nation. Dell is a sympathetic, honest character caught in the midst of it all, quite decided by the end of the story that she does not want to be Harry's wife, nor would he marry her, but undecided about everything else. She is a seeker with no goal.

The awful Kim, on the other hand, who turns up in several stories, is always all too clear about goals. He belongs to that most dangerous breed, those who are expert in self-deception, but who lose touch with humanity by pursuing rigid theories that are allegedly for the benefit of humanity and the extension of knowledge.

Another intractable country town is the background for the story, "The Revolutionary Kidney Punch", which is clearly about the Trotskyist schoolteacher Kim and his wife Sylvia. Kim is going to make the town sing revolutionary songs and (again like the politician Fuller) has imported a folk singing group who will perform in the Memorial Hall. Kim has a vision of the town's young people all coming and joining in to sing "We Shall Overcome". But no one turns up. The hall is almost empty. "What could you do with a town like this? It would have to be dragged into line. A few platoons of worker militia would run the town. Perhaps the farm workers. The teachers would be OK. Would the

THE BEAUTIFUL ONE IS HERE (detail) *Mike Brown*

FRANK MOORHOUSE
1939-

Frank Moorhouse was born in 1939 and educated at high school in Nowra on the New South Wales south coast, and the University of Queensland. For some years he worked as a journalist, beginning as a cadet with the Sydney *Daily Telegraph* and then as a reporter for the *Wagga Wagga Advertiser* and the *Riverina Express*. He was a reporter and sub-editor for the ABC news service, and a columnist and contributor with the *Bulletin*. He was also, for a time, editor of the *Australian Worker*. He has been the Australian Journalists' Association's representative on the Australian Press Council, and President of the Australian Society of Authors. He visited India in 1980 and China in 1983 as a cultural exchange writer under the auspices of the Department of Foreign Affairs.

All these activities represent an interesting contrast to the frequently accepted image of Moorhouse as a Balmain Bohemian of the 1970s, an image of course indirectly reinforced by his own writing.

In the Preface to his book, *Days of Wine and Rage* (1980), edited by Moorhouse and partly made up of his own writings, Moorhouse writes, "I found as I wrote the book and selected the pieces, that it was becoming also a homage to Sydney, where I had lived for twenty years. More particularly to the Sydney 'community of ideas and arts' which had nurtured me creatively, supported me financially, and sometimes protected me. It is also, to narrow it down even further, a homage to my suburb, Balmain, which, for all its posturing and for all the satire it invites, was a significant part of the pageant."

It is this pageant of Sydney (and country towns) that forms the subject matter of the six collections of stories, including *The Americans, Baby* (1972) and *The Electrical Experience* (1974), novellas, including *Conference-ville* (1976) and *The Everlasting Secret Family and Other Secrets* (1980), and "discontinuous narratives" that Moorhouse published between 1969 and 1980. Many of them have been reprinted several times, a tribute to his success as a chronicler of the desires and uncertain aims of his times.

Moorhouse has been much involved as a writer with film and television. He has written the scripts for several short films and for the feature film *Between Wars* with director Michael Thornhill. *Conference-ville*, based on the novella, appeared as a 120-minute telemovie in 1984.

Three of the stories in *The Americans, Baby* won the Henry Lawson, Banjo Paterson and State of Victoria prizes. When the collection was set in Victoria for final year high school, the government rushed to put an R certificate on it. Despite the protests of professors of English at all Victorian universities, at that time the book could not be read by people under 18 and it was removed from library shelves.

It was also the key book in the photocopying test case against the University of New South Wales which led to a High Court case, a Royal Commission and subsequent new legislation, which afforded extra copyright protection for authors.

Rotarians have to be eliminated? The Lions?" It was a time when people thought in such inhuman clichés, and spoke of people having to be "eliminated". All Kim can do is go to Sydney for a demonstration against President Johnson and manage to punch a policeman in the kidney.

In an alarming story, "The Machine Gun", another revolutionary activist, Turvey, reveals to the narrator, Kim, that he has bought a Bren gun from a criminal. They go to a clifftop and fire off a magazine. Turvey is convinced that the machine gun will be needed because "things could get hot" with secret Chinese infiltration. They go to a party. The drunken Turvey comes in with the machine gun. Unknown to him, there is a cartridge still left in the breech, which goes off when he pulls the trigger. Fortunately, despite the screams, no one is killed.

In several stories Moorhouse enjoys bringing a woman on to the scene who will humiliate such humourless and egocentric people as Kim and an American visiting professor, neatly satirised in "A Person of Accomplishment". In "Anti-Bureaucratisation and the Apparatchiki", Dell, at this stage still an earthy, straightforward country town girl, is being instructed in sex and revolutionary principles by Kim, and finding life with him more and more intolerable. The last straw comes when Kim tells her that he and his friend Carl want to tape an interview with her about her sex life in Coolamon, "a case history of sexual taboo". "Go to hell," she says at last, and leaves him. There is a neat ending involving a simpler sexuality.

The Americans, Baby has a lot of sex in encounters both heterosexual and homosexual, but it is seldom joyful and never triumphant. The situations are often comic, but edging towards black. However, Moorhouse is, in this book at least, a good-natured writer who is afflicted with symptoms of desperation, but who avoids bitterness.

Moorhouse specialises in taking people over the limits. Sometimes they are pushed to the edge by dogma or theory, at other times by their own human fallibility. As Becker desperately asks himself, having become involved with a lusty temporary secretary called Terri, "Why did he skirt the odorous abyss so perilously?" Becker goes over the edge twice, once nearly fatally. Needled by Kim, he drunkenly tries to hang himself. It is not explained why Becker wants to take his own life; there are enough hints. In "Soft Drink and the Distribution of Soft Drink" Terri is taken by Becker to a business party and misbehaves herself, finally writing obscenities about Becker with Texta colour on the bathroom mirror. In the end Becker is caught at work in an outrageous sexual scene with Terri, loses his job with Coca-Cola and goes to play jazz piano at Surfer's Paradise.

In Moorhouse's later books his range becomes narrower, but in *The Americans, Baby*, he brilliantly mixes the trendies and the intellectuals (albeit self-appointed) with the ordinary world of Coca-Cola and Rotary. The trendies are sometimes one jump ahead of what is thought to be trendy: " 'Alcohol is a bore and pot and LSD are affectations,' she said . . . 'The new sophistication,' he said tightly."

Such wry incidents are typical of the way Moorhouse manages to write about the contemporary without producing something that ends by being dated. Even at moments of close involvement, he manages to achieve a classic objectivity of distance.

George Farwell

SQUATTER'S CASTLE

MELBOURNE 1973

There were no further signs of devilry among the tribes. The Ogilvies were on excellent terms with them. Young Pundoon was back with his relatives. Men, women and their piccaninnies had set up semi-permanent gunyahs beside the long reach. Their leader and spokesman was the tall, muscular Toolbillibam. The masters of Yulgilbar had developed an easy friendship, based partly on respect for tribal attitudes, partly on physical competitiveness.

Both Edward and Fred challenged the sturdiest tribesmen to bouts of wrestling. Even the redoubtable Toolbillibam. They ran foot races against them. They challenged them to swimming and diving contests along Yulgilbar Reach. It was great sport. The blacks hugely enjoyed it. But all this had begun as something more than sport. There had been elements of real hostility in those vigorous and exhausting bouts. For the powerfully built chief and his supporters this was a testing of the white men. They had to win; or at least to prove themselves. They had to prove their strength if they wanted to be

masters of this country.

There is a family story, told by later generations, that Edward, after the first wrestling bout, was shut in a gunyah for the night, during which the tribal elders debated whether or not he should be allowed to live. Had he not fought so gamely, so the story goes, he would have been killed. Next morning he was relieved to see Toolbillibam's wife approaching the gunyah, leading one of her piccaninnies. It was well known that, when violence was planned, women and children were withdrawn from a camp.

Only later did these fierce and resolute combats descend to the level of more even-tempered play. Even Tindal was drawn into them. As a new chum he, too, was expected to display his manliness.

In November he wrote to his father,

"This afternoon we had some wrestling matches with the blacks. I began with Toolbillibam. He is the biggest man about here. The first round was undecided. In the second he managed to throw me. After this Edward Ogilvie threw his brother Charlie twice out of thrice. Some time back we wrestled with a black named Jemmy. Edward Ogilvie and I threw him, but he had the best of Fred Ogilvie."

The entire scene was almost unimaginable anywhere else in the country. These hardy, outgoing young Ogilvies had created a sense of harmony no other outback squatters enjoyed. It had achieved more than muskets could ever do. The outcome was made clear by a further entry in Tindal's letter: "I have just been making a bargain with a black for a belt, which he had round his loins, and which constitutes his only clothing. He gave it to me for a fish hook. It is made from the hair of his own head. Another is to get me some of their baskets, and I hope to have some of their weapons by and by."

As a story, George Farwell's account of the Ogilvies, pastoralists in New South Wales in the nineteenth century, is as gripping as any novel, but *Squatter's Castle* may also be read as biography or social and economic history. An immense amount of background detail has been skilfully introduced into the basic family history, so that the reader has a sense of living in Australia in the period, of enduring the same hardships, enjoying the good times and suffering the losses.

Farwell, of course, chose his protagonists well. The Ogilvies did not eventually lose their souls, like Brian Penton's Cabell in *Landtakers*. They were radical conservatives who kept communications flowing between themselves and the Aborigines, and the men who worked for them, while at the same time maintaining an awareness of the landscape and the civilisation they came from. In the case of Edward, the metaphysical boundaries were extended from British tradition to Italian culture, especially that of renaissance Florence.

Apart from the interest of their lives as pioneers, the Ogilvies are notable in Australian pastoral history for their enlightened attitude towards the Aborigines. Living at the time of some of the worst conflicts between black and white, in which the Myall Creek massacre was by no means unique, the Ogilvies maintained good relations with the resident Aborigines. This was for a variety of reasons. They always treated them with respect, and without fear. No interference with Aboriginal women was allowed by those who worked for them. Most important of all, perhaps, was that the Ogilvie boys spoke the local Aboriginal language. This was accepted as a token of goodwill and of course made misunderstandings much less likely.

William Ogilvie (husband of Mary and father of the three boys, Edward, William and Frederick, and their sister Ellen) was an ex-naval officer who, on being retired, set up as a farmer at Merton, the village near London where Lord Nelson also intended to retire. In 1824 the Ogilvies travelled to Australia and William took up a land grant of 810 hectares at a place he called Merton on the Upper Hunter River. Ogilvie had 58 convicts and a resident "scourger" assigned to him. Although the system was feudal, and the convicts were in fact unpaid serfs, the outlay for rations was considerable. Some observers claimed that the convicts lived better than labourers in England, on a weekly ration consisting of "a sufficiency of flour to make four quartern loaves at least, of seven pounds of beef, two ounces of tea, one pound of sugar and two ounces of tobacco".

William obtained his first sheep in 1827, and a list of improvements made at that time, estimated to be worth £2000, included eight kilometres of rail fence, "150 acres of land cleared and enclosed for cultivation", a stone house, a barn, a general store, a dairy, a cottage and 17 lesser buildings, and an orchard and garden.

An act of treachery by the local constable and soldiers caused a horde of armed Aborigines to come to Merton one day when the two Williams and Edward were away in Sydney. They surrounded two of the soldiers and seemed about to kill them when, according to a contemporary account, Mary ran in among them and "with a firm persuasive manner awed and soothed them. In half an hour they left on the most cordial terms, the leaders even shaking hands all around, rattling their spears and shouting warnings to 'tell sodja not come meddle Massa Ogilvie blacks.'" Governor Darling's report to London said that:

> Mrs Ogilvie, who appears to have acted with much judgement and spirit, then gave them some maize and tobacco, and they left the premises without being guilty of any irregularity. They then proceeded to Mr Lethbridge's place where, I presume, not being managed with the same spirit, they fell on the overseer and stockmen, killed and speared four men.

Mary's courage on this occasion was typical of her whole life. Her boys grew up with the same ability to take command, allied to a then atypical consciousness of the dignity of the Aborigines as human beings.

The entire scene was almost unimaginable anywhere else in the country. These hardy, outgoing young Ogilvies had created a sense of harmony no other outback squatters enjoyed. It had achieved more than muskets could ever do.

By now Merton was a town, ruled over by Commander Ogilvie as local landowner and resident magistrate. When Charles Tindal, son of an old naval comrade of Ogilvie's, came to Merton for "colonial experience", he wrote that Ogilvie was:

> Very particular about the natives, and the tribe call themselves his blacks. One day I was introduced to them by Mary Ogilvie as another son of hers from England, and therefore brother to all blackfellows. They are finer and more intelligent than I expected, the best are employed at the outstations to track cattle.

Merton was in fact now only the base of operations, and Ogilvie had nine other cattle stations in the district. The Ogilvies and their neighbours were living well, if simply, and were growing grapes to produce their own wine – the Merton hock and the Wyndham's Dalwood claret being particularly well thought of.

But Edward was becoming bored managing his father's sheep, and was well aware that his father, despite apparent prosperity, was still in debt. At 25 Edward was in the full flush of his youth and strength. He was described as "a born bushman, one of those who can go straight to anywhere they wish . . . a small, wiry man, of great strength of character and body, a first-rate rider and very athletic. He could best even the blacks at sprint running and long distance diving."

Now there was talk of excellent new country to the north on what was then known only as "The Big River" (later called the Clarence). An overlanding party was to be guided there by the ex-convict Richard Craig, but for some reason the Ogilvies did not join this party. Instead they rode on ahead in 1840 by themselves: Edward, Fred, a third European and an Aboriginal stockman, all wearing bright red flannel shirts above their moleskins, and long blucher boots.

After some 640 kilometres of extreme hardship crossing the valleys and ranges, they came on a magnificent reach of water, surrounded by hills, which the Aborigines called Yulgilbar. This, with its 90-kilometre river frontage, was Edward's choice for a head station. The party rode on further and then went to the Crown Lands Commissioner's headquarters on the Beardy River, at what now is Armidale, and Edward filed his claim to the land.

Unfortunately the first settlement on the Clarence was attended by conflict with the Aborigines, mostly a result of white misunderstandings. There were punitive expeditions and massacres, such as the one following the alleged murder of a hutkeeper. The murder was in fact committed by a white man. Edward said that the Aborigines were so terrified by these reprisals that it took him two years to gain their confidence.

One of the most dramatic moments in *Squatter's Castle* occurs when Edward and his brother at last make contact with a mountain tribe. By this time they have living with them an Aboriginal boy, Pundoon, whom Edward has discovered hiding after a massacre by a force under Major Oakes. The Ogilvie brothers come upon a camp in the hills and try to talk to a terrified woman who, with a child, is the only person there. Shortly after this they hear shouts, and then see two armed, tall, naked men on the heights above them. "Begone, begone and take away your horses . . . leave the mountains to the black people. . . . Go, go, begone!" they call. Edward shouts out that he is not armed, and urges the men to approach. One of them does, delighted that the white man speaks his language. His name is Toolbillibam, and he calls to Pundoon's father to come to meet the Ogilvies. Edward tells them that they want nothing but the grass for their stock, and that the blacks can keep all the game and the fish. They part good friends. Soon the Aborigines come down to the station, and regularly engage in wrestling matches, racing and diving competitions with the white men.

It was a lonely life, with the inevitable tribulations of drought and flood and diseases of the stock. But soon the flocks were up to 2000 sheep and Edward was making 800 gallons of his own wine. They still lived very simply, and spent months in the saddle, but the squatter's life was good. Then came the Bathurst gold rush and the stations were deserted. Edward got Germans and Chinese to work for him, and even a married couple (the wife was the first white woman to live on Yulgilbar). But he had further plans, which

THE STATION BOUNDARY *A. H. Fullwood*

GEORGE FARWELL
1911-1976

George Farwell was born in Bath, England, on 30 October 1911, and educated at Forest School. His grandmother, Rosanna Magrath, was the first daughter of pioneer settlers to be born at St Kilda, Melbourne.

After working at a variety of jobs in England Farwell considered that there were few exciting prospects ahead in that country and consequently signed up on an expedition to hunt Spanish treasure in the Tuamoto Islands in the Pacific. He has recounted the misfortunes of the expedition in his autobiography, *Rejoice in Freedom* (1976).

Farwell spent two years in the South Seas, mainly in Tahiti, after which he cashed in his return ticket and went to Sydney. "However euphoric it was, Tahiti lacked social involvement, a creative life, the stimulus of art." He considered that "the still, calm eye of beauty" was not enough.

The Australian alternatives in those days were frequently expressed as "Sydney or the Bush", but, as Farwell put it, in the Depression there were jobs in neither. Farwell eventually signed on as a sailor on the trans-Pacific run before settling in Sydney and managing a sketchy living from writing anything from journalism to stories, plays and travel books. He also began his many journeys around outback Australia.

Farwell joined the Communist Party in the early 1940s and worked for the cause during the heady days of the Australia–Russia Friendship League. (ASIO would subsequently blackball him when he applied for various jobs in later years.) Farwell was more of a romantic democrat than a hard-headed political activist. One of his more quixotic efforts, after Malcolm Ellis had written in the *Bulletin* that "the Russian Army couldn't fight its way out of a paper bag", was to borrow a Nazi flag from the New Theatre and hoist it on the flagpole above the *Bulletin* building. It made a good story in the midday *Sun*, with the headline "*Bulletin* flies Nazi Flag".

Farwell was Editor of *Australasian Book News, Library Journal* and *Air Travel* in the late 1940s, and was a feature writer with the Commonwealth News and Information Bureau from 1952 to 1958. From 1958 to 1962 he was on the staff of the Adelaide *Advertiser* and concurrently public relations officer for the Adelaide Festival of Arts. He also did public relations for the Australian Government Pavilion in the Montreal Expo in 1967.

He won first prize in the ABC Australian Radio Play Competition in 1940, and the Rothman-Moomba Award for Australian Literature in Melbourne in 1967. The most popular of his many books about the outback are probably *Land of Mirage* and *Vanishing Australians*.

He had a son and a daughter by his first marriage, which was dissolved in 1953. In 1958 he married Noni Rowland.

After his period with the Adelaide Festival Farwell made a second visit to Tahiti. On his return to Sydney he explained himself to John Gunther as a refugee from the middle class: " 'Then why live in Australia?' asked the American. *Touché.* Yet there were good reasons. The Australian sun; nature still undomesticated; the vast interior reaching beyond time. Besides, where else in this polluted and congested world was there to live?"

George Farwell died in Adelaide in 1976.

---

began with a trip to Europe in 1854. Nothing was hurried until he was in Ireland in 1858 where, after a rapid courtship at the age of 44, he married Theodosia de Burgh, just 20.

He had told her he would build a big house for her when they sailed for Australia shortly after the wedding. Edward imported German masons and bought furniture and a fountain in Italy for what was to be known to him as "The Big House" and to others as "The Castle".

In the meantime, in 1859, the old Commander died, and to everyone's astonishment left £75,000. Merton was leased to Edward White of Edenglassie who subsequently purchased the property.

As the mansion of 40 rooms and its outbuildings went up, Theodosia began producing children; she was to have 11 by the time she was 35. Edward Ogilvie designed the extraordinary house himself with its crenellated walls and towers, and its courtyard around the Italian fountain, employing first-rate craftsmen to complete it.

All this grandeur and success, however, seems to have made Edward more and more remote and quarrelsome. He took no part in the life of Grafton, the capital of the district, and although a Member of the Legislative Council, he put in few appearances in parliament. His private life became more confined when Theodosia was crippled by a broken hip at the birth of her last child, a boy who died a few weeks later.

What makes Edward Ogilvie interesting is the artistic side to the tough old bushman. Taking his family to Florence, he became good friends with the poet Robert Browning. He continued on to London so that Theodosia could see medical specialists, but despite this she died in 1886. In London he saw Browning again, and when his eight daughters sang for him, Browning called them his "Australian Octave".

Yulgilbar, under a manager, fell into a decline while Edward lived in splendour in Florence. Later his eldest son William returned from Oxford to the station. However, he could not get on with the manager, and soon left to buy a place of his own. In the 1890s, with bad economic and social tidings from Australia, Edward returned home with a new wife after nine years in Florence.

Edward Ogilvie died in Bowral in 1896 and was buried at Yulgilbar. The Aborigines gathered in mourning on the flats as the station hands carried the coffin up the hill to the grave. Despite Edward's plans for a Yulgilbar dynasty of Ogilvies, and despite his motto, *Tout Jour* (Forever), following family quarrels Yulgilbar was sold to a syndicate within 30 years and the Castle was allowed to fall into ruins, although it was later restored to some of its former splendour.

It has happened often in pastoral Australia that within three or four generations any semblance of permanence has collapsed. Whatever style of life the squatters achieved, in the end it seems to have proved alien to the Australian environment. And the Aborigines, whose home it has been for thousands of years, have also been destroyed, physically and spiritually, even by those, like the Ogilvies, who cared about them.

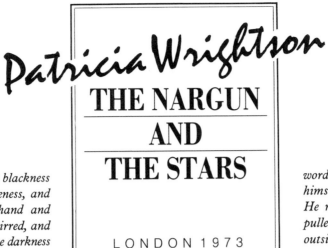

Patricia Wrightson

THE NARGUN AND THE STARS

LONDON 1973

There was a tree close by in the blackness of the hillside. He felt its closeness, and found it by putting out a hand and touching wet bark. Branches stirred, and drops pelted on his raincoat. The darkness and the slow groping made him colder.

Something moved; he felt it close to him. Invisible against the mountain something big and solid moved a little. Simon stood still and listened: no snort from Pet, no breathing, no twitch of ear or tail. He listened as he had not known he could, listened with every inch of his skin: he heard nothing. No pumping heart, no quietly streaming blood. Only the unhearable sound of earth taking a weight, only the universe shifting to balance a small movement. He wanted to put out a hand to discover what moved close by—but the dark places in his mind told his hand to be still, as they told his heart to beat quietly.

The moon's edge lifted from the cloud; there was soft polished light, and he saw a crooked shape. About a yard away—leaning forward—a hard, craggy, blunt-muzzled head and the smallest, most secret movement of a limb. Something without heart or blood, the living earth in a squat and solid shape, reached very secretly, a very little, for Simon.

He wasted no energy to yell or gasp. His stretched nerves twanged, he shot ten feet in one leap and kept on running. Away behind him something cried out savagely in anger—Nga-a-a! The wild, fierce cry laid its echo like a trail along the mountain. The dogs barked for a moment and were silent. Simon raced in among them and crouched there, and the dogs whimpered, and he whimpered with them. They listened together, and peered into the moonlight. Silence. Nothing moved on the ridge.

After a time Simon whispered shaky words of comfort to the dogs and forced himself to go the little way to the house. He raised the window and climbed in, pulled off his wet shoes and dropped them outside and shut the window. He tore off coat and shorts and plunged into bed.

The cooling hot-water bag felt scorching, he was so cold. He tried not to shake the bed by shivering. It was very quiet; no sound at all except the creek and the river. Moonlight lay gently on his red felt mat, and only the pine-tree whispered against the stars.

It was the moon coming out like that, he decided. He was excited by those crazy, wonderful, weird creatures at the swamp; and then groping through the dark, and the moon coming out, and an owl or something screeching. He had seen some rock and imagined the horror. And thinking this he fell into exhausted sleep.

He didn't hear the sound that woke Charlie and brought him to the window: the shrill, terrified bleating of sheep.

The strengths of *The Nargun and the Stars* are immediately evident in the quality of the writing and the imaginative power of the story. It is a novel for adults as well as children. Patricia Wrightson's ability to write with equal authority about mythical earth-creatures and machinery, about nameless fears and precise practical problems, makes it most unusual. The book could just as well have been called *The Nargun and the Bulldozer*.

Her handling of the details of rural life is impeccable. She can even write with sympathy and precision about a grader:

Like every grader Simon had ever seen it was orange-yellow, long and lanky, slow, noisy, and fussy. It fumbled along, blade clanking and grating on the gravel. . . . It backed clumsily, crept around, backed again, with a lot more grumbling and clanking, to go back over the section of road it had just done. Simon was not surprised; he knew the habits of graders.

This is not just a piece of virtuoso writing but a description of the grader as perceived by Simon. The grader is familiar; a consolation to a bereft, sullen and lonely boy.

Simon, the hero of the book, has been orphaned by a car crash, and has gone to live with his uncle Charlie and his aunt Edie. Patricia Wrightson is a perceptive observer:

She said, "Edie'll do me and Charlie'll do Charlie, but I suppose you might want to put an auntie and uncle between us. Suit yourself."

So he didn't call either of them anything.

There are two forms of existence in *The Nargun and the Stars*. One is familiar and contemporary—recognisable people on a 2000-hectare farm, Wongadilla, in mountainous country, somewhere "up the Hunter". The other is the ancient presence of Australia, something aboriginal if not clearly Aboriginal, although the Rainbow Snake does make an appearance.

The book opens with the Nargun, a black bulk as old as earth, that kills and eats "sometimes once in ten years, sometimes in fifty". It blunders north from Victoria about 1880, seeking cool, dark gorges, made uneasy by sunny places. By the late 1920s the Nargun has reached Goulburn, having recently killed a horse and a dog. For decades it goes north, occasionally killing humans or a beast. In the 1960s it turns west along a range and comes to Wongadilla, Charlie's sheep-run.

It is here that Charlie and Edie bring the orphaned Simon. He is suspicious and silent, hating the whole weird place. The sound of a bulldozer clearing scrub up the mountain is the first thing that lifts his heart a little; not the beauty of the surroundings or the calm kindness of his uncle and aunt. The sounds of blasting, trees falling and the bulldozer working making him look longingly up the mountain.

When he does sneak off, he finds the swamp which has already been beautifully described at the beginning of the book. And there as he wades on the edge of the deep water, a swamp creature, the Potkoorok, stirs, chuckling, its golden eyes gleaming. As he wades deeper, "It curled a coldness around his ankle." Simon soon gets over his fright. The Potkoorok is a joker; for it, "a good trick was something to chuckle over for a hundred years". It trips Simon up. He throws a stick at it; it swallows the stick in a whirlpool. "That's where it lives," he says to himself.

That night at bedtime he hears "a sad, high howling, far away and lost". Edie frowns as if she heard it too.

There was a tree close by in the blackness of the hillside. He felt its closeness, and found it by putting out a hand and touching wet bark. Branches stirred, and drops pelted on his raincoat. The darkness and the slow groping made him colder.

The vague growing menace hanging over Wongadilla fills the book with suspense. The Nargun is a threatening stranger. The Potkoorok and the other earth creatures Simon meets are friendly, humorous and local. Simon meets the Potkoorok in person. The creature talks to him, and in answer to Simon's query informs him that the "three grey shadows with straggling beards scuttling like spiders round the trunks of trees" are Turongs, creatures of the trees. They play jokes; they used to like to play them on the Aboriginal hunters, but since there are no more hunters they play them on sheep, or on machines. It is they who sink the grader in the swamp, as later it is the Nyols who steal the bulldozer. There is something old, innocent and free about the Turongs and the Potkoorok. But apart from age they have nothing in common with the Nargun, a companion of rage and terror.

Simon scratches his name on two rocks, SIMON BRENT. When he comes back to the gully the next day the rock with

SIMON on it is gone. It was a big rock, very big, and it is no longer there. He sees marks, grooves, scrapes, crushed ferns and moss, going *up* the valley. "It's mad!" he cries angrily. Then he climbs up and finds the rock, a "queer crouching shape that looked as if it were pressing itself against the side of the gully, hiding its face".

Like the Minotaur or Beowulf, the Nargun is a lost creature; it knows not what it does when it kills, and it hides its face in darkness. In this way Patricia Wrightson gives the monster the classic ability to inspire both terror and pity.

The Potkoorok is not willing to discuss the Nargun. Simon talks to Charlie about it. Charlie doesn't think the boy is mad. In fact he and Edie know all about the Potkoorok and the Turongs, but have never heard of the Nargun. But he is prepared to look, saying calmly, "I'll be surprised if any of the old things have any real harm in 'em, Nargun or not."

The Nargun and the Stars is really a book about belonging. The humans, whether Aboriginal or white, are, of course, more recent occupants of the land; Charlie himself has been there 60 years or so. Simon begins at Wongadilla as a stranger; by the end of the book it is his home.

The benign creatures of swamp, trees and caves are accepted by the humans and bring them together as Simon drops his guard. They belong to an older time-span; there are several references to this.

The Potkoorok, the Turongs and the Nyols are local creatures. The Nargun, in the Potkoorok's words, "doesn't belong here". When Simon asks the Potkoorok if the Nargun is good, it answers, "Good? . . . What is good? It is the Nargun. It came from a long way south. It should go back."

So the Nargun is an older, menacing presence that does not belong in any sense that either the earth creatures or the humans do. It is one of the triumphs of the book that this Nargun, this ancient piece of rock, should suggest both loss and longing. Its cry is "full of hate that was love, of love that was hate, centuries of emptiness, anger hungry to destroy", and makes Simon feel "something curl up inside him. He had always thought it was naked fear, but now he was not sure. It might be naked pity."

The Potkoorok advises Simon to go and see the Nyols, who live in rocks and earth. Climbing the mountain, he is pulled by little dry hands through a crack in the rock, and soft happy voices talk to him. He has found the Nyols, or they him, and they show him the bulldozer, which they have stolen and imprisoned in the mountain. The Nyols won't help, but they show him a way out through a passage. Meanwhile Charlie has been watching the Nargun, for four hours, and noticed that it shivers when the workers clearing the forest blast a tree. Clearly it does not like noise or vibrations through the ground. They go and get the tractor, which is very noisy because of a cracked muffler, and drive it around the Nargun, which makes it move. It was waiting for the silence of the stars, and they have made it angry.

As Simon, Edie and Charlie talk that night Charlie remembers that Simon had said that the bulldozer's muffler, sticking up like a chimney, was broken off when the Nyols put it in the mountain. If the bulldozer was started and the engine kept roaring . . . maybe the noise and vibration would be such that the Nargun would move away.

But the Nyols would never let Charlie near their buried

From **THE NARGUN AND THE STARS** *the original jacket painting by Joan Saint*

PATRICIA WRIGHTSON

Patricia Wrightson tells her own story in an account especially written for this book:

Although I was one of a family of six, I was a lonely child. I was isolated between two older sisters and three younger brothers. My father was a solicitor who preferred the country to law, and so I grew up in country areas of the north coast of New South Wales. My many schools ranged from a two-teacher country school to an important demonstration school; by far my favourite was the State Correspondence School for isolated children. I was really educated in literature, philosophy and wonder by my father; and in the social sciences by my mother. My most profitable year of schooling was the one in which I abandoned the syllabus altogether and spent the year, without permission or guidance, in discovering Shakespeare.

All of my schools assumed I would become a writer, but I very nearly didn't. I was not sure how to begin, was awed by the great writers, and couldn't believe there was any excuse for trying. Only after I had been married and divorced and had two children of my own (Jenny and Peter) did I dare to begin by producing stories for them. I was very lucky to begin by accident in so demanding a school.

I was for many years a hospital administrator and was on the staff of the New South Wales Education Department's *School Magazine* for about 10 years, for the last five of these as editor. At the end of 1975 I gave up my jobs in order to give more time to writing. I was then living in Turramurra, having spent about 15 years in and about Sydney.

Once I had given up work in the city there was not much point in living there. I returned to the north coast in 1978 and now live on the Clarence River, some kilometres out of Maclean. I have a narrow strip of stony ridge, about a mile long and six chains wide, on which to encourage the natural growth of ironbark, stringybark and blackbutt.

The Nargun and the Stars was awarded the Australian Children's Book of the Year Award in 1974. Patricia Wrightson has written seven other books of fiction for children.

---

treasure, the bulldozer. If there were only a way of overcoming this, then something might be done. And to head the enraged Nargun away from the house, which it might smash to pieces, Edie could drive the tractor up and down with its muffler off and the lights on, between the house and the Nargun. It is monster against monster.

Simon was enthralled. This would have been right, he knew. The bulldozer—another monster—dim and secret inside the mountain, unleashing its full roar. The whole mountain shaking: that was a plan big enough for the Nargun, if only it could have been done.

It is done, with the help of the Potkoorok. The climax of the book is too ingenious and exciting to give away. The final imprisonment of the monster Nargun in the mountain once again arouses terror and pity, and returns this ancient creature, child of darkness, to the womb of time.

The Nargun, that was both hostile and sad, has liberated Simon from his silent resentment and suspicion. Now it is clear that Simon belongs, he has been made welcome by the Potkoorok, the Turongs and the Nyols, and he will stay.

"Monster against monster" *Darian Causby*

Helen Garner

MONKEY GRIP

MELBOURNE 1977

So, an hour later I was home in my clean bed, looking after the kids while Rita went to the art school ball. And I kept wondering, what did Javo think in the street tonight? Which of us tries harder to be cool? or in control? Will he come back to sleep with me tonight? Will I care if he doesn't? Should I scramble back out to the solitary life I led when he was away in Asia? Can I live without being loved? Is it true what Lillian said once, years ago, that I've always been too good at giving it all away? And on a practical level, is there a supper show tomorrow night? And if there is, can Rita and I find someone to stay home with the kids so we can dance the night away?

I wanted to get stoned and forget what I looked like and dance till I was loose all over.

"Dear Javo, you said you wondered if the trip we're supposed to be going on is worth it for such a short time. Well, I'm definitely going on Monday, and if you feel doubtful about going, please say so now. Know what I think? I think you see me as not much more than a lump on the other side of the bed. I think maybe you want to fall in love. I think you've got the look of someone who's on the make.

I think that, if I'm right about this, it's high time for us to call it a day . . .

I am afraid of painful, long-drawn-out endings to things. I got a fright, the other day, at the gloom I experienced when we talked about Lillian; and you talked once again about Jessie in the way that makes me feel you are saying, 'My relationship with Jessie was the high point, the great love of my life', and that's OK, it really is, only I get to feel a bit like some kind of charlady keeping the home fires burning after the princess has passed by.

I want to be with you, laugh and mooch round, travel if we can. But I'm not getting anything back, I'm running out, I need love. And if you don't want to give it any more, will you please say so? I'm telling you, Javo! I'm lonely! Are you reading me? . . . over . . . Nora."

I asked the I Ching, "What about my feeling that it is all hopeless with Javo?"

It replied, "Times change, and with them their demands. Changes ought to be undertaken only when there is nothing else to be done. A premature offensive will bring evil results."

I left the letter for him, just the same.

He came in the middle of the night and read it downstairs while I dozed. He came up to my room again and sat on the end of my bed, pulling off his boots.

"Did you read it?"

"Yeah. We'll talk about it tomorrow."

"No, that won't do—because when I have to leave, you'll be asleep."

He got into bed. Before he had come in, I had been fast asleep, and comfortably warm; but when he was coming down, his awful coldness drew the warmth out of my body and left me lying in a chilly envelope of discomfort. He did talk, for an hour or so. Every few minutes he'd groan and roll over, complaining of restlessness and pain. He said,

"One trouble is, that you like me best when I'm off dope, but I'm always happier when I'm into it."

"No, no, you're quite wrong," I said, throwing caution to the winds. "The times I'm most comfortable with you—and it's because of your own attitude to yourself—are when you've just started back into dope, before it gets you by the throat."

"Maybe I never really liked myself much," he said, with a faint bitterness, "before I found dope."

I tried to talk about needing love.

He said, "Sometimes, when you're giving out affection and love towards me, it's . . . missing. I don't mean absent, I mean . . ."

"You mean not hitting the mark?"

"Something like that."

I didn't understand what he meant, and, discouraged, thought better of asking. There was a long silence. He heaved a great sigh.

"Well . . ." I said, "what about going to Sydney, Javes? Will we still go?"

"Yeah, I reckon. We both need to get out of here for a while."

We both needed something, that was certain, but neither of us knew what it was. I wished stupidly for something steady and complete. For someone steady and complete. What's that? No such thing, no such person.

On publication, *Monkey Grip* immediately took its place, and has retained it, as the classic novel of drifting big-city life in the mid-1970s, of men and women in their twenties or thirties, of drugs and drink and joy and despair, of lone mothers with one child, of the day-to-day shapes of lives without pattern. Nora, the narrator, flashes around Melbourne on her bicycle, often with her daughter Gracie hanging on like a monkey behind her, to the baths, to the theatres and places where there is part-time work in plays or films, to the houses of friends. It is very much a novel of friends, and is historically important for that alone, being the first Australian novel of women reacting to each other and to lovers as individuals outside the old social conventions.

"Life's a struggle." The women laugh with each other at the implications, between bouts of feeling desperate. Outside sex, drugs and drink there are few comforts; these people are not sustained by support from families or nature.

The *I Ching* is the nearest Nora gets to the support of a religion. There are a few brief and vivid excursions into the country, some of which help to restore balance, but these are city people, always on the move. The story is told in quick, sharp flashes; Helen Garner has an outstandingly deft and clear style that never clogs even when dealing with highly emotional issues.

That these issues can be taken seriously is perhaps the most remarkable achievement of *Monkey Grip*. Among these people, in and out of each other's beds, forswearing permanence and avoiding commitments, who would suspect the presence of love? At a time, in the 1970s, when romantic love was under siege both in life and in literature, Helen Garner created a character who shows all the characteristics of romantic love and yet is completely convincing. Of course, it is a 1970s version of an ancient theme. In the Middle Ages, love was often unconsummated and usually doomed; the maiden was either lonely in her tower or else she was Tristan's Isolde or Troilus' Criseyde. Later, death did not spare Juliet. Nora is in this tradition. Even though she (most successfully on many occasions) gets to bed with Javo, there is an obstacle just as hopelessly insurmountable as those which doomed those famous heroines.

Javo is a junkie. Heroin is the monkey gripping his back, as love (which includes Gracie) is Nora's. And death, as in those earlier tragedies, always hovers around Javo's thin, wasted body with the lantern head and the brilliant blue eyes.

Those earlier heroines were victims of a fashion in love. Nora is remarkable in that she is both in the fashion and out of it, not only in her attitudes to love but also in her attitudes to drugs. Early in the book she makes a resolution: "to root out of myself two tendencies: to romanticise dope, and to treat junkies with an exaggerated respect". She is harsh on herself. "Terminal naivety was my disease." Yet she knows both the tricks of contemporary sophistication and the brutal facts of how badly junkies behave. She can act tough and uncaring. "I was well-disciplined by the orthodoxy, a fast faker."

The discipline cracks a little when Javo is taken to

From the film *Monkey Grip*

hospital with septicaemia from a dirty hit; he escapes and comes to her house which earlier he had rejected as "too homely". She does not want to mother him. Already they are, surprisingly, highly sexually successful together. But she lets him stay because – she has to apologise to herself – she supposes she loves him.

*W*e both needed something, that was certain, but neither of us knew what it was. I wished stupidly for something steady and complete. For someone steady and complete. What's that? No such thing, no such person.

Whereas Isolde or Juliet totally accepted that love, with all its dangers, was a great and worthy force, Nora is a true child of her time, doing her best to deny it and expecting to hear others do the same. Javo returns from a visit to Bangkok, lucky not to have been jailed there for longer than he was; incredibly this was only for stealing a pair of sunglasses. Javo and Nora are soon together in bed again.

"My heart's full for you," I whispered, ashamed of the words but having to say them.

He smiled at me out of his lantern head, his eyes shone way back in their caverns:

"I don't ever want to stop loving you."

But almost immediately they begin to misunderstand each other. Later, driving down the street, they all smile at seeing a couple kiss in the street. Cheerfully, Nora says, "They must be in love!"

Gracie writhed with laughter. "I hate love! I'm never going to be in love!"

"Good on you, Grace," said Javo, grinning. "Love . . . makes you forget your friends."

Perhaps Javo also means, "It makes you forget you *are* friends." In any case, he finds friendships with men are easier than relationships with women.

The trouble is that it is impossible to be either a friend or a lover to a junkie, as Nora finds out, left with her "Fear of being loved; fear of not being loved". A few days after they are telling each other they love each other, Javo is asking Nora to drive him around to the sinisterly named Easey Street, his old junkie haunt. He has only been back five days when he tells her that he can't have an honest relationship with her, "when that desire's still there. You said you wanted *me*, not me and a bunch of . . . chemicals." And although a moment later they are reassuring each other of their love, he demands to be taken back to Easey Street.

He cannot promise to give up heroin. She never asks him to. After his hits, he is too wasted to make love to her. Then he is acting in a Brecht play and comes home at all hours in the morning to sleep in her bed, which she usually deserts for another bed upstairs.

He cannot give up the heroin; she cannot give him up. She says, "Nobody knows what I get out of Javo, or out of knowing him. I don't know how to explain." But she knows that sometimes when they make love or are peaceful, "*we touch each other*. No-one else gets that close to me. He behaves

THE LOVERS *Charles Blackman*

HELEN GARNER
1942-

Helen Garner (her maiden name was Ford) was born in Geelong, Victoria, in 1942, the eldest of six children. She has described her household as "an ordinary Australian home – not many books and not much talk". She was educated at state primary schools and at the Hermitage CEGGS, Geelong. She matriculated in 1960.

From 1961 to 1965 she studied Arts (English and French literature) at Melbourne University and graduated BA Honours in 1965. She taught in Victorian secondary schools (Werribee High, Upfield High, Fitzroy High) with time off for travelling, for getting married and for the birth of a daughter, until 1972, when she was, in her own words, "sacked from the Education Department for answering students' questions about sex".

She then worked as a journalist and collective member on *Digger* magazine until mid-1974. After an illness in 1974 she lived on a supporting mother's benefit and brought up her daughter.

In 1977 she published her first novel, *Monkey Grip*, which won the 1978 National Book Council Award. In 1978 she also received the first of a series of three Writer's Fellowships from the Literature Board of the Australia Council. For a time she lived in Paris, working on a new book.

In 1979 she returned to Australia and lived for a while with her daughter in Moonee Ponds; they now live in North Carlton. Her second book, two novellas, *Honour and Other People's Children* was published in 1980. In that year she also collaborated on the screenplay of *Monkey Grip*. Both her books were published in the USA and *Monkey Grip* also in the UK.

In 1981 and 1982 she worked as a freelance feature writer for various publications, including the *Age*, and as feature writer and theatre critic for the *National Times*.

In 1982 she translated from the French Richard Demarcy's play *The Stranger in the House* which was performed that year in Melbourne at the Anthill Theatre. In 1983 she published with co-author Jennifer Giles a novelisation of the film *Moving Out*. She also received another Writer's Fellowship from the Literature Board. In 1984 she published another novel, *The Children's Bach*.

Interviewed in 1979 (*National Times*, 2-8 December) she said that she felt "very Australian" in Paris, and she prefers "the terrific freedom of movement" that Australia offers. Back home she was "actually really glad I was here in a physical way, and I feel like that quite often".

In another *National Times* interview (4-10 January 1981) she says of her working habits, "I like to start early in the morning. Morning is my best time. It's something to do with being a mother, I think: your free hours tend to be school hours." She has very particular working habits, and "carries a small lined notebook everywhere, in which she jots down description, ideas, snatches of overheard conversations".

She remembers thankfully that at school she had a teacher, Mrs Grace Dunkley, who "thumped syntax into me". She was a shy girl, but one day summoned up courage to ask how an adverb can modify an adjective. "A look of delight and pleasure crossed her face and she said, 'Well, I'll give you an example: The water was frightfully cold', and I thought, 'This is wonderful.' I was so interested that I was able to overcome my fear."

She says of *Monkey Grip*, "The thing about *Monkey Grip* was that it was so unconscious. I look at it and think, gosh, it's as if it had been written in a dream . . . Your first book comes out and you're never the same again: I mean, it's all over for spontaneity."

towards me, then, with tenderness, holds me when I'm half asleep, he says my name and looks into my face."

Monkey Grip is a book about loneliness, and how love creates loneliness as well as obliterating it. When Javo has gone, Nora says, "The loneliness was drying me out." She has Grace, a multitude of friends, an involvement with making a movie, but she is haunted by loneliness, as the mirror in W. H. Auden's poem: "My dear one is mine as mirrors are lonely."

Once again she is a victim of her time. As she says near the beginning of the book: "I blushed in shame for us women whose guns are too big these days, who learned ten years ago to conduct great sexual campaigns with permanency in mind, while today it is a matter of skirmishes, fast and deft."

Of course, permanency with a junkie is impossible, and equally intransigent is the fate of a romantic attempting the fast, deft skirmish. Nora can neither stay nor escape.

And so she makes do with old, friendly lovers, Clive or Bill, and when she sees Javo, says some terrible things, such as that his life is "*sordid*". In the argument that follows he says what she already knows; when their love-making succeeds it is because of dope. Cold, he will not let her touch him. So she writes him a letter saying that by "sordid" she meant that his life has no centre. But she ends with loving messages, although she thinks that it is really the end.

She is lonely in her body, but her fantasies are of *love*. She, as narrator, underlines the word. Nevertheless, she attempts friendship when she meets Javo again, "a rough

companionableness". By little touches Helen Garner manages to convey that this much is possible, a remarkable achievement considering the mostly unpleasant and humourless reality of Javo.

But rough, simple friendship can be treated too roughly. Javo comes back for a night with Nora and in the morning steals the last $5 from the food kitty. Not much later, he steals the $80 that Nora's friend Rita has put away for the rent for her studio. Eventually Javo is forgiven and the old life goes on. Nora in her distress is comforted by her friends; they all go together for good times at the baths and Javo tries to give up smack and looks better for it. He confesses that he is going to bed with another girl in the group, Claire. Although that later leads to jealous misery, Nora sees in him and herself, "the beginnings of a small stream of happiness . . . the happiness was for the mother in me, watching him gather himself and take off".

But the new Javo is not much different from the old. Inviting himself to dinner, he does not turn up. Nora leaves the house. "I went to the Kingston to hear Jo Jo Zep and danced till the floor was too packed for me to move, and then I danced on a chair."

The book ends with Nora at Anglesey, lying naked in the meagre sunlight with her friend Selena, talking about Javo. "I laughed wholeheartedly about it for the first time."

In a medieval or Renaissance story, both lovers would have died. In *Monkey Grip* both live and love dies, although often it seems that Javo may die, not of love, but of chemicals.

Manning Clark

A HISTORY
OF
AUSTRALIA

VOL. IV

MELBOURNE 1978

Adam Lindsay Gordon toyed with the idea of elevating the bushman's creed to the role of the bible for humanity in Australia. Gordon was one of those exiles from the mother country whose poetry was in part a melancholy elegy about the ache in his own heart and in part a threnody for the death of God. He belonged by birth to those eccentric Gordons who had been driven down to England in the early seventeenth century for all the barbaric cruelties they had practised on their foes in Scotland during the wars of religion. He was born at Fayal in the Azores on 19 October 1833. After a wild youth in England he was exiled by his parents for an offence he had probably not committed. His parents had accused him of staining his pedigree and belying his blood as a Gordon. From that time he became the man with wild eyes and wild words. His loves were idyllic in their chastity. He had loved a man, Charley Walker. He had loved a woman, Jane Bridges, with such purity that he could not bring himself to declare his love for her until it was too late. He was also afraid that she would ridicule him or shun him or wound him in ways he could not bear. He sought relief in a wild life, which always led to agonies of remorse, self-lacerations, and vows of future continence which he could not possibly observe.

In November 1853, some two weeks after his arrival in Adelaide, he took up an appointment as a trooper in the mounted police in the Mount Gambier district of South Australia. After leaving that profession, he became a station-hand at Lake Hawdon. By day he helped to train horses for the armed services in India and by night pursued the life of a man of letters, writing poetry, and reading late by the light of a panican lamp—a honeysuckle cone stuck in clay—in a tiny stone hut in a country where courage, pluck and resource had become part of the bushman's bible. At Robe he entertained the drinkers at the Caledonian Hotel with "glimpses of his own waywardness". He also met Father Julian Edmund Tenison-Woods, a scientist, a mystic with a thirst for the spiritual life, a believer in poverty and simplicity—a man of God with a deep inner life which Gordon was attracted to but unable to emulate. They were both men of talent in whom the gods or chance had planted a kink. Woods suffered from petit mal, Gordon from being an eccentric solitary who spoke to himself. Gordon had a great desire for things spiritual, which was always coming into collision with descents into Hell, wild debauches with drink and women, followed by remorse and self-disgust. He had the wild look in his eyes of a man who never knew any inner peace, and an expression on his face of a thinker, a pilgrim and a seeker for the means of grace. To the delight of Woods, this rather moody and silent man, who did not mix much with the common man, this wearer of the usual bush costume, joined him on a ride in the Australian bush during which Gordon recited to him long passages from Virgil, Ovid and Homer, passages from Racine and Corneille, and uncovered that shy and sensitive man who was doomed to go under in the struggle for life in the Australian colonies. No man could help Gordon: he remained a victim of the cruel joke nature had played on him; he went on tormenting himself for what he was, and tormenting himself for being tormented.

A man who, in his own words, was "as game as a pebble", who could tame wild horses, and confront danger with a courage that surrounded him with a hero's halo even in his lifetime, could not manage the world of men and women. At Penola he had been refused permission to ride in the race for the Ladies' Purse on the grounds that he was not a gentleman. He had been drawn to a woman who was the wife of another man, but had been so frightened of another hurtful rejection slip that he had held his tongue, though it was grief and agony to him. He married a woman beneath his class from the Caledonian Hotel, Margaret Park, on 20 October 1862. She admired him as a horse-rider, but had no interest in Gordon's other quest to find someone who would tell him what it was all about. He entered the House of Assembly in Adelaide as a member for the Victoria district in March 1865. In parliament he asked for mercy to and sympathy with the squatters, and the building of local roads, but he was far too vulnerable to survive in the bear-pit of colonial politics in Adelaide. He barely lasted five months. He invested his inheritance of £7000 from England in land and stock, only to find that he and money had as much affinity with each other as a frog and feathers.

Manning Clark's great *History of Australia* needs to be read as a whole for its tremendous sweep to be fully apparent, for Clark is a historian of ideas who is never content with a mere chronicle. Yet he also loves to tell a story, with the result that there is a constant interplay between thought and action. At the same time he is much too aware of human frailty and greed not to notice that the moralists and the story-tellers are left alone, talking to each other, when someone shouts "Gold!" at the bottom of the gully.

Volume IV of the *History* is a classic that may be singled out because the years it covers, 1851-1888, allow immense scope for all aspects of Clark's mind, including both his enthusiasm and sceptical melancholy. It is a particularly rich period: the gold diggers and the men of Eureka; the squatters and the selectors; the settlers and the Aborigines; the explorers and the bushrangers; the nationalist politicians, and the birth of the *Bulletin*. Behind all these elements are the great themes Clark is always responsive to: the decline of religion and the emergence of self-sufficient man; the decay of that other semi-divine right, the British hold on Australia; and the social revolution, the triumph of the democrat over the gentleman. And Clark also listens to the poets and writers, to those tragic Australians haunted by drink and poverty: Gordon, Harpur, Kendall, Clarke, Lawson.

Above all, the themes of the collapse of religion as a believable miracle, and the "merciles beaute" (to borrow Chaucer's phrase) of the Australian environment, and our attempts to live in it as Australians rather than Britishers, not only give the huge book a sense of unity but also a continuing resonance.

Clark the historian is also very much Clark the Australian. He loves the bush and knows how to live with it. He has taken the trouble to go to Cooper Creek when writing about Burke and Wills, or to Swinton under the Grampians where Marcus Clarke galloped, watching the parrots before dawn and reading Lermontov and Balzac by night. This, incidentally, is another of Clark's virtues as a historian—the reader knows that as well as having ploughed through documents and acts of parliament he has read Lermontov and Balzac.

Another mark of a great historian, and one which Manning Clark shares with Edward Gibbon, is the ability to allow an alert irony to play over the solemnities of a major theme, while never trivialising it with smug hindsight or cynical detachment. Clark's chapters on gold are masterly. He traces the unexpected effects of the greatest mixed blessing ever to fall on Australia. It "put the last nail in the coffin of convict transportation". It corrupted the Sabbath, and at the same time caused bishops to build churches in panic at the ungodliness abroad. It corrupted society as well. Governors and such-like could not "look upon it . . . as a lucky event for the Colony", as it would "spread equality over the whole of society". The antipathies caused by the licensing system soon became a clash between authority and democracy.

Even where there was no gold, as in South Australia's case, gold emptied the colony of labour. Just when it seemed to be giving the individual his great chance, it accelerated Australian capitalism by bringing in complex mining machinery which replaced the pick and shovel.

Clark is especially good on what Parkes called the "un-British error" of the 15 minutes' fighting at the Eureka Stockade. Without exaggerating the tiny scale of Eureka, Clark follows it through to the melancholy end, and the collapse into insignificance of those heroes from so many nations other than the English. "The bourgeoisie were the victors in the battle for wealth on the fields: the Humffray, Seekamp, Carboni, Vern and Kennedy dream of a glorious future for humanity had fallen on stony ground in Australia."

Clark's chapter "A Colonial Bourgeoisie" traces the contradictions of Australia's home-grown leaders who, on the one hand, wanted to rule themselves and, on the other, wanted to stay as British as possible. It is extraordinary how slow to change those bourgeois contradictions have been in the 120 years since the Reverend Doctor John Dunmore Lang, that fearless democrat and republican, was urging independence on Australia as "a Law of Nature and Ordinance of God". Manning Clark's comment on the negative reaction to Lang's appeal could also refer to many late manifestations of the same malaise: "Again the bourgeoisie of the Australian colonies preferred to remain colonial and provincial rather than sail over those uncharted waters of independence, partly because of the influence of the immigrants and partly because independence was tainted with radicalism and socialism."

There is a profound melancholy running through this volume of the *History*, perhaps deepened by Manning Clark's unhappy awareness that by 1978 so little had changed in the quality of Australian leadership: "in Australia the upstart conservative, the mean man, often defeats the generous man and the visionary." It is also given emphasis by those whom Clark has chosen to illustrate his sad theme: the poets Henry Kendall and Adam Lindsay Gordon, and the novelist and essayist Marcus Clarke. All three battered themselves with drink and despair, and Gordon committed suicide.

All of them, as Clark says of Kendall, were "worn out in part" by what Kendall had called in his "In Memoriam—Marcus Clarke":

> . . . the lot austere
> That ever seems to wait upon
> The man of letters here.

The same shadows are gathering around Lawson at the end of the book.

Moving and true though the melancholy is, and aggravated by the "Weird Melancholy" of the land itself, it is a pity that Manning Clark does not make more of the cheerful acceptance and the unabashed humour that enabled ordinary people not only to survive in Australia but to rear children who, despite their leaders, thought of themselves instinctively as Australians. There is not much evidence in Clark's book of the ordinary Australians mildly censured by the visiting English historian, James Froude: "It is hard to quarrel with men who only wish to be innocently happy."

Of course, it is hard to pinpoint happiness, and Clark does give many examples of that unmistakable Australian humour which had its fullest expression in the *Bulletin*. As Clark says:

> It was Australian because it treated life as a cruel joke. . . . It was wicked in its irreverence—a tearer-down, a remover of masks, a stripper-away of all those elaborate forms and ceremonies with which men had protected themselves against each other down the ages. The *Bulletin* was not so much the bushman's bible, as the bible for the men who believed in and trafficked in the low-down view of life.

Clark's love of Australia does not lead him to gloss over the faults of Australians or the harshness of the country. The *Bulletin*'s mockery of the Aborigines and hostility to the Chinese is only an expression of that Australian racism that led to the anti-Chinese riots at Lambing Flat or the many

PANNING FOR GOLD *S. T. Gill*

MANNING CLARK
1915-

Charles Manning Hope Clark was born at Burwood, Sydney, on 3 March 1915. His father, the Reverend C. H. W. Clark, was born in England, the son of a carpenter. His mother was a direct descendant of the famous Reverend Samuel Marsden. Clark says that he is not sure of his father's religious opinions, but he is emphatic about his love of cricket ("he always barracked for England, the country of his birth") and football (he barracked for Geelong because his wife's family had been pioneers in that district). Clark inherited both loves. His mother was a deeply religious person and an excellent pianist. "That precious gift of faith . . . has not been given to me, though she probably planted in me the thirst to believe. Who knows?"

The family moved around a lot when Manning was young. From 1922 to 1924 they lived at Cowes, on Phillip Island, and then in Belgrave, Victoria. Manning was educated at Cowes and Belgrave State Schools, Mont Albert Central School and Melbourne Grammar School. At Melbourne Grammar he was greatly influenced by the headmaster, R. P. Franklin, "who planted in my mind not only the idea of being an historian, but also his own faith that one day I would master all that was required for such a vocation".

Clark went on to the University of Melbourne and Balliol College, Oxford. He taught at Blundell's School in England from 1939 to 1940, and then at Geelong Grammar School from 1940 to 1944. After this he became Lecturer in Political Science at the University of Melbourne, a position he held until 1946 when he became Lecturer in History (1946-48). In 1949 he was appointed Professor of History in the School of General Studies, Australian National University.

The profound questions which Clark asked about Australia and himself, and his hopes and doubts, are expressed in some of the essays and articles collected in *Occasional Writings and Speeches* (1980). In "A Letter to Tom Collins" (1943) he asked for something beyond mateship, while being thankful for the ideal. He suggested that Furphy and Lawson had not noticed "the queer relationship between man and earth in Australia".

In the classic "Rewriting Australian History" (1954) he called for a new attitude to the past. "First, let us drop the idea that our past has irrevocably condemned us to the role of cultural barbarians". He pointed to the differences in ideas in the Australian people, past and present, between those who believed in the Apostles' Creed and those who believed in the Enlightenment or in the Communist Manifesto. He stressed the differences in their view of the world between those brought up Catholic and those brought up Protestant. He suggested Australians drop "the comforter" that the convicts who came to Australia were victims and wronged: "The great majority of the convicts were professional criminals." He questioned all the current ideas on nationalism and exposed the way in which "this belief in a radical tradition distorts and warps our writing of Australian history". He clearly outlined the flaws in mateship: the prejudices against "coloured people", Jews and of course the Aborigines.

All these themes were present in his mind when he began to write *A History of Australia*, with the added emphasis from peering "into the heart of a great darkness" when he arrived in Germany in 1938 at Bonn after Hitler's Storm Troopers had smashed up all the Jewish business houses in Germany as reprisal for the shooting of a German military attaché in Paris by a Jewish exile.

Clark married Dymphna Lodewyckx in 1939 and they have five sons and one daughter. He has retained his enthusiasm for fishing, cricket and football.

Clark has also published short stories. He was a foundation member of the Literature Board of the Australia Council. He is now Emeritus Professor of the Australian National University, and spends his time between Canberra and a house at Wapengo on the south coast of New South Wales.

Ian Turner, one of Australia's most distinguished historians and original thinkers, called Clark "the most original and provocative of contemporary Australian historians".

---

massacres of the Aborigines that Clark chronicles. Nor does Clark's interest in religion lead him to spare the Church for its attitudes to the Aborigines, which were sometimes narrow and sometimes downright unchristian.

Australia was founded on the human cruelty of the convict system and the settlers were constantly reminded of the indifference of nature by the cruelty of the seasons— especially the devastating droughts. Clark sees the violence of the bushrangers as part of an Australian tradition, and notes that although Ben Hall or Ned Kelly were hunted down by authority they were accepted by the bush people. Fresh flowers were frequently renewed on Ben Hall's grave. Also Ned Kelly

> lived on as a man who had been aware of the violence in the Australian tradition, a man who had sensed that the fist and the gun were the keys to power in a society that owed its very existence to an act of violence against the land and its original tenants, the aborigines.

Of necessity Clark writes at length about the powerful or the exceptional, but being a scrupulous historian as well as a humane man he makes great efforts to show the involvement of ordinary people in all stages of his story. The brutish habits ("swinish" is a favourite word of Clark's) of both city and country dwellers give Clark the background to what is perhaps the most profound of his great themes, "that religion could no longer be used to work the great marvel of taming the wild beast in man". Clark is sometimes criticised for the frequency of biblical metaphors in his prose style. But in this setting they help create the atmosphere of the time, when the souls of Australians were slipping out of the control of the churches.

The old class system was also losing its control, in both economic and social spheres. Clark relishes the emergence, so clearly traced in this volume, of those like Henry Lawson who, referring to Australian school children, "wanted an antidote to Australian groveldom. He wanted them to believe in Australia for the Australians."

Clark is well aware that cruelty and greed are all too prominent in Australian history, and that drought may settle on the hearts of human beings as well as over the land. But there is always hope. Although 1888 was a bad year—a great dry—Clark allows himself the liberty of turning the page towards his next volume. In December 1889 the drought broke. "Another great dry was over; there was to be another green year in Australia."

Christopher Koch

THE YEAR OF LIVING DANGEROUSLY

MELBOURNE 1978

He saw a light, from the corner of his eye. Looking past the end of the line of shops, he found that it was the screen of a wayang kulit *show, floating in the dark near the kampong.*

He had seen these before, from the car, but had always passsed them by: he knew that the wayang *was in old Javanese, and thus completely incomprehensible. It had never occurred to him to look at one; they had not interested him, and anyway he had felt vaguely that they were out of bounds, an experience he could not enter. But tonight he had a sudden desire to approach the screen and watch with the village crowd: he was drawn towards the light.*

The wayang *had been set up in a clearing beyond the last shop, its lit screen hanging in the dark like that of a drive-in cinema. Approaching, Hamilton heard the gonging of* gamelan *instruments, and the guttural cries of the puppets. When he came to the edges of the crowd, brown faces turned and studied him briefly; then, grave and intent, they turned back to the screen, re-entering their ancient dream of the Kingdom of Dwarawati, Gate of the World, Kresna's kingdom, whose mountains are highest, women most beautiful, soil most fertile, men most noble. This had been their cinema since the time of Java's ancient Hindu kingdoms, and it seemed to Hamilton to have a weird modernity: a video-machine from an unknown civilisation. At the edges of the* wayang *show's arc of light*

were other small lights, where little stalls sold saté *and cigarettes. People laughed together; came and went; children dodged among their legs. A line of flying-foxes glided overhead, like magic animals which had escaped from the screen into the air.*

He had approached from the side of the screen where the priestly puppet-master worked, with his humble gamelan *orchestra behind him. Three white-clad men played a wooden xylophone, a fiddle, and drums, while a thin woman with an infant at the breast and a cigarette slanting from her mouth worked with her free hand on a set of bronze gongs. The* dalang *was a small, stern man in spectacles and a ceremonial cap of midnight blue: above his head, a pressure-lamp, the source of the radiance, hung from a rope; rows of* wayang *puppets were stuck into yellow-green banana logs below the screen, waiting for their entrances, from the left and the right. Sheaves of rice (tribute for Dewi Sri) hung from each end of the screen. In the* dalang's *upraised hands two of the flat, ornate figures in which Billy Kwan had tried vainly to interest Hamilton were moving now with uncanny life. With a chock held between his toes, the master of the shadows*

knocked constantly for attention on the side of his puppet-box: tun-tun; tuk-tuk.

People pressed close to watch the sacred theatre's mysteries; but Hamilton drifted away to the other side of the screen, to the magic side, where only the filigreed silhouettes could be seen, their insect profiles darting, looming into hugeness, or dwindling to vanishing-point. Their voices chattered things he could never understand, rising into the warm dark: but the schoolroom rapping on the puppet-box commanded his attention. Standing behind solemn elders from the kampong, for whom chairs had been placed on the grass, he seemed to be watching the deeply important activity of dreams.

The dalang *was singing. His wailing, almost female voice climbed higher and higher, while the little drum pattered on underneath, and the gongs bubbled. On one wavering note, his voice was drawn out and out, until Hamilton, transfixed, seemed to see it like a bright thread against eternal sky; until it connected with Heaven. What was the* dalang *singing about? He would never know. Usually bored by things he could not understand, he could not now bring himself to return to the car; he lingered, locked in delight. The figures of this dream of Java's childhood tantalised him with the notion that he ought to know them, ought to recall them, from some other life. And they woke in him now a long-buried memory of his own.*

A novel of public affairs and private lives, *The Year of Living Dangerously* is set in 1965, in the corrupt and collapsing Indonesia of President Sukarno. It plays out the themes of the epigraph quoted from the great Indian epic, the *Bhagavad Gita*: "God dwells in the hearts of all beings, Arjuna: thy God dwells in thy heart. And his power of wonder moves all things — puppets in a play of shadows — whirling them onwards on the stream of time."

The novel's narrator is Cook, an Australian wire-service man. The foreign correspondents who gather in the half-darkness of the Wayang Bar in the Hotel Indonesia have their own stories as well as the stories they have come to cover. And all are symbolised by the Javanese *wayang* shadow puppets. As Billy Kwan, the dwarf cameraman, says to the Australian journalist Hamilton, "If you want to understand Java, Ham, you'll have to understand the *wayang*." Among the leather puppets, "with their black and gold faces, elongated limbs and grotesquely long noses", he points to the hero Prince Arjuna, "who has to master himself before he can master others", and to Semar, the dwarf who serves Arjuna, who is also " 'a god in disguise . . . My patron,' he said lightly. 'The patron of all dwarfs.' "

The tall, courageous, handsome Guy Hamilton is the Arjuna of the novel and Billy Kwan, the half-Australian, half-Chinese dwarf, is his Semar, as long as Hamilton remembers the words of King Krishna to Prince Arjuna, "Greedy lust and anger: this is the enemy of the soul."

Sukarno, "a baffling mixture of menace and playboy appeal", gives each year a name; this one is called "The Year of Living Dangerously". In Indonesian terms this means *Konfrontasi*, confrontation with the Western powers and Malaysia and India, which looks like being followed by a total commitment to a Jakarta-Peking axis. Aidit, the head of the PKI (the Communist Party) is a man of great and growing power. Through Billy Kwan's mysterious influence Hamilton gets a vital interview for his employers, the Australian Radio and Television Corporation, which establishes his position in Jakarta as a top correspondent.

Sir Guy, as the other journalists ironically call him, towers over his faithful dwarf Billy. Koch brilliantly conveys the bottomless cynicism of the journalists, which must coexist with their own hopes and fears. Sukarno has expelled almost all foreign journalists. A few Australians remain, Australia still being accepted by Sukarno and Aidit because of its early support of the revolution against Indonesia's former Dutch colonial masters. Doyen of the bar is the 140-kilogram Wally O'Sullivan, correspondent for a Sydney daily. Pete Curtis, the red-haired Canadian correspondent for the *Washington Post*, unpleasant when drunk, is always trying to stir up trouble. And Guy Hamilton, who travels on an Australian passport, was in fact born in England; he has grown up in Singapore and Australia. He is a hybrid.

People pressed close to watch the sacred theatre's mysteries; but Hamilton drifted away to the other side of the screen, to the magic side, where only the filigreed silhouettes could be seen, their insect profiles darting, looming into hugeness, or dwindling to vanishing-point.

There are two *wayangs* occurring in this novel; the puppet show of the great prince Bung Karno who is also full of "greedy lust and anger" and the shadow play of the journalists—Wally with his unfortunate passion for little boys, the other correspondents who haunt the cemetery where the boy and girl prostitutes gather, and all hungry for the scoop that will set them ahead of their fellows. Koch is particularly good at charting the ebb and flow of enmity and good fellowship among the journalists. One day Curtis and the English journalist Sloane can engineer a really unpleasant practical joke about dwarfs on Hamilton and Billy, while the next night at Wally's housewarming party Curtis and Billy can horse around happily together.

Surprisingly, Billy has a girlfriend, a divorced English girl who works with Colonel Henderson, the British Military Attache. "Here's my little Jillie!" says Kwan, introducing her to Hamilton, although around the swimming pool it rather looks as if she is the colonel's mistress. Koch is very adept at showing the odd workings of male rivalry. There is a biting scene by the swimming pool in which Henderson, much older than Hamilton, humiliates him by executing a perfect back somersault dive from the high board while Hamilton can only perform a simple dive, and even then his legs go over. But when challenged by the colonel to a race over a length of the pool, Hamilton lets the older man win.

The tensions are both complex and common to all in this novel. No one can escape living dangerously. Hamilton's impressive Indonesian assistant, Kumar, is probably a member of the PKI; he saves Hamilton's life in a bad episode with a crowd when Hamilton is slashed on the leg with a bush knife. Kwan in his bungalow keeps mysterious files on everyone, and even on more general subjects, such as "women". Can he be PKI? ASIO? CIA? Yet Billy also profoundly admires Sukarno as a champion of the people, the poor, suffering people of Indonesia who form the background of the novel and sometimes, horrifically, erupt into the foreground.

Billy Kwan is himself, as he says to Hamilton, a hybrid. He is Australian-Chinese, but is unable to speak Chinese. He is a man in a dwarf's body. He is an artist with his camera who can engineer important interviews, but he is only a stringer cameraman; it is not his name that goes over the air nor his face that is seen on the television screen. However, he has certain profound advantages "in our age of conformist tolerance", being "one who was not only racially but physically underprivileged". Kwan, a fascinating mixture of worldly scepticism and poetic idealism, enjoys being able to make use of these advantages, and also being able to manipulate the shadow puppets of his world.

He, as it were, gives Jillie (who was never the colonel's mistress) to Guy Hamilton. He even lends them his house, for Jakarta under curfew is an impossible place for lovers to find any privacy. When Hamilton is on his own in this bungalow one day, waiting for Billy to arrive, he finds one of Kwan's filing cabinets open. Lying on top is a file on Jill, which includes two nude photographs Kwan has taken of her. At the end of the written file is a very recent entry: "7 July. So you are pregnant. Is the child Hamilton's? And if so, what will you do? Of course it's his; it must be." Over scotch that night in his room at the Hotel Indonesia, Hamilton tells Cook of his discovery (except the entry about Jill's pregnancy). The simple, honourable Sir Guy is repelled by his faithful cameraman's secret dossiers, and is also distanced from Jill. Cook tells him not to worry; if Kwan is playing God, then he may be "a benevolent little god". But Cook also is observing Hamilton and seeing "that touching puzzlement of the man of action for whom the complexities of other people have suddenly become too much. Not to take action—not to simply smash something, or begin something new—is unbearable to such a man at such a point."

The irony of this subtly constructed book is that Hamilton's uncontrollable urge to take action destroys his relationship with Kwan and almost with Jill, while Kwan, who is not a man of action but one who should be in the shadows, managing the puppets, destroys himself by taking action.

As Billy says to Guy, there is weakness even in the hero. When Jill and Guy are lying on Billy's divan after making love, she tells him that some extremely important news has

ASSASSIN *Albert Tucker*

C. J. KOCH
1932-

Christopher John Koch was born in Hobart in 1932, of mixed German-English-Irish descent. His great-grandfather, Johann Koch, was a Lutheran German who emigrated to South Australia in the nineteenth century; he later became a prominent architect in Melbourne during the boom period. (His buildings include Labassa, built for the proprietor of Cobb and Co., which is mentioned in Kenneth Slessor's great poem, "Five Bells".)

Koch was educated in Hobart at Clemes College, St Virgil's College, Hobart State High School and the University of Tasmania, where he graduated BA in 1954. He spent the next two years abroad, mostly in London, where he worked in a variety of jobs, including school teaching. His first novel, *The Boys in the Island,* was published in London in 1958, and a revised edition appeared in Sydney in 1974.

Koch had also been writing poetry, and his first published poem appeared in the *Bulletin* in 1951, just after he left school. In the same year as *The Boys in the Island* was first published, three poems by Koch appeared in the *Penguin Book of Modern Australian Verse,* edited by John Thompson, Kenneth Slessor and R. G. Howarth.

The editors wrote:

> Koch's poetry, like that of Vivian Smith, is peculiarly regional. It conveys a feeling of antiquity and silence, of aguish winds and empty beaches, which is as powerfully evocative of the Tasmanian landscape as some of John Blight's poems are of the blaze and rain of Queensland.

Returning to Australia, Koch joined the ABC in 1957 as a producer in the Radio Education department. In 1960 he left the ABC on being awarded the Stanford Writing Fellowship which took him to California for a year. After that he spent a year in Italy, where he taught English.

He rejoined the ABC in 1962, remaining with the organisation until 1972. In 1968, when he was Federal Head of Radio for Schools, he was seconded to UNESCO to advise on the introduction of educational broadcasting to Indonesia. His report was published by UNESCO. Since leaving the ABC he has worked at part-time jobs in order to devote himself as fully as possible to writing. His novel *Across the Sea Wall* was published in London in 1965, with a revised edition in Sydney in 1982.

The Year of Living Dangerously was published in London, New York and Australia in 1978. It won the *Age* Book of the Year Award, and the National Book Council Award for Australian Literature. The MGM film of it, directed by Peter Weir, was released in 1982.

Koch now lives in Sydney, and his latest novel, *The Doubleman,* was published in 1985.

---

broken at the colonel's office; a ship full of Chinese arms destined for the PKI has just left Shanghai. With those arms Aidit can take over the government of Indonesia. Jill warns Guy that she will lose her job if this information gets out.

A spy element enters the story here, which could easily have been disastrous, with the James Bond-like stock-in-trade of a beautiful Vera from the Russian Embassy. Kumar has organised a rest trip for Guy at cool Bogor in the hills. He has also arranged that Vera should accompany them; Guy is disturbed to discover that his assistant speaks Russian. At the swimming pool by the bungalow Guy, sexually aroused by the Russian girl, watches her dive into the pool. Two minutes go by and she has still not surfaced from the dim, dark green water. Guy dives in to rescue her. She has only been fooling and pushes him under, holding him by the hair and almost drowning him. "Just a joke," she says when they are out of the pool again.

It is a tiny incident, but it immediately recalls the race with the colonel in Jakarta. There, Guy was magnanimous, with Jill watching. Now he is in danger of foolishly losing his power to this Russian girl who later, at Bandung, dopes him to worm out from him the date on which the arms ship arrives. Jill, to whom he should by now have been committed, is betrayed.

Before Bandung, where Guy goes in the course of covering the PKI Long March and also to meet Vera, he and Billy have their first and almost final row. Guy has told Billy he does not need a cameraman on this trip. Billy challenges him: "It's that Russian bitch, isn't it? That's who you're meeting in Bandung." Billy asks Guy to give him back the keys to the bungalow.

The "Russian bitch" is not a James Bond doll after all. She is the catalyst to the final section of the book, in which the personal dramas of Guy, Billy and Jill come to a climax.

Kwan's growing disillusion with Sukarno, who is no longer feeding his people, is no longer their saviour and true leader, leads him to attempt Sukarno's assassination, although, like everything to do with Kwan, there is a mystery to this. Maybe Kwan has only intended to unroll his great banner, SUKARNO, FEED YOUR PEOPLE, from a high window of the Hotel Indonesia as Sukarno arrives for a reception. Maybe the security men shoot Kwan and push his body out of the window, as Hamilton accuses them of doing; maybe, as the security men say, he jumps. Whichever way, it does not matter, for Kwan has lost control of himself and his shadow puppets, and his death is no more than an angry protest.

Sukarno is overthrown and many of his generals are murdered by the Communists, who in their turn are overthrown and butchered, perhaps half a million of them, by Suharto. Like a leaf in a storm, Kumar appears briefly, revealed now as an important member of the PKI; he disappears into the hills in search of Aidit. He will probably be one of Suharto's victims.

In the last meeting between Kwan, now estranged from all the journalists, and Hamilton, Kwan has shouted at him, "*I created you!*" In some respects it is true. Kwan has given him his first break as a journalist. He has given him Jill, with whom Hamilton, his eye badly injured by a soldier's rifle in the confused events after Kwan's death, finally escapes to what will be a happy ending. Kwan says he put Hamilton on course as a man, not just as a journalist.

But the relationship between fate, or God, and the *wayang* remains as mysterious as ever. All we know is that "God's power of wonder moves all things".

AN IMAGINARY LIFE

LONDON AND
NEW YORK 1978

How can I give you any notion—you who know only landscapes that have been shaped for centuries to the idea we all carry in our souls of that ideal scene against which our lives should be played out—of what earth was in its original bleakness, before we brought to it the order of industry, the terraces, fields, orchards, pastures, the irrigated gardens of the world we are making in our own image.

Do you think of Italy—or whatever land it is you now inhabit—as a place given you by the gods, ready-made in all its placid beauty? It is not. It is a created place. If the gods are with you there, glowing out of a tree in some pasture or shaking their spirit over the pebbles of a brook in clear sunlight, in wells, in springs, in a stone that marks the edge of your legal right over a hillside; if the gods are there, it is because you have discovered them there, drawn them up out of your soul's need for them and dreamed them into the landscape to make it shine. They are with you, sure enough. Embrace the tree trunk and feel the spirit blow back into you, feel the warmth of the stone enter your body, lower yourself into the spring as into some liquid place of your body's

other life in sleep. But the spirits have to be recognized to become real. They are not outside us, nor even entirely within, but flow back and forth between us and objects we have made, the landscape we have shaped and move in. We have dreamed all these things in our deepest lives and they are ourselves. It is our self we are making out there, and when the landscape is complete we shall have become the gods who are intended to fill it.

It is as if each creature had the power to dream itself out of one existence into a new one, a step higher on the ladder of things. Having conceived in our sleep the idea of a further being, our bodies find, slowly, painfully, the physical process that will allow them to break their own bonds and leap up to it. So that the stone sleeping in the sun has once been molten fire and became stone when the fire was able to say, in its liquid form: "I would

be solid, I would be stone"; and the stone dreams now that the veins of ore in its nature might become liquid again and move, but within its shape as stone, so that slowly, through long centuries of aching for such a condition, for softness, for a pulse, it feels one day that the transformation has begun to occur; the veins loosen and flow, the clay relaxes, the stone, through long ages of imagining some further life, discovers eyes, a mouth, legs to leap with, and is toad. And the toad in turn conceives the possibility, now that it can move over the earth, of taking to the air, and slowly, without ever ceasing to be toad, dreams itself aloft on wings. Our bodies are not final. We are moving, all of us, in our common humankind, through the forms we love so deeply in one another, to what our hands have already touched in lovemaking and our bodies strain towards in each other's darkness. Slowly, and with pain, over centuries, we each move an infinitesimal space towards it. We are creating the lineaments of some final man, for whose delight we have prepared a landscape, and who can only be god.

This book is an extraordinary tour-de-force. David Malouf, in writing about the old age of the Roman poet Publius Ovidius Naso, exiled to Tomis on the Black Sea, has achieved a fable that is beyond history. The book has an intense reality—of the terrible cold, of the wolves, the great frozen river five thousand paces across, the barbarians huddled in their villages, and the "real barbarians", the Dacians, riding their horses across the ice to shoot poisoned arrows over the wooden walls. This alone is an achievement. In deeper human terms, so too is the portrait of the worldly, "modern", exiled poet Ovid, having to learn a new language, forced into primitive duties (he, who had wriggled out of all those things at home), learning the workings of nature at last instead of elegantly observing them.

The life that Ovid has been used to, and the Italy he lived in, were together a created civilisation, and the gods were there "because you have discovered them there, drawn them up out of your soul's need for them and dreamed them into the landscape to make it shine".

Now, amongst the barbarians by the Black Sea, Ovid has lost all these comforts, physical, cultural, spiritual. Everything has been stripped from him. He cannot even speak the language.

I know how far we have come because I have been back to the beginnings. I have seen the unmade earth . . . It is a place of utter desolation, the beginning.

The poet has to learn to understand this harsh place and its simple people, who are not unkind to him. It is as if he has to relearn the language of poetry itself, the most difficult and yet the simplest language of all, to let the earth and animals and trees speak through him instead of him speaking to them. The translator, the pupil who becomes the teacher, is the Child, a wild boy who lives among the deer and is captured and brought back to the village for Ovid to tame and teach.

The idea of a wild child, as Malouf says in his Afterword, "has no basis in fact", but his description is "verified from the best account we have . . . J. M. G. Itard's painstaking observations of Victor, the wild boy of Aveyron". Of course, as Ovid himself points out, Romulus and Remus, the founders of Rome, were wild children suckled by a wolf, though they were the sons of Mars and a Vestal Virgin. For English-speaking readers the most famous of all wild children is Mowgli, of the *Jungle Books*, also brought up by a wolf. Malouf is a great admirer of Kipling, but he makes no attempt to place his Child amongst the animals, or to state his authority over them, if it existed. Nor is his Child particularly handsome.

For Ovid he is also the Wild Child he had known when he was three or four years old, who also lived among wolves "in the ravines to the east, beyond the cultivated farms and villas of our well-watered valley". He asks himself, was he a wolf-boy, one of those "who change painfully at the moon's bidding?"

Ovid's most famous book was the *Metamorphoses* (the Changes). It was the inspiration of countless medieval and renaissance poets and painters, Chaucer and Shakespeare amongst others. Malouf ends his Afterword by saying that in his book he has given Ovid "a capacity for belief that is nowhere to be found in his own writings. But that is exactly the point. My purpose was to make this glib fabulist of 'the changes' live out in reality what had been, in his previous existence, merely the occasion for dazzling literary display."

Ovid first sees the Child's footprints when he is on a hunting expedition in the birchwoods. "The old man nods gravely and explains with signs. It *is* a child, a boy of ten or so, a wild boy, who lives with the deer." Ovid catches a glimpse of him; he immediately "goes bounding away into the woods" so swiftly that the old poet wonders whether he was real or a vision of the wild boy he had known in his youth.

*O*ur bodies are not final. We are moving, all of us, in our common humankind, through the forms we love so deeply in one another, to what our hands have already touched in lovemaking and our bodies strain towards in each other's darkness.

The soft Roman is getting tougher. He survives the winter and attacks by the Dacians. He now understands the language of the people he lives with, and has begun to teach the old man's grandson Latin and to recite poems, some of them his own. Then, one afternoon in the birchwoods, Ovid

and the men see the Child again, "An ugly boy of eleven or twelve with a bird's nest of dirty hair". The men are afraid of him; he may be an evil spirit. Ovid puts out a bowl of food for him, and, in hiding, sees him eat it. He is confident that the Child will come to his fellow-humans. "Next year there will be no need to hunt him. He will seek us out."

As the year passes the poet grows stronger and healthier, his attitude to the environment changes as he begins to notice all the details of the life of nature around him in what at first he had dismissed as desolation. He even plants a garden for pleasure. "For these people it is a new concept, play. How can I make them understand that till I came here it was the only thing I knew?"

The Child does not come into the world of humans easily. He has to be captured and tied up; he howls terribly, "like nothing I have ever heard from a human throat".

Some of the most searching and sympathetic writing in *An Imaginary Life* is the section where Ovid gradually tames the Child. The women will not touch him and his presence creates tension and fear of spirits in the village. But for Ovid, he is a delight as they learn from each other. Language is the immediate problem, for the Child can talk to birds and animals but not to human beings. When Ovid sets about teaching him, the crucial question is what language should he learn? Ovid, the great Latin poet, the civilised man, decides to teach him not Latin but the language of the barbarians. This would, ironically, really have been Greek, but Malouf does not attempt any historical connections. Tomis, the Romanian Constanza where marvellous works of art are being excavated today, was actually Greek, a colony of Miletus; and the nomadic Dacians, Malouf's outer barbarians, had high standards of art. In the book, one just has to accept an infinitely receding scale of barbarity.

For a poet, this decision about language should be a betrayal. For what should a poet be if not the guardian of his language? But Malouf's Ovid is, through the Child, learning a new freedom, if he has the imagination; the freedom to transcend himself and go beyond the limits.

Though Malouf's fable is splendidly convincing, it can only be really understood by reference to other poets. Ovid tries to teach the Child the barbarians' tongue, and when the Child falls sick, in the delirium of his fever, he at last cries out a few words. The local people are terrified; they think, by speaking, he has snatched away another soul.

But it is really Ovid he is speaking to, for he is teaching Ovid how to speak the language of the earth itself. An odd pair of poets, Wordsworth and Whitman, would have understood what Malouf is aiming for. Wordsworth, with his "The Child is father of the Man", saying of the Poet, "Thy Art be Nature", and in the Lucy poems feeling that empathy with nature in which Lucy herself is finally "Rolled round in earth's diurnal course,/ With rocks, and stones, and trees". Whitman, with his soul bathed in God, "transcendent, Nameless, the fibre and breath", and finding (almost an exact description of what happens to Malouf's Ovid):

I incorporate gneiss, coal, long-threaded moss, fruits, grains, esculent roots,
And stucco'd with quadrupeds and birds all over,
And have distanced what is behind me for good reasons,
But call any things back again when I desire it.

THE IDIOT *David Strachan*

DAVID MALOUF
1934-

David Malouf was born in Brisbane in 1934. His father's family had come to Australia in the 1880s from Lebanon, and his mother's family from London just before World War I. He was educated at Brisbane Grammar School and the University of Queensland. He went to the United Kingdom in 1959, and returned to Australia for six months in 1961. From 1962 to 1968 he taught in England at Birkenhead at St Anselm's Christian Brothers Grammar School. In 1968 he was appointed Lecturer in English at the University of Sydney and he taught there until 1978 when he resigned to devote all his time to writing. Since then he has alternated between living in Italy and paying return visits to Australia; in 1984 he was Writer in Residence at Macquarie University in Sydney.

Malouf established himself as a writer with three books of poetry, "Interiors" from *Four Poets* (1962), *Bicycle and Other Poems* (1969) and *Neighbours in a Thicket* (1974); the latter won several awards. His first novel, *Johnno*, based on his youth in Brisbane, was published in 1975. *An Imaginary Life* (1978) was awarded the New South Wales Premier's Literary Award for Fiction in 1979.

From his house in Italy, he writes about some of his feelings and thoughts about living in Italy:

Italy I've discovered (or re-discovered) is a magic world—it represents to all sorts of people an ideal world; they have all, at some time, had the dream of having a little place there. They read all sorts of things into my being here that I don't *feel*.

Over the past six years I have spent approximately half my time in Australia. Italy has become for me a place to "get away to" for quiet work—as other writers get away to a beachhouse on the South Coast or into the hills.

Also one's head is not always where the body is: most of *Bicycle*, which includes some of my most Australian pieces, was written in England between 1962 and 1968; *Johnno* was written in Italy in 1972. *An Imaginary Life* (which people often assume—especially after they have seen this village—is the fruit of my "Italian exile") was written in Sydney in 1976. *Fly Away Peter* was written here, and so was my new book, *Harland's Half Acre*, which is set entirely in Queensland.

I should have thought it was obvious from the writing—but people insist on seeing a problem or a paradox. For me—I may be peculiar—there is no problem at all.

Malouf is deeply interested in music, especially opera, and has written a libretto from Patrick White's *Voss* for Richard Meale's music.

When the Child recovers from his fever, it passes to Lullo, the old man Ryzak's grandson. He recovers, but Ryzak dies, and now there is no protection for either Ovid or the Child. When the rituals of death are over, the people will think of vengeance. So the old poet evolves a desperate plan: he and the Child will cross the frozen river and escape into the Steppes.

*B**ut the spirits have to be recognized to become real. They are not outside us, nor even entirely within, but flow back and forth between us and objects we have made, the landscape we have shaped and move in.*

Thanks to the Child's knowledge of nature, they survive into the spring. This is the final metamorphosis, Ovid becoming the earth, the Child's body straining towards "his own nature as a god". Ovid ponders the question: "Is he, in fact, as the villagers thought (their view was always simpler than mine, and perhaps therefore nearer the truth) some foundling of the gods?"

The mysterious gods which troubled the edges of the Roman empire of rational law are very much present in *An Imaginary Life*. Perhaps the whole book is also given an added edge by a suspicion that Malouf may be writing a kind of autobiography (a very different one from that touched on in his other novel, *Johnno*) of the poet of a European tradition exiled in barbarous Australia. Though Australians as a whole are determined to make a virtue of not going beyond the limits, the mysteries of Australia itself, and its strange unknown gods, remain. Malouf's Ovid painfully realises that here in exile is his true fate, "the one I spent my whole existence trying to escape . . . Here is your second chance." The Child is the guide.

Roger McDonald

1915

ST LUCIA, QLD, 1979

Billy angled his body a little to the left of the line of fire, clasping the weapon loosely in his hands, allowing the ground to take the weight. He imagined a taut wire stretching along his line of sight to the mark opposite. At this moment of preparation Billy was always able to look away, and again look back to find the wire still there. He slowly worked the bolt. The faint metallic slide and click blended with the noise of insects. The insides of his feet gripped firmly against the hospitable ground. He wriggled for ease and comfort and firmness, and for the pleasure of what he was about to do. Now came the moment for absolute steadiness when he would become vulnerable to any unseen watcher who might happen to stare at his hide and see the unnatural straight line of the rifle lift against the scalloped curves of nature, and the man-shape declare itself like a figure in a picture puzzle book.

As he raised the rifle his chest, head and arms rose in obedience. His entire being moved to the imperatives of the rifle. As always he was held by the magic of its weighted but manoeuvrable length, its invisible power over nearby horizons. He jutted his left arm slightly outwards so that his elbows formed stays, as in timber work. He was ready, alert in that state where the devoted marksman knows the whole visible world subservient to his next move. As Billy felt the first pressure of

the trigger he took a deep slow breath and held it. It was a moment for tasting the perfect stillness of death as he had never tasted it before. Excitement like the tickle from a low voltage battery sat at the tip of his tongue. He wiped it away with a quick pointed lick. What other name but "murderer" was there for a person who in the eternity before the second pull found satisfaction for a deep appetite?

But there still seemed a chance for the distant Turk to shift an inch one way or the other and save his own life. Billy could never predict the crucial moment. That was where the other man's chance lay. Split fractions of fractions of seconds were available, and it was then that Billy imagined another person's finger reaching down and flicking the pin forward— igniting the powder, jolting the braced shell, sending the spiralling projectile on its way.

The word "murderer" would never fit. It was as if Billy were the instrument of a greater power, the force that made the rifle and put a man behind it.

After firing he held the rifle steady, "following through" while an alarming

echo lashed the still valley. Then it weakened against the constant battle rumbling from higher up. Only then did Billy let out his breath. Everything had been done right and he knew, as always, that someone at the end of the taut wire lay dead. The trick now was to find the spot with the naked eye, but the wire had twanged towards the target along with the bullet, forming part of the destructive force now spent.

He lowered the rifle and set his eye to the telescope. He was now able to take a leisurely look at the target, an indulgence that the deadly fire on the heights during previous weeks had not permitted.

The man's head protruded only a few inches forward of its previous position. The face, having struck the earth, seemed to have ploughed outwards into a patch of sunlight. Just this detail of humiliation touched Billy. Blood gathered on a temple, black as the hair surrounding it, but catching the light.

It took Billy some time to realize that his killing of the Turkish sniper had taken place in one of those moods of personal obliteration he had sworn to be rid of. But the mood had changed its character. It now brought great elation instead of anger, a sense of timelessness in the midst of necessity. The killer, having erased the object of his passion, thinks he will then be free from the burden of the passion for ever.

Nineteen-fifteen was the fateful year of Gallipoli, but Roger McDonald's novel begins several years earlier, with the two protagonists as boys playing war games in the country. Walter Gilchrist and Billy Mackenzie are neighbours on properties near Parkes in New South Wales; the Gilchrists are better off and more sober than the Mackenzies. Walter goes to school in Sydney, but Billy in his rough way has accumulated more sophistication in Parkes and Forbes.

Between them they are a sort of composite of the Australian character, not much older than Federation, deeply rooted in the country, pitifully ignorant of the world overseas. There is a violent, cruel streak in Billy; a respectful

and respectable one in Walter. They have their share of fights, as Billy says, but their friendship comes together again. They are both good with horses and of course know a great deal about farming and running stock. Walter does not want to go on the land but is resigned to his father forcing him into it. Billy is knowing with women and while still at school is having an affair with a widow. He would like to have an affair with Frances, the daughter of a publican at Forbes; when she does not co-operate, he rapes an Aboriginal girl in the darkness outside the hotel.

It is as if Billy has some of the original Australian crimes on his shoulders, but he is a typical amalgam of stoical good and ignorant bad. He did not intend to rape Frances. His maltreatment of the Aboriginal girl is an instinctive racism which is only half conscious. He has not reached the stage of understanding the humanity of the Aborigines. And he is already, by the time of this episode, established in the reader's favour by an affecting incident when he is walking his horse over the rocky ridge on his way to the Gilchrists. He is thinking of his drunken father and his weary, unhappy mother. "'Who ain't unhappy?' Billy asked the stars . . . But when you fitted it all together, there they were, all three proud of each other. They kept their chins up."

The Gilchrists are, to Mrs Mackenzie, a civilising influence. Mr Gilchrist doesn't drink. They believe in education. The opening sentence of the book is: "It was inconceivable to Walter that a person could be well educated yet morally bad." Billy is not surprised when something sparks between Walter and Frances, who also goes to school in Sydney, after Walter had promised to promote Billy's interests on the train journey to Sydney. " 'But you'd be near enough her type for starters.' Billy struck a match which popped and hissed. With the cigarette wedged in his mouth he now looked Walter in the eye: 'The educated type,' he enunciated."

*H*e slowly worked the bolt. The faint metallic slide and click blended with the noise of insects. The insides of his feet gripped firmly against the hospitable ground. He wriggled for ease and comfort and firmness, and for the pleasure of what he was about to do.

But it is not a strong spark; Frances does not defend Walter when her bitchy mother caricatures him as a future boring farmer. She hankers for concepts like "art", and the world of "overseas", and is excited by her schoolfriend Diana's daring frankness about sex. It is Billy, not Walter, who kisses her and slips his hand up her leg. Never mind her indignation, which is not all that genuine. Billy has come to Sydney to do what he has done, and he is thinking: "*I've beaten Wally good and smart.*" And Frances's mother thinks he is "terrific".

This drifting of unshaped characters, with Billy's undirected strength jutting through it, is the extent of life until the outbreak of war. Suddenly there is a stoush to drink to, to go to. "What about you two?" says an urger in the pub to Billy and Walter; "We're going, too right!" Even so, it takes five beers before Walter is on fire. Back home again, he is encouraged by Mr Gilchrist, but asked for reasons by his mother.

There are Germans in the district, old, respected settlers. "I don't hate the Germans. None of us do," says Mrs Gilchrist. But it is not a matter for logic or even sense, and the conversation finishes when Mrs Gilchrist says dully, "Nobody can tell me why."

The forces working on Australia are not to be analysed until much later by those most affected by them. *1915* is a novel of fate, of stumbling destiny, of 21-year-old men falling from innocence into evil. By the time they begin to question it all they are breathing the stench of corpses.

Billy, without losing any of his independence of mind,

is the perfect soldier. He is a superb horseman when the Light Horse still have their mounts; when they are turned into footsloggers at Gallipoli, his skill with a rifle establishes him as a legendary sniper, known as "The Murderer".

However, it is Walter who carries the weight of the novel for the 100-odd pages before the two young men are reunited at Gallipoli. Billy's glimpse of enlightenment does not come till later, but Walter is taught to think by his odd friends, the older English Ollie and the talkative, questioning ex-schoolteacher Hurst. An officer is blown to bits by a bomb alongside Hurst and Walter in a trench; the blast clears away some of Hurst's personae, which were partly compensating for the death of his young brother a few days before. The lessons Walter learns from Hurst are overlaid by questions asked after a profound experience of beauty with Ollie in a mosque in Alexandria.

> Again Walter caught at the discovery made in the mosque. And an absurd, fanciful thing it was, at the gangling age of twenty-one to have grasped this idea of art and his destiny being intertwined. . . . What a bastard fate was to pluck him from Australia, set him on the rails to war, then give him a vivid glimpse of the what-might-be before tossing him wastefully into the realm of never-shall.

At the same time the unfortunate Walter is undergoing another more humiliating lesson. Frances, who was, he thought, "his girl", suddenly sends him a cold letter. We learn later that the rich Robert Gillen, from a large property 80 kilometres out of Forbes, who has not joined the army, has with his specious glamour and tales of South America won her away from "the sombre Walter Gilchrist".

Walter's deepest initiation into hell comes when, soon after Hurst's death from shrapnel while swimming, his old western New South Wales friend Frank is mortally wounded by a freak accident. Digging, he had lifted his shovel over the trench parapet and a stray bullet ricocheted down and opened up his stomach.

Frank takes a long time to die, long enough for someone to find a priest. This turns out to be "Potty" Fox, who had buried Hurst's brother Roy, but whom the reader remembers having first met at Parkes. He had preached a fire-eating sermon, "Germany's policy, the Long Arm and the Mailed Fist". The soldiers do not care for parsons, but within his limits Fox is a changed man, good with the living and the dead. Walter and a soldier called Bluey are detailed to help him bury the dead after they had been collected during a brief cease-fire. Frank is amongst them, amongst the luckier whole bodies, so recently killed as still to be looking like "stone knights in a makeshift tomb".

As they talk Fox admits he was not a Christian back in Australia. "Are you now?" asks Bluey. "The Christian truth is bedrock. Such a simple lesson to come from pain," Fox replies. He continues that he was no stranger to pain, but "It's just that I failed when I tried to apply faith to the intellect, rather than to the world."

Suddenly he turns to Walter and says, "*You've* changed!" Walter is reassured by this recognition, by the knowledge that his "agonised self-questioning" did not seem so wasteful after all. And in answer to Fox's question as to what he wants to do after the war he finally, after several false leads, blurts out, "Art." As he says the word he realises, almost with anger,

THE AMATEUR ("Who's cutting this hair, you or me?") *Will Dyson*

ROGER McDONALD
1941-

Roger McDonald was born at Young in New South Wales on 23 June 1941. His father was Presbyterian minister at nearby Bribbaree. Later the family moved to Temora, where Roger began his primary education, and then to Bourke on the river Darling in far western New South Wales, where he finished it. His secondary schooling was undertaken at the Scots College at Bellevue Hill in Sydney, an abrupt change from those quiet western country towns.

He attended Sydney University from 1959 to 1962, where amongst other things he was a foundation member of the Sydney University Mountaineering Club. By this stage of his life he was writing poetry, but he showed it to nobody except a few non-literary friends.

For two years after graduation he was a teacher for the NSW Education Department, first at Murrumburrah-Harden and then at Wellington. In 1964 he moved to the ABC where he worked in Brisbane and Hobart as a producer for the schools' broadcast section. In 1968 his first book of poetry, *Citizens of Mist*, was published by University of Queensland Press.

In 1969 he wrote the following personal statement for his poems published in Tom Shapcott's anthology, *Australian Poetry Now* (1970).

I lived my childhood in country towns; my earliest thoughts are evoked by dry grass and peppercorn trees. I got into the habit, when very young, of regarding nature as a friendly place where I could lean away from the dissident voices of people who confused my silent purposes. When I started to write poems I found myself doing the same thing—stepping into a territory where words could clarify and heal the obscure and broken edges of experience.

In 1969 McDonald went to work for University of Queensland Press, where he edited a large number of books until the start of 1977 when he resigned to take up full-time writing with the aid of a one-year Senior Fellowship from the Literature Board of the Australia Council. He also moved to Canberra.

Apart from *Airship* (1975) he has published no poetry since he began to write novels. His first novel was *1915* (1979). Although the story is imaginary, to ensure that the background would be authentic he talked to several veterans of Gallipoli and made use of the books, diaries and letters held in the Australian War Memorial in Canberra, and other libraries.

1915 was *Age* Book of the Year in 1979, and won the South Australian Government's Biennial Literary Prize in 1980. In 1982 it was made into a television series by the ABC. In 1980 it was published in New York by George Braziller and in 1983 in London by Faber. It has also been translated into Swedish.

McDonald's second novel, *Slipstream*, about an early Australian aviator in some ways reminiscent of Kingsford Smith, was published by the University of Queensland Press in 1982, and in Boston by Little, Brown, and in London by Faber in the same year.

McDonald writes: "One of the realities of writers' incomes in Australia is that despite this apparent success I have continued to need support from Australia Council Fellowships."

He lives on a small farm in New South Wales near Braidwood, with his wife and three daughters. He moved there in 1980.

---

that this comes not only from the experience in the mosque but from hearing Frances talk, so many times, "on and on about art". He resents the fact that "he was still bonded insanely to *her*".

McDonald is very skilful in keeping the threads of ordinary life, and the fragmented hopes of a future life, moving through the dreadful impasse of war. It is a moving paradox that the totally demanding presence of this grotesque Gallipoli campaign can still liberate or at least illuminate the souls and minds of those caught in it, even those, like Bluey, who are not keen on too much thinking or talking.

The horrors of war have not drained McDonald's men of emotion. Even Bluey cries after the nightmare of the burying, which often meant, when they got to the decomposed bodies, throwing limbs and heads into the grave. "Here one was compelled to walk to the mucked heart of matter, reach for a hand, plunge it into the black pulp and grasp for a slimy bone which itself was only the outer casing of something deeper, darker, more horrible and endless." In the morning, however, talking with Fox, he grows angry. "Go and complain to your God about the buggered bodies."

McDonald reveals another thread running from New South Wales to Gallipoli, that between Frances's friend Diana Benedetto and Billy. There is a series of flashbacks, agonisingly sharp in their contrast with the burying which has immediately preceded them in the book's sequence.

Now Captain Benedetto, Diana's father, finds Billy and, surprisingly amicable, they talk over the fact that Diana is going to have Billy's child. The reader goes back with Billy and Diana, Walter and Frances, to the hotel where those whole, beautiful, sweet-smelling bodies had made love.

But the threads are running two ways. The deaths in Gallipoli are joined to the death of Diana and her unborn baby, in a clean but no less cruel way, drowned in a river, with Frances blaming herself for the accident.

In a further paradox, Billy, so proud of being about to become a father, is revealed to have been made whole by the war, his violence cured by violence.

> Nothing but a practical equation arranged itself in his mind: the death of the enemy equalled the security of his place in the world . . . Billy's rarity as a soldier came from this atypical union of private thoughts and military function.

The climax of the book, in which Walter and Billy are fatally drawn together by chance, is deliberately ambiguous. At the end a headwound leaves Billy, the survivor, insane. Frances, whose wounds are more complex, long since parted from Robert Gillen, is left with a letter about Walter from Ollie, which may be misleading.

McDonald intends the book to end on a question mark, as to whether friend kills friend; he can offer no further comment on the senselessness of war, and of the Gallipoli campaign in particular. Written two generations after Anzac Day, *1915* offers a harsh tribute to sacrifice.

Jessica Anderson

THE IMPERSONATORS

MELBOURNE 1980

"Rosamond, I am an old woman."

"I wondered when that was coming."

"I am an old woman," said Greta with resolution, "and if it turns out that I have only the house, I'll still have enough for my needs. And all you children are all right."

"Were," said Rosamond.

"What does that mean?"

"You must have seen this morning's paper."

"I did. But Ted's been saying for years—"

"This time it's true. The wolf is real."

"He's really losing—?"

"Hand over fist. Wow."

"In that case he can sell the boat."

"He has."

"What did he get for it?"

"Nothing yet. But he's sure he has a buyer."

"Oh," said Greta, "I see. Well, I think you'll find that Ted's all right. Ted's the kind of man who's always all right. I wish I felt as happy about Steven and Hermione. They'll never get out of that flat. How can they borrow money in times like these? Enough money for what Hermione wants? When they sold the Baulkham Hills house Steven made a very bad deal."

"It's no use blaming Steve, mother, when it's always Min who craves so much to move. And you can't blame her, either, because she can't help it."

"I don't believe in people not being able to help things."

"No, but if God made Minnie looking like a goddess, he ought to have made a marble hall to put her in."

"Goddesses! Marble Halls! They had a perfectly good house. Anyone could see hard times coming. And then to go and have another child, even if it is Imogen." But Greta's voice had lost its sharpness, and was taking on its croon. "Oh, Rosie, what a lovely child she is. Those eyes!"

"I would like to keep Imogen's eyes exactly as they are," said Rosamond, smiling, watching the ship. "It's not fair that they must change."

But Greta's repose, her sudden expelled breath, almost a hiss, made Rosamond sit straight in her chair, and move her eyes quickly to right and left. "Mother?" she said with caution.

There was no reply. Rosamond darted glances of alarm all over the big plate glass window, at one point or another of the sky, the harbour, and the northern shores. "Mother, what's the matter?"

Greta spoke in a flat, drained voice. "Nothing I can explain."

"It's my fault," said Rosamond. "I shouldn't have started talking about hard times, and Min and Steve. But Min and Steve are like Ted and me, mother. One way or another, they'll be all right. I wouldn't have mentioned what's happening to Ted, either, only I knew you would have read it in the paper. And Harry's fine, now that he's stopped pining for Margaret. And Guy, well, worrying doesn't help, does it? Yesterday, did you say he went?"

"Yes, yesterday. He won some money on some sort of gambling."

"He'll be back in a week. You'll see. Next week you'll be keeping his meals hot again, on that gadget."

"I don't want him to come back. I have to shed things. I have to be light."

But Rosamond, though she looked startled, would not relinquish the safety of her mock bullying. "That gadget you bought especially to keep Guy's meals hot. I throw Ted's out, but not Dominic's and Matthew's, because they're growing boys, and if I did, they might stop."

Greta's voice was regaining resonance. "How are the boys, Rosamond?"

"They've just come in. Hullo, darlings."

Rosamond turned in her chair to look at the two school-boys who had dawdled in from the hall, and stood banging their straw hats against their legs. "How are they?" asked Greta's voice again.

Rosamond surveyed her two sons from head to foot. Fifteen and sixteen, they were of similar appearance, both dark, with not an angle of face or figure lacking in harmony. She turned again to the phone. "They have changed into their summer hats."

"Give them my love," said Greta in her croon.

"Nan sends her love," shouted Rosamond at her sons' departing backs. "They send theirs," she said into the phone. "They've gone to feed their faces, the pigs, and then they'll go and smoke a joint, or whatever it's called these days."

Greta spoke in a hushed voice. "They don't really smoke marijuana?"

One of the most intricate and precisely constructed of modern novels, *The Impersonators* is so easy to read that sometimes one has to watch out that a vital clue to the story or to a character has not been passed over. Much of it is accomplished by dialogue, and it is as intimate as a play. At the same time, passages of pure narrative or description create the scene that lies beyond the window of the room.

This scene is Sydney in the 1970s and many contrasting aspects of Sydney are evoked with great mastery. Jessica Anderson can do this without contrivance because she is writing a novel about a family, all the members of which live in different circumstances; it is also a novel about money.

However, it is impossible to make any restrictive definitions of what this subtle novel is "about". There is a constant interaction between the characters who are not only different in themselves but who have different motives and ambitions. So as well as being about a family, it is also a novel about love and affection, or the lack of them, between men and women, children and parents.

On the deepest level of all, the title gives the reader a clue. Scarcely anyone is quite what they seem, and the ones that are are all the more to be valued. Neither houses nor clothes are reliable guides to what people really are, and even when they are lovers and all their clothes are gone they may still be searching for a true self.

Jessica Anderson has thoughtfully provided the reader with a family tree at the beginning of the novel, but the members of the family are introduced with such skill that it is difficult to get lost among them.

The action of the book is sparked between a dying man, Jack Cornock, who has had a severe stroke, and the arrival from Europe of his daughter Sylvia, who has been an expatriate for 20 years. Jack is rich. There is a sort of malevolence between him and his second wife Greta. The rumour is that although he has left her the fine house in Wahroonga he is going to leave his money to Sylvia, his daughter by his first wife Molly, whom he conveniently divorced for adultery when he so badly wanted to marry Greta. Those members of the family with less charity assume that Sylvia is coming home to make sure she gets the money. Jack has rough origins. He was "an ignorant bush boy", and it seems that the roots of his wealth are in some grubby war-time black-marketeering. Nevertheless, with Greta's elegance and determined help, he has achieved some sort of North Shore respectability. Not so Molly, out in Burwood, who is still the original, unimproved version, with her lack of grammar and her fondness for a drop, married to a wiry old carpenter called Ken Fiddies. One of the beauties of *The Impersonators* is that Jessica Anderson is equally at home with the idiom and the surroundings of each different group.

"*Mother?*" she said with caution. There was no reply. Rosamond darted glances of alarm all over the big plate glass window, at one point or another of the sky, the harbour, and the northern shores. "Mother, what's the matter?"

In Jack Cornock's extended family there is plenty of room for variety. By Molly he had Sylvia, who is divorced from her English husband and leads a nomadic life around Europe,

with Italy as her favourite country, conducting tours, writing travel articles, teaching Italian in England or English in Italy. A legacy from an old lady she had conducted around Scotland and Eire enables her to visit Australia for the first time since she left. Jack's other child by Molly is Stewart, a very successful bachelor real estate agent, who confidentially tells Sylvia he probably has more money than Jack.

There are emotional links between Jack's family and that of Greta by her first husband, Hugh Polglaze, dead 31 years ago. Their children are Harry, Rosamond, Hermione and Guy. Harry, Greta's eldest son, now divorced, has had a muted love affair with Sylvia that now may well begin to flourish. Stewart thinks he may be in love with Hermione, who is married to Steven Fyfe, and has three children. He certainly wants to go to bed with her. She is beautiful but not well off; they live at Wollstonecraft. Hermione seems not to be interested in Stewart except in his capacity as a real estate agent; she is always getting Stewart to show her new houses she cannot afford. As her elder sister Rosamond says, "If God made Minnie [Hermione] looking like a goddess, he ought to have made a marble hall to put her in." When Stewart propositions Hermione with money and potential marble halls as well as sex, she does give it some deep thought.

Rosamond is married to a business man, Ted Kitching, and has two sons. With a yacht and a house in Point Piper, they seem to be the richest members of the family, but in fact Ted is in dire financial troubles. To get out of them, he is not the sort of man who would mind becoming even more of a corporate crook than he is already.

Apart from Jack Cornock, described by his lawyer as "a terrible man", the nastiest character in the book is Guy, the youngest of Greta's children. He lives on his wits and, at times, on what he steals from his mother's house. Harry describes him as poison.

The impersonators are at their worst when it comes to love, or what passes for love. At first Rosamond and Ted seem to be the ideal couple, and if ever they have any differences they are settled in bed. "Apart from one accident early in their marriage", Rosamond is faithful to Ted, and Ted "had sexual relations with no other woman in Sydney, and when he was away, only with first-class professionals".

The hollowness there is soon revealed; it is not such a fault with Hermione and Steven and their young children. But Hermione—"Beautiful. Touchy. Restless as hell", in Rosamond's words—is in private not too good at impersonating the happy wife.

Even Harry and Sylvia, who seem to be having a true love affair, are threatened by Sylvia's inability to decide between being an expatriate or an Australian at home.

Only Molly and Ken, with all their raucous limitations, are not pretending to be other than they are; although even straightforward Molly has been a deceiver. Sylvia, visiting her after all those years away, suddenly realises that she is illiterate, although she has always managed to disguise it.

Dominating all these lives is money, at least temporarily, as Jack, unable to speak, sits in his wheel chair and writes misspelled notes and summons his lawyer to make a new will. Hermione puts it most clearly, forgetting she is quoting Herodotus, "It is impossible to be honest in a corrupt society." Jack's ill-gotten money helped make her blood and

DREAMING IN THE STREET *Charles Blackman*

JESSICA ANDERSON

Jessica Anderson was born in Gayndah in Queensland. Her father, Charles Queale, and her mother Alice (née Hibbert) were respectively from Irish and English immigrant families. Her father was a veterinarian who worked in the Queensland Department of Agriculture and Stock. Her mother's father was a violin teacher in Toowoomba and Brisbane, and both he and her mother played violin in the Queensland Orchestra.

Jessica was the youngest of four children. The family lived in a Brisbane suburb with enough land to keep a horse and to grow most of their own fruit and vegetables. Both her parents were active in Labor politics, and there was much talking, debating and reading in the Queale home.

Jessica went to Yeronga State School and Brisbane High School and was horrified by them both. She writes, "I couldn't believe it was happening to me . . . the dull dull classrooms. Looking back at what was taught in Queensland state schools at the time, I think I had some reason on my side. I remember what a difference it made when for one year I had an enthusiastic and original teacher."

She left school at 16 and went to art school for one year. Her father died. She writes:

One day, having amassed £3, I left Brisbane and went to Sydney on a little coastal steamer. Here at once I made many friends, mostly wild young refugees from suburbia like myself. I went to London to join a lover who afterwards became my first husband. As London was the recognised Mecca of those days, I was surprised to find myself so homesick for Sydney. We were there for two years.

I had been writing since I was a child, beginning with doggerel verse and plays in which I myself took no part because I stammered. In my youth I wrote stories. Some were published. None satisfied me. My reason for writing them was that I always needed the money. I always intended to stop doing them and instead put my whole heart into writing and see what I could really do. This I started to do when I was forty. I usually say I was able to do it then because for the first time in my adult life I had financial security (in a second marriage), but an added and perhaps more important reason was that by that time I had been sobered and matured by personal tragedy and by the post-war revelations of the holocaust in Europe.

Jessica Anderson has had five novels published between *An Ordinary Lunacy* (1963) and *The Impersonators* (1980). In between writing her novels she has done adaptations and radio drama for the ABC. She has had two one-year fellowships from the Literature Board, and spent a term as a writer in residence at the University of New England.

The Commandant (1975) is an historical novel of great quality set at the time of the convict settlement at Moreton Bay. *Tirra Lirra by the River* (1978) and *The Impersonators* both won the Miles Franklin Award; the latter also won the NSW Premier's Literary Award.

Jessica Anderson lives alone at Darling Point, Sydney. She writes, "Like my parents, I am politically Labor, and like them, Republican." She has a daughter, Laura Jones (a film and television script writer), and a granddaughter. She is the last of her immediate Queale family.

---

flesh and bones. It bought the necklace of pearls (symbol of purity) which he gives Sylvia. Amongst the others, Ted is used to living with corruption; Rosamond and one of the sons cannot take it any more, and move out.

After Jack dies, Jessica Anderson gathers all her characters together in a brilliant scene to hear the will read. Greta does indeed get the house, but nothing else, not even the furniture or a car. Everything else, apart from one small legacy, goes to Sylvia after her mother dies, but Molly is to have the interest on it in her lifetime.

Nobody knows the reason, but perhaps Jack just wants to make amends to Molly for having treated her so badly. The trigger to it all, Sylvia thinks, is that she betrayed to Jack the secret of Molly's illiteracy. At the time Jack wrote "I KNEW". "But she had seen his stupefaction, and believed this to be a lie. They were still in the old act." The reader never finds out whether Jack did not know, or whether his stupefaction was due to Sylvia's uncovering such a well-hidden secret.

"The old act" is what keeps most people in *The Impersonators* going, and also most people anywhere in real life, one would conclude after finishing the book and looking around at the world of Sydney or beyond.

The city of Sydney, with its far-spread suburbs, is like another character in the book, modifying the way people live; it is far more than a skilfully drawn-in background. The first eight pages of Chapter Three, when the path of Sylvia, walking up from Woolloomooloo to the Botanic Gardens, intersects with those of Steven and Ted jogging in the Domain, is a model of the novelist's skill, giving a perfect integration of people and place, from which the reader learns more than he could from pages of explanation.

When Sylvia learns the truth about herself at the end of the book, and decides to stay in Sydney with Harry, she realises that the attitudes she had selected to criticise in Australians were in fact aspects of herself. "It was she who had repudiated tragedy, and she who needed other people's rituals." Sydney's lack of wholeness, its lack of heart, have been hers.

Hermione does not leave Steven, and they start another baby. Stewart gives Rosamond a job. Molly goes to the races with "that bludger" Guy, as Ken calls him, on the $100 a week she keeps for betting. The death of that "terrible man" Jack Cornock has lifted a number of masks, and let others fall happily in place.

Although she was already an author of some notable books, *The Impersonators* established Jessica Anderson as one of the most accomplished writers of modern fiction in English. Her individual contribution is a bringing together of an acute perception of the hidden motives behind people's actions with an illuminating sense of place and time.

Murray Bail

HOMESICKNESS

LONDON AND
MELBOURNE 1980

"I don't understand it," his uncle was saying. "If you people stayed in the one place you would see more, a million times more. The biggest, the smallest, the worst, the best, the tallest, the most expensive. Such questions come from remoteness and emptiness. Then when you do see something extreme or rare you think you've experienced it. Which of course is not the case; quite the opposite. Incidentally, Karl Marx and Casanova de Seingalt lived in that street you see. Not together, of course."

Returning to the chair Borelli still glanced at the window.

His uncle kept shaking his head. "Cocky over-fed country. You've produced lantern jaws and generalizations. Tourists are a natural follow on. You people are very demanding."

"Travelling," Borelli waved his arms, "there is the time factor to consider. We, ah travellers, operate in a condensed unreal time. For us, even time is summarized."

Not bad: but as he glanced for a reaction he shook his head and began laughing. It didn't matter.

Like Marat in the bath his uncle rested his head back in the pillows.

"See if my socks are under the bed.

There's something seriously wrong if they're not."

And from a nail in the wall he lifted a greatcoat, surplus from one of the Armed Forces. Its outline remained on the wall, a lighter grey, as if the wall had been sprayed around it. His pyjama top was Garibaldi red and as he fitted a tie, added a scarf, and finally a beret, his appearance altered from bedridden pensioner in the bare room to bulky livewire with penetrating stare and the clear skin of a child.

Outside he was recognized by the stall-holders who waved and called out, and many girls in fur coats. To them all he introduced his nephew, twisting Borelli's head to point out the vague resemblance, and showing how they had both used the same walking stick without knowing it.

Borelli pointed across his uncle's chin. "What?"

Funny: a truck there waiting at the lights carried in its back two sets of traffic lights. And that young woman with a crippled leg. Attractive; but see how the leg had pulled down one side of her mouth; already a deep crease had established, by remote action.

His uncle nodded, and Borelli kept his head cocked listening.

"One thing I've decided, after my years of study, is that we behave differently with women. You'll say everyone knows that. But it's a strange thing, isn't it? With women we subtract or multiply our faults."

Borelli shrugged knowingly, "So?"

An iron ball passed through an empty building and a tall wall fell in a complete straight edge, as in World War Two.

"Don't be stupid! Think of the change in your behaviour. By measuring it—measuring the falsity—you define your own character. Sometimes the results aren't very pleasant. I'm saying, if you care to, you'll learn more about yourself from women, than from men. It doesn't hurt," he added, "to spend a lot of time with them."

New districts, new intersections.

The bus emptied. They waited under an umbrella shop and caught another.

All novels are concerned with illusion and reality, not only with what is happening behind the action, but with the emerging outlines of truth and deception that exist in the characters themselves. When characters seem most confident, they may still be undermined by what the reader knows about them.

In *Homesickness* Murray Bail has had the brilliant idea of exposing a group of Australian tourists not only to the strangeness of foreign countries but to a series of museums which suddenly dislocate their attempts to adjust and tax their abilities to understand.

Thirteen men and women on a package tour go to an unnamed African country, to England, to Ecuador, to the USA, and to Russia. Some of them reveal new aspects of themselves, others defiantly parade caricatures of themselves. The tourists are a skilfully mixed bunch. The Kaddoks, in their fifties, are held together by his blindness, which ironically enough does not stop him taking endless photographs. "There is always one who knows the names of things." This also describes Kaddok, identifying an Australian gum tree in Africa. Dr Phillip North is a scientist. Garry Atlas is an Ocker, the one who can always be relied on to make the tactless remark or chat up the girls. Doug ("Howdy") Cathcart and his wife are Ordinary Decent People. Louisa Hofmann is an attractive, sensitive woman in her thirties, married to an unpleasant, egotistical dentist. James Borelli is an intelligent young man who prefers people to artefacts. Shiela, who comes from the country, is always travelling. Violet Hopper is a tough ex-actress with an amiably silly friend Sasha. Gerald Whitehead is a serious older man who is not very impressed by most things he sees abroad.

There is no obvious thread to join such a varied lot together, except their common tongue and a respect for

Australian athletic prowess. They are all rather pleased to find "REMEMBER – DAWN – FRASER" scratched with a knife on the end of a diving board in Africa.

Although Bail incorporates some sharp descriptive writing in this novel, he is careful not to turn it into a travelogue. Nevertheless, each new country is clearly defined both in itself and in its relation to Australia. The novel is not called *Homesickness* for nothing; at some stage or other, most of the tourists would rather be home, and they are always comforting themselves by recalling some aspect of home. In Africa:

> It could almost have been their own country: these sections with the gums briefly framed like a traditional oil painting by the slowly passing window. The colours were as brown and parched; that chaff-coloured grass. Ah, this dun-coloured realism. Any minute now the cry of a crow or a cockatoo; but no.

One recalls Patrick White (*Australian Letters*, Vol. 1, No. 3, p. 39) writing in 1958, "Above all I was determined to prove that the Australian novel is not necessarily the dreary, dun-coloured offspring of journalistic realism."

When they find, to their surprise, an Italian in charge of a museum in Quito, Ecuador, Mrs Cathcart is at home. " 'We have them living next door,' Mrs C. stepped back: this one had been eating garlic too."

Shiela has endless supplies of postcards to send home. Sometimes she is given more news than she had expected, as when the tourists go to one of the oddest of the museums, the Corrugated Iron Museum. This of course immediately evokes Australia, but when the guide shows a series of photographs one of them turns out to be one of "the gracious old spacious homesteads: the iron blended in". " 'Oh,' said Shiela, so matter-of-fact, 'they've got our place.' " Shiela has to confess that she owns it, but has a manager there, and an uncle. "I'm fond of it, but it's quiet."

"*I* *don't understand it,*" his uncle was saying. "*If you people stayed in the one place you would see more, a million times more. The biggest, the smallest, the worst, the best, the tallest, the most expensive . . .*"

It is interesting that this is the only precise evocation of Australia amongst the tourists, and then it is of a place that the Australian, Shiela, goes away from. Borelli in Ecuador says, "Gum trees and heat and an expanse of beach give me back the required colour." Garry of course finds the beer in every country "piss-weak" compared with Australian beer. But there is no attempt to show a deep identification with any particular place in Australia; homesickness is pervasive rather than acute, general rather than specific.

At one level, *Homesickness* is a profound and often very amusing essay on tourism. Tourists are numbered in millions, spending millions of dollars all over the world. Why do they travel? What are they looking for? The characters of *Homesickness* offer, implicitly or explicitly, a number of different explanations. The fastidious and learned Gerald speaks for many who affect to despise tourists while themselves still being tourists. He says, "I usually go to places

where there are no tourists – places that haven't been spoilt. But it's getting to the stage now where even the size of a city or a country is no longer a defence. You know how mobs pour in and stand around, taking up room, and asking the most ludicrous basic questions. They've ruined a place like Venice."

One of the finest comic episodes in the book occurs in the Museum of Legs in Quito, run by the genial Italian, Agostinelli. Among the exhibits is one that appears "finally to summarize the entire museum, LEG OF TOURIST (ENG.) It was thin, bony and experienced. It was thick-skinned. It had corns." The passage that follows, developing the thoughts of Agostinelli, defines tourists as well as legs.

> Of all legs, the tourist's is the most interesting; by far. He, Agostinelli, oughta know. Not only *his* museum lived off them; *all* museums do. . . .
>
> Consider, he went on, the pressure. Feel it. More than most the tourist is made aware of his limits, not only in mileage terms, but the limits of comprehension and tolerance. Tired? There you are, you see. It was a measure of something. And yet you don't stop. The tourist keeps going, one leg after the other, or stands waiting, queued. You embody the Human Condition. Stop. Keep going. Searching. For what?

Homesickness, which seems at first to be a picaresque comedy, turns out to be a most original study of the human condition, both in its travelling appearance and in more permanent aspects of its reality.

Museums were a brilliant choice for revelations of this reality. Bail has not made his selection, either of the museums or of their contents, at random, any more than a sculptor like Robert Klippel in his selection of bits and pieces which he welds together. In Africa there is the Museum of Handicrafts, the architecture of which is Western-gone-wrong and the contents colonial bric-a-brac, ranging from motor bikes to lawn mowers. There is no sign of the native handicrafts the tourists have come to see.

The second museum to "baffle and annoy" the tourists is the Collection of Pygmies, another colonial gathering, not of pygmies but of little figures like Winston Churchill or Bob Menzies. (Six lines encapsulate Churchill's infamies.) The Cathcarts won't hear a word against Menzies. It seems the tourists have to go to ex-colonial countries to learn about the workings of Empire.

When they reach England and the "instant gaiety" of good old London, their hotel, fittingly enough, is a converted wing of the British Museum. After odd experiences at the National, National Portrait and Tate Galleries, where X-ray photographs of the artists' underpainting, or photographs of the subjects, have replaced the paintings, the tourists go to a queen of genealogists, Lady Pamela Hunt-Gibbons. Her museum is history. As she reveals their past to all of them, embarrassing more often than flattering, imagination can throw light on their present.

After the Corrugated Iron Museum, and the Museum of Legs in Ecuador, comes New York, where the first museum they see is the world around them, handily revealed by the telescopes in the windows of their hotel rooms in a tall building. What they see is further revealed in a museum-in-action in Westchester County, the Institution of Marriage

CORRUGATED GIOCONDA *Jeffrey Smart*

MURRAY BAIL
1941-

Although Murray Bail has given a surprising number of interviews, he is not a writer who gives much away about himself.

He was born in Adelaide in 1941, and later lived in Melbourne before moving to Bombay where he lived for two years. He says of this time, "In the early Sixties, Australian literature was so dry and dusty and flat, it was just like the Nullarbor Plain. The place was boring, at least to me, and so was the literature."

He began writing fiction in 1965. In a *Meanjin* interview he elaborates on the effect on his work and attitudes to writing that came from living overseas. He says that India made bourgeois life in Australia seem trivial. "That's what I like in other literatures, the Russians, for example. They don't really fool around with local problems at all. It seems to me that a lot of Australian literature — and painting too — is still primarily concerned with getting ourselves on our own two feet, of establishing our Australianness."

The search for wide horizons, both intellectual and physical, led Bail from Bombay to London where he lived from 1970 to 1974. While there he wrote for various journals including *Transatlantic Review* and *The Times Literary Supplement*.

He now lives in Balmain, Sydney. He is married. *Homesickness* is dedicated to his wife, Margaret. For some years he was on the Council of the Australian National Gallery. In 1981 he published a book on the paintings of Ian Fairweather; he says he was fascinated by Fairweather "as one of the few who looks good here and who would also stand up very easily out of the country".

Fairweather, of course, painted almost nothing specifically "Australian", and Bail's subject matter, too, could be said to be tangential, touching Australia at points but swinging out far beyond it, as in the structure of *Homesickness*.

He was at first much influenced by Ernest Hemingway's short stories: "Reading them in a sleep-out in Adelaide on a hot afternoon,

you certainly liked Hemingway more and more." He went on to the Russian writers, whom he admires still because of "their high seriousness. But if I had to declare one writer as a major influence it would have to be Kafka. He demonstrated what was possible. For the same reason I was much affected by Patrick White." Of late Bail has been deeply interested in French writers, Proust, Roussel, Michel Tournier. Tournier he cherishes for the largeness of his vision; Bail is always in protest against the local or the provincial.

A volume of stories, *Contemporary Portraits and Other Stories*, was published in 1975 to high critical acclaim. Bail now prefers to work on novels. He has even referred to short story writing as "a sort of light relief, to relieve the pain and labour of novel writing". When an interviewer in *Aspect* (June 1981) remarked that this seemed to be "a cruel put-down of the short story", Bail replied: "Not so much a put-down, but common enough in any writer of novels. For after spending several years composing something long and complicated, a return to short fiction comes as pleasant relief. Whoever said short story writing is more difficult than novel writing, is, in my view, wrong. (It was Somerset Maugham: that may explain.)"

When the same interviewer asked Bail whether his theories, and practice, of fiction might make so many demands on the reader that he would be left with a smaller audience, he replied:

> Serious literature unfortunately has a confined committed audience. I am resigned to that. But I would see it as a serious limitation if *Homesickness* appealed only to other writers, to structuralists or academics with their magnifying glass. That would be too arid. At the same time the writer is entitled to make demands on the reader. Sentimentality, banality, laziness of content or style should be resisted. The ideal reader should be tolerant, lofty and yet concerned. I stand by the notion that nothing is simple. Readers who want that can turn to the trash, which is readily available, or better still, television.

As of course any study of the greatest writers will demonstrate, apparent simplicity can often lead to the utmost complexity. With Bail, at the moment at least, the breakdown of simplicity begins with the single word.

(nice pun), and, horrendously, in a tree-hide reminiscent of a Kenyan National Park from which they are forced to watch the rape of a young woman in a fur coat by five Puerto Ricans. This incident, perhaps more than any other in the book, reveals the true characters of the tourists.

By now the sexual patterns of the tourists have changed, some perhaps permanently (as in the case of Louisa and Borelli who seem to be genuine lovers), some temporarily, as mere diversion.

Some readers may have trouble with the last two chapters of *Homesickness,* although in an interview (*Meanjin,* June 1982) Murray Bail has declared: "Needless to say, though perhaps I shouldn't be saying it, those Russian chapters are the key to *Homesickness*." In Chapter 6 Bail unexpectedly intrudes to give his own tourist-impressions of Russia, which are confined to Leningrad and are not particularly memorable. The tourist group then goes to Moscow, where they visit the Centre of Gravity (another pun, this time on the solemnity of Russians). The activities here seem somewhat forced, as do the happenings when the tourists find themselves in a vulgar and almost surrealist encounter with the embalmed corpse of Lenin.

In a brief episode at the end of Chapter 7, the tourists

find themselves in a museum (perhaps still in Russia) which contains nothing at all but the tourists themselves, exposed by row after row of dazzling lights, and some words along the wall. They look at the words, and "Gradually, standing quietly, they began to see themselves."

It is the Human Condition, rather than a number of individuals, that we have come to see more clearly. The way, and the word, are mysterious but the sign posts are clear, and on one occasion made obvious, in an extension of Shakespeare's figure of the world as a stage.

> The world itself is a museum; and within its circumference the many small museums, the natural and the man-built, represent the whole. The rocks of Sicily, the Uffizi, the corner of a garden, each are miniatures of the world at large. Look, the sky at night: the most brilliantly displayed and ever-changing museum of harmonic mathematics and insects, of gods and mythological figures, agricultural machinery. The catalogue is endless.

Bail himself should be allowed the last word on *Homesickness:* "*Homesickness* consists of not one but a number of central themes; indeed that principle may be the central theme."

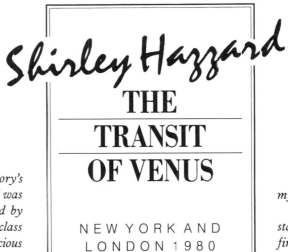

THE TRANSIT OF VENUS

NEW YORK AND
LONDON 1980

You asked me about Paul Ivory's play. I saw it only last month. I was impressed, and perhaps surprised by his ease in handling the working-class milieu. I think you might be suspicious of it—some of the effects spurious, and a pat, clever ending that was nevertheless breathtaking. It looks as if it will run forever, so you may see it when you get back from France.

Caro stopped writing, and read the passage over. How sincere, judicious. How much easier it is to sound genuine when being derogatory.

Caro sat at her office desk remembering Paul Ivory's play and how, for an instant at the end of the final act, the audience had remained silent after its ordeal. Here and there in the theatre a click or tick, a slight crackle such as one hears at potteries among baked wares cooling from the furnace. And then the fracturing applause.

Good that you can go to the Rome conference before returning here—I saw something about it in the papers. In Rome I remember a palace designed on a nobleman's horoscope—that is to say, decorated with representations of planets and pagan gods. Mere astrology, but perhaps you'll manage to see it all the same.

It was thus assured that Ted Tice would pass his happiest hour in Rome in frescoed rooms on the bank of the Tiber.

There will scarcely be time to write again before you get back to England.

Thank you for asking me to dinner, that will be lovely. Until one month, then, from today.

Caroline Bell posted this letter on her way home at noon. Saturday was a half-day at her office, and she stopped to buy food to provide lunch for Paul. She was living at that time in a top-floor furnished flat, rented from an office friend who had been posted abroad. It was near the Covent Garden market, in a building otherwise let to printers and publishers.

Noon came like glory into the narrow sooty brick of Maiden Lane, and expanded with architectural intention at the market. The city rose to the sun's occasion. And Caroline Bell was grateful for a bodily lightness never felt before, which she knew to be her youth. She walked with paper bags in her arms, smiling to think of her lost youth, discovered at the ripe and adult age of twenty-two.

Paul was in her doorway. He waited for her to come up to him, then leaned down from the step to embrace her. With the paper bags and a bunch of red flowers she made quite a bundle. "Why is this woman smiling?"

"I was thinking about adulthood, and adultery."

"Funny, I was thinking about adultery myself. Have you got the key?"

She gave it. They went up linoleum stairs, past doorways sealed with weekend finality. In an old building like this, dust settled quickly, and the unlocking of these small businesses each Monday was a mere deferral, each time surprising, of eventual, ordained oblivion.

Paul said, "Saturday afternoon in England is a rehearsal for the end of the world."

When they paused on a landing to breathe, he said, "These have been the best weeks of my life."

The flat was a large room with windows along one side and a blotched skylight at the far end. One wall was entirely covered by books on warped shelves, and the uneven floor was obscured by a big blue rug, nearly ragged, in which traces of reddish design could still be discerned, like industrial gases in a twilit sky or bloodstains inexpertly removed. A downward sag of ceiling, shelves, and floor was reproduced in a slump of studio couch that stood against the books and was covered by a new blue counterpane. There was a fine old table, scarred, and two chairs. The only picture was Caro's angel from Seville, on a wall near the kitchen door.

Everything was worn, or worn-out, even the smirched sky. The books supplied humanity, as they are supposed to do. Otherwise you might have said dingy, or dreary.

A storm is raging as *The Transit of Venus* opens. It is the early 1950s. Ted Tice, an impecunious young scientist, his cheap suitcase dissolving in the downpour, has made his way to the house of Professor Sefton Thrale, one of England's most distinguished astronomers. Mrs Thrale lets him in the door, and at the top of the stairs he sees a young woman, her face in shadow.

The Transit of Venus always has a strong narrative keeping it going, but the reader is also offered a richness that demands a close attention to detail. Shirley Hazzard is a highly accomplished writer of fiction, but she has often declared her deep allegiance to poetry. *The Transit of Venus* is thick with the allusiveness of poetry, its hints, subtle repetitions, links formed by image or metaphor, its concern with all the unseen forces that impinge on everyday reality.

Australia is of interest in *The Transit of Venus* but not of great importance, except that it has made Caroline and Grace different from English girls. Although clearly of the same racial family as the English, they are both open and vulnerable, having come from so far away, and also free of the inhibitions of English class structure. Of course it is speedily established that they have disadvantages, being Australian. Grace is engaged to marry Professor Thrale's son Christian. "Professor Thrale did not much care for the fact that Grace came from Australia. Australia required apologies, and was almost a subject for ribaldry."

Christian, however, limited though he is, appreciates what is different about the sisters.

> These women provided something new to Christian – a clear perception unmingled with suspiciousness. Their distinction was not only their beauty and their way with one another, their crying need of a rescue for which they made no appeal whatever; but a high humorous candour for which – he could frame it no other way – they would be willing to sacrifice.

It later becomes apparent that they are not at all the same, despite being "indissolubly bound" together, in their attitude to sacrifice, either in offering it or accepting it. Caro has already made the discovery ("not original") that "truth has a life of its own". And warnings have already been given by the title of the book and a later explanation of it, that life cannot be predicted. Captain Cook went all the way to Tahiti in 1769 to observe the planet Venus crossing the face of the sun, but, as Tice says, "The calculations were hopelessly out . . . Calculations about Venus often are." Professor Thrale adds the comment: "Venus cannot blot out the sun." Much later in the book, Caro in the despair of love recalls that confident scientific statement. "There are dying conditions as well as living conditions. Venus can blot out the sun." It is as well to remember these two extremes; *The Transit of Venus* is a novel about aspects of love, set in a frame of science. It is particularly relevant that the science is astronomy, and that in ancient and medieval and renaissance times people thought of astrology as more of a science than astronomy; poetry is full of references to love and the stars.

*P*aul was in her doorway. He waited for her to come up to him, then leaned down from the step to embrace her. With the paper bags and a bunch of red flowers she made quite a bundle. "Why is this woman smiling?"

In *The Transit of Venus* the relations between men and women are almost entirely those of love, or lack of love, or failed, unrequited love. Almost at the end of the book, when the sisters meet across the gulfs of many griefs, Caro says, " 'I don't know that suspense ever ends.' . . . By suspense, women meant the desire to love, be loved: great expectations." A moment or two later, Grace reflects that "men prefer not to go through with things. When the opposite occurred, it made history."

Ted Tice is one of those exceptions. His love for Caroline endures, from long rejection to tragically brief acceptance, right through the book. He provides, as Caro early observed, with a mixture of approval and exasperation, "the indispensable humanity".

Caro will not have Ted, but takes instead the elegant and heartless Paul Ivory, a successful young playwright who does not intend to let his affair with Caro interfere with his marriage into the aristocracy. In the most brilliant tragicomic scene in the book, Caro and Paul, in bed in an empty house, suddenly hear the noise of an approaching car, a particular car. It is the beautiful pre-war Bentley of Tertia Drage, Paul's fiancée. As she gets out of the car and calls up to the window he puts on a shirt and a tie and calls back to her, naked legs and thighs hidden. She is suggesting they go for a drive, of course knowing nothing of Caro's presence. At that moment Paul knows "from the fixing of Tertia's limbs that Caro stood beside him".

> He did not turn, but, as if he himself were Tertia Drage, saw Caro standing naked beside him at the high window and looking down; looking down on the two of them.

What happens is equally damning. Tertia, with aristocratic (or perhaps corrupt) sang-froid ignores Caro and waits for Paul, who comes, and they drive off. Much later we learn that Tertia had made Paul stop by a wood a few minutes later and take her, on the grass. Whereas Caro goes to London and to bed with a Guards officer whom she has met briefly and whom she meets again on the train. It is a double betrayal.

For a moment, at the window, Paul was in Caro's power and he much later confesses to her that "I could see my entire construction falling apart".

At this time he has just explained to her that the construction of his life is based on the fact that he is secretly homosexual. His pleasure has been to deceive both Tertia (a tough enough victim) and Caro. The bed in the inn near Avebury (a sacred site) in which he, recently engaged to Tertia, takes Caro's virginity, is the same one in which he had been with his lover Victor. Caro, learning of it years later, thinks of "her ignorance of his deepest pleasure".

An added pleasure, even more complex, was in possessing the woman Ted Tice loved. There is a strange bond between Tice and Ivory (the surnames are suggestive of warmth and coldness), and an even stranger link between two fateful incidents in their lives.

When Ted was a boy of 16 he found an escaped German prisoner on the beach and let him go. Caro is the first person he tells of this. "A conscious act of independent humanity is what society can least afford." It turns out that the German is a scientist with missile installations, and after his escape is responsible for the rockets which fall on England. This is an ironic variation on the phrase that comes to Caro a few pages later in the book, of Ted's "indispensable humanity".

It seems that Caro can inspire, even in the vile Paul, that love or at least confidence that enables men to confess their secrets. Paul's is that, with his "construction" threatened by a homosexual scandal, he leaves the sleeping Victor to be drowned in a river flooding from a burst dam.

At the last moment he realises that a man on the other side of the river has seen him walk away without waking Victor. That man was Ted. He had been on a walking tour of the West Country, and had stopped to see the Stones of Avebury Circle. And a few weeks later there he is again, at the astronomer's house where Paul first meets Caro. Ted

THE LOVERS *Jon Molvig*

SHIRLEY HAZZARD
1931-

Shirley Hazzard was born in Sydney in 1931 and was brought up in Mosman. With her family she left Australia in 1947 to live first in Hong Kong, and subsequently in New Zealand, before travelling to Europe in 1951. Her father was an Australian Trade Commissioner. She arrived in New York late in 1951, and soon afterwards joined the United Nations Secretariat there. Her 10 years at the United Nations, in New York and abroad, were to provide material for a work of satirical fiction, *People in Glass Houses* (1967), and for her only non-fiction book, *Defeat of an Ideal* (1973).

She has sometimes commented severely on the cultural climate in the Australia of her youth. In an "Author's Statement" in the special issue of *Australian Literary Studies* (October 1981) devoted to "The Contemporary Australian Short Story" she wrote:

> . . . it is hard to reproduce in few words the cultural aridity of the Australia in which I spent my childhood. It is also hard to say why a child should be aware of that condition, as it were, from earliest consciousness, particularly when there is no strong attachment to the life of culture in the immediate family. . . . It may be that gender has to do with this—the arts, though forceful enough in their way, being (or being seen as) part of the "feminine" aspect of humanity; and for this reason lying under particular proscription in a country whose "maleness" was a matter of strident and even panic-stricken assertion.

She says that she did not achieve freedom from this content of hostility, and "repressiveness towards pleasure that lurks, however much subdued, in the Anglo-American-Australian ethos", until she went to live in Italy. "Two years after I went to live in Italy, I began to write. In my first several years as a writer, I produced only short stories."

She achieved a modest but precarious financial independence by selling her short stories to magazines, in particular *The New Yorker*. She has published collections of stories, *Cliffs of Fall* (1963) and *People in Glass Houses* (1967).

She is married to the biographer and French scholar Francis Steegmuller; she met him at a small party given by Muriel Spark to which she recalls, "I almost didn't go". She and her husband have a house in Italy where they live in early summer; they return to New York in August "to write in peace, as no one is there", and go back to the Mediterranean in the autumn. She has written two novels set in Italy, *The Evening of the Holiday* (1966) and *The Bay of Noon* (1970).

She has been a guest lecturer at New York, Columbia, and Princeton Universities, and gave the Boyer Lectures on the ABC in 1984. She has published a number of articles on international affairs, but regards these as a duty, saying of them, "it is a terrible process for me. I'd rather write a book than an article." She has also written articles on cultural matters, one of the most notable being a long piece on Australian life published in *The New Yorker* after her visit to Australia in connection with Writers Week at the Adelaide Festival of Arts in 1976. Commenting on this visit, she said in an interview with Jenny Palmer (the *Bulletin* Literary Supplement 13 October 1981):

> When I was in Australia in 1976, after a long absence, and saw how Australia had come to life, it gave me a wider hopefulness. When you find that a people has enlarged its ideas—its tolerance, its imagination, its curiosity, all its possibilities—in a relatively short time, it gives hope that other favourable things are taking place in the world, even if they are obscured or overshadowed by contemporary dangers.

The Transit of Venus (1980) was on the *New York Times* best-seller list, and won the 1981 USA National Book Critics' Circle Award.

In 1982 Shirley Hazzard was elected to the American Academy and Institute of Arts and Letters.

---

never tells anyone what he knows, not even Caro.

Despite that moment at the window, Caro is a victim in her relationship with Paul. When she breaks away (there are some brilliant vignettes of Caro's life working in an office in London) she marries a rich American, Adam Vail, who is involved in various humanitarian enterprises. The evil of Paul is balanced against Adam's goodness; in the background, like a statement of nature, is the goodness of Ted, whom Caro continues to correspond with and occasionally meet. He, in despair at her marriage, himself marries, without love, the daughter of a scientist; one is left to wonder whether this impairs his goodness and humanity. Even more so, after Adam's death when he leaves his wife for Caro, breaking the news to her over the telephone, when Caro is at last prepared to admit his love.

The Transit of Venus is so tightly constructed, so full of enriching detail, that in a short space it is impossible to do more than indicate where the treasures lie outside the main lodes of Caro, Paul, Adam and Ted. There is a dreadful half-sister, Dora, who supplies anguish and grotesque comedy. There is the sharply ironic account, tragi-comic, of the affair between Grace's pompous husband Christian and a girl in his office. There is an early picture of the sisters' life in Australia, which contrasts subtly with the later one of Caro's life in New York and her relationship with Adam's daughter. And time and again, if one reads the text with an open memory, there are recurrences of a phrase, an image or a mood which add depth and meaning to the story.

As in a classic play, the tragic deaths of Caro (in a plane crash) and Ted (by suicide) take place off stage. The catastrophe has to be set in place entirely in the reader's imagination, by the exercise of a retentive memory for detail, which will recall the only three clues: the mention of Ted's suicide in Chapter 2, an allusion to Caro's fate in a letter she writes to Ted in Chapter 29, and the preview of Caro's New York eye-doctor's death in a plane crash in Chapter 35. In the final pages of the book Caro notices him at the Stockholm airport, boarding the plane in front of her.

The ending would be unreasonably cruel if we did not already know that calculations about Venus are often hopelessly out. And on the last morning, talking to Caro on the phone, Ted is finally able to say, "I am happier than I have ever been." To which Caro answers, "That might be enough. That is fulfilment." Where the mirrored door of a wardrobe hung open, she saw herself reflected. She said, "Some of that will last."

Peter Carey

BLISS

ST LUCIA, QLD, 1981

It was one of those hot still mornings that come in the beginning of the wet season: the sky a brilliant cobalt blue, and beneath it legions of green all freshly washed or newly born and only the rustling dry leaves hanging like giant dried fish from the banana trees might suggest death, and then only to someone hunting eagerly for its signs. The air that blew through the open windows of the old wooden house was sweet and warm, and honeysuckle and frangipani lent their aromatic veils, which billowed like invisible curtains in the high-ceilinged rooms.

Harry Joy whistled and spread the old newspapers across the kitchen table and set up the boot polish (dark tan, light tan, black and neutral) and the matching brushes and the polishing cloths. He brought to his goodness the slightly obsessive concern with method which is the hallmark of the amateur. He picked up the first pair of shoes and was pleased to see them muddy. He took an old knife and scraped them carefully; then a slightly damp cloth to wipe them; then the brush and polish; now the cloth. Then considering he had rushed the job and perhaps done it badly, he removed the laces and began again.

In the hour before eight o'clock he had cleaned the whole family's shoes, and none

of them had so much as stirred. He allowed himself the luxury of a cup of tea and while the kettle boiled he watched a family of honey-eaters attack the last of the previous season's pawpaws on the tree outside the kitchen window. He tried to memorize the form and colours of the birds but he knew he had no talent for it. In three minutes' time the honey-eaters would be a crude blur in his memory and all he would know was that they had a yellow marking near the eye.

When he had finished his tea he began to clean the windows, beginning in the kitchen where a fine layer of grease lay across the surface of the glass. He was engaged in rubbing this dry with old newspaper when David, already dressed with his wet hair combed neatly, came into the kitchen.

"Morning," said Harry.

David took in the shoes which were now lined up on the back doorstep, the clean window, and Harry Joy resplendent in bare scarred chest and Balinese sarong,

his taut body glistening with sweat, his yellowed teeth biting his lower lip in concentration. He didn't know what to be indignant about first.

He picked up his shoes. "Did you do this?"

"Yes."

"Dad, please, you mustn't."

"It's O.K., it gave me pleasure."

It was true. He couldn't remember ever having had so nice a time as this morning, alone with his family's shoes. He had enjoyed everything about it.

"You must not," his son said.

"They were dirty." He rubbed the window until the smeary marks had all gone. "It gave me pleasure," he said. "I liked cleaning them for you."

David's dark eyes shone. "No. I should clean your shoes."

"If you want to. . ."

"But it's wrong for you to clean mine."

"David, I enjoyed it."

He was not displeased with his son's irritation. It seemed to indicate the efficacy of the ritual.

"But you mustn't, Dad, you mustn't. Don't you understand? Why don't you understand?" He started shaking his head and smoothing down his wet hair.

The sustained originality of *Bliss* comes from the disturbing clash of experiences in the life of its hero, Harry Joy. He is a successful advertising man, that most twentieth century of professions, who is obsessed by an ancient, irrational belief in Hell. A theologian might argue that Harry is nearer to Purgatory than Hell, but Harry firmly believes he is in Hell, right here in Queensland. It is Hell after death, for at the beginning of the book he is dead for a few minutes after a heart attack. Detached from his body, he starts to learn about the world.

The opening sentence of the book begins: "Harry Joy was to die three times, but it was his first death which was to have the greatest effect on him. . . ." He thinks he is going to die again when he is to be operated on for a heart bypass. But although he does die again, the operation is successful, and during his convalescence, "Harry Joy became totally

convinced that he was actually in Hell."

This refocus on reality is the essence of *Bliss*, and enlarges on Carey's previous demonstrations in his short stories of his ability not only to mix fantasy with ordinary life but to explore the extent of the fantastic in the lives of ordinary people. Harry Joy's name, and the title of the novel, give an ironical warning about human happiness, but also, if irony can be discarded, suggest further possibilities. Perhaps joy, even bliss, may be at least sometimes attainable. Harry's third, and final, death takes meaning in the life of that possibility.

The electric shock that revives him after his first death and leads him towards Hell is a product of the industrialised world in which Harry seems to have attained enviable success. He runs a lucrative advertising agency, he has a wife Bettina and two children, David, 17, "who in his father's words is a 'good boy, going to be a doctor'," and Lucy, 15, who is a bright, healthy girl. But Harry has not seen his family as the reader has in the first 30-odd pages. Some 200 more pages elapse before, in Harry's circuits of Hell, he comes to full knowledge of them and their friends.

Bettina is the mistress of Harry's partner Joel; she has frustrated ambitions to work in the agency. David is a singularly unpleasant young man who will do anything for money, of which he has already accumulated a lot by working for drug-runners. Lucy, when not getting drugs by some devious means or other from her brother, is a Communist.

Of all this, and more, Harry was ignorant in the days when he used to settle himself down at his regular table at Milanos restaurant and watch with pleasure while his friend the proprietor, Aldo, opened a bottle of fine French wine. It was the same easy-going story with the advertising agency, where Harry did not concern himself with the effects, harmful or otherwise, of the products he was selling.

Yet it is very soon apparent in the book that Harry is neither mindless nor menial, and that his "good bloke" charm is not calculated. He has little vanities, such as silk shirts and tailored suits, but he drives a battered red Fiat 500 Bambino and leaves the Jaguar for Bettina. He has imagination and a gift for storytelling, inherited (with the stories, on which he improves) from his father, who "had been born in New York State and had travelled the world". His parents were "charming, beautiful, educated, eccentric . . . aristocrats of a sort". Harry has a similar distinction, "this feeling that he belonged to an elite", and the bony features not obscured by his large moustache remind some people of Krishna.

. . . The sky a brilliant cobalt blue, and beneath it legions of green all freshly washed or newly born and only the rustling dry leaves hanging like giant dried fish from the banana trees might suggest death, and then only to someone hunting eagerly for its signs.

There are strong North and South American links in the book, apart from Harry's father. Joel, in his late twenties, is an American. Bettina longs to live in New York. David has dreams of drug-running in Bogotá. And for others in the book, industrial, big-business America is the source of all evil. Australia itself is seen as an outpost of an empire; not the old British one, but the conquering American one.

After his second "death", and his conviction he is now in Hell, Harry starts to watch and make notes on the "three sorts of people in Hell. Captives, like us. Actors. And Those in Charge." The Actors work for Those in Charge, persecuting the Captives.

For a while, even in adversity, Harry retains his native optimism. In a section that is both very funny and harrowing, an elephant sits on the little Fiat while Harry is having lunch at Milanos, and the police who pick him up struggling home in the battered car of course do not believe his story. After beating him up in a desultory way the two policemen invite him to tell a story, "something interesting . . . something we haven't heard before", they say maliciously. So he

extemporises, "the only original story he would ever tell", and, ironically, they let him go. *Bliss* is in fact not only a story (and a highly readable one) but also a series of stories told by Harry who is the father of truth as well as lies.

His attempts to understand life in Hell soon lead to trouble. He thinks he should begin by trying to be good. He begins by telling his old friend Alex Duval, Account Director at the Agency, that he intends to close their account with Krappe Chemicals (worth over $300,000 a year) because of their harmful products. Alex, a closet radical, is appalled, fearing for his job.

Harry then goes home and starts cleaning the children's shoes, the bathroom and the windows, to the consternation of Bettina and the children. " 'Don't you damn well make me tea.' Bettina was stumbling to her feet. 'Don't you dare. . . . Don't try and be a martyr with me.' " Bettina is a tough lady, with a swift retort. " 'Does it cause you pain?' He tried to be disinterested. 'In the arse, yes.' "

In a flashback that follows this scene the source of Bettina's obvious unhappiness is revealed: "She was going to be a hot-shot but she met Harry Joy and fell in love with him." She is a receptionist at Ogilvy & Mather, advertising is her whole life; she gives up her ambitions for love of Harry, but does not abandon her interest in advertising. Ten years later it is a different story. She longs to work in the agency. Harry will not let her. "In Bettina's view, it was that rejection which had produced their present unhappiness." But even at this stage, there are still some flickers of love left between Harry and Bettina and the children.

However, they are all worried by the notes he has been taking about what is going on around him. They are part of his somewhat eccentric plan that he should conduct a number of "Tests". The last one of these is to climb the figtree by the house at night, having first pretended to fly to another State, and observe his family. He does not know that Joel has already outlined his plan to Bettina that they should have Harry committed—he has been acting "loony" enough—and take over the agency.

He sees incest and adultery from his perch in the tree; falls out and is left hanging by his trousers. When he is finally cut down he faces the family, the Final Test, and formally curses them. "I curse you all, for all time, without exception."

Harry retires to a suite at the top of the Hilton, where he drinks his expensive wines while his own son offers to put up the $5000 which will enable him to be committed. In the meantime a splendid new character enters the book, one of the most original and forceful women in Australian fiction. Honey Barbara is a callgirl, who for two months in the year goes whoring to earn money for her commune of hippies in the far rainforest. She carries a jar of leatherwood honey with her, the key to the diet that gives her extraordinarily beautiful eyes. One look at Harry's eyes is enough to establish how appalling his diet is.

When he tells her he thinks they are in Hell, "she did not, for an instant, think that he meant it metaphorically. She understood him perfectly." The people she lives with have even queerer notions about the nature of reality. Nor does she think him crazy when he tells her that there are moves to commit him. She gives him, from experience, a list of things not to do with psychiatrists and police—a manual on how to survive in Hell. Harry is in love with her.

SEXTON *Gareth Sansom*

PETER CAREY
1943-

Peter Carey was born on 7 May 1943 at Bacchus Marsh, Victoria. His parents had a Ford dealership operating out of the same street Frank Hardy lived in. His sister and brother were respectively 11 and 10 years older than him.

He attended Bacchus Marsh State School until the end of sixth grade, and then went to Geelong Grammar School in 1954, where he passed his Matriculation exam intending to be a scientist. In 1961 he began to study for a BSc at Monash University.

In some notes especially written for this book he says:

I wrote poetry, drew a cartoon strip, got drunk a lot, fell in love, failed my exams, had a car accident, got three supps, failed them all, and went to get a job.

Advertising seemed an interesting thing to do. Sir Robert Menzies seemed like a good bloke. I was, in short, ready to get my education.

In my first job I met Barry Oakley and Morris Lurie. I began to read. I learned all about such esoteric matters as moral dilemmas. I announced my intention to write a novel.

I got married in 1964 and stayed married until about 1974.

In the eary 1960s Jacaranda Press published an extract from an unpublished novel ("Contracts") in an anthology, *Under 25*. Carey comments, "Thank God they published so little." His first short story, "She Wakes", which later appeared in *The Fat Man in History* (1974), was published in *Australian Letters*. His second, third and fourth novels remain unpublished.

In 1974 I went to live in Sydney. I knew nothing about Balmain Writers, but I went to live in Balmain because it was close to the city and you could still get a place on the water at a reasonable rent. *The Fat Man in History* was then published and I was suddenly a Balmain Writer.

The short stories in *The Fat Man in History* were very well received in Australia and in London. *The Times Literary Supplement*'s comment is particularly apt.

Carey's non-realistic stories, which tend towards fable, owe something to surrealism, something to science fiction, and something to an older tradition of the imaginative and Gothic tale (particularly Poe) . . . He is also notable for his supposedly old-fashioned ability to hold the reader's attention.

Meanwhile, until 1977, Carey worked very hard in an advertising agency, in which he was a partner, in Sydney. Then he went to live in an alternative community in Yandina, Queensland. He lived there for most of the next three years. During that time he wrote his second book of stories, *War Crimes* (1979), which established him as one of the finest writers of stories in the English language, and *Bliss* (1981), his first published novel.

Two days after I finished *Bliss* we packed up the ute and drove to Sydney. The plan was to stay a year while I helped establish McSpedden Carey, the business I run in partnership with Bani McSpedden. The one year became two years. . . .

He has received many awards, including the New South Wales Premier's Award for both *War Crimes* and *Bliss*, and the Miles Franklin Award and the National Book Council Award for *Bliss*.

Carey's new novel, *Illywhacker*, which he began in 1981, was published in 1985. He now lives in Sydney and was married again in 1985.

She rather likes him, an innocent in the poisoned city.

In scenes typical of Carey, both comic and horrifying, Harry is locked up in an institution for the insane. He is eventually released from there with the assistance of the resourceful Honey Barbara and the use of his own money, brought by Bettina on the condition that he works with her in the agency. Honey Barbara abandons them in disgust.

In an unexpected extension of the reader's sympathies, Harry realises from the work his wife has prepared that she has outstanding talents in advertising, which he has prevented her from using. With him selling her copy, they achieve tremendous success. Honey Barbara comes to live in and cook for the strange household, where she and Harry, Bettina and Joel, Lucy and her semi-literate friend Ken share beds while David looks angrily at them all.

Honey Barbara's strictness at supervising their food and aspects of their morality is being undermined by the household. "What alarmed her silent Victorian heart was that she was starting to enjoy the life." She even, against her principles, is not only drinking wine but becoming a connoisseur. But Harry is making his own Hell with this corrupt life, two-sevenths good, five-sevenths devoted to fear and anger. After allowing herself to be seduced by the cunning David (who had planned this humiliation for a long time), Honey Barbara goes back to the rainforest.

In a series of cataclysms Harry's false world comes apart.

Bettina and Joel kill themselves, David has a fantasy-death. In a purgatorial journey Harry reaches the rainforest. Although Honey Barbara is at first cold to him he proves himself by becoming a fit and resourceful man, and all ends happily. The scar of his heart operation had been his initiation into a new life.

He had a glimpse of it when hovering above his body after his first death.

Ecstasy touched him. He found he could slide between the spaces in the air itself. He was stroked by something akin to trees, cool, green, leafy. His nostrils were assailed with the smell of things growing and dying, a sweet fecund smell like the valleys of rain forests. . . . It was only later that he felt any wish to return to his body, when he discovered that there were many different worlds, layer upon layer, as thin as filo pastry, and that if he might taste bliss he would not be immune to terror.

Carey does not sentimentalise Harry Joy's life in the rainforest, which initially subjects him to a number of terrors. The life there is not a fanciful retreat from the world, it is tough and practical. Yet it should not be taken too literally. Harry becomes the storyteller of the rainforest, and *Bliss* is a fable, however realistic and entertaining, about the oldest of fable subjects, the battle between good and evil.

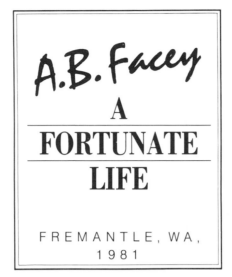

A.B. Facey

A

FORTUNATE

LIFE

FREMANTLE, WA,
1981

Early next morning Grandma came to me and said, "You go, and if you don't like it you can come back home again." Grandma had been the only mother I had known and I loved her, and I believed in her judgement. She had taken us in and worked hard to feed and look after us when our mother had deserted us. So, on this darling old lady's advice, I agreed to take the job. Grandma told the man. He had just returned with his horse and my pony from where they had been grazing tethered out for the night.

I had a problem now. I had to ride the pony and this troubled me. I was frightened, being so young—although I was big for my age I was still under nine years old. (I would turn nine in August but still had three months to go.) The man's name was Bob—"Short for Robert," he said. "They all call me Bob." He put the saddle on the pony, then he helped me into it and led the pony around by the reins with me on its back. I grabbed the front of the saddle and held on. The pony didn't mind a bit, and it didn't seem too bad. Then Bob put the saddle on his horse and got on its back and trotted it around in a circle to show me how to rise to a trot. I got the idea of this, but not before I had fallen off several times, to the amusement of Uncle, Aunt, Grandma and the other kids.

So about ten o'clock that morning we set off. Grandma gave me a single red blanket. She put all my clothes and things in the blanket, wrapping it up like a swag. Then the man strapped it on to the front of the saddle. This made it safer for me to ride, at least I thought it did.

It was hard leaving Grandma and the rest of the kids. After we had been travelling for a while Bob suddenly wanted to go faster. He explained to me that when you made a horse go faster than trotting it was called cantering. He set his horse into a canter, and my pony responded at once, but I didn't. I started to lose my balance and let go of the reins and held on like blazes to the saddle. The pony was off, going as fast as it could. We were on a bush-track which wasn't straight, and the pony didn't bother to keep to it. A limb of a tree caught me, lifted me clean out of the saddle and dumped me on the ground. The pony didn't bother to stop. I felt sure that it was glad to get rid of me.

The fall shook me up badly, but I wasn't hurt. Bob told me to wait while he went after the pony. I waited a long time before Bob came back with the pony, and it took a long time before I plucked up enough courage to get back into the saddle. Finally I did and we were on our way, but we didn't try to canter again.

It was past midday when Bob said we had better rest the horses. He picked a place where there was plenty of good grass for the horses and tethered them, and we had a rest ourselves and ate some food that Bob had with him. When we got going again I found that riding horseback wasn't all fun. My bottom and legs were getting very sore, in fact so sore that I had to hold all of my weight up out of the saddle by standing up in the stirrups.

The sun was going down and it was near dark when we rested the horses again. Bob undid my blanket and spread it over my saddle. This was soft and would make it better for me. How sore I was. My legs were red raw. After awhile we got going again and arrived at Bob's mother's place about nine o'clock that night.

The old lady was waiting for us. I was too tired to notice much about the place, and after having some supper, I was asleep almost as soon as my head hit the pillow. I never even knew the old lady had rubbed some kind of ointment on my sore legs and bottom until next morning.

Albert Facey's *A Fortunate Life* is an outstanding example of how difficult simplicity is to achieve in literature, and how rewarding simplicity is when it has been achieved. Facey has an extraordinary story to tell, but he treats it with the cool detachment of a born writer, although he had no education and had to teach himself to read and write. *A Fortunate Life* also demonstrates the delicate balance that exists between literature and emotion. The terrible events of Facey's childhood would not have made their impact in the telling if not for the calm simplicity with which they are told. Phrases of Wordsworth's come to mind: "emotion recollected in tranquillity"; "a man speaking to men".

One might expect that a man who had endured so much and could still call his autobiography *A Fortunate Life* would be hiding his wounds under a mask of toughness or sardonic humour, and that would be a very Australian way of handling it. But Facey, who is redoubtably Australian, has no qualms about admitting his feelings. He frequently admits fear, and he is not afraid of telling us that he burst into tears. For instance, in 1912, when he is about 18, he is working with two mates on windmills and wells for the Western Australian Water Supply, near Corrigin in the central wheatbelt of Western Australia. The Inspector asks them to clean up a well which is 42 metres deep. It is obviously a very dangerous well, with gaps between sets of rough timber.

Facey laconically says, "Jock and Bentley refused to go down the well, so that left me." When he is near the bottom of the well, timbers and earth suddenly give way and crash around him. Miraculously he is not killed, but he is on his own. (He does not know it, but his mates, thinking him dead, have gone for help.) The rest of the well is about to collapse. Striking matches and climbing up the timbers, he reaches the cave-in, about 20 metres from the top. It is a death-trap. Then he sees the windlass rope

> . . . hanging down on the east side of the shaft, still intact. My hopes mounted. I stepped gently across and got hold of that precious rope and pulling on it, I went up and out in a few minutes.
>
> When I was well away – about twenty yards or so – I couldn't help it, I cried bitterly and couldn't stop. Yet while I was down the well in great danger and scared stiff, crying was the furthest thing from my mind.

Note the instinctive details that make Facey such a good storyteller – the rope was on the east side of the shaft (a bushman's notation), and he cried when he was safe, but not when he was in danger.

It is a wonder that he has any tears left after what he has had to endure as a child. Born in Victoria in 1894, he is one of seven children. His father, taking the two older brothers, Joseph and Vernon, has gone to Western Australia looking for gold. Instead of finding it, he catches typhoid fever and dies when Bert is two. His mother leaves for Western Australia, allegedly to look after the teenage sons, and depositing the other five children with their grandparents in Castlemaine. Grandpa dies in 1898 and tiny Grandma decides to sell her property and take the children to their mother in the West.

There is no one at Fremantle to meet them, so they take the train to the goldfields and – so they think – to their mother. But in the dark they are wakened at Northam station and "Grandma said we had to get off the train as that was as far as her money would take us". So they build bush *mia-mias* in a government reserve and live there for three weeks, kept alive by gifts of food from generous neighbours. After three weeks a letter comes from Aunt Alice in Kalgoorlie (nothing from "our mother") with a money order.

Original illustration by Robert Juniper (*A Fortunate Life*)

Grandma and the children live with Aunt Alice and Uncle Archie and their brood of children in a hut with hessian walls in Kalgoorlie. Then Uncle gets a 405-hectare block of land under the government conditional purchase scheme about 40 kilometres from Narrogin. There is only room in the cart for the driver (Uncle, Aunt and Grandma take it in turns to drive) so the barefoot children walk from York to "Uncle's 'dream land'". It takes them three weeks.

A limb of a tree caught me, lifted me clean out of the saddle and dumped me on the ground. The pony didn't bother to stop. I felt sure that it was glad to get rid of me.

At nine Bert has to go to work, leaving Grandma ("the darling old lady") and his other relatives, at a farm at Cave Rock, some 50 kilometres away. Uncle, who has recommended the move, does not know that these people are cattle thieves who have been in gaol; they are drunkards and layabouts. Bert is nearly killed by one of the men who whips him with a stockwhip; his life is saved by a neighbour who has been a nurse. When he recovers his strength, he makes himself boots out of wheat bags and walks home.

Bert not only has to suffer this physical assault but to endure, with these and other people, the humiliation of not being paid for his work. He says that by the age of 12, "My experience up to now made me doubt the word of everyone."

Bert admits in later years to disliking his mother. She excuses herself by saying that the man with whom she was living would not allow her to have her children near her, but she seems to have been entirely devoid of maternal instincts. She reached her lowest point as a mother when Bert was 13 and the childless couple for whom he was working, named Phillips, wanted to adopt him. He was delighted – he already called Mrs Phillips "Mum" – and the papers were duly filled in at the police station at Narrogin. Bert's mother refused to sign the adoption papers. Not only that, "I think she probably asked for money in exchange for me." Whatever it was, the Phillips' attitudes towards him completely changed, and after a row with Mr Phillips Bert left. Fortunately, he found work with some good people nearby called Bibby.

> I set out along the track leading to Bibby's house. My swag was heavy so I rested several times . . . I arrived at Bibby's place before lunchtime . . . Mrs Bibby came out to see what the dogs were barking at. She said, "I didn't know you. Your swag is bigger than you are."

One of the fascinations of *A Fortunate Life* is to speculate what it is in Facey's character that enables him, throughout his life, to call it "fortunate". He seems a good advertisement for the humanist cause. He is not sustained by a belief in God; in fact, his later experiences at Gallipoli, and the events of World War II, make him doubt the truth of the Bible and the powers of God, if one exists. He then comes right out and says, "No sir, there is no God, it is only a myth."

If Facey denies the love of God, he believes in the love of human beings, despite his mother. (Even so, he has his first major fight with a man for calling him a bastard, and

UNTITLED *Hal Gye*

A. B. FACEY
1894-1982

Albert Facey was born in 1894 at Maidstone in Victoria, one of a family of seven children. Shortly after Albert's birth his father left for the Western Australian goldfields, taking the two oldest sons. He died there in 1896. Albert's mother then went to the West, leaving the children with their grandparents. The grandfather died in 1898, and in 1899 the grandmother took the five children to Western Australia. The mother refused to see them; they were taken in by the children's Aunt Alice and her husband Archie McColl.

The two families eventually settled on McColl's 405-hectare block near Wickepin, about 240 kilometres south-east of Perth, where they cleared the land and built a house, or rather a humpy; until the land became productive they lived off the sale of possum skins.

Albert never went to school; eventually he taught himself to read and write. He first went to work at the age of eight, and had several unfortunate experiences with farmers who promised him wages that he never received. At his first place of work a man almost beat him to death with a stockwhip; the man was never charged by the police, witnesses being afraid to give evidence.

After working for two families who paid him his wages he saved enough money to go to Perth in 1908 to see his mother, "although she hadn't been much of a mother to us". He found her at Subiaco and met his stepfather. "With that we all sat down to dinner. This was the first meal I could remember having with my mother."

For a short time he worked in Perth, paying his mother £1 a week board, but then left for Geraldton where he signed up as cook's assistant at £1 a week and keep with a drover bringing cattle down from the Ashburton River country to Geraldton. They left on 10 January 1909 to ride the 960 kilometres to collect the cattle. They

reached Geraldton in July and Bert earned £50; he also nearly died when he was lost in the bush for seven days between the Ashburton and Lyons Rivers. He was saved by the Aborigines. "A person would have to be lost like I was to really know what it was like – it was dreadful."

Back in Perth he saw his mother again, worked for a while and then took a job on a property not far from the last farm where he had worked. Various jobs followed, including clearing 57 hectares in 11 weeks, felling trees.

With the money he had saved, he went in 1912 to see his sister Laura at Castlemaine in Victoria; he also visited Melbourne and Sydney. Returning to Perth he went to the Burns' boxing school, and then took a job with the Western Australian Water Supply. He nearly lost his life down a well when the timbers collapsed. After a spell as a dogger hammering spikes on the Merredin-Wickepin railway in 1913, he became a prizefighter, winning 25 fights and travelling to Adelaide and Sydney with Mickey Flynn's boxing troupe. By this time he was exactly six feet tall (1.8 metres) and weighed 82 kilograms.

At the outbreak of war, he enlisted in the AIF and sailed for Egypt in February 1915. He was slightly wounded at Gallipoli but returned to action; later he was severely wounded and invalided out of the army. He eventually got a job as a tram driver, and later became President of the Tramways Union. In 1916 he married Evelyn Gibson. When she died in 1976, "We had been married for fifty-nine years, eleven months and twelve days."

In 1922 he took up land near Wickepin as a soldier settler, and grew wheat and wool, but was forced off the land by the Depression. He returned to the city in 1934 and eventually found a job as a trolley-bus driver. His grandmother died in 1932, aged 100.

He was a member of four different Metropolitan and Country Roads Boards, and in 1953 was appointed a Justice of the Peace. He retired on a full army pension, and died in 1982.

The huge manuscript of *A Fortunate Life* was skilfully edited by Wendy Jenkins and published by Fremantle Arts Centre Press in 1981. It won the NSW Premier's Literary Award for 1981, and has since been enormously successful in Penguin paperback.

---

casting a slur on his mother.) Grandma is a potent influence on his life, and he has a lot of affection for his brothers and sisters, even though he hardly ever sees them. He simply has an indomitably friendly nature. He likes men and women who "understand people's feelings", people such as hefty Mrs Stafford, the landlady of the Coffee Palace. He sees her cutting the wood and offers to do it for her. She watches him expertly do it, and offers him a reduced board as "cutting that wood is killing me".

As a child he has been told terrible tales about wild Aborigines, but his life is saved by them when he is lost for seven days in wild country when droving cattle from Mundiwindi in the Ophthalmia Range to Geraldton. "You would have thought I was a special king or something, the fuss they made."

And then of course there is Bert's quiet sense of humour. When he is lost, he tries to emulate his pony Dinnertime in eating grass, of which there is plenty. "Dinnie was in clover; she didn't seem to mind if we were lost for ever."

All the major threads of Facey's life and character come together at Gallipoli, where his capacity for affection and for getting on well with his mates who "understand people's feelings" enable him to write, without any conscious artifice, one of the finest accounts in existence of comradeship in

battle. His account of Gallipoli is also noteworthy for the deep element of controlled disgust that underlies his observations. Although, apart from a few caustic portraits of British officers and NCOs, he does not complain about those in authority, he makes it quite clear that, in his opinion and from his experience, men should never have been subjected to what they had to endure at Gallipoli.

Bert is no stock figure of the boozing, lawless Australian soldier. He is a teetotaller who does not go near women, and although at one stage he had been a professional boxer he never seeks out a fight. He certainly resents the pompous formalities of British discipline, but he is clearly a fine soldier. After the war, however, he says, "I'd have stayed behind if I'd known."

After being wounded and invalided home he makes the perfect marriage – with the girl who had knitted the socks he has received from a Red Cross parcel at Gallipoli. Finding work with the tramways, he eventually becomes President of the Tramways Union.

The story of the last 50 years of Bert's life is told quickly and neatly, up to his wife's death in 1976. It is the story of the first 25 years that gives *A Fortunate Life* its rare quality, full of poignant humanity, devoid of bitterness or sentimentality.

MELBOURNE 1981

MOONLITE

The ropes are still in the tunnel, and the men collect them and proceed to that cliff known as Glacan Mor on the west face of Mullach Mor. This is the biggest cliff close to the tunnel, falling nine hundred feet in two hundred yards to the ocean south-west of Boreray. Donald tags along.

Though the fledgling fulmar is easily caught and partly preferred for that reason, the people feel a strange affinity with this bird, and actually worshipped it before the druids came. They are silent now, and guilt-ridden, having failed in their duty to slaughter the young at the proper time. The steward's son Murdo thirteen, that being the number of the house he inhabits—it could be coincidence, but the village has as many men as a MacEsau has fingers and toes—slips the rope round his waist, ties a knot of rash simplicity and drops over the edge. Two colleagues hold the other end. This is Murdo thirteen's cliff, and he must go first, though at times of real crisis property is ignored.

The last young birds will soon be gone, but the adults return in November. The immature young spend years at sea before mating and their breeding cycle is prolonged and delicate. A single egg is laid in May, and the fulmar neither lays again nor returns to the nest if disturbed. Nonetheless, eggs are taken. Each man protects his own cliff from gulls, bonxies and sheep, and by mid-August the fledglings are fat with regurgitated plankton and ready to fly. At this stage their parents leave them, and the climbers descend.

The fulmar is not a large bird, being rather like a stout common gull with salient tube nostrils and a thick neck. It is easily seized, being more inclined to fight than flee, but if its precious oil is not to be lost, its neck must be broken before it can draw forward its wings.

Murdo, a hundred feet down, grabs a ledge with his prehensile toes. There are several young birds to his left. The fledglings laugh, but make no attempt to move: Murdo has been careful not to land too close to them. He judges the distance from the corner of an eye, then lunges with his left hand like a boxer. The crunch that follows is not the impact of his fist on the rock, but the sound of the birds' neck being snapped. It's over before the neighbours know what's happened; as they respond to an aural alarm, they don't even move. Slowly and deliberately Murdo removes the dead bird and tucks it under his belt. In this way he clears the ledge, then signals, by a tug at the rope, he is going down. With a kick he repels himself and scampers down the cliff face backwards. Donald feels ill at the sight: the open sea is so far below it looks strangely peaceful, and a bird on the wave is no more than a white dot; but there are birds leaving nests at some eight hundred different levels, and the stereoptic confusion this creates in the brain results in a kind of hypnosis. With difficulty Donald distracts his gaze and turns to the rope.

Each family owns a ten fathom horsehair rope, though the last horse on Hiphoray, a shaggy brute the size and disposition of a Shetland pony, died some centuries back. The role of the horse has since been assumed by the women, who now carry peat and provide hair. So far no rope is entirely of human hair, but all are mended and reinforced with it, and it's no exaggeration to say that a man's life depends on the strength of his wife's keratin. Indeed a fine head of hair is as much esteemed in a woman as a well turned ankle in a man, and for this reason if no other, it seems unlikely that Flora with her fine, flaxen hair, will ever find a new husband. In addition to these family heirlooms there are three heavy duty ropes, each twenty fathoms long and covered in rawhide. Despite all precautions, ropes break, and each mend in the rope marks the death of a man.

This is perhaps the most original of all Australian novels, the demonic energy of its style projecting the albino hero, Finbar (Moonlite) MacDuffie, from a tiny island in the Hebrides, north-west of Scotland, to the other end of the world in New West Highlands, a version of Australia in the goldrush days.

Moonlite is a comedy of such range and diversity that it is hard to find parallels in literature to give the reader a frame of reference. There are strong elements of ribald farce, especially in the satire of religion, high society, university life and the free-for-all of colonial scrambling for gold. Yet there are also hauntingly beautiful and profoundly serious moments of which images remain, such as the keening of women (and Finbar himself on hearing of his mother's death), the appallingly dangerous fowling on the 300-metre high cliffs of the island, or Finbar's first sight of a rainbow. And Finbar himself, with his brilliant mind and his vulnerable body, his capacity for affection and his sexual deprivation, is a tragi-comic figure, a cross between Don Quixote and Charlie Chaplin. He remains a searcher for truth, but life foils him.

"Life is a sequence of disparate events strung together by whim," he explains. "There was a time I might have been glad to impute a causal relationship; a time before that when I should have preferred one, to another, reaction. But now . . ."

The "disparate events" occur on the island of Mugg before Finbar is born early in the nineteenth century, when the tyrannical chief of the MacIshmael clan—"one of only four chiefs in the world entitled to be addressed by the definite article—the others being The King, The Pope and The Chisolm"—orders the recently widowed Lamech MacDuffie to marry his cousin Flora. On the day of the wedding the MacDuffies, Flora, her father Donald and her new husband Lamech, are evicted by The MacIshmael to the furthermost island, Hiphoray.

After a terrible voyage the boat reached "the island on the edge of the world", an island of birds, fulmars, auks, puffins, shearwaters, shags and petrels, also occupied by a few pagan human beings and their sheep and cattle. Although the people run these decrepit animals and plant a few hectares of windblown crops, they are pre-eminently fowlers who live on the export of oil and feathers from the birds. When she finds out the strange customs of the island Flora says to her father, "My God it's a pagan place."

Foster gives a number of extraordinarily powerful descriptions of the gathering of the fulmar chicks and eggs from the sheer cliffs down which the islanders descend on ropes of human hair, holding on to the rock with their prehensile toes. There are weird customs, as the one in which the men one by one hurl themselves off a 50-metre cliff, relying on the Atlantic gale to blow them back to land again.

Life is so primitive and superstitious on Hiphoray that the islanders are constantly battling with starvation. Flora, "to the men's impotent fury", teaches the women to collect shellfish. But Donald cannot persuade the men to catch fish. "The MacEsaus have all sorts of answers. Fish are unlucky, unhealthy, not fit to eat, dirty feeders, too soft, too dangerous, too hard to catch. In fact, MacEsaus don't like to sit in a boat when they could be climbing a cliff."

Though the fledgling fulmar is easily caught and partly preferred for that reason, the people feel a strange affinity with this bird, and actually worshipped it before the druids came.

Flora gives birth to a son, who is "very pale, with strange eyes". Soon after, a boat arrives with a passenger who has come to stay. He is the Reverend Stewart Campbell, a middle-aged bachelor come to convert the islanders; Hiphoray will never be the same again.

Donald, staunchly anti-religious, tells Campbell to take himself off; Flora on the other hand, welcomes him, no doubt also thinking that he can educate her son Finbar. Campbell sets the MacEsaus to rebuilding the village, and he makes them slaughter their sheep and eat fish to avert starvation, not forgetting to pound them into submission with his sermons. It is, after all, his island, given to his Church by The MacIshmael.

Foster's portrait of Campbell is richly humorous. Flora's conversations with him are models of innocence at the feet of experience. Flora says, "I thought you had to forgive your enemies?" The minister answers, "Aye, forgive them by all means but don't *spare* them on that account!"

The next invasion of Hiphoray, which itself is becoming a symbol of primitive innocence being destroyed by cunning experience, is by rich tourists and philanthropists, organised by Campbell through Captain Fadden, in whose boat he had arrived. Hiphoray goes downhill rapidly. "Within a few short years the island will be irredeemably spoilt, and the islanders, squatting like gulls on a garbage tip, sufficiently greedy and lazy to repel even a steerage class tourist."

After the tourists come the scientists, and Foster ironically observes that both groups are fundamentally not in the least concerned with the welfare of the islanders, only with their own justification. In the struggle between scientists and tourists for dominion of the island, "the tourists bring gifts of food, which the scientists do everything in their power to prevent the islanders from eating . . . At the new jetty . . . a large sign confronts the tourist, saying 'Please do not feed these islanders. It is both unkind and unnecessary.'"

By the time Finbar is six infanticide is being practised and the island has become dependent on imports. But in a few years time it is Finbar, who can see in the dark, who leads the islanders back to prosperity by taking geese from the cliffs at night.

Campbell sends Finbar to a colleague on Conmore, and from there he makes his way down to England; "he lives like a fox, avoiding towns". By a series of lucky chances he is admitted, on the lowest level, to Jesus Christ College at Newbridge University; one of those chances is that the Warden is, like him, an albino. So was Noah, the Warden tells him. Finbar does not want to hear this, as he knows from the Bible that Noah was a drunkard, and he is a teetotaller.

Finbar reveals an extraordinary talent for mathematics, but has no time for the university's "seminars in sophistry" and is appalled at the rich and idle undergraduates. He is even repelled by his fellow-Scot, Mungo MacQueen, who is a terrible drunkard. Finbar finds that not being a drinker in such a society also imposes severe strains on a man. The strain is finally too much and Finbar disgraces himself at a dinner party by an outburst of foul language. As Mungo says to him afterwards of that vulgar performance, "if it did nothing else it proved one thing, and that's your need of a drink".

At this low ebb, Finbar discovers rainbows (with the help of the dark glasses the Warden has lent him), and immerses himself in the problems of optics. After being told of the death of his mother, and terrifying Mungo by an outbreak of keening, he begins to drink, and "For the sake of his work he must keep drinking". His personal habits begin to degenerate, his theories have led him over the edge of the

MAN AND BIRD, BASS STRAIT *Russell Drysdale*

DAVID FOSTER
1944-

David Foster was born in 1944 and spent his early childhood at Katoomba in the Blue Mountains of New South Wales: he has described this landscape in his first novel, *The Pure Land* (1974). After attending a variety of schools, he graduated BSc from the University of Sydney in 1967, winning the University Medal for Inorganic Chemistry, and PhD from the Australian National University in 1970. He then did a year's postdoctoral work in the USA, as a Fellow of the US National Institute of Health.

In 1973 he gave up scientific research in order to write full-time. Since then he has published seven books of fiction, one of poetry and four radio plays. *The Pure Land* (1974) shared the *Age* award for the best Australian book of the year, and *Moonlite* won the 1981 National Book Council Award. Foster has held several writer's fellowships from the Literature Board since 1974, and also won the Marten Bequest travelling scholarship, which enabled him to visit the Hebrides to research *Moonlite*.

Foster and his Dutch-born second wife, Gerda, a singer, live in a century-old stone house in a small town in the NSW Southern Highlands, with the four youngest of their eight combined-family children. They live as self-sufficiently as they can, and provide their own fuel, vegetables, honey, eggs and dairy products. Since he left home at the age of 16, Foster has worked in many jobs besides science: labourer, truck driver, swimming pool attendant, drummer in a rock band. Many of these experiences have provided material for his stories and novels, giving him a grasp of Australian working conditions and different idioms that makes him unique among the younger Australian writers of fiction.

He is a precise craftsman who can involve himself totally in the writing of a book for up to two years at a time. He works in the morning, writing in pencil. "You can believe in it then. By lunchtime that belief is gone," he says. In the afternoon he works outside and at night revises and types what he has written.

Of Foster's other novels, the strangest is *Christian Rosy Cross*, a work about medieval and Renaissance gnosticism and alchemy, a retelling of the Rosicrucian myth as comedy. This work occupied Foster, on and off, for 10 years. *The Empathy Experiment* (1975), written with neurophysiologist Des Kirk, under the pseudonym D. Lyall, is science fiction. *Plumbum* (1983) describes the adventures, in Australia and Asia, of a five-member heavy metal rock band; lead vocalist Sharon, apart from Flora in *Moonlite*, is Foster's first significant woman character. His most recent novel, *Dog Rock* (1985), is a murder mystery spoof set in a small country town.

Interviewed by Alison Broinowski for the *National Times* (17-23 January 1982), David Foster made some comments on himself and his work which are very much to the point. Broinowski wrote, "He admits to being schizophrenic. He and his characters exemplify the contradictions which he sees as a condition of modern life. He and they are acted upon by science and mysticism, comedy and deep seriousness, civilization and disintegration, the boredom of isolation and the search for a greater empathy with their surroundings."

---

world, and there is nothing the Warden can do but expel him from College.

Returning to Scotland he soon finds himself, in appalling squalor, on an emigrant ship going to Australia, or rather to what Foster calls the New West Highlands, where the gold rush is on.

The last section of the book is conducted at breakneck speed as a farce in a world that is literally upside down. On his first night ashore, Finbar sees an opera where "the thief appeared to be the hero and the policeman the villain!" Finbar can now hold his own as a drinker, but he has to watch what is taken for a Pommie accent, and his Hiphoray habit of calling everyone "my dear". An obliging man tells him, "Listen, son: I know you mean well but you musta come out with a boatload of Poms. Talk like that creates the wrong impression."

Finbar makes friends with a fellow gold-digger, the Aboriginal Sunbeam, and runs into his old Newbridge companion, Mungo. To his astonishment, the rich butcher Grogstrife wants to put him up for parliament. Sunbeam, on the other hand, sees his mate Moonlite (as Finbar is now known) as a spirit who must die and be born again. "The Rainbow Fella's gonna rip you apart, take out your gizzards, clean an dry'm, then stuff'm back with a quartz crystal." After strange ceremonies of death and rebirth, Moonlite ("a future premier") makes his way back to Boomtown, a man of destiny.

"Friends . . . I am a man utterly without human emotion of any kind! Nothing! *Nothing*! can stand between me and the will of the people I represent. Not common sense — not love nor hate — not fear for the future, not guilt for the past — nothing. I have no soul of my own, no heart, to intrude upon my judgements."

Finbar/Moonlite has become the perfect politician and the hardships of his youth will stand him in good stead.

Stabbed through the throat by a Chinaman that night, Finbar is immortal, though "extinct". The book ends with an apocalyptic warning that God's patience with the New West Highlands is running out.

Moonlite is so carefully crafted that it could survive on the style alone, as *Tristram Shandy* can. It is constantly illuminated by flashes of satire, explosions of wit, jumping-jacks of farce, Roman candles of high drama. On an allegorical level, Hiphoray is doomed primitivism, Newbridge is the decay of civilisation, the New West Highlands is an upside-down world where life is a vulgar parody of dying. It is there that Finbar/Moonlite, who can see in the dark, by pure accident finds his true home, the outcome of strange links between Celtic pre-history and Aboriginal myth.

Acknowledgements

*The publishers gratefully acknowledge
the co-operation of the following writers, artists, copyright holders and
publishers who have given permission for text extracts
from copyright works and for copyright paintings and illustrations to
appear in this book. While every effort has been made to
trace and acknowledge copyright holders, the publishers tender their apologies
for any unintended infringement where the copyright holder
has proved untraceable.*

Text extracts

Jessica Anderson for *The Impersonators*; The Macmillan Company of Australia Pty Ltd, Penguin Books Australia Ltd.

Thea Astley for *The Slow Natives*; Angus & Robertson Publishers.

Australian War Memorial for *The Story of Anzac, Vol. 1, The Official History of Australia in the War of 1914-1918* by C. E. W. Bean; University of Queensland Press.

Murray Bail and The Macmillan Company of Australia Pty Ltd for *Homesickness*; The Macmillan Company of Australia Pty Ltd, Penguin Books Australia Ltd.

Geoffrey Blainey for *The Tyranny of Distance*; The Macmillan Company of Australia Pty Ltd, Sun Books Ltd.

Mrs Patricia Boyd for *The Australian Ugliness* by Robin Boyd; Penguin Books Australia Ltd.

Jonathan Cape Ltd, London, for *Voss* by Patrick White; Penguin Books Australia Ltd.

Donald E. Charlwood for *All the Green Year*; Angus & Robertson Publishers.

Chatto & Windus, London, for *An Imaginary Life* by David Malouf; Pan Books (Australia) Pty Ltd.

C. Manning Clark for *A History of Australia, Vol. IV*; Melbourne University Press.

William Collins Pty Ltd for
The Timeless Land by Eleanor Dark; William Collins Australia, Angus & Robertson Publishers.
Bottersnikes and Gumbles by S. A. Wakefield; William Collins Australia.
My Brother Jack by George Johnston; William Collins Australia.

Curtis Brown (Aust.) Pty Ltd for
Caddie: The Autobiography of a Sydney Barmaid by Caddie; Angus & Robertson Publishers, Penguin Books Australia Ltd; © C. A. Wright.
Capricornia by Xavier Herbert; Angus & Robertson Publishers; © estate of the late Xavier Herbert.
The Chant of Jimmie Blacksmith by Thomas Keneally; Angus & Robertson Publishers, William Collins Australia; © Thomas Keneally.
Come In Spinner by Dymphna Cusack and Florence James; Angus & Robertson Publishers; © Florence James and James McGrath.
The Complete Adventures of Snugglepot and Cuddlepie by May Gibbs; Angus & Robertson Publishers; © The Spastic Centre of NSW and The NSW Society for Crippled Children.
Coonardoo by Katharine Susannah Prichard; Angus & Robertson Publishers; © R. P. Throssell.
The Harp in the South by Ruth Park; Angus & Robertson Publishers, Penguin Books Australia Ltd; © Ruth Park.
A House Is Built by M. Barnard Eldershaw; Australasian Publishing Co. Pty Ltd, Lloyd O'Neil Pty Ltd; © Marjorie Barnard.
A Little Bush Maid by Mary Grant Bruce; Ward Lock Ltd; © J. E. Bruce.
The Magic Pudding by Norman Lindsay; Angus & Robertson Publishers; © Janet Glad.
The Shiralee by D'Arcy Niland; Angus & Robertson Publishers; Penguin Books Australia Ltd; © Ruth Park.
The Unknown Industrial Prisoner by David Ireland; Angus & Robertson Publishers; © David Ireland.
They All Ran Wild by Eric Rolls; Angus & Robertson Publishers; © Eric Rolls.
Wake In Fright by Kenneth Cook; Angus & Robertson Publishers, Penguin Books Australia Ltd; © Kenneth Cook.

Mrs Marie Davison for *Man-Shy* by Frank Dalby Davison; Angus & Robertson Publishers.

Dr H. A. Derham for *We of the Never Never* by Mrs Aeneas Gunn; Angus & Robertson Publishers, Hutchinson Publishing Group.

Mary Durack for *Kings in Grass Castles*; Transworld Publishers (Australia) Pty Ltd; © Mary Durack Miller.

Faber & Faber Ltd for *The Watcher on the Cast-Iron Balcony* by Hal Porter.

John Farquharson Pty Ltd, London, for
My Crowded Solitude by Jack McLaren; Sun Books Ltd.
The Naked Island by Russell Braddon; T. Werner Laurie Ltd.

Mrs Noni Farwell for *Squatter's Castle* by George Farwell; Angus & Robertson Publishers.

David Foster for *Moonlite*; The Macmillan Company of Australia Pty Ltd, Pan Books (Australia) Pty Ltd.

Nene Gare for *The Fringe Dwellers*; Sun Books Ltd.

Helen Garner for *Monkey Grip*; Penguin Books Australia Ltd.

Hamish Hamilton Ltd, London, for *Cooper's Creek* by Alan Moorehead; The Macmillan Company of Australia Pty Ltd, Thomas Nelson Australia.

Frank Hardy for *Power Without Glory*; Angus & Robertson Publishers.

Shirley Hazzard for *The Transit of Venus*; The Macmillan Company of Australia, Penguin Books Ltd.

William Heinemann Ltd, London, for
The Fortunes of Richard Mahony by Henry Handel Richardson; Angus & Robertson Publishers, Penguin Books Australia Ltd.
Her Privates We (or *The Middle Parts of Fortune*) by Frederic Manning; P. Davies Ltd.

T. A. G. Hungerford for *The Ridge and the River*; Angus & Robertson Publishers.

Hutchinson Publishing Group (Australia) Pty Ltd and Patricia Wrightson for *The Nargun and the Stars* by Patricia Wrightson.

Idriess Enterprises Pty Ltd for *Flynn of the Inland* by Ion L. Idriess; Angus & Robertson Publishers.

Christopher Koch for *The Year of Living Dangerously*; Thomas Nelson Australia.

Lansdowne-Rigby for *They're a Weird Mob* by Nino Culotta (John O'Grady).

Peter Mathers for *Trap*; Thomas Nelson Australia.

Frank Moorhouse and Rosemary Creswell Agency for *The Americans, Baby*; Angus & Robertson Publishers.

Pan Books (Australia) Pty Ltd for *Careful, He Might Hear You* by Sumner Locke Elliott; Pan Books (Australia) Pty Ltd, Victor Gollancz Ltd.

Cyril Pearl for *Wild Men of Sydney*; Angus & Robertson Publishers.

Penguin Books Australia Ltd for
A Fortunate Life by Albert Facey.
Lucinda Brayford by Martin Boyd.
The Lucky Country by Donald Horne.
Picnic at Hanging Rock by Joan Lindsay.

Rigby Publishers for
The Escape of the Notorious Sir William Heans by William Gosse Hay.
The Home of the Blizzard by Douglas Mawson.
No Roads Go By by Myrtle Rose White.
Storm Boy by Colin Thiele.

Kevin D. Ronan for *Vision Splendid* by Tom Ronan; Lloyd O'Neil Pty Ltd.

Olaf Ruhen for *Naked Under Capricorn*; Angus & Robertson Publishers.

Vincent Serventy for *Dryandra*; A. H. & A. W. Reed Pty Ltd.

Ivan Southall for *Ash Road*; Angus & Robertson Publishers, Penguin Books Ltd.

Randolph Stow for *To the Islands*; Angus & Robertson Publishers, Pan Books (Australia) Pty Ltd.

Hugh Stretton for *Ideas for Australian Cities*; Georgian House Pty Ltd.

Kylie Tennant for *The Battlers*; Angus & Robertson Publishers.

Tessa Sayle Literary & Dramatic Agency for *Man of Two Tribes* by Arthur W. Upfield; Angus & Robertson Publishers; © Bonaparte Holdings Pty Ltd.

University of Queensland Press and the authors for
1915 by Roger McDonald; University of Queensland Press.
Bliss by Peter Carey; University of Queensland Press, William Collins Australia.

Ward Lock Ltd, London, for *Seven Little Australians* by Ethel Turner.

Russel Ward for *The Australian Legend*; Oxford University Press.

Judah Waten for *Alien Son*; Angus & Robertson Publishers, Sun Books Pty Ltd.

Angus & Robertson Publishers for
Flying Fox and Drifting Sand by Francis Ratcliffe.
Here's Luck by Lennie Lower.
Jonah by Louis Stone.
Landtakers by Brian Penton.
The Letters of Rachel Henning, ed. David Adams.
The Man Who Loved Children by Christina Stead.
My Brilliant Career by Miles Franklin.
On Our Selection and *Our New Selection* by Steele Rudd.
The Pea-pickers by Eve Langley.
Rum Rebellion by H. V. Evatt.
Wild Cat Falling by Colin Johnson.

ACKNOWLEDGEMENTS

*All photographs of the authors have been supplied
by the authors or their estates, unless mentioned below.*

Illustrations

Page 10 Philip Gidley King. *Native Family of NSW* (c. 1789). Mitchell Library, State Library of NSW.

Page 11 William Bradley. *Sydney Cove, Port Jackson* (1788), watercolour. Mitchell Library, State Library of NSW.

Page 12 Watkin Tench. Mitchell Library, State Library of NSW.

Page 13 Joseph Lycett (1774-1825). *Aborigines resting by a camp fire showing Newcastle Harbour and Nobbys*, watercolour, 17.6 x 27.7 cm, in his *Drawings of the Natives and Scenery of Van Diemen's Land*, 1830. National Library of Australia.

Page 15 Charles Sturt (1795-1869). *The Depot Glen in Lat 29° 40' S. Long 148°E*, wash drawing 16.8 x 28.7 cm. National Library of Australia.

Page 17 Charles Sturt. From Andrew Garran's *Picturesque Atlas of Australasia*. Mitchell Library, State Library of NSW.

Page 19 Eyre and Wylie travel along the coast. From Andrew Garran's *Picturesque Atlas of Australasia*. Mitchell Library, State Library of NSW.

Page 20 Edward Eyre. From Andrew Garran's *Picturesque Atlas of Australasia*. Mitchell Library, State Library of NSW.

Page 21 Edward Charles Frome (1802-90). *First View of the Salt Desert – Called Lake Torrens* (1843), watercolour, 17.8 x 28.1 cm. Art Gallery of South Australia; South Australian Government Grant, Adelaide City Council, public and private donations 1970.

Page 24 *A chain gang. Convicts going to work near Sidney N.S. Wales.* From J. Backhouse's *Narrative of a visit to the Australian Colonies*, London 1843. State Library of NSW.

Page 25 Thomas Rowlandson (1756-1827). *Convicts embarking for Botany Bay*, pen and wash drawing, 17.3 x 15.7 cm. Rex Nan Kivell Collection (NK 228), National Library of Australia.

Page 28 Peter Lalor. Victorian Government Printing Office.

Page 29 J. B. Henderson. *The Eureka Stockade Riot, Ballarat* (1854). Mitchell Library, State Library of NSW.

Page 30 Raffaello Carboni, *Age*, 10/3/1885.

Page 32 Attributed to Rachel Henning. *Exmoor Station, Queensland* (c. 1862-67). Mitchell Library, State Library of NSW.

Page 33 Attributed to Rachel Henning. *The Dwelling at Mt Keira*. Courtesy of the owner.

Page 37 *The Flogging of Charles Maher* from Robert Jones' notebook *Recollections of 13 years' residence in Norfolk Island* (1823). Mitchell Library, State Library of NSW.

Page 38 (top) Marcus Clarke, aged 20. A & R archives.

Page 38 (bottom) From the 1927 film *For the Term of His Natural Life*. National Film & Sound Archive, Canberra.

Page 41 William Strutt (1826-1915). *Bushrangers on St Kilda Road* (c. 1880-87), oil on canvas, 74 x 154.8 cm. University of Melbourne; Grimwade Bequest.

Page 42 Rolf Boldrewood. A & R archives.

Page 44 Giles at Queen Victoria Springs. From Ernest Giles' *Australia Twice Traversed*. Mitchell Library, State Library of NSW.

Page 45 Lloyd Rees (b. 1895). *The Olgas, the Northern Aspect* (1976), wax crayon, watercolour, pencil and charcoal on paper, 38.2 x 56.6 cm. Australian National Gallery.

Page 46 Ernest Giles. From Andrew Garran's *Picturesque Atlas of Australasia*. Mitchell Library, State Library of NSW.

Page 49 Ray Crooke. *Poinsettia Garden*. Courtesy of artist and Holdsworth Galleries. Photograph by Greg Weight.

Page 50 Louis Becke. Mitchell Library, State Library of NSW.

Page 52 *Nursery Tea*. From *Seven Little Australians* (1894). Mitchell Library, State Library of NSW.

Page 53 Frank Mahony (1826-1917). *Untitled* (1896), watercolour, 31.5 x 48.5 cm. Art Gallery of New South Wales; gift of estate of E. H. McIntyre 1983.

Page 54 Ethel Turner (c. 1894). Courtesy of Sir Adrian Curlewis.

Page 57 Tim Storrier. *Campsite 1. Saddle and Equipment for the Primary Surveyor (with axe)* (1982), 152.4 x 152.4 cm, mixed media assemblage. Courtesy of artist. Photograph by Rafe Wayment.

Page 58 (top) David Carnegie. From *Spinifex and Sand* (1878). Mitchell Library, State Library of NSW.

Page 58 (bottom) *Establishing Friendly Relations*. From *Spinifex and Sand* (1878). Mitchell Library, State Library of NSW.

Pages 60, 61, 62 (bottom) Frank Mahony. Original illustrations from *Dot and the Kangaroo*. A & R archives.

Page 62 (top) Ethel Pedley. Mitchell Library, State Library of NSW.

Pages 64 & 65 Percy Lindsay. *Untitled*. A & R archives.

Page 66 Steele Rudd. Mitchell Library, State Library of NSW.

Page 69 Frederick McCubbin (1855-1917). *The Pioneer* (detail) (1904), oil on canvas, centre panel, 224.7 x 122.5 cm, outer panels 223.5 x 86 cm. National Gallery of Victoria; Felton Bequest 1906.

Page 70 Henry Lawson. Mitchell Library, State Library of NSW.

Page 73 Gordon Coutts (c. 1869-1937). *Waiting*, oil on canvas, 90.2 x 59.7 cm. Art Gallery of New South Wales; purchased 1896.

Page 74 Miles Franklin. Mitchell Library, State Library of NSW.

Page 77 Frank Mahony (1862-1916). *The Bullock Team* (1891), watercolour. Art Gallery of New South Wales; purchased 1920.

Page 78 Joseph Furphy. Mitchell Library, State Library of NSW.

Page 81 Sali Herman (b. 1898) *Tropical Garden* (1966), oil on canvas, 153 x 203.1 cm. Art Gallery of New South Wales; gift of the artist 1971.

Page 82 *The Beachcomber* (1922). A & R archives. Photograph by A. W. Pearse.

Page 84 From the film *We of the Never Never*. Courtesy Adams Packer Film Production/Film Corporation of Western Australia.

Page 85 Sidney Nolan. *House* (1978). Courtesy of artist and owner.

Page 86 Mrs Aeneas Gunn. News Ltd.

Page 89 Sydney Long (1871-1955). *Midday* (1896), oil on canvas, 102 x 133 cm. Art Gallery of New South Wales; purchased 1896.

Page 90 (top) Mary Grant Bruce. A & R archives.

Page 90 (bottom) Norah and Bobs. From *A Little Bush Maid*, 1910, published by Ward Lock, illustration by J. McFarlane. Mitchell Library, State Library of NSW.

Page 92 Larrikin and donah. George Ashton. *Bulletin*, 18/4/1891. Mitchell Library, State Library of NSW.

Page 93 Normand Baker (1908-55). *Morning in the Markets*, oil on canvas, 101.5 x 86 cm. Art Gallery of New South Wales; purchased 1932.

Page 94 Louis Stone. Mitchell Library, State Library of NSW.

Page 96 Frank Hurley. *Pushing Against a Gale, Winter Quarters, Cape Denison*. Mawson Institute for Antarctic Research, University of Adelaide.

Page 97 Van Waterschoot van der Gracht. *Sledging in Adelie Land*. The Mawson Institute for Antarctic Research, University of Adelaide.

Page 98 Douglas Mawson (1911). Mawson Institute for Antarctic Research, University of Adelaide.

Pages 100 & 101 May Gibbs. Original illustrations from *Snugglepot and Cuddlepie*. Mitchell Library, State Library of NSW. Courtesy of Gibbs estate.

Page 102 May Gibbs. Mitchell Library, State Library of NSW.

Page 105 Norman Lindsay. Original illustration from *The Magic Pudding*. Courtesy of Lindsay estate.

Page 106 Norman Lindsay. A & R archives.

Page 108 *Hobart from McGregor's Gardens*. From Andrew Garran's *Picturesque Atlas of Australasia*. Mitchell Library, State Library of NSW.

Page 109 Artist unknown. *Port Arthur* (c. 1842), oil on canvas. Tasmanian Museum and Art Gallery.

Page 110 William Gosse Hay. National Library of Australia.

Page 113 Frank Crozier. *The Beach At Anzac* (1919), oil on canvas, 123 x 184.2 cm. Australian War Memorial (2161).

Page 114 George Lambert. *C. E. W. Bean* (1924), oil on canvas, 90.7 x 71.1 cm. Australian War Memorial.

Page 117 Sidney Nolan (b. 1917). *Rain Forest*, oil on canvas, 152.9 x 122.3 cm. National Gallery of Victoria, Melbourne. Courtesy of artist.

Page 118 Jack McLaren. Mitchell Library, State Library of NSW.

Page 121 Frederick Garling. *Circular Quay* (1834). Mitchell Library, State Library of NSW.

Page 122 (top) Marjorie Barnard. News Ltd; (bottom) Flora Eldershaw. Mitchell Library, State Library of NSW. Courtesy of Freeman Studios.

Page 125 Elizabeth Durack. *Leitmotif*. Courtesy of artist.

Page 126 Katharine Susannah Prichard. A & R archives.

Pages 128 & 129 WEP. Original illustrations from *Here's Luck*.

Page 130 Lennie Lower. A & R archives.

Page 133 Frank Crozier. *Dead Beat, Tired Out*, oil on canvas, 40.6 cm x 50.7 cm. Australian War Memorial (214).

Page 134 Frederic Manning. Mitchell Library, State Library of NSW.

Page 136 S. T. Gill. *Ballarat Post Office and Township from Government Enclosure*. From *Victoria Illustrated*. Mitchell Library, State Library of NSW.

Page 137 Robert Ingpen. Original illustration from *Clancy of the Overflow*. Courtesy of artist.

Page 138 Henry Handel Richardson. Mitchell Library, State Library of NSW.

Page 141 Frank Mahony. *Untitled*. Courtesy of owners.

Page 142 Frank Dalby Davison. A & R archives.

Page 144 Courtesy of Royal Flying Doctor Service of NSW.

Page 145 Sam Fullbrook (b. 1922). *Plane Over Dunlop* (c. 1964), oil on canvas on cardboard, 35.5 x 48.2 cm. Australian National Gallery.

Page 146 Ion L. Idriess. A & R archives.

Page 149 Russell Drysdale. *Woman at a Window* (c. 1969). Courtesy of artist's estate and owner.

Page 150 Myrtle Rose White (1961). National Library of Australia. Courtesy of *The News*, Adelaide.

Page 153 Tom Roberts. *The Charcoal Burners (The Splitters)* (1866), oil/canvas/board, 49.5 x 74.3 cm. Ballarat Fine Art Gallery–Ballaarat City Council; acquired 1943, Martha K. Pinkerton Bequest.

Page 154 Brian Penton. A & R archives.

Page 156 William Blight. From Andrew Garran's *Picturesque Atlas of Australasia*. Mitchell Library, State Library of NSW.

Page 157 Raymond Lindsay. *Major Johnston Announcing the Arrest of Governor Bligh*. Geelong Art Gallery.

Page 158 H. V. Evatt. News Ltd.

Page 161 Russell Drysdale. *The Out-Station* (1965). Courtesy of artist's estate, Lister Galleries, Perth and Sotheby's.

Page 162 Xavier Herbert. A & R archives.

Page 165 Hans Heysen (1855-1977). *Drought (Arkaba)* (1929), watercolour, 28.4 x 40.3 cm. National Gallery of Victoria, Melbourne; purchased 1947.

Page 166 Francis Ratcliffe. Courtesy of CSIRO.

Page 169 Noel Counihan (b. 1913). *The Parents*. Courtesy of artist and Reg and Judy McDonald. Photograph by Daryl Pinder.

Page 170 Christina Stead. News Ltd.

Page 173 Thomas Watling. *A Direct North General View of Sydney Cove* (1794). Dixson Galleries, State Library of NSW.

Page 174 Eleanor Dark. Photograph by Max Dupain. Courtesy of Max Dupain.

Page 177 Noel Counihan (b. 1913). *Unemployed Marchers*. Courtesy of artist and David Levine. Photograph by Henry Jolles.

Page 181 Elaine Haxton (b. 1909). *The Pea Pickers* (1944), oil on panel. Art Gallery of New South Wales; purchased 1945.

Page 185 Tom Roberts (1856-1931). *Portrait of Florence* (1898), oil on canvas, 66.6 x 38.7 cm. Art Gallery of New South Wales; bequest of Florence Turner Blake 1959.

Page 189 Sali Herman. *Woolloomooloo*. Art Gallery of Western Australia. Courtesy of artist.

Page 190 Ruth Park. Magazine Promotions.

Page 193 Noel Counihan (b. 1913). *The Lobby, Parliament House* (1956), oil on composition board, 61 x 91.4 cm. National Gallery of Victoria, Melbourne; purchased 1956.

Page 194 Frank Hardy. Courtesy of John Fairfax & Sons Ltd.

Page 198 (top) Dymphna Cusack and (bottom) Florence James. From *Age*. Courtesy of Heinemann Publishers, Australia.

Page 200 Ronald Searle. *Fit Parade for Work on the Railway*. From *The Naked Island*. Courtesy of Russell Braddon.

Page 201 Murray Griffin. *Digging Bore-hole Latrines, Changi Camp* (1942), oil on paper on hardboard, 42.6 x 52.5 cm. Australian War Memorial (24493).

Page 202 Russell Braddon. News Ltd.

Page 205 Harold Abbott. *Life on Slater's Knoll* (1945), oil on canvas, 40.3 x 45.3 cm. Australian War Memorial.

Page 209 Robert Dickerson. *Boy in Street*. Courtesy of artist, owner and Biennale of Sydney. Photograph by Terence Bogue.

Page 210 Judah Waten. News Ltd.

Page 213 Herbert Badham. *Untitled* (1942). Courtesy of John Williams Antiques.

Page 214 Caddie. Courtesy of Curtis Brown (Aust.) Pty Ltd.

Page 217 Frank Mahony (1862-1916). *Rounding up a Straggler* (1889), oil on canvas, 91.5 x 127.6 cm. Art Gallery of New South Wales; purchased 1889.

Page 218 Tom Ronan. Courtesy of John Fairfax & Sons Ltd.

Page 221 Arthur Streeton (1867-1943). *Golden Summer*. Courtesy of artist's estate and owner.

Page 222 D'Arcy Niland. A & R archives.

Page 225 Robert Juniper. *Resting Figure* (1979), acrylic on canvas, 48.2 x 88.9 cm. Courtesy of artist and Diana Johnston.

Page 226 Arthur Upfield. A & R archives.

Pages 228, 229, 230 (bottom) WEP. Original illustrations from *They're a Weird Mob*. Courtesy of Lansdowne-Rigby.

Page 230 (top) John O'Grady. News Ltd.

Page 233 Jon Molvig. *Tree of Man, Sketch II*. Courtesy of artist's estate and G. and K. Collection. Photograph by Ray Fulton.

Page 234 Patrick White. Mitchell Library, State Library of NSW. Photograph by Ern McQuillan.

Page 237 L. H. Hart, tobacconist. From the Holtermann Collection. Hand-coloured. Mitchell Library, State Library of NSW.

Page 238 Cyril Pearl. A & R archives.

Page 241 Ray Crooke. *Palmer River Study*. Courtesy of artist and owner.

Page 245 Ray Crooke. *North Queensland Stockman*. Courtesy of artist and Gallery 460, Green Point, Gosford.

Page 246 Randolph Stow. News Ltd.

Page 248 *Wool-shearing*. Wood engraving published in Victoria, 1873. National Library of Australia.

Page 249 Noel Counihan (b. 1913). *Pub Talk* (1962), oil on composition board, 91.5 x 137.2 cm. Queensland Art Gallery; purchased 1963.

Page 253 S. T. Gill. *Droving*. Dixson Galleries, State Library of NSW.

Page 256 "Visual chaos of advertising." Australian Picture Library.

Page 257 Sydney Ure Smith (1887-1949). *The Bridge from Potts Point*, pencil with watercolour wash, 45.5 x 56.5 cm. Art Gallery of New South Wales; gift of the Society of Artists 1938. Courtesy of Sam Ure Smith.

Page 258 Robin Boyd. Courtesy of Patricia Davies.

Page 261 Russell Drysdale (1912-81). *Road with Rocks* (1949), oil on canvas, 66 x 101.7 cm. Art Gallery of New South Wales; purchased 1949.

Page 262 Kenneth Cook. News Ltd.

Page 265 John Rigby. *Aboriginal Girls At Cunnamulla Show*. Courtesy of artist and Chambers Pty Ltd. Photograph by Ray Fulton.

Page 269 Margaret Preston (1875-1963). *Mosman Bridge* (1925), woodcut, hand-coloured, 18.6 x 25 cm. Australian National Gallery.

Page 270 Sumner Locke Elliott. News Ltd.

Page 273 Ludwig Becker. *Crossing the Terrick-Terrick Plains, August 29, 1860*. La Trobe Collection, State Library of Victoria.

Page 274 Alan Moorehead. News Ltd.

Page 276 Hal Porter. Original illustration from his book *Bairnsdale—Portrait of an Australian Country Town*. Courtesy of John Ferguson Pty Ltd.

Page 278 Hal Porter. A & R archives.

Page 280 Scene from the film *Storm Boy*. Courtesy of South Australian Film Corporation.

Page 281 Robert Ingpen. Original illustration from *Storm Boy*. Courtesy of artist.

Page 285 Charles Meere (1890-1961). *Australian Beach Pattern* (1940), oil on canvas, 91.5 x 122 cm. Art Gallery of New South Wales; purchased 1965.

Page 286 Donald Horne. Courtesy of John Fairfax & Sons Ltd.

Page 289 Russell Drysdale. *Study of a Man* (c. 1937), gouache, 25.4 x 35.5 cm. Courtesy of artist's estate and owners.

Page 290 George Johnston. A & R archives.

Page 293 Tony Tuckson (1921-73). *Family at Table* (c. 1950), oil on canvas, 76 x 152 cm. Art Gallery of New South Wales; gift of Margaret Tuckson 1977.

Page 294 Thea Astley. A & R archives.

Page 297 Arthur Streeton (1867-1943). *Boys Bathing, Heidelberg* (c. 1891), oil on canvas, 30.4 x 62.8 cm. Queensland Art Gallery. Courtesy of artist's estate.

Page 298 D. E. Charlwood. Courtesy of ABC.

Page 301 Robert Boynes. *Limbo* (1979). Courtesy of Macquarie Gallery.

Page 305 Rosamund Heritage. *The Fire*. Courtesy of Rosamund Heritage, Stirling, South Australia.

Page 306 Ivan Southall. Photograph by Rain Ryan.

Page 308 S. T. Gill. *Wool Drays* from *The Australian Sketchbook*. Mitchell Library, State Library of NSW. Photograph by Rafe Wayment.

Page 309 *Clipper Ship* Thyatira *Entering Sydney Heads*, watercolour. Mitchell Library, State Library of NSW. Photograph by Rafe Wayment.

Page 313 Jost Bergner (b. 1920). *Aborigines in Fitzroy* (1941), oil on board, 62 x 49.5 cm. Art Gallery of South Australia; South Australian Government Grant 1978.

Page 314 Peter Mathers. Photograph by Jacqueline Mitelman.

Page 317 J. J. Hilder (1881-1916). *Morning in the Gardens*, watercolour, 23.5 x 20 cm. Art Gallery of New South Wales; gift of Howard Hinton 1917.

Page 318 Joan Lindsay. News Ltd.

Page 320, 321, 322 (bottom) Desmond Digby. Original illustration from *Bottersnikes and Gumbles*. Courtesy of William Collins Pty Ltd.

Page 324 *Rabbit auction at the Melbourne Fish Market* from *Illustrated Australian News*, 13/8/1872. Courtesy of *Age*, Melbourne.

Page 325 *Tens of Thousands of Rabbits Clubbed to Death in a Battue at Corack* from *Illustrated Australian News*, 12/4/1879. Courtesy of *Age*, Melbourne.

Page 326 Eric Rolls. A & R archives.

Page 329 Vincent Serventy. *Dryandra Forest*. Courtesy of Vincent Serventy.

Page 333 John Brack (b. 1920). *Backdrop for* Roundelay, pen, ink, wash, watercolour, 44.5 x 73 cm. National Gallery of Victoria; purchased 1964.

Page 334 Hugh Stretton. News Ltd.

Page 337 Russell Drysdale (1912-81). *Industrial Landscape*. Courtesy of artist's estate and Joseph Brown.
Photograph by Henry Jolles.

Page 338 David Ireland. Courtesy of John Fairfax & Sons Ltd.

Page 341 Arthur Boyd. *Reflected Bride* (1958). Courtesy of artist and owner.

Page 345 Mike Brown (b. 1938). *The Beautiful One is Here* (detail) (1969-70), synthetic polymer paint and collage on hardboard, 121.5 x 121.5 cm. Art Gallery of New South Wales; purchased 1975. Courtesy of artist.

Page 346 Frank Moorhouse. A & R archives.

Page 349 A. H. Fullwood (1863-1930). *The Station Boundary* (1891), oil on canvas, 92 x 61.6 cm. Art Gallery of New South Wales; purchased 1891.

Page 350 George Farwell. A & R archives.

Page 353 Joan Saint. Original jacket painting for *The Nargun and the Stars*. Courtesy of Patricia Wrightson and Hutchinson Publishers. Photograph by Stuart Fox.

Page 356 From the film *Monkey Grip*. Courtesy of Pavillion Films. Photograph by Ian Potter.

Page 357 Charles Blackman (b. 1928). *The Lovers* (1961). Courtesy of artist and owner.

Page 358 Helen Garner. Photograph by Jill Gibb.

Page 361 S. T. Gill. *Panning for Gold* (1874). Mitchell Library, State Library of NSW.

Page 365 Albert Tucker. *Assassin* (1954). Courtesy of artist.

Page 369 David Strachan. *The Idiot*, from *Accent and Hazard* by A. Kershaw. Mitchell Library, State Library of New South Wales. Courtesy of copyright holder.

Page 370 David Malouf. News Ltd.

Page 373 Will Dyson. *The Amateur ("Who's Cutting this Hair, You or Me?")* (1920), oil on cardboard, 61 x 49.9 cm. Australian War Memorial (2434).

Page 374 Roger McDonald. News Ltd.

Page 377 Charles Blackman (b. 1928). *Dreaming in the Street* (1960), oil on composition board, 122.2 x 183.2 cm. National Gallery of Victoria, Melbourne; purchased 1960. Courtesy of artist.

Page 378 Jessica Anderson. News Ltd.

Page 381 Jeffrey Smart (b. 1921). *Corrugated Gioconda* (1975-6), oil on canvas, 80.8 x 116.6 cm. Australian National Gallery, Canberra. Courtesy of artist.

Page 382 Murray Bail. News Ltd.

Page 385 Jon Molvig. *The Lovers*. Courtesy of artist's estate and Pamela Bell. Photograph by Ray Fulton.

Page 386 Shirley Hazzard. News Ltd.

Page 389 Gareth Sansom. *Sexton* (1969). Courtesy of artist. Photograph by Henry Jolles.

Page 390 Peter Carey. Courtesy of John Fairfax & Sons Ltd.

Page 392 Robert Juniper. Original illustration from *A Fortunate Life*. Courtesy of artist.

Page 394 A. B. Facey. News Ltd.

Page 397 Russell Drysdale. *Man and Bird, Bass Strait*. Courtesy of artist's estate and Kerry Packer.

Page 398 David Foster. News Ltd.

INDEX OF AUTHORS

Anderson, Jessica 375
Astley, Thea 291

Bail, Murray 379
Banfield, E. J. 79
Barnard Eldershaw, M. 119
Bean, C. E. W. 111
Becke, Louis 47
Blainey, Geoffrey 307
Boldrewood, Rolf 39
Boyd, Martin 183
Boyd, Robin 255
Braddon, Russell 199
Bruce, Mary Grant 87

Caddie 211
Carboni, Raffaello 27
Carey, Peter 387
Carnegie, David W. 55
Charlwood, D. W. 295
Clark, Manning 359
Clarke, Marcus 35
Cook, Kenneth 259
Culotta, Nino 227
Cusack, Dymphna 195

Dark, Eleanor 171
Davison, Frank Dalby 139
Durack, Mary 251

Elliott, Sumner Locke 267
Evatt, H. V. 155
Eyre, Edward John 18

Facey, A. B. 391
Farwell, George 347
Foster, David 395
Franklin, Miles 71
Furphy, Joseph 75

Gare, Nene 263
Garner, Helen 355
Gibbs, May 99
Giles, Ernest 43
Gunn, Mrs Aeneas 83

Hardy, Frank 191
Hay, William Gosse 107
Hazzard, Shirley 383
Henning, Rachel 31
Herbert, Xavier 159
Horne, Donald 283
Hungerford, Tom 203

Idriess, Ion L. 143
Ireland, David 335

James, Florence 195
Johnson, Colin 299
Johnston, George 287

Keneally, Thomas 339
Koch, Christopher 363

Langley, Eve 179
Lawson, Henry 67
Lindsay, Joan 315

Lindsay, Norman 103
Lower, Lennie 127

McDonald, Roger 371
McLaren, Jack 115
Malouf, David 367
Manning, Frederic 131
Mathers, Peter 311
Mawson, Douglas 95
Moorehead, Alan 271
Moorhouse, Frank 343

Niland, D'Arcy 219

Park, Ruth 187
Pearl, Cyril 235
Pedley, Ethel 59
Penton, Brian 151
Porter, Hal 275
Prichard, Katharine Susannah

Ratcliffe, Francis 163
Richardson, Henry Handel 135
Rolls, Eric 323
Ronan, Tom 215
Rudd, Steele 63
Ruhen, Olaf 239

Serventy, Vincent 327
Southall, Ivan 303
Stead, Christina 167
Stone, Louis 91
Stow, Randolph 243

Stretton, Hugh 331
Sturt, Charles 14

Tench, Watkin 9
Tennant, Kylie 175
Thiele, Colin 279
Tucker, James 23
Turner, Ethel 51

Upfield, Arthur W. 223

Wakefield, S. A. 319
Ward, Russel 247
Waten, Judah 207
White, Myrtle Rose 147
White, Patrick 231
Wrightson, Patricia 351

INDEX OF TITLES

Alien Son 207
All the Green Year 295
Americans, Baby, The 343
Ash Road 303
Australia Twice Traversed 43
Australian Legend, The 247
Australian Ugliness, The 255

Battlers, The 175
Bliss 387
Bottersnikes and Gumbles 319
By Reef and Palm 47

Caddie: The Autobiography of a Sydney
    Barmaid 211
Capricornia 159
Careful, He Might Hear You 267
Chant of Jimmie Blacksmith, The 339
Come In Spinner 195
Complete Adventures of Snugglepot and
    Cuddlepie, The 99
Confessions of a Beachcomber, The 79
Coonardoo 123
Cooper's Creek 271

Dot and the Kangaroo 59
Dryandra 327

Escape of the Notorious Sir William
    Heans, The 107
Eureka Stockade, The 27

Flying Fox and Drifting Sand 163
Flynn of the Inland 143
For the Term of his Natural Life 35
Fortunate Life, A 391
Fortunes of Richard Mahony, The 135
Fringe Dwellers, The 263

Harp in the South, The 187
Her Privates We 131
Here's Luck 127
History of Australia, A, Vol. IV 359
Home of the Blizzard, The 95
Homesickness 379
House is Built, A 119

Ideas for Australian Cities 331
Imaginary Life, An 367
Impersonators, The 375

Joe Wilson Stories, The 67
Jonah 91
Journals of Expeditions of Discovery into
    Central Australia 18

Kings in Grass Castles 251

Landtakers 151
Letters of Rachel Henning, The 31
Little Bush Maid, A 87
Lucinda Brayford 183
Lucky Country, The 283

Magic Pudding, The 103
Man of Two Tribes 223
Man Who Loved Children, The 167
Man-Shy 139
Middle Parts of Fortune, The. See Her
    Privates We
Monkey Grip 355
Moonlite 395
My Brilliant Career 71
My Brother Jack 287
My Crowded Solitude 115

Naked Island, The 199
Naked Under Capricorn 239
Nargun and the Stars, The 351
1915 371
No Roads Go By 147

On Our Selection 63
Our New Selection 63

Pea-pickers, The 179
Picnic at Hanging Rock 315
Power Without Glory 191

Ralph Rashleigh 23
Ridge and the River, The 203
Robbery Under Arms 39
Rum Rebellion 155

Seven Little Australians 51
Shiralee, The 219
Slow Natives, The 291
Spinifex and Sand 55
Squatter's Castle 347
Storm Boy 279
Story of ANZAC, The 111
Such is Life 75
Sydney's First Four Years 9

They All Ran Wild 323
They're a Weird Mob 227
Timeless Land, The 171
To the Islands 243
Transit of Venus, The 383
Trap 311
Two Expeditions into the Interior of
    Southern Australia 14
Tyranny of Distance, The 307

Unknown Industrial Prisoner, The 335

Vision Splendid 215
Voss 231

Wake in Fright 259
Watcher on the Cast-Iron Balcony,
    The 275
We of the Never Never 83
Wild Cat Falling 299
Wild Men of Sydney 235

Year of Living Dangerously, The 363